Lecture Notes in Computer Science   9560

Commenced Publication in 1973
Founding and Former Series Editors:
Gerhard Goos, Juris Hartmanis, and Jan van Leeuwen

Editorial Board

David Hutchison
  Lancaster University, Lancaster, UK
Takeo Kanade
  Carnegie Mellon University, Pittsburgh, PA, USA
Josef Kittler
  University of Surrey, Guildford, UK
Jon M. Kleinberg
  Cornell University, Ithaca, NY, USA
Friedemann Mattern
  ETH Zurich, Zürich, Switzerland
John C. Mitchell
  Stanford University, Stanford, CA, USA
Moni Naor
  Weizmann Institute of Science, Rehovot, Israel
C. Pandu Rangan
  Indian Institute of Technology, Madras, India
Bernhard Steffen
  TU Dortmund University, Dortmund, Germany
Demetri Terzopoulos
  University of California, Los Angeles, CA, USA
Doug Tygar
  University of California, Berkeley, CA, USA
Gerhard Weikum
  Max Planck Institute for Informatics, Saarbrücken, Germany

More information about this series at http://www.springer.com/series/7407

Christian W. Probst · Chris Hankin
René Rydhof Hansen (Eds.)

Semantics, Logics, and Calculi

Essays Dedicated to
Hanne Riis Nielson and Flemming Nielson on the
Occasion of Their 60th Birthdays

 Springer

Editors
Christian W. Probst
Technical University of Denmark
Kongens Lyngby
Denmark

René Rydhof Hansen
Aalborg University
Aalborg
Denmark

Chris Hankin
Imperial College London
London
UK

Photograph on p. V: © private

ISSN 0302-9743   ISSN 1611-3349   (electronic)
Lecture Notes in Computer Science
ISBN 978-3-319-27809-4   ISBN 978-3-319-27810-0   (eBook)
DOI 10.1007/978-3-319-27810-0

Library of Congress Control Number: 2015959793

LNCS Sublibrary: SL1 – Theoretical Computer Science and General Issues

Printed on acid-free paper

This Springer imprint is published by SpringerNature
The registered company is Springer International Publishing AG Switzerland

Hanne and Flemming

Preface

Hanne Riis Nielson and Flemming Nielson turned 60 in 2014 and 2015, respectively. Congratulations! To celebrate the 60th birthdays, and to honor the birthday children, a colloquium was held at the Technical University of Denmark on January 8, 2016, to deliver the Festschrift and presentations of most contributions as our birthday presents.

This volume is dedicated to Hanne and Flemming and to their work. The Festschrift features contributions from colleagues who have worked together with Hanne and Flemming through their scientific life.

We would like to thank all the contributors to this Festschrift—for their hard work, for their both scientifically interesting and individual articles, as well as for their enthusiasm to contribute. The mix of articles resembles very nicely the impressively wide area in which Hanne and Flemming have worked and made fundamental contributions. Both the Festschrift and the colloquium were a wonderful way to celebrate them.

Our thanks also go to all the reviewers whose support made excellent articles even better. We are also indebted to Alfred Hofmann at Springer for his feedback and advice on our project, and to Anna Kramer from Springer for her fast responses to all our questions about Festschrifts and all matters around them.

October 2015

Christian W. Probst
Chris Hankin
René Rydhof Hansen

Contents

Effect Systems Revisited—Control-Flow Algebra and Semantics

Alan Mycroft[1]([⊠]), Dominic Orchard[2]([⊠]), and Tomas Petricek[1]

[1] University of Cambridge, Cambridge, UK
{alan.mycroft,tomas.petricek}@cl.cam.ac.uk
[2] Imperial College London, London, UK
d.orchard@imperial.ac.uk

Abstract. Effect systems were originally conceived as an inference-based program analysis to capture program behaviour—as a set of (representations of) effects. Two orthogonal developments have since happened. First, motivated by static analysis, effects were generalised to values in an algebra, to better model control flow (*e.g.* for may/must analyses and concurrency). Second, motivated by semantic questions, the syntactic notion of set- (or semilattice-) based effect system was linked to the semantic notion of monads and more recently to graded monads which give a more precise semantic account of effects.

We give a lightweight tutorial explanation of the concepts involved in these two threads and then unify them via the notion of an *effect-directed* semantics for a *control-flow algebra* of effects. For the case of effectful programming with sequencing, alternation and parallelism—illustrated with music—we identify a form of *graded joinads* as the appropriate structure for unifying effect analysis and semantics.

1 Introduction and Musical Homily

Instead of the usual introduction explaining effect systems and exemplifying their various forms, we start with a musical example. This motivates a particular algebraic approach to *describing* effects, including concurrency, based around the development of Nielson and Nielson along with Amtoft [2,26].

Section 2 again starts as tutorial, first relating set-based effect systems with *syntactic* labelled monads (due to Wadler and Thiemann [39]) and later with a *semantic* relationship to graded monads [16,28]. This relationship is parallel to that between types as syntax and types as semantic objects such as sets and domains—or that of algebra as symbol-pushing versus algebraic models.

Section 3 is more novel and argues that (graded) monads alone are insufficient to model effects representing parallelism, and even certain forms of conditional. We identify the notion of control-flow effect operators, as opposed to ordinary effect operators, to characterise the situation.

C.W. Probst et al. (Eds.): Nielsons' Festschrift, LNCS 9560, pp. 1–32, 2016.
DOI: 10.1007/978-3-319-27810-0_1

Section 4 continues by showing how the *joinad* structure [29,32], which refines monads, can be "graded" (indexed) to unite the above two orthogonal developments of effect systems—giving a particular control-flow algebra which provides an algebraic-and-semantic model of effect systems including parallelism.

Anyway, enough of this chatter—the show must go on!

```
let happyBirthdayMelody() =
    for line = 1 to 4 do
        play(G, 0.75); play(G, 0.25);
        if line = 3 then play(G2, 1);  play(E2, 1);  play(C2, 1);  play(B, 1);  play(A, 1);
        else  play(A, 1); play(G, 1);
            if line = 2 then play(D2, 1); play(C2, 2); else play(C2, 1); play(B, 2);
```

Fig. 1. Happy birthday to Hanne and Flemming

Motivation: richer effect systems. When writing about effect systems, many authors still consider only set-based systems. However, as shown by Nielson and Nielson [26], richer effect systems are useful. In addition to sequential composition, such systems also capture recursion (looping), choice (to model conditionals), and spawning threads. We demonstrate the importance of such rich effect structures in this section, albeit using parallel composition rather than spawning.

1.1 Effect Systems for Music

In our first example, we honour the celebratory nature of this paper and consider an effect system for music. More specifically, we look at a program (Fig. 1) that plays the melody of the "Happy Birthday to You" song.[1] We use a simple imperative language[2] with a primitive $play(N, l)$ which plays the note N (drawn from the usual CDEFGAB range, with suffix '2' meaning an octave higher, along with the silent note 'rest') for duration l (a rational number) and blocks until l time has elapsed. The function iterates over four phrases of the song. Each phrase starts with notes G G, so these are played always. The third phrase (*Happy birthday dear Hanne and Flemming*) has a different melody, which is handled using the first if. The first two phrases also differ (the second if).

Set-based effect system. The most basic effect system that we could add to the language is shown in Fig. 2. It annotates programs with effects Φ—here the *set* of notes that are played. (We generally use F, G, H to range over effects, but while discussing music—perhaps containing the note F—we use Φ instead. Similarly

---

[1] To slightly shorten the example, the melody of the last phrase repeats that of the first. Musicians are invited to use the correct notes: F2;F2;E2;C2;D2;C2.

[2] This easily maps to the λ-calculus-with-constants formulation used in later sections by replacing the for statement with if and a tail-recursive call, and by treating $e; e'$ as shorthand for let $x = $ e in e for some fresh variable x.

$$(\text{PLAY}) \; \frac{}{\Gamma \vdash \text{play}(N, l) : \text{void}, \; \{N\}} \qquad (\text{IF}) \; \frac{\Gamma \vdash e_0 : \text{bool}, \Phi_0 \quad \Gamma \vdash e_1 : \tau, \Phi_1 \quad \Gamma \vdash e_2 : \tau, \Phi_2}{\Gamma \vdash \text{if } e_0 \text{ then } e_1 \text{ else } e_2 : \tau, \; \Phi_0 \cup \Phi_1 \cup \Phi_2}$$

$$(\text{SEQ}) \; \frac{\Gamma \vdash e_1 : \tau_1, \; \Phi_1 \quad \Gamma \vdash e_2 : \tau_2, \; \Phi_2}{\Gamma \vdash e_1; e_2 : \tau_2, \; \Phi_1 \cup \Phi_2} \qquad (\text{FOR}) \; \frac{\Gamma \vdash e : \text{void}, \; \Phi}{\Gamma \vdash \text{for } i = n_1 \text{ to } n_2 \text{ do } e : \text{void}, \; \Phi}$$

Fig. 2. Simple set-based effect system for music

the singleton type is written void rather than unit to avoid conflict with the monad unit operator later.) The (PLAY) rule annotates play with a singleton set containing the played note, ignoring its duration. Sequential composition (SEQ) and (IF) simply union the sets of sub-expressions and (FOR) ignores the repetition and just uses the annotation of the body. Thus, for the above program, the simple effect systems reports the effect $\{\mathsf{G}, \mathsf{A}, \mathsf{B}, \mathsf{C2}, \mathsf{D2}, \mathsf{E2}, \mathsf{G2}\}$.

This is a good start (we now know the range of notes that our piano needs to have!), but it does not tell us very much about the structure of the song.

Adding Kleene star and choice. If we want to track the effects of our song more precisely, we can follow Nielson and Nielson and use an effect system with a richer structure [26]. For music, we might use annotations of the following structure:

$$
\begin{aligned}
\Phi = \; &\mathsf{C}, \mathsf{D}, \mathsf{E}, \ldots, \mathsf{rest} && (\textit{primitives: notes, including } \mathsf{rest}) \\
&\mid \; \Phi_1 + \Phi_2 && (\textit{choice}) \\
&\mid \; \Phi_1 \bullet \Phi_2 && (\textit{sequencing}) \\
&\mid \; \Phi^* && (\textit{looping})
\end{aligned}
$$

(where (*) binds more tightly than (•) which binds more tightly than (+))

$$(\text{PLAY}) \; \frac{}{\Gamma \vdash \text{play}(N, l) : \text{void}, \; N} \qquad (\text{IF}) \; \frac{\Gamma \vdash e_0 : \text{bool}, \Phi_0 \quad \Gamma \vdash e_1 : \tau, \; \Phi_1 \quad \Gamma \vdash e_2 : \tau, \; \Phi_2}{\Gamma \vdash \text{if } e_0 \text{ then } e_1 \text{ else } e_2 : \tau, \; \Phi_0 \bullet (\Phi_1 + \Phi_2)}$$

$$(\text{SEQ}) \; \frac{\Gamma \vdash e_1 : \tau_1, \; \Phi_1 \quad \Gamma \vdash e_2 : \tau_2, \; \Phi_2}{\Gamma \vdash e_1; e_2 : \tau_2, \; \Phi_1 \bullet \Phi_2} \qquad (\text{FOR}) \; \frac{\Gamma \vdash e : \text{void}, \; \Phi}{\Gamma \vdash \text{for } i = n_1 \text{ to } n_2 \text{ do } e : \text{void}, \; \Phi^*}$$

Fig. 3. A richer effect system for music with Kleene star and choice

The effect system shown in Fig. 3 uses the new structure of effect annotations. Sequential composition (SEQ) annotates the expression $e_1; e_2$ with $\Phi_1 \bullet \Phi_2$. The for loop is annotated with Φ^* meaning that the body is executed zero or more times. The conditional if-then-else is annotated with $\Phi_0 \bullet (\Phi_1 + \Phi_2)$ meaning that it evaluates the guard expression first, followed by one of the branches.

Using the revised effect system, the effect annotation of "Happy Birthday to You" becomes: $(\mathsf{G} \bullet \mathsf{G} \bullet (\mathsf{G2} \bullet \mathsf{E2} \bullet \mathsf{C2} \bullet \mathsf{B} \bullet \mathsf{A} + \mathsf{A} \bullet \mathsf{G} \bullet (\mathsf{D2} \bullet \mathsf{C2} + \mathsf{C2} \bullet \mathsf{B})))^*$. This contains a lot more information about the song! It is still an approximation—we only know there are zero or more repetitions, and not how the choices are made or note durations. However we do know in which order the notes are played and what variations there might be. Such an effect system could be used in a music programming language as an interface to communicate higher-order function (combinator) behaviour (see *e.g.*, effect systems for music live coding [1]).

Why richer effects matter. Effect systems can inform optimisations, aid program understanding, and help reject buggy programs. Richer effect systems therefore let us specify valid transformations/programs more precisely.

The above effect system has two interesting properties. Firstly, in the revised Nielson-Nielson-style system, each syntactic element is annotated with a distinct operation in an abstract effect structure. This means that we are, in some sense, describing the most powerful and general non-dependently-typed effect system for the language. For example, separating sequencing and alternation allows both 'may' and 'must' properties to be analysed. For the effects of if with $\Phi_0 \bullet (\Phi_1 + \Phi_2)$, the usual set-based approach where $\bullet = + = \cup$ gives a 'may' analysis. A 'must' analysis is obtained by instead taking $+ = \cap$, *i.e.* each branch of a conditional must satisfy the minimal requirements specified by the effect.

Secondly, the laws (equational theory) of the programming language imply equations on the effect structure, and vice versa. For example, consider the following program law (inspired by the introduction of Benton *et al.* [4]):

$$\{\text{if } b \text{ then } c \text{ else } c'\};\ c'' \equiv \text{ if } b \text{ then } \{c; c''\} \text{ else } \{c'; c''\}$$

corresponding to effect algebra axiom $(\Phi + \Phi') \bullet \Phi'' = (\Phi \bullet \Phi'') + (\Phi' \bullet \Phi'')$, where sequential composition is right-distributive over alternation. Thus, axioms of the effect algebra make language properties more explicit and easier to understand.

Adding parallelism. These $\bullet/+/(*)$ operators often suffice to summarise program behaviour—indeed they capture a range of classical dataflow analyses when appropriately interpreted. However, languages for expressing music need an additional construct, namely parallel composition, to play multiple phrases at the same time. For example, to accompany "Happy Birthday to You" with chords C, G7 and F, we need a parallel-composition construct e_1 par e_2 and define:

```
let chord_C(l)  = play(C, l) par play(E, l) par play(G, l)
let chord_G7(l) = play(G, l) par play(B, l) par play(D, l) par play(F, l)
let chord_F(l)  = play(F, l) par play(A, l) par play(C, l)
```

Following the methodology of the previous section, we now need a corresponding extension of our effect system. We add a new operation for parallel composition to the effect structure, written $\Phi_1 \& \Phi_2$, and supply the following typing rule:

$$(\text{PAR}) \quad \frac{\Gamma \vdash e_1 : \tau_1,\ \Phi_1 \quad \Gamma \vdash e_2 : \tau_2,\ \Phi_2}{\Gamma \vdash e_1 \text{ par } e_2 : \tau_1 \times \tau_2,\ \Phi_1 \& \Phi_2}$$

We can now write a program that accompanies the melody with the above chords as harmony. For the last two lines, we play C and F chords for line 3 and then

C, G7, C for line 4, giving an effect that is the parallel composition & of the melody program above and the effect of the chords (C&E&G) • ((F&A&C) + ((G&B&D&F) • (C&E&G))). Note that the effect structure above allows us to capture the fact that one chord finishes before the next chord starts. However, we would need to enrich effects with durations to be able to use effect-based reasoning to argue that the melody and harmony synchronise as our ears expect.

Our modelling of music is inspired by Nielson and Nielson who considered spawning processes in CML, in an effect system over what they termed *behaviours*. This included basic effects of channel allocation, sending and receiving (similar to *session types* [11]), a τ action for internal communication, binary effect operators for sequencing and alternation, and unary effect operator SPAWN to denote task spawning. We prefer to use a binary parallel-composition operator instead of SPAWN as commutativity of parallelism is more easily expressed.

Parallelism and other operators. How does the & operator relate to other effect operators? In CCS and the π-calculus, Milner's *interleaving-semantic* view identifies our $(\Phi_1 \& \Phi_2)$ with $(\Phi_1 \bullet \Phi_2) + (\Phi_2 \bullet \Phi_1)$; two concurrent *events* are equivalent to the same two events in some non-deterministic order [22]. In Milner's work, this rests on his assumption that events are atomic and, indeed, the model is sufficient for many purposes (*e.g.* when the primitive operations are serialised into one-at-a-time interactions).

However, doing so is against our aim of providing a fully *general* system and it excludes many effect systems we wish to consider. In music, events have *duration* and so we need to distinguish three basic effect operators: assuming Φ_1 and Φ_2 are notes (or pieces of music) then $\Phi_1 \bullet \Phi_2$ means play Φ_1 then Φ_2, and $\Phi_1 + \Phi_2$ means play Φ_1 or Φ_2, and $\Phi_1 \& \Phi_2$ means play Φ_1 at the same time as Φ_2. This justifies the idea of having three separate effect operators which can, if desired, be interpreted so as to satisfy interleaving, but not to build in interleaving.

1.2   Section Conclusion and Placement

"The methodology of annotated type and effect systems consists of: (*i*) expressing a program analysis by means of an annotated type or effect system, (*ii*) showing the semantic correctness of the analysis, (*iii*) developing an inference algorithm and proving it syntactically sound and complete." (Nielson *et al.* [25])

This paper addresses a particular subset of effect systems (*i*), ones expressible in terms of primitive effects composed with operations for sequential and parallel composition along with alternation (and iteration, considered briefly in Sect. 5). In Sect. 2, we overview some of the literature connecting effect systems to monads, first syntactically and then semantically, and we explain how graded monads [16] provide an *effect-directed semantics*. This refines a usual monadic semantics and aids correctness (*ii*) by unifying analysis and semantics.

Section 3 explores how (graded) monads have limited ability to express non-sequential control flow (choice/parallelism); monads per se capture only *sequential composition* (corresponding to • in effect annotations). For the musical example, we must also capture control flow corresponding to the + and & effect operations. We propose that *joinads* [32] fill this role. Section 4 recalls joinads, introducing a variant that we call *conditional joinads*; these are graded analogously to monads. The resulting *graded conditional joinads* provide an effect-directed denotational semantics for rich effect systems. Relevant work from the literature is scattered throughout, but more is given along with discussion in Sect. 5.

This paper does not consider inference *algorithms* (*iii*), and indeed we do not discuss polymorphism over type or effects, which are precursors to principality, or near principality, of type and effect *inference systems*.

Whilst much of the material here is grounded in category theory, we aim at a more accessible presentation, mostly in terms of set-theoretic or programming concepts. Throughout we assume an underlying Cartesian-closed category for our semantics and so use the λ-calculus as its internal language to aid readability.

Paper outline. The following diagram summarises the big picture of the paper, where ◄ indicates a richer structure to the right:

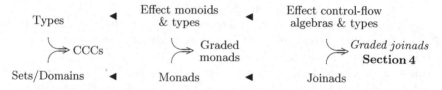

The top line gives syntax of program analyses (types and effects); the bottom gives the related semantic interpretations. The left-hand denotes the use of Cartesian-closed categories to refine a set- or domain-based semantics with types to give a *type-directed semantics*. In a similar way (in the middle part), graded monads unify (refine) a monadic semantics with the information from a traditional monoidal effect system, giving *effect-directed semantics*. The right-hand part expresses our analogous construction, relating the generalisation of monads to joinads with the generalisation of monoidal effects to richer (semiring-like) structures for control flow, by *graded joinads*.

2   Monads and Effect Systems

Effect systems are a class of static analyses for program side-effects [9,18,37]. They are typically inductively defined over the syntax (and types) of a program, presented as augmented typing rules (rather than a flow-based analysis such as dataflow), hence their full title: *type-and-effect systems*. (Another view is that the effect annotations are types of a different *kind*). Effect systems have been used for a variety of applications, including analysing memory access [9], message passing [12], control side-effects and unstructured control primitives (goto/comefrom) encoded as continuations [13], and atomicity in concurrency [7].

We overview effect systems briefly (Sect. 2.1) and relate these to semantics in a gradual way: first syntactically to monadic typing (Sect. 2.2), then semantically in a type-directed way (Sect. 2.3) and finally in an effect-directed way using *graded monads* (Sect. 2.4) (from [16, 28]).

Our base language is the call-by-value simply-typed λ-calculus with constants, conditionals, and parallel composition, with syntax:

$$e ::= x \mid k_\tau \mid \lambda x.e \mid e_1\, e_2 \mid \text{let } x = e_1 \text{ in } e_2 \mid \text{if } e_1 \text{ then } e_2 \text{ else } e_3 \mid e_1 \text{ par } e_2$$

where k_τ are constants of type τ (k_τ of function type can produce effects). Throughout x, y range over variables. The par construct is considered only in Sect. 4; let $x = e_1$ in e_2 is treated as a simple abbreviation for $(\lambda x.e_2)\, e_1$.

Semantics. We mainly use a denotational-semantic framework: the meaning of an expression e is a value $[\![e]\!]$ in a mathematical domain, defined inductively over the structure of e. The meaning of an expression depends on both its free variables and its type derivation, accordingly $[\![\Gamma \vdash e : \tau]\!]$ is typically a value in the space of denotations $[\![\Gamma]\!] \to [\![\tau]\!]$. Free-variable contexts $\Gamma = x_1 : \tau_1, ..., x_n : \tau_n$ are interpreted as environments ranged over by γ. Conventionally these are products $[\![\tau_1]\!] \times ... \times [\![\tau_n]\!]$ indexed by positions but for our purposes we index by variable names written $\langle x_1 : [\![\tau_1]\!], ..., x_n : [\![\tau_n]\!] \rangle$. We write $\gamma[x \mapsto v]$ for the environment γ with variable x updated to value v. Finally, the space of denotations is often presented as a *category*. While this can be a unifying framework, it can impose additional overhead (*e.g.* the need for 'strength' of monads, Appendix A) so here we largely keep to a set-based special-case framework.

Correctness of denotational models is established here relative to an *axiomatic semantics* (equational theory)—a congruence relation $\equiv$ (on e), typically derived from an operational semantics (rewrite rules). A denotational semantics is *sound* when $e \equiv e' \Rightarrow [\![e]\!] = [\![e']\!]$, and *complete* if the converse holds. This extends naturally to equalities $\Gamma \vdash e \equiv e' : \tau, F$ relative to a type (and effect) derivation, and their interpretations $[\![\Gamma \vdash e : \tau, F]\!] = [\![\Gamma \vdash e' : \tau, F]\!]$.

We assume the standard operational and axiomatic semantics of the call-by-value λ-calculus for our base language (with β-reduction on syntactic values $(\lambda x.e)\, v \to e[v/x]$ and its corresponding β-equality). The axiomatic semantics of if and par are given in Sect. 4.2. The denotational and axiomatic semantics are specialised for particular notions of effect and effectful primitives.

2.1 Traditional Effects

Type and effect judgements take the form: $\Gamma \vdash e : \tau, F$ asserting that an expression e has a type τ and at most produces *immediate* effects F, in the context Γ. Effects F are taken from a set $\mathcal{F}$ and types have the form: $\tau ::= \tau_1 \xrightarrow{F} \tau_2 \mid \iota$ where ι ranges over primitive types (*e.g.* bool, int, void). Throughout τ ranges over types and F over effects. Function types give an anchor for the *latent* effects of a function, which arise when the function is applied. In Sect. 1, only immediate effects appeared explicitly, but we can see happyBirthdayMelody as having the latent effect of playing the music when called, but no immediate effects.

$$(\text{VAR}) \frac{}{\Gamma, x{:}\tau \vdash x : \tau,\ \bot} \qquad (\text{LET}) \frac{\Gamma \vdash e_1 : \tau,\ F \quad \Gamma, x{:}\tau \vdash e_2 : \tau',\ G}{\Gamma \vdash \text{let } x = e_1 \text{ in } e_2 : \tau',\ F \sqcup G}$$

$$(\text{CONST}) \frac{}{\Gamma \vdash k_\tau : \tau,\ \bot} \qquad (\text{IF}) \frac{\Gamma \vdash e_0 : \text{bool},\ F \quad \Gamma \vdash e_1 : \tau,\ G \quad \Gamma \vdash e_2 : \tau,\ H}{\Gamma \vdash \text{if } e_0 \text{ then } e_1 \text{ else } e_2 : \tau,\ F \sqcup G \sqcup H}$$

$$(\text{ABS}) \frac{\Gamma, x{:}\tau \vdash e : \tau',\ F}{\Gamma \vdash \lambda x.e : \tau \xrightarrow{F} \tau',\ \bot} \qquad (\text{APP}) \frac{\Gamma \vdash e_1 : \tau \xrightarrow{H} \tau',\ F \quad \Gamma \vdash e_2 : \tau,\ G}{\Gamma \vdash e_1\, e_2 : \tau',\ F \sqcup G \sqcup H}$$

Fig. 4. Gifford-Lucassen effect system for an impure λ-calculus, using semilattice notation (concretely they used sets of effects).

$$(\text{WRITE}) \frac{\Gamma \vdash e_1 : \text{ref}_\rho\, \tau,\ F \quad \Gamma \vdash e_2 : \tau,\ G}{\Gamma \vdash \text{write } e_1\, e_2 : \text{void},\ F \sqcup G \sqcup \text{wr}_\rho} \qquad (\text{READ}) \frac{\Gamma \vdash e : \text{ref}_\rho\, \tau,\ F}{\Gamma \vdash \text{read } e : \tau,\ F \sqcup \text{rd}_\rho}$$

Fig. 5. Effect-specific (derived) rules instantiating k_τ for memory access.

Early definitions of effect systems described a *lattice* structure on effects but rely only on effects forming a join *semi*-lattice, where the least-upper-bound (join) operation combines effect annotations and the least element annotates pure computations [9,18]. This was demonstrated for sets with union: ($\mathcal{F} = \mathcal{P}(S), \cup, \emptyset$). Originally, effects were considered for the polymorphic λ-calculus with type and effect polymorphism. The discussion in this paper is monomorphic. We use meta-variables for effects and types which may be instantiated, giving meta-level polymorphism.

Figure 4 shows a type and effect system for our base language, following Gifford and Lucassen's approach. We generalise from sets to an arbitrary bounded join semilattice $(\mathcal{F}, \sqcup, \bot)$. Figure 5 shows additional rules for an instance of the calculus which tracks memory accesses to memory regions ρ. This instance has additional types ref ρ and effectful primitives read and write with their respective effects rd_ρ and wr_ρ (note, these are derived rules, from (CONST) and (APP)). Figure 6 gives the usual (SUB) rule for *sub-effecting*, over-approximating effects with respect to an ordering [37] and an alternative syntax-directed (COERCE) rule.

2.2 Effects and Monads—Syntactically

We summarise Wadler and Thiemann's work which goes halfway towards a semantic unification of monads and effects [39]. We distinguish the notion of

$$(\text{SUB}) \frac{\Gamma \vdash e : \tau,\ F}{\Gamma \vdash e : \tau,\ G} \text{ if } F \sqsubseteq G \qquad (\text{COERCE}) \frac{\Gamma \vdash e : \tau,\ F}{\Gamma \vdash \text{coerce}^{F,G} e : \tau,\ G} \text{ if } F \sqsubseteq G$$

Fig. 6. Implicit and explicit sub-effecting rules.

syntactic monads (basically a type constructor, written M here) from semantic monads (written T following tradition) which model effectful computation.

Monads are a class of algebraic structure from category theory that have been found to provide a useful model for the sequential composition of computations that have various kinds of side effect, such as state, non-determinism, exceptions, and continuations [23, 24]. The idea is that impure, call-by-value computations can be modelled semantically by functions $A \to TB$ where A and B model input and output types respectively and TB is a structure[3] encoding the side effects which occur during the computation of a B output value. The operations and axioms of a monad provide an (associative) sequential composition $\hat{\circ}$ such that, given functions $f : A \to TB$ and $g : B \to TC$, then $g \hat{\circ} f : A \to TC$ with an identity (modelling a trivially pure computation) $\hat{id} : A \to TA$. Usual presentations of monads decompose the definition of $\hat{\circ}$. A more formal definition is delayed until Definition 1.

Wadler and Thiemann observed that (semilattice) effect systems and monads are *homomorphic*: they have the same shape and carry related information [39]. They show this via two languages: *Effect*, a λ-calculus with an effect system, recursion, and mutable references (for which Figs. 4 and 5 give a similar definition), and *Monad*, a typed λ-calculus for monadic programming without an effect system. The standard monadic approach to programming (such as in Haskell) introduces a parameterised data type M to encapsulate and encode effects, where $M\tau$ represents a computation that may perform some effects to compute a value of type τ. In the *Monad* language, this type constructor M is additionally labelled with a set of effects F denoting the (maximum) set of side effects which may be performed by that computation, written M^F.

The *Monad* language adds the following constructs for manipulating monadic computations, where (RETURN) constructs a pure monadic computation and (BIND) provides composition of monadic computations.

$$(\text{RETURN}) \ \frac{\Gamma \vdash_M e : \tau}{\Gamma \vdash_M \langle e \rangle : M^{\emptyset} \tau} \qquad (\text{BIND}) \ \frac{\Gamma \vdash_M e : M^F \tau \quad \Gamma, x : \tau \vdash e' : M^G \tau'}{\Gamma \vdash_M \text{let } x \Leftarrow e \text{ in } e' : M^{F \cup G} \tau'}$$

Effectful operations in the language are given monadic types, with state-using functions: read : ref $\tau \to M^{\{rd\}} \tau$ and write : ref $\tau \to \tau \to M^{\{wr\}} \tau$, which are composable with (BIND). For example, the following increments location r:

$$r : \text{ref int} \vdash_M \text{let } x \Leftarrow \text{read } r \text{ in write } r \ (x + 1) \ : \ M^{\{rd,wr\}} \text{int}$$

Wadler and Thiemann show that all terms e in the *Effect* language can be translated[4] to terms $[e]$ in the *Monad* language, with type-and-effect judgements

---

[3] Mathematically, T is an *endofunctor*, but languages such as Haskell (and the *Monad* language in this section) expose monads syntactically as *parametric type constructors* M; thus side-effecting functions have analogous types $\tau \to M\tau'$. We try not to labour either this distinction or that between types (often written A, B instead of τ, τ' above) and the categorical objects A, B which model them (more formally $[\![\tau]\!], [\![\tau']\!]$).

[4] We use $[-]$ for *translation* into another language and reserve $[\![-]\!]$ for semantic *interpretation* (denotation) as in the next section.

$\Gamma \vdash e : \tau, F$ of *Effect* mapped to $[\Gamma] \vdash_M [e] : M^F[\tau]$ of *Monad* where $[\tau]$ is defined:

$$[\tau \xrightarrow{F} \tau'] = [\tau] \to M^F[\tau']$$

$$[\mathsf{int}] = \mathsf{int} \quad \text{(and similarly for other base types)}$$

Contexts Γ are translated to $[\Gamma]$ by applying $[\tau]$ pointwise. For expressions e, we show (a simplified version of) Wadler and Thiemann's encoding for variables, abstraction, and application:

$$[x] = \langle x \rangle \qquad [\lambda x.e] = \langle \lambda x.[e] \rangle \qquad [e\,e'] = \mathsf{let}\, f \Leftarrow [e] \text{ in } \mathsf{let}\, x \Leftarrow [e'] \text{ in } f\,x$$

Variables are translated by wrapping them in the "return" construct $\langle - \rangle$, lifting the computation to a trivially effectful monadic value of type $M^{\emptyset}[\tau]$ to keep in step with the type/effect translation. The translation of λ-abstraction translates the body, places it within a (pure) λ-term in *Monad*, and finally wraps this in an effectless $\langle - \rangle$ similarly to variables, thus having type $M^{\emptyset}([\tau] \to M^F[\tau'])$ for effects F in the body of the function. For application, the function term e (say with effect F and latent effect H) and argument term e' (with effect G) are translated and bound to f and x respectively using monadic binding, giving a left-to-right call-by-value evaluation order of the effects. Thus, $f : [\tau] \to M^H[\tau']$ and $x : [\tau]$ by the typing of let and the overall term has type $M^{F \cup G \cup H}[\tau']$.

2.3 Effects and Monads—Weakly Semantically

So far, we discussed effect systems from a purely syntactic perspective. In this section, we interpret families of labelled syntactic monadic types M^F as a single semantic monad T, ignoring the effect label. This gives a semantics that is syntax- and type-directed. In Sect. 2.4, we show how *graded monads* provide a stronger *effect-directed* semantics, where effect labels are part of the semantics—*i.e.* each M^F is separately interpreted as a semantic object T_F.

The *Monad* language is based on a monadic denotational semantics (similar to Moggi's monadic meta language [24]). The translation from *Effect* to *Monad*, coupled with a monadic semantics for *Monad*, provides a monadic semantics for *Effect* (similar to a semantics for an impure λ-calculus [23]). The semantics of *Monad* is given by mapping the monadic let (BIND) and $\langle - \rangle$ (RETURN) constructs into the operations of a monad in the semantic domain. We first define monads, balancing both the categorical and programming language viewpoints:

Definition 1. *A monad* T *is an operator on spaces (here either categories, e.g. semantic domains, or programming language types) along with a family of constants* $\mathsf{unit}_A : A \to \mathsf{T}A$ *and a family of operations* $\mathsf{extend}_{A,B}$ *mapping from space* $A \to \mathsf{T}B$ *to space* $\mathsf{T}A \to \mathsf{T}B$ *satisfying the axioms:*

$$\mathsf{extend}\ \mathsf{unit}\ x = x \quad [\mathrm{M1}] \qquad\qquad \mathsf{extend}\ f\ (\mathsf{unit}\ x) = f\,x \quad [\mathrm{M2}]$$

$$\mathsf{extend}\ (\mathsf{extend}\ g\ (f\ x)) = \mathsf{extend}\ g\ (\mathsf{extend}\ f\ x) \quad [\mathrm{M3}]$$

Given functions $f : A \to \mathsf{T}B$ and $g : B \to \mathsf{T}C$, their composition, given by $g \,\hat{\circ}\, f = (\text{extend } g) \circ f : A \to \mathsf{T}C$, is associative (by axiom [M3]) and has unit as identity (by [M1],[M2]). This definition is the *Kleisli triple* form of a monad.

Remark 1. Mathematically, monads are endofunctors on the category of spaces of semantic values. On the other hand, programming-language monads are unary type constructors with associated polymorphic unit and extend operations. In Haskell, unit is written `return`, and extend is written '`>>=`' (with its two arguments reversed), called *bind*. These are presumed to follow the above equations.

Example 1 (State monad). Let $\mathsf{State}\,A = S \to (A \times S)$ for some store type S, modelling a mapping from a store S to a result value A paired with a new store. State is a monad with the following operations:

$$\text{extend } f\,x = \lambda s.\,\text{let } (a, s') = x\,s \text{ in } (f\,a)\,s' \qquad \text{unit } x = \lambda s.\,(x, s)$$

where $\text{extend } f : A \to (S \to (B \times S))$ and $x : S \to (A \times S)$. The extend operation 'threads' state through a computation. An effectful function, of type $f : A \to \mathsf{State}\,B$, is a *state transformer* (by uncurrying $A \to (S \to (B \times S)) \cong A \times S \to B \times S$, *cf.* small-step operational semantics reductions $\langle e, s\rangle \to \langle e', s'\rangle$ mapping terms paired with stores). The unit operation lifts a value to a pure computation where the state is unchanged (a trivial state transformer).

Here we give a type-directed semantics for *Monad*, mapping type *derivations* to denotations as functions (more generally, morphisms) from the interpretation of the context Γ to that of the resulting type τ, *i.e.* $[\![\Gamma \vdash_M e : \tau]\!] : [\![\Gamma]\!] \to [\![\tau]\!]$.

Monadic Denotational Semantics. For the monadic semantics of *Monad*, the *syntactic* notion of a monad represented by the type constructors M^F is mapped to an abstract *semantic* monad T (note there is a single monad T capturing the meaning of the family of type constructors). Thus, the interpretation of types is:

$$[\![\tau \to \tau']\!] = [\![\tau]\!] \to [\![\tau']\!] \qquad [\![M^F\tau]\!] = \mathsf{T}[\![\tau]\!] \tag{1}$$

We assume some additional interpretation of base types ι into suitable sets in the domain of the semantics (*e.g.*, $[\![\text{int}]\!] = \mathbb{Z}_\perp$).

The interpretation of type(-and-effect) derivations ending in (BIND) and (RETURN) rules are then (omitting the type subscripts on unit and extend):

$$[\![\Gamma \vdash_M \text{let } x \Leftarrow e \text{ in } e' : M^{F \cup G}\tau']\!] : [\![\Gamma]\!] \to \mathsf{T}[\![\tau']\!] =$$
$$\lambda\gamma.\,\text{extend } (\lambda v.\,[\![\Gamma, x:\tau \vdash_M e' : M^G\tau']\!]\,\gamma[x \mapsto v])\,([\![\Gamma \vdash_M e : M^F\tau]\!]\,\gamma)$$

$$[\![\Gamma \vdash_M \langle e \rangle : M^\emptyset\tau]\!] : [\![\Gamma]\!] \to \mathsf{T}[\![\tau]\!] = \text{unit} \circ [\![\Gamma \vdash_M e : \tau]\!]$$

The semantics for *Monad* resembles the desugaring of Haskell's **do**-notation into methods of the `Monad` type class. Seen categorically, the semantics requires some additional structure: the monad T must be *strong*. This is implicit in the category of sets and Cartesian-closed categories and is elided here (see Appendix A).

This monadic semantics for *Monad* (and thus for *Effect* via translation [−])
can be shown sound and complete with respect to the axiomatic semantics (due
to the strong monad axioms, see [23,24] with semantics on similar calculi).

Wadler and Thiemann showed the syntactic correspondence between the
types-and-effects of *Effect* and (annotated) monadic typing of *Monad*, and soundness results on their operational semantics. However they did not give a denotational semantics marrying effect annotations to monads—all labelled monadic
type constructors M^F are interpreted within a single semantic monad T (Eq. (1))
and hence lose the effect information F. While Wadler and Thiemann conjec-
tured that a general 'coherent' denotational semantics can be given to unify
effect systems with a monadic-style semantics, it was Katsumata who provided
the missing piece—*graded monads* [16]. These allow each syntactic type $M^F\tau$ to
be interpreted as a semantic object $\mathsf{T}_F[\![\tau]\!]$ in which only the effects represented
by F are modelled. Thus Eq. (1) is refined to $[\![M^F\tau]\!] = \mathsf{T}_F[\![\tau]\!]$.

2.4   Effects and Monads—Strongly Semantically via Gradedness

Graded monads provide a model of sequential composition for computational
effects similar to monads, but which carry, and can be refined by, effect information. A graded monadic type T has two parameters, an effect (say F) and
a type (say A as usual) written $\mathsf{T}_F A$. Note that we use superscripted effects
on syntactic monads representing effects M^F but write the effects of graded
monads as subscripts. Effects F are drawn from a (partially) ordered[5] monoid
$(\mathcal{F}, \bullet, I, \sqsubseteq)$ generalising a semilattice $(\mathcal{F}, \sqcup, \bot, \sqsubseteq)$. Here $\bullet$ represents sequential
composition of effects and I the trivial, pure effect; ($\bullet$) must be ($\sqsubseteq$)-monotonic.
The ordering $\sqsubseteq$ can capture both sub-effecting (treating a smaller effect as a
larger one giving a 'may' analysis for if-then-else) and super-effecting (giving a
'must' analysis)—see Remark 2. For if-then-else it is often convenient that $\sqsubseteq$ has
least upper bounds; we also return to this point later.

A graded monad structure on T provides (associative) sequential composition
$\hat{\circ}$ for all $f : A \to \mathsf{T}_F B$ and $g : B \to \mathsf{T}_G C$ such that $g\,\hat{\circ}\,f : A \to \mathsf{T}_{F\bullet G}C$ with an
identity $\hat{id} : A \to \mathsf{T}_I A$, constructing a pure computation.

Definition 2 (Graded monads [16,21], without ordering). *Let $(\mathcal{F}, \bullet, I)$
be a monoid. An $(\mathcal{F})$-graded monad T is a family of endofunctors $\mathsf{T}_F A$ (or,
in the programming-language view, an effect-annotated unary type constructor)
along with two families of operations (polymorphic functions): $\mathsf{unit}^I_A : A \to \mathsf{T}_I A$
and extension operations $\mathsf{extend}^{F,G}_{A,B}$ which map functions $g : A \to \mathsf{T}_G B$ to
$\mathsf{extend}^{F,G}_{A,B}\,g : \mathsf{T}_F A \to \mathsf{T}_{F\bullet G}B$, satisfying the following axioms (omitting type
subscripts) for all $F, G, H \in \mathcal{F}$:*

$$\mathsf{extend}^{F,I}\,\mathsf{unit}^I\,x = x \quad \text{[M1]} \qquad\qquad \mathsf{extend}^{I,F}\,f\,(\mathsf{unit}^I\,x) = f\,x \quad \text{[M2]}$$

$$\mathsf{extend}^{F,G\bullet H}\,(\mathsf{extend}^{G,H}\,h\,(g\,x)) = \mathsf{extend}^{F\bullet G,H}\,h\,(\mathsf{extend}^{F,G}\,g\,x) \quad \text{[M3]}$$

---

[5] Katsumata uses 'pre-ordered' but we simply consider $(\sqsubseteq) \cap (\sqsubseteq^{-1})$ equivalence classes.

A graded monad is a homomorphism (*structure-preserving map*) between a monoidal algebra of effects $\mathcal{F}$ and a monoidal structure for effect semantics. The axioms [M1-3] rely on the monoid axioms on $\mathcal{F}$ e.g. [M1–2] as diagrams are:

$$
\begin{array}{ccc}
\mathsf{T}_F A \xrightarrow{\ \ \mathsf{extend}^{F,I}\,\mathsf{unit}^I\ \ } & & A \xrightarrow{\ \ \mathsf{unit}^I\ \ } \mathsf{T}_I A \\
{\scriptstyle id}\downarrow \quad\quad [\mathrm{M1}] \qquad \searrow & & {\scriptstyle f}\downarrow \quad\quad [\mathrm{M2}] \qquad \downarrow {\scriptstyle \mathsf{extend}^{I,F} f} \\
\mathsf{T}_F A =\!=\!=\!=\!=\!=\!= \mathsf{T}_{F\bullet I} A & & \mathsf{T}_F B =\!=\!=\!=\!=\!=\!= \mathsf{T}_{I\bullet F} B
\end{array}
\qquad (2)
$$

The equality edges (double lines) explain the need for the monoid axioms of graded monads: for [M1] that $F = F \bullet I$ for all F and for [M2] that $F = I \bullet F$. The diagram for [M3], not shown for brevity, needs the associativity axiom.

Definition 3 (Graded monads, with ordering). *Katsumata's definition of graded monads includes the pre-ordering $\sqsubseteq$ and subsequently a family of morphisms, which we call $\mathsf{coerce}_A^{F,G} : \mathsf{T}_F A \to \mathsf{T}_G A$ for every $F \sqsubseteq G$ satisfying:*

$$\mathsf{coerce}_A^{F,F} = id_{\mathsf{T}_F A} \ \textit{(reflexivity)} \quad \mathsf{coerce}_A^{G,H} \circ \mathsf{coerce}_A^{F,G} = \mathsf{coerce}_A^{F,H} \ \textit{(transitivity)}$$

$$\mathsf{coerce}_B^{F\bullet X, G\bullet Y} \circ \mathsf{extend}_{A,B}^{F,X} f = \mathsf{extend}_{A,B}^{G,Y}(\mathsf{coerce}_B^{X,Y} \circ f) \circ \mathsf{coerce}_A^{F,G} \ \textit{(monotonicity)}$$

Example 2 (Graded state monad, appears in [27]). Example 1 showed the state monad $\mathsf{State}\,A = S \to (A \times S)$ in which all read and write operations are represented. We now refine this to a graded monad State_F in which only read and write operations expressed by F may be represented. Suppose S is the space of functions from a set of locations Loc, ranged over by ρ, to Val (abusively, we conflate the notions of 'region' and 'location' here.) Take effects $F \in \mathcal{F}$ to be sets of tokens $\mathsf{rd}\,\rho$ and $\mathsf{wr}\,\rho$, giving an ordered effect monoid $(\mathcal{F}, \cup, \emptyset, \subseteq)$. We refine State to $\mathsf{State}_F\,A = (\mathsf{R}_F \to \mathsf{Val}) \to (A \times (\mathsf{W}_F \to \mathsf{Val}))$ where $\mathsf{R}_F = \{\rho \mid \mathsf{rd}\,\rho \in F\}$ and $\mathsf{W}_F = \{\rho \mid \mathsf{wr}\,\rho \in F\}$ are respectively the subsets of Loc where State_F might read and write. The effect-graded operations are then:

$$
\mathsf{extend}^{F,G} f\,x = \lambda s.\,\mathsf{let}\,(a,s') = x\,(s|_{\mathsf{R}_F})\,\mathsf{in} \qquad\qquad \mathsf{unit}^\emptyset\,x = \lambda s.\,(x,s)
$$
$$
\mathsf{let}\,(b,s'') = (f\,a)\,((s \lhd s')|_{\mathsf{R}_G})\,\mathsf{in}\,(b, s' \lhd s'')
$$

The incoming store s of extend is restricted into substore $s|_{\mathsf{R}_F}$ for the reads made by x. Operator $s \lhd s'$ merges stores preferring the right-hand-side mapping for locations $\rho \in \mathrm{dom}\,(s) \cup \mathrm{dom}\,(s')$, which is then restricted by $|_{\mathsf{R}_G}$ to the substore of locations read by $f\,a$. Locations read by $f\,a$ use values in s' in preference ($\lhd$) to those in s. Finally the resulting store prefers writes from s'' over those in s'.

Note that $\mathsf{unit}^\emptyset$ is isomorphic to the identity as $\mathsf{R}_\emptyset = \mathsf{W}_\emptyset = \emptyset$, and so s there is the empty mapping. Hence any denotation in $A \to \mathsf{State}_\emptyset B$ is necessarily a pure function—useful for enabling various optimisations relating to purity.

Graded Monadic Semantics. Graded monads enable effect-directed semantics, where syntactic effect labels are incorporated as semantic objects; type-and-effect judgements are mapped to denotations of the form $\llbracket \Gamma \vdash e : \tau, F \rrbracket : \llbracket \Gamma \rrbracket \to \mathsf{T}_F \llbracket \tau \rrbracket$. This gives a monadic semantics for Wadler and Thiemann's *Monad* language, generalised to a monoidal effect system, where syntactic type constructors $M^F \tau$ are mapped to the (semantic) graded monad $\mathsf{T}_F \llbracket \tau \rrbracket$. The semantics of *Monad* is analogous to that of the previous section:

$$\llbracket \Gamma \vdash_M \text{let} \, x \Leftarrow e \, \text{in} \, e' : M^{F \bullet G} \tau' \rrbracket : \llbracket \Gamma \rrbracket \to \mathsf{T}_{F \bullet G} \llbracket \tau' \rrbracket =$$
$$\lambda \gamma . \, \text{extend}^{F,G} \, (\lambda v. \, \llbracket \Gamma, x \colon \tau \vdash_M e' : M^G \tau' \rrbracket \, \gamma[x \mapsto v]) \, (\llbracket \Gamma \vdash_M e : M^F \tau \rrbracket \, \gamma)$$

$$\llbracket \Gamma \vdash_M \langle e \rangle : M^0 \tau \rrbracket : \llbracket \Gamma \rrbracket \to \mathsf{T}_\emptyset \llbracket \tau \rrbracket = \text{unit}^I \circ \llbracket \Gamma \vdash_M e : \tau \rrbracket$$

Via the translation from *Effect* to *Monad*, this also provides an effect-directed semantics of the effectful simply-typed λ-calculus via graded monads.

The axioms of a (strong) graded monad provide a sound semantics, with respect to a standard β-equational theory, as shown by Katsumata [16].

Grading for Semantics-and-Analysis Co-Design. The correspondence between the effect annotations and the indices of a graded monad provides a kind of *co-design* principle for defining semantics and effect systems: start with a graded monad and follow the shape of a usual monadic semantics; an effect system for the term language emerges from the indices and the inductive definition of the semantics. Conversely, start with an effect system, say the one in the introduction for music. An effect-graded semantics then requires semantic operations annotated by each of the effect operations used,[6] with a structure that reflects that of the effect system. In this way, graded approaches aid a kind of co-design process between analysis and semantics.

This relationship extends to the equational theory of a language and the axioms of its underlying semantic structures. For example, consider the following equation (relative to a type derivation) of the *Monad* language:

$$\Gamma \vdash_M \quad \text{let} \, x \Leftarrow e \, \text{in} \, \langle x \rangle \equiv e \quad : \quad M^F \tau$$

This syntactic equality relies on the monoid axiom $F \bullet I = F$ to ensure that the types of the left- and right-hand side ($M^{F \bullet I} \tau$ and $M^F \tau$ respectively) are equal. Soundness of the semantics, with respect to this equation, thus requires that $\llbracket \Gamma \vdash \text{let} \, x \Leftarrow e \, \text{in} \, \langle x \rangle : M^{F \bullet I} \tau \rrbracket = \llbracket \Gamma \vdash e : M^F \tau \rrbracket$. The proof of this denotational equality uses the graded monad axiom [M1], which itself uses the monoidal axiom $F \bullet I = F$ (see diagram (2)). A proof search procedure (whether by-hand or automatic) can be guided by the link between the syntax of effect annotations and their corresponding indices (grades) in the semantics: the required semantic axioms are those which witness the syntactic axioms.

Terminology. Graded monads have been previously called *parameterised effect monads* by Katsumata [16] (relating to the work of Mellies [20]) and *indexed monads* [28]. We opt for the name *graded monad* here to avoid confusion with the idea of indexed monads in topos theory and the parameterised monads of Atkey [3] or *parametricity*. The *graded* terminology has recently become a popular name for this concept [21,36].

---

[6] Section 3 addresses the subtlety here that if-then-else is reflected with *operation* + in the music effect while Katsumata's graded monads use a *relation* ⊑.

2.5   Type-Directed and Effect-Directed Analysis and Semantics

As noted earlier, the semantics of an expression may depend on its associated type derivation. For example, in the presence of a derivation of $\vdash \lambda x.x : \text{int} \to \text{int}$, the term $\lambda x.x$ is interpreted as the identity function on $\mathbb{Z}$. We call these *type-directed* semantics or analyses (more precisely *type-derivation-directed*).

A type-directed semantics tends to simplify definitions and reasoning. For example, consider an untyped denotational semantics on a Scott domain satisfying $D \cong \mathbb{Z} + (D \to D)$ *vs.* a type-directed semantics where each type has a distinct domain, *e.g.*, $D_{\text{int}} = \mathbb{Z}$ and $D_{\sigma \to \tau} = D_\sigma \to D_\tau$. The former has a more complicated semantics, with injections on sum types and deconstructors to identify semantically meaningful terms, which are unnecessary in the latter.

Our notion of *type-and-effect-directed* semantics (or just *effect-directed* for brevity) naturally extends this idea to effect annotations. In such a language the apply function $\lambda f.\lambda x.f\,x$ has many effects and types, in particular every instance of $(\tau \xrightarrow{F} \tau') \to \tau \xrightarrow{F} \tau'$ for types τ, τ' and effects F. Any expression e of this type can be interpreted monadically as belonging to semantic domain $([\![\tau]\!] \to \mathsf{T}[\![\tau']\!]) \to \mathsf{T}([\![\tau]\!] \to \mathsf{T}[\![\tau']\!])$ for some monad T. Via graded monads, an effect-directed semantic domain refines this to $([\![\tau]\!] \to \mathsf{T}_F[\![\tau']\!]) \to \mathsf{T}_I([\![\tau]\!] \to \mathsf{T}_F[\![\tau']\!])$. So if we knew, for example, that F is the trivial pure effect I and the graded monad is such that $\mathsf{T}_I A = A$ then an effect-directed semantics could simply interpret e as a value in $([\![\tau]\!] \to [\![\tau']\!]) \to [\![\tau]\!] \to [\![\tau']\!]$. This was seen with the State graded monad in Example 2.

3   Control-Flow Effects and Monad Limitations

Section 2 developed, in tutorial style, the theory for effects expressed monadically, including grading (precise denotational models of types and effects)—but limited to the situation where effect annotations form an ordered monoid $(\mathcal{F}, I, \bullet, \sqsubseteq)$, expressing sequential composition. This leaves the additional effect operators $(+, \&)$ for alternation (conditionals) and parallel composition (which Sect. 1 argued were essential for modelling music) and the question of how to incorporate them into an effect algebra and graded semantics. We defer treatment of $(\&)$ to Sect. 4, and here focus on the rather interesting issues centred around the question of how well can monads capture conditionals—both semantically and in terms of relating an $(+)$-enriched effect algebra to monad grading.

We explore three specific issues. Section 3.1 examines how well monads can give a general semantics to if-then-else and similar control-flow operations; Sect. 3.2 shows that while Wadler and Thiemann's work only handles a semilattice of effects, Katsumata's graded monads use an *ordered* monoid of effects and which can very nearly capture $(+)$ as well as $(\bullet)$. These two issues turn out to be two sides of the same coin. Finally, Sect. 3.3 argues that certain operations augmenting the usual monad operations of unit and extend should be characterised as *control-flow operators* and thus merit being operations on the augmented effect monoid too. This all sets the scene for Sect. 4 where *joinads* (a specific extension to monads), graded by a control-flow algebra dubbed *joinoids* (augmenting monoids), complete the development.

3.1 (Graded) Monadic Semantics for Conditionals

Consider a denotational interpretation for (type derivations over) conditionals $[\![\Gamma \vdash \text{if } e \text{ then } e' \text{ else } e'' : \tau]\!]$ where e, e', e'' may be effectful expressions (in a simple system where effects do not form part of judgements). Following the denotational tradition, the denotation of a compound expression is some function of those of its sub-expressions, traditionally expressed for some $\underline{\text{COND}}$ as:

$$[\![\text{if } e \text{ then } e' \text{ else } e'']\!] = \underline{\text{COND}}([\![e]\!], [\![e']\!], [\![e'']\!])$$

Formally, our semantics interprets type derivations, hence is more accurately:

$$[\![\Gamma \vdash \text{if } e \text{ then } e' \text{ else } e'' : \tau]\!] = \underline{\text{COND}}([\![\Gamma \vdash e : \text{bool}]\!], [\![\Gamma \vdash e' : \tau]\!], [\![\Gamma \vdash e'' : \tau]\!])$$

for some $\underline{\text{COND}}_{X,A} : (X \rightarrow \mathsf{T}\mathbb{B}) \times (X \rightarrow \mathsf{T}A) \times (X \rightarrow \mathsf{T}A) \rightarrow (X \rightarrow \mathsf{T}A)$ instantiated at $X = [\![\Gamma]\!]$, the space of environments, and $A = [\![\tau]\!]$. Given that if-then-else does not bind variables, this can be written $\lambda(x, y, z).\lambda\gamma.\text{COND}(x\,\gamma, y\,\gamma, z\,\gamma)$ where $\text{COND}_A : \mathsf{T}\mathbb{B} \times \mathsf{T}A \times \mathsf{T}A \rightarrow \mathsf{T}A$. It is convenient to use the notation COND on computations and $\underline{\text{COND}}$ in semantic rules to avoid the clutter of γ.

In categories which have coproducts (sum types), and hence booleans $\mathbb{B}$, the semantics of effectful if-then-else can be simply *derived* from existing monad operations. Such categories (including our set-based framework) have a parametric operation[7] $\text{cond}_A : \mathbb{B} \times A \times A \rightarrow A$ with axioms: $\text{cond}(\text{true}, x, y) = x$ and $\text{cond}(\text{false}, x, y) = y$. By instantiating cond at $\mathsf{T}A$ to get $\text{cond}_{\mathsf{T}A} : \mathbb{B} \times \mathsf{T}A \times \mathsf{T}A \rightarrow \mathsf{T}A$, we obtain one possible definition for COND using sequential composition:

$$\text{COND}_A(x, y, z) = \text{extend}_{\mathbb{B},A} (\lambda b.\, \text{cond}_{\mathsf{T}A}(b, y, z))\, x$$

This derived semantics is *dichotomous*—it encodes the laws that if-then-else returns one of its branches (*i.e.*, if true then e else $e' \equiv e$ and if false then e else $e' \equiv e'$)—and *sequential*—it encodes the axiom (assuming fresh variable x) that

$$\text{if } e \text{ then } e' \text{ else } e'' \quad \equiv \quad \text{let } x = e \text{ in if } x \text{ then } e' \text{ else } e''$$

There are other reasonable non-dichotomous or non-sequential semantics we may wish to model, thus the derived model above is quite limited. Prolog-style backtracking provides a good example of a non-dichotomous if-then-else as both branches are explored in some fixed order (leading to non-commutative + operator on effects); we could even imagine a variant of if-then-else where the boolean indicates whether the then branch is explored before or after the else branch. Similar non-commutativity arises for case expressions with overlapping

---

[7] Categorically, a natural transformation, derived from coproducts with $\mathbb{B} = 1 + 1$.

patterns. Non-sequential if-then-else is exemplified in *"parallel if"* which satisfies the semantic property (for a system where non-termination is an effect):

$$[\![\text{if } e \text{ then } e' \text{ else } e'']\!] = [\![e']\!] \quad \text{if} \quad [\![e']\!] = [\![e'']\!] \quad (\text{and even if } [\![e]\!] = \bot).$$

Speculative behaviour (with software-transactional memory for rolling-back effects) is a non-sequential if-then-else. Non-dichotomous variants may also give a collecting semantics which captures computation *trees* instead of single traces—the derived semantics using cond_A can only capture a dynamic trace.

In the music example, we used operators $\bullet$, $+$ and $\&$ to model the effects of the sequencing, conditional and parallel language constructs. However, for full generality, we should use a ternary operator $?{+}(F, G, H)$ to capture the effects of conditionals. Nonetheless, sequential semantic variants of if-then-else require that $?{+}(F, G, H) = F \bullet (G + H)$. The $+$ operator can be defined $G + H = ?{+}(I, G, H)$ where I is the identity of $\bullet$. Most interpretations of if-then-else in the rest of the paper are sequential, but not all are dichotomous—Example 4 shows a non-standard 'synchronous' semantics for conditionals in music, where duration of if-then-else is the maximum of both branches. In short, we choose not to require conditionals to have the monadic derived semantics.

A language with effects and parallelism similarly requires a semantic model for how effectful computation are composed in parallel. While we noted *one* interpretation of conditionals can be derived from coproducts in the domain, there is no analogous derived structure to be found for parallelism since the 'obvious' operation $par_{A,B} : A \times B \to A \times B$ can only be the identity function (by parametricity). In contrast, an operation $par'_{A,B} : \mathsf{T}A \times \mathsf{T}B \to \mathsf{T}(A \times B)$ (called **merge** in the next section) for some monad T can perform an effect-specific implementation of parallelism, *e.g.*, arbitrary effect interleaving.

3.2   Effect Operators for Conditional

Until now, monads have been graded by an ordered effect *monoid*. But we now want to model richer effect operators such as that of if-then-else as above, with $F \bullet (G + H)$ or $?{+}(F, G, H)$ for non-sequential variants.

It turns out that a special case for $+$ can nearly be derived from the ordering structure. Katsumata writes: "When giving an effect system, it is desirable to have the join operator on effects (... [augmenting the] monoid structure), because we can use it to unify the effects given to different branches of case expressions." [16] Suppose all joins (least upper bounds) of $\sqsubseteq$ exist (not an existing requirement for graded monads), then we can define $+$ to be the join operator—thus obtaining an effect algebra $(\mathcal{F}, I, \bullet, +)$. Monotonicity of $\bullet$ (w.r.t. $\sqsubseteq$) becomes a distributive law $x \bullet (y + z) = (x \bullet y) + (x \bullet z)$.

A general effect-directed denotational semantics for if (with ternary $?{+}$ on effects) is then captured by a graded version of COND, to wit $\text{COND}_A^{F,G,H}$: $\mathsf{T}_F \mathbb{B} \times \mathsf{T}_G A \times \mathsf{T}_H A \to \mathsf{T}_{?{+}(F,G,H)} A$, lifted on environments $[\![\Gamma]\!]$ to $\underline{\text{COND}}_{[\![\Gamma]\!],A}^{F,G,H}$

$$[\![\Gamma \vdash \text{if } e \text{ then } e' \text{ else } e'' : \tau, ?{+}(F, G, H)]\!]$$
$$= \underline{\text{COND}}_{[\![\Gamma]\!],[\![\tau]\!]}^{F,G,H}([\![\Gamma \vdash e : \text{bool}, F]\!], [\![\Gamma \vdash e' : \tau, G]\!], [\![\Gamma \vdash e'' : \tau, H]\!])$$

We can then analogously construct a graded monadic version of the *derived* (non-general) semantics of if-then-else. Assuming the effect ordered monoid additionally has all least upper bounds (written $+$ as above) we set $?{+}(F, G, H) = F \bullet (G + H)$ and define $\mathsf{COND}_A^{F,G,H}$ by:

$$\mathsf{COND}_A^{F,G,H}(x, y, z) = \mathsf{extend}^{F,G+H}(\lambda b.\ \mathsf{cond}_{\mathsf{T}_{G+H} A}(b, \mathsf{coerce}^{G,G+H}\ y,$$
$$\mathsf{coerce}^{H,G+H}\ z))\ x$$

Remark 2. Note that if we instantiate $\mathcal{F}$ to be *sets* of effects with $(\bullet) = (\cup)$ and $I = \{\,\}$ then interpreting $(+) = (\cup)$ and $(\sqsubseteq) = (\subseteq)$ produces a traditional 'may' set-based effect system, while interpreting $(+) = (\cap)$ and $(\sqsubseteq) = (\supseteq)$ gives a 'must' form of effect system. This does not appear to be generally appreciated, and shows that Katsumata's graded-monad-with-an-ordering approach to effect systems captures both the $(\bullet)$ and $(+)$ operators introduced by the Nielsons.

So, amusingly, monads provide *one* (derived) semantics for conditionals, and semilattice-ordered-monoids provide *one* way of separating the effects for $\bullet$ and $+$, but neither is fully general. Just as we argued that not all semantics for if-then-else could be factored via parametric conditional, we also argue that not all $(+)$ operations on augmented effect monoids can be expressed as the least upper bound of an ordering $(\sqsubseteq)$ originally envisaged as sub-effecting. The required property is merely that $F \sqsubseteq F{+}G$ and $G \sqsubseteq F{+}G$ (we argued in Sect. 3.1 that $+$ may not be commutative, and we also do not require its idempotency). Multisets of effects provide an example: we may naturally define $(+)$ to capture addition on multiplicities, while $(\sqcup)$ captures maximum on multiplicities.

3.3   Control-Flow Operators

The semantics of Sect. 2 is abstract, using a (graded) monad to sequentially compose effects. The semantics can then be specialised to a particular notion of side effect (*e.g.*, state, exceptions) by instantiating the monad and providing effect-specific constants, such as with the state monad (Example 2) and the read and write operations. The denotations of these additional operations are necessarily of the form $A \to \mathsf{T}B$ (a *Kleisli morphism*) so that they can be composed via the monadic structure of the semantics. In a graded setting, these denotations introduce members of $\mathcal{F}$, *e.g.* $[\![\mathsf{read}]\!]_{\tau,\rho} : [\![\mathsf{ref}\ \tau]\!] \to \mathsf{T}_{\{\mathsf{rd}\rho\}}\ [\![\tau]\!]$.

We observe that any function with negative occurrences of the computation type $\mathsf{T}A$ (*i.e.*, left of a function arrow) cannot be the denotation of an expression. This is because the semantics generates only Kleisli morphisms and the interpretation of types only introduces T on the right hand side of an arrow. Instead, such operators are *effect control-flow operators*, *e.g.*, $\mathsf{COND}_A : \mathsf{T}\mathbb{B} \times \mathsf{T}A \times \mathsf{T}A \to \mathsf{T}A$.

From a different perspective, that of control-flow graphs, computation values $\mathsf{T}A$ correspond to closed basic blocks and functions $A \to \mathsf{T}B$ to open blocks with incoming dataflow which are composed by extend; unit constructs an empty block. By contrast, operations whose type has $\mathsf{T}A$ appearing to the left of a function arrow (*e.g.* $\mathsf{T}A \to \ldots$) correspond to control-flow operations. For example, the type $\mathsf{T}A \times \mathsf{T}A \to \mathsf{T}A$ corresponds to an operator which merges basic blocks for branching, and indeed bind (which is extend with its arguments flipped) bind : $\mathsf{T}A \to (A \to \mathsf{T}B) \to \mathsf{T}B$ is the primitive control-flow operator for sequential composition which appends a closed basic block to an open basic block, creating a new composite block.

It is clear from our definition that $\mathsf{COND}_A : \mathsf{T}\mathbb{B} \times \mathsf{T}A \times \mathsf{T}A \to \mathsf{T}A$ is a control-flow operator. Similarly, $\mathsf{cond}_A : \mathbb{B} \times A \times A \to A$ is a control operator when instantiated at $A = \mathsf{T}B$ but can also be a non-control operator: $e.g.$, when $A = \mathbb{Z}$ it is effectively a multiplexer. Due to parametricity, $\mathsf{cond}_{\mathsf{T}B}$ cannot however do any 'interesting control flow', it must either select one branch or another, while a function $\mathsf{cond}'_A : \mathbb{B} \times \mathsf{T}A \times \mathsf{T}A \to \mathsf{T}A$ of the same type but parametric only in A $could$ combine effects from both branches. Similarly, parametricity means instantiations of $par_{A,B} : A \times B \to A \times B$ cannot exhibit observable parallelism—this needs a function typed $par_{A,B} : \mathsf{T}A \times \mathsf{T}B \to \mathsf{T}(A \times B)$.

Control-flow operators also provide a link to abstract interpretation [6]. Primitive effectful operations in the concrete semantics are abstracted to effects in an effect algebra. Control-flow operators compose these primitive effectful operations in the concrete semantics and are abstracted to operations of the effect algebra. This yields effect monoids (or effect $joinoids$ later in the paper). Effect-graded semantics provide a form of concrete "correct by construction" semantic models, corresponding to abstract effect algebras.

4   Joinads and Rich Effect Systems for Control Flow

As discussed in the previous section, for richer languages (with parallelism, music, or speculative evaluation) we need richer semantic structure to model effects, one that provides control combinators additional to sequential composition—most importantly for branching and parallel composition. The structure of a $joinad$ does just this: extending monads with operations for modelling alternation (conditionals) and parallelism [29,32].

This paper introduces a variant of joinads (Sect. 4.1), based on the COND conditional operator of Sect. 3, instead of the classical formulation (Sect. 4.3) based on choose and fail operations. We name these $conditional\ joinads$—more fully "joinads with conditional instead of choose and fail". The choose-and-fail variant is convenient for capturing pattern matching (its original motivation) but the conditional formulation is more flexible and convenient here.

We repeat the development of Sect. 2 showing how conditional joinads provide a $type\text{-}directed$ semantics for conditionals and parallel composition (Sect. 4.2). We compare this with classical joinads (Sect. 4.3) which model conditionals similarly to the derived model of Sect. 3. We then introduce $graded\ conditional\ joinads$ to give a more precise $effect\text{-}directed$ semantics (Sect. 4.4).

4.1   Joinads and Conditional Joinads

Many monads are equipped with additional $combinators$ that provide different ways of composing computations compared to the standard sequential composition guaranteed by a monad. This is particularly so in source-level uses of monads on data types in Haskell. The original motivation for joinads was to capture common combinators for parallel, concurrent, and reactive programming (and then develop a new notation for programming with joinads) [29,32]. This is similar to our aim of capturing additional common ways of composing effectful computations. To quote the original work:

> "We identify *joinads*, an abstract notion of computation that is stronger than monads and captures many [of their] ad-hoc extensions. In particular, joinads are monads with ... additional operations: one of type $M\,a \to M\,b \to M\,(a \times b)$ captures various forms of parallel composition [and] one of type $M\,a \to M\,a \to M\,a$ that is inspired by choice ... Algebraically, [these] operations form a near-semiring with commutative multiplication." (Petricek, Mycroft, Syme [29])

The meaning of the operations differs for various notions of computation. For concurrency effects (the obvious interpretation), parallel composition means running tasks in parallel and choice is non-determinism. However, the operations also make sense for *parsers*— parallel composition means that two parsers both recognise an input, and choice means at least one parser recognises it [29].

The joinad structure appears in many libraries, for example, Mirage, a Library Operating System written in OCaml [19]. Mirage is effectively a large parameterised module, which when applied to modules representing the underlying hardware abstraction, can execute equally well as an application under Linux or as an entire OS on a bare-metal virtual machine. Its core is based on the co-operative threading library Lwt [38], which exhibits the joinad structure. In Lwt, processes are expressed monadically (using return and extend as usual) for their sequential parts; the <&> (called 'merge' here) and <?> ('choose' here) provide parallelism and first-to-arrive alternation respectively.

4.2   Type-Directed Semantics Using Conditional Joinads

As discussed in Sect. 3, the derived (graded) monadic semantics for conditionals is restrictive. Instead, conditional joinads are more flexible, allowing the semantics of conditionals to be parameterised. As an intermediate between monads and conditional joinads, we first extend monads with a conditional operation.

For brevity, we lift operations to environment-passing style, where for some $\mathsf{OP} : A \times B \to C$ then $\underline{\mathsf{OP}}_X = \lambda\gamma.\mathsf{OP}(f\,\gamma, g\,\gamma) : (X \to A) \times (X \to B) \to (X \to C)$. Such X are implicitly instantiated to $[\![\Gamma]\!]$ to avoid clutter.

Definition 4 (Conditional monad). *Given booleans $\mathbb{B}$ in the base category $\mathcal{C}$, a conditional monad extends a monad T on $\mathcal{C}$ with the parametric operation (natural transformation) $\mathsf{mcond}_A : \mathsf{T}\,\mathbb{B} \times \mathsf{T}\,A \times \mathsf{T}\,A \to \mathsf{T}\,A$ satisfying axioms of associativity (3, 4), commutativity (5), units (6, 7), and right-distributivity (8):*

$$\text{mcond}_A(\text{unit}_\mathbb{B}\ b, x, \text{mcond}_A(\text{unit}_\mathbb{B}\ b', y, z)) \tag{3}$$
$$\equiv \text{mcond}_A(\text{unit}_\mathbb{B}\ (b \vee b'), \text{mcond}_A(\text{unit}_\mathbb{B}\ b, x, y), z)$$

$$\text{mcond}_A(\text{unit}_\mathbb{B}\ b, \text{mcond}_A(\text{unit}_\mathbb{B}\ b', x, y), z) \tag{4}$$
$$\equiv \text{mcond}_A(\text{unit}_\mathbb{B}\ (b \wedge b'), x, \text{mcond}_A(\text{unit}_\mathbb{B}\ b, y, z))$$

$$\text{mcond}_A(\text{unit}_\mathbb{B}\ b, x, y) \equiv \text{mcond}_A(\text{unit}_\mathbb{B}\ \neg b, y, x) \tag{5}$$

$$\text{mcond}_A(\text{unit}_\mathbb{B}\ \text{true}, x, \text{unit}_A\ y) \equiv x \tag{6}$$

$$\text{mcond}_A(\text{unit}_\mathbb{B}\ \text{false}, \text{unit}_A x, y) \equiv y \tag{7}$$

$$\text{extend}_{A,B}\ f\ \text{mcond}_A(b, x, y) \equiv \text{mcond}_B(b, \text{extend}_{A,B}\ f\ x, \text{extend}_{A,B}\ f\ y) \tag{8}$$

The idea behind mcond_A is that it generalises the standard conditional cond_A : $\mathbb{B} \times A \times A \to A$ to a true control-flow operator with respect to effects. The two unit axioms (6, 7) are a restricted form of the standard if-β dichotomous behaviour of cond (that is, $\text{cond}_A(\text{true}, x, y) = x$ and $\text{cond}_A(\text{false}, x, y) = y$) when the guard and the unselected branch are both pure (*i.e.*, factor through unit).

The mcond operation provides a general operation for modelling the syntactic if construct from the source language. Given a typing-derivation for the term if e then e' else e'', a type-directed semantics is obtained by directly passing the semantics of sub-expressions to the effect control-flow operator mcond_A:

$$\begin{aligned}
&[\![\Gamma \vdash \text{if } e \text{ then } e' \text{ else } e'' : \tau, F \bullet (G + H)]\!] \\
&\quad = \underline{\text{mcond}}_{[\![\tau]\!]}\ ([\![\Gamma \vdash e : \text{bool}, F]\!], [\![\Gamma \vdash e' : \tau, G]\!], [\![\Gamma \vdash e'' : \tau, H]\!])
\end{aligned} \tag{9}$$

Proposition 1. *A monad* T *on a category* $\mathcal{C}$ *with coproducts (providing booleans* $\mathbb{B}$ *and the* cond_A *operation) is a conditional monad, where* mcond_A *is defined:*

$$\text{mcond}_A(x, y, z) = \text{extend}_{\mathbb{B},A}\ (\lambda b.\ \text{cond}_{TA}\ (b, y, z))\ x$$

The proof follows straightforwardly from the monad and cond_A axioms. This gives the standard derived semantics for conditionals.

Definition 5 (Conditional joinads). *A conditional joinad extends a conditional monad* T *with a parametric operation* $\text{merge}_{A,B} : TA \times TB \to T(A \times B)$ *satisfying associativity (10), commutativity (11), unit (12), and distributivity (13):*

$$\text{merge}_{A \times B, C}(\text{merge}_{A,B}(x, y), z) \equiv \text{map assoc merge}_{A, B \times C}(x, \text{merge}_{B,C}(y, z)) \tag{10}$$

$$\text{merge}_{A,B}(x, y) \equiv \text{map swap } (\text{merge}_{B,A}(y, x)) \tag{11}$$

$$\text{merge}_{A,B}(\text{unit}_A\ x, y) \equiv \text{map } (\lambda y'.(x, y'))\ y \tag{12}$$

$$\text{merge}_{A,B}(\text{mcond}_A(b, x, y), z) \equiv \text{mcond}_A(b, \text{merge}_{A,B}(x, z), \text{merge}_{A,B}(y, z)) \tag{13}$$

where map *is the morphism-mapping of the functor* T, *i.e., given* $f : A \to B$ *then* $\text{map}\ f : TA \to TB$, *and* $\text{assoc } (a, (b, c)) = ((a, b), c)$ *and* $\text{swap } (a, b) = (b, a)$.

Categorically, merge therefore witnesses that T is a symmetric monoidal functor with additional right-distributivity with mcond.

We use the merge operation directly for the semantics of the par construct:

$$[\![\Gamma \vdash e \text{ par } e' : \tau \times \tau', F \& G]\!] = \underline{\text{merge}}_{[\![\tau]\!], [\![\tau']\!]}([\![\Gamma \vdash e : \tau, F]\!], [\![\Gamma \vdash e' : \tau', G]\!]) \tag{14}$$

We now have a fully parameterised semantics for if-then-else and par via conditional joinads. For music, notes can be played in parallel; for concurrency, two tasks can be run in parallel (multiple threads) or using interleaved concurrency.

The axioms of a conditional joinad include the commutativity of merge (as in the original joinad formulation); this has pros and cons. On the one hand, commutativity provides a natural intuition for parallel execution (both true parallelism and non-deterministic interleaving). On the other hand, commutativity forbids various kinds of static scheduling by sequencing, *e.g.*, left-first or right-first scheduling, since sequential composition is typically not commutative.

Theorem 1 (Soundness). *Given a monadic semantics for the simply-effect-and-typed λ-calculus with a conditional joinad semantics for if (Definition 5) and* par *(Definition 5) then, for all e, e', Γ, τ, F:*

$$\Gamma \vdash e \equiv e' : \tau, F \quad \Rightarrow \quad [\![\Gamma \vdash e : \tau, F]\!] = [\![\Gamma \vdash e' : \tau, F]\!]$$

with respect to the following equational theory defined by $\equiv$ (we omit the typing), augmenting CBV β-equality:

$$
\begin{array}{rl}
(\text{IF}\beta1') & \text{if } true \text{ then } e \text{ else } x \equiv e \\
(\text{IF}\beta2') & \text{if } false \text{ then } x \text{ else } e' \equiv e' \\
(\text{IF-DIST-PAR}) & (\text{if } b \text{ then } e \text{ else } e') \text{ par } e'' \equiv \text{if } b \text{ then } (e \text{ par } e'') \text{ else } (e' \text{ par } e'') \\
(\text{IF-DIST-SEQ}) & \text{let } x = (\text{if } e \text{ then } e' \text{ else } e'') \text{ in } e''' \\
& \qquad\qquad \equiv \text{if } e \text{ then } (\text{let } x = e' \text{ in } e''') \text{ else } (\text{let } x = e'' \text{ in } e''') \\
(\text{PAR-PURE}) & x \text{ par } e \equiv (x, e) \\
(\text{PAR-SYM}) & e \text{ par } e' \equiv swap \, (e' \text{ par } e) \\
(\text{PAR-ASSOC}) & e \text{ par } (e' \text{ par } e'') \equiv assoc \, ((e \text{ par } e') \text{ par } e'')
\end{array}
$$

where in (IF-DIST-PAR) *b is pure i.e. $\Gamma \vdash b : \mathbf{bool}, I$. In* (PAR-PURE) *the left-hand side is a pure computation represented with a variable x thus $\Gamma \vdash x : \tau, I$. Further,* (IF-)$\beta1'$ (IF-)$\beta2'$ *have pure terms (variables) in the unselected branches.*

Proof. By induction on $\equiv$ and following from the conditional joinad axioms.

4.3   Classical Joinads

We introduced the conditional variant of joinads. The original joinad structure [29,32] has instead of $\text{mcond}_A : T\,\mathbb{B} \times TA \times TA \to TA$ two operations called choose and fail (also known as the MonadPlus type class in Haskell [10]) of type:

$$\text{choose}_A : TA \times TA \to TA \qquad\qquad \text{fail}_A : \text{void} \to TA$$

The choose operation models a choice between two computations. The fail operation creates a failing computation that is the unit element with respect to choose and choose must be associative, *i.e.* these two operations form a monoid on TA. Furthermore, merge must be right-distributive with choose_A and fail_A absorbing with respect to extend and merge, that is, applying extend to a computation that fails produces a computation equivalent to fail, and failure of one parallel branch makes both fail. Algebraically, this means that operations form a *near-semiring* with choose as addition and merge as multiplication [29]. Similar structure is shown in the work of Rivas *et al.* [35]. This guarantees various desirable syntactic equivalences when used for a language semantics.

These operations (together with their axioms) let us encode conditionals as:

$$\mathsf{mcond}_A(x,y,z) = \mathsf{choose}_A \ (\mathsf{extend}_{\mathbb{B},A} \ (\lambda b. \ \mathsf{cond}_A(b,y,\mathsf{fail}_A)$$
$$(\mathsf{extend}_{\mathbb{B},A} \ (\lambda b. \ \mathsf{cond}_A(b,z,\mathsf{fail}_A)) \ x)$$

Here, both branches are turned into computations that fail if they should *not* be executed (and succeed otherwise). This definition of joinads was inspired by ML-style pattern matching and so the fail operation represents a *commit point*. Given suitable definitions for choose and fail, the above definition of mcond *can* capture the derived (from extend and cond) monadic semantics, but is also rather more general in that it can also use a free joinad (and hence a non-dichotomous conditional semantics)—leading to a trace containing a (free version of) choice at each conditional branch, but where one of the branches is trivially fail.

Remark 3. For atomic/independent computations, parallelism can be modelled as a choice between the two ways of sequencing the computations (see Sect. 1, also Milner [22]) *e.g.* merge (for par) can be defined in terms of choose and extend:

$$\mathsf{merge}_{A,B}(x,y) = \mathsf{choose}_{A \times B} \ (\mathsf{extend} \ (\lambda a. \ \mathsf{extend} \ (\lambda b. \ \mathsf{unit} \ (a,b)) \ y) \ x)$$
$$(\mathsf{extend} \ (\lambda b. \ \mathsf{extend} \ (\lambda a. \ \mathsf{unit} \ (a,b)) \ x) \ y)$$

We might consider this as a candidate for modelling parallel composition, thus requiring fewer semantic primitives for a language with conditionals and parallelism. However, the above does not capture the semantics for our music language (where playing notes in parallel produces a different sound than that of any sequencing) or for languages with parallelism based on multiple threads. More flexibility is therefore provided by making parallelism a separate semantic notion via the joinad (or conditional joinad) merge operation.

The next section generalises conditional joinads to a *graded* form to allow effect systems to refine the semantics of conditionals and parallelism.

4.4   Control-Flow Algebras and Graded Joinads

Traditional set-based 'may' effect systems use a semilattice of effects, which we see as a special case of effect *monoids*. Effect monoids are a simple *control-flow* algebra, capturing just sequential control flow. Monads can be seen as an instance of effect monoids, but over endofunctors (type constructors) encoding effects. These syntactic and semantic descriptions of effects are unified via *graded monads* to give an effect-directed semantics (Sect. 2).

Section 1 defined effect systems capable of capturing choice and parallelism via a rich control-flow algebra of effects, as suggested by Nielson and Nielson.

We formalise this class of control-flow algebra below, calling it a *joinoid*. Both the effect systems of Sect. 1 and conditional joinads (Sect. 4.1) are instances of this control-flow algebra: at the level of syntax (analysis/types) and semantics respectively. However, the link between a joinoid-based effect system and its semantics (via conditional joinads) has only been loosely coupled and intuitive so far. This section introduces the *graded conditional joinad* structure (the joinad analogue of graded monads) to make this correspondence concrete, providing an effect-directed semantics for effect systems over a *joinoid* control-flow algebra.

Definition 6 (Joinoid). *Let $\mathcal{F}$ be a set with $I \in \mathcal{F}$, binary operations $\bullet$ and $\&$, a ternary operator $?+$ and a binary relation $\sqsubseteq$. Then $(\mathcal{F}, \bullet, I, \&, ?+, \sqsubseteq)$ is a joinoid control-flow algebra (joinoid for short) if, letting $F + G = ?+(I, F, G)$:*

- $(\mathcal{F}, \bullet, I)$ *is a monoid, representing sequential composition and purity;*
- $(\mathcal{F}, \&, I)$ *is a commutative monoid, representing parallel composition;*
- $(\mathcal{F}, +)$ *is a semigroup, representing choice between two conditional; branches*
- *with right-distributivity axioms:*

$$(F + G) \bullet H = (F \bullet H) + (G \bullet H) \qquad (F + G) \& H = (F \& H) + (G \& H)$$

- *all operations are monotonic with respect to $\sqsubseteq$.*

Definition 7 (Graded conditional joinads). *Given a joinoid on $\mathcal{F}$, a graded conditional joinad is a graded monad T for the ordered monoid $(\mathcal{F}, \bullet, I, \sqsubseteq)$ together with the following two parametric operations:*

$$\mathsf{merge}_{A,B}^{F,G} : \mathsf{T}_F A \times \mathsf{T}_G B \to \mathsf{T}_{F\&G}(A \times B)$$
$$\mathsf{mcond}_A^{F,G,H} : \mathsf{T}_F \mathbb{B} \times \mathsf{T}_G A \times \mathsf{T}_H A \to \mathsf{T}_{?+(F,G,H)} A$$

which satisfy analogous equations to a conditional joinad (Definition 4, p. 20, and Definition 5) but with the presence of the grades and where $\mathsf{coerce}_A^{F,G}$ commutes with merge and mcond to witness monotonicity.

Remark 4. Graded monads are a lax[8] homomorphism between a monoids of effects $(\mathcal{F}, \bullet, I)$ and monoidal structure over $\mathcal{C}$ (of composing type constructors on $\mathcal{C}$). Similarly, graded joinads are a lax homomorphism, given by T and witnessed by the graded conditional joinad operations, between a joinoid of effects $(\mathcal{F}, \bullet, I, \&, ?+, \sqsubseteq)$ and a joinoid structure over $\mathcal{C}$. Thus, the joinoid axioms are preserved by T. For example, &-commutativity $F\&G = G\&F$ is preserved by T as witnessed by the axiom: (where $x : \mathsf{T}_F A$ and $y : \mathsf{T}_G B$)

$$\mathsf{merge}_{A,B}^{F,G}(x,y) : \mathsf{T}_{F\&G}(A \times B) \equiv \mathsf{map\ swap\ merge}_{B,A}^{G,F}(y,x) : \mathsf{T}_{G\&F}(A \times B)$$

---

[8] Laxity means that the homomorphic map $\mathsf{T} : \mathcal{F} \to [\mathcal{C}, \mathcal{C}]$ from effects to type-constructors (endofunctors) on $\mathcal{C}$ has functions witnessing the mapping between structure on $\mathcal{F}$ and on $[\mathcal{C}, \mathcal{C}]$, e.g., $\mathsf{merge}_{A,B}^{F,G} : \mathsf{T}_F A \times \mathsf{T}_G B \to \mathsf{T}_{F\&G}(A \times B)$, rather than equalities, e.g., $\mathsf{T}_F A \times \mathsf{T}_G B = \mathsf{T}_{F\&G}(A \times B)$.

Example 3 (Graded non-determinism joinad). Non-deterministic computations can be modelled as computations that return a list of possible results. The standard monadic model is to use List $A = \text{void} + (A \times \text{List } A)$. Using a graded joinad, we can be more precise—and add an annotation that captures an *upper bound* on the length of the list resulting from a computation. Thus our graded type is $\text{List}_n A = \sum_{m \leq n} A^m$ which represents a list that has at most n elements.

The associated joinoid control-flow algebra is $(\mathbb{N}, *, 1, *, \lambda(x, y, z).x * (y \max z))$. Sequential composition multiplies the degrees of non-determinism of the two computations as does parallel composition. For conditionals $(?+)$ multiplies the degree of the guard with the maximum of the two branches. These annotations are consistent (sound) with the following graded joinad operations. We write $[v_1, ..., v_n]$ for lists of length n, with :: for *cons* and @ for concatenation:

$$\text{mcond}^{n,m,p}([], x, y) = [] \quad \text{mcond}^{n,m,p}(\text{true} :: g, x, y) = x \,@\, \text{mcond}^{n-1,m,p}(g, x, y)$$
$$\text{mcond}^{n,m,p}(\text{false} :: g, x, y) = y \,@\, \text{mcond}^{n-1,m,p}(g, x, y)$$

$$\text{unit } x = [x]$$
$$\text{merge}^{n,m}([u_1, ..., u_n], [v_1, ..., v_m]) = [(u_1, v_1), ..., (u_1, v_m), (u_2, v_1), ...(u_n, v_m)]$$
$$\text{extend } f \,[u_1, ..., u_n] = f(u_1)@...@f(u_n)$$

The unit operation returns a singleton list and extend concatenates lists produced by applying f to all possible inputs (indeed, $n * 1 = n$). The merge operation takes the cross product and mcond concatenates the results of either the left or right branch depending on each possible guard. Note that merge is commutative up-to isomorphism, or commutative where equality is order-agnostic.

The key point of this example is that the graded conditional joinad structure itself captures the essence of effect annotations. The definition is consistent with respect to the lengths specified in the effect grades. In some way, the semantics *already* entails the effect system for the language. This is made explicit next.

Effect-Directed Semantics Using Graded Joinads. The previous graded monadic semantics connected the structure and axioms of an effect system to a semantics for sequential composition, but did not capture parallelism or all possible forms of alternation. Graded joinads provide the opportunity for more fine-grained semantics and reasoning above conditionals and parallel composition. The following gives the graded conditional joinad effect-directed semantics:

$$[\![\Gamma \vdash e \text{ par } e' : \tau \times \tau', F\&G]\!] = \underline{\text{merge}}^{F,G}_{[\![\tau]\!],[\![\tau']\!]} ([\![\Gamma \vdash e : \tau, F]\!], [\![\Gamma \vdash e' : \tau', G]\!])$$

$$[\![\Gamma \vdash \text{if } e_0 \text{ then } e_1 \text{ else } e_2 : \tau, \,?+(F, G, H)]\!] =$$
$$\underline{\text{mcond}}^{F,G,H}_{[\![\tau]\!]} ([\![\Gamma \vdash e_0 : \text{bool}, F]\!], [\![\Gamma \vdash e_1 : \tau, G]\!], [\![\Gamma \vdash e_2 : \tau, H]\!])$$

As before, the semantics is defined over derivations, hence the left-hand side of each interpretation ends in the (PAR) and (IF) type-and-effect rules respectively. Effect annotations in the judgements correspond to the grades on the operations.

Theorem 2 (Syntactic soundness). *For all judgements $\Gamma \vdash e : \tau, F$ then:* $[\![\Gamma \vdash e : \tau, F]\!] : [\![\Gamma]\!] \to \mathsf{T}_F[\![\tau]\!]$ *where* $[\![\tau \xrightarrow{F} \tau']\!] = [\![\tau]\!] \to \mathsf{T}_F[\![\tau']\!]$ *and there is an interpretation for all base types.*

Proof. A straightforward analysis of the definition of $[\![-]\!]$.

Theorem 3 (Soundness). *Given a graded conditional joinad semantics for the simply-effect-and-typed λ-calculus with if then, for all e, e', Γ, τ, F:*

$$\Gamma \vdash e \equiv e' : \tau, F \quad \Rightarrow \quad [\![\Gamma \vdash e : \tau, F]\!] = [\![\Gamma \vdash e' : \tau, F]\!]$$

with respect to the equational theory for our language, in Theorem 1.

The syntactic soundness theorem (essentially that $[\![-]\!]$ preserves the typing structure and the semantics has corresponding grades) closes the gap between richer type-and-effect systems and semantics based on graded conditional joinads. It demonstrates the usefulness of the general approach advocated in this paper—a language with semantics based on graded conditional joinads comes equipped with an effect systems based on a joinoid control-flow algebra. Conversely, if we start with a joinoid effect system, the annotations can be used to determine the right structure of our semantics.

Example 4 (Graded music joinad). We tie the graded joinad discussion back to our motivating musical example with a simple graded conditional joinad model. As in Sect. 1, we use a joinad control-flow algebra to capture possible notes but not to capture their timing. Recall that music effects were drawn from terms defined by $\Phi = \mathcal{N} \mid \Phi_1 + \Phi_2 \mid \Phi_1 \bullet \Phi_2 \mid \Phi_1 \& \Phi_2$ where $\mathcal{N}$ is the set of all possible notes and rests, *e.g.* $\mathcal{N} = \{C, D, E, \ldots, rest\}$. We adjoin an additional effect ϵ representing a zero-length rest to be the identity for $\bullet$. Equality on Φ terms is defined such that the joinoid axioms hold.

Musical computations are modelled by tuples of a value, a duration d drawn from $\mathbb{R}$, and a *soundtrack*—a function g mapping from time within interval $[0, d] \in \mathbb{R}$ to sets of notes to be played at that time, returning $\emptyset$ outside that interval. This is given by the data type $\mathsf{Music}_F A = A \times \mathbb{R} \times (\mathbb{R} \to \mathcal{P}(\mathcal{N})|_F)$ where sets of notes drawn from $\mathcal{P}(\mathcal{N})$ are restricted to the notes appearing in effect annotation F, written $|_F$. Soundtracks g and g' are combined with a time offset d for g' using the operator $g + g'@d = \lambda t.$if $t \leq d$ then $g(t)$ else $g'(t - d))$.

We provide the following graded conditional joinad definition, with additional effect-specific operation play for modelling note-playing.

$$\mathsf{mcond}^{m,n,p} \ (\mathsf{true}, d, g) \ (v', d', g') \ (v'', d'', g'') = (v', \ d + \mathsf{max}(d', d''), \ g + g'@d)$$

$$\mathsf{mcond}^{m,n,p} \ (\mathsf{false}, d, g) \ (v', d', g') \ (v'', d'', g'') = (v'', \ d + \mathsf{max}(d', d''), \ g + g''@d)$$

$$\mathsf{merge}^{m,n} \ (v, d, g) \ (v', d', g') = ((v, v'), \ \mathsf{max}(d, d'), \ \lambda t. \ g(t) \cup g'(t))$$

$$\mathsf{unit}^\epsilon \ v = (v, 0, \lambda t. \emptyset)$$

$$\mathsf{extend}^{m,n} \ f \ (v, d, g) = \mathsf{let} \ (v', d', g') = f \ v \ \mathsf{in} \ (v', \ d + d', \ g + g'@d)$$

$$\mathsf{play}^n \ (n, d) = ((), \ d, \ \lambda t. \ \mathsf{if} \ 0 \leq t \leq d \wedge n \neq \mathsf{rest} \ \mathsf{then} \ \{n\} \ \mathsf{else} \ \emptyset)$$

For example, $\mathsf{play}(C, 0.75) : \mathsf{Music}_C \ [\![\mathsf{void}]\!]$ which is modelled by the unit value () of type void, the duration 0.75, and the constant function $\lambda t.\{C\}$.

As discussed earlier, there is an important design decision regarding mcond. Consider the expression if b then play$(D, 0.5)$ else play$(E, 1)$. In our semantics, the expression *always* takes time 1: if b is true, it plays D for 0.5 and then rests for 0.5. This is because our mcond operation *implicitly synchronises* the branches. This is only possible because we interpret conditionals using the joinad control-flow operator mcond that has access to computations of both of the branches.

Now consider the *derived* semantics for conditionals obtained via extend along with cond$_A$: $\mathbb{B} \to A \to A \to A$ instantiated at computation types $A = \text{Music}_F[\![\text{void}]\!]$. This leads to quite a different semantics in that we have:

$$\text{mcond (true}, d, g) \; (v', d', g') \; (v'', d'', g'') = (v', \, d + d', \, g + g'@d)$$
$$\text{mcond (false}, d, g) \; (v', d', g') \; (v'', d'', g'') = (v'', \, d + d'', \, g + g''@d)$$

Here, the total time of the if operation is the total time of the executed branch, meaning that the conditional, now being dichotomous, does not perform implicit synchronisation. By turning mcond into a to-be-specified control-flow operator instead of requiring the monad-derived semantics, we get additional flexibility and can choose between the two behaviours. (This example provides another practical use for non-dichotomous semantics for if-then-else.)

4.5   Classical Joinads—Grading and Control-Flow Algebra

Classical joinads (with choose and fail instead of mcond) can similarly be formulated as a control-flow algebra [29]. We briefly give the definitions here.

Definition 8 (Joinad control-flow algebra). $(\mathcal{F}, \bullet, +, \&, 0, I)$ *is a* joinad control-flow algebra *if* $(\mathcal{F}, \bullet, I)$ *is a monoid,* $(\mathcal{F}, +, 0, \bullet)$ *is a near-semiring and* $(\mathcal{F}, +, 0, \&)$ *is a near-semiring with commutative* $\&$. *This can be extended with an ordering* $\sqsubseteq$ *on* $\mathcal{F}$ *w.r.t. which operations* $\bullet, +, \&$ *are required to be monotonic.*

This definition captures the structure and axioms of a joinad. The first near-semiring requirement means that $(\mathcal{F}, +, 0)$ is a monoid, that 0 is the $\bullet$-absorbing element $(0 \bullet F = 0)$, and $(F + G) \bullet H = (F \bullet H) + (G \bullet H)$ (sequencing distributes over alternation). The second near-semiring requirement implies that $(\mathcal{F}, \&)$ is a semigroup, $0\&F = 0$, and & distributes over alternation.

Definition 9 (Graded classical joinads). *Given* $(\mathcal{F}, \bullet, +, \&, 0, I, \sqsubseteq)$—*a* joinad control-flow algebra—*then a* graded joinad *is an ordered graded monad for the ordered monoid* $(\mathcal{F}, \bullet, I, \sqsubseteq)$ *together with the following three operations:*

$$\text{choose}_A^{F,G} : \mathsf{T}_F A \times \mathsf{T}_G A \to \mathsf{T}_{F+G} A \qquad\qquad \text{fail}_A : void \to \mathsf{T}_0 A$$
$$\text{merge}_{A,B}^{F,G} : \mathsf{T}_F A \times \mathsf{T}_G B \to \mathsf{T}_{F\&G}(A \times B)$$

The operations are required to satisfy the joinad control-flow algebra laws (Definition 8), which are syntactically the same as standard joinad laws, but annotated with corresponding effects. We omit these for brevity.

This structure provides a useful effected-directed model for effectful pattern matching, in contrast to standard if-then-else conditionals. All examples of joinads [29,32] can be turned into graded joinads via the trivial (single element) joinoid control-flow algebra or by adding some suitable effect algebra which refines the existing semantics. For parsers, annotations may capture the degree of non-determinism (how many choices there are) and the length of the required input. In parallel programming, the annotations on graded joinads can estimate the maximal evaluation time (with $\bullet$ as addition; $+$ and $\&$ taking the maximum) or the minimal evaluation time (same, with $+$ as minimum).

5   Discussion

Kleene Algebras and Recursion. In our musical introduction, we introduced iteration (for loops) and modelled this in the effect system by a Kleene-star-like unary operator $\varPhi^*$. Recursion, or iteration, is another useful control-flow operator that we may wish to distinguish in an effect system and its semantics.

Similarly to conditionals, we can give a derived semantics for effectful recursion in terms of underlying operations in the semantic domain. Given fix which maps every $f : A \to A$ to $\mathsf{fix}_A f : A$, we can derive an effectful fixed-point: $\mathsf{mfix}_A = \mathsf{fix}_{TA}\ (\mathsf{extend}_{A,A}\ f)$ operator mapping $f : A \to TA$ to $\mathsf{mfix}_A f : TA$ (*i.e.*, a fixed point is taken over the monadic extension of f, *i.e.*, $\mathsf{mfix}_A f = (\mathsf{extend}_{A,A}\ f) \circ (\mathsf{extend}_{A,A}\ f) \circ ...)$. This is similar to the approach of Kleene monads [10]. Interestingly, replacing extend with the graded monad version in the above fixed-point definition forces an additional requirement on the effect algebra, that $\bullet$ is idempotent; that is, $f : A \to \mathsf{T}_F A$ is mapped to $\mathsf{mfix}_A^F f : \mathsf{T}_F A$ where $\mathsf{mfix}_A^F f = \mathsf{fix}_{\mathsf{T}_F A}(\mathsf{extend}_{A,A}^{F,F} f)$ where $\mathsf{extend}_{A,A}^{F,F} : \mathsf{T}_F A \to \mathsf{T}_{F \bullet F} A$ and thus $F \bullet F = F$. For some effect systems this would suffice, but for others we may want to introduce an effect element ω ('repeat forever') or traces via regular languages. We see this as a maxim: *give a semantic operator for every effect operator; sometimes these can be derived from existing operators but we should avoid building in this as a requirement.*

Following the philosophy of this paper, an abstract effect-directed semantics for recursion is best served by a control-flow algebra for effect annotations with F^* and a graded operation mfix_A^F which maps $f : A \to \mathsf{T}_F A$ to $\mathsf{mfix}_A^F f : \mathsf{T}_{F^*} A$. This provides a more general model for static analysis and semantics.

Other Related Work. Benton *et al.* previously defined an effect-directed semantics for state, similar in motivation to the work on graded monads but specialised [4]. This is used for precise semantic reasoning based on refinements from effect analysis. They show various effect-driven transformations, which are proven sound in their semantics. Their work gives a deep treatment to some of the themes we have touched on here more broadly. We focused more on the idea of generalising the treatment of control-flow operators in the presence of effects.

The work on *algebraic effects* and *handlers* provides an alternative approach, connecting effect systems and monads [15,34]. This approach focuses on effectful operations (read/write/*etc.*) and equations between them. This is a change of perspective to monads, which consider first an encoding of effects rather than the effectful operations. The work of Power and Plotkin starts with the effectful operations and generates an encoding as the free structure arising from the operations quotiented by their equational theory [33]. Recent work by Kammar *et al.* has used these approaches to give effect-dependent optimisations with a sound semantics [14,15]. That work can be similarly described as *effect-directed semantics*, but from a different perspective to that laid down by the line of work of Wadler-Thiemann, Katsumata, and this paper. The work on algebraic effects largely focuses on the *building blocks* of effects: the effectful operations and their algebraic theories. We have instead focused on the *scaffolding*: control-flow structures which compose effectful computations.

Coeffects, the dual of effects, which track how a program depends on its context or how it consumes resources have been similarly given a *coeffect*-directed categorical denotational semantics [5,30,31]. Coeffect structures tend to comprise some form of resource semiring with a semiring-graded *comonad* in the semantics [8].

Conclusions and Further Work. The semantic understanding of effect systems and their use for static analysis has rather diverged. Nielson and Nielson developed richer effect algebras, but left the proof of correctness (with respect to semantics) to users of these algebras. By contrast, Wadler, Thiemann, Katsumata *et al.*, (and Atkey via parameterised monads [3]) have developed models which link (semilattice-based) effects directly to semantic models, so that a model of a computation only includes elements consistent with their effect annotations.

We showed that monads and graded monads do not capture richer control flow (in particularly parallelism and some forms of conditional). We argued that certain operators in extensions of monads are *control-flow operators* distinguishable by their type, and provided a link between such types and control-flow graphs. We showed that joinads (monads extended with operations for alternation and parallelism, on top of the existing monadic sequential composition) provide a practical example of these control-flow algebras, and that they express concepts similar to those of Nielson and Nielson. Joinads can also be graded in a similar manner to Katsumata's graded monads, thus providing a framework where semantic models can only express values appropriate to syntactic effects.

Further work might explore other control-flow algebras that could be similarly "graded", beyond those discussed here, such as backtracking [17]. Another avenue is to establish the conditions under which the graded connection between syntax and semantics induces soundness, or even goes as far as completeness.

Acknowledgements. We thank Matthew Danish, Ohad Kammar, Shinya Katsumata, Jeremy Yallop, and the anonymous referees for their helpful comments. Any remaining errors are our own. The second author is funded by EPSRC EP/K011715/1 and thanks Nobuko Yoshida for her support.

A Issues Surrounding Monadic Strength

A monadic semantics for an effectful simply-typed λ-calculus requires that monads are *strong*. This captures the idea (implicit in the category of sets, but not in all categories) that a free variable may be captured by an outer λ-binding. Strong monads have an additional operation: $\mathsf{str}_{A,B} : A \times \mathsf{T}B \to \mathsf{T}(A \times B)$ satisfying various axioms (see [23,24]) which amount to saying that the effects encoded in the result of str are the effects encoded by the second argument.

The monadic semantics for (BIND) in *Monad* (shown in Sect. 2.3), omitting the type subscripts on extend and str, is then:

$$[\![\Gamma \vdash_M \mathsf{let}\, x \Leftarrow e\, \mathsf{in}\, e' : M^{F \bullet G} \tau']\!] \; : \; [\![\Gamma]\!] \to \mathsf{T}[\![\tau']\!]$$
$$= \lambda \gamma . \; \mathsf{extend}\; [\![\Gamma, x\!:\!\tau \vdash_M e' : M^G \tau']\!] \; (\mathsf{str}\,(\gamma,\, [\![\Gamma \vdash_M e : M^F \tau]\!]\,\gamma))$$

The str operation turns an environment $\gamma : [\![\Gamma]\!]$ and a result $\mathsf{T}[\![\tau]\!]$ into $\mathsf{T}([\![\Gamma]\!] \times [\![\tau]\!])$ for composition with extend $[\![\Gamma, x\!:\!\tau \vdash_M \ldots]\!] : \mathsf{T}([\![\Gamma]\!] \times [\![\tau]\!]) \to \mathsf{T}[\![\tau']\!]$.

Graded monads can be similarly strong with operation $\mathsf{str}^F_{A,B} : A \times \mathsf{T}_F B \to \mathsf{T}_F(A \times B)$, satisfying analogous axioms to the usual strong monad axioms [16]. The graded semantics is then the analogous one to the above.

We might consider adding an effect operation $\mathsf{S} : \mathcal{F} \to \mathcal{F}$ corresponding to use of strength in the semantics *e.g.*, $\mathsf{str}^F_{A,B} : A \times \mathsf{T}_F B \to \mathsf{T}_{\mathsf{S}F}(A \times B)$. However, an axiom of (non-graded) strong monads is that for all $x \in A, y \in \mathsf{T}B$ then $\mathsf{map}\,\mathsf{fst}\,(\mathsf{str}_{A,B}(x,y)) = y$ which for graded strength would imply that $\mathsf{S}\,F = F$. We accordingly exclude S from the effect algebra since it is necessarily identity.

References

1. Aaron, S., Orchard, D., Blackwell, A.F.: Temporal semantics for a live coding language. In: Proceeding 2nd ACM SIGPLAN International Workshop on Functional Art, Music, Modelling and Design, pp. 37–47. ACM (2014)
2. Amtoft, T., Nielson, F., Nielson, H.: Type and Effect Systems Behaviours for Concurrency. Imperial College Press (1999)
3. Atkey, R.: Parameterised notions of computation. Cambridge University Press. In: Proceedings of MSFP (2006)
4. Benton, N., Kennedy, A., Hofmann, M.O., Beringer, L.: Reading, writing and relations. In: Kobayashi, N. (ed.) APLAS 2006. LNCS, vol. 4279, pp. 114–130. Springer, Heidelberg (2006)
5. Brunel, A., Gaboardi, M., Mazza, D., Zdancewic, S.: A core quantitative coeffect calculus. In: Shao, Z. (ed.) ESOP 2014 (ETAPS). LNCS, vol. 8410, pp. 351–370. Springer, Heidelberg (2014)
6. Cousot, P., Cousot, R.: Abstract interpretation: a unified lattice model for static analysis of programs by construction or approximation of fixpoints. In: Proceedings of POPL, pp. 238–252. ACM (1977)
7. Flanagan, C., Qadeer, S.: A type and effect system for atomicity. In: Proceedings of PLDI 2003. ACM (2003)
8. Ghica, D.R., Smith, A.I.: Bounded linear types in a resource semiring. In: Shao, Z. (ed.) ESOP 2014 (ETAPS). LNCS, vol. 8410, pp. 331–350. Springer, Heidelberg (2014)

9. Gifford, D.K., Lucassen, J.M.: Integrating functional and imperative programming. In: Proceedings of Conference on LISP and Functional Programming, LFP 1986 (1986)
10. Goncharov, S., Schröder, L., Mossakowski, T.: Kleene monads: handling iteration in a framework of generic effects. In: Kurz, A., Lenisa, M., Tarlecki, A. (eds.) CALCO 2009. LNCS, vol. 5728, pp. 18–33. Springer, Heidelberg (2009)
11. Honda, K., Vasconcelos, V.T., Kubo, M.: Language primitives and type discipline for structured communication-based programming. In: Hankin, C. (ed.) ESOP 1998. LNCS, vol. 1381, pp. 122–138. Springer, Heidelberg (1998)
12. Jouvelot, P., Gifford, D.K.: Communication Effects for Message-Based Concurrency. Technical report, Massachusetts Institute of Technology (1989)
13. Jouvelot, P., Gifford, D.K.: Reasoning about continuations with control effects. In: Proceedings of PLDI 1989. ACM (1989)
14. Kammar, O.: Algebraic theory of type-and-effect systems, Ph.D. dissertation. The University of Edinburgh (2014)
15. Kammar, O., Plotkin, G.D.: Algebraic foundations for effect-dependent optimisations. In: Proceedings of POPL 2012, pp. 349–360. ACM (2012)
16. Katsumata, S.: Parametric effect monads and semantics of effect systems. In: Proceedings of POPL 2014, pp. 633–645. ACM (2014)
17. Kiselyov, O., Shan, C.C., Friedman, D.P., Sabry, A.: Backtracking, interleaving, and terminating monad transformers (functional pearl). In: Proceedings of ICFP 2005, pp. 192–203. ACM (2005)
18. Lucassen, J.M., Gifford, D.K.: Polymorphic effect systems. In: Proceedings of the 15th ACM SIGPLAN-SIGACT symposium on Principles of programming languages, pp. 47–57. ACM (1988)
19. Madhavapeddy, A., Mortier, R., Rotsos, C., Scott, D., Singh, B., Gazagnaire, T., Smith, S., Hand, S., Crowcroft, J.: Unikernels: library operating systems for the cloud. SIGPLAN Not. **48**(4), 461–472 (2013)
20. Mellies, P.A.: Parametric monads and enriched adjunctions (2012) http://www.pps.univ-paris-diderot.fr/mellies/tensorial-logic.html
21. Milius, S., Pattinson, D., Schröder, L.: Generic trace semantics and graded monads. In: Proceedings of 6th International Conference in Algebra and Coalgebra in Computer Science (2015)
22. Milner, R.: Communication and Concurrency, vol. 84. Prentice Hall, New York (1989)
23. Moggi, E.: Computational lambda-calculus and monads. In: Fourth Annual Symposium on Logic in Computer Science, pp. 14–23. IEEE (1989)
24. Moggi, E.: Notions of computation and monads. Inf. Comput. **93**(1), 55–92 (1991)
25. Nielson, F., Cousot, P., Dam, M., Degan, P., Jouvelot, P., Mycroft, A., Thomsen, B.: Logical and operational methods in the analysis of programs and systems. In: Dam, M. (ed.) LOMAPS-WS 1996. LNCS, vol. 1192, pp. 1–12. Springer, Heidelberg (1997)
26. Nielson, F., Riis Nielson, H.: Type and Effect Systems. In: Olderog, E.-R., Steffen, B. (eds.) Correct System Design. LNCS, vol. 1710, pp. 114–136. Springer, Heidelberg (1999)
27. Orchard, D., Petricek, T.: Embedding effect systems in Haskell. In: Proceedings of ACM SIGPLAN symposium on Haskell, pp. 13–24. ACM (2014)
28. Orchard, D.A., Petricek, T., Mycroft, A.: The semantic marriage of monads and effects. CoRR, abs/1401.5391 (2014)
29. Petricek, T., Mycroft, A., Syme, D.: Extending monads with pattern matching. In: Proceedings of Haskell Symposium, Haskell (2011)

30. Petricek, T., Orchard, D., Mycroft, A.: Coeffects: unified static analysis of context-dependence. In: Fomin, F.V., Freivalds, R., Kwiatkowska, M., Peleg, D. (eds.) ICALP 2013, Part II. LNCS, vol. 7966, pp. 385–397. Springer, Heidelberg (2013)
31. Petricek, T., Orchard, D., Mycroft, A.: Coeffects: a calculus of context-dependent computation. In: Proceedings of the 19th ACM SIGPLAN international conference on Functional programming, pp. 123–135. ACM (2014)
32. Petricek, T., Syme, D.: Joinads: a retargetable control-flow construct for reactive, parallel and concurrent programming. In: Rocha, R., Launchbury, J. (eds.) PADL 2011. LNCS, vol. 6539, pp. 205–219. Springer, Heidelberg (2011)
33. Plotkin, G., Power, J.: Notions of computation determine monads. In: Nielsen, M., Engberg, U. (eds.) FOSSACS 2002. LNCS, vol. 2303, pp. 342–356. Springer, Heidelberg (2002)
34. Plotkin, G., Pretnar, M.: A logic for algebraic effects. In: Logic in Computer Science, LICS 2008, pp. 118–129. IEEE (2008)
35. Rivas, E., Jaskelioff, M., Schrijvers, T.: From monoids to near-semirings: the essence of monadplus and alternative. In: Proceeding of International Symposium on Principles and Practice of Declarative Programming, pp. 196–207. ACM (2015)
36. Smirnov, A.L.: Graded monads and rings of polynomials. J. Math. Sci. 151(3), 3032–3051 (2008)
37. Talpin, J.P., Jouvelot, P.: The type and effect discipline. In: Logic in Computer Science, LICS 1992, pp. 162–173. IEEE (1992)
38. Vouillon, J.: Lwt: a cooperative thread library. In: Proceedings of ACM SIGPLAN Workshop on ML, pp. 3–12. ACM, New York (2008)
39. Wadler, P., Thiemann, P.: The marriage of effects and monads. ACM Trans. Comput. Logic 4, 1–32 (2003)

Last Mile's Resources

Chiara Bodei[(⊠)], Pierpaolo Degano, Gian-Luigi Ferrari, and Letterio Galletta

Dipartimento di Informatica, Università di Pisa, Pisa, Italy
{chiara,degano,giangi,galletta}@di.unipi.it

Abstract. We extend an existing two-phase static analysis for an adaptive programming language to also deal with dynamic resources. The focus of our analysis is on predicting how these are used, in spite of the different, ever changing operating environments to which applications automatically adapt their behaviour. Our approach is based on a type and effect system at compile time, followed by a control flow analysis carried on at loading time. Remarkably, the second analysis cannot be anticipated, because information about availability, implementation and other aspects of resources are unknown until the application is injected in the current environment.

1 Introduction

Today's software systems are expected to operate *every time, everywhere* within a *highly dynamic and open operational environment*. Also *software is eating the world* by pervading the objects of our everyday life, such as webTV, coffeemakers, wearable devices, cars, smartphones, ebook readers, and Smart Cities, on a broader scale. The operational environment of software systems, often referred to as the *context*, has indeed turned to be a *virtual computing platform* that provides access to groups of heterogeneous *smart* resources. The main distinguishing characteristic of these resources is that in principle they are always connected to the Internet, possibly linking to it through different access points, so to coordinate and interact each other. For instance, your smart alarm clock can activate your coffeemaker to prepare you a cup of coffee. In general, the Internet of Things scenario is the most significant example of this computing framework. In this vision, the physical resources (e.g. the coffeemaker) are difficult to tell apart from the virtual ones (e.g. your wireless network), in that they are potentially unlimited and "virtualised" in order to appear fully dedicated to their users. In addition, they can choose on their own *where, when* and to *whom* they are visible and in *which* portions of their context. A further important feature is that smart resources can collect and exchange information of various kind. According to their knowledge, smart resources can perform actions that also modify the environment.

A key challenge is designing software systems that run without compromising their intended behaviour or their non-functional requirements, e.g. quality of

---

Work partially supported by the MIUR-PRIN project Security Horizons.

C.W. Probst et al. (Eds.): Nielsons' Festschrift, LNCS 9560, pp. 33–53, 2016.
DOI: 10.1007/978-3-319-27810-0_2

service, when injected in highly dynamic and open operational environments. Programming these systems thus requires new programming language features and effective mechanisms to sense the modifications of the actual context and to properly *adapt* to changes. We refer to [2] for a comprehensive discussion on the software engineering challenges of the *open world assumption* and *adaptation*.

Several approaches have been considered for adapting applications according to the resources currently available in their running context, and to the form these resources assume. In this paper, we address this issue from a language-based perspective, by relying on ML_{CoDa} [5,8,9], a core ML with Context-Oriented Programming features [13,17]. Its main novelty is to be a two-component language: a declarative part for handling the context and a functional one for computing. The context in ML_{CoDa} is a knowledge base implemented in Datalog, and queries to the context return information about resources, as well as handles to access them.

The ML_{CoDa} context has been designed to hide the complexity of the operational environment and to provide an abstraction from low level details such as protocol handling, data marshalling, networking technologies, and so on. Consequently, it masks the heterogeneity of the virtual computing infrastructure to facilitate the design and the development of applications.

As usual, applications are assumed to know in advance the kind of smart resources that are possibly hosted in the environment. However, the resources that are actually present in the context and their form can only be discovered when the application enters the context and is about to run. Technically, each resource is supposed to come equipped with a resource manager and with a public API. An application can manipulate a resource through a *handle* provided by its manager, that also governs the life-cycle of the resource, its availability, etc. The handle enables the application to operate over a resource through the mechanisms declared by the API. Actually, this contains information about the kind of the resource, such as the available operations, their signatures etc. In particular, by querying the context, an ML_{CoDa} application can operate on a resource both *explicitly* by retrieving its handle, and *implicitly* by inspecting its current status through system predicates. For example, a home automation system controlling the house can query the alarm clock to retrieve the level of battery. In the ML_{CoDa} programming model, the running context consists of two parts: the *system* and the *application* context. The first one is provided by the ML_{CoDa} virtual machine through its API, while the other one stores specific knowledge of the application, filled in by the programmer. In the execution model the actual state of a resource, as well as its usage constraints, is completely known only at runtime. A relevant goal is therefore to ensure that an application that enters into a context finds all the needed resources and uses them correctly. This assurance can offer the basis for providing highly "reliable" service management for virtual computing platforms such as the Internet of Things.

In this paper we suitably extend the two-step static analysis of [9] to take care of resources. We call our proposal *last mile* analysis, right because full knowledge on the context is only available at runtime.

Technically, the ML_{CoDa} compiler produces a triple (C, e, H) consisting of the application context, the object code and an effect over-approximating the behaviour of the application. The third component H describes resource usage, independently of the possible context running the application, so it contains parameters to be instantiated when available. Using the above triple, the ML_{CoDa} virtual machine performs a linking and a verification phase at loading time: the last mile. During the linking phase, the initial context is constructed, by merging the application and the system contexts. Then the verification phase checks whether the application adapts to all evolutions of the initial context that may occur at runtime (a *functional* property), and whether it respects the constraints on the usage of the resources (a *non-functional* property). Only programs that pass this verification phase will be run.

To efficiently perform the last mile analysis, we build a graph $\mathcal{G}$ describing the possible evolutions of the initial context. Technically, we compute $\mathcal{G}$ from H, through a static analysis specified in terms of Flow Logic [14,16]. The evolution graph facilitates checking functional and non-functional properties, reducing them to reachability. The non-functional properties are similar to those expressible in CTL* [1], in that they predicate over nodes, i.e. contexts, and paths of $\mathcal{G}$.

This paper is organised as follows. The next section intuitively introduces ML_{CoDa} and our approach, with the help of some illustrative examples. The syntax and the operational semantics of our extension of ML_{CoDa} are formally given in Sect. 3. The next two sections describe our two-phase static analysis: Sect. 4 presents the type and effect system, while Sect. 5 presents the loading time analysis. Section 6, summarises our results and discusses some future work.

2 An Example

Consider a mobile application used for accessing to some databases of a company. The vendors, among which Jane and Bob, can access the databases from both inside and outside the office. The access control policies are part of the context of the application, so they are stored as Datalog facts and predicates. For example, the following facts specify which databases Bob and Jane can access, whereas the predicate allows an administrator to grant permissions:

```
has_auth(Bob,DB1).
has_auth(Jane,DB1).
has_auth(Jane,DB2).
has_auth(x,db) ← delegate(z,x,db), is_admin(z)
```

The context typically includes other information ranging on a wide collection, e.g. users, administrators, location of users and company offices, information about the company ICT services, etc. Also, the context contains information about the application state, e.g. the application is connected to the database through the company intranet or through an external proxy.

The following ML_{CoDa} code implements a simple application which accesses a database and performs a query to retrieve data about customers. The execution depends on the location and on the capabilities of the user: when inside the office, the user can directly connect to and query the database. Otherwise, the communication exploits a proxy which allows getting the database handle.

```
1  fun main () =
2    let records = (table){
3      ← office(),current_usr(name),has_auth(name,handle).
4        let c = open_db(handle) in
5          query(c, select * from table)
6      ← ¬office(),current_usr(name),has_auth(name,handle),
7        proxy(ip),crypto_key(k).
8        let chan = connect(ip) in
9        let c = get_db(chan) in
10       let data = crypto_query(c, k, select * from table) in
11         decrypt(k, data)
12   } in let result =  #(records customers) in
13       display(result);
14       let balance_customer = choose_customer(result)
15       let socket = connect(server1) in
16         write(socket, balance_customer)
```

The core of the snippet above is the behavioural variation (lines 2–11) bound to records that downloads the table of customers. The behavioural variation is a construct similar to pattern matching where goals replace patterns and whose execution triggers a dispatching mechanism. In our case, there are two alternatives which depend on the location and on the capabilities of the current user. Note that every resource available to the application is only accessible through a handle provided by the context and only manipulated through system functions provided by the API. As an example, when outside the office the IP address of an available proxy is retrieved by the predicate proxy that binds the handle to the variable ip. Then the application calls the API function connect to establish a communication through chan. By exploiting this channel the application gets a handle to the database (the API function get_db at line 9) in order to obtain the required data. Note that the third argument of the call to crypto_query is a lambda expression (in a sugared syntax) that invokes another API function select-from (as common, we assume that the cryptographic primitives are supplied by the system). Other resources occur in the snippet above: the database connection c at line 4, a cryptographic key k at line 7, the address and a connection to the server1 at line 15. Other API functions are: open_db at line 4, query at line 5, decrypt at line 11 and write at line 16. (Note that at line 14 we assume that the function choose_customer interactively asks the name of the customer to the user.)

To dynamically update the context, we use the constructs tell and retract, that add and remove Datalog facts, respectively. For example, the following code transfers the right to access the database DB2 from Jane to Bob:

```
retract has_auth(Jane,DB2)
tell has_auth(Bob,DB2)
```

An application fails to adapt to a context (*functional failure*), when the dispatching mechanism fails. Another kind of failure happens when an application does not manipulate resources as expected (*non-functional failure*).

As an example of non-functional failure, assume that the company at a certain point decides to protect data about its customers. To do that, it constraints a vendor's application to open no further connections once connected to the company proxy, when out of the office — inside, a firewall is assumed to do the job. The application above violates this constraint because it computes the balance of a customer and sends it to `server1`.

Our two-phase static analysis prevents programs from experiencing either kind of failures. It consists of a type and effect system at compile time and of a control flow analysis at loading time.

The compilation results in a triple (C_p, e, H) made of the application context, the object code and an effect. Types are (almost) standard, and H is an over-approximation, called *history expression*, of the actual runtime behaviour of e. The effect abstractly represents the changes and the queries performed on the context and the invocations to the API functions at runtime.

For example, the type of function `main` is `unit` $\rightarrow$ `unit`, and the history expression of the fragment between lines 6 and 11 is

$$H = ask\, G \cdot connect(address)\langle H_c\rangle \cdot get\_db(channel)\langle H_g\rangle \cdot$$
$$crypto\_query(database)\langle H_q\rangle \cdot decrypt(key)\langle H_k\rangle$$

where $ask\, G$ represents (a call to the Datalog deduction machinery on) the goal in lines 6 and 7, followed by four abstract calls, corresponding to the API invocations in lines 8–11 ($\cdot$ stands for sequential composition). The abstract calls have the form $f(k)\langle H\rangle$, where k is the kind of the resource affected by f and the history expression H is its latent effect as declared by the API. For example, $get\_db(channel)\langle H_g\rangle$ corresponds to the invocation at line 9, and indicates that the resource is a channel, and that H_g is the latent effect of the system function `get_db`. Note that the function f changes the resource state *and* the context, e.g. through a `tell/retract`. Consequently, the latent effect registers these modifications. Indeed, most likely H_g will contain an element *tell connected(Jane, DB2)* to record in the context that the system function connected the current user to the selected database, say Jane to DB2.

At loading time, the virtual machine of ML_{CoDa} performs two steps: linking and verification. The first step links the API to its actual implementation, and it constructs the initial context C, by combining the one of the application C_p with the system context that includes information on the actual state of the system, e.g. available resources and their usage constraints. Of course, the context C is checked for consistency. Then our last mile verification begins: it checks whether no functional failure occurs, i.e. whether the application adapts to all evolutions of C that may occur at runtime. And then it checks non-functional failures, i.e. whether resources are used in accordance with the rules established by the system that loads the program. Only those which pass the verification will be run. To do that conveniently and efficiently, we build a graph $\mathcal{G}$ describing the

Fig. 1. Two evolution graphs showing a functional failure (top) and a non-functional failure (bottom) (Colour figure online)

possible evolutions of the initial context C, through a control flow analysis of the history expression H. The nodes of $\mathcal{G}$ over-approximate the context arising at runtime and its edges are labelled by the action which carried out the context change. A distinguished aspect of our analysis is that it depends on the initial context C, right because our application may behave correctly in one context and fail in another.

The example above is rather simple, but suffices to show a functional and a non-functional failure. For the first, consider Alan who runs the application above. The graph shown in Fig. 1 (top) results from our analysis, where C_a is the initial context. Since he is not authorised to access the company database, the behavioural variation records fails (the predicate has_auth is false in C_a). The failure is shown in the graph of Fig. 1 because the failure node (dotted and in red in the pdf) ✻ is reachable.

A non-functional failure occurs when Jane runs the application outside the office. The initial context now is different from C_a, and the graph in Fig. 1 (bottom) displays how this context evolves when the API calls in the code are carried out. Since Jane is outside, the second case of the behavioural variation records is selected. The application violates the constraint informally introduced above (once connected from outside, no other connections are allowed), because the function connect attempts to establish a new connection to server1 at line 15 (represented by the dotted edge and the node, drawn in blue in the pdf).

3   ML$_{\text{CoDa}}$ with Resources

We briefly define the syntax and the operational semantics of our extension of ML$_{\text{CoDa}}$ to explicitly deal with resources; we mainly concentrate on its peculiar constructs, as those inherited by Datalog and ML are standard.

Syntax. ML$_{\text{CoDa}}$ consists of two sub-components: a Datalog with negation to describe the context and a core ML extended with COP features.

The Datalog part is standard: a program is a set of facts and clauses. We assume that each program is safe [7]; to deal with negation, we adopt *Stratified Datalog* under the Closed World Assumption.

The functional part inherits most of the ML constructs. Besides the usual ones, our values include Datalog facts F, behavioural variations and resource handles r. Also, we introduce the set $\tilde{x} \in DynVar$ of *parameters*, i.e. variables assuming values depending on the properties of the running context, while $x, y \in Var$ are standard identifiers, disjoint from parameters. Our COP constructs include behavioural variations $(x)\{Va\}$, each consisting of a variation Va, i.e. a list $G_1.e_1, \ldots, G_n.e_n$ of expressions e_i guarded by Datalog goals G_i (x possibly free in e_i). At runtime, the first goal G_i satisfied by the context determines the expression e_i to be selected (*dispatching*). The *dlet* construct implements the context-dependent binding of a parameter $\tilde{x}$ to a variation Va. The *tell/retract* constructs update the context by asserting/retracting facts. The append operator $e_1 \cup e_2$ concatenates behavioural variations, so allowing for dynamic composition. The application of a behavioural variation $\#(e_1, e_2)$ applies e_1 to its argument e_2. To do so, the dispatching mechanism is triggered to query the context and to select from e_1 the expression to run, if any. We assume that the programmer can invoke a set of functions provided by the API, by writing $f(e_1, \ldots, e_n)$. The syntax follows:

$$\tilde{x} \in DynVar \ (Var \cap DynVar = \emptyset) \quad C, C_p \in Context \quad r \in Res \quad f \in API$$
$$Va ::= G.e \mid G.e, Va$$
$$v ::= c \mid \lambda_y x.e \mid (x)\{Va\} \mid F \mid r$$
$$e ::= v \mid x \mid \tilde{x} \mid e_1 e_2 \mid let \ x = e_1 \ in \ e_2 \mid if \ e_1 \ then \ e_2 \ else \ e_3 \mid$$
$$dlet \ \tilde{x} = e_1 \ when \ G \ in \ e_2 \mid tell(e_1) \mid retract(e_1) \mid e_1 \cup e_2 \mid \#(e_1, e_2) \mid$$
$$f(e_1, \ldots, e_n)$$

Semantics. For the Datalog evaluation, we adopt the top-down standard semantics for stratified programs [7]. Given a context $C \in Context$ and a goal G, $C \vDash G \ with \ \theta$ means that the goal G, under the substitution θ replacing constants for variables, is satisfied in the context C.

The small-step operational semantics of ML_{CoDa} is defined for expressions with no free variables, but possibly with free parameters, allowing for openness. For that, we have an environment $\rho : DynVar \to Va$, mapping parameters to variations. A transition $\rho \vdash C, e \to C', e'$ says that in the environment ρ, the expression e is evaluated in the context C and reduces to e' changing C to C'. We assume that the initial configuration is $\rho_0 \vdash C, e_p$ where ρ_0 contains the bindings for all system parameters, and C results from linking the system and the application contexts.

Figure 2 shows the inductive definitions of the reduction rules for the constructs typical of ML_{CoDa}; the other ones are standard, and such are the congruence rules that reduce subexpressions, e.g. $\rho \vdash C, tell(e) \to C', tell(e')$ if $\rho \vdash C, e \to C', e'$. See [11] for full definitions. Below, we briefly comment on the rules displayed.

The rule for $tell(e)/retract(e)$ evaluates the expression e until it reduces to a fact F, which is a value of ML_{CoDa}. Then, the evaluation yields the unit value () and a new context C', obtained from C by adding/removing F. The following

(TELL1)
$$\frac{\rho \vdash C,\, e \to C',\, e'}{\rho \vdash C,\, tell(e) \to C',\, tell(e')}$$

(TELL2)
$$\overline{\rho \vdash C,\, tell(F) \to C \cup \{F\},\, ()}$$

(RETRACT1)
$$\frac{\rho \vdash C,\, e \to C',\, e'}{\rho \vdash C,\, retract(e) \to C',\, retract(e')}$$

(RETRACT2)
$$\overline{\rho \vdash C,\, retract(F) \to C\backslash\{F\},\, ()}$$

(DLET1)
$$\frac{\rho[G.e_1, \rho(\tilde{x})/\tilde{x}] \vdash C,\, e_2 \to C',\, e_2'}{\rho \vdash C,\, dlet\ \tilde{x} = e_1\ when\ G\ in\ e_2 \to C',\, dlet\ \tilde{x} = e_1\ when\ G\ in\ e_2'}$$

(DLET2)
$$\overline{\rho \vdash C,\, dlet\ \tilde{x} = e_1\ when\ G\ in\ v \to C,\, v}$$

(PAR)
$$\frac{\rho(\tilde{x}) = Va \quad dsp(C, Va) = (e,\, \{\,\overrightarrow{\overline{c}\,/\,\overrightarrow{y}}\})^\frown}{\rho \vdash C,\, \tilde{x} \to C,\, e\{\overrightarrow{\overline{c}\,/\,\overrightarrow{y}}\}^\frown}$$

(APPEND1)
$$\frac{\rho \vdash C,\, e_1 \to C',\, e_1'}{\rho \vdash C,\, e_1 \cup e_2 \to C',\, e_1' \cup e_2}$$

(APPEND2)
$$\frac{\rho \vdash C,\, e_2 \to C',\, e_2'}{\rho \vdash C,\, (x)\{Va_1\} \cup e_2 \to C',\, (x)\{Va_1\} \cup e_2'}$$

(APPEND3)
$$\frac{z\ fresh}{\rho \vdash C,\, (x)\{Va_1\} \cup (y)\{Va_2\} \to C,\, (z)\{Va_1\{z/x\},\, Va_2\{z/y\}\}}$$

(VAAPP1)
$$\frac{\rho \vdash C,\, e_1 \to C',\, e_1'}{\rho \vdash C,\, \#(e_1, e_2) \to C',\, \#(e_1', e_2)}$$

(VAAPP2)
$$\frac{\rho \vdash C,\, e_2 \to C',\, e_2'}{\rho \vdash C,\, \#((x)\{Va\}, e_2) \to C',\, \#((x)\{Va\}, e_2')}$$

(VAAPP3)
$$\frac{dsp(C, Va) = (e,\, \{\overrightarrow{\overline{c}\,/\,\overrightarrow{y}}\})^\frown}{\rho \vdash C,\, \#((x)\{Va\}, v) \to C,\, e\{v/x,\, \overrightarrow{\overline{c}\,/\,\overrightarrow{y}}\}^\frown}$$

(RES1)
$$\frac{\rho \vdash C, e_i \to C', e_i'}{\rho \vdash C,\, f(v_1, \ldots, e_i, \ldots, e_n) \to C',\, f(v_1, \ldots, e_i', \ldots, e_n)}$$

(RES2)
$$\frac{v = syscall(f, r, v_2, \ldots, v_n)}{\rho \vdash C,\, f(r, v_2, \ldots, v_n) \to C', v}$$

Fig. 2. The reduction rules for the constructs peculiar of ML$_{\text{CoDa}}$

example shows the reduction of a *tell* construct, where we apply the function $foo = \lambda x.\ if\ e_1\ then\ F_2\ else\ F_3$ to unit, assuming that e_1 reduces to false without changing the context:

$$\rho \vdash C,\, \texttt{tell(foo ())} \to^* C,\, \texttt{tell(}F_3\texttt{)} \to C \cup \{F_3\},\, ()$$

The rules (DLET1) and (DLET2) for the construct *dlet*, and the rule (PAR) for parameters implement our context-dependent binding. To simplify the technical development we assume here that e_1 contains no parameters. The rule (DLET1) extends the environment ρ by appending $G.e_1$ in front of the existent binding for $\tilde{x}$. Then, e_2 is evaluated under the updated environment. Notice that the *dlet* does *not* evaluate e_1 but only records it in the environment. The rule (DLET2) is standard: the whole *dlet* yields the value which eventually e_2 reduces to.

The (PAR) rule looks for the variation Va bound to $\tilde{x}$ in ρ. Then the dispatching mechanism selects the expression to which $\tilde{x}$ reduces by the following partial function:

$$dsp(C, (G.e, Va)) = \begin{cases} (e, \theta) & \text{if } C \vDash G \text{ with } \theta \\ dsp(C, Va) & \text{otherwise} \end{cases}$$

A variation is inspected from left to right to find the first goal G satisfied by the context C ($C \vDash G$), under a substitution θ. If this search succeeds, the dispatching returns the corresponding expression e and θ. Then $\tilde{x}$ reduces to $e\,\theta$. Instead, if the dispatching fails because no goal holds, the computation gets stuck since the program cannot adapt to the current context.

As an example of context-dependent binding consider the expression $\mathtt{tell}(\tilde{x})$, in an environment ρ that binds the parameter $\tilde{x}$ to $e' = \mathsf{G_1.F_5, G_2.foo}\,()$ (foo is defined above) and in a context C that satisfies the goal G_2 but not G_1:

$$\rho \vdash C, \mathtt{tell}(\tilde{x}) \ \rightarrow \ C, \mathtt{tell}(\mathsf{foo}\,()) \ \rightarrow^* \ C, \mathtt{tell}(\mathsf{F_3}) \ \rightarrow \ C \cup \{\mathsf{F_3}\}, ()$$

In the first step, we retrieve the binding for $\tilde{x}$ (recall it is e'), where $dsp(C, e') = dsp(C, \mathsf{G_1.F_5, G_2.foo}\,()) = (\mathsf{foo}\,(), \theta)$, for a suitable substitution θ.

The rules for $e_1 \cup e_2$ sequentially evaluate e_1 and e_2 until they reduce to behavioural variations. Then, they are concatenated (bound variables are renamed to avoid name captures, see rule (APPEND3)). As an example of concatenation, let T be the goal always true, and consider the function $doo = \lambda x.\lambda y.\,x \cup (w)\{\mathsf{T}.y\}$. It takes as arguments a behavioural variation x and a value y, and it extends x by adding a default case which is always selected when no other case applies. In the following computation we apply doo to the behavioural variation $bv = (x)\{G_1.c_1, G_2.x\}$ and to c_2 (c_1, c_2 constants):

$$\rho \vdash C, doo\,p\,c_2 \ \rightarrow \ C, (x)\{G_1.c_1, G_2.x\} \cup (w)\{\mathsf{T}.c_2\} \ \rightarrow \ C, (z)\{G_1.c_1, G_2.z, \mathsf{T}.c_2\}$$

The behavioural variation application $\#(e_1, e_2)$ evaluates the subexpressions until e_1 reduces to $(x)\{Va\}$ and e_2 to a value v. Then the rule (VAAPP3) invokes the dispatching mechanism to select the relevant expression e from which the computation proceeds after v replaced x. Also in this case the computation gets stuck if the dispatching mechanism fails. As an example, consider the above behavioural variation bv and apply it to the constant c in a context C that satisfies the goal G_2 but not G_1. Since $dsp(C, bv) = dsp(C, (x)\{G_1.c_1, G_2.x\}) = (x, \theta)$ for some substitution θ, we get

$$\rho \vdash C, \#((x)\{G_1.c_1, G_2.x\}, c) \ \rightarrow \ C, c$$

The rules for API invocation first evaluate the arguments, and then run the code of f through the meta function $syscall$, possibly affecting the context. For simplicity, we assume that a single resource handle occurs in an API invocation, as its first argument.

4   Types

4.1   History Expressions

History Expressions [3] are a basic process algebra used to soundly abstract the set of execution histories that a program may generate. Here, history expressions approximate the sequence of actions that a program may perform over the

$$\overline{C, \epsilon \cdot H \to C, H} \qquad \overline{C, \mu h.H \to C, H[\mu h.H/h]} \qquad \frac{C, H_1 \to C', H_1'}{C, H_1 + H_2 \to C', H_i'}$$

$$\frac{C, H_2 \to C', H_2'}{C, H_1 + H_2 \to C', H_2'} \qquad \frac{C, H_1 \to C', H_1'}{C, H_1 \cdot H_2 \to C', H_1' \cdot H_2} \qquad \overline{C, tell\, F \to C \cup \{F\}, \epsilon}$$

$$\overline{C, retract\, F \to C \backslash \{F\}, \epsilon} \qquad \frac{C, H \to C', H'}{C, f(k)\langle H \rangle \to C', f(k)\langle H' \rangle} \qquad \overline{C, f(k)\langle \epsilon \rangle \to C, \epsilon}$$

$$\frac{C \vDash G}{C, ask\, G.H \otimes \Delta \to C, H} \qquad \frac{C \nvDash G}{C, ask\, G.H \otimes \Delta \to C, \Delta}$$

Fig. 3. Semantics of History Expressions

context at runtime, i.e. asserting/retracting facts and asking if a goal holds, as well as how behavioural variations will be "resolved". In addition, we record a call to an API function, together with its abstract behaviour, represented as a history expression.

The syntax of history expressions is the following

$$H ::= \epsilon \mid h \mid \mu h.H \mid H_1 + H_2 \mid H_1 \cdot H_2 \mid tell\, F \mid retract\, F \mid f(k)\langle H \rangle \mid \Delta$$
$$\Delta ::= ask\, G.H \otimes \Delta \mid fail$$

The empty history expression ϵ abstracts programs which do not interact with the context; $\mu h.H$ represents possibly recursive functions, where h is the recursion variable; the non-deterministic sum $H_1 + H_2$ stands for the conditional expression $if\text{-}then\text{-}else$; the concatenation $H_1 \cdot H_2$ is for sequences of actions that arise, e.g. while evaluating applications; the "atomic" history expressions $tell\, F$ and $retract\, F$ are for the analogous expressions of $\mathrm{ML_{CoDa}}$; the history expression for an API invocation is rendered by $f(k)\langle H \rangle$, where f acts on a resource of type k, and H is the history expression declared in the API; Δ is an *abstract variation*, defined as a list of history expressions, each element H_i of which is guarded by an $ask\, G_i$, so to mimic our dispatching mechanism. For an example of abstract variation, see the history expression H in Sect. 2.

Given a context C, the behaviour of a closed history expression H (i.e. with no free variables) is formalised by the transition system inductively defined in Fig. 3. A transition $C, H \to C', H'$ means that H reduces to H' in the context C and yields the context C'. Most rules are similar to the ones in [3], and below we briefly comment on them.

The recursion $\mu h.H$ reduces to its body H substituting $\mu h.H$ for the recursion variable h. The sum $H_1 + H_2$ non-deterministically reduces to the history expression obtained by reducing either H_1 or H_2. The sequence $H_1 \cdot H_2$ reduces to H_2, provided that H_1 step-wise becomes ϵ. An action $tell\, F$ reduces to ϵ and yields a context C' where the fact F has just been added; similarly for $retract\, F$. The rules for an API invocation evaluate the body H until termination.

The rules for Δ scan the abstract variation and look for the first goal G satisfied in the current context; if this search succeeds, the overall history expression reduces to the history expression H guarded by G; otherwise the search continues on the rest of Δ. If no satisfiable goal exists, the stuck configuration $C, fail$ is reached, representing that the dispatching mechanism fails.

4.2   Types and Effects

We extend in Figs. 5 and 4 the logical presentation of a type and effect system for ML_{CoDa} of [9] by introducing a family of types $res(k)$ for every kind k of resource. As done there, we assume a Datalog typing function γ that given a goal G returns a list of pairs $(x, \text{type-of-}x)$, for all the variables x of G (γ is used e.g. in the rule TVARIATION in Fig. 5).
The syntax of types is

$$\tau_b ::= \tau_c \mid res(k) \qquad \tau_c \in \{int, bool, unit, \dots\} \qquad k \in ResFamily$$

$$\tau ::= \tau_b \mid \tau_1 \xrightarrow{K|H} \tau_2 \mid \tau_1 \xRightarrow{K|\Delta} \tau_2 \mid fact_\phi \qquad \phi \in \wp(Fact)$$

We have types for constants (int, $bool$, $unit$, $\dots$), resource types, functional types, behavioural variations types, and facts. Some types are annotated to support our static analysis. In the type $fact_\phi$ the set ϕ soundly contains the facts that an expression can be reduced to at runtime (see the rules of the semantics (TELL2) and (RETRACT2)). In the type $\tau_1 \xrightarrow{K|H} \tau_2$ associated with a function f, the environment K is a precondition needed to apply f. The environment K maps a parameter $\tilde{x}$ to a pair consisting of a type and an abstract variation Δ, used to resolve the binding for $\tilde{x}$ at runtime, formally $K ::= \emptyset \mid K, (\tilde{x}, \tau, \Delta)$. As an annotation, K stores the types and the abstract variations of parameters occurring inside the body of f. The history expression H is the latent effect of f, i.e. the sequence of actions that may be performed over the context during the function evaluation. Analogously, in the type $\tau_1 \xRightarrow{K|\Delta} \tau_2$ associated with the behavioural variation $bv = (x)\{Va\}$, K is a precondition for applying bv and Δ is an abstract variation representing the information that the dispatching mechanism uses at runtime to apply bv.

We now introduce the orderings $\sqsubseteq_H, \sqsubseteq_\Delta, \sqsubseteq_K$ on H, Δ and K, respectively (often omitting the indexes when unambiguous). We define $H_1 \sqsubseteq H_2$ iff $\exists H_3$ such that $H_2 = H_1 + H_3$; $\Delta_1 \sqsubseteq \Delta_2$ iff $\exists \Delta_3$ such that $\Delta_2 = \Delta_1 \otimes \Delta_3$, (note that we assume $fail \otimes \Delta = \Delta$, so Δ has a single trailing term $fail$); $K_1 \sqsubseteq K_2$ iff $((\tilde{x}, \tau_1, \Delta_1) \in K_1$ implies $(\tilde{x}, \tau_2, \Delta_2) \in K_2 \wedge \tau_1 \leq \tau_2 \wedge \Delta_1 \sqsubseteq \Delta_2)$.

Typing judgements $\Gamma; K \vdash e : \tau \triangleright H$ mean that in the standard type environment Γ and in the *parameter environment* K, the expression e has type τ and effect H. Furthermore, we assume that the type of every API function f is stored in the typing environment Γ, i.e. $\Gamma(f) = res(k) \times \tau_2 \times \cdots \times \tau_n \xrightarrow{\epsilon; H} \tau_b$, where, by abuse of notation, we use a tuple type for the domain of f (see the rule (TRES) below).

$$\text{(Stconst)} \over \tau_b \le \tau_b$$

$$\text{(Sfact)} \over {\phi \subseteq \phi' \over fact_\phi \le fact_{\phi'}}$$

(Sfun)

$$\frac{\tau_1' \le \tau_1 \quad K \sqsubseteq K'}{\tau_2 \le \tau_2' \quad H \sqsubseteq H'} \over {\tau_1 \xrightarrow{K|H} \tau_2 \le \tau_1' \xrightarrow{K'|H'} \tau_2'}$$

(Sva)

$$\frac{\tau_1' \le \tau_1 \quad K \sqsubseteq K'}{\tau_2 \le \tau_2' \quad \Delta \sqsubseteq \Delta'} \over {\tau_1 \xRightarrow{K|\Delta} \tau_2 \le \tau_1' \xRightarrow{K'|\Delta'} \tau_2'}$$

Fig. 4. The subtyping relation

We now briefly comment on the most interesting rules; more comments and examples can be found in [9]. As expected the rules for subtyping and subeffecting (Fig. 4) say that the subtyping relation is reflexive (rule (Srefl)); that a type $fact_\phi$ is a subtype of a type $fact_{\phi'}$ whenever $\phi \subseteq \phi'$ (rule (Sfact)); that functional types are contra-variant in the types of arguments and covariant in the type of the result and in the annotations (rule (Sfun)); analogously for the types of behavioural variations (rule (Sva)).

The rule (Tsub) allows us to freely enlarge types and effects by applying the subtyping and subeffecting rules. The rule (Tfact) says that a fact F has type $fact$ annotated with the singleton $\{F\}$ and empty effect. The rule (Ttell)/(Tretract) asserts that the expression $tell(e)/retract(e)$ has type $unit$, provided that the type of e is $fact_\phi$. The overall effect is obtained by concatenating the effect of e with the non-deterministic summation of $tell\,F/retract\,F$ where F is any of the facts in the type of e. Rule (Tpar) looks for the type and the effect of the parameter $\tilde{x}$ in the environment K. In the rule (Tvariation) we guess an environment K' and the type τ_1 for the bound variable x. We determine the type for each subexpression e_i under K' and the environment Γ extended by the type of x and of the variables $\overrightarrow{y_i}$ occurring in the goal G_i (recall that the Datalog typing function γ returns a list of pairs $(z, \text{type-of-}z)$ for all variable z of G_i). Note that all subexpressions e_i have the same type τ_2. We also require that the abstract variation Δ results from concatenating $ask\,G_i$ with the effect computed for e_i. The type of the behavioural variation is annotated by K' and Δ. The rule (Tvapp) type-checks behavioural variation applications and reveals the role of preconditions. As expected, e_1 is a behavioural variation with parameter of type τ_1 and e_2 has type τ_1. We get a type if the environment K', which acts as a precondition, is included in K according to $\sqsubseteq$. The type of the behavioural variation application is τ_2, i.e. the type of the result of e_1, and the effect is obtained by concatenating the ones of e_1 and e_2 with the history expression Δ, occurring in the annotation of the type of e_1. The rule (Tappend) asserts that two expressions e_1, e_2 with the same type τ, except for the abstract variations Δ_1, Δ_2 in their annotations, and effects H_1 and H_2, are combined into $e_1 \cup e_2$ with type τ, and concatenated annotations and effects. More precisely, the resulting annotation has the same precondition of e_1 and e_2 and abstract

(TSUB)
$$\frac{\Gamma; K \vdash e : \tau' \triangleright H' \qquad \tau' \leq \tau \qquad H' \sqsubseteq H}{\Gamma; K \vdash e : \tau \triangleright H}$$

(TCONST)
$$\frac{}{\Gamma; K \vdash c : \tau_c \triangleright \epsilon}$$

(TFACT)
$$\frac{}{\Gamma; K \vdash F : fact_{\{F\}} \triangleright \epsilon}$$

(TVAR)
$$\frac{\Gamma(x) = \tau}{\Gamma; K \vdash x : \tau \triangleright \epsilon}$$

(TIF)
$$\frac{\Gamma; K \vdash e_1 : bool \triangleright H_1 \qquad \Gamma; K \vdash e_2 : \tau \triangleright H_2 \qquad \Gamma; K \vdash e_3 : \tau \triangleright H_3}{\Gamma; K \vdash if\, e_1\, then\, e_2\, else\, e_3 : \tau \triangleright H_1 \cdot (H_2 + H_3)}$$

(TLET)
$$\frac{\Gamma; K \vdash e_1 : \tau_1 \triangleright H_1 \qquad \Gamma; x : \tau_1, K \vdash e_2 : \tau_2 \triangleright H_2}{\Gamma; K \vdash let\, x = e_1\, in\, e_2 : \tau_2 \triangleright H_1 \cdot H_2}$$

(TTELL)
$$\frac{\Gamma; K \vdash e : fact_\phi \triangleright H}{\Gamma; K \vdash tell(e) : unit \triangleright H \cdot \left(\sum_{F \in \phi} tell\, F \right)}$$

(TRETRACT)
$$\frac{\Gamma; K \vdash e : fact_\phi \triangleright H}{\Gamma; K \vdash retract(e) : unit \triangleright H \cdot \left(\sum_{F \in \phi} retract\, F \right)}$$

(TABS)
$$\frac{\Gamma, x : \tau_1, f : \tau_1 \xrightarrow{K'|H} \tau_2; K' \vdash e : \tau_2 \triangleright H}{\Gamma; K \vdash \lambda_f x.e : \tau_1 \xrightarrow{K'|H} \tau_2 \triangleright \epsilon}$$

(TVARIATION)
$$\frac{\forall i \in \{1, \ldots, n\} \qquad \gamma(G_i) = \overline{y_i : \tau_i} \quad \Gamma, x : \tau_1, \overline{y_i : \tau_i}; K' \vdash e_i : \tau_2 \triangleright H_i \qquad \Delta = ask\, G_1.H_1 \otimes \cdots \otimes ask\, G_n.H_n \otimes fail}{\Gamma; K \vdash (x)\{G_1.e_1, \ldots, G_n.e_n\} : \tau_1 \xrightarrow{K'|\Delta} \tau_2 \triangleright \epsilon}$$

(TAPPEND)
$$\frac{\Gamma; K \vdash e_1 : \tau_1 \xrightarrow{K'|\Delta_1} \tau_2 \triangleright H_1 \qquad \Gamma; K \vdash e_2 : \tau_1 \xrightarrow{K'|\Delta_2} \tau_2 \triangleright H_2}{\Gamma; K \vdash e_1 \cup e_2 : \tau_1 \xrightarrow{K'|\Delta_1 \otimes \Delta_2} \tau_2 \triangleright H_1 \cdot H_2}$$

(TVAPP)
$$\frac{\Gamma; K \vdash e_1 : \tau_1 \xrightarrow{K'|\Delta} \tau_2 \triangleright H_1 \qquad \Gamma; K \vdash e_2 : \tau_1 \triangleright H_2 \qquad K' \sqsubseteq K}{\Gamma; K \vdash \#(e_1, e_2) : \tau_2 \triangleright H_1 \cdot H_2 \cdot \Delta}$$

(TAPP)
$$\frac{\Gamma; K \vdash e_1 : \tau_1 \xrightarrow{K'|H_3} \tau_2 \triangleright H_1 \qquad \Gamma; K \vdash e_2 : \tau_1 \triangleright H_2 \qquad K' \sqsubseteq K}{\Gamma; K \vdash e_1\, e_2 : \tau_2 \triangleright H_1 \cdot H_2 \cdot H_3}$$

(TPAR)
$$\frac{K(\tilde{x}) = (\tau, \Delta)}{\Gamma; K \vdash \tilde{x} : \tau \triangleright \Delta}$$

(TDLET)
$$\frac{\Gamma, \overline{y : \tau}; \overrightarrow{K} \vdash e_1 : \tau_1 \triangleright H_1 \qquad \Gamma; K, (\tilde{x}, \tau_1, \Delta') \vdash e_2 : \tau_2 \triangleright H_2}{\Gamma; K \vdash dlet\, \tilde{x} = e_1\, when\, G\, in\, e_2 : \tau_2 \triangleright H_2} \qquad \begin{array}{l} where\, \gamma(G) = \overline{y : \tau} \\ \Delta' = \begin{cases} (G.H_1 \otimes \Delta) & if\, K(\tilde{x}) = (\tau_1, \Delta) \\ (G.H_1 \otimes fail) & if\, \tilde{x} \notin K \end{cases} \end{array}$$

(TRES)
$$\frac{\Gamma(f) : res(k) \times \tau_2 \times \cdots \times \tau_n \xrightarrow{\emptyset; H} \tau_b \qquad \Gamma; K \vdash e_i : \tau_i \triangleright H_i}{f(e_1, \ldots, e_n) : \tau_b \triangleright H_1 \cdot \ldots \cdot H_n \cdot f(k)\langle H \rangle} \qquad where\, \tau_1 = res(k)$$

Fig. 5. Type and effect system

variation $\Delta_1 \otimes \Delta_2$, and effect $H_1 \cdot H_2$. The rule (TDLET) requires that e_1 has type τ_1 in the environment Γ extended with the types for the variables $\overrightarrow{y}$ of the goal G. Also, e_2 has to type-check in an environment K extended with information on the parameter $\tilde{x}$. The type and the effect for the overall *dlet* expression are those of e_2. Finally, the rule (TRES) retrieves the type of f from Γ and type-checks its arguments. The resulting type is the retrieved one for f and the overall effect is the concatenation of the effects of the arguments and $f(k)\langle H\rangle$, where k denotes the kind of the resource affected and H is the latent effect of f. For simplicity we assume that f manipulates a single resource occurring in first position and that f can always be applied so its type has no preconditions.

As an example, consider the behavioural variation $bv_1 = (x)\{G_1.f(e_1), G_2.e_2\}$. Let Γ' be the environment $\Gamma, x : int, f : res(k_1) \to \tau$ (goals have no variables) and K' be the parameter environment. Then assume that under these environments e_1 has type $res(k_1)$ and effect H_r, and that the two cases of this behavioural variation have type τ and effects $H_1 = f(k_1)\langle H_r\rangle$ and H_2, respectively. Hence, the type of bv_1 will be $int \xrightarrow{K'|\Delta} \tau$ with $\Delta = ask\, G_1.H_1 \otimes ask\, G_2.H_2 \otimes fail$, while the effect will be empty.

Our type and effect system is sound with respect to the operational semantics of ML$_{\text{CoDa}}$. To concisely state soundness, it is convenient to introduce the following technical definition and to exploit the following results.

Definition 1 (Type of dynamic environment). *Given the type and parameter environments Γ and K, we say that the dynamic environment ρ has type K under Γ (in symbols $\Gamma \vdash \rho : K$) iff $dom(\rho) \subseteq dom(K)$ and $\forall \tilde{x} \in dom(\rho)$ such that $\rho(\tilde{x}) = G_1.e_1, \ldots, G_n.e_n$ and $K(\tilde{x}) = (\tau, \Delta)$, $\forall i \in [1, n]$ the following hold:*
(a) $\gamma(G_i) = \vec{y_i} : \vec{\tau_i}$ and (b) $\Gamma, \vec{y_i} : \vec{\tau_i}; K \vdash e_i : \tau' \triangleright H_i$ and (c) $\tau' \leq \tau$ and (d) $\bigotimes_{i \in [1,n]} G_i.H_i \sqsubseteq \Delta$.

Theorem 1 (Preservation). *Let e_s be a closed expression; and let ρ be a dynamic environment such that $dom(\rho)$ includes the set of parameters of e_s and such that $\Gamma \vdash \rho : K$. If $\Gamma; K \vdash e_s : \tau \triangleright H_s$ and $\rho \vdash C, e_s \to C', e_s'$ then $\Gamma; K \vdash e_s' : \tau \triangleright H_s'$ and $C, H_s \to^* C', H$ for some $H \sqsubseteq H_s'$.*

This theorem is quite standard: types are preserved under computations and the effect statically determined includes the one reached by the considered computation. However, the Progress Theorem assumes that the effect H does not reach *fail*, i.e. that the dispatching mechanism succeeds at runtime. We take care of ensuring this property in Sect. 5 (below $\rho \vdash C, e \not\to$ means that there exist no C' and e' such that $\rho \vdash C, e \to C', e'$). The following corollary ensures that the history expression obtained as an effect of e over-approximates the actions that may be performed over the context during the evaluation of e.

Theorem 2 (Progress). *Let e_s be a closed expression s.t. $\Gamma; K \vdash e_s : \tau \triangleright H_s$; and let ρ be a dynamic environment s.t. $dom(\rho)$ includes the set of parameters of e_s, and $\Gamma \vdash \rho : K$. If $\rho \vdash C, e_s \not\to \wedge C, H_s \not\to^+ C', fail$ then e_s is a value.*

Corollary 1 (Over-approximation). *Let e_s be a closed expression. If $\Gamma; K \vdash e_s : \tau \triangleright H_s \wedge \rho \vdash C, e_s \to^* C', e'$, for some ρ such that $\Gamma \vdash \rho : K$, then $\Gamma; K \vdash e' : \tau \triangleright H_s'$ and there exists a sequence of transitions $C, H_s \to^* C', H'$ for some $H' \sqsubseteq H_s'$.*

The following theorem ensures the correctness of our approach.

Theorem 3 (Correctness). *Let e_s be a closed expression such that $\Gamma; K \vdash e_s : \tau \triangleright H_s$; let ρ be a dynamic environment such that $dom(\rho)$ includes the set of parameters of e_s, and that $\Gamma \vdash \rho : K$; finally let C be a context such that $C, H_s \twoheadrightarrow^+ C', fail$. Then either the computation of e_s terminates yielding a value $(\rho \vdash C, e_s \to^* C'', v)$ or it diverges, but it never gets stuck.*

5   Loading Time Analysis

As anticipated in Sect. 1, the $\mathrm{ML_{CoDa}}$ compiler produces a triple (C_p, e_p, H_p) made of the application context C_p, the object code e_p, and an effect H_p over-approximating the behaviour of the application. Using it, the virtual machine of $\mathrm{ML_{CoDa}}$ performs a linking and a verification phase at loading time. During the linking phase, system variables are resolved and the initial context C is constructed, combining C_p and the system context, provided that the result is consistent. Still, the application is "open" with respect to its parameters. This calls for the last mile verification phase: we check whether the application adapts to all the evolutions of C that may occur at runtime, i.e., that all dispatching invocations will always succeed. And then we check that resources are used in accordance with the rules established by the system loading the program. Only programs which pass this verification phase will be run. To do that conveniently and efficiently, we build a graph $\mathcal{G}$ describing all the possible evolutions of the initial context, exploiting the history expression H_p. Technically, we compute $\mathcal{G}$ through a static analysis of history expressions with a notion of validity; intuitively, a history expression is valid for an initial context if the dispatching mechanism always succeeds. Our static analysis is specified in terms of Flow Logic [14, 16], a declarative approach borrowing from and integrating many classical static techniques. Flow Logic has been applied to a wide variety of programming languages and calculi of computation including calculi with functional, imperative, object-oriented, concurrent, distributed, and mobile features, among many see [4, 6, 10, 12, 15].

To support the formal development, we assume that history expressions are mechanically labelled from a given set $Lab = Lab_H \uplus Lab_S$, with typical element l. The elements of Lab_H label the abstract counterparts of $\mathrm{ML_{CoDa}}$ constructs, while those of Lab_S occur in the declared latent effects of the API functions (sometimes, with $\hat{l}$ as typical element). Formally:

$$H ::= \ni \mid \epsilon^l \mid h^l \mid (\mu h.H)^l \mid tell\, F^l \mid retract\, F^l \mid f(k)^l \langle H^{\hat{l}} \rangle \mid$$
$$(H_1 + H_2)^l \mid (H_1 \cdot H_2)^l \mid \Delta$$
$$\Delta ::= (ask\, G.H \otimes \Delta)^l \mid fail^l$$

For technical reasons, we introduce a new empty history expression $\ni$ which is unlabelled. This is because our analysis is syntax-driven, and we need to distinguish when the empty history expression comes from the syntax (ϵ^l) and when it is instead obtained by reduction in the semantics ($\ni$). The semantics of history expressions is accordingly modified, by always allowing the transition $C, \epsilon^l \to C, \ni$. Furthermore, w.l.o.g. we assume that all the bound variables occurring in a history expression are distinct. To keep track of a bound variable h^l introduced in $(\mu h.H_1^{l_1})^{l_2}$, we shall use a suitable function $\mathbb{K}$.

The static approximation is represented by an *estimate* $(\Sigma_\circ, \Sigma_\bullet)$, given by the pair of functions $\Sigma_\circ, \Sigma_\bullet : Lab \to \wp(Context \cup \{*\})$, where $*$ is the distinguished "failure" context representing a dispatching failure. For each label l, the *pre-set* $\Sigma_\circ(l)$ and the *post-set* $\Sigma_\bullet(l)$ over-approximate the set of contexts possibly arising *before* and *after* the evaluation of H^l, respectively.

We inductively specify our analysis in Fig. 6 by defining the validity relation

$$\vDash \; \subseteq \; \mathcal{AE} \times \mathbb{H}$$

where $\mathcal{AE} = (Lab \to \wp(Context \cup \{*\}))^2$ is the domain of the results of the analysis and $\mathbb{H}$ the set of history expressions. We write $(\Sigma_\circ, \Sigma_\bullet) \vDash H^l$, when the pair $(\Sigma_\circ, \Sigma_\bullet)$ is an acceptable analysis estimate for the history expression H^l. The notion of acceptability will then be used in Definition 3 to check whether H, hence the expression e it is an abstraction of, will never fail in a given initial context C. Below, we briefly comment on the inference rules, where $\mathcal{E} = (\Sigma_\circ, \Sigma_\bullet)$ and immaterial labels are omitted.

The rule (ANIL) says that every pair of functions is an acceptable estimate for the semantic empty history expression $\ni$. The estimate $\mathcal{E}$ is acceptable for the syntactic ϵ^l if the pre-set is included in the post-set (rule (AEPS)). By the rule (ATELL), $\mathcal{E}$ is acceptable if for all contexts C in the pre-set, the context $C \cup \{F\}$ is in the post-set. The rule (ARETRACT) is similar. The rules (ASEQ1) and (ASEQ2) handle the sequential composition of history expressions. The rule (ASEQ1) states that $(\Sigma_\circ, \Sigma_\bullet)$ is acceptable for $H = (H_1^{l_1} \cdot H_2^{l_2})^l$ if it is valid for both H_1 and H_2. Moreover, the pre-set of H_1 must include that of H and the pre-set of H_2 includes the post-set of H_1; finally, the post-set of H includes that of H_2. The rule (ASEQ2) states that $\mathcal{E}$ is acceptable for $H = (\ni \cdot H_1^{l_2})^l$ if it is acceptable for H_1 and the pre-set of H_1 includes that of H, while the post-set of H includes that of H_1. By the rule (ASUM), $\mathcal{E}$ is acceptable for $H = (H_1^{l_1} + H_2^{l_2})^l$ if it is valid for H_1 and H_2; the pre-set of H is included in the pre-sets of H_1 and H_2; and the post-set of H includes both those of H_1 and H_2. The rules (AASK1) and (AASK2) handle the abstract dispatching mechanism. The first states that the estimate $\mathcal{E}$ is acceptable for $H = (askG.H_1^{l_1} \otimes \Delta^{l_2})^l$, provided that, for all C in the pre-set of H, if the goal G succeeds in C then the pre-set of H_1 includes that of H and the post-set of H includes that of H_1. Otherwise, the pre-set of Δ^{l_2} must include the one of H and the post-set of Δ^{l_2} is included in that of H. The rule (AASK2) requires $*$ to be in the post-set of $fail$. By the rule (AREC) $\mathcal{E}$ is acceptable for $H = (\mu h.H_1^{l_1})^l$ if it is acceptable for $H_1^{l_1}$ and the pre-set of H_1 includes that of H and the post-set of H includes that of H_1. The rule (AVAR) says that a pair $(\Sigma_\circ, \Sigma_\bullet)$ is an acceptable estimate for a variable h^l if the pre-set of the history expression introducing h, namely $\mathbb{K}(h)$, is included in that of h^l, and the post-set of h^l includes that of $\mathbb{K}(h)$. Finally, the rule (ARES) handles

(ANIL)
$$\frac{}{(\Sigma_\circ, \Sigma_\bullet) \vDash \ni}$$

(AEPS)
$$\frac{\Sigma_\circ(l) \subseteq \Sigma_\bullet(l)}{(\Sigma_\circ, \Sigma_\bullet) \vDash \epsilon^l}$$

(ATELL)
$$\frac{\forall C \in \Sigma_\circ(l) \qquad C \cup \{F\} \in \Sigma_\bullet(l)}{(\Sigma_\circ, \Sigma_\bullet) \vDash tell\ F^l}$$

(ARETRACT)
$$\frac{\forall C \in \Sigma_\circ(l) \qquad C \backslash \{F\} \in \Sigma_\bullet(l)}{(\Sigma_\circ, \Sigma_\bullet) \vDash retract\ F^l}$$

(ASEQ1)
$$\frac{(\Sigma_\circ, \Sigma_\bullet) \vDash H_1^{l_1}}{(\Sigma_\circ, \Sigma_\bullet) \vDash H_2^{l_2} \quad \Sigma_\circ(l) \subseteq \Sigma_\bullet(l_1) \quad \Sigma_\bullet(l_1) \subseteq \Sigma_\circ(l_2) \quad \Sigma_\bullet(l_2) \subseteq \Sigma_\bullet(l)}{(\Sigma_\circ, \Sigma_\bullet) \vDash (H_1^{l_1} \cdot H_2^{l_2})^l}$$

(ASEQ2)
$$\frac{(\Sigma_\circ, \Sigma_\bullet) \vDash H_2^{l_2} \quad \Sigma_\circ(l) \subseteq \Sigma_\bullet(l_2) \quad \Sigma_\bullet(l_2) \subseteq \Sigma_\bullet(l)}{(\Sigma_\circ, \Sigma_\bullet) \vDash (\ni \cdot H_2^{l_2})^l}$$

(ASUM)
$$\frac{\begin{array}{l}(\Sigma_\circ, \Sigma_\bullet) \vDash H_1^{l_1} \quad \Sigma_\circ(l) \subseteq \Sigma_\circ(l_1) \quad \Sigma_\bullet(l_1) \subseteq \Sigma_\bullet(l) \\ (\Sigma_\circ, \Sigma_\bullet) \vDash H_2^{l_2} \quad \Sigma_\circ(l) \subseteq \Sigma_\circ(l_2) \quad \Sigma_\bullet(l_2) \subseteq \Sigma_\bullet(l)\end{array}}{(\Sigma_\circ, \Sigma_\bullet) \vDash (H_1^{l_1} + H_2^{l_2})^l}$$

(AASK1)
$$\frac{\forall C \in \Sigma_\circ(l) \quad \begin{array}{l}(C \vDash G \implies (\Sigma_\circ, \Sigma_\bullet) \vDash H^{l_1} \quad \Sigma_\circ(l) \subseteq \Sigma_\circ(l_1) \quad \Sigma_\bullet(l_1) \subseteq \Sigma_\bullet(l)) \\ (C \nvDash G \implies (\Sigma_\circ, \Sigma_\bullet) \vDash \Delta^{l_2} \quad \Sigma_\circ(l) \subseteq \Sigma_\circ(l_2) \quad \Sigma_\bullet(l_2) \subseteq \Sigma_\bullet(l))\end{array}}{(\Sigma_\circ, \Sigma_\bullet) \vDash (askG.H^{l_1} \otimes \Delta^{l_2})^l}$$

(AASK2)
$$\frac{* \in \Sigma_\bullet(l)}{(\Sigma_\circ, \Sigma_\bullet) \vDash fail^l}$$

(AREC)
$$\frac{(\Sigma_\circ, \Sigma_\bullet) \vDash H^{l_1} \quad \Sigma_\circ(l) \subseteq \Sigma_\circ(l_1) \quad \Sigma_\bullet(l_1) \subseteq \Sigma_\bullet(l)}{(\Sigma_\circ, \Sigma_\bullet) \vDash (\mu h.H^{l_1})^l}$$

(AVAR)
$$\frac{\mathbb{K}(h) = (\mu h.H^{l_1})^{l'} \quad \Sigma_\circ(l) \subseteq \Sigma_\circ(l') \quad \Sigma_\bullet(l') \subseteq \Sigma_\bullet(l)}{(\Sigma_\circ, \Sigma_\bullet) \vDash h^l}$$

(ARES)
$$\frac{(\Sigma_\circ, \Sigma_\bullet) \vDash H^{\hat{l}} \quad \Sigma_\circ(l) \subseteq \Sigma_\circ(\hat{l}) \quad \Sigma_\bullet(\hat{l}) \subseteq \Sigma_\bullet(l)}{(\Sigma_\circ, \Sigma_\bullet) \vDash f(k)^l \langle H^{\hat{l}} \rangle}$$

Fig. 6. Specification of the analysis for History Expressions

the abstraction $f(k)^l \langle H^{\hat{l}} \rangle$ of an API function. It requires that $(\Sigma_\circ, \Sigma_\bullet)$ is an acceptable estimate for $H^{\hat{l}}$ and that the pre-set of $\hat{l}$ includes that of l, while the inverse relation holds for the post-sets.

We are now ready to introduce when an estimate for a history expression is valid for an initial context.

Definition 2 (Valid analysis estimate). *Given H^l and an initial context C, we say that a pair $(\Sigma_\circ, \Sigma_\bullet)$ is a valid analysis estimate for H and C iff $C \in \Sigma_\circ(l_p)$ and $(\Sigma_\circ, \Sigma_\bullet) \vDash H^l$.*

The set of estimates can be partially ordered in the standard way, and shown to form a Moore family. Therefore, there always exists a minimal valid analysis estimate [16] (see [9] Th. 4). The correctness of our analysis follows from subject reduction.

Theorem 4 (Subject Reduction). *Let H^l be a closed history expression such that $(\Sigma_\circ, \Sigma_\bullet) \vDash H^l$. If for all $C \in \Sigma_\circ(l)$ such that $C, H^l \rightarrow C', H^{l'}$ then $(\Sigma_\circ, \Sigma_\bullet) \vDash H^{l'}$ and $\Sigma_\circ(l) \subseteq \Sigma_\circ(l')$ and $\Sigma_\bullet(l') \subseteq \Sigma_\bullet(l)$.*

Now we can define when a history expression H_p is viable for an initial context C, i.e. when it passes the verification phase. In the following definition, let $lfail(H)$ be the set of labels of the *fail* sub-terms in H:

Definition 3 (Viability). *Let H_p be a history expression and C be an initial context. We say that H_p is viable for C if there exists the minimal valid analysis estimate $(\Sigma_\circ, \Sigma_\bullet)$ such that $\forall l \in dom(\Sigma_\bullet) \setminus lfail(H_p)$, $* \notin \Sigma_\bullet(l)$.*

Table 1. An estimate for the history expression H_a in the context $C = \{F_2, F_5\}$.

	$\Sigma_\circ^1$	$\Sigma_\bullet^1$
1	$\{\{F_2, F_5\}\}$	$\{\{F_1, F_2, F_5\}\}$
2	$\{\{F_1, F_2, F_5\}\}$	$\{\{F_1, F_5\}\}$
3	$\{\{F_1, F_5\}\}$	$\{\{F_1\}\}$
4	$\{\{F_1, F_5\}\}$	$\{\{F_1\}\}$
5	$\{\{F_1, F_2, F_5\}\}$	$\{\{F_1\}\}$
6	$\{\{F_2, F_5\}\}$	$\{\{F_1\}\}$
7	$\{\{F_2, F_5\}\}$	$\{\{F_1, F_5\}\}$
8	$\{\{F_2, F_5\}\}$	$\{\{F_2, F_5, F_8\}\}$
9	$\{\{F_2, F_5, F_8\}\}$	$\{\{F_1, F_2, F_5, F_8\}\}$
10	$\{\{F_2, F_5\}\}$	$\{\{F_1, F_2, F_5, F_8\}\}$
11	$\emptyset$	$\emptyset$
12	$\emptyset$	$\emptyset$
13	$\emptyset$	$\emptyset$
14	$\{\{F_2, F_5\}\}$	$\{\{F_1, F_2, F_5, F_8\}\}$
15	$\{\{F_2, F_5\}\}$	$\{\{F_1\}, \{F_1, F_2, F_5, F_8\}\}$

As an example of viability checking, consider the context $C = \{F_2, F_5\}$, consisting of facts only, and the following history expression H_a:

$$H_a = ((tell\ F_1^1 \cdot (retract\ F_2^2 \cdot f(k_1)^3 \langle retract\ F_5^4 \rangle)^5)^6\ +$$
$$g(k_2)^7 \langle (ask\ F_5.(tell\ F_8^8 \cdot tell\ F_1^9)^{10} \otimes (ask\ F_3.retract\ F_4^{11} \otimes fail^{12})^{13})^{14} \rangle)^{15}$$

For each label l occurring in H_a, Table 1 shows the corresponding values of $\Sigma_\circ^1(l)$ and $\Sigma_\bullet^1(l)$, respectively.

Now we exploit the result of the above analysis to build the evolution graph $\mathcal{G}$, that describes how the initial context C evolves at runtime. The virtual machine can use $\mathcal{G}$ to predict how the application interacts with and affects the context and the resources.

In the following let $Fact^*$ and $Lab^* = Lab_H^* \uplus Lab_S^*$ be the set of facts and the set of labels occurring in H_p, the history expression under verification. Intuitively, $\mathcal{G}$ is a direct graph, the nodes of which are the set of contexts reachable from an initial context C, while running H_p. There is a labelled arc between two nodes C_1 and C_2 if C_2 is obtained from C_1 either through telling or removing a fact F, or through telling a set of facts and removing another set, when executing an API f. In the definition below the function $\mu : Lab_H^* \to \mathbb{H}$ recovers a construct in a given history expression $H \in \mathbb{H}$ from its label. Also let $\mathcal{A} = \{tell\ F^l, retract\ F^l, f(k)^l \langle H^{\hat{l}} \rangle \mid F \in Fact^* \wedge l, \hat{l} \in Lab^*\}$.

Definition 4 (Evolution Graph). *Let H_p be a history expression, C be a context, and $(\Sigma_\circ, \Sigma_\bullet)$ be a valid analysis estimate. The evolution graph of C is $\mathcal{G} = (N, E, L)$, where*

$N = \bigcup_{l \in Lab_H^*} (\Sigma_\circ(l) \cup \Sigma_\bullet(l))$
$E = \{(C_1, C_2) \mid \exists l \in Lab_H^*\ s.t.\ \mu(l) \in \mathcal{A} \wedge C_1 \in \Sigma_\circ(l) \wedge (C_2 \in \Sigma_\bullet(l) \vee C_2 = *)\}$
$L\ :\ E \to \mathcal{P}(\mathcal{A})$ *is such that* $\mu(l) \in L(t)$ *iff* $t = (C_1, C_2) \in E \wedge C_1 \in \Sigma_\circ(l)$

We can use the evolution graph $\mathcal{G}$ to verify that there are no functional or non-functional failures. The first case verifies viability, and simply consists in checking that the failure context $*$ is not reachable from the initial one. The non-functional properties, a sort of CTL* formulae [1], constrain the usage of resources and predicate over nodes, i.e. contexts, and paths in the evolution graph. We can naturally check this kind of properties by visiting the graph.

Figure 7 depicts the evolution graph of the context C and the history expressions H_a introduced above. It is immediate checking that the node $*$ is not reachable, thus showing in another way that H_a is viable for C. As an example of non-functional property, assume that the system requires that the program is not allowed to invoke the API function f on a resource of kind k_1 when the fact F_5 holds in the context. Verifying this property requires to visit the graph and to check that there is no arc labelled $f(k_1)$ from every node in which F_5 is true. We can easily detect that the node $\{F_1, F_5\}$ double circled (blue in the pdf) violates the requirement. One can also require a property on the context target of an API function. For instance, if the constraint is "after f the fact F_2 must hold" the target of f would be marked as a non-functional failure.

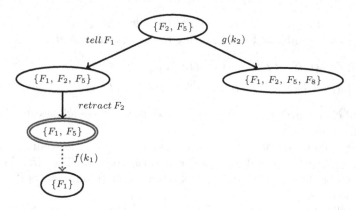

Fig. 7. The evolution graph for the context $C = \{F_2, F_5\}$ and the history expression H_a (only the nodes reachable from C are shown). (Color figure online)

6   Conclusions

We considered the problem of managing resources in adaptive systems. In these systems the context, i.e. the working environment, contains different kinds of resources and makes them available to applications, typically through specific handles. The actual capabilities of the available resources, their permitted usage and their number depend on the hosting system and are only known at runtime. To address these issues, we extended ML_{CoDa}, a two-component language for programming adaptive systems, with a notion of API providing programmers with a set of functions that allow them to manipulate resources.

When entering in a context an application can fail for two reasons: either because it is unable to adapt to the context or because it misuses a resource. To prevent this kind of non-functional failures to occur, we extended the type and effect system and the control flow analysis of [9]. Since parts of the context are unknown at compile time, the control flow analysis can only be carried out (on the effect) at loading time after the linking step. Indeed, full information about resources is only available when in the current context.

As future work we will study how to express the constraints over the usage of resources, e.g. in the form of CTL* formulas. A natural candidate approach for verifying that resources are correctly handled, would then be model-checking the evolution graph built at loading time.

References

1. Baier, C., Katoen, J.P.: Principles of Model Checking. MIT Press, Cambridge (2008)
2. Baresi, L., Di Nitto, E., Ghezzi, C.: Toward open-world software: issue and challenges. Computer **39**(10), 36–43 (2006)
3. Bartoletti, M., Degano, P., Ferrari, G.L., Zunino, R.: Local policies for resource usage analysis. ACM Trans. Program. Lang. Syst. **31**(6), 23 (2009)

4. Bodei, C., Buchholtz, M., Degano, P., Nielson, F., Nielson, H.R.: Static validation of security protocols. J. Comput. Secur. **13**(3), 347–390 (2005)

5. Bodei, C., Degano, P., Galletta, L., Salvatori, F.: Linguistic mechanisms for context-aware security. In: Ciobanu, G., Méry, D. (eds.) ICTAC 2014. LNCS, vol. 8687, pp. 61–79. Springer, Heidelberg (2014)

6. Bodei, C., Degano, P., Nielson, F., Nielson, H.R.: Static analysis for the Pi-calculus with applications to security. Inf. Comput. **168**(1), 68–92 (2001)

7. Ceri, S., Gottlob, G., Tanca, L.: What you always wanted to know about Datalog (and never dared to ask). IEEE Trans. Knowl. Data Eng. **1**(1), 146–166 (1989)

8. Degano, P., Ferrari, G.L., Galletta, L.: A two-component language for COP. In: Proceeding 6th International Workshop on Context-Oriented Programming. ACM Digital Library(2014). doi:10.1145/2637066.2637072

9. Degano, P., Ferrari, G.-L., Galletta, L.: A two-phase static analysis for reliable adaptation. In: Giannakopoulou, D., Salaün, G. (eds.) SEFM 2014. LNCS, vol. 8702, pp. 347–362. Springer, Heidelberg (2014)

10. Degano, P., Levi, F., Bodei, C.: Safe ambients: control flow analysis and security. In: Kleinberg, R.D., Sato, M. (eds.) ASIAN 2000. LNCS, vol. 1961, pp. 199–214. Springer, Heidelberg (2000)

11. Galletta, L.: Adaptivity: linguistic mechanisms and static analysis techniques. Ph.D. thesis, University of Pisa (2014). http://www.di.unipi.it/galletta/phdThesis.pdf

12. Gasser, K.L.S., Nielson, F., Nielson, H.R.: Systematic realisation of control flow analyses for CML. In: Proceeding of the 1997 ACM SIGPLAN International Conference on Functional Programming (ICFP 1997), pp. 38–51 (1997)

13. Hirschfeld, R., Costanza, P., Nierstrasz, O.: Context-oriented programming. J. Object Technol. **7**(3), 125–151 (2008)

14. Nielson, F., Nielson, H.R., Hankin, C.: Principles of Program Analysis. Springer, 1st edn. 1999. corr. 2nd printing, 1999 edn. Heidelberg (2005)

15. Nielson, F., Nielson, H.R., Hansen, R.R.: Validating firewalls using flow logics. Theor. Comput. Sci. **283**(2), 381–418 (2002)

16. Riis Nielson, H., Nielson, F.: Flow logic: a multi-paradigmatic approach to static analysis. In: Mogensen, T.Æ., Schmidt, D.A., Sudborough, I.H. (eds.) The Essence of Computation. LNCS, vol. 2566, pp. 223–244. Springer, Heidelberg (2002)

17. Salvaneschi, G., Ghezzi, C., Pradella, M.: Context-oriented programming: a software engineering perspective. J. Syst. Softw. **85**(8), 1801–1817 (2012)

Formal Modelling and Analysis of Socio-Technical Systems

Christian W. Probst[1]($\boxtimes$), Florian Kammüller[2], and René Rydhof Hansen[3]

[1] Technical University of Denmark, Kongens Lyngby, Denmark
cwpr@dtu.dk
[2] Middlesex University, London, UK
f.kammueller@mdx.ac.uk
[3] Aalborg University, Aalborg, Denmark
rrh@cs.aau.dk

Abstract. Attacks on systems and organisations increasingly exploit human actors, for example through social engineering. This non-technical aspect of attacks complicates their formal treatment and automatic identification. Formalisation of human behaviour is difficult at best, and attacks on socio-technical systems are still mostly identified through brainstorming of experts. In this work we discuss several approaches to formalising socio-technical systems and their analysis. Starting from a flow logic-based analysis of the insider threat, we discuss how to include the socio aspects explicitly, and show a formalisation that proves properties of this formalisation. On the formal side, our work closes the gap between formal and informal approaches to socio-technical systems. On the informal side, we show how to steal a birthday cake from a bakery by social engineering.

1 Introduction

Applying formal methods [1] to an informal world is difficult. It often requires to loosen the precision of analysis results, or to overly restrict the aspects that can be modelled. This dilemma causes many approaches that try to understand events in the real world to abstract away its difficult parts. In this paper we present an application of formal methods to organisations to analyse socio-technical systems, and illustrate how aspects of the informal world can be handled in formal analyses.

Socio-technical systems, as the name implies, are a mix of social and technical aspects. Organisations are a good example for socio-technical systems, since they combine technical infrastructure and policies with human actors, who operate (in) this infrastructure and interact with it. An increasing number of attacks against organisations exploit this mix and involve attack steps on the "socio" part, for example, through social engineering. Security in socio-technical systems should therefor not only consider both individual parts, but also their interactions.

C.W. Probst et al. (Eds.): Nielsons' Festschrift, LNCS 9560, pp. 54–73, 2016.
DOI: 10.1007/978-3-319-27810-0_3

The recent attack on a German steel mill [2] was a combination of both targeted phishing emails and social engineering attacks. The phishing helped the hackers extract information they used to gain access to the plant's office network and then its production systems. As a result, the technical infrastructure of the mill suffered severe damage. Traditional and well-established risk assessment methods often identify potential threats against socio-technical systems, but often abstract away the internal structure of an organisation and ignore human factors.

Actually, only few, if any, approaches to systematic risk assessment take such "human factor"-based attacks into consideration. Probably the strongest threat against socio-technical systems is the insider threat [3,4]. Insiders have access to parts of the organisation's infrastructure and assets, and they are trusted to perform certain operations on these. Starting from a flow logic [5] based analysis of the insider threat, we discuss how to include the socio aspects explicitly, and show a formalisation that proves properties of this formalisation.

On the formal side, our work closes the gap between formal and informal approaches to socio-technical systems. On the informal side, we show how to steal a birthday cake from a bakery by social engineering.

Our work thereby closes the gap by developing models and analytic processes that support assessing both the socio *and* the technical side of organisations as socio-technical systems, thus combining human factors and physical infrastructure. Our approach simplifies the identification of possible attacks and provides qualified assessment and ranking of attacks based on the expected impact.

The rest of this chapter is structured as follows. After introducing the bakery example as our socio-technical system, Sect. 3 presents a formalisation of such systems followed by a flow logic-based analysis in Sect. 4. A discussion of the limitations of this formal approach when facing human actions leads to a more general identification of possible attacks in Sect. 5, followed by an attempt to formalise human behaviour in Sect. 6. After discussing related work Sect. 7, we conclude the paper with an outlook on future developments.

2   The Drama of the Birthday Cake in Three Pictures

In this section, we provide a case study of a very recent insider attack where a baker's wife socially engineered her husband the baker with the malicious intention to steal Hanne and Flemming's birthday cake. What is worse, is that she succeeded—due to the lack of formal analysis in this bakery. In the rest of this paper we will illustrate the attack and then show different formalisations to identify this attack. Figures 1, 2, and 3 illustrate the sequence of events that lead to the devastating outcome. The part of the bakery that is not illustrated is presented in the next section.

Fig. 1. The baker bakes a cake for Hanne and Flemming's birthday and protects it by putting it in the cake locker—but his wife sees it all.

Fig. 2. The baker's wife uses a social engineering attack on the baker to get his credentials: the key to the cake locker.

Fig. 3. Disaster: Hanne and Flemming's birthday cake vanished from cake locker!

3   Modelling Socio-Technical Systems

Our model represents the infrastructure of organisations, in this case the bakery, as nodes in a directed graph [6], representing *rooms*, access control points, and similar locations. *Actors* are represented by nodes and can possess *assets*, which model data and items that are relevant in the modelled scenario. Assets can be annotated with a value and a metric, *e.g.*, the likelihood of being lost. Nodes representing assets can be attached to locations or actors; assets attached to actors move around with that actor. Actors perform *actions* on locations, including physical locations or other actors. These actions are restricted by *policies* that represent both access control and the behaviour as expected by an organisation from its employees. Policies consist of required credentials and enabled actions, representing what an actor needs to provide in order to enable the actions in a policy, and what actions are enabled if an actor provides the required credentials, respectively.

Our modelling approach is based on Klaim [7]. In contrast to Klaim, we attach processes and actors to special nodes that move around with the process. This makes the modelling of actors and items carried by actors more intuitive and natural, but can easily be mapped back to original Klaim. The metrics mentioned above can represent any quantitative knowledge about components, for example, likelihood, time, price, impact, or probability distributions. The latter could describe behaviour of actors or timing distributions.

3.1   Semantics of Socio-Technical Models

In the following we briefly summarise the formal semantics of our socio-technical models. The calculus follows previous presentations closely and we will therefore not go deep into details here, merely refer to [8]. As already mentioned, the semantics is based on a variant of the Klaim calculus [7], called bacKlaim, which in turn is based on acKlaim [6,8]. The Klaim calculus uses the *tuple space* paradigm, in which systems are composed of a set of distributed nodes that communicate and interact by reading and writing tuples in shared tuples spaces. The following presentation of bacKlaim is an adaptation and simplification of the calculus presented in [8].

In keeping with tradition, the semantics of the bacKlaim calculus is split into three layers: nets, processes, and actions. Nets define the overall, distributed structure of the system by specifying where individual nodes and tuple spaces are located. Processes and actions define the actual behaviour of the nodes. The syntax of nets, processes, and actions is shown in Fig. 4. In the bacKlaim calculus there are two actions for reading a tuple in a remote tuple space: **in** for destructive read and **read** for non-destructive read. Both these input actions allow for *template* specifications of the tuple(s) to be read, facilitating a simple form of pattern matching with variable binding. The syntax for templates is shown in Fig. 5 and the corresponding semantics is shown in Fig. 7.

One of the key differences between classic Klaim and bacKlaim is the explicit support for access control policies in the latter, through a *reference monitor*

$$
\begin{array}{llll}
\ell ::= l & \text{locality} & N ::= l ::^{\delta} P & \text{single node} \\
\quad | \; u & \text{locality variable} & \quad | \; l ::^{\delta} \langle et \rangle & \text{located tuple} \\
& & \quad | \; N_1 \parallel N_2 & \text{net composition} \\
\\
P ::= \textbf{nil} & \text{null process} & a ::= \textbf{out}\,(t)@\ell & \text{output} \\
\quad | \; a.P & \text{action prefixing} & \quad | \; \textbf{in}\,(T)@\ell & \text{input} \\
\quad | \; P_1 \,|\, P_2 & \text{parallel composition} & \quad | \; \textbf{read}\,(T)@\ell & \text{read} \\
\quad | \; A & \text{process invocation} & \quad | \; \textbf{eval}\,(P)@\ell & \text{migration} \\
& & \quad | \; \textbf{move}\,(\ell) & \text{move}
\end{array}
$$

Fig. 4. Syntax of nets, processes, and actions.

$$
\begin{array}{llll}
T ::= F \mid F, T & \text{templates} & et ::= ef \mid ef, et & \text{evaluated tuple} \\
F ::= f \mid !x \mid !u & \text{template fields} & ef ::= V \mid l & \text{evaluated tuple field} \\
t ::= f \mid f, t & \text{tuples} & e ::= V \mid x \mid \ldots & \text{expressions} \\
f ::= e \mid l \mid u & \text{tuple fields} & &
\end{array}
$$

Fig. 5. Syntax for tuples and templates.

embedded in the semantics. Before going further into the semantics of bacKlaim, we first need to define these *access control policies*. In the bacKlaim calculus, the kind of access that is relevant to control, is whether or not a process at a given location is allowed to perform a specific action at a remote location. Thus we can formalise access control policies as follows:

$$
\pi \subseteq \text{AccMode} = \{\textbf{i}, \textbf{r}, \textbf{o}, \textbf{e}, \textbf{n}, \textbf{m}\}
$$
$$
\delta \in \text{Policy} = (\text{Loc} \cup \{\star\}) \rightarrow \mathcal{P}\,(\text{AccMode})
$$

where the *access modes* correspond to the actions that can be taken in the semantics: **i** for (destructively) reading a tuple, **r** for (non-destructively) reading a tuple, **o** for outputting (writing) a tuple, **e** for remote evaluation of a process, and **n** for the capability to create new locations. The special '$\star$' location is used to denote default policies, i.e., access modes that are allowed from all locations not specifically mentioned.

We can now continue with the semantics for bacKlaim, by defining the reduction relation for processes and actions, shown in Fig. 6. In general, a process is composed of sequences of actions, (sub-)processes that execute in parallel, or a recursive invocation through a place-holder variable. The actions a process can perform are: **out**, that writes a tuple to the specified tuple space; **in**, that reads a tuple (at the specified tuple space) matching the template and then *removes* the tuple in question; **read** that also reads a tuple (at the specified tuple space) matching the given template but does *not* remove the tuple; **eval** that evaluates the given process at the specified (remote) location. Finally, the **move** action relocates the node representing the actor or process. However, we only wish to allow certain moves between nodes, e.g., a node representing a (physical) actor

$$\frac{[\![t]\!] = et \quad \boxed{(l,l') \in \mathcal{I} \wedge \mathbf{o} \in \delta(l')}}{l ::^\delta \mathbf{out}\,(t)@l'.P \parallel l' ::^{\delta'} P' \longmapsto_{\mathcal{I}} l ::^\delta P \parallel l' ::^{\delta'} P' \parallel l' ::^{\delta'} \langle et \rangle}$$

$$\frac{match([\![T]\!], et) = \sigma \quad \boxed{(l,l') \in \mathcal{I} \wedge \mathbf{i} \in \delta(l')}}{l ::^\delta \mathbf{in}\,(T)@l'.P \parallel l' ::^{\delta'} \langle et \rangle \longmapsto_{\mathcal{I}} l ::^\delta P\sigma \parallel l' ::^{\delta'} \mathbf{nil}}$$

$$\frac{match([\![T]\!], et) = \sigma \quad \boxed{(l,l') \in \mathcal{I} \wedge \mathbf{r} \in \delta(l')}}{l ::^\delta \mathbf{read}\,(T)@l'.P \parallel l' ::^{\delta'} \langle et \rangle \longmapsto_{\mathcal{I}} l ::^\delta P\sigma \parallel l' ::^{\delta'} \langle et \rangle}$$

$$\frac{\boxed{(l,l') \in \mathcal{I} \wedge \mathbf{e} \in \delta(l')}}{l ::^\delta \mathbf{eval}\,(Q)@l'.P \parallel l' ::^{\delta'} P' \longmapsto_{\mathcal{I}} l ::^\delta P \parallel l' ::^{\delta'} Q \parallel l' ::^{\delta'} P'}$$

$$\frac{\boxed{\{(l,l''),(l'',l')\} \in \mathcal{I} \wedge \mathbf{m} \in \delta(l')}}{l ::^\delta \mathbf{move}\,(l').P \parallel l' ::^{\delta'} P' \longmapsto_{\mathcal{I}'} l ::^\delta P \parallel l' ::^{\delta'} P'} \quad \mathcal{I}' = \mathcal{I} \setminus (l, \_) \cup \{(l,l')\}$$

$$\frac{L \vdash N_1 \longmapsto_{\mathcal{I}} L' \vdash N_1'}{L \vdash N_1 \parallel N_2 \longmapsto_{\mathcal{I}} L' \vdash N_1' \parallel N_2} \qquad \frac{N \equiv N_1 \quad L \vdash N_1 \longmapsto_{\mathcal{I}} L' \vdash N_2 \quad N_2 \equiv N'}{L \vdash N \longmapsto_{\mathcal{I}} L' \vdash N'}$$

Fig. 6. Reduction semantics for bacKlaim.

$$match(V, V) = \epsilon \quad match(!x, V) = [V/x] \quad match(l, l) = \epsilon \quad match(!u, l') = [l'/u]$$

$$\frac{match(F, ef) = \sigma_1 \quad match(T, et) = \sigma_2}{match((F,T), (ef, et)) = \sigma_1 \circ \sigma_2}$$

Fig. 7. Semantics for template matching.

should only be able to move between nodes representing physical localities. We formalise this in the form of the so-called *infrastructure* of the underlying nets:

$$\mathcal{I} \in \mathsf{Infrastructure} = \mathcal{P}\,(\mathsf{Locality} \times \mathsf{Locality})$$

Essentially, the infrastructure is a graph, relating the pairs of nodes between which moves are allowed (still subject to access control rules).

In addition to the reduction relation, the semantics also incorporates a structural congruence, simplifying (re-)presentation of, computation with, and reasoning about processes and nets. The congruence is shown in Fig. 8.

$$N_1 \parallel N_2 \equiv N_2 \parallel N_1 \qquad (N_1 \parallel N_2) \parallel N_3 \equiv N_1 \parallel (N_2 \parallel N_3)$$

$$l ::^\delta P \equiv l ::^\delta (P \,|\, \mathbf{nil}) \qquad l ::^\delta A \equiv l ::^\delta P \quad \text{if } A \overset{\triangle}{=} P$$

$$l ::^\delta (P_1 \,|\, P_2) \equiv l ::^\delta P_1 \parallel l ::^\delta P_2$$

Fig. 8. Structural congruence on nets and processes.

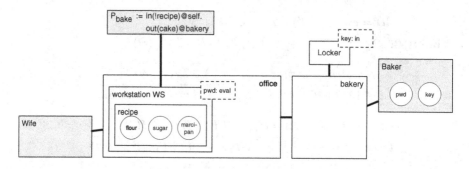

Fig. 9. Graphical representation of the crime scene, the bakery. The rectangles represent actors, locations, assets, and processes. The baker is (still) in possession of the key and the password for the computer.

3.2 The Bakery Model

The bakery example introduced in Sect. 2 is based on the baker and his wife, and of course the cake. The assets in this example are the key to the cake locker, the cake itself, and, to add to the excitement, a computer with the recipe for the cake. The recipe is input to a process on the computer that outputs a cake in the bakery.[1] We assume the baker to have an (internalised) policy that forbids the cake to leave the bakery prematurely. Figure 9 shows the formalisation of the bakery, consisting of the baker shop, the office, the cake locker, and the outside world. The baker has the key and the Password to his computer. The policies in the model require, *e.g.*, the key to enter the cake locker and the password to log into the computer. Actor nodes also represent processes running on the corresponding locations. The process at the computer represents the "creation" of a cake, that is output at the bakery.

4 Flow Logic-Based Analysis of Processes

The first analysis for catching the thief is a flow logic analysis similar to [8]. This analysis takes a sequence of actions and performs a static control flow analysis to compute and assess its effect by a conservative approximation of the possible flow between actors, processes, and tuple spaces. Following the Flow Logic framework [9], we specify a *judgements* for nets, processes, and actions that determine whether or not an analysis estimate correctly describes all configurations that are reachable from the initial state. The definitions are shown in Fig. 10.

The tuple spaces and variable values are collected in $\hat{T}$ and $\hat{\sigma}$. For space reasons we do not consider the **newloc** action that dynamically creates new locations. Similar to [8] we could use canonical names. For the pattern matching we reuse the Flow Logic specification, shown in Fig. 11 from [8].

---

[1] To simplify treatment we assume the bakery to be high-tech. A different approach would have been to model the baking process at the baker or the bakery, requiring the recipe as input.

$$(\hat{T}, \hat{\sigma}, \hat{\mathcal{I}}) \models_{\text{N}} l ::^{\delta} P \qquad \text{iff} \qquad (\hat{T}, \hat{\sigma}, \hat{\mathcal{I}}) \models_{\text{P}}^{\lfloor l \rfloor} P$$

$$(\hat{T}, \hat{\sigma}, \hat{\mathcal{I}}) \models_{\text{N}} l ::^{\delta} \langle et \rangle \qquad \text{iff} \qquad \langle et \rangle \in \hat{T}(\lfloor l \rfloor, \delta)$$

$$(\hat{T}, \hat{\sigma}, \hat{\mathcal{I}}) \models_{\text{N}} N_1 \parallel N_2 \qquad \text{iff} \qquad (\hat{T}, \hat{\sigma}, \hat{\mathcal{I}}) \models_{\text{N}} N_1 \wedge (\hat{T}, \hat{\sigma}, \hat{\mathcal{I}}) \models_{\text{N}} N_2$$

$$(\hat{T}, \hat{\sigma}, \hat{\mathcal{I}}) \models_{\text{P}}^{l} \textbf{nil} \qquad \text{iff} \qquad \textit{true}$$

$$(\hat{T}, \hat{\sigma}, \hat{\mathcal{I}}) \models_{\text{P}}^{l} P_1 \mid P_2 \qquad \text{iff} \qquad (\hat{T}, \hat{\sigma}, \hat{\mathcal{I}}) \models_{\text{P}}^{l} P_1 \wedge (\hat{T}, \hat{\sigma}, \hat{\mathcal{I}}) \models_{\text{P}}^{l} P_2$$

$$(\hat{T}, \hat{\sigma}, \hat{\mathcal{I}}) \models_{\text{P}}^{l} A \qquad \text{iff} \qquad (\hat{T}, \hat{\sigma}, \hat{\mathcal{I}}) \models_{\text{P}}^{l} P \quad \text{if } A \stackrel{\triangle}{=} P$$

$$(\hat{T}, \hat{\sigma}, \hat{\mathcal{I}}) \models_{\text{P}}^{l} a.P \qquad \text{iff} \qquad (\hat{T}, \hat{\sigma}, \hat{\mathcal{I}}) \models_{\text{A}}^{l} a \wedge (\hat{T}, \hat{\sigma}, \hat{\mathcal{I}}) \models_{\text{P}}^{l} P$$

$$(\hat{T}, \hat{\sigma}, \hat{\mathcal{I}}) \models_{\text{A}}^{l} \textbf{out}\,(t)@\ell' \qquad \text{iff} \qquad \forall \hat{l} \in \hat{\sigma}(\ell'): (\textbf{o} \in \delta(\hat{l}) \Rightarrow \hat{\sigma}[\![t]\!] \subseteq \hat{T}(\hat{l}))$$

$$(\hat{T}, \hat{\sigma}, \hat{\mathcal{I}}) \models_{\text{A}}^{l} \textbf{in}\,(T)@\ell' \qquad \text{iff} \qquad \forall \hat{l} \in \hat{\sigma}(\ell'): (\textbf{i} \in \delta(\hat{l}) \Rightarrow \hat{\sigma} \models_1 T : \hat{T}(\hat{l}) \triangleright \hat{W}_{\bullet})$$

$$(\hat{T}, \hat{\sigma}, \hat{\mathcal{I}}) \models_{\text{A}}^{l} \textbf{read}\,(T)@\ell' \qquad \text{iff} \qquad \forall \hat{l} \in \hat{\sigma}(\ell'): (\textbf{r} \in \delta(\hat{l}) \Rightarrow \hat{\sigma} \models_1 T : \hat{T}(\hat{l}) \triangleright \hat{W}_{\bullet})$$

$$(\hat{T}, \hat{\sigma}, \hat{\mathcal{I}}) \models_{\text{A}}^{l} \textbf{eval}\,(Q)@\ell' \qquad \text{iff} \qquad \forall \hat{l} \in \hat{\sigma}(\ell'): (\textbf{e} \in \delta(\hat{l}) \Rightarrow (\hat{T}, \hat{\sigma}, \hat{\mathcal{I}}) \models_{\text{P}}^{\hat{l}} Q)$$

$$(\hat{T}, \hat{\sigma}, \hat{\mathcal{I}}) \models_{\text{A}}^{l} \textbf{move}\,(\ell') \qquad \text{iff} \qquad \forall \hat{l} \in \hat{\sigma}(l): \forall \hat{l'} \in \hat{\sigma}(\ell'): (\textbf{m} \in \delta(\hat{l'}) \Rightarrow (\hat{l}, \hat{l'}) \in \hat{\mathcal{I}})$$

Fig. 10. Flow logic specification for control flow analysis of bacKlaim.

$$\hat{\sigma} \models_i \epsilon : \hat{V}_{\circ} \triangleright \hat{V}_{\bullet} \qquad \text{iff} \qquad \{\hat{et} \in \hat{V}_{\circ} | |\hat{et}| = i\} \subseteq \hat{V}_{\bullet}$$

$$\hat{\sigma} \models_i V, T : \hat{V}_{\circ} \triangleright \hat{W}_{\bullet} \qquad \text{iff} \qquad \hat{\sigma} \models_{i+1} T : \hat{V}_{\bullet} \triangleright \hat{W}_{\bullet} \wedge \{\hat{et} \in \hat{V}_{\circ} | \pi_i(\hat{et}) = V\} \subseteq \hat{V}_{\bullet}$$

$$\hat{\sigma} \models_i l, T : \hat{V}_{\circ} \triangleright \hat{W}_{\bullet} \qquad \text{iff} \qquad \hat{\sigma} \models_{i+1} T : \hat{V}_{\bullet} \triangleright \hat{W}_{\bullet} \wedge \{\hat{et} \in \hat{V}_{\circ} | \pi_i(\hat{et}) = V\} \subseteq \hat{V}_{\bullet}$$

$$\hat{\sigma} \models_i x, T : \hat{V}_{\circ} \triangleright \hat{W}_{\bullet} \qquad \text{iff} \qquad \hat{\sigma} \models_{i+1} T : \hat{V}_{\bullet} \triangleright \hat{W}_{\bullet} \wedge \{\hat{et} \in \hat{V}_{\circ} | \pi_i(\hat{et}) \in \hat{\sigma}(x)\} \subseteq \hat{V}_{\bullet}$$

$$\hat{\sigma} \models_i u, T : \hat{V}_{\circ} \triangleright \hat{W}_{\bullet} \qquad \text{iff} \qquad \hat{\sigma} \models_{i+1} T : \hat{V}_{\bullet} \triangleright \hat{W}_{\bullet} \wedge \{\hat{et} \in \hat{V}_{\circ} | \pi_i(\hat{et}) \in \hat{\sigma}(u)\} \subseteq \hat{V}_{\bullet}$$

$$\hat{\sigma} \models_i !x, T : \hat{V}_{\circ} \triangleright \hat{W}_{\bullet} \qquad \text{iff} \qquad \hat{\sigma} \models_{i+1} T : \hat{V}_{\bullet} \triangleright \hat{W}_{\bullet} \wedge \hat{V}_{\circ} \subseteq \hat{V}_{\bullet} \wedge \pi_i(\hat{W}_{\bullet}) \subseteq \hat{\sigma}(x)$$

$$\hat{\sigma} \models_i !u, T : \hat{V}_{\circ} \triangleright \hat{W}_{\bullet} \qquad \text{iff} \qquad \hat{\sigma} \models_{i+1} T : \hat{V}_{\bullet} \triangleright \hat{W}_{\bullet} \wedge \hat{V}_{\circ} \subseteq \hat{V}_{\bullet} \wedge \pi_i(\hat{W}_{\bullet}) \subseteq \hat{\sigma}(u)$$

Fig. 11. Flow logic specification for pattern match analysis [8].

Having specified the analysis it remains to be shown that the information computed by the analysis is correct. In the Flow Logic framework this is usually done by establishing a *subject reduction* property for the analysis:

Theorem 1 (Subject Reduction). *If* $(\hat{T}, \hat{\sigma}, \hat{\mathcal{I}}) \models_N N$ *and* $L \vdash N \rightarrowtail_{\mathcal{I}} L' \vdash N'$ *then* $(\hat{T}, \hat{\sigma}, \hat{\mathcal{I}}) \models_N N'$.

Proof. (Sketch) By induction on the structure of $L \vdash N \rightarrowtail_{\mathcal{I}} L' \vdash N'$ and using auxiliary results for the other judgements.

4.1 Analysing the Bakery Example

Before we conclude this section, we quickly want to see whether the flow logic analysis can help the baker in protecting the cake. We consider the two processes shown in Fig. 12; the first process represents the baker going to the office and starts the "bake" process on the workstation. As a result, the cake appears in the bakery, the baker goes there and picks up, goes to the Locker and puts it down, and then returns to the bakery. The wife meets the baker somewhere, in

$P_{baker} :=$ **move** (*office*) .**eval** (P_{bake})@ *WS*.**move** (*bakery*) .**in** (*cake*)@*bakery*.
move (*Locker*) .**out** (*cake*)@*Locker*.**move** (*bakery*)

$P_{wife} :=$ **move** (*bakery*) .**in** (*key*)@*baker*.
move (*Locker*) .**in** (*cake*)@*Locker*.**move** (*bakery*)

Fig. 12. The two processes for the Flow logic analysis. The baker bakes the cake and brings it to the Locker, and his wife picks the key from him, goes also to the Locker, and steals the cake.

our case in the bakery, picks the key from his pocket, goes to the Locker, gets the cake, and returns to the bakery.

The result of the flow logic analysis of the two processes shown in Fig. 12 is that the cake will be at the baker, the bakery, and the Locker. However, it will also be at the wife, which is what the baker wanted to prevent, knowing her sweet tooth. This means that from the flow logic analysis, the baker can learn that his wife has stolen the cake.

5   Attack Generation

Unfortunately, there is a problem with the processes described in the previous section. Processes are a suitable abstraction for programs, but we are in general not able to obtain processes describing human behaviour. If the baker knew, which actions his wife had performed, he also would know that she stole cake— without any analysis or tool support.

If we cannot obtain processes to identify attacks, we need a different method to do so. In this section we present a recent development to attack generation based on the negation of policies [10,11]. The policies we consider describe global system states that should be fulfilled at all times; our approach identifies sequences of actions that results in a policy violation.

In the bakery example, the baker could have the global policy that only the birthday children or he should get the cake, or more concretely, that his wife should *not* have the cake. Since she is determined to obtain the cake, she would violate this global policy by obtaining it.

We choose attack trees as a succinct way of representing attacks. In attack trees [12,13], the root represents a goal, and the children represent sub-attacks. Sub-attacks can be alternatives for reaching the goal (disjunctive node) or they must all be completed to reach the goal (conjunctive node). We assume an implicit, left to right order for children of conjunctive nodes. For example, an attacker first needs to move to a location before being able to perform an action. Leaf nodes represent the basic actions in an attack. The operators $\oplus_\vee$ and $\oplus_\wedge$ combine attack trees by adding a disjunctive or conjunctive root, respectively.

In the remainder of this section we present the rules for generating attack trees from models. The rules take as arguments the infrastructure $\mathcal{I}$ and an actor component $\mathcal{A}$, which stores reached locations, obtained data, and acquired identities for the attacker. The rules either succeed and return an (possibly empty) attack tree, or they block if no valid result can be computed. Our approach for invalidating a policy consists of four basic steps:

Identify Attackers: Choose the policy to invalidate, and identify the possible actors who could invalidate it.

Target Locations: Identify a set of locations where the prohibited actions can be performed.

Goto Target Location: Generate attacks for reaching target locations. This will identify and obtain required assets to perform any of these actions, and obtain all assets required to reach the target location.

Move to Target Location and Perform Action: Finally, move to the location identified in the second step and perform the action.

In the first step we identify possible attackers and locations where the action violating the global policy can be applied (see Fig. 13). These are the goals for the attacker, and are the basis for generating attack trees (Fig. 14). For each goal we generate a tree for moving to the location and another one for performing the action. While moving to the location new credentials may be required, which recursively invoke the attack generation again. The resulting new knowledge is added to the actor component $\mathcal{A}$.

The rules in Figs. 15 and 16 generate attack trees for moving around, performing actions, and obtaining credentials, resulting in attack trees for every single action of the attacker. The function *missingCredentials* uses the unification described above to match policies with the assets available in the model. The attack generation then generates one attack for each of these assets and combines the resulting trees with a disjunctive node.

$$\frac{\sigma = \mathit{unify}_{\mathcal{I}}(\mathit{Actors}, \mathit{credentials})}{\mathit{attackers} = \mathit{getAttacker}_{\mathcal{I}}(\mathit{actor}, \sigma) \qquad \mathit{goals} = \mathit{applicableAt}_{\mathcal{I}}(\mathit{credentials}, \mathit{enabled}, \sigma)}$$
$$\frac{\mathcal{I}, \mathit{attackers}, \mathit{goals} \vdash_{\mathit{goal}} \mathit{trees} \qquad\qquad \mathcal{T} := \oplus_{\vee} \mathit{trees}}{\mathcal{I}, \mathit{not}(\mathit{actor}, \mathit{credentials}, \mathit{enabled}) \vdash_{P} \mathcal{T}}$$

Fig. 13. Attack generation starts from the global policy *not(actor, credentials, enabled)*. Attack trees are generated for all possible policy violations. As every attack tree represents a violation of the policy, the resulting attack trees are combined by an *or* node.

$$\frac{\mathcal{I}, \mathcal{A}, \mathit{goto}(\mathit{location}) \wedge \mathit{perform}(\mathit{action}) \vdash_{GP} \mathcal{T}}{\mathcal{I}, \mathcal{A}, (\mathit{location}, \mathit{action}) \vdash_{\mathit{goal}} \mathcal{T}}$$

$$\frac{\mathcal{I}, \mathcal{A}, \mathit{goto}(l) \vdash_{\mathit{goto}} \mathcal{T}_{\mathit{goto}}, \mathcal{A}' \qquad \mathcal{I}, \mathcal{A}', \mathit{perform}(a) \vdash_{\mathit{perform}} \mathcal{T}_{\mathit{action}}, \mathcal{A}''}{\mathcal{I}, \mathcal{A}, \mathit{goto}(l) \wedge \mathit{perform}(a) \vdash_{GP} \mathcal{T}_{\mathit{goto}} \oplus_{\wedge} \mathcal{T}_{\mathit{action}}, \mathcal{A}''}$$

Fig. 14. For each identified goal (consisting of a location and an action) an attacker moves to the location and performs the action. The rules result in an attack tree and a new state of the attacker, which includes the obtained keys and reached locations.

$$paths = getAllPaths_{\mathcal{I}}(\mathcal{A}, l) \qquad \mathcal{I}, \mathcal{A}, paths \vdash_{path} trees, \mathcal{A}'$$
$$\frac{\mathcal{T} := \oplus_{\vee} trees}{\mathcal{I}, \mathcal{A}, goto(l) \vdash_{goto} \mathcal{T}, \mathcal{A}'}$$

$$missing = missingCredentials_{\mathcal{I}}(\mathcal{A}, path) \qquad \mathcal{I}, \mathcal{A}, missing \vdash_{credential} trees, \mathcal{A}'$$
$$\frac{\mathcal{T} := \oplus_{\wedge} trees}{\mathcal{I}, \mathcal{A}, path \vdash_{path} \mathcal{T} \oplus_{\wedge} \mathcal{N}^{\text{pass } path}, \mathcal{A}'}$$

Fig. 15. Going to a location and performing an action results in two attack trees. The function *getAllPaths* returns all paths from the current locations of the actor to the goal location l, and the resulting attack trees are alternatives for reaching this location.

$$\frac{i \notin identities \implies \mathcal{T} = \mathcal{N}^{\text{obtain identity } i}}{\mathcal{I}, (identities, locations, assets), identity\ i \vdash_{credential} \mathcal{T}, (identities \cup \{i\}, locations, assets)}$$

$$\frac{\mathcal{A} = (identities, locations, assets) \wedge a \notin assets \implies}{goals = availableAt_{\mathcal{I}}(a) \qquad \mathcal{I}, \mathcal{A}, goals \vdash_{goal} trees, \mathcal{A}' \qquad \mathcal{T} := \oplus_{\vee} trees}$$
$$\overline{\mathcal{I}, \mathcal{A}, asset\ a \vdash_{credential} \mathcal{T}, \mathcal{A}'}$$

$$\frac{\mathcal{I}, \mathcal{A}, predicate\ p(arguments) \vdash_{predicate} trees, \mathcal{A}' \qquad \mathcal{T} := \oplus_{\vee} trees}{\mathcal{I}, \mathcal{A}, predicate\ p(arguments) \vdash_{credential} \mathcal{T}, \mathcal{A}'}$$

Fig. 16. Depending on the missing credential, different attacks are generated. If the actor lacks an identity, an attack node representing an abstract social engineering attack is generated, for example, social engineering or impersonating. If the missing credential is an asset, the function *availableAt* returns a set of pairs of locations from which this asset is available, and the according **in** actions. If the missing credential is a predicate, a combination of credentials fulfilling the predicate must be obtained.

Attack generation also considers triggering processes to obtain assets. We do not present this interaction between actors and processes for space reasons, as it follows the rules presented above.

5.1 Post-Processing Attack Trees

The generated attack trees only represent the factual attack steps for reaching the final goal. The trees do not contain any annotation or metrics about the likelihood of success of actions such as social engineering, or the potential impact of actions. Also the likelihood of a given attacker to succeed or fail is not considered.

Computing qualitative and quantitative measures [14,15] on attack trees is orthogonal to our approach and beyond the scope of this work. The generated attack trees also often contain duplicated sub-trees, due to similar scenarios being encountered in several locations, for example, the social engineering of the same actor, or the requirement for the same credentials. This is not an inherent limitation, but may clutter attack trees. Similar to [16], a post-processing of attack trees can simplify the result.

5.2   Attack Tree for the Bakery Example

Figure 17 shows part of the attack tree generated for the bakery example. The first attack is the one described in the previous section and shown in Fig. 12: the wife steals the key from the baker and gets the cake from the Locker after it has been baked. A variant of this attack is that she breaks the Locker door open. In the second attack, she social engineers the baker to bake the cake, and then picks up the cake in the bakery *before* the baker does so. In the third attack, she gets the password to the work station from the baker, and then starts P_{bake} herself. Finally, she can social engineer the baker to give her the cake, maybe promising him to share it. All attacks, where assets are stolen also occur in a variant where actors with access to the asset are social engineered to obtain the asset and give it to the attacker.

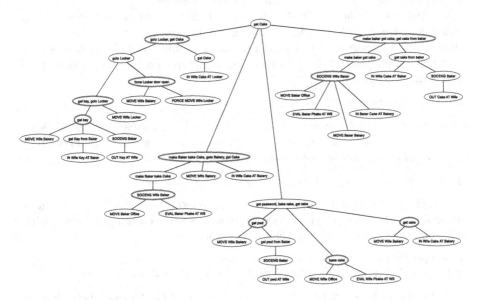

Fig. 17. Attack tree generated for the bakery example. The double-lined borders indicate disjunctive nodes.

6   Analysis of Socio-Technical Attacks in Isabelle

We now consider a third approach to modelling socio-technical systems using the interactive theorem prover Isabelle. We first illustrate the attack and then we discuss how the socio-technical model can be transfered to the modeling and verification of insider threats using our Isabelle framework [17]. Finally, we extend the Isabelle technique here further to Isabelle Attack Trees.

6.1   Social Explanation for Insider Threats in Isabelle

In earlier work [17], we have used the process of sociological explanation based on Max Weber's *Grundmodell* and its logical interpretation to explain insider threats by moving between societal level (macro) and individual actor level (micro). The interpretation into a logic of explanation is formalized in Isabelle's Higher Order Logic thereby providing a tool to prove global security properties with machine assistance [17]. Isabelle/HOL is an interactive proof assistant based on Higher Order Logic (HOL). It enables specification of so-called object-logics for an application. Object-logics comprise new types, constants and definitions and reside in theory files, e.g., the file `Insider.thy` contains the object-logic we define for social explanation of insider threats below. We construct our theory as a conservative extension of HOL guaranteeing consistency. I.e., we do not introduce new axioms that could lead to inconsistencies.

We first provide here only the elements of this Insider theory necessary as a basis for attack trees and for modeling the bakery application. For a more complete view, please refer to [17] and the related online Isabelle resources [18].

In the Isabelle/HOL theory for Insiders, we express policies over actions `get`, `move`, `eval`, and `put`.

```
datatype action = get | move | eval | put
```

We abstract here from concrete data – actions have no parameters. Policies describe prerequisites for actions to be granted to actors given by pairs of predicates (conditions) and sets of (enabled) actions.

```
type_synonym policy = ((actor ⇒ bool) × action set)
```

We integrate policies with a graph into the infrastructure providing an organisational model where policies reside at locations and actors are adorned with additional predicates to specify their 'credentials'.

```
datatype infrastructure = Infrastructure
"node graph" "location ⇒ policy set" "actor ⇒ bool"
```

These local policies serve to provide a specification of the 'normal' behaviour of actors but are also the starting point for possible attacks on the organisation's assets. The `enables` predicate specifies that an actor a can perform an action a'∈ e at location l in the infrastructure I if a's credentials (stored in the tuple space `tspace I a`) imply the location policy's (stored in `delta I l`) condition p for a.

```
enables I l a a' ≡
∃ (p,e) ∈ delta I l. a' ∈ e ∧ (tspace I a ⟶ p(a))
```

For the application to the bakery senario, we only model two identities, `Baker` and `Wife` representing the baker and his wife. We define the set of bakery actors as a local definition in the locale `scenarioBakerNN`. We show here in a first instance the full Isabelle/HOL syntax but in all subsequent definitions we omit the `fixes` and `defines` keywords and also drop the types for clarity of the exposition. The double quotes `''s''` create a string in Isabelle/HOL.

```
fixes bakery_actors :: identity set
defines bakery_actors_def: bakery_actors ≡ {''Baker''}
```

The graph representing the infrastructure of the bakery case study contains only the minimal structure: (1) Kitchen, (2) Cake locker, (3) Home.

```
bakery_locations ≡ {Location 1, Location 2, Location 3}
```

The global policy is 'no one except bakery employees can get anything from the cake locker'.

```
global_policy I a ≡  a ∉ bakery_actors ⟶
                        ¬(enables I (Location 2) (Actor a) get)
```

Next, we have to provide the definition of the infrastructure. We first define the graph representing the organisation's locations and the positions of its actors. Locations are wrapped up with the datatype constructor NL and actors using the corresponding constructor NA to enable joining them in the datatype **node** and thus creating the following **node graph** as a set of pairs between locations or actors.

```
ex_graph ≡ Graph {(NA (''Baker''), NL (Location 3)),
                  (NL (Location 3), NL(Location 1)),
                  (NL (Location 2), NL(Location 1)),
                  (NA (''Wife''), NL (Location 1))}
```

Policies are attached to locations in the organisation's graph using a function that maps each location to the set of the policies valid in this location. The policies are again pairs. The first element of these pairs are credentials which are defined as predicates over actors, *i.e.*, boolean valued functions describing, for example, whether an actor inhabits a role, or, whether an actor possesses something, like an identity or a key. The second elements are sets of actions that are authorised in this location for actors authenticated by the credentials.

```
local_policies ≡
(λ x. if x = Location 1 then
  {(λ x. (ID x ''Baker'')∨(ID x ''Wife''), {get,put}), (λ x. True, {move})}
              else (if x = Location 2 then
                      {((λ x. has (x, ''key'')), {get,put,move})}
                    else (if x = Location 3 then
                      {((λ x. True, {get,put,move}))}
                    else {})))
```

The final component of any infrastructure is the credentials contained in a **tspace**. We define the assignment of the credentials to the actors similarly as a predicate over actors that is true for actors that have the credentials.

```
ex_creds ≡ (λ if x = Actor ''Baker'' then has (x, ''key'') else False)
```

Finally, we can put the graph, the local policies, and the credential assignment into an infrastructure.

```
Bakery_scenario ≡ Infrastructure ex_graph local_policies ex_creds
```

Note, that all the above definitions have been implemented as local definitions using the locale keywords `fixes` and `defines`. Thus they are accessible whenever the locales `scenarioBakerNN` is invoked but are not axioms that could endanger consistency. We now also make use of the possibility of locales to define local assumptions. This is very suitable in this context since we want to emphasize that the following formulas are not general facts or axiomatic rules but are assumptions we make in order to explore the validity of the infrastructure's global policy. The first assumption provides that the precipitating event has occurred which leads to the second assumption that provides that Charly can act as an insider.

```
assumes Bakers_Wife_precipitating_event: tipping_point (astate ''Wife'')
assumes Insider_Wife : Insider ''Charly_comp'' {''Charly_priv''}
```

So far, we have specified the model. Based on these definitions and assumptions we can now state theorems about the security of the model and interactively prove them in our Isabelle/HOL framework. We can now first prove a sanity check on the model by validating the infrastructure for the "normal" case. For the baker as a bakery actor, everything is fine: the global policy does hold. The following is an Isabelle/HOL theorem `ex_inv` that can be proved automatically followed by the proof script of its interactive proof. The proof is achieved by locally unfolding the definitions of the scenario, e.g., `Bakery_scenario_def` and applying the simplifier.

```
lemma ex_inv:
  global_policy Bakery_scenario (''Baker'')
by (simp add: Bakery_scenario_def global_policy_def bakery_actors_def)
```

However, since the baker's `Wife` is at tipping point, she will ignore the global policy. This insider threat can now be formalised as an invalidation of the global company policy for ''Wife'' in the following "attack" theorem named `ex_inv1`.

```
theorem ex_inv1:
  ¬ global_policy Bakery_scenario ''Wife''
```

The proof of this theorem consists of a few simple steps largely supported by automated tactics. Thus `Wife` can get access to the cake leading to devastating outcomes (see Fig. 3). The attack is proved above as an Isabelle/HOL theorem. Applying logical analysis, we thus exhibit that under the given assumptions the organisation's model is vulnerable to an insider. This overall procedure corresponds to the approach of invalidation of a global policy based on local policies for a given application scenario [10].

However, to systematically derive the actual attack vector the present paper provides a more constructive approach. We will next see how we can extend the Isabelle Insider framework to this.

6.2   Attack Trees in Isabelle

We now extend the theory Insider by Attack trees. The base attacks figure in an attack sequence (see Sect. 5). We represent them in Isabelle/HOL as a datatype and a list over this datatype.

```
datatype baseattack = None | Goto ''location''
                    | Perform ''action''| Credential ''location''
type_synonym attackseq = ''baseattack list''
```

The following definition of attack tree, really defines the nodes of an attack tree. The simplest case is when a node in an attack tree is a base attack. Attacks can also be combined as the "and" of other attacks as defined in Sect. 5. This prescribes that the third element of type **attree** is a **baseattack** (usually a **Perform** action) that represents this attack, while the first element is an attack sequence and the second element is a label describing the attack (here a string).

```
datatype attree = BaseAttack ''baseattack'' (''N (_)'') |
                  AndAttack ''attackseq'' ''string'' ''baseattack'' (''_ ⊕^(-)_∧ _'')
```

As the corresponding projection functions for **attree** we define **get_attseq** and **get_attack** returning the entire attack sequence or the final base attack, respectively.

The following inductive predicate **get_then_move** shows how we represent the static analysis rules for the derivation of attack sequences. It translates the two rules of Fig. 15 and formalizes how the impossible base attack **Goto l'** can be achieved by first going to location **l** and getting the credential from there. Logically, this is justified if an actor **a** can get to location **l'** in the extended infrastructure **add_credential I a s** where he possesses the credential **s** – as is expressed by the third **enables** proviso.

```
⟦ enables I l a move; enables I l a get;
  enables (add_credential I a s) l' a get ⟧
⟹ get_then_move I s
   (get_attackseq ([Goto l, Credential l, Goto l'] ⊕^{get-move}_∧ Perform get))
   (Goto l')
```

An attack tree is constituted from the above defined nodes of type **attree** but children nodes must be refinement of their parents. Refinement means that some portion of the attack sequence has been extended according to rules like the above **get_then_move**. We formalize this constructor relation of the attack trees by the following refinement. The rules **trans** and **refl** make the refinement a preorder; the rule **get_moveI** shows how the **get_then_move** rule is integrated: If we replace the attack **a** by the **get_then_move** sequence **l** we get refine the attack sequence **A** into **A'** (the auxiliary function **sublist_rep** replaces a symbol in list by a list).

```
inductive
refines_to :: ''[attree, infrastructure, attree] ⟹ bool'' (''_ ⊑(-) _'')
where
```

```
get_moveI: ⟦ get_then_move I s l a;
              sublist_rep l a (get_attseq A) = (get_attseq A');
              get_attack A = get_attack A' ⟧ ⟹ A ⊑_I A' |
trans: ⟦ A ⊑_I A'; A' ⊑_I A '' ⟧ ⟹ A ⊑_I A'' |
refl : A ⊑_I A
```

The refinement of attack sequence allows the expansion of top level abstract attacks into longer sequences. Ultimately, we need to have a notion of when a sufficiently refined sequence of attacks is valid. This notion is provided by the final inductive predicate is_and_attack_tree. It integrates the base cases where base attacks can be directly logically derived from corresponding enables properties; it states that an attack sequence is valid if all its constituent attacks are so and it allows to transfer validity to shorter attacks if a refinement exists.

```
inductive
is_and_attack_tree :: [infrastructure, actor, attree] ⇒ bool ("_, _ ⊢ _")
where
att_act: enables I l a a' ⟹ I , a ⊢ 𝒩(Perform(a')) |
att_goto: enables I l a (move) ⟹ I, a ⊢ 𝒩(Goto l) |
att_cred: enables I l a (get) ⟹ I, a ⊢ 𝒩(Credential l) |
att_list: ⟦ ∀ a ∈ (set(as)). I, a' ⊢ 𝒩(a) ⟧ ⟹ I, a' ⊢ as ⊕_∧^s a'' |
att_ref: ⟦ A ⊑_I A'; I, a ⊢ A' ⟧ ⟹ I, a ⊢ A
```

The Isabelle/HOL theory library provides a lot of list functions. We can thus simply define the "or" of attack trees by folding the above validity over a list of attacks.

```
I, a  ⊢_G⊕∨ al ≡ fold (λ x y. (I, a ⊢ x) ∨ y) al False
```

To validate this formalisation of the attack trees, we now show how the bakery scenario attack can be derived.

First, we prove the following get_then_move property.

```
lemma get_move_lem: get_then_move Bakery_scenario ''key''
  (get_attseq ([Goto (Location 1), Credential (Location 1), Goto (Location 2)]
  ⊕_∧^{get-move} Perform get))
  (Goto (Location 2))
```

After reducing with the defining rule of get_then_move above, proof requires resolving three "enables" subgoals; the final one uses the add_credential for Wife. This lemma rather immediately implies the following refines property.

```
([Goto (Location 2)] ⊕_∧^{get-cake} Perform get)
⊑_Bakery-scenario
([Goto (Location 1), Credential (Location 1), Goto (Location 2)]
  ⊕_∧^{get-move} Perform get)
```

We can show this refined attack as valid mainly showing that each step in it is valid.

```
lemma final_attack: Bakery_scenario, Actor ''Wife'' ⊢
([Goto (Location 1), Credential (Location 1), Goto (Location 2)]
  ⊕_∧^{get-move} Perform get)
```

The last lemma together with the refinement gives us finally that the top level abstract attack is a valid attack.

```
theorem bakery_attack:
Bakery_scenario, Actor ''Wife'' ⊢ ([Goto (Location 2)] ⊕_∧^{get-cake} Perform get)
```

7 Related Work

System models such as ExASyM [6,8] and Portunes [19] also model infrastructure and data, and analyse the modelled organisation for possible threats. However, Portunes supports mobility of nodes, instead of processes, and represents the social domain by low-level policies that describe the trust relation between people to model social engineering. Pieters *et al.* consider policy alignment to address different levels of abstraction of socio-technical systems [20], where policies are interpreted as first-order logical theories containing all sequences of actions and expressing the policy as a "distinguished" prefix-closed predicate in these theories. In contrast to their use of refinement for policies we use the security refinement paradox, *i.e.*, security is *not* generally preserved by refinement.

Attack trees [21] specify an attacker's main goal as the root of a tree; this goal is then disjunctively or conjunctively refined into sub-goals until the reached subgoals represent basic actions that correspond to atomic components. Disjunctive refinements represent alternative ways of achieving a goal, whereas conjunctive refinements depict different steps an attacker needs to take in order to achieve a goal. Techniques for the automated generation of attack graphs mostly consider computer networks only [22,23]. While these techniques usually require the specification of atomic attacks, in our approach the attack consists in invalidating a policy, and the model just provides the infrastructure and methods for doing so.

8 Conclusion

Modelling socio-technical systems with formal methods is a difficult undertaking. Due to the unpredictability of human behaviour, formal methods are often too restrictive to capture essential aspects. This results in the human factor often being ignored in these formalisations, since it cannot be represented in the model used.

In this work we have presented different techniques for modelling and analysing systems *including* human factors using recent advances in system models. Our approach supports all kinds of human factors that can be instantiated once an attack has been identified. The presented techniques address different aspects of analysing socio-technical systems. The flow-logic based approach (Sect. 4) supports analysis of observed actions; this can be compared to an a posteriori analysis to identify what has happened, or in combination with logged information, what might have happened. The attack generation (Sect. 5) identifies *all possible* attacks with respect to the model; this constitutes an a priori analysis of the modelled system. Finally, the formalisation with Isabelle (Sect. 6) provides a different view on system models and attacks, and a proof that the contributes the soundness of attack generation.

The attacks generated by the last two techniques include all relevant steps from detecting the required assets, obtaining them as well as any credentials needed to do so, and finally performing actions that are prohibited in the system. The generated attacks are precise enough to illustrate the threat, and they are general enough to hide the details of individual steps. The generated attacks are also complete with respect to the model; whenever an attack is possible in the model, it will be found.

Acknowledgments. Part of the research leading to these results has received funding from the European Union Seventh Framework Programme (FP7/2007-2013) under grant agreement no. 318003 (TRE$_S$PASS). This publication reflects only the authors' views and the Union is not liable for any use that may be made of the information contained herein.

References

1. Nielson, F., Nielson, H.R., Hankin, C.: Principles of Program Analysis. Springer, Heidelberg (2004)
2. BBC News: Hack attack causes 'massive damage' at steel works (2014). http://www.bbc.com/news/technology-30575104. Accessed 15 October 2015
3. Cappelli, D.M., Moore, A.P., Trzeciak, R.F.: The CERT Guide to Insider Threats: How to Prevent, Detect, and Respond to Information Technology Crimes (Theft, Sabotage, Fraud). Addison-Wesley Professional, Boston (2012)
4. Hunker, J., Probst, C.W.: Insiders and insider threats–an overview of definitions and mitigation techniques. J. Wirel. Mob. Netw. Ubiquitous Comput. Dependable Appl. **2**(1), 3–25 (2011)
5. Nielson, H.R., Nielson, F., Pilegaard, H.: Flow logic for process calculi. ACM Comput. Surv. **44**(1), 3 (2012)
6. Probst, C.W., Hansen, R.R.: An extensible analysable system model. Inf. Secur. Tech. Rep. **13**(4), 235–246 (2008)
7. de Nicola, R., Ferrari, G.L., Pugliese, R.: KLAIM: a kernel language for agents interaction and mobility. IEEE Trans. Softw. Eng. **24**(5), 315–330 (1998)
8. Probst, C.W., Hansen, R.R., Nielson, F.: Where can an insider attack? In: Dimitrakos, T., Martinelli, F., Ryan, P.Y.A., Schneider, S. (eds.) FAST 2006. LNCS, vol. 4691, pp. 127–142. Springer, Heidelberg (2007)
9. Riis Nielson, H., Nielson, F.: Flow logic: a multi-paradigmatic approach to static analysis. In: Mogensen, T.Æ., Schmidt, D.A., Sudborough, I.H. (eds.) The Essence of Computation. LNCS, vol. 2566, pp. 223–244. Springer, Heidelberg (2002)
10. Kammüller, F., Probst, C.W.: Invalidating policies using structural information. In: Proceedings of the 2nd International IEEE Workshop on Research on Insider Threats (WRIT 2013), pp. 76–81, May 2013
11. Kammüller, F., Probst, C.W.: Combining generated data models with formal invalidation for insider threat analysis. In: Proceedings of the 3rd International IEEE Workshop on Research on Insider Threats (WRIT 2014), pp. 229–235, May 2014
12. Schneier, B.: Secrets and Lies: Digital Security in a Networked World. Wiley, New York (2004)

13. Kordy, B., Piètre-Cambacédès, L., Schweitzer, P.: Dag-based attack and defense modeling: don't miss the forest for the attack trees. Comput. Sci. Rev. **13–14**, 1–38 (2014)
14. Aslanyan, Z., Nielson, F.: Pareto efficient solutions of attack-defence trees. In: Focardi, R., Myers, A. (eds.) POST 2015. LNCS, vol. 9036, pp. 95–114. Springer, Heidelberg (2015)
15. Buldas, A., Lenin, A.: New efficient utility upper bounds for the fully adaptive model of attack trees. In: Das, S.K., Nita-Rotaru, C., Kantarcioglu, M. (eds.) GameSec 2013. LNCS, vol. 8252, pp. 192–205. Springer, Heidelberg (2013)
16. Vigo, R., Nielson, F., Nielson, H.R.: Automated generation of attack trees. In: Proceedings of the 27th Computer Security Foundations Symposium (CSF), pp. 337–350. IEEE (2014)
17. Kammüller, F., Probst, C.W.: Modeling and verification of insider threats using logical analysis. IEEE Syst. J., Special issue on Insider Threats to Information Security, Digital Espionage, and Counter Intelligence. Accepted for publication (2016)
18. Kammüller, F.: Isabelle formalisation of an insider threat framework with examples entitled independent and ambitious leader (2015). https://www.dropbox.com/sh/rx8d09pf31cv8bd/AAALKtaP8HMX642fi04Og4NLa?dl=0
19. Dimkov, T.: Alignment of Organizational Security Policies - Theory and Practice. University of Twente (2012)
20. Pieters, W., Dimkov, T., Pavlovic, D.: Security policy alignment: a formal approach. IEEE Syst. J. **7**(2), 275–287 (2013)
21. Salter, C., Saydjari, O.S., Schneier, B., Wallner, J.: Toward a secure system engineering methodology. In: Proceedings of the 1998 Workshop on New Security Paradigms (NSPW). pp. 2–10, September 1998
22. Phillips, C., Swiler, L.P.: A graph-based system for network-vulnerability analysis. In: Proceedings of the 1998 Workshop on New security paradigms (NSPW 1998), pp. 71–79 (1998)
23. Sheyner, O., Haines, J., Jha, S., Lippmann, R., Wing, J.M.: Automated generation and analysis of attack graphs. In: Proceedings of the 2002 IEEE Symposium on Security and Privacy (S&P 2002), vol. 129, pp. 273–284 (2002)

Static Timing Analysis – What is Special?

Jan Reineke and Reinhard Wilhelm[(✉)]

Informatik, Saarland University, Saarbrücken, Germany
{reineke,wilhelm}@cs.uni-saarland.de

Abstract. Abstract interpretation is successfully used for determining execution-time bounds of real-time programs. The particular problem it solves is the determination of invariants at all program points that describe the set of all execution states that are possible at these program points. These invariants are then used to exclude some of the possible costly executions of instructions, thereby reducing the execution-time bounds. This article considers the properties of this application of abstract interpretation that differ from those in the standard applications of abstract interpretation in compilation and in verification. It also shows how some particular designs of the underlying abstract domains made efficient timing analysis possible.

1 Introduction

1.1 Timing Analysis

Timing analysis of embedded real-time programs attempts to determine tight upper, and sometimes also lower bounds on the execution times of the programs. Ideally, one would find out the worst-case and best-case execution times. This is possible in principle since real-time programs are programmed in a way that termination is guaranteed, and since the execution platform has only finite resources. However, the complete exploration of the associated state space would take far too long to be practically feasible.

It was therefore clear that *abstraction* would need to be applied to arrive at sound execution-time bounds in acceptable times. Our entry into the timing-analysis area started with the (quite successful) attempt to predict the cache behavior by abstract interpretation [3,10]. Abstract interpretation had not been applied to the timing-analysis problem. The existing approaches were rather ad hoc and of doubtful correctness. It turned out that using abstract interpretation was the recipe for success.

1.2 What is Different?

The standard textbook on static program analysis, authored by Flemming Nielson, Hanne Riis Nielson, and Chris Hankin, covers most needs of a designer of abstract

---

Work reported herein was supported by the Deutsche Forschungsgemeinschaft in the Transregional Research Center AVACS, Automatic Verification and Analysis of Complex Systems.

C.W. Probst et al. (Eds.): Nielsons' Festschrift, LNCS 9560, pp. 74–87, 2016.
DOI: 10.1007/978-3-319-27810-0_4

interpretations. At least this was what we thought when we started out to design static analyses of the cache behavior of real-time programs. However, it turned out that timing analysis offers a number of challenges that were not foreseen by the existing theory or not used in previous practice. Here is a list, some items more absent from the Nielson/Nielson/Hankin book than others, some that could be covered by adaptations of the theory. Some concern cache analysis, others more general timing analysis.

- All traditional static program analyses we found in the literature were, in the best case, based on a semantics of the programming language that abstracted from the underlying execution platform. However, any timing analysis needs to *talk about* architectural behavior. Hence, the behavior of the execution platform must be an integral part of the semantics of the programming language, on which the static analysis is based.
- Any timing analysis is composed of many component analyses, one for each architectural component contributing to the timing behavior of programs. These component analyses interact in possibly complex ways, essentially originating from the dependencies of the architectural components on each other. Worst are cyclic dependencies since they render separate analyses of component behavior more or less impossible [18]. An adequate design of the individual analyses and of the composition is needed to arrive at overall timing analyses that are both precise and efficient.

This composition of timing analysis of many component analyses is in contrast with the application of static program analysis in compilation, where typically one static analysis checks the applicability of one program transformation [26]. It is also different from the composition of abstract domains as in [5] used to increase precision of one static analysis by using information from another one.

- Timing analyses need to analyze programs on the executable level since the source level does not contain the information on memory allocation of instructions and data, indispensable for cache analyses, nor the information on when memory is accessed, needed for the analysis of bus-access conflicts.
- The replacement strategy of a cache architecture always needs some bookkeeping mechanism about past memory accesses. The state representation of this mechanism is optimized for the speed and the size of the update logic. Cache analysis, however, is interested in the state itself, not its representation. The design of cache analyses therefore starts with a lossless abstraction of the HW implementation of the cache.

This is somewhat comparable to the situation in *shape analysis* [24], which is based on a *storeless semantics* abstracting from actual heap addresses, but keeping connectivity information.

- The cache semantics shows many *indirect effects* of state changes of one object on another independent object, e.g. memory block a is loaded into the cache, thereby replacing memory block b.

  These indirect effects are different from the ones caused by manipulations through pointers: These may also have side-effects, however, only on *aliases*, i.e. pointer expressions reaching the same object. So, these indirect effects result from program execution.
  In contrast, cache loads have indirect effects on objects related by the execution platform, i.e., by the cache-set mapping.

- A particularly hard problem is the static analysis of *write-back caches*. Here a modification of the contents of a memory block a residing in the cache leads to a temporary inconsistency in the value of a in the memory hierarchy. This inconsistency is repaired by a write back, possibly much later, when a is evicted by loading some other memory block b. These delayed cause-effect chains are quite unusual in the semantics of programming languages and therefore also in traditional static program analyses.

- The *invariant* at a program point, computed by some static analysis, may have different expressivity (precision), depending on whether the invariant is to hold for all executions reaching this program point or only for a subset corresponding to a particular context and/or a particular control flow. Traditional static program analyses may therefore be *context-* and/or *flow sensitive* or *insensitive* depending on the desired precision of the results and the required effort. The notion of *context* is defined by some abstraction of the set of call strings.

  Timing analyses must be flow-sensitive in order to obtain any precision at all. In addition, timing analyses need and use a generalized notion of *context* to be precise. Different iterations of a loop may have vastly different execution times. Hence, they have to be considered as contexts for the instructions in the body. This is an instance of trace partitioning, invented before trace partitioning was proposed in the literature [21].

- Static analyses of *concurrent systems* focus on the interaction of the concurrently executed tasks on *global variables*. In contrast to this, cache analysis, and more general timing analysis, has to determine safe approximations of the *resource-occupancy interaction* [1]. An additional complication, compared to the static analysis of concurrent systems, is the non-transparency of which objects compete with which other objects for resources.

- Cache analysis, and more general timing analysis, determines invariants about execution states at program points and derives safety properties from these invariants, i.e., certain timing accidents like a cache miss will never happen at a program point. The proof of such safety properties allows reducing the execution-time bound by the timing penalty corresponding to the excluded timing accident. This use is different from that in traditional static program analyses used in verification, where such a safety property typically proves the absence of a run-time error.

– The profitability of code optimizations involving static analyses as check for
their applicability is seldom clear. In contrast, excluding a timing accident by
a strong invariant computed by a timing analysis is often associated with the
elimination of a very clear penalty.

2 From Microarchitectures to Abstractions for Timing Analysis

When developing a timing analysis, the first task is to obtain a faithful *model* of
the microarchitecture that the analysis is targeted at. This can be very challenging because documentation at the required level of detail is seldom available. One
promising approach is to start from cycle-accurate models in hardware description languages like VHDL or Verilog if those are made available by the hardware
manufacturer [25]. If such models are not provided by the manufacturer, they
have to be constructed manually based on processor manuals and extensive measurements on evaluation boards. For some microarchitectural features, such as
caches the modeling process can be partially automated [2]. In the remainder of
this section, we assume that a cycle-accurate model of the microarchitecture has
already been obtained by one of the ways described above.

Mathematically, a cycle-accurate model is a transition relation $R \subseteq S \times S$
that captures the behavior of the processor in a single execution cycle. Programs
and their input data are part of the states S of the processor. So the initial states
of a program P under all possible inputs are a subset I_P of S. The goal of timing
analysis is then to determine a bound on the number of cycles from any possible
state in I_P to the program's termination, i.e., until it reaches one of its final
states F_P. Brute-force exploration of all possible reachable states from the set
of initial states is practically infeasible due to its large number. Therefore, a
number of abstractions have been introduced to arrive at safe approximations
of the worst-case execution time. In the following, we will discuss the two most
important such abstractions.

2.1 Analysis Framework

Microarchitectures implement instruction set architectures (ISA). The semantics
of binary programs in terms of the computed values in registers and memory are
governed by the instruction set architecture. In particular, they are independent
of its microarchitectural implementation.

As a consequence, analysis at the ISA level can be separated from analyses specific to a microarchitecture. This separation has led to the high-level
structure of WCET analysis tools depicted in Fig. 1. For a given instruction
set, in a preprocessing step, a *value analysis* [4] determines the possible values
of registers and memory locations, usually based on interval and congruence
abstractions. The control-flow graph of the program under analysis is annotated
with the results of value analysis for use in the subsequent analysis steps. They
are required for precise data-cache analysis within microarchitectural analysis,

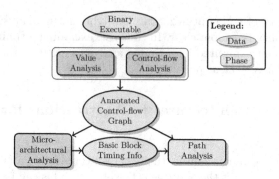

Fig. 1. Main components of a timing-analysis framework and their interaction.

as well as in control-flow analysis. *Control-flow analysis* [7,9,19,27] determines loop bounds and other characterizations of the set of semantically-feasible paths through the control-flow graph.

The task of *microarchitectural analysis* [6,8,11,12,29], which we will illuminate further in the following section, is to determine bounds on the execution times of small program fragments such as basic blocks. These bounds, together with the results of the control-flow analysis are then used in *path analysis* [20,28] to determine an upper bound on the execution time of the program as a whole. Path analysis is usually performed using integer linear programming formulations.

2.2   Separation into Value and Microarchitectural Analysis

Microarchitectural analysis first computes an overapproximation of the set of all reachable microarchitectural states. From this approximation and the transitions between the different reachable states, execution time bounds for basic blocks can be determined.

A relatively simple microarchitecture may consist of the following components: pipeline control, pipeline datapath, register file, branch predictor, cache, and main memory. The microarchitecture's space can be modeled as the cartesian product of the state spaces of its components:

$$S = \text{PipelineControl} \times \text{PipelineDatapath} \times \text{RegisterFile}$$
$$\times \text{BranchPredictor} \times \text{Cache} \times \text{Memory}$$

The set of reachable states of program P is the least fixed point of the *next* operator containing the initial states I_P of program P:

$$Col(P) = I_P \cup next(I_P) \cup next^2(I_P) \cup \ldots,$$

where *next* captures the effect of one execution cycle:

$$next(M) = \{s' \mid (s, s') \in R\}$$

The first abstraction, discussed informally in the previous section, is to perform *value analysis* separately, prior to *microarchitectural analysis*. Value analysis can be formalized as abstracting values in the register file and the memory.

Let $\text{VALUE}^{\#}$ be the abstract domain used in value analysis. A concretization function $\gamma_{VA} : \text{VALUE}^{\#} \to \mathcal{P}(\text{REGISTERFILE} \times \text{MEMORY})$ provides the meaning of a result of value analysis. Such analyses are flow- or even context-sensitive so that information about registers and memory is available for each program location separately. Formally,

$$\text{VALUE}^{\#} = (\text{LOC} \times \text{CONTEXT}) \to (\text{REGISTER}^{\#} \times \text{MEMORY}^{\#}),$$

where LOC and CONTEXT are sets of program locations and contexts, and $\text{REGISTER}^{\#}$ and $\text{MEMORY}^{\#}$ are abstractions of the register file and memory, respectively. For reasons of brevity we cannot further elaborate on these abstractions. A correct abstract $next_{VA}^{\#} : \text{VALUE}^{\#} \to \text{VALUE}^{\#}$ operator guarantees global correctness of the value analysis.

Given value analysis results, microarchitectural analysis can thus focus on the remaining parts of the microarchitecture, pipeline control, as well as the state of the branch predictor and the cache. The state of the pipeline datapath can be inferred from the state of the pipeline control and the values of registers and memory, and is thus *not explicitly* represented by either value analysis or by microarchitectural analysis.

Let $\mu\text{ARCH}^{\#}$ be the abstract domain used in microarchitectural analysis, and let $\gamma_{\mu A} : \mu\text{ARCH}^{\#} \to \mathcal{P}(\text{PIPELINECONTROL} \times \text{BRANCHPREDICTOR} \times \text{CACHE})$ be its concretization function. While value analysis does not depend on microarchitectural analysis, the converse is not true. In particular, $next_{\mu A}^{\#}$ depends on the results of value analysis: $next_{\mu A}^{\#} : \mu\text{ARCH}^{\#} \times \text{VALUE}^{\#} \to \mu\text{ARCH}^{\#}$. For example, upon a memory access, microarchitectural analysis will query the results of value analysis, which have been annotated to the program's control-flow graph, to determine which memory block is being accessed to be able to classify the access as a cache hit or a cache miss.

For a correctness argument, the abstract operators $next_{VA}^{\#}$ and $next_{\mu A}^{\#}$ can be combined to obtain the abstract $next^{\#}$ operator as follows:

$$next^{\#}(v^{\#}, m^{\#}) := (next_{VA}^{\#}(v^{\#}), next_{\mu A}^{\#}(m^{\#}, v^{\#})).$$

Given correctness of $next_{VA}^{\#}$ and $next_{\mu A}^{\#}$, it can be shown that $next^{\#}$'s least fixed point,

$$Col^{\#}(P) = (i_v^{\#}, i_m^{\#}) \sqcup next^{\#}(i_v^{\#}, i_m^{\#}) \sqcup next^{\#^{2}}(i_v^{\#}, i_m^{\#}) \dots,$$

overapproximates the set of reachable states $Col(P)$, with the combined concretization function

$$\gamma(v^{\#}, m^{\#}) := \{(pc, pd, rf, bd, c, m) \in S \mid$$
$$(rf, m) \in \gamma_{VA}(v^{\#}) \wedge (pc, bd, c) \in \gamma_{\mu A}(m^{\#}), \}$$

given that $\gamma(i_v^{\#}, i_m^{\#}) \supseteq I_P$.

From the formalization it is apparent that value analysis can be performed in a preprocessing step, as it does not depend upon the results of microarchitectural analysis. This preprocessing step produces a control-flow graph annotated with the results of value analysis, which is then used by microarchitectural analysis.

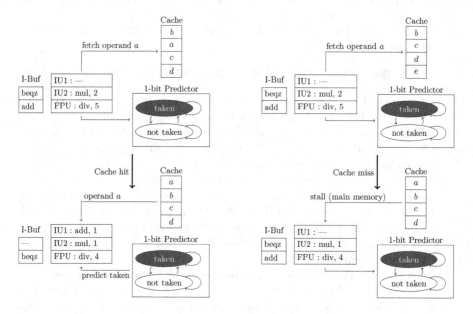

Fig. 2. Transitions from two different initial states of a simple processor consisting of an in-order pipeline, a 2-way fully-associative cache, and a 1-bit branch predictor.

2.3 Microarchitectural Analysis

Now let us turn to the internal structure of μARCH$^{\#}$. Can the pipeline control, the branch predictor, and the cache be analyzed independently of each other? Unfortunately, this is not the case due to the mutual dependencies of the three components. This is best explained with the help of Fig. 2. At the top, we see two microarchitectural states of a simple processor, consisting of an in-order pipeline containing an instruction fetch buffer, two integer units, one floating-point unit, a cache, and a 1-bit branch predictor. The two processor states initially only differ in their cache states. The pipeline is about to dispatch the *add* instruction from the instruction fetch buffer to integer unit 1. Assume this *add* instruction adds the contents of a memory address to the contents of a register. Then, the instruction can be dispatched as soon as the memory operand is available. In the state on the left, the operand *a* is in the cache, and so *add* is dispatched immediately. On the other hand, in the state on the right, operand *a* needs to be fetched from memory, as it is not in the cache, and the *add* instruction cannot be dispatched yet. So the cache state has an influence on the pipeline state.

Now consider the successor states. On the left, the next instruction from the instruction fetch buffer to execute is a *branch equal zero* instruction. As the condition upon which the branch depends has not yet been evaluated, the pipeline queries the branch predictor to decide in which direction to speculate. The prediction influences which instruction to fetch next, which in turn will affect the cache contents. So the future cache state depends on the current state of the pipeline and the branch predictor. Due to this tight coupling of the three components, they need to be analyzed relationally to obtain reasonably precise results.

The example also demonstrates that pipeline states cannot easily be ordered in terms of "progress": Intuitively, the successor state on the left has progressed further than the state on the right, as the *add* instruction has already been dispatched in this case. However, if speculative execution proceeds in the wrong direction, the pipeline state on the left may result in a longer execution time than the state on the right, which has no potential to speculate. Due to this lack of a natural ordering, which are usually the basis of abstractions[1], no efficient and precise abstractions are known so far for sets of pipeline states. In Sect. 3, we speculate about the design of abstractable pipelines and its abstraction.

The analysis essentially operates on the power-set domain of sets of concrete pipeline states, where only the datapath is abstracted away, as discussed earlier. For the cache, however, precise and efficient abstractions have been found.

2.4 Two Abstractions for Caches

The abstraction described in the following applies to caches with least-recently-used (LRU) replacement and was originally proposed by Ferdinand and Wilhelm [12]. For simplicity we assume a fully-associative cache, i.e., the cache consists of a single cache set, as the example cache in Fig. 2. The extension to set-associative caches is straightforward, as set-associative caches can be seen as cartesian products of multiple independent fully-associative caches, each of which can be abstracted independently of the others.

A Lossless Logical Abstraction. The first abstraction to perform in the analysis of caches is a cache's physical implementation to a formal, logical model of its behavior. In physical implementations, caches consists of multiple memories containing data, tags, and status bits. In particular, each cache line is associated with a tag to keep track of which memory block is cached in the respective line. In addition, a number of status bits are maintained in each cache set to record the "logical" state of the replacement policy.

For instance, an implementation of least-recently-used replacement needs status bits to remember in which order the cache lines of each set have been used. Abstracting from the data stored in the cache, a model of a fully-associative cache with LRU replacement fairly close to the physical implementation might thus consist of two functions: (1) a function $cl : \{1, \ldots, k\} \to \mathcal{B}$ that captures

---

[1] In interval analysis for example a set of values is abstracted by its least and their greatest element.

which memory block is stored in each of the k cache lines, and (2) a function $age_{cl} : \{1, \ldots, k\} \rightarrow \{0, \ldots, k-1\}$ that maintains the "age" of each cache line, i.e., the number of distinct cache lines that have been accessed since the last access to the given cache line.

For cache analysis it is irrelevant in which physical cache line a memory block is stored; only the relative ages of different cached memory blocks are required to predict the future cache hit behavior. Thus, a lossless abstraction can be applied that captures the age of each memory block $age : Cache = \mathcal{B} \rightarrow \{0, \ldots, k-1, k\}$, where uncached blocks assume age k. One can relate the two models by an abstraction function α defined as follows:

$$\alpha(cl, age_{cl}) := \lambda b \in \mathcal{B} : \begin{cases} age_{cl}(i) & : if \, cl(i) = b \\ k & : if \, cl(i) \neq b \forall i \in \{1, \ldots, k\} \end{cases}$$

Upon a load of memory block b, the ages are updated as follows:

$$up(age, b) := \lambda b' \in \mathcal{B} : \begin{cases} 0 & : if \, b' = b \\ age(b') & : if \, age(b) \leq age(b') \\ age(b') + 1 & : if \, age(b) > age(b') \end{cases}$$

An Interval Abstraction. Cache analysis needs to represent sets of cache states. In particular, at program start no knowledge about the cache state may be available, and so cache analysis needs to represent all possible cache states. Obviously, explicit representations are practically infeasible in such cases. A further abstraction is required to compactly represent large sets of cache states with little precision loss.

Fortunately, such abstractions are possible in the case of LRU. This is because LRU exhibits a form of *monotonicity*. Intuitively, the "younger" a memory block, i.e., the lower its age, the better. Thus, it is sufficient to maintain upper and lower bounds on the age of each memory block *independently* of the ages of the other memory blocks. This yields the following abstract domain

$$\widehat{CacheInterval} = \{(l, u) \mid l, u \in \mathcal{B} \rightarrow \{0, \ldots, k-1, k\} \\ \wedge \forall b \in \mathcal{B} : l(b) \leq u(b)\}$$

storing a lower and an upper bound on the age of each memory block.

In the literature, the two analyses have been proposed separately, where lower bounds are maintained in what is called *may analysis* and upper bounds are maintained in *must analysis*. Lower bounds can be used to reason about which memory blocks *may* be cached, whereas upper bounds can be used to reason about which memory blocks *must* be cached.

$\widehat{CacheInterval}$ forms a join semi-lattice with the following order:

$$(\widehat{a}_{may}, \widehat{a}_{must}) \sqsubseteq (\widehat{a}'_{may}, \widehat{a}'_{must}) :\Leftrightarrow \widehat{a}_{may} \sqsubseteq_{may} \widehat{a}'_{may} \wedge \widehat{a}_{must} \sqsubseteq_{must} \widehat{a}'_{must}$$

$$\widehat{a}_{may} \sqsubseteq_{may} \widehat{a}'_{may} :\Leftrightarrow \forall b \in \mathcal{B} : \widehat{a}_{may}(b) \geq \widehat{a}'_{may}(b)$$

$$\widehat{a}_{must} \sqsubseteq_{must} \widehat{a}'_{must} :\Leftrightarrow \forall b \in \mathcal{B} : \widehat{a}_{must}(b) \leq \widehat{a}'_{must}(b)$$

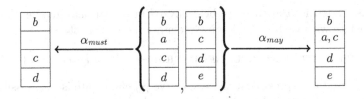

Fig. 3. Must and may cache abstractions.

Abstract cache states are related to sets of concrete cache states by a *Galois connection* via the following abstraction and concretization functions:

$$\alpha(C) := (\alpha_{may}(C), \alpha_{must}(C)), \text{ with}$$

$$\alpha_{may}(C) := \lambda b \in \mathcal{B} : \min_{age \in C} age(b)$$

$$\alpha_{must}(C) := \lambda b \in \mathcal{B} : \max_{age \in C} age(b)$$

and

$$\gamma(\widehat{age}_{may}, \widehat{age}_{must}) := \gamma_{may}(\widehat{age}_{may}) \cap \gamma_{must}(\widehat{age}_{must}), \text{ with}$$

$$\gamma_{may}(\widehat{age}) := \{age \mid \forall b \in \mathcal{B} : \widehat{age}(b) \le age(b)\}$$

$$\gamma_{must}(\widehat{age}) := \{age \mid \forall b \in \mathcal{B} : age(b) \le \widehat{age}(b)\}$$

In Fig. 3, the two abstractions are illustrated at the example of the set of cache states found in the two initial states of Fig. 2. In the concrete cache states the ith row contains the memory block with age i. In the abstract cache states the ith row contains all memory blocks with age bound i.

The abstract update functions for the lower and upper bounds closely resemble the concrete update function and can be proven correct rather easily:

$$up_{may}(\widehat{age}, b) := \lambda b' \in \mathcal{B} : \begin{cases} 0 & : \text{if } b' = b \\ age(b') & : \text{if } \widehat{age}(b) < \widehat{age}(b') \\ age(b') + 1 & : \text{if } \widehat{age}(b) \ge \widehat{age}(b') \ne k \\ k & : \text{if } \widehat{age}(b') = k \end{cases}$$

$$up_{must}(\widehat{age}, b) := \lambda b' \in \mathcal{B} : \begin{cases} 0 & : \text{if } b' = b \\ age(b') & : \text{if } \widehat{age}(b) \le \widehat{age}(b') \\ age(b') + 1 & : \text{if } \widehat{age}(b) > \widehat{age}(b') \end{cases}$$

Integration of Cache Analysis Within Microarchitectural Analysis. As discussed earlier, no good abstractions for sets of pipeline control states are known, and so they are analyzed using a power-set domain. How can the analysis of the pipeline be integrated with the analysis of the cache behavior? Due to their mutual dependencies they need to be analyzed in a relational manner. The idea is to associate with each possible pipeline state, *one* cache state:

$$\mu\text{ARCHITECTURE} := \text{PIPELINECONTROL} \to (\widehat{CacheInterval} \cup \{\bot\}),$$

where $\bot$ is used to express that the respective pipeline state is not possible. For simplicity, here, we omit branch predictors, which can be treated similarly to caches.

Other Replacement Policies. We have seen a precise and efficient abstraction for caches with LRU replacement. For other replacement policies, similarly efficient abstractions have been developed [13–17,22]. However, they do not reach the same level of precision as the replacement policies are less predictable [23].

3   An Abstractable Pipeline

We have seen in the previous section that pipelines in modern high-performance microprocessors don't provide for compact abstractions similar to abstract cache states. This forced the pipeline analysis to work with a power-set domain [29]. We now speculate about an abstractable instruction pipeline, i.e. an instruction pipeline that has a compact abstract domain, simple update and join functions, and thereby admits efficient and precise pipeline analysis. The goal is to have an abstract instruction pipeline which looks much like a concrete instruction pipeline. The concrete state of an instruction pipeline contains a set of instructions of a given program, each in one particular pipeline stage. In addition, the pipeline is connected to a set of queues, buffers, and functional units holding instructions to be fetched next, stores to still be executed, or operations under execution.

The progress in executing a given program, as given by a particular concrete pipeline state, consists in

- which instructions of the program have already retired from the pipeline,
- how far other instructions of the program have progressed in the pipeline,
- how many instructions to be executed next have been prefetched into prefetch queues,
- how far operations dispatched by instructions currently in the pipeline have progressed in the pipelined functional units,
- how many outstanding stores are still in the store buffer.

An abstract state of an instruction pipeline, as we envision it, should look much like a concrete pipeline state. However, the interpretation (*concretization*) is different:

- Any progress of an instruction in the abstract pipeline state is a guaranteed progress of the instruction.
- the contents of the abstract prefetch queue is a sequence of instructions, guaranteed to have been prefetched,

– the progress of dispatched operations in the functional units is guaranteed progress, and
– the stores removed from the store buffer have definitely been performed, the ones still in the store buffer may be still outstanding.

This notion of progress is the basis for defining a partial order of the abstract pipeline domain.

Let us discuss the implication for the pipeline architecture. It means that the pipelines should be an *in-order pipeline*, i.e., without reordering of instructions. An out-of-order pipeline admits several dynamically selected schedules of a given sequence of instructions. The join function would be applied to the different schedules resulting in an abstract pipeline state where each instruction is recorded with its slowest possible progress. Thus the effect of out-of-order execution would be completely lost in the pipeline analysis.

A first step towards *abstractable* pipelines has been done in [18]. We proposed a *strictly in-order* pipeline, i.e., one where no phase of a later instruction can block execution of a phase of an earlier instruction. This restriction excludes timing anomalies, which were still possible in in-order pipelines, against common beliefs. The simple pipeline design admits a compact abstract domain based on the maximally guaranteeable progress.

Pipeline analysis is typically performed on basic blocks. For each predecessor block of a basic block to be analyzed it has produced a final abstract state. These final states need to be combined to an initial state by applying the join function of the abstract domain. Different predecessor basic blocks will consist of different instruction sequences, such that their final abstract states will have different subsequences of instructions in the pipeline. Joining the set of abstract final states would roughly correspond to flushing the pipeline, a costly approach if the pipeline is deep. The efficiency gain of overlapping execution across basic-block boundaries would always get lost. A way out of this dilemma could consist in delaying the join at the beginning of basic blocks until the remaining instructions of the predecessor blocks have retired.

4   Conclusions

We have shown how the architectural basis of static timing analysis influences the character of static timing analysis, which includes a particular instance of abstract interpretation as its most important component. In particular, we have described how two important transformations of the underlying complex cartesian-product domain were needed and successfully used to arrive at efficient analyses.

References

1. Abel, A.: Impact of resource sharing on performance and performance prediction: a survey. In: D'Argenio, P.R., Melgratti, H. (eds.) CONCUR 2013 – Concurrency Theory. LNCS, vol. 8052, pp. 25–43. Springer, Heidelberg (2013). http://dx.doi.org/10.1007/978-3-642-40184-8_3

2. Abel, A., Reineke, J.: Measurement-based modeling of the cache replacement policy. In: RTAS, April 2013. http://embedded.cs.uni-saarland.de/publications/CacheModelingRTAS2013.pdf

3. Alt, M., Ferdinand, C., Martin, F., Wilhelm, R.: Cache behavior prediction by abstract interpretation. In: Static Analysis, Third International Symposium, SAS 1996, pp. 52–66 (1996). http://dx.doi.org/10.1007/3-540-61739-6_33

4. Cousot, P., Cousot, R.: Abstract interpretation: a unified lattice model for static analysis of programs by construction or approximation of fixpoints. In: Proceedings of the 4th ACM SIGACT-SIGPLAN Symposium on Principles of Programming Languages, pp. 238–252. ACM Press, New York (1977)

5. Cousot, P., Cousot, R.: Systematic design of program analysis frameworks. In: Aho, A.V., Zilles, S.N., Rosen, B.K. (eds.) Conference Record of the Sixth Annual ACM Symposium on Principles of Programming Languages, pp. 269–282. ACM Press (1979). http://doi.acm.org/10.1145/567752.567778

6. Cullmann, C.: Cache persistence analysis: theory and practice. ACM Trans. Embed. Comput. Syst. 12(1s), 40:1–40:25 (2013)

7. Cullmann, C., Martin, F.: Data-flow based detection of loop bounds. In: Rochange, C. (ed.) 7th International Workshop on Worst-Case Execution Time Analysis (WCET 2007), Dagstuhl, Germany (2007). http://drops.dagstuhl.de/opus/volltexte/2007/1193

8. Engblom, J.: Processor Pipelines and Static Worst-Case Execution Time Analysis. Ph.D. thesis, Uppsala University, Sweden (2002). http://citeseerx.ist.psu.edu/viewdoc/summary?doi=10.1.1.19.5355

9. Ermedahl, A., Gustafsson, J.: Deriving annotations for tight calculation of execution time. In: Lengauer, C., Griebl, M., Gorlatch, S. (eds.) Euro-Par 1997. LNCS, vol. 1300. Springer, Heidelberg (1997)

10. Ferdinand, C.: Cache Behavior Prediction for Real-Time Systems. Ph.D. thesis, Saarland University, Saarbruecken, Germany (1997). ISBN: 3-9307140-31-0

11. Ferdinand, C., Heckmann, R., Langenbach, M., Martin, F., Schmidt, M., Theiling, H., Thesing, S., Wilhelm, R.: Reliable and precise WCET determination for a real-life processor. In: Henzinger, T.A., Kirsch, C.M. (eds.) EMSOFT 2001. LNCS, vol. 2211, pp. 469–485. Springer, Heidelberg (2001)

12. Ferdinand, C., Wilhelm, R.: Efficient and precise cache behavior prediction for real-time systems. Real-Time Syst. 17(2–3), 131–181 (1999)

13. Grund, D., Reineke, J.: Abstract interpretation of FIFO replacement. In: Palsberg, J., Su, Z. (eds.) SAS 2009. LNCS, vol. 5673, pp. 120–136. Springer, Heidelberg (2009)

14. Grund, D., Reineke, J.: Precise and efficient FIFO-replacement analysis based on static phase detection. In: Proceedings of the 22nd Euromicro Conference on Real-Time Systems (ECRTS), pp. 155–164, July 2010

15. Grund, D., Reineke, J.: Toward precise PLRU cache analysis. In: Lisper, B. (ed.) 10th International Workshop on Worst-Case Execution Time Analysis (WCET 2010), pp. 23–35 (2010). http://drops.dagstuhl.de/opus/volltexte/2010/2822

16. Guan, N., Lv, M., Yi, W., Yu, G.: WCET analysis with MRU cache: challenging LRU for predictability. ACM Trans. Embed. Comput. Syst. 13(4s), 123:1–123:26 (2014). http://doi.acm.org/10.1145/2584655

17. Guan, N., Yang, X., Lv, M., Yi, W.: FIFO cache analysis for WCET estimation: a quantitative approach. In: Proceedings of Design, Automation Test in Europe Conference Exhibition (DATE), 2013, pp. 296–301, March 2013

18. Hahn, S., Reineke, J., Wilhelm, R.: Toward compact abstractions for processor pipelines. In: Meyer, R., Platzer, A., Wehrheim, H. (eds.) Correct System Design. LNCS, vol. 9360, pp. 205–220. Springer, Heidelberg (2015). http://dx.doi.org/10.1007/978-3-319-23506-6_14

19. Healy, C., Sjödin, M., Rustagi, V., Whalle, D., van Engelen, R.: Supporting timing analysis by automatic bounding of loop iterations. Real-Time Syst. 18(2), 129–156 (2000)

20. Li, Y.T.S., Malik, S.: Performance analysis of embedded software using implicit path enumeration. In: Proceedings of the 32nd ACM/IEEE Design Automation Conference, pp. 456–461 (1995)

21. Mauborgne, L., Rival, X.: Trace partitioning in abstract interpretation based static analyzers. In: Sagiv, M. (ed.) ESOP 2005. LNCS, vol. 3444, pp. 5–20. Springer, Heidelberg (2005). http://dx.doi.org/10.1007/978-3-540-31987-0_2

22. Reineke, J., Grund, D.: Relative competitive analysis of cache replacement policies. In: Proceedings of the 2008 ACM SIGPLAN-SIGBED Conference On Languages, Compilers, And Tools For Embedded Systems, LCTES 2008, pp. 51–60. ACM, June 2008. http://rw4.cs.uni-saarland.de/grund/papers/lctes08-rel_comp.pdf

23. Reineke, J., Grund, D., Berg, C., Wilhelm, R.: Timing predictability of cache replacement policies. Real Time Syst. 37(2), 99–122 (2007)

24. Sagiv, M., Reps, T.W., Wilhelm, R.: Parametric shape analysis via 3-valued logic. ACM Trans. Program. Lang. Syst. 24(3), 217–298 (2002). http://doi.acm.org/10.1145/514188.514190

25. Schlickling, M., Pister, M.: Semi-automatic derivation of timing models for WCET analysis. In: Proceedings of the ACM SIGPLAN/SIGBED 2010 Conference on Languages, Compilers, and Tools For Embedded Systems, pp. 67–76. ACM, April 2010

26. Seidl, H., Wilhelm, R., Hack, S.: Compiler Design - Analysis and Transformation. Springer, Heidelberg (2012). http://dx.doi.org/10.1007/978-3-642-17548-0

27. Stein, I., Martin, F.: Analysis of path exclusion at the machine code level. In: Rochange, C. (ed.) 7th International Workshop on Worst-Case Execution Time Analysis (WCET 2007). OpenAccess Series in Informatics (OASIcs), Dagstuhl, Germany (2007). http://drops.dagstuhl.de/opus/volltexte/2007/1196

28. Theiling, H.: ILP-based interprocedural path analysis. In: Sangiovanni-Vincentelli, A.L., Sifakis, J. (eds.) EMSOFT 2002. LNCS, vol. 2491, pp. 349–363. Springer, Heidelberg (2002)

29. Thesing, S.: Safe and Precise WCET Determinations by Abstract Interpretation of Pipeline Models. Ph.D. thesis, Saarland University, Saarbrücken, Germany (2004). http://scidok.sulb.uni-saarland.de/volltexte/2005/466/

An Automata-Based Approach to Trace Partitioned Abstract Interpretation

Mads Christian Olesen, René Rydhof Hansen[✉], and Kim Guldstrand Larsen

Department of Computer Science, Aalborg University, Aalborg, Denmark
{mchro,rrh,kgl}@cs.aau.dk

Abstract. Trace partitioning is a technique for retaining precision in abstract interpretation, by partitioning all traces into a number of classes and computing an invariant for each class. In this work we present an automata-based approach to trace partitioning, by augmenting the finite automaton given by the control-flow graph with abstract transformers over a lattice. The result is a lattice automaton, for which efficient model-checking tools exist. By adding additional predicates to the automaton, different classes of traces can be distinguished.

This shows a very practical connection between abstract interpretation and model checking: a formalism encompassing problems from both domains, and accompanying machinery that can be used to solve problems from both domains efficiently.

This practical connection has the advantage that improvements from one domain can very easily be transferred to the other. We exemplify this with the use of multi-core processors for a scalable computation. Furthermore, the use of a modelling formalism as intermediary format allows the program analyst to simulate, combine and alter models to perform ad-hoc experiments.

1 Introduction

The formal connection between model checking and static analysis is well known and was first explored by Schmidt and Steffen, showing how data flow analysis can be reformulated as a model checking problem [33–35], and more recently by Nielson and Nielson, showing how certain model checking problems can be reformulated as static analyses [30].

In this paper we exploit and further explore this deep connection between static analysis and model checking, and show that it is not only of theoretical interest, but also useful in practice. In particular, we develop an automata-based approach to *trace partitioning*, a technique used to improve precision of analyses based on abstract interpretation. In our approach the control flow graph of the program under analysis is transformed into an equivalent *lattice automaton*, that captures the control flow of a program and combines it with information drawn from a lattice. The lattice automaton can then be model checked efficiently [11] and thereby yield program analysis information. An overview of our method can be seen in Fig. 1.

© Springer International Publishing Switzerland 2016
C.W. Probst et al. (Eds.): Nielsons' Festschrift, LNCS 9560, pp. 88–110, 2016.
DOI: 10.1007/978-3-319-27810-0_5

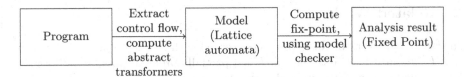

Fig. 1. Overview of the proposed method.

Our approach opens a direct route for implementing static analyses based on abstract interpretation and trace partitioning through the use of state-of-the-art model checking engines. This allows not only for efficient implementations, but it also enables analyses to automatically take advantage of any performance improvements in the underlying model checking engine(s). In the following, we illustrate this point by taking advantage of recent advances in model checking on multi-core platforms [12] to obtain an efficient multi-core implementation of abstract interpretation through trace partitioning.

In addition to providing efficient implementations, our approach also simplifies the often difficult and underestimated task of using, adapting, and fine-tuning trace partitioning in abstract interpretation. This is due to the use of automata not only for representing control flow graphs, but also for specifying the particulars of a given trace partitioning. These automata have an intuitive and well-known graphical representation facilitating easy, interactive specification and modification using a graphical editor.

Finally, a further advantage of our approach is that programs, or rather their control flow graphs, are represented as expressive high-level models, namely lattice automata. This is an often overlooked or unappreciated feature that is useful in a wide range of scenarios, e.g., for running simulations of the program; modelling the environment in which the program will run; modelling other systems, devices, or services that the program will interact with. These additional models can be as concrete or abstract as needed, e.g., using abstract specifications to model services that have not yet been implemented. As a concrete example, consider whether this program fragment is buggy or not:

```
1    char str[40];
2    gets(str);
3    printf("%s", str);
```

The answer is of course: it depends. Since the 'gets()' function does not constrain the size of the input it copies to the 'str' buffer, a correct and conservative answer would be that the fragment contains a potential buffer overrun, *if nothing is known* about the environment in which the fragment will be run. However, it may be the case that this fragment is only ever run in an environment that can only input strings with strictly fewer than 40 characters. Such a restriction in the environment is trivial to model using our approach.

2 Related Work

In essence, the work in this paper is concerned with the mathematical structure $A \times L$, where A is a finite set and L is a partially ordered, possibly infinite set. This structure is well-known and also occurs in:

- model checking of infinite state systems, e.g., timed automata [12], where A comprises the states of a finite automaton, enhanced with a symbolic part L where each element represents an infinite set of clock valuations;
- static analysis using abstract interpretation [6], where L is a lattice representing a program invariant over a set of traces, and A is used to divide the set of all traces into partitions (most commonly partitioning on the end-state of the trace) [26].

Furthermore, by equipping L with a least upper-bound operator, the classic presentation of abstract interpretation can be realised [6]; interestingly this structure also captures the convex hull abstraction used in model checking of timed automata [13]. Because the structure is so commonly occurring, it is infeasible to list all related work; consequently we focus mainly on related work in the area of program analysis.

The formalism we propose in this paper has been derived from the formalism used for model checking networks of timed automata in the UPPAAL [3] model checker, but it could equally well have been based on the notion of well-structured transition systems [14]. The addition of a least upper-bound operator, or *join* operator, on the state space sets our definition apart from both, but the definition of abstraction operators has previously been done, e.g., for timed automata [13] with the convex-hull abstraction for zones, or for finite lattices in finite automata in αSPIN [25]. In this work we address cases where the lattice has no infinite ascending chains, or where widening is applied to eliminate such chains.

In the classic presentation of abstract interpretation, abstract transformers are derived from the concrete semantics of a program relative to a lattice defining the abstraction [6]. This abstraction lattice is typically defined in terms of a Galois connection or by using widening and narrowing where the latter is considered more powerful [9]. In this work we follow the approach taken in [33] and focus on using Galois connections, with an implicit application of widening in place of joining to eliminate infinite ascending chains.

Much work within abstract interpretation has centered on finding abstract domains that are powerful enough to prove invariants of interest in real programs, while still being computationally affordable [7]. One technique for gaining precision without changing domain or sacrificing performance is *trace partitioning* [17,19,26,32], or the related technique of *property-oriented expansion* [36]. In later sections we show how trace partitioning corresponds directly to instrumenting a finite automaton with additional predicates. Other work in this areas includes [4] which describes a series of program analyses, configurable in precision by a partial join operator, mimicking aspects of trace partitioning, and implemented on top of a model checking engine.

As mentioned in the introduction, the formal connection between abstract interpretation and model checking has been explored by Schmidt and Steffen [33], where it was shown how data-flow queries for a given program can be answered using a parameterised variant of computation tree logic (CTL) model checked over an abstract interpretation of the program, following the work of [34,35], which was implemented in [37]. In order for this to work, the abstract model must be finite. The work in this paper was heavily inspired by the work of Schmidt and Steffen but focus on showing that the formal machinery developed by Schmidt and Steffen can solve *both* model checking problems and static analysis problems, also for models where joining or widening is required for termination. In [10] it was shown how abstract interpretation can be used to reduce the state space needing to be searched by a model checker.

Model checking was initially only available for small finite state automata [2]. The state-space explosion problem meant that abstractions were needed to reduce the state space to practical size [5]. The case of finite domains allows the methods for finite state automata to be applied to these abstract models directly [1,5]. In general, infinite domains are avoided because termination is not guaranteed.

In model checking software the counter-example guided abstraction refinement (CEGAR) approach allows model checking of increasingly more detailed abstractions of the program, starting from the control flow graph [18]. Based on found error traces additional boolean predicates are added to the lattice domain. CEGAR works very well in practice, but termination is not guaranteed.

Very efficient implementations of model checking algorithms for models with lattices exist, mostly in the area of timed automata model checking [12,24]. In particular model checkers such as LTSMIN [23] exploit the multiple processing cores of modern shared-memory processors to do the work in parallel. The multi-core backend of LTSMIN has recently been extended to the timed automata setting [12], and has been shown to scale up to 48 cores. The static analyser Astrée also has a parallel version [28], for which timings on a distributed cluster architecture (non-shared memory) are reported scaling up to 3–4 machines.

The work on lattice automata in [21] is unrelated to our definition of lattice automata, in that we allow arbitrary transitions as long as the transitions are monotonically enabled with regards to the lattice ordering, and [21] only allows transitions to affect the "value of a run" using the meet operator, which does not allow abstract transformers such as those of assignments.

3 Abstract Interpretation and Trace Partitioning

In this section we briefly review and define concepts and terminology related to trace partitioning in abstract interpretation, following Mauborgne and Rival [26].

A *program* is taken to be a transition system $(S, A, \rightarrow, s_0)$ where S is the set of states, A is the set of actions (representing statements), $\rightarrow \subseteq S \times A \times S$ is the transition relation, and s_0 is the initial state. Following convention, we write $s \xrightarrow{a} s'$ for the transition $(s, a, s') \in \rightarrow$.

A finite *trace* over a program is a finite sequence of states: $\sigma = s_0 \dots s_n$, such that for $0 \leq i \leq n$, $s_i \in S$ and $s_i \xrightarrow{a_i} s_{i+1}$ for some $a_i \in \mathcal{A}$. We denote the final state of a trace σ as $\sigma_\dashv$. The set of all (finite) traces of a program P is denoted $[\![P]\!] = \{\sigma \in S^* \mid \sigma \text{ is a finite trace of } P\}$ where S^* is the set of all sequences of states in S.

In "classic" abstract interpretation safety properties for a given program can be verified using approximations of the set of states that are reachable by the program. In later sections we shall need a generalisation of this approach, using approximations of sets of *traces*. The approximation of the set of traces for a given program $P = (S, \mathcal{A}, \rightarrow, s_0)$ is represented by an abstract domain, $(L, \sqsubseteq_L)$, with a concomitant (concretisation) function $\gamma : L \rightarrow 2^{S^*}$ that maps an abstract representation of a trace, $\ell \in L$, to the set of corresponding concrete program traces. This gives rise to a *Galois connection*, comprising α and γ such that $\alpha(X) \sqsubseteq_L \ell \iff X \sqsubseteq_{2^{S^*}} \gamma(\ell)$. This Galois connection can be used to induce an *abstract model* of the program P by defining for each concrete action, $a \in \mathcal{A}$, a corresponding abstract action, $f_a : L \rightarrow L$, that safely approximates the concrete semantics by requiring that for all $s, s' \in S$ it holds that if $s \xrightarrow{a} s'$, $s_1 s_2 \cdots s \in X$ and $\alpha(X) = \ell$ then $f_a(\ell) = \ell'$ and $s_1 s_2 \cdots s s' \in \gamma(\ell')$ [33]. For any program, P, we denote this abstract model of (all the actions of) a program: $\mathcal{M}_P = \{f_a \mid a \in \mathcal{A}\}$.

In the above approach to abstract interpretation, all traces (corresponding to a given abstract value) are treated in the same way, since it is not possible to discern where the different traces originate from, e.g., whether or not a given trace corresponds to a 'then' branch of a conditional or to the 'else' branch. This may lead to an increased number of false positives when attempting to verify safety properties.

As shown in [26], it is possible to extract more information from the traces by *partitioning* the set of traces and thereby increase the precision of the analysis by treating each partition separately. Partitioning is performed through the use of a partitioning function:

Definition 1 (Partitioning Function [26]). *A function $\delta : L \rightarrow 2^{S^*}$ is called a partitioning function if and only if it is covering:*

$$\bigcup_{l \in L} \delta(l) = 2^{S^*}$$

and it is a partitioning *of 2^{S^*}:*

$$\forall l, l' \in L : l \neq l' \implies \delta(l) \cap \delta(l') = \emptyset$$

In [26] it is proven that using trace partitioning leads to more precise analyses.

An example of a trace partitioning is the *final control state partition* that partitions traces based on their final state. This partitioning is commonly built into the abstract semantics in "standard" abstract interpretation. Following [26], we define a state to be a pair consisting of a control location, and a memory

Algorithm 1. The worklist algorithm for computing the MFP_P [29, p. 75], given abstract model $\mathcal{M}_P = \{f_a | a \in \mathcal{A}\}$, and initial lattice element ℓ_0. In the algorithm $s, t \in \mathcal{S}$ and $a \in \mathcal{A}$.

```
 1: procedure WORKLIST
 2:     W := {(s, a, t)|(s, a, t) ∈→}
 3:     Analysis(·) := ⊥, Analysis(s₀) := ℓ₀
 4:     while W ≠ ∅ do
 5:         Remove some (s, a, t) from W
 6:         if fₐ(Analysis(s)) ⋢ Analysis(t) then
 7:             Analysis(t) := Analysis(t) ⊔ fₐ(Analysis(s))
 8:             for all a', t' where t ─a'→ t' do
 9:                 W := W ∪ {(t, a', t')}
10:     MFP := Analysis
```

state: $\mathcal{S} = LOC \times MEM$. The final control state partitioning function is then $\delta_{LOC} : LOC \to 2^{\mathcal{S}^*}$, such that:

$$\delta_{LOC}(l) = \{\sigma \in S^* | \sigma_{\dashv} = (l, m) \text{ for some } m \in MEM\}$$

We can now define the result of a static analysis using abstract interpretation under a trace partitioning. Note that we follow the approach and terminology of [29] and call this the *maximal fixed point solution*, although this name is mainly used for historic reasons:

Definition 2 (Maximal Fixed Point Solution [29]). *Let* $P = (\mathcal{S}, \mathcal{A}, \to, s_0)$ *be a program,* $\mathcal{M}_P$ *an abstract model of* P *over the lattice* $\mathcal{L} = (L, \sqsubseteq)$*, and* $\delta : E \to 2^{\mathcal{S}^*}$ *a partitioning function. The* maximal fixed point solution *(MFP) for the set of monotone framework equations for* P *is then a mapping* $MFP_P : E \to L$*, such that for any element in the partitioning,* $e \in E$*, the mapping,* $MFP_P(e) \in L$*, represents the least solution to the monotone framework equations for the given partition.*

The *MFP* is typically calculated using a worklist algorithm; for the final control state partitioning the instantiation is as shown in Algorithm 1.

More specialised partitioning functions can be defined, resulting in a more precise *MFP*. In [26] a number of partitioning functions are defined and discussed, partitioning on control flow and values, these will be treated in Sect. 5. A distinction should be made between static partitioning (where the trace partitioning is decided before the analysis, and does not change during the analysis) and dynamic partitioning (where the trace partitioning can change during the analysis). In Sect. 5 we will see how static partitioning allows for a more efficient encoding into an abstract model.

4 Lattice Automata

In the following we introduce the concept of *lattice automata* and define the corresponding notion of model checking for lattice automata. Model checking is a well-known technique for verification purposes: it takes as input a model of the intended target system, e.g., a representation of a program, typically in the form of an automaton, and then computes the unfolded transition system of the automaton on-the-fly while checking all encountered states against the properties to be verified (usually formulated in a special logic). In this paper we will focus on model checking *reachability properties*, namely whether a state with a certain property can be reached.

We start by defining *lattice transition systems*, a formalism that subsumes many other types of transition systems traditionally used in model checking, such as finite automata and timed automata.

Definition 3 (Lattice Transition System). *A* lattice transition system *is a triple* $\mathcal{T} = (S, \mathcal{L}, \longrightarrow)$ *where S is a finite set of states, $\mathcal{L} = (L, \sqsubseteq, \sqcup)$ is a lattice and* $\longrightarrow \subseteq S \times L \times S \times L$ *is a transition relation which has the monotonicity property: for all $s_1, s_2 \in S$ and $\ell_1, \ell_2, \ell_1' \in L$:*

$$if\ (s_1, \ell_1) \longrightarrow (s_2, \ell_2)\ and\ \ell_1 \sqsubseteq \ell_1'$$
$$then\ \exists \ell_2' \in L : (s_1, \ell_1') \longrightarrow (s_2, \ell_2')\ with\ \ell_2 \sqsubseteq \ell_2'$$

Transitions are usually written as $(s, \ell) \longrightarrow (s', \ell')$ whenever $(s, \ell, s', \ell') \in \longrightarrow$. Configurations are pairs of the form (s, ℓ) where $s \in S$ and $\ell \in L$.

Definition 4 (Path). *A finite path in a lattice transition system $\mathcal{T}$ is a finite sequence $\sigma = (s_0, \ell_0)(s_1, \ell_1) \cdots (s_n, \ell_n)$ such that $(s_i, \ell_i) \longrightarrow (s_{i+1}, \ell_{i+1})$ for all $i, 0 \leq i \leq n - 1$.*

We extend the $\sqsubseteq$ ordering to configurations such that $(s, \ell) \sqsubseteq (t, \ell') \iff s = t \wedge \ell \sqsubseteq \ell'$. Given a set of configurations X and a configuration (s, ℓ) we shall write $(s, \ell) \sqsubseteq X$ to mean $\exists (s, \ell') \in X : \ell \sqsubseteq \ell'$, and $(s, \ell) \not\sqsubseteq X$ to mean $\neg((s, \ell) \sqsubseteq X)$.

To describe a lattice transition system in a concise way we will use *networks of extended lattice automata* (analogous to networks of timed automata as in UPPAAL [3]). An extended lattice automaton is a finite automaton extended with a finite set of integer variables defined over a finite domain. In UPPAAL, and our implementation in opaal, a restricted subset of the C programming language can be used to describe the conditions guarding a transition, and how a transition updates the integer variables. For a network of n automata with state sets S_i (for $i = 0, \ldots, n$), and m integer variables over the finite domain $\{0, \ldots, N\}$, the set of states S of the network product is given by the crossproduct $S_0 \times \cdots \times S_n \times \{0, \ldots, N\}^m$, which is equivalent to a (large) finite automaton. For the full semantics see [31].

Denoting lattice elements by ℓ, ℓ', transitions can also be guarded by expressions over the lattice, e.g., $\ell \sqcap \ell' \neq \bot$, as long as the *monotonicity property* is satisfied. Note that the monotonicity property does not apply to guards or updates of the discrete variables. We will describe how a transition updates the lattice element from ℓ to ℓ' by an assignment of a expression using ℓ to ℓ', e.g. $\ell' = \ell \sqcap \ell''$. To describe an abstract transformation of an action a of the lattice element ℓ we will use the notation $\ell[\![a]\!]$, equivalent to applying the abstract transformer $f_a(\ell)$.

In a network of automata, different automata can synchronise over channels, such that one automaton initiates a synchronisation over channel ch using the syntax ch!, while another receives on the same channel: ch?. Synchronisations can either be one-to-one (handshake), or one-to-many (broadcast). Handshake synchronisation is blocking, and chooses a receiver non-deterministically among the enabled receivers. Unless otherwise noted all synchronisations are handshake. An example of a network of extended lattice automata is shown in Fig. 2.

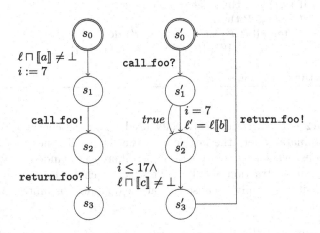

Fig. 2. An example of a network of two lattice automata, with integer variable i, initial states s_0 and s_0', and two channels call_foo and return_foo.

With the basic notions in place, we now turn to (reachability) model checking: model checking of lattice automata asks whether a model, $\mathcal{M}$, satisfies a formula ϕ, expressed in some appropriate logic, written $\mathcal{M} \models \phi$ if and only if some reachable state $(s, \ell) \models \phi$. The result of solving a model checking problem instance [2] is either a negative answer and a *counter-example* path, σ, or a positive answer and a set of configurations $\{(s_0, \ell_0), \ldots\}$ such that for any reachable state (s, ℓ) there exists some (s_i, ℓ_i) such that $(s, \ell) \sqsubseteq (s_i, \ell_i)$.

The requirement that a positive answer is accompanied by a set of configurations that cover all reachable configurations can be viewed as providing a *certificate*. It typically comprises the set of configurations examined during the model checking, the so-called *passed set* of all explored configurations. We call the set of configurations returned a *covering set*. Traditionally, the covering set is not presented to the user, because its size may be exponential in the size of the input model. The covering set is related to the *coverability* problem of well-structured transition systems [15]. In the following we are only interested in using model checking to find a covering set, and thus assume the formula $\phi = false$, which is never satisfied.

We will now give two algorithms for solving the model checking problem for a lattice transition system.

Algorithm 2. Algorithm to compute a covering set or a counter-example, given a model in the form of a lattice transition system $\mathcal{M} = (S, \mathcal{L}, \rightarrow)$, initial configuration (s_0, ℓ_0) and formula ϕ, if the set of reachable configurations of $\mathcal{M}$ is finite.

```
 1: procedure MC-COVER(M, (s₀, ℓ₀), φ)
 2:     W := {(s₀, ℓ₀)}, P := ∅
 3:     while W ≠ ∅ do
 4:         Remove some (s, ℓ) from W
 5:         if (s, ℓ) ⊭ φ then return counterexample
 6:         if (s, ℓ) ⋢ P then
 7:             for all (t, ℓ') s.t. (s, ℓ) → (t, ℓ') do
 8:                 W := (W \ {(t, ℓ'')|ℓ'' ⊑ ℓ'}) ∪ {(t, ℓ')}
 9:                 P := (P \ {(s, ℓ')|ℓ' ⊑ ℓ}) ∪ {(s, ℓ)}
10:     return Covering set P
```

Algorithm 2 is the algorithm typically used for model checking reachability for timed automata, where the lattice $\mathcal{L}$ is the set of all zones (convex sets of clock valuations, efficiently representable as difference-bounded matrices), and $\sqsubseteq$ is the inclusion abstraction of [13]. If the set of reachable configurations in the model $\mathcal{M}$ is finite (typically because the lattice domain L is finite), Algorithm 2 will terminate.

Lemma 1. *Given a lattice transition system $\mathcal{M} = (S, \mathcal{L}, \rightarrow)$ and initial configuration (s_0, ℓ_0): if Algorithm 2 returns a covering set P, then the covering set is exact, i.e. some (s, ℓ) is covered by a reachable configuration if and only if $(s, \ell) \sqsubseteq P$.*

$$(s_0, \ell_0) \rightarrow^* (s, \ell') : (s, \ell) \sqsubseteq (s, \ell') \iff (s, \ell) \sqsubseteq P$$

Proof (Sketch). For the if direction assume that some (s, ℓ) is covered by a reachable configuration. The algorithm will eventually visit some state (s, ℓ') with $\ell \sqsubseteq \ell'$ because of the monotonicity of $\rightarrow$, and add this to P, so eventually $(s, \ell) \sqsubseteq P$. To see that this holds invariantly afterwards notice that the only configurations removed from P in line 9, are covered by the newly added state thus preserving the invariant.

For the only if direction assume $(s, \ell) \sqsubseteq P$. Since the algorithm only adds a configuration (s, ℓ) to P if it is reachable and not already covered by P, the lemma holds.

Algorithm 2 is only useful for finite state spaces, but provides exact answers. If a sound but over-approximated answer is sufficient, Algorithm 3 can be used. Algorithm 3 is the algorithm used for over-approximate reachability checking of timed automata using the convex-hull abstraction [13]. If the lattice $\mathcal{L}$ has no infinite ascending chains Algorithm 3 will terminate. If $\mathcal{L}$ has infinite ascending chains (occasional) widening will have to be used instead of joining, as suggested by [33].

Lemma 2. *If Algorithm 3 returns a covering set it is sound, i.e. if some (s, ℓ) is covered by a reachable configuration then $(s, \ell) \sqsubseteq P$.*

Algorithm 3. Algorithm to compute a covering set or a counter-example, given a model in the form of a lattice transition system $\mathcal{M} = (S, \mathcal{L}, \rightarrow)$, initial configuration (s_0, ℓ_0) and formula ϕ, and using lattice join as abstraction.

```
1:  procedure MC-JOIN(M, (s₀, ℓ₀), φ)
2:      W := {(s₀, ℓ₀)}, P := ∅
3:      while W ≠ ∅ do
4:          Remove some (s, ℓ) from W
5:          if (s, ℓ) ⊭ φ then return counterexample
6:          if (s, ℓ) ⋢ P then
7:              for all (t, ℓ') s.t. (s, ℓ) → (t, ℓ') do
8:                  ℓ_joined := ℓ' ⊔ {ℓ'''|(t, ℓ''') ∈ W ∪ P}
9:                  W := (W \ {(t, ℓ''')|ℓ''' ⊑ ℓ_joined}) ∪ {(t, ℓ_joined)}
10:             P := (P \ {(s, ℓ')|ℓ' ⊑ ℓ}) ∪ {(s, ℓ)}
11:     return Covering set P
```

Proof (Sketch). Assume (s, ℓ) is covered by a reachable configuration. Then at some point an (s, ℓ') with $\ell \sqsubseteq \ell'$ has been removed from W at line 4, because of the monotonicity of $\rightarrow$. At line 10 the invariant $(s, \ell') \sqsubseteq P$ (implying $(s, \ell) \sqsubseteq P$) will be established. Future modifications to P at line 10 preserves this invariant.

Algorithm 2 was implemented in the multi-core backend of LTSMIN with the purpose of model checking timed automata [12], using a scheme of lockless data structures, state compression and swarm-like workers with work stealing, for details see [22]. The performance and scalability of this algorithm was shown to scale almost linearly up to 48 processors, primarily limited by the size/structure of the model [12].

For the implementation of Algorithm 2 the disjunctive completion [8] of the lattice $\mathcal{L}$ generally needs to be stored; for details see [31, Chap. 2]. In the implementation [12] this is done by storing states (s) in a shared passed-waiting hash table, and for each state storing a linked list of lattice elements $(\ell, \ell', \ldots)$ forming configurations $((s, \ell), (s, \ell'), \ldots)$, and a number of bits for each lattice element marking whether it is waiting or passed. For models where there are many reachable configurations compared to the number of reachable states, this results in sub-linear scaling of the model checking.

In this work we have extended the implementation to also include a join operator, providing a multi-core implementation of Algorithm 3. Because the implementation actually works on the disjunctive completion we can allow the join operator $\sqcup$ to be selective: it can select to keep two elements separate if so desired. This will be important for implementing dynamic partitioning. Note how Lemma 2 still holds in this case; on lines 9 and 10 only configurations actually covered by the joined lattice element are discarded.

5   Abstract Interpretation as Lattice Model Checking

In this section we describe how to concretely transform the problem of computing an *MFP* given a program $P = (\mathcal{S}, \mathcal{A}, \rightarrow, s_0)$, an abstract model of the program

$\mathcal{M}_P$ over a domain L, and a trace partitioning function δ, into a problem of computing a covering set for a lattice automaton. The presentation below is divided into four parts, depending on the nature of the trace partitioning function. Even though the most general way to perform trace partitioning, namely *dynamic partitioning*, naturally covers simpler cases, the simpler trace partitioning functions are crucial for obtaining good performance of the model checking.

5.1   Final Control Location Partitioning

The most abstract partitioning function we consider in this paper is the *final control state partitioning* with δ_{LOC} as defined in Sect. 3. Recall that it partitions traces, based on the control location of the last state of the trace. Given a trace, it is thus sufficient to keep track of which control location the trace ends in, to know which trace partition the current memory state should be put in. Also recall that we assume program states are pairs in $LOC \times MEM$.

A finite automaton that accepts valid traces of the program P and at the same time keeps track of the current control location is trivially obtained from the control flow graph of the program, given by the set of locations LOC and the set of edges $E \subseteq LOC \times LOC$ such that $(s, s') \in E$ iff $\exists a \in \mathcal{A}$ such that $s \xrightarrow{a} s'$. Consider the program in Fig. 3a, for which the control flow graph is shown in Fig. 3b.

Given the abstract semantics for the program P, $\mathcal{M}_P$ over some lattice $\mathcal{L} = (L, \sqsubseteq, \sqcup)$, we construct a lattice automaton $\mathcal{T} = (S, L, \Rightarrow)$ based on the control flow graph:

- S is the set of control locations LOC
- L is the abstract domain as given by the lattice $\mathcal{L}$
- $\Rightarrow$ is the transition relation such that for a pair of configurations (s, ℓ) and (s', ℓ') it holds that $(s, \ell) \Rightarrow (s', \ell')$ if and only if $\exists a \in \mathcal{A}$ such that $s \xrightarrow{a} s'$ and $f_a(\ell) = \ell'$.

The lattice automaton for the program in Fig. 3a is shown in Fig. 3c, with the abstract transformers written on the edges as transformations of a lattice element ℓ into another ℓ'. Using Algorithm 3 a covering set can be computed for this lattice automaton.

The soundness of this construction can now be formulated:

Theorem 1. *Given a program $P = (\mathcal{S}, \mathcal{A}, \rightarrow, s_0)$ and abstract semantics $\mathcal{M}_P$ over a domain L and the final control trace partitioning function δ_{LOC}, the MFP as computed by Algorithm 1 is the same as the covering set P computed by Algorithm 3 on the lattice automaton $\mathcal{T} = (S, L, \Rightarrow)$ constructed as described above.*

Proof (Sketch). For simplicity we assume the case of $\sqcup$ being a total function. The cardinality of the covering set, and *MFP* are then the same: one lattice element in LOC. We can therefore view P as a mapping $P : LOC \rightarrow L$, where $P(s) = \bot$ if there is no $(s, \ell) \in P$. Similarly, we can consider the waiting list W

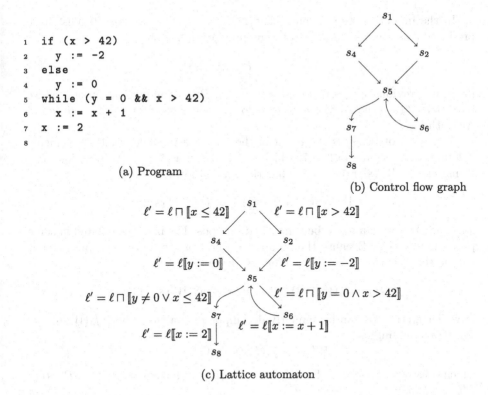

```
1   if (x > 42)
2       y := -2
3   else
4       y := 0
5   while (y = 0 && x > 42)
6       x := x + 1
7   x := 2
8
```

(a) Program

(b) Control flow graph

(c) Lattice automaton

Fig. 3. (a) Program, (b) Control flow graph of the program, and (c) constructed lattice automaton.

as a function $W : LOC \rightarrow L$, because at any point in the algorithm there will be only one $(s, \ell) \in W$.

We show the proof in two parts: first we show that each iteration of Algorithm 3 can be simulated by a finite number of iterations in Algorithm 1. From [29, Sect. 2.4] we have that $Analysis \sqsubseteq MFP$ after each iteration of Algorithm 1. In the second part we show that at termination $P(s)$ is a fixed-point.

First part: each update of $P(s)$ in Algorithm 3 can be simulated by a finite number of updates of $Analysis(s)$ in Algorithm 1. Note that line 10 can be written as $P(s) := P(s) \sqcup \ell$, where (s, ℓ) was removed from W. Also, line 9 can be written as $W(s) := W(s) \sqcup P(s) \sqcup f_a(\ell)$ for some abstract transformer f_a.

We proceed by induction on the number of iterations in Algorithm 3. For the base case we have that the first update of P at line 10 must be of s_0, and because $P(s_0) = \bot$ we have that

$$P(s_0) := \bot \sqcup \ell_0 = \ell_0$$

This is simulated by the initial value of $Analysis(s_0)$ in Algorithm 1. In the first iteration, the configurations added to W in line 9 of Algorithm 3 are equivalent to adding the transitions to W in Algorithm 1.

In the inductive step we have that $P(s) := P(s) \sqcup \ell$ at line 10 must have produced ℓ as follows, on line 9 of some previous iteration:

$$\ell = W'(s) \sqcup P'(s) \sqcup f_b(\ell') \tag{1}$$

for some previous values of $W'(s)$ and $P'(s)$. By the induction hypothesis we have that $P'(s)$ is equal to $Analysis(s)$ for some iteration for some execution of Algorithm 1.

The value of $W'(s)$ is the result of the join of a number of lattice elements ℓ' found as successors in line 7, which is calculated as $\ell' = f_a(W'(s'))$ for some transition $(s', W'(s')) \Rightarrow (s, \ell')$. Thus the general form of $W'(s)$ is:

$$W'(s) = f_a(W'(s')) \sqcup W'(s) \sqcup P'(s)$$

for which $W'(s')$ can again be similarly decomposed as being calculated in some previous iteration. Because the number of iterations is finite, at some point it will be the case that $W'(s) = \bot$. Then we have that:

$$W'(s) = f_a(W'(s')) \sqcup \bot \sqcup P'(s) = f_a(W'(s')) \sqcup P'(s)$$

in which $f_a(W'(s'))$ can be similarly decomposed to a case where $f_a(W'(s')) = f_a(P''(s'))$, giving us

$$W'(s) = f_a(P''(s')) \sqcup P'(s)$$

which substituted back into Eq. (1) gives (because of the monotonicity of $P''(s) \sqsubseteq P'(s) \sqsubseteq P(s)$):

$$\ell = f_a(P''(s')) \sqcup P'(s) \sqcup P'(s) \sqcup f_b(\ell'') \tag{2}$$
$$P(s) := P(s) \sqcup f_a(P''(s')) \sqcup P'(s) \sqcup P'(s) \sqcup f_b(\ell'') \tag{3}$$
$$P(s) := P(s) \sqcup f_a(P''(s')) \sqcup f_b(\ell'') \tag{4}$$

This last equation is equivalent to two iterations of Algorithm 1 updating $P(s)$ given two different transitions, concluding the proof of this part.

Second part: At termination $P(s)$ is a fixed-point. Assume, towards a contradiction, that for some transition $s \xrightarrow{a} t$ it is the case that $f_a(P(s)) \not\sqsubseteq P(t)$. $P(s)$ was last updated in line 10, but before $P(s)$ was updated the abstract successor corresponding to the transition $s \xrightarrow{a} t$ was considered and a configuration $(t, f_a(\ell) \sqcup W'(t) \sqcup P'(t))$ was put on the waiting list W. Any update of $W(t)$ afterwards is monotonically increasing, until at some point later the configuration was removed from W, and either was already covered by $P(t)$ or $P(t) := P(t) \sqcup f_a(\ell) \ldots$ at line 10. Thus we have a contradiction.

Combining the two parts we have that after each iteration $P \sqsubseteq MFP$, and eventually P reaches a fixed-point: as MFP is the least fixed-point, $P = MFP$. $\square$

Modelling of Functions. Having shown how partitioning on control location can be handled, we will briefly mention how function calls can be modelled mono- or poly-variantly. Functions are naturally modelled using one automaton

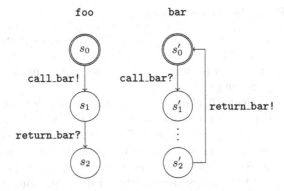

Fig. 4. The general pattern for poly-variant modelling of function calls.

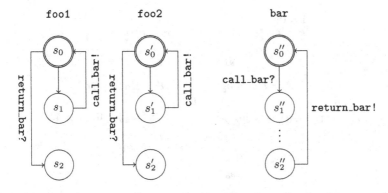

Fig. 5. The general pattern for mono-variant modelling of function calls.

per function, in a poly-variant [29] way using *channel synchronisation* between the automata to model the actual function call and concomitant return from the function call. The general pattern is shown in Fig. 4, where foo calls bar over the channel call_bar. When bar is done, it returns by synchronising back over the channel return_bar. This approach is limited to only modelling bounded recursion, as the discrete state will contain an entry for the call-site location, as well as the location within the function, effectively analysing the function call in the context of the current call-site.

In Fig. 5 the pattern for mono-variant modelling of functions is shown. When a function is invoked, the caller returns to it's initial state. From the initial state of all callers of a function bar there are transitions to the return-sites for such function calls synchronising on return_bar. When bar is returning, the caller to return to is picked non-deterministically.

If unbounded recursion is encountered these modelling patterns will cause the execution trace to deadlock, causing an overall unsound result. This condition can be detected and flagged, if desired.

5.2   Control Flow Based Partitioning

Another class of trace partitioning functions put forth is trace partitioning based on control flow [17,26]. In general, control flow partitioning partitions traces based on their history of control flow choices, possibly merging the partitions at a later point during execution.

Lattice automata elegantly allow the recording of a limited amount of control flow history, by using discrete finitely valued integer variables. For each control flow partitioning point a discrete variable i is added, such that each branch of the control flow point sets i to a unique value. If the partitions should later be merged [26] the variable is simply reset to one value. Consider the example lattice automata in Fig. 6a, where traces are partitioned depending on the control flow at s_1, and merged at s_7.

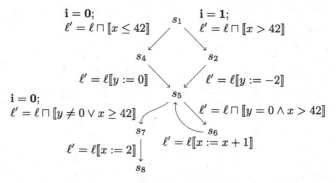

(a) Lattice automaton with control flow partitioning, the only addition compared to Fig. 3c being the updates of the variable i, as highlighted.

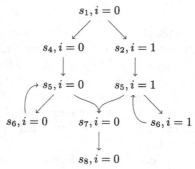

(b) Reachable locations for the lattice automaton in Fig. 6a.

Fig. 6. Control flow partitioning of the program in Fig. 3a.

Similarly loops can be unrolled any finite number of times by adding a loop counter variable that is reset on entry to the loop, and incremented on backedges until a certain limit is reached. As an example unrolling the (s_5, s_6) loop at most

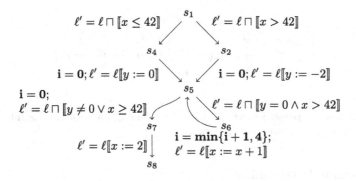

Fig. 7. Loop unrolling of order four, for the program in Fig. 3a

four times is exemplified in Fig. 7. The first four iterations are treated separately as $i \in \{0, 1, 2, 3\}$, while the subsequent iterations are joined together as $i = 4$. At the loop exit, the partitions are merged, as i is set to 0.

In fact, any iteration pattern that can be described by a finite automaton can be partitioned in this manner, e.g., partitioning the loop into whether the iteration count is even or odd: add variable i and annotate the backedge with $i = i + 1$ modulo 2.

An advantage of using an intermediate format, such as lattice automata used here, is that the program analyst can easily experiment with different control flow partitionings by manually adding discrete variables and setting their value at different locations in a model editor. As long as no guards depend on the introduced variables, the soundness of properties is preserved, as no trace is excluded.

5.3 Value Based Partitioning

Another class of trace partitioning is based on partitioning different values into different partitions, akin to *property-oriented expansion* [36]. This can be handled similarly to the control flow partitioning case, by splitting control flow into a finite set of value classes (covering the entire range of the variable) using the general pattern shown in Fig. 8. For partitioning into $v_0, \ldots, v_n$ different values a discrete variable i with range $[0, n]$ is added. At each partitioning point n transitions are added, each following the pattern in Fig. 8. Each transition has a guard of the form $\ell \sqcap [\![x = v_1]\!] \neq \bot$ meaning that the transition can only be taken if at s the invariant $x = v_1$ is possible; there is no reason to explore a partition if it is already proven that no execution can have this value. If the transition is taken the partition is recorded in the discrete variable i, and the value v_i of the partition is assigned using the abstract transformer. If merging is desired at a later point, i is simply set to a constant value.

As the additional edges cover the entire range for the value partitioned variable no trace is excluded, and thus soundness is preserved while precision is increased.

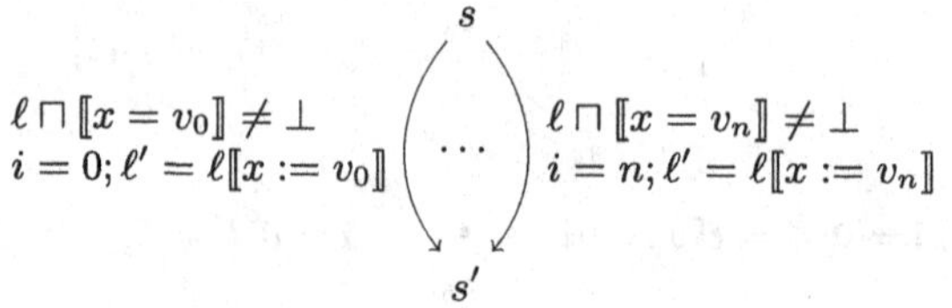

$$\ell \sqcap [\![x = v_0]\!] \neq \bot \quad \left(\underset{s'}{\overset{s}{\cdots}}\right) \quad \ell \sqcap [\![x = v_n]\!] \neq \bot$$
$$i = 0; \ell' = \ell[\![x := v_0]\!] \qquad \qquad i = n; \ell' = \ell[\![x := v_n]\!]$$

Fig. 8. The general pattern of value based partitioning on a variable x into a finite number of partitions of values $v_0, \ldots, v_n$.

5.4 Dynamic Partitioning

The most general class of trace partitioning functions is allowing for the partitioning to be changed during computation [32]. In our setting this is realised using a *joining strategy* [11], namely allowing the $\sqcup$ function to be selective in which elements to join.

Definition 5 (Joining Strategy). *A joining strategy is a function*

$$\delta : (S \times \mathcal{L}) \times (S \times \mathcal{L}) \rightarrow \{true, false\}$$

detailing whether two states in a lattice transition system are allowed to be joined, or should be kept separate.

In our work we assume that states of different locations are never joined, i.e. $s \neq t \Rightarrow \delta((s, \ell), (t, \ell'))) = false$, which is always the case in our typical use cases. However, with a slight modification of Algorithm 3, it is possible to lift also this assumption. A joining strategy can then be used to define a partial join operator as follows

Definition 6 (Partial Join Operator). *A joining strategy δ implies a partial join operator for a lattice transition system:*

$$\sqcup_\delta(s)(\ell, \ell') \begin{cases} (s, \ell \sqcup \ell') & if \ \delta((s, \ell), (s', \ell')) = true \\ (s, \ell) & otherwise \end{cases}$$

As mentioned in Sect. 4, Algorithm 3 is already designed for this; it does the joining and removing of covered configurations in two separate steps, and only joins to the left, so a simple modification of line 8 to be:

8: $\ell_{joined} := \ell' \bigsqcup_\delta(t)\{\ell'''|(t, \ell''') \in W \cup P\}$

is enough to incorporate a partial join operator of a joining strategy.

During the analysis the joining strategy can be changed. One direction is to make the analysis coarser, based on the current analysis result or on extra-analysis information such as runtime and memory usage. A joining strategy δ_1 is (possibly) coarser than another δ_2 iff:

$$\forall s, \ell, s', \ell' : \delta_2((s, \ell), (s', \ell')) = true \implies \delta_1((s, \ell), (s', \ell')) = true$$

This is analogous to the ordering defined in [32], however it does suggest that the basis is a "completely partitioned system" and partitions are then merged to ensure termination. Note that changing the joining strategy to a coarser strategy does not affect soundness.

A dynamically calculated joining strategy is however only limited by the answers it has already given and can be thought of as a sort of oracle. It can dynamically give answers that in turn create partitions, as long as no partitions overlap. This allows a joining strategy to exactly mimic the mechanisms put forth in [32]. It should be noted that static partitioning provides better performance than dynamic partitioning, because of the data structures used: more configurations stored per location affects the performance negatively [12].

6   Experiments

To evaluate the feasibility and performance of the described approach, we have implemented a prototype for a small subset of C. The prototype is written in Python using the pycparser library, and generates models compatible with the opaal model checking framework [11]. One of the tools in opaal exports models to the multi-core model checker in the LTSMIN toolset [23], previously developed for timed automata in [12]. The models can be edited in the UPPAAL [24] GUI, to introduce static partitionings.

We have furthermore implemented support for using the octagon domain [27] from the APRON library [20] (using the standard widening) in opaal models, and made the required changes to implement Algorithm 3 in the multi-core model checker LTSMIN; the change to the core algorithm implementation is 6 lines of code.

```
1   void main() {
2       unsigned int a1, a2, a3,
3           a4, a5, a6; int r;
4       while (a1 < 20) {
5           a1++; }
6       while (a2 < 20) {
7           a2++; }
8       while (a3 < 20) {
9           a3++; }
10      while (a4 < 20) {
11          a4++; }
12      while (a5 < 20) {
13          a5++; }
14  }
```

Fig. 9. The explode.c program from [7]; with full control flow trace partitioning there is an exponential (in the size of the model) number of traces to explore.

In order to test and experiment with our prototype implementation, we took a "tricky" example program snippet (shown in Fig. 9) from [7] that was reported by the Astrée developers to lead to a state space explosion with an exponential number of traces to explore. One can observe that given no initial constraints for the program variables, the variables a1 through a5 can in succession be incremented by any value between 0 and 20. Tracking the relationship (as the octagon domain does) between all variables leads to one partition per possible value assignment, thus giving the state explosion. One can choose to partition on a number of the loops only, leading to a more coarse but faster analysis.

Applying our prototype implementation to this program snippet[1] and calculating the fix-point with increasingly more precise control flow trace partitioning results in the runtimes shown in Fig. 10.

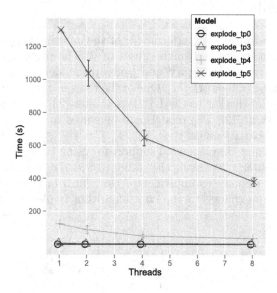

Fig. 10. Benchmark timings (mean and standard deviation) for the explode.c program with full trace partitioning on the first 0, 3, 4 or 5 loops, run on 1, 2, 4 and 8 cores.

The LTSMIN model checker was invoked with the following command line: 'opaal2lts-mc --state=table -s 25 --threads=N -o bfs -u3 -prr' directing LTSMIN to use a hashtable for passed-waiting list of size 2^{25}, run with N threads, use a breadth-first search order, do joining and choose a local successor state at random. Each experiment has been repeated four times and the mean is plotted, to account for the inherent non-determinism of the search order between multiple threads. As noted in [12] the search order can have a large effect on the runtime, because one worker can find a "large" (according to the $\sqsubseteq$ ordering) state quickly, enabling another worker to skip part of the state space.

---

[1] Experiments were performed on a 8-core Intel Xeon X5570 machine, with 74Gb of RAM.

Table 1. Mean benchmark runtimes in seconds for the `explode.c` program with control-flow trace partitioning of the first 0, 3, 4 or 5 loops, run on 1, 2, 4 or 8 cores. (Relative speedups are in parentheses)

	$Time_1$	$Time_2$	$Time_4$	$Time_8$
explode_tp0	0.02 s (1.00)	0.06 s (0.39)	0.10 s (0.25)	0.09 s (0.26)
explode_tp3	6.34 s (1.00)	3.41 s (1.86)	3.01 s (2.11)	2.18 s (2.91)
explode_tp4	122.99 s (1.00)	87.62 s (1.40)	49.68 s (2.48)	34.93 s (3.52)
explode_tp5	1301.92 s (1.00)	1038.70 s (1.25)	645.40 s (2.02)	379.44 s (3.43)

As can be seen in Fig. 10 and Table 1 the use of more cores improves the runtime, in all cases except for no trace partitioning where the analysis time is so low that the thread initialisation is more expensive than the computation itself. Note that our runtimes cannot be compared to those in [7], as the domain in Astrée is more advanced than ours. The speedup is sub-linear, yielding speedups up to 3.5 using 8 cores. In [12], where the abstract domain was quite similar to the octagon domain namely Difference-Bound Matrices using UPPAAL's DBM library, the speedup was shown to be up to 40 using 48 cores. The difference in scalability can be attributed to two factors: implementation details affecting the multi-core performance[2] and the structure of the models allowing for less parallelism – as can be seen by the smaller speedup of models with little trace partitioning.

The main sources of theoretically exploitable parallelism is (i) multiple execution paths due to non-determinism in the control-flow, and (ii) multiple trace partitionings that result in separate execution paths. There is an inherent risk of redundant work being performed, as the workers do not wait for all relevant joins to have been performed before proceeding. Theoretically the amount of work increases exponentially with the number of orthogonal partitionings, while parallelism only provides a linear speedup.

7   Conclusion

We have shown the connection between abstract interpretation and model checking at a very practical level: by defining a formalism of lattice automata encompassing both domains, showing how this formalism can be used to compute a fix-point of an abstract semantics defined by a Galois connection, and showing how trace partitioning is modelled very simply in this formalism. A common formalism as an intermediate format has the advantage that the intermediate format can be edited, debugged and simulated by a program analyst, e.g., to add components modelling the environment external to the program.

---

[2] E.g. increased usage of the dynamic memory allocator: APRON uses dynamic resizing of some data structures, whereas the UPPAAL DBM library does not. In general dynamic memory allocation is more expensive in a multi-core shared-memory setting, because it potentially requires synchronisation.

A common formalism allows using the same machinery for solving problems from both domains. This approach has the advantage that improvements from one domain can immediately be transfered to the other, exemplified by using a multi-core model checker. This yields significant speedups, reducing analysis times by up to a factor 3.5 on a 8-core machine.

We plan to implement support for a much more complete subset of C, in order to perform more complete experiments. In addition we plan to implement support for more input programming languages; an especially exciting perspective is the ability to combine models extracted from different programming languages and model the interaction of e.g. Python code with C-code, or C-code with assembly, as outlined in [31].

Since the search order has a large impact on the speed-up, another interesting topic for future work is to see how techniques from model checking, or from static analysis [16] can influence the performance — especially also in a multi-core setting, where different workers can employ different strategies.

Finally, with programs represented as models, it would also be of interest to investigate if it is possible to use the underlying model checker directly to check properties of programs. For example checking whether an error state or an assert is reachable or possibly even more elaborate properties such as (bounded) liveness. However, the corresponding queries would likely yield very large formula to be model checked, again stressing the need for good multi-core scalability.

Acknowledgments. We would like to thank the LTSMIN and APRON developers for making their excellent code available to others in the research community.

References

1. Alur, R.: Timed automata. In: Halbwachs, N., Peled, D.A. (eds.) CAV 1999. LNCS, vol. 1633, pp. 8–22. Springer, Heidelberg (1999)
2. Baier, C., Katoen, J.P.: Principles of Model Checking. The MIT Press, New York (2008)
3. Behrmann, G., David, A., Larsen, K.G.: A tutorial on UPPAAL. In: Bernardo, M., Corradini, F. (eds.) SFM-RT 2004. LNCS, vol. 3185, pp. 200–236. Springer, Heidelberg (2004)
4. Beyer, D., Henzinger, T.A., Théoduloz, G.: Configurable software verification: concretizing the convergence of model checking and program analysis. In: Damm, W., Hermanns, H. (eds.) CAV 2007. LNCS, vol. 4590, pp. 504–518. Springer, Heidelberg (2007). http://dx.doi.org/10.1007/978-3-540-73368-3_51
5. Clarke, E.M., Grumberg, O., Long, D.E.: Model checking and abstraction. ACM Trans. Programm. Lang. Syst. (TOPLAS) **16**(5), 1512–1542 (1994)
6. Cousot, P., Cousot, R.: Abstract interpretation: a unified lattice model for static analysis of programs by construction or approximation of fixpoints. In: Proceedings of the 4th ACM SIGACT-SIGPLAN Symposium on Principles of Programming Languages (POPL 1977), pp. 238–252 (1977)
7. Cousot, P., Cousot, R., Feret, J., Mauborgne, L., Miné, A., Rival, X.: Why does ASTRÉE scale up? Formal Meth. Syst. Des. **35**(3), 229–264 (2009)

8. Cousot, P., Cousot, R.: Systematic design of program analysis frameworks. In: Conference Record of the Sixth Annual ACM Symposium on Principles of Programming Languages (POPL 1979), pp. 269–282. ACM Press, San Antonio (1979). http://dblp.org/db/conf/popl/popl79.html#CousotC79

9. Cousot, P., Cousot, R.: Comparing the Galois connection and widening/narrowing approaches to abstract interpretation. In: Bruynooghe, M., Wirsing, M. (eds.) PLILP 1992. LNCS, vol. 631, pp. 269–295. Springer, Heidelberg (1992)

10. Cousot, P., Cousot, R.: Refining model checking by abstract interpretation. Autom. Softw. Eng. 6, 69–95 (1999). http://dblp.org/db/journals/ase/ase6.html#CousotC99

11. Dalsgaard, A.E., Hansen, R.R., Jørgensen, K.Y., Larsen, K.G., Olesen, M.C., Olsen, P., Srba, J.: opaal: a lattice model checker. In: Bobaru, M., Havelund, K., Holzmann, G.J., Joshi, R. (eds.) NFM 2011. LNCS, vol. 6617, pp. 487–493. Springer, Heidelberg (2011). http://dblp.org/db/conf/nfm/nfm2011.html#DalsgaardHJLOOS11

12. Dalsgaard, A.E., Laarman, A., Larsen, K.G., Olesen, M.C., van de Pol, J.: Multi-core reachability for timed automata. In: Jurdziński, M., Ničković, D. (eds.) FORMATS 2012. LNCS, vol. 7595, pp. 91–106. Springer, Heidelberg (2012). http://dblp.org/db/conf/formats/formats2012.html#DalsgaardLLOP12

13. Daws, C., Tripakis, S.: Model checking of real-time reachability properties using abstractions. In: Steffen, B. (ed.) TACAS 1998. LNCS, vol. 1384, pp. 313–329. Springer, Heidelberg (1998)

14. Finkel, A., Schnoebelen, P.: Well-structured transition systems everywhere!. Theor. Comput. Sci. 256(1–2), 63–92 (2001)

15. Geeraerts, G., Raskin, J.F., Van Begin, L.: Expand, enlarge and check: new algorithms for the coverability problem of WSTS. J. Comput. Syst. Sci. 72(1), 180 (2006)

16. Gopan, D., Reps, T.: Guided static analysis. In: Riis Nielson, H., Filé, G. (eds.) SAS 2007. LNCS, vol. 4634, pp. 349–365. Springer, Heidelberg (2007). http://dl.acm.org/citation.cfm?id=2391451.2391475

17. Handjieva, M., Tzolovski, S.: Refining static analyses by trace-based partitioning using control flow. In: Levi, G. (ed.) SAS 1998. LNCS, vol. 1503, pp. 200–214. Springer, Heidelberg (1998). http://dblp.org/db/conf/sas/sas98.html#HandjievaT98

18. Henzinger, T.A., Jhala, R., Majumdar, R., Sutre, G.: Lazy abstraction. In: Proceedings of the 29th ACM SIGPLAN-SIGACT Symposium on Principles of Programming Languages (POPL 2002), pp. 58–70. ACM (2002)

19. Jeannet, B., Halbwachs, N., Raymond, P.: Dynamic partitioning in analyses of numerical properties. In: Cortesi, A., Filé, G. (eds.) SAS 1999. LNCS, vol. 1694, pp. 39–50. Springer, Heidelberg (1999). http://dblp.org/db/conf/sas/sas99.html#JeannetHR99

20. Jeannet, B., Miné, A.: APRON: a library of numerical abstract domains for static analysis. In: Bouajjani, A., Maler, O. (eds.) CAV 2009. LNCS, vol. 5643, pp. 661–667. Springer, Heidelberg (2009). http://dblp.org/db/conf/sas/sas99.html#JeannetHR99

21. Kupferman, O., Lustig, Y.: Lattice automata. In: Cook, B., Podelski, A. (eds.) VMCAI 2007. LNCS, vol. 4349, pp. 199–213. Springer, Heidelberg (2007)

22. Laarman, A.: Scalable multi-core model checking. Ph.D. thesis, University of Twente (2014)

23. Laarman, A., van de Pol, J., Weber, M.: Multi-core LTSMIN: marrying modularity and scalability. In: Bobaru, M., Havelund, K., Holzmann, G.J., Joshi, R. (eds.) NFM 2011. LNCS, vol. 6617, pp. 506–511. Springer, Heidelberg (2011). http://dblp.org/db/conf/nfm/nfm2011.html#LaarmanPW11

24. Larsen, K.G., Pettersson, P., Yi, W.: UPPAAL in a nutshell. Int. J. Softw. Tools Technol. Transfer (STTT) **1**(1), 134–152 (1997)

25. del Mar Gallardo, M., Martinez, J., Merino, P., Pimentel, E.: aSPIN: Extending SPIN with abstraction. In: Model Checking Software, pp. 241–252 (2002)

26. Mauborgne, L., Rival, X.: Trace partitioning in abstract interpretation based static analyzers. In: Sagiv, M. (ed.) ESOP 2005. LNCS, vol. 3444, pp. 5–20. Springer, Heidelberg (2005)

27. Miné, A.: The octagon abstract domain. High. Order Symbolic Comput. (HOSC) **19**(1), 31–100 (2006)

28. Monniaux, D.: The parallel implementation of the Astrée static analyzer. In: Yi, K. (ed.) APLAS 2005. LNCS, vol. 3780, pp. 86–96. Springer, Heidelberg (2005). http://dx.doi.org/10.1007/11575467_7

29. Nielson, F., Nielson, H.R., Hankin, C.: Principles of Program Analysis. Springer-Verlag New York Inc., Secaucus (1999)

30. Nielson, F., Nielson, H.R.: Model checking *Is* static analysis of modal logic. In: Ong, L. (ed.) FOSSACS 2010. LNCS, vol. 6014, pp. 191–205. Springer, Heidelberg (2010)

31. Olesen, M.C.: Program analysis as model checking. Ph.D. thesis, Aalborg University (defended December 2013)

32. Rival, X., Mauborgne, L.: The trace partitioning abstract domain. ACM Trans. Program. Lang. Syst. (TOPLAS) **29**(5), 26 (2007). http://dblp.org/db/journals/toplas/toplas29.html#RivalM07

33. Schmidt, D.A., Steffen, B.: Program analysis *as* model checking of abstract interpretations. In: Levi, G. (ed.) SAS 1998. LNCS, vol. 1503, pp. 351–380. Springer, Heidelberg (1998)

34. Steffen, B.: Data flow analysis as model checking. In: Ito, T., Meyer, A.R. (eds.) TACS 1991. LNCS, vol. 526, pp. 346–365. Springer, Heidelberg (1991). http://dx.doi.org/10.1007/3-540-54415-1_54

35. Steffen, B.: Generating data flow analysis algorithms from modal specifications. Sci. Comput. Program. **21**(2), 115–139 (1993). http://dx.doi.org/10.1016/0167-6423(93)90003-8

36. Steffen, B.: Property-oriented expansion. In: Cousot, R., Schmidt, D.A. (eds.) SAS 1996. LNCS, vol. 1145, pp. 22–41. Springer, Heidelberg (1996). http://dblp.org/db/conf/sas/sas96.html#Steffen96

37. Steffen, B., Classen, A., Klein, M., Knoop, J., Margaria, T.: The fixpoint-analysis machine. In: Lee, I., Smolka, S.A. (eds.) CONCUR 1995. LNCS, vol. 962, pp. 72–87. Springer, Heidelberg (1995). http://dblp.org/db/conf/concur/concur1995.#htmlSteffenCKKM95

Probabilistic Abstract Interpretation: From Trace Semantics to DTMC's and Linear Regression

Alessandra Di Pierro[1] and Herbert Wiklicky[2(✉)]

[1] Dipartimento di Informatica, Università di Verona, Verona, Italy
alessandra.dipierro@univr.it
[2] Department of Computing, Imperial College London, London, UK
herbert@doc.ic.ac.uk

Abstract. In order to perform *probabilistic program analysis* we need to consider probabilistic languages or languages with a probabilistic semantics, as well as a corresponding framework for the analysis which is able to accommodate probabilistic properties and properties of probabilistic computations. To this purpose we investigate the relationship between three different types of probabilistic semantics for a core imperative language, namely Kozen's Fixpoint Semantics, our Linear Operator Semantics and probabilistic versions of Maximal Trace Semantics. We also discuss the relationship between Probabilistic Abstract Interpretation (PAI) and statistical or linear regression analysis. While classical Abstract Interpretation, based on Galois connection, allows only for worst-case analyses, the use of the Moore-Penrose pseudo inverse in PAI opens the possibility of exploiting statistical and noisy observations in order to analyse and identify various system properties.

1 Introduction

In this contribution we will address a topic which we believe is dear to the hearts of Hanne and Flemming, namely Abstract Interpretation based techniques in program analysis [1–4]. We will concentrate on the treatment of the probabilistic setting where either the program or its semantics or both contain an element of chance that can be used to refine the possible nondeterminism associated with their models. As program analysis is essentially based on the semantics of programs, we will first describe three different probabilistic semantics that could be used as a basis for probabilistic analysis by clarifying the differences and relationship between them, and discussing their potential for the construction of precise program analyses. As a result of this comparison it will be clear that the Probabilistic Abstract Interpretation framework originally introduced in [5,6] is not an instance of a probabilistic application of classical Abstract Interpretation as recently suggested in [7] in order to analyse probabilistic programs.

The use of linear operators on vector spaces – more concretely on Hilbert spaces – for the definition of a probabilistic semantics is an important feature

C.W. Probst et al. (Eds.): Nielsons' Festschrift, LNCS 9560, pp. 111–139, 2016.
DOI: 10.1007/978-3-319-27810-0_6

of the Probabilistic Abstract Interpretation framework for several reasons: (i) it provides a well-defined notion of generalised inverse that enjoys properties similar to the concretisation/abstraction functions in the Galois connection framework; (ii) it allows us to exploit a well-defined metric (the Euclidean distance) in order to achieve quantitative results for our static analyses; (iii) it is an appropriate setting where statistical models can be used to enhance the power of static analysis techniques with information gathered via observations.

While we have variously addressed the first two points in our previous work, the potentiality of Probabilistic Abstract Interpretation for performing a kind of *statistical* program analysis was never completely explored before. As another result we will show in this paper that, contrary to the typical computer scientist approach that constructs observations from models, it is sometimes useful to define a model starting from observations, as typically done in statistics. To this end, the particular notion of generalised inverse defining Probabilistic Abstract Interpretation – namely the Moore-Penrose pseudo-inverse [8–10] – makes it very natural to use statistical techniques such as linear regression [10,11] for constructing abstractions that are as close as possible to the actual system with respect to the observed behaviour.

2 Probabilistic Semantics

There exist a number of proposals for probabilistic languages. These can be based on procedural languages, e.g. [12–14], functional ones, e.g. [15–17], but also declarative ones, like [5,18]. Besides this there is also a substantial work in probabilistic process algebras [19,20]. It would be impossible to discuss or even to mention all these approaches here in detail, so we will only concentrate on a small (core) procedural language, which will call **pWhile** and which is essentially the same as the one in [12].

Similarly, a number of approaches have been proposed for defining a semantics for probabilistic programs, not least in order to allow for some form of static program analysis. Usually, it is straightforward to define an operational semantics for a probabilistic extension of a deterministic language; this can be achieved for example by replacing the original (unlabelled) transition relation of an SOS semantics with a weighted version, where the weights represent the probabilities associated with random choices or assignments. Some arguably more useful kinds of semantics are, for example, Kozen's Fixed-Point Semantics (KFS) [12], the Linear Operator Semantics (LOS) introduced by the authors in [21], and the probabilistic Maximal Trace Semantics (MTS) of [7]. We will concentrate in the following on these three models but again stress that many other approaches exist, which are based e.g. on domain theory [22–24], weakest preconditions [25,26], and the monadic approach in [16,27].

2.1 A Probabilistic Language

The syntax of the language we consider is a straightforward extension of an imperative language with a probabilistic assignment "x ?= ρ" where ρ represents a probability distribution on the set **Value** of possible values of x which associates to every $v_i \in$ **Value** a probability p_i. As usual we require for distributions that $0 \leq p_i \leq 1$ and $\sum_i p_i = 1$; these probabilities are all constant, i.e. we do not consider here dynamical changes of distributions. For so-called sub-probability distributions we require $0 \leq p_i \leq 1$ but only $\sum_i p_i \leq 1$. We denote (sub-)probability distributions by sets of pairs $\{\langle v_i, p_i \rangle\}_i$ which express the fact that a constant value v_i has probabilities p_i (pairs with probability $p_i = 0$ can be omitted).

The syntax of statements is given below. We also provide a labelled version of this syntax (cf. [4]) in order to be able to refer to certain program points in a program analysis context. For details on (arithmetic) expressions $f(x_1, \ldots, x_n)$ (sometimes denoted simply by e or a) and (Boolean) expressions or tests b, etc. we refer to e.g. [4,14].

$$
\begin{array}{ll}
S ::= \texttt{skip} & S ::= [\texttt{skip}]^\ell \\
\quad | \quad x := f(x_1, \ldots, x_n) & \quad | \quad [x := f(x_1, \ldots, x_n)]^\ell \\
\quad | \quad x \; \texttt{?=} \; \rho & \quad | \quad [x \; \texttt{?=} \; \rho]^\ell \\
\quad | \quad S_1 ; S_2 & \quad | \quad S_1 ; S_2 \\
\quad | \quad \texttt{if } b \texttt{ then } S_1 \texttt{ else } S_2 \texttt{ fi} & \quad | \quad \texttt{if } [b]^\ell \texttt{ then } S_1 \texttt{ else } S_2 \texttt{ fi} \\
\quad | \quad \texttt{while } b \texttt{ do } S \texttt{ od} & \quad | \quad \texttt{while } [b]^\ell \texttt{ do } S \texttt{ od}
\end{array}
$$

It would also be possible to allow for a probabilistic choice construct of the form "$\texttt{choose } p_1 : S_1 \texttt{ or } p_2 : S_2 \texttt{ ro}$", but in order to keep things simple we omit it in our treatment. This statement can be implemented, for example, as $c \; \texttt{?=} \; \rho$; $\texttt{if } c == 0 \texttt{ then } S_1 \texttt{ else } S_2 \texttt{ fi}$ with $\rho = \{\langle 0, p_1 \rangle, \langle 1, p_2 \rangle\}$. Further details on the (intuitive and operational) semantics of this language can be found for example in [14,21,28].

Though we only deal with constant probabilities in the following we will implicitly always normalise probabilities in a distribution (we cannot assume that a programmer provides the correct probabilities), and we will only allow for rational values (non-rational real values for p_i raise issues of computability we will avoid). This means that we can also require that the p_i are integers indicating the probability ratio between different alternatives.

Example 1. We will consider the following **pWhile** program as a running example throughout the paper (its labelled version can be found below in Example 5):

```
while true do
    if (x == 1)
        then x ?= {⟨0, p⟩, ⟨1, 1 − p⟩}
        else x ?= {⟨0, 1 − q⟩, ⟨1, q⟩}
    fi
od
```

This program may be thought of implementing a scheduler in some protocol where $x \mapsto 0$ and $x \mapsto 1$ determines which of two processes has, for example, control over a communication channel.

Clearly the execution of this program never terminates: a random switching between the state $x \mapsto 0$ and $x \mapsto 1$ is performed indefinitely according to the probabilities p and q.

In the following we will assume that the state space (and thus the set of configurations) is finite. This makes the treatment substantially simpler as we can avoid topological and measure theoretic details (for which we refer to [28]) and work with just linear algebraic notions instead of functional analytical or operator algebraic ones, cf. [29,30] etc. This finiteness condition is fulfilled by the example above. It should be noted that the finiteness of the state space however still allows for infinite executions.

2.2   Kozen's Fixed-Point Semantics (KFS)

A well-known denotational semantics for probabilistic programs was introduced by Kozen in the 1980s [12] based on bounded Banach space operators. This is a fixed-point I/O semantics that describes how an input probability distribution (or in general a measure) is transformed into an output sub-probability distribution/measure. It only records contributions of terminating processes. The probabilities of non-terminating, i.e. infinite, computations "gets lost" so the final outcome is no longer normalised or a full probability distribution/measure. As a consequence the semantics of all non-terminating processes is the same (cf. also [28]).

In Kozen's language in [12] the element of chance is introduced via random assignments. In the semantical interpretation of this language, all the actual executions of a program are however deterministic, as all possible choices are made beforehand [12, Section 3.2.2,p336]. More precisely, before the execution of a program commences, all later probabilistic choices have already been resolved by picking an $\omega \in \Omega$ with $(\Omega, \mathcal{E}, \mu)$ an appropriate measure space ($\mathcal{E}$ the σ-algebra of measurable events and μ a probability measure). The semantics of a program is then parametric in this event or scenario ω which determines the probability that the otherwise deterministic execution of a program may effectively happen.

Example 2. Consider the following simple program:

$$x \;?= \{\langle 0, \tfrac{1}{3}\rangle, \langle 1, \tfrac{2}{3}\rangle\}; \; x \;?= \{\langle 0, \tfrac{1}{2}\rangle, \langle 1, \tfrac{1}{2}\rangle\}.$$

The minimal event space we need for defining a semantics for this program is $\Omega = \{0,1\} \times \{0,1\}$ and, because this is a finite set, we can take the whole power-set $\mathcal{E} = \mathcal{P}(\Omega)$ as the σ-algebra of measurable sets. The probability measure of the elements in Ω is then: $\mu(\{(0,0)\}) = \tfrac{1}{6}$, $\mu(\{(0,1)\}) = \tfrac{1}{6}$, $\mu(\{(1,0)\}) = \tfrac{1}{3}$, and $\mu(\{(1,1)\}) = \tfrac{1}{3}$.

After a scenario ω has been picked, the program behaves exactly as one of the following deterministic programs:

for $\omega = (0,0)$ we execute "$x := 0; \; x := 0$" with probability $\tfrac{1}{6}$,
for $\omega = (0,1)$ we execute "$x := 0; \; x := 1$" with probability $\tfrac{1}{6}$,
for $\omega = (1,0)$ we execute "$x := 1; \; x := 0$" with probability $\tfrac{1}{3}$,
for $\omega = (1,1)$ we execute "$x := 1; \; x := 1$" with probability $\tfrac{1}{3}$.

In the Kozen semantics we can identify a state with a distribution on $\mathbf{Value}^n$, where n is the number of variables and $\mathbf{Value}$ is the set of possible values of a variable which we assume here – as said before – to be finite. Thus, a probabilistic state (as a distribution $\sigma \in \mathcal{D}(\mathbf{Value}^n)$) can be seen as a normalised element (in the sense of the 1-norm) in the vector space $\mathcal{V}(\mathbf{Value}^n)$. The space $\mathcal{V}(X)$, which allows for the representation of distributions as well as sub-distributions on X, is defined as the set of linear combinations of elements in X, i.e.

$$\mathcal{V}(X) = \left\{ \sum_i \lambda_i x_i \mid x_i \in X \wedge \lambda_i \in \mathbb{R} \right\}.$$

This space is isomorphic to $\mathbb{R}^{|X|}$ with $|X|$ the cardinality of X. Vector addition and scalar product are defined pointwise. We can identify $x_i \in X$ with the base vectors of $\mathcal{V}(X)$ and any element in $\mathcal{V}(X)$ with its coordinates, i.e. the tuple $(\lambda_i)_i$. This space is equipped with an inner product $\langle (\lambda_i)_i | (\nu_i)_i \rangle = \sum_i \lambda_i \nu_i$ and one of various norms, e.g. $\|(\lambda_i)_i\|_1 = \sum_i |\lambda_i|$ and $\|(\lambda_i)_i\|_2 = \sqrt{\sum_i |\lambda_i|^2} = \sqrt{\langle (\lambda_i)_i | (\lambda_i)_i \rangle}$. The choice of one norm or another is nevertheless largely irrelevant in the finite dimensional case where all norms are equivalent. In fact, the topology on finite dimensional vector spaces is uniquely determined by the algebraic structure, cf. e.g. [31, 1.22].

The Kozen semantics of a program P is then given by the linear operator $[\![P]\!]_{KFS} \in \mathcal{L}(\mathcal{V}(\mathbf{Value}^n))$ where $\mathcal{L}(X)$ is the set of linear maps $\mathbf{T}$ on X, i.e. $\mathbf{T}(x + y) = \mathbf{T}(x) + \mathbf{T}(y)$ and $\mathbf{T}(\lambda x) = \lambda \mathbf{T}(x)$:

$$[\![P]\!]_{KFS} : \mathcal{V}(\mathbf{Value}^n) \to \mathcal{V}(\mathbf{Value}^n),$$

which is the solution to the following set of equations:

$$[\![\text{skip}]\!]_{KFS} = \mathbf{I}$$
$$[\![x := f(x_1, \ldots, x_n)]\!]_{KFS} = \mathbf{U}(x \leftarrow f(x_1, \ldots, x_n))$$
$$[\![x \mathrel{?=} \rho]\!]_{KFS} = \sum_v \rho(v) \mathbf{U}(x \leftarrow v)$$
$$[\![S_1; S_2]\!]_{KFS} = ([\![S_1]\!]_{KFS}[\![S_2]\!]_{KFS})$$
$$[\![\text{if } b \text{ then } S_1 \text{ else } S_2 \text{ fi}]\!]_{KFS} = (\mathbf{P}(b)[\![S_1]\!]_{KFS} + \mathbf{P}(\neg b)[\![S_2]\!])$$
$$[\![\text{while } b \text{ do } S \text{ od}]\!]_{KFS} = (\mathbf{P}(b)[\![S]\!]_{KFS}[\![\text{while } b \text{ do } S \text{ od}]\!]_{KFS} + \mathbf{P}(\neg b)).$$

The operator $\mathbf{I}$ is the identity on $\mathcal{V}(\mathbf{Value}^n)$ represented by a matrix with $(\mathbf{I})_{vv} = 1$ and 0 otherwise for $v = (v_1, \ldots, v_n) \in \mathbf{Value}^n$. The matrix representation of the test or projection operators $\mathbf{P}$ is given by a diagonal matrix with $(\mathbf{P}(b))_{vv} = 1$ if $b(v)$ holds for $v \in \mathbf{Value}^n$ and 0 otherwise. Note that $\mathbf{P}(\text{true}) = \mathbf{I}$ and that $\mathbf{P}(\neg b) = \mathbf{I} - \mathbf{P}(b)$. The assignment or update operator $\mathbf{U}$ is given by a matrix with entries $(\mathbf{U}(x_i \leftarrow f(x_1, \ldots, x_n)))_{v, F(v)} = 1$ for all $v \in \mathbf{Value}^n$ and 0 otherwise, where $F : \mathbf{Value}^n \to \mathbf{Value}^n$ is defined as

$$F(v_1, \ldots, v_{i-1}, v_i, v_{i+1}, \ldots, v_n) = (v_1, \ldots, v_{i-1}, f(v_1, \ldots, v_n), v_{i+1}, \ldots, v_n).$$

This definition is equivalent to that given in [12, p339]).

The *existence* of a solution to these equations is guaranteed in general (i.e. also for infinite state spaces) by the Brouwer-Schauders fixed-point theorem (see e.g. [30,32]). The least fixed-point can be *constructed* iteratively via a "super-operator" $\tau : \mathcal{L}(\mathcal{V}(\mathbf{Value}^n)) \rightarrow \mathcal{L}(\mathcal{V}(\mathbf{Value}^n))$ which encodes the above equations and by exploiting the lifted point-wise order on distributions/measures.

Example 3. Consider again the program P in Example 1. As no executions of this program will ever terminate, there is no proper (sub-)probability distribution describing the final state. Thus Kozen's semantics, which describes the I/O behaviour, is trivial:

$$[P]_{KFS} = \begin{pmatrix} 0 & 0 \\ 0 & 0 \end{pmatrix} = \mathbf{O}$$

i.e. the zero operator $[P]_{KFS} : \mathcal{V}(\{x \mapsto 0, x \mapsto 1\}) \rightarrow \mathcal{V}(\{x \mapsto 0, x \mapsto 1\})$.

This is also justified by the fixed-point construction described in [12, p 341]. The semantics of the statement S given by

```
if (x == 1) then x ?= {⟨0,p⟩,⟨1,1-p⟩} else x ?= {⟨0,1-q⟩,⟨1,q⟩} fi
```

forming the body of the loop is easily computed as:

$$[S]_{KFS} = \begin{pmatrix} p & 1-p \\ 1-q & q \end{pmatrix},$$

but whatever the semantics $[S]_{KFS}$ of the body of loop is, the Kozen semantics of the whole program P is the (appropriate) supremum of a sequence of matrices $\tau^n(\mathbf{O})$ with $n = 1, 2, 3, \ldots$ (starting with the zero matrix $\mathbf{O}$):

$$\tau^n(\mathbf{O}) = \sum_{k=0}^{n-1} (\mathbf{P}(\texttt{true})[S]_{KFS})^k \mathbf{P}(\texttt{false}) = \sum_{k=0}^{n-1} (\mathbf{I}[S]_{KFS})^k \mathbf{O} = \mathbf{O}.$$

That is, for all $n = 1, 2, 3, \ldots$ we have $\tau^n(\mathbf{O}) = \mathbf{O}$ and thus $[P]_{KFS} = \mathbf{O}$.

We also represent (sub-)probability distributions as row vectors; the application of an operator or linear map $\mathbf{T}(x)$ is thus expressed by *post-multiplication* $x \cdot \mathbf{T}$ rather than *pre-multiplication* as it can be found elsewhere (e.g. [12]).

Example 3 describes the situation of a program that never terminates on all inputs. More interestingly, Kozen's semantics also allows us to model programs that terminate with probability $0 < p < 1$, as shown in the following example.

Example 4. Consider the programs Q, Q' and Q'' which incorporate the program P in Example 3:

```
if (x == 1)          x := 1;              x ?= {⟨0,½⟩,⟨1,½⟩};
    then x := 0      if (x == 1)          if (x == 1)
    else P               then x := 0          then x := 0
fi                       else P               else P
                     fi                   fi
```

The operator $[\![Q]\!]_{KFS}$ of the first program can be easily computed (based on $[\![P]\!]_{KFS}$ in Example 3). We have the Kozen semantics of the two branches of the if statements:

$$[\![x := 0]\!]_{KFS} = \begin{pmatrix} 1 & 0 \\ 1 & 0 \end{pmatrix} \quad [\![P]\!]_{KFS} = \begin{pmatrix} 0 & 0 \\ 0 & 0 \end{pmatrix}$$

as well as for the tests guarding the if statement:

$$[\![x = 0]\!]_{KFS} = \begin{pmatrix} 1 & 0 \\ 0 & 0 \end{pmatrix} \quad [\![x = 1]\!]_{KFS} = \begin{pmatrix} 1 & 0 \\ 0 & 0 \end{pmatrix} = \mathbf{I} - [\![x = 0]\!]_{KFS}$$

Thus by the fifth equation in the definition of the KFS (or section (3.3.4) in [12, p 340]) we get:

$$[\![Q]\!]_{KFS} = [\![x = 1]\!]_{KFS}[\![x := 0]\!]_{KFS} + [\![x = 0]\!]_{KFS}[\![P]\!]_{KFS} = \begin{pmatrix} 1 & 0 \\ 0 & 0 \end{pmatrix}$$

This means that if we have an initial state $\sigma = (p, 1 - p)^t$ which describes the fact that the initial value of x is zero with probability p, and one with probability $1 - p$, then $\sigma[\![Q]\!]_{KFS} = (p, 0)^t$ (where $.^t$ denotes vector transposition). This is in general (unless $p = 1$) only a sub-probability distribution expressing the fact that this program will terminate with probability p with a zero value for x and that with probability $1 - p$ we have non-termination.

If we consider instead the second program Q' then we have

$$[\![x := 1]\!]_{KFS} = \begin{pmatrix} 0 & 1 \\ 0 & 1 \end{pmatrix} \quad \text{and thus} \quad [\![Q']\!]_{KFS} = [\![x := 1]\!]_{KFS}[\![Q']\!]_{KFS} = \begin{pmatrix} 1 & 0 \\ 1 & 0 \end{pmatrix}$$

That means that independently of the initial value of x we always get (i.e. with probability one) a termination and a zero value for x.

Finally, if we consider the program Q'' we get

$$[\![Q'']\!]_{KFS} = \left(\frac{1}{2}[\![x := 0]\!]_{KFS} + \frac{1}{2}[\![x := 1]\!]_{KFS} \right)[\![Q]\!]_{KFS} = \begin{pmatrix} \frac{1}{2} & 0 \\ \frac{1}{2} & 0 \end{pmatrix}$$

Here we terminate (again with the resulting x being zero) with a half probability, independently from the initial value of x.

2.3   Linear Operator Semantics (LOS)

The Linear Operator Semantics in [21,28] constructs the generator of a Discrete Time Markov Chain (DTMC) in a syntax directed fashion. Like Kozen's semantics we can represent the LOS as an operator on the vector space of probabilistic states. However, differently from Kozen's semantics, the definition of this operator is based on the syntax rather than on a denotational domain. Moreover, in order to provide a suitable base for static analysis, we do not construct the LOS of a program by simply translating the SOS transition relation into a DTMC generator. Instead, we define it in a *structured* way by composing the operators associated with each syntactic elementary components of the program by means of the tensor (or Kronecker) product operation "$\otimes$" on vector spaces (cf. e.g. [33, 34] or [21]).

The state space is constructed starting from the classical states, i.e. states that associate concrete values in $v_i \in$ **Value** to variables $x_i \in$ **Var** $= \{x_1, \ldots, x_n\}$. The classical state space can therefore be defined as **State** $=$ **Var** $\rightarrow$ **Value** or equivalently **State** $=$ **Value**$_1 \times \ldots \times$ **Value**$_n =$ **Value**^{n}.

In order to describe the probabilistic state of a computation we consider (probability) distributions over (classical) states again – as in Kozen's construction – as elements in $\mathcal{V}($**Value**$^n)$. However, we can use the tensor product operation "$\otimes$" to decompose this probabilistic state space, i.e. $\mathcal{V}(X \times Y) = \mathcal{V}(X) \otimes \mathcal{V}(Y)$ and represent probabilistic states thus as elements in $\mathcal{V}($**Value**$^n) = \mathcal{V}($**Value**$_1) \otimes \mathcal{V}($**Value**$_2) \otimes \ldots \otimes \mathcal{V}($**Value**$_n) = \mathcal{V}($**Value**$)^{\otimes n}$.

The LOS is based on the labelled version of the syntax of **pWhile**. This allows us to record not only the values of all variables but also the current point in the program we are executing, i.e. the "program counter". Thus, the state space of the corresponding DTMC is a space of configurations which also contain information about the current label. This is defined as the space **Conf** $=$ **State**$\times$ **Label** of distributions in $\mathcal{D}($**Conf**$) \subseteq \mathcal{V}($**Conf**$) = \mathcal{V}($**State**$) \otimes \mathcal{V}($**Label**$) = \mathcal{V}($**Value**$)^{\otimes n} \otimes \mathcal{V}($**Label**$)$.

The LOS $[\![P]\!]_{LOS}$ of a program P is then an operator in $\mathcal{L}(\mathcal{V}($**Conf**$))$ or, more precisely

$$[\![P]\!]_{LOS} : \mathcal{V}(\textbf{Value}^n) \otimes \mathcal{V}(\textbf{Label}) \rightarrow \mathcal{V}(\textbf{Value}^n) \otimes \mathcal{V}(\textbf{Label}).$$

It is constructed by means of a set $\{\!\{P\}\!\}_{LOS}$ of linear operators describing local changes (at individual labels) as follows:

$$[\![P]\!]_{LOS} = \sum \{\!\{P\}\!\}_{LOS} = \sum \{\mathbf{G} \mid \mathbf{G} \in \{\!\{P\}\!\}_{LOS}\}.$$

The $\{\!\{S\}\!\}_{LOS}$ associated to a statement S is given by a set of global and local operators, i.e. $\{\!\{.\}\!\}_{LOS} :$ **Stmt** $\rightarrow \mathcal{P}(\Gamma \cup \Lambda)$. Global operators are linear operators on $\mathcal{V}($**Conf**$)$ i.e. $\Gamma = \mathcal{L}(\mathcal{V}($**Value**$^n) \otimes \mathcal{V}($**Label**$)) = \mathcal{L}(\mathcal{V}($**Conf**$))$, and local operators are pairs of operators on $\mathcal{V}($**State**$)$ and labels $\ell \in$ **Label**, i.e. $\Lambda = \mathcal{L}(\mathcal{V}($**Value**$^n)) \times$ **Label**.

Global operators provide information about how the computational state changes at a label as well as the control flow; in other words, they define the label of the next statement to be executed. Local operators represent statements for which a "continuation" is not yet known. In order to transform local operators into global ones, we define a continuation operation $\langle \mathbf{F}, \ell \rangle \rhd \ell' = \mathbf{F} \otimes \mathbf{E}(\ell, \ell')$ which we extend in the obvious way to sets of operators by $\{\langle \mathbf{F}_i, \ell_i \rangle\} \rhd \ell' = \{\mathbf{F}_i \otimes \mathbf{E}(\ell_i, \ell')\}$ (for global operators, clearly, we have $\mathbf{G} \rhd \ell' = \mathbf{G}$). Here, $\mathbf{E}(i, j)$ denotes the matrix unit with $(\mathbf{E}(i, j))_{ij} = 1$ and 0 otherwise.

The set $\{\!\{S\}\!\}_{LOS}$ of operators for a statement S is defined inductively on the syntactic structure of S as follows:

$$\{\![\texttt{skip}]^\ell\}\!\}_{LOS} = \{\langle \mathbf{I}, \ell \rangle\}$$

$$\{\![x := e]^\ell\}\!\}_{LOS} = \{\langle \mathbf{U}(x \leftarrow e), \ell \rangle\}$$

$$\{\![x \texttt{ ?= } \rho]^\ell\}\!\}_{LOS} = \{\langle \sum_{\langle v,p \rangle \in \rho} p \cdot \mathbf{U}(x \leftarrow v), \ell \rangle\}$$

$$\{\![S_1;\ S_2]\!\}_{LOS} = (\![S_1]\!] \triangleright init(S2)) \cup [\![S_2]\!]$$

$$\{\![\texttt{if } [b]^\ell \texttt{ then } S_1 \texttt{ else } S_2 \texttt{ fi}]\!\}_{LOS} = \{\langle \mathbf{P}(b), \ell \rangle\} \triangleright init(S_1)\} \cup \{\![S_1]\!\}_{LOS} \cup$$
$$\{\langle \mathbf{P}(b)^\perp, \ell \rangle\} \triangleright init(S_2)\} \cup \{\![S_2]\!\}_{LOS}$$

$$\{\![\texttt{while } [b]^\ell \texttt{ do } S \texttt{ od}]\!\}_{LOS} = \{\langle \mathbf{P}(b), \ell \rangle\} \triangleright init(S)\} \cup \{\![S]\!\}_{LOS} \cup \{\langle \mathbf{P}(b)^\perp, \ell \rangle\}$$

We use elementary update and test operators $\mathbf{U}$ and $\mathbf{P}$ (and its complement $\mathbf{P}^\perp = \mathbf{I} - \mathbf{P}$) as in Kozen's semantics. However, the tensor product structure allows us to define these operators in a different (although equivalent) way.

For a *single* variable the assignment to a constant value $v \in \mathbf{Value}$ is represented by the operator on $\mathcal{V}(\mathbf{Value})$ given by $\mathbf{U}(v) = 1$ if $v = i$ and 0 otherwise. Testing if a *single* variable satisfies a Boolean test b is achieved by a projection operator on $\mathcal{V}(\mathbf{Value})$ with $(\mathbf{P}(b))_{ii} = 1$ if $b(i)$ holds and 0 otherwise.

We extend these to the multivariable case, i.e. for $|\mathbf{Var}| = n > 1$ by defining the following operators on $\mathcal{V}(\mathbf{Value})^{\otimes n}$:

$$\mathbf{P}(s) = \bigotimes_{i=1}^{n} \mathbf{P}(\mathbf{x}_i = s(\mathbf{x}_i)) \qquad \mathbf{P}(e = v) = \sum_{\mathcal{E}(e)s=v} \mathbf{P}(s),$$

where $\mathbf{P}(s)$ is for testing if we are in a classical state $s \in \mathbf{Value}^n$ while $\mathbf{P}(e = v)$ checks if an expression e evaluates to a constant v (assuming an appropriate evaluation function $\mathcal{E} : \mathbf{Expr} \to \mathbf{State} \to \mathbf{Value}$).

Operators for updating a variable $\mathbf{x}_k$ in the context of other variables to a constant v or to the value of an expression e are defined on $\mathcal{V}(\mathbf{Value})^{\otimes n}$ by:

$$\mathbf{U}(\mathbf{x}_k \leftarrow v) = \bigotimes_{i=1}^{k-1} \mathbf{I} \otimes \mathbf{U}(v) \otimes \bigotimes_{i=k+1}^{n} \mathbf{I} \qquad \mathbf{U}(\mathbf{x}_k \leftarrow e) = \sum_v \mathbf{P}(e = v)\mathbf{U}(\mathbf{x}_k \leftarrow v)$$

As we model the semantics of a program as a DTMC, we need to add a final loop ℓ^* (for ℓ^* a fresh label not appearing already in P) when we consider a complete program. This is because a DTMC never terminates and thus we have to simulate termination by an infinite repetition of the final state. We will therefore use $(\{\!P]\!\}_{LOS} \triangleright \ell^*) \cup \{\mathbf{I} \otimes \mathbf{E}(\ell^*, \ell^*)\}$ for the construction of $[\![P]\!]_{LOS}$. In this way we also resolve all open or dangling control flow steps, i.e. we deal ultimately with a set containing only global operators.

Example 5. Consider the labelled version of the program in Example 1

```
while [true]¹ do
    if [(x == 1)]²
        then [x ?= {⟨0, p⟩, ⟨1, 1 − p⟩}]³
        else [x ?= {⟨0, 1 − q⟩, ⟨1, q⟩}]⁴
    fi
od
```

In order to define the LOS of this program we construct the state space as $\mathcal{V}(\{x \mapsto 0, x \mapsto 1\}) = \mathbb{R}^2$ (since we have only one variable we do not need the tensor product for this). The space of configurations is $\mathcal{V}(\{x \mapsto 0, x \mapsto 1\}) \otimes \mathcal{V}(\{1, 2, 3, 4, 5\})$, where label 5 is the label of the additional final loop. We will omit the final label (which in this program we actually never reach) in order to deal with smaller matrices. The set $\{\!\{P\}\!\}_{LOS}$ of P will contain the following operators:

$$\{\!\{P\}\!\}_{LOS} = \{\mathbf{P}(\mathbf{true}) \otimes \mathbf{E}(1,2), \mathbf{P}(x=1) \otimes \mathbf{E}(2,3), \mathbf{P}(x=1)^\perp \otimes \mathbf{E}(2,4),$$
$$(p \cdot \mathbf{U}(x \leftarrow 0) + (1-p) \cdot \mathbf{U}(x \leftarrow 1) \otimes \mathbf{E}(3,1)),$$
$$((1-q) \cdot \mathbf{U}(x \leftarrow 0) + q \cdot \mathbf{U}(x \leftarrow 1) \otimes \mathbf{E}(4,1))\}$$

The concrete matrices representing the operators on $\mathcal{V}(\{x \mapsto 0, x \mapsto 1\}) \otimes \mathcal{V}(\{1, 2, 3, 4\})$ are of the form

$$\{\!\{P\}\!\}_{LOS} = \left\{ \begin{pmatrix} 1 & 0 \\ 0 & 1 \end{pmatrix} \otimes \mathbf{E}(1,2), \begin{pmatrix} 0 & 0 \\ 0 & 1 \end{pmatrix} \otimes \mathbf{E}(2,3), \begin{pmatrix} 1 & 0 \\ 0 & 0 \end{pmatrix} \otimes \mathbf{E}(2,4), \right.$$
$$\left(\begin{pmatrix} p & 0 \\ p & 0 \end{pmatrix} + \begin{pmatrix} 0 & (1-p) \\ 0 & (1-p) \end{pmatrix} \right) \otimes \mathbf{E}(3,1), \left(\begin{pmatrix} (1-q) & 0 \\ (1-q) & 0 \end{pmatrix} + \begin{pmatrix} 0 & q \\ 0 & q \end{pmatrix} \right) \otimes \mathbf{E}(4,1) \right\}$$

or, explicitly

$$\{\!\{P\}\!\}_{LOS} = \left\{ \begin{pmatrix} 1 & 0 \\ 0 & 1 \end{pmatrix} \otimes \begin{pmatrix} 0&1&0&0 \\ 0&0&0&0 \\ 0&0&0&0 \\ 0&0&0&0 \end{pmatrix}, \begin{pmatrix} 0 & 0 \\ 0 & 1 \end{pmatrix} \otimes \begin{pmatrix} 0&0&0&0 \\ 0&0&1&0 \\ 0&0&0&0 \\ 0&0&0&0 \end{pmatrix}, \begin{pmatrix} 1 & 0 \\ 0 & 0 \end{pmatrix} \otimes \begin{pmatrix} 0&0&0&0 \\ 0&0&0&1 \\ 0&0&0&0 \\ 0&0&0&0 \end{pmatrix}, \right.$$
$$\left. \begin{pmatrix} p & (1-p) \\ p & (1-p) \end{pmatrix} \otimes \begin{pmatrix} 0&0&0&0 \\ 0&0&0&0 \\ 1&0&0&0 \\ 0&0&0&0 \end{pmatrix}, \begin{pmatrix} (1-q) & q \\ (1-q) & q \end{pmatrix} \otimes \begin{pmatrix} 0&0&0&0 \\ 0&0&0&0 \\ 0&0&0&0 \\ 1&0&0&0 \end{pmatrix} \right\}$$

The sum of these 8×8 matrices gives the operator $[\![P]\!]_{LOS}$, i.e. the generator of the corresponding DTMC. By including also the final label $\ell^* = 5$, we obtain a 10×10 matrix, which we depict in the following for the case $p = q = \frac{1}{2}$:

$$[P]_{LOS} = \begin{pmatrix} 0 & 1 & 0 & 0 & 0 & 0 & 0 & 0 & 0 & 0 \\ 0 & 0 & 0 & 1 & 0 & 0 & 0 & 0 & 0 & 0 \\ \frac{1}{2} & 0 & 0 & 0 & 0 & \frac{1}{2} & 0 & 0 & 0 & 0 \\ \frac{1}{2} & 0 & 0 & 0 & 0 & \frac{1}{2} & 0 & 0 & 0 & 0 \\ 0 & 0 & 0 & 0 & 1 & 0 & 0 & 0 & 0 & 0 \\ 0 & 0 & 0 & 0 & 0 & 0 & 1 & 0 & 0 & 0 \\ 0 & 0 & 0 & 0 & 0 & 0 & 0 & 1 & 0 & 0 \\ \frac{1}{2} & 0 & 0 & 0 & 0 & \frac{1}{2} & 0 & 0 & 0 & 0 \\ \frac{1}{2} & 0 & 0 & 0 & 0 & \frac{1}{2} & 0 & 0 & 0 & 0 \\ 0 & 0 & 0 & 0 & 0 & 0 & 0 & 0 & 0 & 1 \end{pmatrix} \quad \begin{matrix} \ldots x \mapsto 0, \ell = 1 \\ \ldots x \mapsto 0, \ell = 2 \\ \ldots x \mapsto 0, \ell = 3 \\ \ldots x \mapsto 0, \ell = 4 \\ \ldots x \mapsto 0, \ell = 5 \\ \ldots x \mapsto 1, \ell = 1 \\ \ldots x \mapsto 1, \ell = 2 \\ \ldots x \mapsto 1, \ell = 3 \\ \ldots x \mapsto 1, \ell = 4 \\ \ldots x \mapsto 1, \ell = 5 \end{matrix}$$

The entries of this matrix represent the probability of the configuration (i.e. value of x and current label ℓ) each row and column corresponds to. It is perhaps worth noting that this – as one would expect for a DTMC – is indeed a stochastic matrix (i.e. all row sums are one) representing the SOS transition relation.

There is a close relationship between the KFS and the LOS. For basic blocks B – i.e. (random) assignments, tests and skips – the LOS operator is the same as the KFS operator except for an additional control flow step. That means that $\{\!\{\ldots [B]^i \ldots\}\!\}_{LOS} = \{\ldots, \langle [B]_{KFS}, i \rangle, \ldots\}$ or $\{\!\{\ldots [B]^i \ldots\}\!\}_{LOS} = \{\ldots, [B]_{KFS} \otimes \mathbf{E}(i,j), \ldots\}$ for some label j.

Example 6. For the programs in Example 4 with the following labelling

```
if [(x == 1)]^1          [x := 1]^0;              [x ?= {⟨0,½⟩,⟨1,½⟩}]^0;
  then [x := 0]^2          if [(x == 1)]^1          if [x == 1]^1
  then P                     then [x := 0]^2          then [x := 0]^2
fi                          then P                     then P
                          fi                         fi
```

(the labels of P are as in the previous example shifted by an offset of 2), we can describe the LOS using the KFS operators as follows:

$$\{\!\{Q\}\!\}_{LOS} = \{ [x = 1]_{KFS} \otimes \mathbf{E}(1,2), [x = 0]_{KFS} \otimes \mathbf{E}(1,3),$$
$$\langle [x := 0]_{KFS}, 2 \rangle, \langle [\mathtt{false}]_{KFS}, 3 \rangle \} \cup \{\!\{P\}\!\}_{LOS}$$
$$\{\!\{Q'\}\!\}_{LOS} = \{ [x := 1]_{KFS} \otimes \mathbf{E}(0,1) \} \cup \{\!\{Q\}\!\}_{LOS}$$
$$\{\!\{Q''\}\!\}_{LOS} = \{ (\frac{1}{2}[x := 1]_{KFS} + \frac{1}{2}[x := 1]_{KFS}) \otimes \mathbf{E}(0,1), \} \cup \{\!\{Q\}\!\}_{LOS}$$

where we can re-use the LOS semantics of program P (with shifted labelling):

$$\{\!\{P\}\!\}_{LOS} = \{ [\mathtt{true}]_{KFS} \otimes \mathbf{E}(3,4), [x = 1]_{KFS} \otimes \mathbf{E}(4,5), [x = 0]_{KFS} \otimes \mathbf{E}(4,6),$$
$$(p[x := 0]_{KFS} + (p-1)[x := 1]_{KFS}) \otimes \mathbf{E}(5,3),$$
$$((q-1)[x := 0]_{KFS} + q[x := 1]_{KFS}) \otimes \mathbf{E}(6,3) \}$$

Note that the LOS of the three small programs contain not just global but also local operators, namely $\langle [\![x := 0]\!]_{KFS}, 2 \rangle$ and $\langle [\![\mathtt{false}]\!]_{KFS}, 3 \rangle$. This is because we still have to add a terminal label $\ell^* = 7$ for the construction of the complete DTMC generators $[\![Q]\!]_{LOS}$, $[\![Q']\!]_{LOS}$ and $[\![Q'']\!]_{LOS}$. The terminal label can be reached from both branches of the if statement labelled 2 and 3. However, as $[\![\mathtt{false}]\!]_{KFS}$ is $\mathbf{O}$ this operator (which would correspond to a terminating program P) does not actually contribute to the DTMC generator.

2.4   Maximal Trace Semantics (MTS)

Maximal Trace Semantics for non-probabilistic programs has been discussed in [35, 36] and shown to be the most concrete semantics in a hierarchy of various semantics for (non-)deterministic programs. In [7] the MTS is extended to the probabilistic case.

Similar to the Kozen semantics, the conceptual idea is to ban any probabilistic steps from the actual execution of the program and resolve all probabilistic choices (coin flips, rolling of dices) beforehand. The actual execution of a program is therefore purely (non-)deterministic but parameterised by the results of the "pre-run" choices (cf. [7, p 171]). These outcomes represent the events or scenarios of a probability space Ω, which the execution traces depend on.

Given a set of states Σ, a *trace* $\sigma = s_1 s_2 \ldots$ is a finite or infinite sequence of elements $s_i \in \Sigma$. Concatenation of traces is juxtaposition, i.e. for $s \in \Sigma$ we have $s\sigma = s s_1 s_2 \ldots$ and for $\sigma_1 = s_{11} \ldots s_{1n}$ and $\sigma_2 = s_{21} \ldots$ we have $\sigma_1 \sigma_2 = s_{11} \ldots s_{1n} s_{21} \ldots$. We denote by Σ^+ the set of finite traces, by Σ^* the set $\Sigma^+ \cup \{\varepsilon\}$, where ε is the empty trace of length 0, by Σ^∞ the infinite traces, by $\Sigma^{+\infty}$ the set $\Sigma^+ \cup \Sigma^\infty$ and by $\Sigma^{*\infty}$ the set $\Sigma^* \cup \Sigma^\infty$. For sets of traces $X, Y, \ldots$ in $\Sigma^{*\infty}$, we can define the following operations: $X^\infty = X \cap \Sigma^\infty$, $X^+ = X \cap \Sigma^+$, $X|_Y = \{s\sigma_X \in X \mid \exists \sigma : \sigma s \in Y^+\}$, and $X; Y = X^\infty \cup \{\sigma_X s \sigma_Y \mid \sigma_X s \in X^+ \wedge s\sigma_Y \in Y\}$.

The MTS is defined as a function $[\![S]\!]_{MTS} : \mathbf{Stmt} \to \Omega \to \mathcal{P}(\Sigma^{+\infty})$ where $\Sigma = \mathbf{State}$. In order to combine non-determinism with probabilities each scenario $\omega \in \Omega$ is associated to a whole set of possible traces. Thus $[\![S]\!]_{MTS}$ is defined by

$$
\begin{aligned}
[\![\mathtt{skip}]\!]_{MTS}(\omega) &= \{ss \mid s \in \Sigma\} \\
[\![x := e]\!]_{MTS}(\omega) &= \{ss[x \mapsto [\![e]\!](\omega)s] \mid s \in \Sigma\} \\
[\![S_1; S_2]\!]_{MTS}(\omega) &= [\![S_1]\!]_{MTS}(\omega); [\![S_2]\!]_{MTS}(\omega) \\
[\![b]\!]_{MTS}(\omega) &= \{s \mid [\![b]\!](\omega)s\} \\
[\![\mathtt{if}\ b\ \mathtt{then}\ S_1\ \mathtt{else}\ S_2\ \mathtt{fi}]\!]_{MTS}(\omega) &= [\![b]\!]_{MTS}(\omega); [\![S_1]\!]_{MTS}(\omega) \cup [\![\neg b]\!]_{MTS}(\omega); [\![S_2]\!]_{MTS}(\omega) \\
[\![\mathtt{while}\ b\ \mathtt{do}\ S\ \mathtt{od}]\!]_{MTS}(\omega) &= \mathrm{lfp}\lambda X.[\![b]\!]_{MTS}(\omega) \cup [\![\neg b]\!]_{MTS}(\omega); [\![S]\!]_{MTS}(\omega); X
\end{aligned}
$$

According to the definition in [7, Example 4] the evaluation $[\![e]\!]$ of an expression e depends on the scenario ω, i.e. $[\![e]\!] : \Omega \to (\Sigma \to \Sigma)$. The language considered in [7] does actually not have either random assignments or a choice construct; the former is instead implemented via a kind of "system call", i.e. $\mathtt{x := random(\rho)}$.

We can reformulate the MTS in the case of the **pWhile** language where no non-determinism is present: Once a scenario ω is fixed there is only one trace for every initial state or configuration which is actually executed. We are not interested in the scenarios $\omega \in \Omega$ themselves but only in their probabilities $\mu(\omega)$, i.e. the probability that a certain trace gets executed. Thus, for a fixed initial state or configuration s the MTS of a program in **pWhile** can be seen as a distribution over traces. The probability for each trace σ is inherited from the scenario ω it depends on. We will use in the following the notation $\{\langle \sigma, \mu(\omega)\rangle\}$ to express that a trace σ is executed with probability $\mu(\omega)$.

We can define the map $[\![.]\!]_{MTS} : \mathbf{Stmt} \to \mathcal{V}(\Sigma^{+\infty})$ implicitly, i.e. as solution to the following equations:

$$[\![\mathtt{skip}]\!]_{MTS} = \{\langle ss, 1\rangle \mid s \in \Sigma\}$$
$$[\![x := e]\!]_{MTS} = \{\langle ss[x \mapsto [\![e]\!]s], 1\rangle \mid s \in \Sigma\}$$
$$[\![x\ \mathtt{?=}\ \rho]\!]_{MTS} = \{\langle ss[x \mapsto v], \rho(v)\rangle \mid s \in \Sigma \wedge \rho(v) \neq 0\}$$
$$[\![S_1; S_2]\!]_{MTS} = [\![S_1]\!]_{MTS}; [\![S_2]\!]_{MTS}$$
$$[\![\mathtt{if}\ b\ \mathtt{then}\ S_1\ \mathtt{else}\ S_2\ \mathtt{fi}]\!]_{MTS} = \{\langle s, 1\rangle \mid \text{for } [\![b]\!](s) = \mathtt{true}\}; [\![S_1]\!]_{MTS}$$
$$\cup \{\langle s, 1\rangle \mid \text{for } [\![b]\!](s) = \mathtt{false}\}; [\![S_2]\!]_{MTS}$$
$$[\![\mathtt{while}\ b\ \mathtt{do}\ S\ \mathtt{od}]\!]_{MTS} = \{\langle s, 1\rangle \mid \text{for } [\![b]\!](s) = \mathtt{true}\}; [\![S; \mathtt{while}\ b\ \mathtt{do}\ S\ \mathtt{od}]\!]_{MTS}$$
$$\cup \{\langle s, 1\rangle \mid \text{for } [\![b]\!](s) = \mathtt{false}\};$$

Clearly, the evaluation of deterministic functions or expressions is independent of the scenario ω. For random assignments we produce a set of weighted traces, one trace for each $v \in \mathbf{Value}$ with non-vanishing probability according to the distribution ρ. We extend the concatenation operation for traces to probabilistic ones in the obvious way: $\langle X, p_X\rangle; \langle Y, p_Y\rangle = \langle X; Y, p_X p_Y\rangle$ in order to define the semantics of sequential statements. The operation ";" also extends pointwise to sets of weighted traces in $\mathcal{V}(\Sigma^{+\infty})$. The union construction $\cup$ of sets of weighted tuples corresponds to a sum if we take them as elements in the vector space $\mathcal{V}(\Sigma^{+\infty})$.

It should be noted that this formulation of the MTS for a purely probabilistic language eliminates the dependency on the scenarios $\omega \in \Omega$ but not on the initial state $s \in \Sigma$. This means that for a statement S the weighted set of traces $[\![S]\!]_{MTS} \in \mathcal{V}(\Sigma^{+\infty})$ does in general itself *not* represent a distribution (on traces) but just a (positive) vector in $\mathcal{V}(\Sigma^{+\infty})$. However, if we collect all those traces which start with the same state s then we obtain a distribution over traces, i.e. $\sum\{p \mid \langle \sigma, p\rangle \text{ with } \sigma = s \ldots\} = 1$.

It would be possible to formulate the MTS also as a map which expresses the dependency on the initial state explicitly and returns directly distributions over traces, i.e. $[\![.]\!]_{MTS} : \mathbf{Stmt} \to \Sigma \to \mathcal{D}(\Sigma^{+\infty}) \subseteq \mathcal{V}(\Sigma^{+\infty})$, in which case $[\![S]\!]_{MTS}(s)$ would simply represent a distribution over traces. However, our aim is to stay as close as possible to the formulation in [7], which is based on the typing $[\![.]\!]_{MTS} : \mathbf{Stmt} \to \Omega \to \mathcal{P}(\Sigma^{+\infty})$ rather than, for example, $[\![.]\!]_{MTS} : \mathbf{Stmt} \to \Omega \to \Sigma \to \mathcal{P}(\Sigma^{+\infty})$.

Example 7. In order to illustrate the basic construction of the MTS we consider the following program in both its unlabelled and labelled version, with $x, y \in \{0, 1\}$:

```
if  (y < 1)                        if  [(y < 1)]¹
  then x ?= {⟨0,p⟩,⟨1,1 − p⟩}        then [x ?= {⟨0,p⟩,⟨1,1 − p⟩}]²
  else x := 0                        else [x := 0]³
fi;                                fi;
if  (x < 1)                        if  [(x < 1)]⁴
  then y ?= {⟨0,q⟩,⟨1,1 − q⟩}        then [y ?= {⟨0,q⟩,⟨1,1 − q⟩}]⁵
  else y := 0                        else [y := 0]⁶
fi                                 fi
```

In this example we have no loops or recursions, so we know that we will need (at most) two "coin flips". Thus, the space of scenarios Ω is defined via the two choices, one for x and one for y, i.e. as $\Sigma = \{x \mapsto 0, x \mapsto 1\} \times \{y \mapsto 0, y \mapsto 1\}$, which we will denote by $\Sigma = \{[00], [01], [10], [11]\}$ with $[00]$ the state $x \mapsto 0$, $y \mapsto 0$, etc. Following the reformulation of the MTS we have:

$$[\![x := 0]\!]_{MTS} =$$
$$= \{\langle[00][00], 1\rangle, \langle[01][01], 1\rangle, \langle[10][00], 1\rangle, \langle[11][01], 1\rangle\}$$
$$[\![y := 0]\!]_{MTS} =$$
$$= \{\langle[00][00], 1\rangle, \langle[01][00], 1\rangle, \langle[10][10], 1\rangle, \langle[11][10], 1\rangle\}$$
$$[\![x ?= \{\langle0,p\rangle,\langle1,1 − p\rangle\}]\!]_{MTS} =$$
$$= \{\langle[00][00], p\rangle, \langle[01][01], p\rangle, \langle[10][00], p\rangle, \langle[11][01], p\rangle,$$
$$\langle[00][10], 1 − p\rangle, \langle[01][11], 1 − p\rangle, \langle[10][10], 1 − p\rangle, \langle[11][11], 1 − p\rangle\}$$
$$[\![y ?= \{\langle0,q\rangle,\langle1,1 − q\rangle\}]\!]_{MTS} =$$
$$= \{\langle[00][00], q\rangle, \langle[01][00], q\rangle, \langle[10][10], q\rangle, \langle[11][10], q\rangle,$$
$$\langle[00][01], 1 − q\rangle, \langle[01][01], 1 − q\rangle, \langle[10][11], 1 − q\rangle, \langle[11][11], 1 − q\rangle\}$$

With these sets of weighted traces we can now construct the MTS for the two if statements:

$$[\![\text{if } (y < 1) \text{ then } x ?= \{\langle0,p\rangle,\langle1,1 − p\rangle\} \text{ else } x := 0 \text{ fi}]\!]_{MTS} =$$
$$= \{\langle[00][00][00], p\rangle, \langle[10][10][00], p\rangle, \langle[00][00][10], 1 − p\rangle,$$
$$\langle[10][10][10], 1 − p\rangle, \langle[01][01][01], 1\rangle, \langle[11][11][01], 1\rangle\}$$
$$[\![\text{if } (x < 1) \text{ then } y ?= \{\langle0,q\rangle,\langle1,1 − q\rangle\} \text{ else } y := 0 \text{ fi}]\!]_{MTS} =$$
$$= \{\langle[00][00][00], q\rangle, \langle[01][01][00], q\rangle, \langle[00][00][01], 1 − q\rangle,$$
$$\langle[01][01][01], 1 − q\rangle, \langle[10][10][10], 1\rangle, \langle[11][11][10], 1\rangle\}$$

Note that some traces which we constructed for the branches disappear because when we apply the operator ";" the last state of the first (one step) trace (representing the test) and the first state of the continuation (in one of the two branches) do not match.

The traces for the whole program are then given by:

$$[P]_{MTS} = \{\langle[00][00][00], p\rangle; \langle[00][00][00], q\rangle, \langle[00][00][00], p\rangle; \langle[00][00][01], 1-q\rangle,$$
$$\langle[10][10][00], p\rangle; \langle[00][00][00], q\rangle, \langle[10][10][00], p\rangle; \langle[00][00][01], 1-q\rangle,$$
$$\langle[00][00][10], 1-p\rangle; \langle[10][10][10], 1\rangle, \langle[10][10][10], 1-p\rangle; \langle[10][10][10], 1\rangle,$$
$$\langle[01][01][01], 1\rangle; \langle[01][01][00], q\rangle, \langle[01][01][01], 1\rangle; \langle[01][01][01], 1-q\rangle,$$
$$\langle[11][11][01], 1\rangle; \langle[01][01][00], q\rangle, \langle[11][11][01], 1\rangle; \langle[01][01][01], 1-q\rangle\},$$

where again the matching condition eliminates a number of possible traces. Finally we get:

$$[P]_{MTS} = \{\langle[00][00][00][00][00], pq\rangle, \langle[00][00][00][00][01], p(1-q)\rangle,$$
$$\langle[10][10][00][00][00], pq\rangle, \langle[10][10][00][00][01], p(1-q)\rangle,$$
$$\langle[00][00][10][10][10], 1-p\rangle, \langle[10][10][10][10][10], 1-p\rangle,$$
$$\langle[01][01][01][01][00], q\rangle, \langle[01][01][01][01][01], 1-q\rangle,$$
$$\langle[11][11][01][01][00], q\rangle, \langle[11][11][01][01][01], 1-q\rangle\}.$$

Here we have three possible traces starting with the initial state $s = [00]$ or $s = [10]$ but only two for $s = [01]$ and $[11]$. We also observe that the probabilities associated to the traces starting with each of the four initial states sum up to one, e.g. for $s = [00]$ we have the probabilities $(pq) + (p - pq) + (1 - p) = 1$.

In this presentation of the MTS the states only record the values of the variables but not the current label (or program counter). This makes it possible to obtain the same trace for completely different executions of the program. To keep track of the control flow through the program, its labelled version allows to record in the labels the information about the configurations executed and not just the states. For the labelled version of the program we would then replace a trace like $[00][00][00][00][00]$ by $\langle[00], 1\rangle\langle[00], 2\rangle\langle[00], 4\rangle\langle[00], 5\rangle\langle[00], \ell^*\rangle$ with ℓ^* the final label indicating termination.

3   Probabilistic Vs Classical Abstract Interpretation

Abstract Interpretation (AI) is a well known mathematical theory at the base of a number of static analysis techniques [4]. Because of the need to consider computable domains for performing the analysis of program properties, abstraction and approximation are essential features of any static analysis technique. The theory of AI establishes when the approximation is such that an analysis can be safely performed on an abstract rather than the concrete domain of computation. More precisely, the correctness of an abstract semantics is guaranteed by ensuring that a pair of functions α and γ can be defined which form a *Galois connection* between two lattices C and D representing concrete and abstract properties. This classical theory originally introduced for (non-)deterministic programs can be extended so as to include the treatment of probabilistic programs by considering the appropriate (abstract and concrete) domains as recently shown in [7] (see also [37]).

Though the approximations allowed by the AI theory will always be safe, they might also be quite unrealistic, addressing a *worst case* scenario rather than the *average case* [38]. This latter is typically the aim of a probabilistic analysis which is therefore hardly correct in the classical sense of the AI theory. However, although such an average case analysis is not guaranteed to 'err on the safe side', we can still define it so as to reduce the error margin. In order to provide a mathematical framework for probabilistic analysis, we have previously introduced in [5,6], a theory of linear operators on Hilbert spaces (i.e. here just finite dimensional spaces as discussed before) where the notion of approximation is characterised in terms of *least square approximation*, which we have called *Probabilistic Abstract Interpretation* (PAI).

The PAI approach is based, as in the classical case, on a concrete and abstract domain $\mathcal{C}$ and $\mathcal{D}$ – except that $\mathcal{C}$ and $\mathcal{D}$ are now vector spaces instead of lattices. We assume that the pair of abstraction and concretisation function $\mathbf{A} : \mathcal{C} \to \mathcal{D}$ and $\mathbf{G} : \mathcal{D} \to \mathcal{C}$ are again structure preserving, i.e. in our setting they are (bounded) linear maps represented by matrices $\mathbf{A}$ and $\mathbf{G}$. Finally, we replace the notion of a Galois connection by the notion of *Moore-Penrose pseudo-inverse* [8,10].

Definition 1. *Let $\mathcal{C}$ and $\mathcal{D}$ be two finite dimensional vector spaces, and let $\mathbf{A} : \mathcal{C} \to \mathcal{D}$ be a linear map between them. The linear map $\mathbf{A}^\dagger = \mathbf{G} : \mathcal{D} \to \mathcal{C}$ is the* Moore-Penrose pseudo-inverse *of $\mathbf{A}$ iff*

$$\mathbf{A} \circ \mathbf{G} = \mathbf{P}_A \quad and \quad \mathbf{G} \circ \mathbf{A} = \mathbf{P}_G$$

where $\mathbf{P}_A$ and $\mathbf{P}_G$ denote orthogonal projections (i.e. $\mathbf{P}_A^* = \mathbf{P}_A = \mathbf{P}_A^2$ and $\mathbf{P}_G^* = \mathbf{P}_G = \mathbf{P}_G^2$ where . denotes the adjoint [33, Ch 10]) onto the ranges of $\mathbf{A}$ and $\mathbf{G}$.*

Alternatively, if $\mathbf{A}$ is Moore-Penrose invertible (and all finite dimensional operators or matrices are), its Moore-Penrose pseudo-inverse, $\mathbf{A}^\dagger$ satisfies the following:

(i) $\mathbf{A}\mathbf{A}^\dagger\mathbf{A} = \mathbf{A}$,
(ii) $\mathbf{A}^\dagger\mathbf{A}\mathbf{A}^\dagger = \mathbf{A}^\dagger$,
(iii) $(\mathbf{A}\mathbf{A}^\dagger)^* = \mathbf{A}\mathbf{A}^\dagger$,
(iv) $(\mathbf{A}^\dagger\mathbf{A})^* = \mathbf{A}^\dagger\mathbf{A}$.

It is instructive to compare these equations with the classical setting. For example, a Galois connection (α, γ) satisfies the properties $\alpha \circ \gamma \circ \alpha = \alpha$ and $\gamma \circ \alpha \circ \gamma = \gamma$ which are similar to conditions (i) and (ii) in Definition 1. Moreover, we also have in a similar way as in the AI setting that $\mathbf{A}$ and $\mathbf{A}^\dagger$ determine each other uniquely, i.e. $(\mathbf{A}^\dagger)^\dagger = \mathbf{A}$ (cf. e.g. [10]).

The Moore-Penrose pseudo-inverse allows us to construct the closest (i.e. least square) approximation $\mathbf{T}^\# : \mathcal{D} \to \mathcal{D}$ of a concrete semantics $\mathbf{T} : \mathcal{C} \to \mathcal{C}$ as:

$$\mathbf{T}^\# = \mathbf{G} \cdot \mathbf{T} \cdot \mathbf{A} = \mathbf{A}^\dagger \cdot \mathbf{T} \cdot \mathbf{A} = \mathbf{A} \circ \mathbf{T} \circ \mathbf{G}.$$

In [5] we show how we can transform a Probabilistic Abstract Interpretation into a classical Abstract Interpretation by forgetting the concrete values of probabilities and only considering the support set of a distribution as the set of "possibilities". One can also lift (in a non-unique way) a classical Abstract Interpretation to a Probabilistic Abstract Interpretation (e.g. by using uniform distributions). This method is conceptually equivalent to the probabilistic version of Abstract Interpretation presented in [7], although the result does not refer explicitly to the Maximal Trace Semantics. However, AI and PAI are not equivalent in terms of the analyses that they support. Besides the relaxation of the safety constraint for the analysis results, PAI is also a suitable mathematical framework for *testing*, as we will show in Sect. 5.

4   Comparison of Probabilistic Semantics

For the language **pWhile**, the Kozen semantics describes the I/O behaviour of programs, the LOS semantics gives the generator for a step-wise execution of the program (as a DTMC), and the MTS determines the possible traces and their corresponding probabilities (inherited from the scenarios of the probability space). In this section we will discuss in some detail the relationship between them with the aim of clarifying their different role in the static analysis of programs.

Kozen's Semantics and LOS. One important difference between the LOS and Kozen's semantics (Semantics 2 in [12]) is the use of labels (as a kind of program counter) to model the computational steps.

As already mentioned, in Kozen's semantics all non-terminating executions are treated equally, i.e. have a trivial or zero semantics. Another difference is that Kozen's semantics is based on a state space $\mathcal{V}(\mathbf{Value}^n)$ as opposed to the LOS state space $\mathcal{V}(\mathbf{Value})^{\otimes n}$ which allows for an independent treatment of each variable. In general, the tensor construction of the LOS allows for a kind of 'compositional' program analysis where the various syntactic components of a program can be analysed individually, which is not possible with Kozen's semantics.

In [28] we have shown that Kozen's operator $[P]_{KFS}$ is an abstraction of a limit of iterations of the LOS semantics $[P]_{LOS}$. This abstraction is defined by the PAI operator which "forgets" about the computational state at all labels except ℓ:

$$\mathbf{A}_\ell = \mathbf{I} \otimes \ldots \otimes \mathbf{I} \otimes e_\ell,$$

where e_ℓ is a unit or base vector in $\mathcal{V}(\mathbf{Label})$ corresponding to label $\ell \in \mathbf{Label}$, i.e. $e_\ell = (0, 0, \ldots, 0, 1, 0 \ldots, 0)$ with only one non-zero entry for the coordinate ℓ. This can also be seen as $1 \times |\mathbf{Label}|$ matrix. This operation keeps all the information about the state, i.e. values of the variables, but only when the execution is in label ℓ. If we take $\ell = \ell^*$, i.e. the terminal looping state in the semantics of a program, then this gives the probabilities of the values of all variables for those computations which have already reached the end. So for any initial (classical) state s_0 and initial label $\ell = 0$ we can obtain the computational state in the final label ℓ^* by iteration. The following propositions hold (cf. [28]):

Proposition 1. *Given a **pWhile** program P and initial state s_0 in $\mathcal{V}(\textbf{Value})^{\otimes n}$, then $(s_0 \otimes e_0)[\![P]\!]_{LOS}^t \mathbf{A}_{\ell^*}$ corresponds to the distributions over all states on which P terminates in t or fewer computational steps.*

This covers all finite computations of t steps or fewer. In order to get the I/O behaviour for all terminating computations, i.e. the Kozen semantics, we need just to consider the limit of all computations of any length:

Proposition 2. *Given a **pWhile** program P and initial state s_0 in $\mathcal{V}(\textbf{Value})^{\otimes n}$, let $[\![P]\!]_{KFS}$ be Kozen's semantics of P and $[\![P]\!]_{LOS}$ the DTMC generator for P. Then*

$$(s_0 \otimes e_0)(\lim_{t\to\infty} [\![P]\!]_{LOS}^t)\mathbf{A}_{\ell^*} = s_0[\![P]\!]_{KFS}.$$

Maximal Trace Semantics and LOS. The probabilistic semantics in [7] is a classical abstraction of the probabilistic MTS corresponding to a "strongest postcondition semantics". This is in effect an operator semantics which maps input distributions into some output distributions (cf. formula (2) in [7, 7.4]). A common interpretation of the claims made in Sect. 7.3 of [7] is that the LOS is just an abstraction of the probabilistic MTS. We show here that this interpretation is incorrect.

In order to investigate the relationship between LOS and MTS in more detail we will look at a concrete construction of probabilistic traces by means of the LOS. It is somewhat unclear if the MTS in [7] should be based on $\Sigma = \textbf{State}$ or $\Sigma = \textbf{Conf}$. In the first case it is straightforward to see that the LOS actually contains more information than an MTS based only on state information. We will thus consider the MTS based on $\Sigma = \textbf{Conf}$, i.e. the reformulation of the probabilistic MTS as an element in $\mathcal{V}(\textbf{Conf}^{+\infty})$, which associates with every possible trace a probability that this is indeed the trace which will be executed during the program run. We will then relate this set of 'weighted' traces to the LOS as an operator on $\mathcal{V}(\textbf{Conf})$ where we also provide the initial distribution $s_0 \otimes e_0 = \rho_0 \in \mathcal{V}(\textbf{Conf})$.

The LOS allows for the construction of a *sequence of distributions* over states (fronts): Given an initial state we can calculate for every t the probabilities of reaching any state after t steps by applying the LOS operator t times to the initial state. The MTS does not construct fronts but rather a *distribution over sequences* (traces): given an initial state we can calculate the probabilities of all the execution traces starting from that initial state. The two notions are thus somewhat orthogonal. However, they turn out to be equivalent for languages that, like **pWhile**, can be modelled via a DTMC. This is because DTMC's abstract from the history of a computation as only the current configuration determines the probabilities of the successor configurations. Transition probabilities are exactly what is specified in the generator matrix of the DTMC and is all one needs to reconstruct both the fronts and the computational traces with their probabilities.

Instantiated for purely probabilistic languages the classical abstraction given by formula (2) in [7, 7.4] is an operator from distributions over traces to distribution transformers (for a fixed initial configuration s), i.e.

$$\alpha_s : \mathcal{V}(\mathbf{Conf}^{+\infty}) \to \mathcal{L}(\mathcal{V}(\mathbf{Conf}))$$

rather than $(\Omega \to \mathcal{P}(\mathbf{Conf}^{+\infty})) \to (\mathcal{V}(\mathbf{Conf}) \to \mathcal{V}(\mathbf{Conf}))$ as in [7, 7.4]. In this purely probabilistic case, the abstraction map becomes:

$$((\alpha_s(\{\langle p, X\rangle\})(\delta))(s')) = \sum_{s \in \Sigma} \{\delta(s) \cdot p \mid \text{for } s\sigma s' \in X^+\}.$$

In other words, we associate to every distribution over traces $\{\langle p, X\rangle\}$ a linear operator $(\alpha_s(\{\langle p, X\rangle\})) \in \mathcal{L}(\mathcal{V}(\mathbf{Conf}))$. To see how this operator transforms a distribution $\delta \in \mathcal{V}(\mathbf{Conf})$ into another distribution $\alpha_s(\{\langle p, X\rangle\})(\delta) = \delta' \in \mathcal{V}(\mathbf{Conf})$ we describe the probability of every configuration $s' \in \mathbf{Conf}$ in the new distribution δ'. This is the sum of all products of the probabilities associated with all the traces which, starting from any s, reach s' in finitely many steps and the probability $\delta(s)$ that we start indeed with s. The probability $\delta'(s')$ is the probability that we terminate with s'. Therefore this abstraction gives the Kozen I/O semantics. However, it does not give the LOS which instead would require a classical abstraction of the form

$$((\bar{\alpha}_s(\{\langle p, X\rangle\})(\delta))(s')) = \sum_{s \in \Sigma} \{\delta(s) \cdot p \mid \text{if } ss' \ldots \in X\}$$

i.e. an operator that collects the probabilities that we reach s' in one step rather than eventually. Note that this abstraction does not require that s' is a terminating state. The question is now whether $\bar{\alpha}_s$ is indeed an abstraction or not. If we consider the dimension of the spaces involved, the answer is positive as there is obviously a loss of information when considering the space $\mathcal{L}(\mathcal{V}(\mathbf{Conf}))$ of $n \times n$ matrices (for $\mathbf{Conf}$ with n states) with dimension n^2 in place of the space of distributions $\mathcal{V}(\mathbf{Conf})^{\otimes t}$ (on traces of finite length t) whose dimension is n^t. However, due to the memory-less property of DTMC, we only need to consider traces of length 2 (i.e. transition steps) and thus a space $\mathcal{V}(\mathbf{Conf}) \otimes \mathcal{V}(\mathbf{Conf})$ whose dimension is n^2. Thus, no information is lost and the abstraction is not really an abstraction but only a recasting of the MTS. If the MTS is the most concrete semantics (in the sense of [36]) then so is the LOS. In fact, we can show the following proposition.

Proposition 3. *Given a* **pWhile** *program P, then the LOS $[\![P]\!]_{LOS}$ and the MTS $[\![P]\!]_{MTS}$ are equivalent, i.e. it is possible to construct either semantics from the other one.*

It is straightforward to construct the LOS operator out of the MTS by considering for all initial configurations (i.e. point-distributions) the single step traces (or single step trace-prefixes) starting from each initial configuration. In fact, the probability associated to these traces is exactly the transition probability recorded in the DTMC generator, i.e. the LOS – this is indeed what the map $\bar{\alpha}_s$ above achieves. On the other hand, the probability associated with a trace $s_{i_1}s_{i_2}s_{i_3}\ldots$ is the product of the transition probabilities $(\llbracket P \rrbracket_{LOS})_{i_1 i_2}$, $(\llbracket P \rrbracket_{LOS})_{i_2 i_3}$ etc. – i.e. $\prod_j (\llbracket P \rrbracket_{LOS})_{i_j i_{j+1}}$ – times the probabilities given by the initial distribution $\delta(s_{i_1})$.

As already mentioned, these constructions require that the semantics of **pWhile** is modelled by a *homogeneous* DTMC, i.e. that the transition probabilities from one configuration to another one do not change over time. This and the memory-less property of DTMC's seems to be a reasonable requirement for a programming language.

5   Statistical Analysis of Probabilistic Programs via PAI

Probabilistic semantics provides the basis for the static analysis of probabilistic programs. While both the AI and the PAI framework allow us to use traces as a basis for constructing more abstract semantics, there is an important difference between the two frameworks. In the AI setting these traces are assumed to be *ideal* traces, i.e. traces that are actually obtained when a program is executed. In the PAI setting – similar to the situation in statistical analysis, learning etc. – we can attempt to utilise not just ideal traces but also experimentally *observed*, maybe *corrupted*, i.e. *distorted* by noise, traces in order to reconstruct the most plausible underlying abstract semantics.

In this section we show an approach where the probabilistic information about the program executions is inferred by *observing* some sample runs. This establishes a link between static program analysis and testing and demonstrates the use of PAI to calculate best estimates for program's properties in a way similar to the so-called *linear statistical model* or *linear regression* method.

The approach we are going to present is based on the idea of identifying observations with a linear combination of a set of random variables x_i, whose weights are chosen with the method of least squares so as to minimise the distance from the observations and the actual model expressing the program behaviour. Thus the framework of Probabilistic Abstract Interpretation is particularly appropriate as a base of this approach.

5.1   The Linear Statistical Model

In several contexts it is often useful to predict or estimate a variable β (or a vector of variables), given that we have the opportunity to observe variables $y_1, y_2, \ldots, y_n$ that somehow (statistically) depend on β. This is a very important statistical problem which is typically faced by using so-called linear regression analysis, also known as linear statistical model (cf e.g. [11], [10, Section 8.3] or [8, Section 6.4]). This widely used statistical technique applies to situations such as the one mentioned above, where a random vector y depends *linearly* on a vector of parameters β, i.e. (using post-multiplication)

$$y = \beta \mathbf{X} + \varepsilon, \tag{1}$$

where y represents some measurement results, the parameters β are unknown, the matrix $\mathbf{X}$ is the *design matrix*, and ε is a random vector representing the errors of observing y. This error is conventionally assumed to have expected value equal to zero and some further statistical conditions regarding its variance and co-variance are typically imposed. These requirements mean that there is no underlying or systematic reason for the distortions ε and this is only due to random noise.

The role of least square approximations and the Moore-Penrose pseudo-inverse in this context is of particular relevance for the well-known Gauss-Markov theorem (cf. [10, Section 8.3, Thm. 1]).

Theorem 1 (Gauss-Markov). *Consider the linear model $y = \beta \mathbf{X} + \varepsilon$ with $\mathbf{X}$ of full column rank and ε fulfilling the conditions in [10, Section 8.3]. Then the* Best Linear Unbiased Estimator *(BLUE) is given by*

$$\hat{\beta} = y\mathbf{X}^{\dagger}.$$

In its simplest version, the Gauss-Markov theorem thus asserts that the best estimate $\hat{\beta}$ of the unknown parameters β can be obtained from some experimentally observed y by calculating $y\mathbf{X}^{\dagger}$, i.e. via the Moore-Penrose pseudo-inverse of the design matrix $\mathbf{X}$, cf. [10, Section 8.3, eqn (35)].

5.2   Application to Security Analysis

We discuss the relevance of the reconstruction of unknown parameters or properties of a system in the field of computer security by presenting a simplified version of the well-known Kocher's attack on crypto-protocols [39].

Modular exponentiation is a basic operation for computing the private key in crypto-systems using the Diffie-Hellman or the RSA protocols. In [39], it is shown that by carefully measuring the time required to perform such an operation, an attacker may be able to find the Diffie-Hellman exponents or factor the RSA keys and break the crypto-systems.

The crucial point is the estimation of a single bit b in the secret key k. Since modular exponentiation takes very different execution times depending on the value of a certain bit b being 0 or 1, what the attacker needs are good estimate of these execution times in order to deduce the value of each bit of the key. Thus, linear statistical models play a crucial role in the analysis of security. We show how the problem of the timing attacks can be described as a statistical analysis problem, by using as an example a simplified implementation of the RSA exponentiation algorithm. This will also highlight the relationship between PAI and linear regression.

Suppose that t_0 is the time it takes to perform multiplication in the modular exponentiation procedure if a single bit b of the cryptographic key k is $b = 0$ and t_1 if $b = 1$. We thus need to consider two possible DTMC models, one for the case $b = 0$ and one for $b = 1$. In realistic situations we also need to take into account the noise due for example to the fact that the physical device we observe is also involved in other tasks/threads such as network communication. The aim is to guess correctly which of the two models is actually being executed, i.e. the value of b, by observing the (possibly distorted) running time. We can also set the vector β to represent the strength/weights/probabilities that in a given model we have $b = 0$ or $b = 1$, respectively. More concretely, we can set the vector $\beta_0 = (1,0)$ to represent the models of the system where the bit b of the key is $b = 0$ and $\beta_1 = (0,1)$ to the key with $b = 1$. We can now define a linear statistical model by constructing a design matrix $\mathbf{X}$ (in the PAI sense a concretisation operator), which maps a model (element in the abstract domain) onto its timing behaviour (element in the concrete domain). As an example, we can consider the situation where we can observe ten possible execution times t_i that we enumerate and use as column indices for $\mathbf{X}$. Suppose that t_0 corresponds to the 3rd and t_1 to the 7th column in this enumeration. In this case we obtain a design matrix of the form:

$$\mathbf{X} = \begin{pmatrix} 0\,0\,1\,0\,0\,0\,0\,0\,0\,0 \\ 0\,0\,0\,0\,0\,0\,1\,0\,0\,0 \end{pmatrix},$$

and we can calculate

$$\beta_0 \mathbf{X} = (1,0) \cdot \mathbf{X} = (0,0,1,0,0,0,0,0,0,0)$$

which tells us that for $b = 0$ the chances of observing any other time signature than t_0 is zero, and that t_0 will definitely be observed. A similar calculation can be done for $\beta_1 = (0,1)$.

If we begin instead by observing the time behaviour, i.e. if we test the program and obtain, for example, an (undistorted) observation vector of the form

$$y = (0,0,1,0,0,0,0,0,0,0),$$

then, by calculating $y\mathbf{X}^\dagger = (1,0)$ we will get that b is definitely 0. If we now add a (Gaussian) error to our experiment then the observed times, corresponding to an estimate y would perhaps be something like (cf. Figures 1 and 2 in [39]):

$$\hat{y} = (0.1, 0.2, 0.7, 0.2, 0.1, 0, 0, 0, 0, 0),$$

because, for example, in 10 measurements we have observed once the first possible time, twice the second, etc. The estimation based on these observations leads to a guess of the weights of the parameters in β that we calculate as $\hat{y}\mathbf{X}^\dagger = (0.7, 0)$. This result reflects the fact that it is very likely that the value of bit b is 0 as we have observed, although with some errors, a time behaviour where the times cluster around the value t_0.

5.3   Abstraction and Linear Regression

Statistics can be used in static analysis in all those cases where we have some observations at hand and we want to use them in order to improve the precision of the analysis. To this purpose the theory of linear regression provides us with a useful means to determine a best estimate of the model underlying those observations, e.g. the DTMC generator that with highest probability produces the traces that we observe.

Note that classical abstract interpretation cannot be used in this scenario even in its probabilistic re-formulation as given e.g. in [7]; this is because the safety constraint at the base of the framework does not permit the consideration of expectation values in the analysis result, as these would not guarantee the correctness of the analysis (cf. Section 3).

In the setting of linear statistical models, the concretisation operator $\mathbf{G}$ of the PAI framework corresponds to a mapping from an abstract domain consisting of all possible DTMC models for the observed program to all possible observable traces corresponding to the different runnings of the program. Thus, $\mathbf{G}$ plays the role of the design matrix of the statistical model. If y is a vector defining the probabilities of certain traces according to some observations and β represents a parameterised DTMC model, then we can use the linear statistical Eq. (1) in its simplest instance, i.e. with $\varepsilon = 0$, $y \in \mathbb{R}^n$, $\mathbf{X} \in \mathbb{R}^{n \times p}$ and $\beta \in \mathbb{R}^p$, in order to obtain the best estimate of the concrete DTMC model by $\hat{\beta} = y\mathbf{X}^\dagger$.

Example 8. Consider the following simple examples of DTMC's:

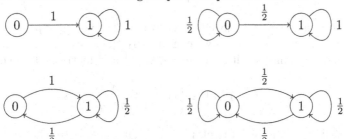

with generator matrices

$$\mathbf{T}_{0,1} = \begin{pmatrix} 0 & 1 \\ 0 & 1 \end{pmatrix} \quad \mathbf{T}_{\frac{1}{2},1} = \begin{pmatrix} \frac{1}{2} & \frac{1}{2} \\ 0 & 1 \end{pmatrix} \quad \mathbf{T}_{0,\frac{1}{2}} = \begin{pmatrix} 0 & 1 \\ \frac{1}{2} & \frac{1}{2} \end{pmatrix} \quad \mathbf{T}_{\frac{1}{2},\frac{1}{2}} = \begin{pmatrix} \frac{1}{2} & \frac{1}{2} \\ \frac{1}{2} & \frac{1}{2} \end{pmatrix}.$$

Clearly with $\mathbf{T}_{\frac{1}{2},\frac{1}{2}}$ we can generate all infinite 0/1 sequences. Note that since these are uncountably many, the probability structure on the maximal trace space will require a measure theoretical treatment. By restricting ourselves to traces of finite length we can however stay withing a finite-dimensional setting.

These DTMC's are in essence the processes which, for different values of p and q, describe the core (loop body) of Example 1 in the LOS or Kozen semantics (cf. also $[\![S]\!]_{KFS}$ in Example 3).

The processes above depend on the parameters p and q in the real interval $[0,1]$ which we can see as the probability to remain in state 0 and state 1, respectively. They are represented by the parametric DTMC

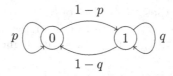

with generator

$$\mathbf{T}_{pq} = \begin{pmatrix} p & 1-p \\ 1-q & q \end{pmatrix}$$

Any property of a program whose behaviour can be described as above will depend on the parameters p and q. Moreover, observing the property may be influenced by some distorted execution of $\mathbf{T}_{pq}$. Applying the statistical linear model to find best estimates for the parameters p and q corresponds to performing a statistical analysis based on PAI, as shown in the the following example.

Example 9. Consider the DTMC in Example 8 with generator

$$\mathbf{T}_{pq} = \begin{pmatrix} p & 1-p \\ 1-q & q \end{pmatrix}.$$

This system is completely specified when both the values of p and q and the initial state s are specified. Thus we can identify the abstract semantic domain with the set of all pairs of initial states $s \in \{0,1\}$ and matrices $\mathbf{T}_{pq}$, i.e.

$$\mathcal{M} = \{\langle s, \mathbf{T}_{pq} \rangle\} = \left\{ \left\langle s, \begin{pmatrix} p & 1-p \\ 1-q & q \end{pmatrix} \right\rangle \right\}$$

or equivalently with the set of triples $\mathcal{M} = \{\langle s, p, q \rangle \mid s \in \{0,1\}, p, q \in [0,1]\}$.

Note that this parametric DTMC generator encodes the same information as the set of all parametric traces starting from any initial state (cf. Section 4). In order to apply PAI we consider the distributions over $\mathcal{M}$, i.e. the space $\mathcal{D} = \mathcal{V}(\mathcal{M})$ of all normalised, positive elements in the vector space over $\mathcal{M}$.

The concrete computational space consists of the set of all sequences of 0 and 1 in $\mathcal{T} = \{0,1\}^{+\infty}$, representing the execution traces resulting from fixing actual values of the parameters p and q and the input state. The concrete domain of PAI is therefore the space of distributions on traces $\mathcal{C} = \mathcal{V}(\mathcal{T})$.

Numerical Experiments. Even for the simple example given above, the sets involved are uncountably infinite. In order to be able to compute an analysis of the system in Example 8 we will consider here the simple case where transition probabilities can only assume values in a finite set, i.e. $p, q \in \{p_0, \ldots, p_n\}$ and where traces can only be of length t, for a given t. We report below some of the results we obtained from numerical experiments performed using the Octave system [40]. In these experiments we considered $p, q \in \{0, \frac{1}{2}, 1\}$, thus obtaining 9 possible semantics, with possible initial states either 0 or 1. This corresponds to an abstract domain $\mathcal{D} = \mathcal{V}(\{0,1\}) \otimes \mathcal{V}(\{0,\frac{1}{2},1\}) \otimes \mathcal{V}(\{0,\frac{1}{2},1\}) = \mathbb{R}^2 \otimes \mathbb{R}^3 \otimes \mathbb{R}^3 = \mathbb{R}^{18}$.

For different models – i.e. different values of p and q – as well as different noise levels we simulated 10000 executions of the system and observed traces of length $t = 10$. In this setting, concrete domain is therefore $\mathcal{C} = \mathcal{V}(\{0,1\}^{10}) = \mathcal{V}(\{0,1\})^{\otimes 10} = (\mathbb{R}^2)^{\otimes 10} = \mathbb{R}^{1024}$, i.e. there are about one thousand possible traces that can be observed.

The concretisation/design matrix $\mathbf{G} : \mathcal{D} \to \mathcal{C}$ associates to each of the 18 instance models and initial inputs one of the distributions over the 1024 traces, namely the one representing those traces that are obtained in that model. As it is impossible to reproduce here the actual 18×1024 matrix $\mathbf{G}$ (due to its size) we give in Fig. 1 the matrix G for the restricted case of 8 possible traces of 3 steps, with rows representing the possible instance models and columns the possible traces. The entries of this matrix specify the probabilities that a given model (row) generates a certain trace (column). For example, the entry $\mathbf{G}_{33} = \frac{1}{2}$ means that with the third model in the enumeration given above, i.e. for initial state $s = 0$, $p = \frac{1}{2}$ and $p = 0$, we get the third trace, i.e. 010, with probability $\frac{1}{2}$.

In order to calculate the best estimators of the parameters p and q, we computed the Moore-Penrose pseudo-inverse $\mathbf{G}^\dagger$ of $\mathbf{G}$, which is also reported in Fig. 1 for the restricted case. Intuitively, $\mathbf{G}^\dagger$ gives us the probabilities that when a certain trace is observed this comes from a certain model.

In our experiments we considered systems without distortion, i.e. no error, as well as the cases where a noise of "strength" ε was applied according to a normal distribution (cf. randn() in Octave 3.8.0 [40, p391]).

The observations were aggregated to a distribution over all 2^{10} possible traces. The probability associated to each trace σ_i is the ratio between the number of times σ_i was actually observed and the number of experiments we ran (i.e. 10000 in our case). For the undistorted case we denote this distribution vector by y, for $\varepsilon = 0.01$ by y', for $\varepsilon = 0.1$ by y'', and for $\varepsilon = 0.25$ by y'''. The initial state was always chosen with probability $\frac{1}{2}$ as state 0 or state 1.

Model $p = 0 = q$: The vectors we obtained in the case when the true model is given by $p = 0 = q$ are for the different noise levels:

$$y\mathbf{G}^\dagger = \begin{pmatrix} 0.50\ 0.50\ 0\ 0\ 0\ 0\ 0\ 0\ 0\ 0\ 0\ 0\ 0\ 0\ 0\ 0\ 0\ 0 \end{pmatrix}$$

$$y'\mathbf{G}^\dagger = \begin{pmatrix} 0.47\ 0.49\ 0.02\ 0.01\ 0\ 0\ 0.01\ 0.03\ -0.02\ -0.02\ 0\ 0\ 0\ 0\ 0\ 0\ 0\ 0 \end{pmatrix}$$

$$y''\mathbf{G}^\dagger = \begin{pmatrix} 0.33\ 0.34\ 0.17\ 0.11\ 0\ 0\ 0.11\ 0.18\ -0.12\ -0.12\ 0\ 0\ 0\ 0\ 0\ 0\ 0\ 0 \end{pmatrix}$$

$$y'''\mathbf{G}^\dagger = \begin{pmatrix} 0.18\ 0.17\ 0.28\ 0.18\ 0\ 0\ 0.18\ 0.26\ -0.13\ -0.12\ 0\ 0\ 0\ 0\ 0\ 0\ 0\ 0 \end{pmatrix}$$

Model $p = \frac{1}{2} = q$: The same observations for the case that $p = \frac{1}{2} = q$ gave us:

$$y\mathbf{G}^\dagger = \begin{pmatrix} 0\ 0\ 0\ 0\ 0\ 0\ 0\ 0\ 0.51\ 0.50\ 0\ 0\ 0\ 0\ 0\ 0\ 0\ 0 \end{pmatrix}$$

$$y'\mathbf{G}^\dagger = \begin{pmatrix} 0\ 0\ 0\ 0\ 0\ 0\ 0\ 0\ 0.51\ 0.49\ 0\ 0\ 0\ 0\ 0\ 0\ 0\ 0 \end{pmatrix}$$

$$y''\mathbf{G}^\dagger = \begin{pmatrix} 0\ 0\ 0\ 0\ 0\ 0\ 0\ 0\ 0.51\ 0.49\ 0\ 0\ 0\ 0\ 0\ 0\ 0\ 0 \end{pmatrix}$$

$$y'''\mathbf{G}^\dagger = \begin{pmatrix} 0\ 0\ 0\ 0\ 0\ 0\ 0\ 0\ 0.50\ 0.50\ 0\ 0\ 0\ 0\ 0\ 0\ 0\ 0 \end{pmatrix}$$

$$
G = \begin{pmatrix}
0 & 0 & 1 & 0 & 0 & 0 & 0 & 0 \\
0 & 0 & 0 & 0 & 0 & 1 & 0 & 0 \\
\frac{1}{4} & \frac{1}{4} & \frac{1}{2} & 0 & 0 & 0 & 0 & 0 \\
0 & 0 & 0 & 0 & \frac{1}{2} & \frac{1}{2} & 0 & 0 \\
1 & 0 & 0 & 0 & 0 & 0 & 0 & 0 \\
0 & 0 & 0 & 0 & 1 & 0 & 0 & 0 \\
0 & 0 & \frac{1}{2} & \frac{1}{2} & 0 & 0 & 0 & 0 \\
0 & 0 & 0 & 0 & 0 & \frac{1}{2} & \frac{1}{4} & \frac{1}{4} \\
\frac{1}{4} & \frac{1}{4} & \frac{1}{4} & \frac{1}{4} & 0 & 0 & 0 & 0 \\
0 & 0 & 0 & 0 & \frac{1}{4} & \frac{1}{4} & \frac{1}{4} & \frac{1}{4} \\
1 & 0 & 0 & 0 & 0 & 0 & 0 & 0 \\
0 & 0 & 0 & 0 & \frac{1}{2} & 0 & \frac{1}{4} & \frac{1}{4} \\
0 & 0 & 0 & 1 & 0 & 0 & 0 & 0 \\
0 & 0 & 0 & 0 & 0 & 0 & 0 & 1 \\
\frac{1}{4} & \frac{1}{4} & 0 & \frac{1}{2} & 0 & 0 & 0 & 0 \\
0 & 0 & 0 & 0 & 0 & 0 & 0 & 1 \\
1 & 0 & 0 & 0 & 0 & 0 & 0 & 0 \\
0 & 0 & 0 & 0 & 0 & 0 & 0 & 1
\end{pmatrix}
$$

$s\ p\ q$	$s\ p\ q$	$trace$
$0\ 0\ 0$	$1\ \frac{1}{2}\ \frac{1}{2}$	$0\ 0\ 0$
$1\ 0\ 0$	$0\ 1\ \frac{1}{2}$	$0\ 0\ 1$
$0\ \frac{1}{2}\ 0$	$1\ 1\ \frac{1}{2}$	$0\ 1\ 0$
$1\ \frac{1}{2}\ 0$	$0\ 0\ 1$	$0\ 1\ 1$
$0\ 1\ 0$	$1\ 0\ 1$	$1\ 0\ 0$
$1\ 1\ 0$	$0\ \frac{1}{2}\ 1$	$1\ 0\ 1$
$0\ 0\ \frac{1}{2}$	$1\ \frac{1}{2}\ 1$	$1\ 1\ 0$
$1\ 0\ \frac{1}{2}$	$0\ 1\ 1$	$1\ 1\ 1$
$0\ \frac{1}{2}\ \frac{1}{2}$	$1\ 1\ 1$	

$$
G^\dagger = \begin{pmatrix}
0 & 0 & 0 & 0 & \frac{1}{3} & 0 & 0 & 0 & 0 & 0 & \frac{1}{3} & 0 & 0 & 0 & 0 & 0 & \frac{1}{3} & 0 \\
-\frac{2}{3} & 0 & \frac{4}{3} & 0 & -\frac{1}{3} & 0 & -\frac{2}{3} & 0 & \frac{4}{3} & 0 & -\frac{1}{3} & 0 & -\frac{2}{3} & 0 & \frac{4}{3} & 0 & -\frac{1}{3} & 0 \\
\frac{11}{15} & 0 & \frac{1}{5} & 0 & 0 & 0 & \frac{1}{3} & 0 & 0 & 0 & 0 & -\frac{1}{15} & 0 & -\frac{1}{5} & 0 & 0 & 0 & 0 \\
-\frac{1}{15} & 0 & -\frac{1}{5} & 0 & 0 & 0 & \frac{1}{3} & 0 & 0 & 0 & 0 & \frac{11}{15} & 0 & \frac{1}{5} & 0 & 0 & 0 & 0 \\
0 & -\frac{1}{15} & 0 & \frac{1}{3} & 0 & \frac{11}{15} & 0 & -\frac{1}{5} & 0 & 0 & 0 & \frac{1}{5} & 0 & 0 & 0 & 0 & 0 & 0 \\
0 & \frac{11}{15} & 0 & \frac{1}{3} & 0 & -\frac{1}{15} & 0 & \frac{1}{5} & 0 & 0 & 0 & -\frac{1}{5} & 0 & 0 & 0 & 0 & 0 & 0 \\
0 & -\frac{2}{3} & 0 & -\frac{2}{3} & 0 & -\frac{2}{3} & 0 & \frac{4}{3} & 0 & \frac{4}{3} & 0 & -\frac{1}{3} & 0 & -\frac{1}{3} & 0 & -\frac{1}{3} & 0 \\
0 & 0 & 0 & 0 & 0 & 0 & 0 & 0 & 0 & 0 & 0 & \frac{1}{3} & 0 & \frac{1}{3} & 0 & \frac{1}{3}
\end{pmatrix}
$$

Fig. 1. Relating models (s, p, q) and traces of length 3

Model $p = 0, q = \frac{1}{2}$: Finally, for the case of an underlying model with $p = 0$ and $q = \frac{1}{2}$ we obtained:

$$y G^\dagger = \begin{pmatrix} 0\ 0\ 0\ 0\ 0\ 0\ 0.50\ 0.49\ 0\ 0.01\ 0\ 0\ 0\ 0\ 0\ 0\ 0 \end{pmatrix}$$

$$y' G^\dagger = \begin{pmatrix} 0\ 0\ 0\ 0\ 0\ 0\ 0.49\ 0.50\ 0.01\ 0\ 0\ 0\ 0\ 0\ 0\ 0\ 0 \end{pmatrix}$$

$$y'' G^\dagger = \begin{pmatrix} 0\ 0\ 0\ 0\ 0\ 0\ 0.43\ 0.43\ 0.07\ 0.06\ 0\ 0\ 0\ 0\ 0\ 0\ 0 \end{pmatrix}$$

$$y''' G^\dagger = \begin{pmatrix} 0\ 0\ 0.01\ 0\ 0\ 0\ 0.33\ 0.35\ 0.16\ 0.16\ 0\ 0\ 0\ 0\ 0\ 0\ 0 \end{pmatrix}$$

These results demonstrate that if we observe the *undisturbed* DTMC in order to obtain experimentally the probabilities y for all possible 2^{10} traces then we can identify the underlying model more or less uniquely. The abstract distribution $\hat{\beta} = y G^\dagger$ (i.e. when $\varepsilon = 0$) gives an estimate which corresponds precisely to the true parameters p and q and the probability $\frac{1}{2}$ for the initial states 0 and 1 (cf. the enumeration of models in Fig. 1).

For $\varepsilon = 0.01$ we can also identify the unknown system with high probability. However, there are coordinates of $y' G^\dagger$ which are non-zero although they do not correspond to the actual system. These stem from the fact that y' has non-zero probability for traces which actually should not be realised but due to the noise distortion are nevertheless observed.

If we increase the error term in the simulation, i.e. for the distortion $\varepsilon = 0.1$ or $\varepsilon = 0.25$, the possibility of a wrong identification of the actual model(s) is (as expected) higher: The weights associated to the actual system tends to decrease further, while other possible models get stronger. If we further increase ε the estimate $\hat{\beta}$ will still be the optimal one (BLUE) but ultimately it will not allow any meaningful identification of the actual system – we will get only (white) noise. We obtained similar results also for other choices of p and q.

6   Conclusions

We have presented a comparison of three different probabilistic semantics: (i) Kozen's I/O Fixed-Point Semantics, (ii) the Linear Operator Semantics previously introduced by the authors, and (iii) a probabilistic version of the Maximal Trace Semantics. We have argued that Kozen's semantics can be recovered as an abstract limit from the LOS (cf. [28]) and that the abstraction α_s in [7, Section 7.4] in fact gives Kozen's semantics (by collecting the information/probability along finite traces in the MTS). We also demonstrated that LOS contains more information than MTS, namely information about the control flow, but that otherwise LOS and MTS are equivalent.

The second part of this paper relates the Probabilistic Abstract Interpretation framework introduced in [5] with the most widely used statistical technique, namely Linear Regression. As already shown in [5], classical Abstract Interpretations can be recovered from a Probabilistic Abstract Interpretation by means of a forgetful functor that restricts probabilistic domains to their support sets. In this paper we have extended the (re)construction of the LOS from the MTS alluded to in [7] – though this involves the "abstraction" $\bar{\alpha}_s$ rather than α_s – to deal also with distorted observations of traces. This provides a bridge between statistics (testing) and static program analysis. Intended application areas include problems in computer security like covert channels and non-interference notions reinterpreted as process equivalence.

Our presentation was restricted to finite state spaces. However a full treatment of the different semantical models is possible though slightly more complex as it involves a deeper study of the underlying measure-theoretic notion (e.g. the σ-algebras generated by trace pre-fixes) as well as topological notions (e.g. Hilbert vs Banach spaces and their operators, weak limits etc., cf. [28]).

Finally, it might be worth pointing out the rich literature on filtering, system identification, Hidden Markov Models (e.g. [41–43]), and related topics which we did not discuss but are clearly related. Our approach to Linear Regression could be considered to be very simple and basic. However, we think it is worth highlighting the relationship between PAI and statistics. Given the role that least square methods – i.e. the Moore-Penrose pseudo-inverse – play in control theory etc. – for example, for the well-known and celebrated technique of Kalman filters [11] – we aim to further explore this field.

References

1. Jones, N.D., Nielson, F.: Abstract interpretation: a semantics-based tool for program analysis. In: Handbook of Logic in Computer Science, pp. 527–636. Clarendon Press, Oxford (1985)
2. Nielson, F.: Strictness analysis and denotational abstract interpretation. Inf. Comput. **76**(1), 29–92 (1988)
3. Nielson, F., Nielson, H.R.: Infinitary control flow analysis: a collecting semantics for closure analysis. In: Proceedings of POPL 1997, pp. 332–345 (1997)
4. Nielson, F., Nielson, H.R., Hankin, C.: Principles of Program Analysis. Springer, Heidelberg (1999)
5. Di Pierro, A., Wiklicky, H.: Concurrent constraint programming: towards probabilistic abstract interpretation. In: Proceedings of PPDP 2000, pp. 127–138 (2000)
6. Di Pierro, A., Wiklicky, H.: Measuring the precision of abstract interpretations. In: Lau, K.-K. (ed.) LOPSTR 2000. LNCS, vol. 2042, pp. 147–164. Springer, Heidelberg (2001)
7. Cousot, P., Monerau, M.: Probabilistic abstract interpretation. In: Seidl, H. (ed.) Programming Languages and Systems. LNCS, vol. 7211, pp. 169–193. Springer, Heidelberg (2012)
8. Campbell, S.L., Meyer, C.D.: Generalized Inverses of Linear Transformations. Pitman - Dover, London (1979)
9. Deutsch, F.: Best Approximation in Inner-Product Spaces. Springer, New York (2001)
10. Ben-Israel, A., Greville, T.N.E.: Gereralized Inverses - Theory and Applications. CMS Books in Mathematics, 2nd edn. Springer, New York (2003)
11. Albert, A.: Regression and the Moore-Penrose Pseudoinverse. Mathematics in Science and Engineering. Elsevier, New York (1972)
12. Kozen, D.: Semantics of probabilistic programs. J. Comput. Syst. Sci. **22**(3), 328–350 (1981)
13. Di Pierro, A., Sotin, P., Wiklicky, H.: Relational analysis and precision via probabilistic abstract interpretation. In: Proceedings of QAPL 2008. vol. 220(3) of ENTCS, pp. 23–42. Elsevier (2008)
14. Di Pierro, A., Hankin, C., Wiklicky, H.: Probabilistic semantics and program analysis. Formal Methods for Quantitative Aspects of Programming Languages. LNCS, vol. 6154, pp. 1–42. Springer, Heidelberg (2010)
15. Di Pierro, A., Hankin, C., Wiklicky, H.: Probabilistic lambda calculus and quantitative program analysis. J. Logic Comput. **15**(2), 159–179 (2005)
16. Ramsey, N., Pfeffer, A.: Stochastic lambda calculus and monads of probability distributions. ACM SIGPLAN Notices **37**(1), 154–165 (2002)
17. Pfeffer, A.: Practical Probabilistic Programming. Manning, Shelter Island (2015)
18. Di Pierro, A., Hankin, C., Wiklicky, H.: Probabilistic linda-based coordination languages. In: de Boer, F.S., Bonsangue, M.M., Graf, S., de Roever, W.-P. (eds.) FMCO 2004. LNCS, vol. 3657, pp. 120–140. Springer, Heidelberg (2005)
19. Priami, C.: Stochastic π-calculus. Comput. J. **38**(7), 578–589 (1995)
20. Hillston, J.: A Compositional Approach to Performance Modelling. Cambridge University Press, Cambridge (1996)
21. Di Pierro, A., Hankin, C., Wiklicky, H.: A systematic approach to probabilistic pointer analysis. In: Shao, Z. (ed.) APLAS 2007. LNCS, vol. 4807, pp. 335–350. Springer, Heidelberg (2007)

22. Jones, C., Plotkin, G.D.: A probabilistic powerdomain of evaluations. In: Proceedings of LICS 1989, pp. 186–195. IEEE (1989)
23. Jones, C.: Probabilistic non-determinism. Ph.D. thesis, University of Edinburgh (1989)
24. Jung, A., Tix, R.: The troublesome probabilistic powerdomain. ENTCS **13**, 70–91 (1998)
25. Morgan, C., McIver, A., Seidel, K.: Probabilistic predicate transformers. ACM Trans. Program. Lang. Syst. **18**(3), 325–353 (1996)
26. Gretz, F., Katoen, J.P., McIver, A.: Operational versus weakest pre-expectation semantics for the probabilistic guarded command language. Perform. Eval. **73**, 110–132 (2014)
27. Park, S., Pfenning, F., Thrun, S.: A probabilistic language based upon sampling functions. In: Proceedings of POPL 2005, 171–182 (2005)
28. Di Pierro, A., Wiklicky, H.: Semantics of probabilistic programs: a weak limit approach. In: Shan, C. (ed.) APLAS 2013. LNCS, vol. 8301, pp. 241–256. Springer, Heidelberg (2013)
29. Lax, P.D.: Functional Analysis. Pure and Applied Mathematics. Wiley, New York (2002)
30. Kubrusly, C.S.: The Elements of Operator Theory, 2nd edn. Birkhäuser, Boston (2011)
31. Greub, W.H.: Linear Algebra, vol. 97. Springer, Heidelberg (1967)
32. Goebel, K., Kirk, W.: Topics in Metric Fixed Point Theory. Cambridge Studies in Advanced Mathematics. Cambridge University Press, Cambridge (1990)
33. Roman, S.: Advanced Linear Algebra. Graduate Texts in Mathematics, vol. 135, 2nd edn. Springer, New York (2005)
34. Kadison, R., Ringrose, J.: Fundamentals of the Theory of Operator Algebras: Elementary Theory. AMS (1997). Reprint from Academic Press edition 1983
35. Cousot, P., Cousot, R.: Systematic design of program transformation frameworks by abstract interpretation. In: Proceedings POPL 2002, pp. 178–190 (2002)
36. Cousot, P.: Constructive design of a hierarchy of semantics of a transition system by abstract interpretation. Theoret. Comput. Sci. **277**(1–2), 47–103 (2002)
37. Monniaux, D.: Abstract interpretation of probabilistic semantics. In: Palsberg, J. (ed.) SAS 2000. LNCS, vol. 1824, pp. 322–339. Springer, Heidelberg (2000)
38. Di Pierro, A., Hankin, C., Wiklicky, H.: Abstract interpretation for worst and average case analysis. In: Reps, T., Sagiv, M., Bauer, J. (eds.) Wilhelm Festschrift. LNCS, vol. 4444, pp. 160–174. Springer, Heidelberg (2007)
39. Kocher, P.C.: Timing attacks on implementations of Diffie-Hellman, RSA, DSS, and other systems. In: Koblitz, N. (ed.) CRYPTO 1996. LNCS, vol. 1109, pp. 104–113. Springer, Heidelberg (1996)
40. Eaton, J.W., Bateman, D., Hauberg, S.: GNU Octave - A High-Level Interactive Language For Numerical Computations, 3rd edn. Cambridge University Press, New York (2007)
41. Crassidis, J.L., Junkins, J.L.: Optimal Estimation of Dynamic Systems. Chapman & Hall/CRC Applied Mathematics & Nonlinear Science. CRC Press, Boca Raton (2004)
42. Verhaegen, M., Verdult, V.: Filtering and System Identification: A Least Squares Approach. Cambridge University Press, New York (2007)
43. Rao, C.R., Toutenburg, H., Shalabh, Heumann, C.: Linear Models and Generalizations: Least Squares and Alternatives. Springer Series in Statistics. Springer, Heidelberg (2008)

Abstract Interpretation of PEPA Models

Stephen Gilmore, Jane Hillston$^{(\boxtimes)}$, and Natalia Zoń

Laboratory for Foundations of Computer Science,
University of Edinburgh, Edinburgh, Scotland
`jane.hillston@ed.ac.uk`

Abstract. This paper relates the fluid-flow semantics of the stochastic process algebra PEPA (Performance Evaluation Process Algebra) to the static analysis technique of *abstract interpretation*. The explanation in the paper is illustrated through the example of a *distributed denial of service* (DDoS) attack which is being launched against a server. DDoS attacks are mounted by a large population of attackers, who are coordinating and working together in attacking a specific server. The scale of the attack is crucial to its success, but the resulting large number of states in the system makes it difficult to model and analyse using the conventional discrete-state interpretation of PEPA.

1 Introduction

Discrete-state modelling of computer systems is the bedrock of our attempts to gain intellectual control of informatic systems by building precise models of their behaviour and reasoning about these models. For some types of reasoning, such as identifying contention problems or finding deadlocks, it can be sufficient to work with a model with a small number of components, and show that the problem arises there. *Resource-constrained networks* [1] are an example of this, where several processes compete for resources from a limited pool, as are the so-called *feature interaction* problems which arise in telephony networks.

For other types of problems, such as distributed denial of service attacks (DDoS), it is *not* possible to scale down the analysis: the problem only arises when large-scale systems are involved. The case in point here is whether a service endpoint providing a service can continue to maintain the robustness of that service if larger and larger numbers of attackers threaten to overwhelm the server. This sentiment has been expressed very well in [2] where the authors write: "We believe that with quantitative information on the robustness, it will be possible to better determine whether or not the software continues to deal appropriately with risks and threats as their application environment changes." To analyse these problems in large-scale systems we need to use scalable modelling methods.

Concurrency in informatic systems effectively thwarts our attempts to reason about large-scale systems using a concrete interpretation of our models because the asynchronous interleaving of concurrent processes gives rise to state spaces which are too large to be represented. With the scalable, virtualised services

© Springer International Publishing Switzerland 2016
C.W. Probst et al. (Eds.): Nielsons' Festschrift, LNCS 9560, pp. 140–158, 2016.
DOI: 10.1007/978-3-319-27810-0_7

which are in use today components are replicated to provide resilience and application scalability to serve growing numbers of clients using the service. In order to reason about systems with replicated components it is essential to move away from discrete-state models and use representations which provide efficient representations of populations of components [3].

The PEPA stochastic process algebra [4] supports such reasoning about large-scale systems by providing a formal language which allows system behaviour to be captured as a discrete-state model, and verification methods which scale to allow the analysis of models which are composed of replicated components. This is achieved through an abstract interpretation of PEPA models via a representation in terms of ordinary differential equations over a continuous-state space. This is an over-approximation of the true discrete state-space, and this relaxation of the strict small-step interleaving semantics of PEPA allows efficient analysis of models which could not be contemplated by other means.

Structure of this paper: Our goal here is to describe a formal dynamic analysis approach which is based on a continuous-space abstraction of discrete-space systems. We illustrate the use of this analysis method in practice by developing a PEPA model of a server system which is trying to withstand a distributed denial of service attack. We use our continuous approximation of the model to investigate effective ways to defend against such attacks. The rest of the paper is organised as follows. In Sect. 2 we relate the subject matter of the present paper to other research and give pointers to important work in this area. In Sect. 3 we present the relevant technical background for this paper, with an introduction to the PEPA stochastic process algebra and its concrete small-step operational semantics. Section 4 explains the abstract interpretation of PEPA models with reference to the scalable differential semantics of PEPA. Section 5 presents the case study of the paper, involving a PEPA model of a DDoS attack. Finally, Sect. 6 concludes the paper.

2   Related Work

Static analysis of PEPA models has first been presented in 2007, in [5], where the author developed an approach based on data flow analysis. A transfer function is defined and then the classical worklist algorithm is used to construct a finite automaton capturing all possible interactions between components, on which deadlock detection can be based. Here we take an alternative approach based on abstract interpretation rather than data flow analysis [6]. The interpretation of PEPA models as a set of ordinary differential equations was initiated in [7]. Similar work has been done for the KAPPA modelling language [8].

Three recent papers are very directly relevant to our presentation here because they also use process algebra and quantitative methods to model denial-of-service attacks. They are [9–11], as discussed next. Each builds on the Quality Calculus [12], a process algebra in the family of CCS and the π-calculus, intended to study the behaviour of software components in distributed systems when the communication has vulnerabilities; similar to the type of system considered at the end of this paper. In particular, one motivation for the Quality Calculus is seeking to ensure that messages are correctly received, and denial of service attacks are a major challenge in this context. In [9], the authors introduce the Applied Quality Calculus which extends the Quality Calculus. The Applied Quality Calculus is used in modelling secure systems which must operate in the context of low computational power devices which communicate by broadcast communication in a challenging computational context where communication failures cannot be ignored. The Applied Quality Calculus has an executable semantics which is implemented in the Maude term-rewriting system, resulting in a simulation engine which can be used both directly for prototyping and for solving bounded reachability problems. Here, the notion of denial of service centres on the distinction between data and *optional data* introduced by the Quality Calculus. A rewrite rule-based mechanism is used to implement both an input selection mechanism and cryptographic reasoning in addition to designing *quality guards* which are more expressive than traditional predicates which are used in propositions.

In [10], the authors extend the Hybrid CSP language of He Jifeng with the notion of *binders* from the Quality Calculus. The modelling domain of interest here is *hybrid systems* which bring together discrete-state computational controllers and continuous-time physical systems into a dynamic assembly. A small-step transition semantics is presented for the language, in a timed, discrete-event context. The purpose of the modelling is to show that error configurations are not reachable and that the (continuous) velocities of the moving objects in the hybrid system cannot be degraded out of the safe range of operation. In [11], the same authors place greater emphasis on the safety aspects of the problem.

In [13], Zeng *et al.* extend the Quality Calculus with quantitative information capturing explicit timing and probability of actions. Unlike PEPA, where the probability distributions governing the delays associated with actions are restricted to follow an exponential distribution, the Stochastic Quality Calculus supports generally distributed delays but with the associated cost that the semantics gives rise to a Generalised Semi-Markov Decision Process in general, and a Generalised Semi-Markov Process when non-determinism can be eliminated. Both these mathematical structures are very difficult to analyse.

PEPA has previously been used to analyse security in [14], but in that paper the focus was on securing systems against timing attacks, where an attacker gains information about the activity on secure channels through eavesdropping on the timing characteristics of message exchanges. In the model developed in this paper we are specifically considering the case of a denial of service attack, where the strategy of the attacker is much more brute force, relying on scalability vulnerabilities of the service under attack.

3   Background

3.1   PEPA

PEPA is a compact formal modelling language which provides the appropriate abstract language constructs to represent many dynamic systems. It has stochastically-timed activities which can be used to encode activities which take time to complete, such as data processing and a probabilistic choice operator to express the likelihood of different outcomes, for example in the presence of communication failures. Different patterns of behaviour are encoded in recursive process definitions. Features such as these are found in many modelling formalisms [15] but a distinctive strength of the PEPA language is that populations of components, encoded as arrays of process instances, are both convenient to express in the language and efficiently supported by the dynamic analysis which reveals the collective behaviour which emerges from the interactions of the populations of components. The PEPA language has found application in many modelling problems such as scalable and quantitative analysis of web-services [16–18], software performance engineering with UML-based models [19,20], secure key distribution [21], internet worms [22], and peer-to-peer systems [23].

As a process calculus, PEPA has CSP-style multiway communication, and actions in PEPA have durations. A PEPA model consists of a collection of *components* (also known as *processes*) which undertake actions [4]. A component may perform an action autonomously, *independent actions*, or in synchronisation with other components, *shared actions*. PEPA models are generated by the following two-level grammar:

$$S ::= (\alpha, r).S \quad | \quad S + S \quad | \quad A_S, A_S \stackrel{def}{=} S$$

$$C ::= S \quad | \quad C \bowtie_L C \quad | \quad C/L \quad | \quad A_C, A_C \stackrel{def}{=} C$$

The first production defines *sequential components*, i.e., processes which only exhibit sequential or branching behaviour (by means of prefix, ".", or choice, "+", respectively). The second production defines *model components*, in which the interactions between the sequential components are expressed through the cooperation (" $\bowtie_L$ ") and hiding ("/") operators. Within a cooperation, the set L specifies which action types must be shared; components can proceed independently and concurrently on other action types. A *system equation* specifies all the components within a system and how they must interact.

Typically, each sequential component corresponds to a component of the system and the performance of the system is constrained by the interactions between components as imposed by the cooperations. For example for a client-server system, some number of clients may compete for access to a limited number of servers. This may be written as the system equation

$$System \stackrel{def}{=} Client[N_c] \bowtie_{\{request\}} Server[N_s]$$

where $Client[N_c]$ is shorthand for $Client \bowtie_{\emptyset} \cdots \bowtie_{\emptyset} Client$ for a population of N_c clients, and similarly for $Server[N_s]$.

3.2 Concrete Semantics

Stochastic process algebras, such as PEPA, are typically given a semantics in terms of a labelled transition system, derived from small-step operational semantics. In other words, a set of semantic rules, shown in Fig. 1, detail the possible evolutions of a term in the language based on the syntactical construction of the term. The transitions which are derived are labelled by the activities and thus contain information about the dynamic behaviour in terms of the expected rate of the transition in addition to the type of activity performed. This inclusion of information about the rates within the labelled transition system means that a multi-transition system must be used in order to correctly reflect the dynamics of the system, i.e., if there are multiple instances of the same transition the resulting action will occur at a faster rate than if there is only a single instance, because each instance contributes to the apparent rate of the action.

The rules in Fig. 1 correspond to the operators of the language introduced in the previous section. Most of the rules are straightforward, and presented here without comment. Rule C_2 is the fundamental inference for the characterisation of the dynamic behaviour of a shared action. It implements the semantics of *bounded capacity*: informally, the overall rate of execution of a shared activity is the minimum between the rates of the synchronising components. The rule relies

Prefix

$$S_0 : \frac{}{(\alpha, r).E \xrightarrow{(\alpha,r)} E}$$

Choice

$$S_1 : \frac{E \xrightarrow{(\alpha,r)} E'}{E + F \xrightarrow{(\alpha,r)} E' + F} \qquad S_2 : \frac{F \xrightarrow{(\alpha,r)} F'}{E + F \xrightarrow{(\alpha,r)} E + F'}$$

Cooperation

$$C_0 : \frac{E \xrightarrow{(\alpha,r)} E'}{E \underset{L}{\bowtie} F \xrightarrow{(\alpha,r)} E' \underset{L}{\bowtie} F}, \alpha \notin L \qquad C_1 : \frac{F \xrightarrow{(\alpha,r)} F'}{E \underset{L}{\bowtie} F \xrightarrow{(\alpha,r)} E \underset{L}{\bowtie} F'}, \alpha \notin L$$

$$C_2 : \frac{E \xrightarrow{(\alpha,r_1)} E' \quad F \xrightarrow{(\alpha,r_2)} F'}{E \underset{L}{\bowtie} F \xrightarrow{(\alpha,R)} E' \underset{L}{\bowtie} F'}, \alpha \in L$$

$$R = \frac{r_1}{r_\alpha(E)} \frac{r_2}{r_\alpha(F)} \min\left(r_\alpha(E), r_\alpha(F)\right)$$

Hiding

$$H_0 : \frac{E \xrightarrow{(\alpha,r)} E'}{E/L \xrightarrow{(\alpha,r)} E'/L}, \alpha \notin L \qquad H_1 : \frac{E \xrightarrow{(\alpha,r)} E'}{E/L \xrightarrow{(\tau,r)} E'/L}, \alpha \in L$$

Constant

$$A_0 : \frac{E \xrightarrow{(\alpha,r)} E'}{A \xrightarrow{(\alpha,r)} E'}, A \stackrel{def}{=} E$$

Fig. 1. Markovian semantics of PEPA.

on the notion of *apparent rate* to compute the total capacity of a cooperating component, according to the following definition.

The *apparent rate* of action α in process E, denoted by $r_\alpha(E)$, indicates the overall rate at which α can be performed by E. It is recursively defined as follows:

$$r_\alpha((\beta,r).E) = \begin{cases} r \text{ if } & \beta = \alpha \\ 0 \text{ if } & \beta \neq \alpha \end{cases}$$

$$r_\alpha(E + F) = r_\alpha(E) + r_\alpha(F)$$

$$r_\alpha\left(E \bowtie_L F\right) = \begin{cases} \min\left(r_\alpha(E), r_\alpha(F)\right) \text{ if } \alpha \in L \\ r_\alpha(E) + r_\alpha(F) \qquad \text{ if } \alpha \notin L \end{cases}$$

$$r_\alpha(E/L) = \begin{cases} r_\alpha(E) \text{ if } & \alpha \notin L \\ 0 \qquad \text{ if } & \alpha \in L \end{cases}$$

According to this definition, for the array of sequential components $Client[N_C]$, where $Client \stackrel{def}{=} (comm, r_d).Client'$, the apparent rate of $comm$ is

$$r_{comm}(Client[N_C]) = N_C\, r_{comm}(Client) = N_C \times r_d. \tag{1}$$

Similarly, for $Server \stackrel{def}{=} (comm, r_u).Server'$,

$$r_{comm}(Server[N_S]) = N_S\, r_{comm}(Server) = N_S \times r_u. \tag{2}$$

Once the labelled transition system, or *derivation graph*, corresponding to a PEPA model has been constructed then it can be interpreted as the state transition diagram of a continuous time Markov chain (CTMC). In this CTMC each state corresponds to a distinct syntactic form of the PEPA expression, as the model evolves according to the semantics. The CTMC is stored as an infinitesimal generator matrix, a matrix which captures the rates of transitions between states. From this the probability distribution over the states of the model at any given time, or at steady state, can be readily derived using standard linear algebra algorithms.

4   Abstract Interpretation of PEPA Models

4.1   Overview

As we saw in the previous section the concrete semantics of a PEPA model gives rise to a mathematical object, a continuous time Markov chain (CTMC). For model analysis the CTMC is encoded as an *infinitesimal generator matrix*, $\mathbf{Q}$. If the model has N distinct states in the derivation graph, $\mathbf{Q}$ will be an $N \times N$ matrix, with each entry $q(i,j)$ storing the rate of the exponential distribution governing transitions from state s_i to state s_j. The behaviour of the CTMC is captured in terms of its probability distribution, typically denoted $\pi(t)$, the N-dimensional vector in which the i-th entry denotes the probability to be in state i at time t. For steady state properties of a system we are interested in $\pi(\infty)$, usually denoted simply as π, which can be found by linear algebra as the solution to the equations

$$\pi\mathbf{Q} = \mathbf{0} \qquad \sum_i \pi_i = 1$$

where the equation on the left represents the *global balance equations*, ensuring that at equilibrium the probability distribution is stable, and the equation on the right represents the normalisation condition, capturing that π is indeed a probability distribution.

Considering the operation of the modelled system, each possible behaviour can be regarded as a possible trajectory through the state space. In contrast to solving the CTMC, as described above, to find the probability distribution over states, simulating the CTMC generates a single trajectory. Thus the CTMC itself encodes all possible trajectories, and the state probability distribution gives the relative likelihood of each one. This is a complete encapsulation of all possible behaviours of the model of the system, and thus the concrete semantics can be regarded as being exhaustive with respect to the possible executions. However, this exhaustive view relies on being able to construct and manipulate the whole CTMC, i.e., its infinitesimal generator matrix, something that is not possible when the size of N grows too large (say $> 10^8$ states). The alternative, based on simulation amounts to *sampling* trajectories/behaviours. This is computationally costly especially as many repeated samples are needed in order to derive statistically sound results.

A continuous *space* alternative has been proposed which makes an abstract interpretation of the CTMC underlying a PEPA model [24]. Instead of a probability distribution over a set of possible trajectories, the model gives rise to a single system of ordinary differential equations (ODEs). These ODEs can be regarded as representing the expectation over the probability distribution over possible trajectories, or as the single trajectory that captures the average behaviour of the system. The seminal theorem by Kurtz [25], establishes that if we consider a sequence of CTMCs, with increasing populations of components interacting in the same proportions, then as the population increases, behaviour of the CTMCs converges to this single ODE trajectory. This corresponds to a functional form of the law of large numbers. Instead of a sequence of random variables, i.e., the sample mean, converging to a deterministic value, i.e., the true mean, here we have a sequence of CTMCs or trajectories for increasing population size which converge to a deterministic trajectory, given by the ODEs. Thus the ODE semantics provide an abstract semantics for PEPA, which can be regarded as an over-approximation since it summarises all possible behaviours obtained via the concrete semantics. Details of the abstract semantics are given in the following subsection.

4.2 Scalable Differential Semantics

In [26] the authors explain how the ODEs of the abstract semantics can be inferred statically from the PEPA model. This is done via a more abstract representation of the underlying CTMC in terms of generating functions, which are then approximated from discrete functions, to functions over continuous variables, the ODEs. This approach allows the consistency between the concrete semantics, now encoded in generating functions, and the abstract semantics, to be readily proved. Moreover it is shown that the ODEs generated are indeed those consistent with Kurtz's theorem, implying correctness of the abstract semantics as explained above. Furthermore in a subsequent paper it is shown how the abstract semantics may be used to derive performance measures from PEPA models, in addition to the evolution of population counts, giving the expectations of measures over trajectories rather than simply the expectation of the trajectories themselves [27].

Construction of the abstraction semantics proceeds in three steps:

1. **Context reduction:** identifying the component *types* in operation in the model and the local state space of each type, resulting in a reduced state representation based on a counting abstraction;
2. **Identify the jump multiset:** characterising the effect of each type of action in terms of a symbolic update on the reduced state representation;
3. **Define generating functions:** expressing the rate of transitions in the state space as a function of the state.

Context reduction: The aim of context reduction is to statically reduce the state representation of the PEPA model to its most compact form. Previous work [28], Gilmore *et al.*, showed how a static analysis could find lumpable partitions in the underlying state space of a PEPA model and find a reduced state space based on a canonical form of the PEPA model expressions. In [26] the syntax of the PEPA expression is discarded in the state representation and a numerical vector is used to capture the state of the model. The objective of the context reduction is to identify the entries which are needed for the representation. Roughly speaking, two components are considered to have the same *type* if they have the same derivation graph *and* they are subject to the same cooperation sets in the expression of the model. For each component type there is one entry in the numerical vector for each of the states in its derivation graph. For the definition of the semantics the entries of the numerical vector are represented symbolically $\xi = (\xi_1, \ldots, \xi_n)$. Note that this is a list of the *local* states of each of the component types considered in isolation, and consequently much smaller than a list of all the possible *global* states that could be encountered through their interleaving. This is an important distinction. A system of ODEs, the Chapman-Kolmogorov equations, describing the evolution of the system based on the concrete interpretation of the CTMC can also be constructed. In these equations the variables are the probability mass associated with each *global* state, i.e., there is one equation corresponding to every global state of the system. This system equation becomes unmanageable for models of any reasonable size.

The *reduced context* of a PEPA component P, denoted by $red(P)$, is recursively defined as follows:

$$red\left((\alpha, r) . P\right) = (\alpha, r) . P$$
$$red\left(P + Q\right) = P + Q$$
$$red(A \stackrel{def}{=} P) = red(P)$$
$$red(P \bowtie_L P') = \begin{cases} red(P), & \text{if } L = \emptyset \wedge P = P' \\ & \wedge P, P' \text{ are sequential components} \\ red(P) \bowtie_L red(P'), & \text{otherwise} \end{cases}$$
$$red(P/L) = red(P)/L$$

The jump multiset: Once we have the symbolic representation of a prototypical state of the system we can consider the transitions induced on this state representation by the actions in the PEPA model. For each action type, from the model specification, we can identify the impact that completing the action will have on the counts of component types involved in the action: if a component enables an action, then completing the action will decrease the corresponding count by 1; conversely if a component is a one-step derivative of the action, then its corresponding count will be increased by one. Thus for each action type in the model we can build an update vector which will make the appropriate change to the symbolic state vector whenever the action is completed. For example if the update vector or *jump* associated with an action α is $\mathbf{u}_\alpha$, and a state ξ completes an action α, then the resulting state will be $\xi + \mathbf{u}_\alpha$.

Generating functions: Finally, in order to capture the dynamics of the process we need to know the rate at which actions will be completed. In general this will depend on the state of the system since, as remarked earlier, when an action is enabled multiple times its apparent rate increases. However, the (symbolic) state representation gives us the information needed to deduce the multiplicities of actions enabled in any state and consequently the rates of actions can be expressed symbolically too. For example, if (α, r) is an individual action of the component P_j whose count is captured by the variable ξ_j, then the rate of α in an arbitrary state will be $\xi_j \times r$. The generating function would then be expressed as $f_\alpha(\xi, \mathbf{u}_\alpha) = \xi_j \times r$.

These functions are parametrised by action types to keep track of the additional information about which action type is associated with a transition. Let $\mathbf{u}_\alpha \in \mathbb{Z}^d$ be the *transition jump*. The generating functions are denoted by $f_\alpha(\xi, \mathbf{u}_\alpha) : \mathbb{R}^d \to \mathbb{R}$ and give the transition rate for a jump $\mathbf{u}_\alpha$ and an activity of type $\alpha \in \mathcal{A}$. Thus, the entry in the generator matrix corresponding to the transition from ξ to $\xi + \mathbf{u}$, denoted by $q_{\xi, \xi + \mathbf{u}}$, can be written as

$$q_{\xi, \xi + \mathbf{u}} = \sum_{\alpha \in \mathcal{A}} f_\alpha(\xi, \mathbf{u}_\alpha).$$

The summation across $\mathcal{A}$ captures the fact that distinct action types may contribute to a transition to the same target state, e.g., $(\alpha, r).P + (\beta, s).P$.

These transitions are kept distinct in the labelled transition system of PEPA, because it records the action type as well as the transition rate, but they collapse onto the same entry in the underlying generator matrix. We use the notation

$$f(\xi, \mathbf{u}) \equiv \sum_{\alpha \in \mathcal{A}} f_\alpha(\xi, \mathbf{u}_\alpha)$$

to indicate the overall contribution to the transition. The extraction of the generating functions from the PEPA model usually presents very little computational challenge because the environment collected via the inference rules in our operational semantics abstracts away from the (potentially very large) actual population levels of the system under study.

As stated above, when the generating functions are instantiated with a state representation based on integer counts and updates of the component types, they may be used to derive the state space of a CTMC corresponding to a PEPA model instantiated with that many copies of each component type. This is a template for all possible trajectories over the reduced state space. But when the functions are treated as continuous functions (we replace ξ by a vector of real values $\mathbf{x}$, and allow them to evolve continuously) they give rise to a vector field which defines the evolution of the expectation over the trajectories. Thus from $f(\xi, \mathbf{u})$ it is possible to construct a vector field $F : \mathbb{R}^d \to \mathbb{R}^d$ defined as

$$F(x) = \sum_{\mathbf{u} \in \mathbb{Z}^d} \mathbf{u} f(x, \mathbf{u}) \tag{3}$$

and an associated ODE

$$\frac{dx(t)}{dt} = F(x(t)). \tag{4}$$

5   Modelling a Distributed Denial of Service Attack

In this section, we turn to the case study of the paper: a *Distributed Denial of Service* (DDoS) attack. Such attacks on server-based systems are particularly challenging because they are fundamentally different in nature from attacks which exploit logical weaknesses in the design of communication protocols. Protocol breaking-attacks are fundamentally *qualitative* in nature. In contrast, DDoS attacks are fundamentally *quantitative* in nature. A Dolev-Yao attack requires ingenuity and cunning; a DDoS attack simply requires a large enough pool of attackers to take down the server by brute force.

We present the model in three instances, each of which builds on the model which came before. In every model, components are replicated to form populations of components. There are multiple clients, multiple servers, multiple attackers, and so forth. Populations are numerous. There are hundreds of instances of each component, not just five or ten. The three versions of the model are explained below.

– In the first version of our DDoS model we present only the *servers* and the *clients*. There are no attackers in the first model: the purpose of this first model is only to show idealised *optimal* service, and thereby to serve as a basis against which to compare *sub-optimal* service. We are mostly interested in how connections are made and held, so we focus on the Servers on the server side, and the process of connecting and disconnecting.

– In the second version of our model we add the *attackers*, showing how they impede the use of the server, making it much more difficult for genuine clients to get any service at all. Creating this form of unproductive interference is the essence of a distributed denial of service attack.

– In the third version of our model we introduce new components: the *defenders* try to impede the attackers, by monitoring each socket. As we will see, the defenders are not able to restore the optimal level of service which was enjoyed in the absence of the attackers but they lessen the effectiveness of the DDoS attack by impeding the attackers. This is done by introducing a *delay* which monitors the connection to the server and ejects a connection if it appears to be taking too long. Unfortunately this means that genuine clients may also be ejected sometimes but as we will see, although the attackers continue to frequently connect to the server, the number of clients trying unsuccessfully to connect is significantly reduced.

We encoded our model in PEPA and analysed it with the PEPA Eclipse Plug-in [29], a modelling tool developed in the European project SENSORIA (Software Engineering for Service-Oriented Overlay Computers) and subsequently used in teaching and research internationally. It incorporates a custom editor for PEPA models, model visualisation and static analysis tools, a model debugger, Markov chain analysis tools, stochastic simulation and discrete analysis tools, a model compiler which delivers a continuous representation of the system, efficient ODE-based solvers, and plotting functions for analysis results.

5.1   Model Parameters, for All Models

PEPA models have both continuous variables and discrete variables. The continuous variables are *rate parameters* which are used to model the exponentially-distributed *rate* at which actions (more properly, *activities*) occur. The discrete variables are *population counts* which count the number of copies of each PEPA component in the model. Multiplicities are important in all models, but they are important in DDoS models in particular. A DDoS attack which has been launched by 10 hostile bots somewhere on the Internet is not anywhere near as troubling as a DDoS attack which is being launched by 10,000,000 hostile bots.

5.2   First Model: Server and Clients only

The basic model is formed as the cooperation of a population of servers with a population of clients on some work to be done. There is a protocol of interaction observed by both servers and clients, as shown in Figs. 3 and 4.

Model number	Rate variable	Rate value	Variable description	Used by PEPA component(s)
1,2,3	r_z	0.02	the client's *think* rate	*Client*
1,2,3	r_c	1.0	the *connect* rate	*Client, Server*
1,2,3	r_h	10	*handshake* rate (if innocent)	*Client, Server*
1,2,3	r_a	0.001	*handshake* rate (if attackers)	*Client, Attacker*
1,2,3	r_s	0.1	the server's *serve* rate	*Server*
1,2,3	r_d	5	the *disconnect* rate	*Client, Server*
1,2,3	r_t	0.01	a general *timeout* rate	*Client, Server*
3 only	r_d	0.5	*delay* rate	*Defender*
3 only	r_y	10	*eject* rate when under attack	*Defender*

Fig. 2. Parameters of the model

$$Server_{free} \stackrel{def}{=} (connect, r_c).Server_{claimed}$$
$$Server_{claimed} \stackrel{def}{=} (handshake, r_h).Server_{ready}$$
$$Server_{ready} \stackrel{def}{=} (serve, r_s).Server_{idle} + (timeout, r_t).Server_{free}$$
$$Server_{idle} \stackrel{def}{=} (disconnect, r_d).Server_{free}$$

Fig. 3. The *Server* component of the PEPA model

Figure 3 is the *Server* process, which, if viewed from an automata-theoretic perspective, would accept all and only the sentences of the formal language (*connect, handshake,* (*serve, disconnect*) | *timeout*)* and that of course means that the *Server* component can give rise to only two possible *traces*, which are

- (*connect*; *handshake*; *serve*; *disconnect*); or
- (*connect*; *handshake*; *timeout*).

Figure 4 shows the *Client* process, which, if viewed from an automata-theoretic perspective, would accept all and only the sentences of the formal language (*think, connect, handshake,* (*serve, disconnect*) | *timeout*)* and that of course means that the *Server* component can give rise to only two possible *traces*, which are

- (*think*; *connect*; *handshake*; *serve*; *disconnect*); or
- (*think*; *connect*; *handshake*; *timeout*).

In a normal interaction there is a two-stage connection, with the client first connecting to the server, and the server then confirming the connection with a handshake, before providing the required service. At the end of service the client disconnects, freeing the server. Between service interactions the client operates independently, indicated by the *think* action, appearing idle from the server's

$$Client_{idle} \stackrel{def}{=} (think, r_z). Client_{enter}$$

$$Client_{enter} \stackrel{def}{=} (connect, r_c). Client_{connected}$$

$$Client_{connected} \stackrel{def}{=} (handshake, r_h). Client_{waiting}$$

$$Client_{waiting} \stackrel{def}{=} (disconnect, r_d). Client_{idle}$$
$$+ (timeout, r_t). Client_{enter}$$

Fig. 4. The *Client* component of the PEPA model

perspective. To guard against dropped connections and other communication difficulties there is also the possibility for the server to timeout a connection which seems inactive. The components are combined as:

$$System_0 \stackrel{def}{=} Server_{free}[200] \underset{\mathcal{L}}{\bowtie} Client_{idle}[1000]$$
$$\text{where } \mathcal{L} = \{ \ connect, handshake, disconnect, timeout \ \}.$$

The use of array notation syntax in PEPA (say, for example, $P[2]$) indicates a PEPA component *array*, which is syntactic sugar for $P \parallel P$, which is itself syntactic sugar for $P \underset{L}{\bowtie} P$ when L, the *cooperation set*, is $\emptyset$ (meaning the empty set, as usual).

The behaviour of $System_0$, with the rate parameters given in Fig. 2, is shown in Fig. 5.

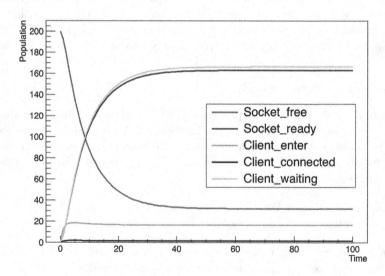

Fig. 5. The evolution of $System_0$ with the rate parameters given in Fig. 2

$$
\begin{aligned}
Attacker_{idle} &\stackrel{def}{=} (connect, r_c).Attacker_{connected} \\
Attacker_{connected} &\stackrel{def}{=} (handshake, r_a).Attacker_{hold} \\
Attacker_{hold} &\stackrel{def}{=} (timeout, r_t).Attacker_{idle} + (disconnect, r_d).Attacker_{idle}
\end{aligned}
$$

Fig. 6. The *Attacker* component of the PEPA model

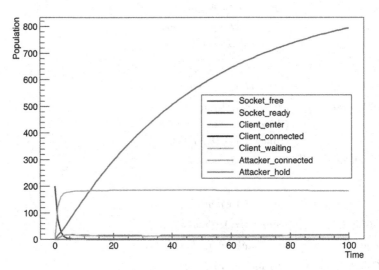

Fig. 7. The evolution of $System_1$ incorporating 250 attackers with the rate parameters given in Fig. 2

5.3   Second Model: Adding the Attackers

The objective of the attackers is to occupy the server for as long as possible so that it is unable to undertake any genuine service interactions. We might say that the attackers are 'tricking' the server. In any case, the semantics are very clear: the attacker initiates the protocol for requesting server-side computation masquerading as a genuine client. Only the initial part of the protocol is executed by the attacker: specifically, the sequential composition of actions which is (*connect*; *handshake*). The attacker has no intention of executing the second part of the protocol which performs the server-side computation cleanly (*serve*; *disconnect*). Moreover, in contrast to the *brisk* handshake of the genuine client, the attacker uses a *slow* handshake at a slower rate, r_a. Note that, *any* additional delay is of interest to the attacker because it impedes the progress of the genuine clients, and that is the attacker's priority. The behaviour of the attacker is shown in Fig. 6. The revised system becomes:

$$Server_{free} \stackrel{def}{=} (connect, r_c).Server_{claimed}$$

$$Server_{claimed} \stackrel{def}{=} (handshake, r_h).Server_{ready}$$

$$Server_{ready} \stackrel{def}{=} (serve, r_s).Server_{idle}$$
$$+ (timeout, r_t).Server_{free}$$
$$+ (eject, r_e).Server_{free}$$

$$Server_{idle} \stackrel{def}{=} (disconnect, r_d).Server_{free}$$
$$+ (eject, r_e).Server_{free}$$

$$Defender \stackrel{def}{=} (connect, r_c).Defender_1$$

$$Defender_1 \stackrel{def}{=} (delay, r_y).Defender_2$$
$$+ (disconnect, r_d).Defender$$
$$+ (timeout, r_t).Defender$$

$$Defender_2 \stackrel{def}{=} (eject, r_e).Defender$$

$$Client_{idle} \stackrel{def}{=} (think, r_z).Client_{enter}$$

$$Client_{enter} \stackrel{def}{=} (connect, r_c).Client_{connected}$$

$$Client_{connected} \stackrel{def}{=} (handshake, r_h).Client_{waiting}$$

$$Client_{waiting} \stackrel{def}{=} (disconnect, r_d).Client_{idle}$$
$$+ (timeout, r_t).Client_{enter}$$
$$+ (eject, r_e).Client_{idle}$$

$$Attacker_{idle} \stackrel{def}{=} (connect, r_c).Attacker_{connected}$$

$$Attacker_{connected} \stackrel{def}{=} (handshake, r_a).Attacker_{hold}$$

$$Attacker_{hold} \stackrel{def}{=} (timeout, r_t).Attacker_{idle}$$
$$+ (disconnect, r_d).Attacker_{idle}$$
$$+ (eject, r_e).Attacker_{idle}$$

$$System_2 \stackrel{def}{=} (Server_{free}[200] \underset{\mathcal{L}_1}{\bowtie} Defender[200])$$
$$\underset{\mathcal{L}_2}{\bowtie} (Client_{idle}[1000] \parallel Attacker_{idle})$$
$$\text{where } \mathcal{L}_1 = \{ connect, disconnect, timeout, eject \}$$
$$\text{and } \mathcal{L}_2 = \{ connect, handshake, disconnect, timeout, eject \}.$$

Fig. 8. Modified model containing the DDoS defence

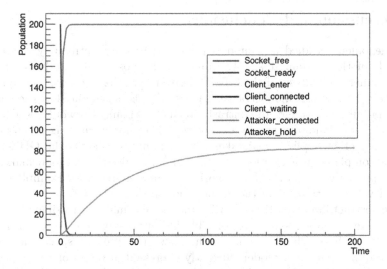

Fig. 9. The evolution of $System_2$ incorporating defence mechanisms with the rate parameters given in Fig. 2

$$System_1 \stackrel{def}{=} Server_{free}[200] \bowtie_{\mathcal{L}} Client_{idle}[1000]$$
$$\text{where } \mathcal{L} = \{ \, connect, handshake, disconnect, timeout \, \}.$$

The behaviour of $System_1$, with the attackers incorporated and with the rate parameters given in Fig. 2, is shown in Fig. 7. In contrast to the behaviour seen in Fig. 5, we can see that the system does not reach a steady state behaviour, as a growing number of clients are in the state waiting for connection to the server. It can be seen that very quickly after the start of the attack, most of the sockets are held by an attacker, leaving almost no capacity for the genuine clients.

5.4   Third Model: Adding the Defenders

In order to defend against the DDoS attack we introduce a *Defender* which monitors each socket. When a connection appears to be consuming too much time it ejects the connection, allowing a fresh competition for connection between attackers and clients. The new model is shown in Fig. 8. Note that the *delay* in the *Defender* is raced against the on-going socket connection and aborts the interaction if the *delay* completes before either a *disconnect* or a *timeout*.

The results of analysis of the model are shown in Fig. 9 with all parameters values as shown in Fig. 2, i.e., the characteristics of the servers, users and attackers are unchanged except for the addition of the rapid *eject* action. We can see that the attackers are still successful in gaining access to the server, but there is much more turnover meaning that clients are also able to gain connections. This is evident because the number of clients in the $Client_{enter}$ state, waiting to form a connection, is significantly reduced compared to the growing value in Fig. 7.

6   Discussion and Conclusions

The phenomena studied and models presented here are intimately related to the scale of the system. It simply would not be possible to study the model with a numerical analysis of the CTMC derived from the discrete-state concrete semantics of the PEPA models because the state spaces generated by these models are prohibitively large. In contrast, stochastic simulation would be possible but much more computationally expensive. For example, running a simulation of $System_2$ (1000 replications) takes several minutes whereas the ODE-based analysis completes in a fraction of a second. This speed of solution makes the ODE-approach very suitable for exploring parameter space, for example to find the best value for the rate of the *delay* action in the *Defender*.

The abstract interpretation of PEPA models also makes it feasible to address the problem of model synthesis. In [30] the authors present an extension to the PEPA Eclipse Plug-in tool, which allows the user to specify a performance requirement for a model, currently expressed in terms of response time or throughput. From this specification the tool automatically searches parameter space to find the "smallest" model which is able to satisfy the performance requirement. Here "smallest" is essentially taken to mean the smallest number of components, but a user-defined cost function allows the modeller to weight different types of components differently (see [30] for details). The particle swarm optimisation (PSO) meta-heuristic [31] is used to efficiently explore parameter space. Nevertheless this approach would not be tractable if based on the discrete-state space representation of the PEPA models except for very small models.

Acknowledgements. This work is supported by the EU project QUANTICOL, 600708. The authors thank Mirco Tribastone for useful discussions.

References

1. Yüksel, E., Nielson, H.R., Nielson, F.: Key update assistant for resource-constrained networks. In: 2012 IEEE Symposium on Computers and Communications, ISCC 2012, Cappadocia, 1–4 July 2012, pp. 75–81. IEEE (2012)
2. Nielson, F., Nielson, H.R., Zeng, K.: Stochastic model checking of the stochastic quality calculus. In: De Nicola, R., Hennicker, R. (eds.) Wirsing Festschrift. LNCS, vol. 8950, pp. 522–537. Springer, Heidelberg (2015)
3. Hillston, J.: The benefits of sometimes not being discrete. In: Baldan, P., Gorla, D. (eds.) CONCUR 2014. LNCS, vol. 8704, pp. 7–22. Springer, Heidelberg (2014)
4. Hillston, J.: A Compositional Approach to Performance Modelling. Cambridge University Press, New York (1996)
5. Yang, F.: Static Analysis of Stochastic Process Algebras. MSc dissertation (2007)
6. Cousot, P.: Abstract interpretation based formal methods and future challenges. In: Wilhelm, R. (ed.) Informatics: 10 Years Back, 10 Years Ahead. LNCS, vol. 2000, p. 138. Springer, Heidelberg (2001)
7. Hillston, J.: Fluid flow approximation of PEPA models. In: Proceedings of the Second International Conference on the Quantitative Evaluation of Systems, pp. 33–43. IEEE Computer Society Press, Torino, September 2005

8. Danos, V., Feret, J., Fontana, W., Krivine, J.: Abstract interpretation of cellular signalling networks. In: Logozzo, F., Peled, D.A., Zuck, L.D. (eds.) VMCAI 2008. LNCS, vol. 4905, pp. 83–97. Springer, Heidelberg (2008)
9. Vigo, R., Nielson, F., Nielson, H.R.: Broadcast, denial-of-service, and secure communication. In: Johnsen, E.B., Petre, L. (eds.) IFM 2013. LNCS, vol. 7940, pp. 412–427. Springer, Heidelberg (2013)
10. Wang, S., Nielson, F., Nielson, H.R.: A framework for hybrid systems with denial-of-service security attack. CoRR, abs/1403.6367 (2014)
11. Wang, S., Nielson, F., Nielson, H.R.: Denial-of-service security attack in the continuous-time world. In: Ábrahám, E., Palamidessi, C. (eds.) FORTE 2014. LNCS, vol. 8461, pp. 149–165. Springer, Heidelberg (2014)
12. Nielson, H.R., Nielson, F., Vigo, R.: A calculus for quality. In: Păsăreanu, C.S., Salaün, G. (eds.) FACS 2012. LNCS, vol. 7684, pp. 188–204. Springer, Heidelberg (2013)
13. Zeng, K., Nielson, F., Nielson, H.R.: The stochastic quality calculus. In: Kühn, E., Pugliese, R. (eds.) COORDINATION 2014. LNCS, vol. 8459, pp. 179–193. Springer, Heidelberg (2014)
14. Buchholtz, M., Gilmore, S., Hillston, J., Nielson, F.: Securing statically-verified communications protocols against timing attacks. In: Bradley, J., Knottenbelt, W. (eds.) Proceedings of the First International Workshop on Practical Applications of Stochastic Modelling, pp. 61–79. England, London (2004)
15. Clark, A., Gilmore, S., Hillston, J., Tribastone, M.: Stochastic process algebras. In: Bernardo, M., Hillston, J. (eds.) SFM 2007. LNCS, vol. 4486, pp. 132–179. Springer, Heidelberg (2007)
16. Gilmore, S., Tribastone, M.: Evaluating the scalability of a Web service-based distributed e-learning and course management system. In: Bravetti, M., Núñez, M., Zavattaro, G. (eds.) WS-FM 2006. LNCS, vol. 4184, pp. 214–226. Springer, Heidelberg (2006)
17. Bravetti, M., Gilmore, S., Guidi, C., Tribastone, M.: Replicating Web services for scalability. In: Barthe, G., Fournet, C. (eds.) TGC 2007. LNCS, vol. 4912, pp. 204–221. Springer, Heidelberg (2008)
18. Cappello, I., Clark, A., Gilmore, S., Latella, D., Loreti, M., Quaglia, P., Schivo, S.: Quantitative analysis of services. In: Wirsing, M., Hölzl, M. (eds.) SENSORIA. LNCS, vol. 6582, pp. 522–540. Springer, Heidelberg (2011)
19. Tribastone, M., Gilmore, S.: Automatic extraction of PEPA performance models from UML activity diagrams annotated with the MARTE profile. In: Proceedings of the 7th International Workshop on Software and Performance (WOSP2008), pp. 67–78. ACM Press, Princeton (2008)
20. Tribastone, M., Gilmore, S.: Automatic translation of UML sequence diagrams into PEPA models. In: 5th International Conference on the Quantitative Evaluation of Systems (QEST 2008), pp. 205–214. IEEE Computer Society Press, St Malo (2008)
21. Zhao, Y., Thomas, N.: Approximate solution of a PEPA model of a key distribution centre. In: Kounev, S., Gorton, I., Sachs, K. (eds.) SIPEW 2008. LNCS, vol. 5119, pp. 44–57. Springer, Heidelberg (2008)
22. Bradley, J.T., Gilmore, S., Hillston, J.: Analysing distributed Internet worm attacks using continuous state-space approximation of process algebra models. J. Comput. Syst. Sci. **74**(6), 1013–1032 (2008)
23. Duguid, A.: Coping with the parallelism of BitTorrent: conversion of PEPA to ODEs in dealing with state space explosion. In: Asarin, E., Bouyer, P. (eds.) FORMATS 2006. LNCS, vol. 4202, pp. 156–170. Springer, Heidelberg (2006)

24. Hillston, J.: Fluid flow approximation of PEPA models. In: Second International Conference on the Quantitative Evaluaiton of Systems (QEST 2005), 19–22 September 2005, pp. 33–43. IEEE Computer Society, Torino (2005)
25. Kurtz, T.G.: Solutions of ordinary differential equations as limits of pure jump markov processes. J. Appl. Probab. **7**, 49–58 (1970)
26. Tribastone, M., Gilmore, S., Hillston, J.: Scalable differential analysis of process algebra models. IEEE Trans. Softw. Eng. **38**(1), 205–219 (2012)
27. Tribastone, M., Ding, J., Gilmore, S., Hillston, J.: Fluid rewards for a stochastic process algebra. IEEE Trans. Softw. Eng. **38**(4), 861–874 (2012)
28. Gilmore, S., Hillston, J., Ribaudo, M.: An efficient algorithm for aggregating PEPA models. IEEE Trans. Softw. Eng. **27**(5), 449–464 (2001)
29. Tribastone, M., Duguid, A., Gilmore, S.: The PEPA eclipse plug-in. Perform. Eval. Rev. **36**(4), 28–33 (2009)
30. Williams, C.D., Hillston, J.: Automated capacity planning for PEPA models. In: Horváth, A., Wolter, K. (eds.) EPEW 2014. LNCS, vol. 8721, pp. 209–223. Springer, Heidelberg (2014)
31. Poli, R., Kennedy, J., Blackwell, T.: Particle swarm optimization; an overview. Swarm Intell. **1**(1), 33–57 (2007)

Static Analysis of Parity Games:
Alternating Reachability Under Parity

Michael Huth[1]([✉]), Jim Huan-Pu Kuo[1], and Nir Piterman[2]

[1] Department of Computing, Imperial College London, London SW7 2AZ, UK
{m.huth,jimhkuo}@imperial.ac.uk
[2] Department of Computer Science, University of Leicester, Leicester LE1 7RH, UK
nir.piterman@leicester.ac.uk

Abstract. It is well understood that solving parity games is equivalent, up to polynomial time, to model checking of the modal mu-calculus. It is a long-standing open problem whether solving parity games (or model checking modal mu-calculus formulas) can be done in polynomial time. A recent approach to studying this problem has been the design of *partial solvers*, algorithms that run in polynomial time and that may only solve *parts* of a parity game. Although it was shown that such partial solvers can completely solve many practical benchmarks, the design of such partial solvers was somewhat ad hoc, limiting a deeper understanding of the potential of that approach. We here mean to provide such robust foundations for deeper analysis through a new form of game, *alternating reachability under parity*. We prove the determinacy of these games and use this determinacy to define, for each player, a monotone fixed point over an ordered domain of height linear in the size of the parity game such that all nodes in its greatest fixed point are won by said player in the parity game. We show, through theoretical and experimental work, that such greatest fixed points and their computation leads to partial solvers that run in polynomial time. These partial solvers are based on established principles of static analysis and are more effective than partial solvers studied in extant work.

1 Introduction

Model checking [9,24] is an approach to formal methods in which a system is represented as a model M, system behavior of interest is represented as a formula ϕ of a suitable temporal logic, and the question of whether the model satisfies that property (written $M \models \phi$) is decided using an algorithm parametric in M and ϕ. For infinite models, this question often is undecidable and may therefore require the abstraction of models to finite ones [2].

Program analyses (see e.g. [23]) consider programs P and aim to answer questions such as "Are there portions of code in P that can never be reached during execution?". Since exact answers may be undecidable, abstraction is often used to under-approximate or over-approximate such answers, for example, the set of program points that can never be reached. Many program analyses can be

© Springer International Publishing Switzerland 2016
C.W. Probst et al. (Eds.): Nielsons' Festschrift, LNCS 9560, pp. 159–177, 2016.
DOI: 10.1007/978-3-319-27810-0_8

computed by a static analysis that computes a least fixed point of a monotone function over a complete lattice; see for example Chapter 6 in [23] for more details on this approach based on worklist algorithms.

These two approaches, model checking and static analysis, appear to be quite different even though they share the need for abstraction. For example, it is not immediately clear whether each program analysis might correspond to a property ϕ of some suitable logic. But there is a body of research that points out a close relationship and connections between these approaches. For example, in [26] it is shown how data-flow analyses can be seen as instances of model checking: if programs are represented as models of a modal logic, one can capture a data-flow analysis as a formula in that modal logic, and then partially evaluate the model checker for that logic to thus implement the data-flow analyzer. This insight led to an actual methodology: in [25] one converts a program into a transition system as program model – using its operational semantics, then applies abstraction [3,4] to eliminate details of that model that are irrelevant to the analysis/formula in question, and finally one can do model checking on the abstract model using formulas that capture the analysis in question.

These contributions furthered the understanding of how program analysis can be seen within the framework of model checking. Conversely, it turns out that the central question of model checking, whether $M \models \phi$ holds, can be computed with techniques from static analysis. In [22], an alternation-free fixed-point logic was defined and it was shown how static analysis over the resulting flow logic can decide model-checking instances for modal logics such as computation tree logic (CTL) [9]. The flow logic in [22] was also demonstrated to have applications in data-flow analysis and constraint solving [11]. In later work [28], this alternation-free least fixed-point logic was extended so that one could capture model checking of the modal mu-calculus [18] (not just of CTL) in this manner, and a Moore family result was proved for this logic; Moore families are the set of closed sets of a closure operator.

The temporal logic CTL and the linear-time temporal logic LTL can be seen as subsets of the temporal logic CTL* (see e.g. [15]). The logic CTL* can in turn be embedded into the modal mu-calculus [5], although at an exponential cost [19]. LTL and CTL capture many practically important property patterns [7] and are therefore very useful. But some have argued that these logics are mathematically somewhat ad hoc. The modal mu-calculus, on the other hand, is more canonical since it does not limit the manner in which fixed-point patterns can be composed (apart from syntactic restrictions that ensure monotonicity of meaning). It is therefore apt to understand the connections between static analysis and model checking over the modal mu-calculus as well, and the work reported in [28] shows how static analysis in the form of flow logics can capture model checking of the modal mu-calculus.

There is another important aspect to the study of such connections though. It is well understood [8,10,27] that model checking of the modal mu-calculus is equivalent (within polynomial time) to the solving of parity games. These are directed graphs whose nodes are owned by one of two players and colored by a natural number. In this chapter, we assume that such graphs are finite. Plays between these players generate infinite paths in these graphs whose winners are decided by minimal colors of cycles generated by these paths. A player wins a node if she can play such that all plays beginning in that node are won by her in this manner. A central result for parity games states that these games are determined [8,21,29]: each node is won by exactly one of the two players. Deciding which player wins which nodes, and how they can achieve these wins is what one means by solving parity games.

Using the aforementioned results in [8,10,27], we can therefore understand how to use static analysis for model checking by understanding how static analyses may solve parity games. Known approaches of solving parity games in this manner, for example the ones based on *small progress measures* [17], all suffer from the fact that the height of the ordered domain derived from the parity game may be exponentially larger than that game – leading to exponential worst-case running times of least fixed-point computations in the resulting worklist algorithm that implements a static analysis. In fact, the decision problem of whether a given node in a parity game is won by a given player is in UP ∩ coUP [16], and its exact complexity has been an open problem for over twenty years now.

The work that we report here means to combine static analysis with *abstraction*. The analyses we design below run in polynomial time by construction. But this efficiency is gained by possibly *under-approximating* the solution of a parity game: the used static analysis may not decide the winners of all (or indeed some) nodes although they often solve games completely. Furthermore, in *local* modal checking (see e.g. [27]) it suffices to know whether one or several designated states satisfy a property. In the setting of parity games, this means that it may suffice to statically decide the winner of one or several nodes – which the static analyses we present here may often achieve.

Outline of Chapter: In Sect. 2, we recall background on parity games. Our new type of alternating reachability game is defined and studied in Sect. 3. In Sect. 4, we show how this game induces monotone functions for each player of a parity game, and that we can use these functions to build static analyses of parity games that repeatedly compute greatest fixed points of such functions on (residual) games. We discuss, in Sect. 5, how this approach generalizes our earlier work on fatal attractors in [13]. Our experimental results are reported in Sect. 6, related work not discussed above already is presented in Sect. 7, and the chapter concludes in Sect. 8.

2   Background

In this section, we define key concepts of parity games, and fix technical notation used in this chapter. We write $\mathbb{N}$ for the set $\{0, 1, \dots\}$ of natural numbers. A parity game G is a tuple (V, V_0, V_1, E, c), where V is a set of nodes partitioned into possibly empty node sets V_0 and V_1, with an edge relation $E \subseteq V \times V$ (where for all v in V there is a w in V with (v, w) in E), and a coloring function

$c\colon V \to \mathbb{N}$. In figures, $c(v)$ is written within nodes v, nodes in V_0 are depicted as circles and nodes in V_1 as squares. For v in V, we write $v.E$ for node set $\{w \in V \mid (v,w) \in E\}$ of successors of v. Below we write $\mathsf{C}(G)$ for the set of colors in game G, i.e. $\mathsf{C}(G) = \{c(v) \mid v \in V\}$, and $\mathsf{C}(G)_\perp$ for set $\mathsf{C}(G) \cup \{\perp\}$.

Throughout, we write p (or sometimes p') for one of 0 or 1 and $1-p$ for the other player. In a parity game, player p owns the nodes in V_p. A play from some node v_0 results in an infinite play $\pi = v_0 v_1 \ldots$ in (V, E) where the player who owns v_i chooses the successor v_{i+1} such that (v_i, v_{i+1}) is in E. Let $\mathsf{Inf}(\pi)$ be the set of colors that occur in π infinitely often:

$$\mathsf{Inf}(\pi) = \{k \in \mathbb{N} \mid \forall j \in \mathbb{N}\colon \exists i \in \mathbb{N}\colon i > j \text{ and } k = c(v_i)\}$$

Player 0 wins play π iff $\min \mathsf{Inf}(\pi)$ is even; otherwise player 1 wins play r.

A strategy for player p is a total function $\sigma_p\colon V^* \cdot V_p \to V$ where the pair $(v, \sigma_p(w \cdot v))$ is in E for all v in V_p and w in V^*. A play π conforms with σ_p if for every finite prefix $v_0 \ldots v_i$ of π with v_i in V_p we have $v_{i+1} = \sigma_p(v_0 \ldots v_i)$. A strategy σ_p is memoryless if for all w, w' in V^* and v in V_p we have $\sigma_p(w \cdot v) = \sigma_p(w' \cdot v)$ and such a σ_p can be seen to have type $V_p \to V$.

It is well known that each parity game is determined [8,21,29]: (i) node set V is the disjoint union of two, possibly empty, sets W_0 and W_1, the winning regions of players 0 and 1 (respectively); and (ii) there are memoryless strategies σ_0 and σ_1 such that all plays beginning in W_0 and conforming with σ_0 are won by player 0, and all plays beginning in W_1 and conforming with σ_1 are won by player 1. Solving a parity game means computing such data $(W_0, W_1, \sigma_0, \sigma_1)$.

Throughout this chapter, we write G for a parity game (V, V_0, V_1, E, c), denote by p one of its players, and let X be a non-empty set of nodes of G. We write $x\%2$ for x modulo 2 for an integer x, and $\mathsf{Attr}_p[G, X]$ to denote the attractor of node set X for player p, which computes the standard alternating reachability of X for that player in the game graph of G (see e.g. Definition 1 in [13]).

Example 1. In the parity game G depicted in Fig. 1, the winning regions are $W_1 = \{\}$ and $W_0 = V$. The memoryless strategy σ_0, defined by $\sigma_0(v_1) = v_2$, is a winning strategy for player 0 on W_0.

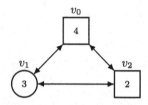

Fig. 1. A parity game: circles denote nodes in V_0, squares denote nodes in V_1.

3   Alternating Reachability Under Parity

In this section, we generalize alternating reachability in parity game graphs, so that this reachability is aware of minimal colors encountered en route:

Definition 1. *Given parity game G, player p, and non-empty node set X, let $\pi = v_0 v_1 \ldots$ be an infinite play in G.*

1. *Player p wins play π in the* reachability game for (X, p) under parity *iff there is some $j > 0$ such that v_j is in X and $\min(\{c(v_i) \mid 0 \leq i \leq j\})\%2 = p$. Dually, player $1 - p$ wins play π in that reachability game iff she detracts from (X, p) under parity, that is to say iff for all $j > 0$ we have that v_j in X implies that $\min(\{c(v_i) \mid 0 \leq i \leq j\})\%2 = 1 - p$.*
2. *A strategy for player p' in this game is defined like a strategy for that player in the parity game G. Also, the definition of when plays conform with strategies in this game is the same as for parity game G.*
3. *Player p' wins a node v for reachability of (X, p) under parity iff she has a strategy $\sigma_{p'}$ such that all plays starting from v and conforming to $\sigma_{p'}$ are winning for player p' in the reachability game for (X, p) under parity.*
4. *We write $\mathsf{W}_r^p(G, X)$ for the set of nodes that player p wins in this manner (we won't need notation for the set of nodes won by player $1 - p$).*

This acceptance condition binds p to X: it is player p who wants to reach (X, p) under parity. Also, starting from X in a play does not yet mean that X has been reached. In particular, player $1-p$ wins all plays that don't visit X after the initial node. An immediate question is whether such games are determined and how complex it is to solve them. We answer these questions next.

Lemma 1. *For all parity games G, players p, and non-empty node sets X, the derived game in G of reaching (X, p) under parity is determined.*

Proof. For a color i in $\mathsf{C}(G)$ and node set $S \subseteq V$ let $S_i = \{v \in S \mid c(v) = i\}$ and $S_{\geq i} = \{v \in S \mid c(v) \geq i\}$. Also, let $C = \{c \in \mathsf{C}(G) \mid c\%2 = p\}$. The set of winning plays for player p in the reachability game for (X, p) under parity is the union of $(V_{\geq i}^* \cdot V_i \cdot V_{\geq i}^* \cdot X_{\geq i} \cdot V^\omega) \cup (V_{\geq i}^+ \cdot X_i \cdot V^\omega)$ over all i in C. Note that, for each such i, both expressions in this union capture the non-deterministic choice of reaching X in Definition 1. The difference in these expressions is merely that the minimal color i may be witnessed before that non-deterministic choice of reaching X. The set of winning plays for player p is thus a Borel definable set of paths. From the Borel determinacy of turn-based games [20] it therefore follows that the game is determined. $\square$

Next, we derive from parity game G and node set X a game graph that reduces reachability of (X, p) under parity to (the usual alternating) reachability in the derived game graph. This derived game has nodes of form (v, l) where l records the history of the minimal color encountered so far. In particular, we use $l = \bot$ to model that a play is just beginning.

Definition 2. *For parity game* $G = (V, V_0, V_1, E, c)$, *player* p, *and non-empty node set* X, *game graph* $G_X^p = (V \times C(G)_\perp, E')$ *is defined as follows: For* c *in* $C(G)_\perp$, *player 0 owns all nodes* (v, c) *with* $v \in V_0$. *Player 1 owns all nodes* (v, c) *with* $v \in V_1$. *And the edge relation* $E' \subseteq (V \times C(G)_\perp) \times (V \times C(G)_\perp)$ *is defined as*

$$E' = \{((v, \perp), (v', \min(c(v), c(v')))) \mid (v, v') \in E\} \cup \qquad (1)$$
$$\{((v, c), (v', \min(c, c(v')))) \mid (v, v') \in E, c \in C(G), (v \notin X \text{ or } c\%2 \neq p)\}$$

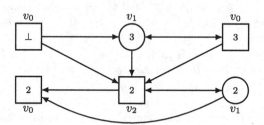

Fig. 2. Game graph G_X^p for G from Fig. 1 and X being $\{v_0\}$; only nodes and edges reachable (in non-alternating sense) from $X \times \{\perp\}$ in G_X^p are shown, as this is all that is needed for deciding which nodes in X are contained in $W_r^p(G, X)$. The winning strategy for player 0 requires her to make different choices from the same nodes of G when they are combined with different colors: player 0 needs to move from $(v_1, 3)$ to $(v_2, 2)$ and from $(v_1, 2)$ to $(v_0, 2)$ in G_X^p

Note that relation E' is even contained in $(V \times C(G)_\perp) \times (V \times C(G))$ and contains dead ends (nodes that don't have outgoing edges in the game graph). The latter is not an issue since all dead ends in G_X^p are target nodes for the alternating reachability in G_X^p. Figures 2 and 3 show examples of this construction.

The intuition of game graph G_X^p is that player p can win node v in G for reaching (X, p) under parity iff player p can win the (alternating) reachability game in G_X^p for target set $X \times \{c \in C(G) \mid c\%2 = p\}$. We state this formally:

Theorem 1. *For* G *and* G_X^p *as above, let* Z *be* $X \times \{c \in C(G), c\%2 = p\}$ *and* W *be* $\{v \in V \mid (v, \perp) \in \text{Attr}_p(G_X^p, Z)\}$. *Then* W *is the winning region of player* p *in* G *for reachability of* (X, p) *under parity.*

Proof. First, let $W_p = W_r^p(G, X)$ be the winning region of player p in G for reachability of (X, p) under parity. Since this game has a Borel defined winning condition, there exists a strategy $\tau \colon V^* \times V_p \to V$ such that all plays conforming with τ and starting in W_p are won by player p for reachability of (X, p) under parity.

We write τ' for the same strategy but applied to G_X^p whilst ignoring the second component of nodes in G_X^p. (We note that E' updates the second component of nodes in G_X^p deterministically.) Consider a play π in G_X^p that starts in

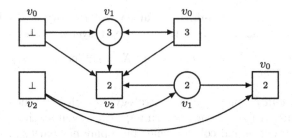

Fig. 3. Game graph G^p_X for G from Fig. 1 and X being $\{v_0, v_2\}$. As in Fig. 2, only nodes and edges reachable (in non-alternating sense) from $X \times \{\bot\}$ in G^p_X are shown. The winning strategy for player 0 allows her to make choices that do not depend on the color annotating the states. She can move from (v_1, c) to $(v_2, 2)$ regardless of the value of c.

$W_p \times \{\bot\}$ and conforms with τ'. The projection of π onto the first components of its nodes is a play in G that starts in W_p and conforms with τ. Therefore, that play is won by player p in G, and so it is also won by player p in G^p_X.

Second, it remains to show that $\{v \mid (v, \bot) \in \mathsf{Attr}_p(G^p_X, Z)\}$ is contained in W_p. Let δ' be a winning (attractor) strategy for player p in G^p_X for the attractor $\mathsf{Attr}_p(G^p_X, Z)$. As an attractor strategy, δ' is memoryless. That is, for every node $(v, c) \in V_p \times \mathsf{C}(G)_\bot$ we can write $\delta'(v, c)$ and this is in $V \times \mathsf{C}(G)$. For a sequence of nodes $\pi = v_0, \ldots, v_n$, let $c(\pi)$ denote $\min\{c(v_i) \mid 0 \le i \le n\}$. Let $\delta \colon V^* \cdot V_p \to V$ be the strategy obtained from δ' by setting $\delta(\pi \cdot v) = \delta'(v, c(\pi \cdot v))$. Then δ is a strategy in G. Every play that begins in $W = \{v \mid (v, \bot) \in \mathsf{Attr}_p(G^p_X, Z)\}$ and conforms with δ in G can be extended to a play in G^p_X that begins in $\mathsf{Attr}_p(G^p_X, Z)$ and conforms with δ' by adding the deterministic second components. Therefore, this play is winning for player p in G^p_X. It follows from the construction of E' that player p reaches X from $W = \{v \mid (v, \bot) \in \mathsf{Attr}_p(G^p_X, Z)\}$ such that the minimal color encountered on the way in G has parity p. □

This theorem also gives us an upper bound on the complexity of solving games for reachability of (X, p) under parity, noting that alternating reachability is linear in the number of edges of the game graph, and that G^p_X has at most $|E| \cdot |\mathsf{C}(G)|$ many edges.

Corollary 1. *For G, p, and X as above, the reachability game in G for (X, p) under parity can be solved in time $O(|E| \cdot |\mathsf{C}(G)|)$.*

We later consider the issue of whether memoryless strategies suffice for winning in G for reachability of (X, p) under parity (they do not). However, from the proof of Theorem 1 it follows that the size of memory required is bounded by the number of colors in the game (plus 1).

4   Monotone Functions for a Partial Solver

Let player p win node v for reaching (X, p) under parity in G. Then player p can make sure that X is reached from v, and that X can be reached from v such that the minimal color encountered so far has color parity p. If all nodes in X are won by player p, node set X is then won by player p in the parity game G:

Lemma 2. *For all G, X, and p such that X is contained in $W_r^p(G, X)$, player p wins all nodes from X in parity game G.*

Proof. For each v in X, player p has a strategy σ_v with finite memory such that all plays beginning at node v and conforming with σ_v will reach again some node in X such that the minimal color of that finite play has parity p. Because X is contained in $W_r^p(G, X)$, player p can compose all these strategies to a strategy σ_p with finite memory as follows:

From v_0 in X, she plays conform with σ_{v_0} until a finite play $v_0 \ldots v_k$ is generated such that v_k is in X and $\min\{c(v_j) \mid 0 \le j \le k\}$ has color parity p. We know that such a finite subplay will be generated by σ_{v_0} as it is a winning strategy for player p witnessing that v is in $W_r^p(G, X)$. At node v_k, player p now continues to play conform with strategy σ_{v_k}. She can continue this composition pattern to generate an infinite play $\pi = v_0 \cdots v_k \cdots$ that is partitioned into infinitely many finite sub-plays $(\pi^i)_{i \ge 0}$ that begin and end in X (and may contain other nodes in X) and that each have some minimal color c_i with parity p.

Since G has only finitely many nodes, this means that all colors that occur infinitely often in π are greater than or equal to some color that occurs as minimal color in infinitely many sub-plays π^i (and so has parity p and also occurs infinitely often in π). Therefore, player p wins π in the parity game G and so the described strategy is also winning for player p on node set X in parity game G.   □

We now put this lemma to use by characterizing such winning node sets as fixed points of a monotone function. For that, let V^p be the (possibly empty) set of nodes of G that have color parity p, that is V^p equals $\{v \in V \mid c(v)\%2 = p\}$. Let us consider the function F_G^p, defined by

$$F_G^p \colon \mathbb{P}(V^p) \to \mathbb{P}(V^p), \qquad F_G^p(X) = X \cap W_r^p(G, X) \tag{2}$$

Lemma 2 then says, in particular, that all non-empty fixed points of F_G^p are node sets won by player p in parity game G. That function is monotone:

Lemma 3. *For all G and p, function F_G^p defined in (2) is monotone.*

Proof. Let X and Y be subsets of V^p such that X is contained in Y. We need to show that $F_G^p(X)$ is contained in $F_G^p(Y)$ as well. By definition of F_G^p, monotonicity follows if X or Y is empty. So let X and Y be non-empty. Since $X \subseteq Y$ and since intersection is monotone, it suffices to show that $W_r^p(G, X)$ is contained in $W_r^p(G, Y)$. So let v be in $W_r^p(G, X)$. Then player p has a winning strategy that ensures that all plays from node v reach X such that the minimal color encountered thus far has parity p. Since X is contained in Y, this means that all such plays will also reach Y with minimal color encountered en route. Therefore, the winning strategy for $v \in W_r^p(G, X)$ is also a winning strategy for $v \in W_r^p(G, Y)$, and so v is in $W_r^p(G, Y)$ as claimed.   □

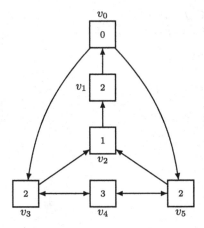

Fig. 4. Function F_G^0 is no longer always monotone when $W_r^p(G, X)$ has acceptance condition that looks at the minimal color of the prefix for the *first* reached element of X instead of a non-deterministically chosen first or future element of X. For G above and $X = \{v_3, v_5\}$ and $Y = V^0$, we would then have $X \subseteq Y$ but $F_G^0(X) = \{v_3, v_5\}$ would not be contained in $F_G^0(Y) = \{v_0, v_1\}$ under that modified acceptance condition

Neither the monotonicity of F_G^p nor the result of Lemma 2 depend on the fact that all nodes in X have color parity p, nor that anything is known about colors in X; for Lemma 2, it only matters that all nodes in X are also in $W_r^p(G, X)$. It is of interest to note that function F_G^p would not be monotone if we were to change the acceptance condition for reaching (X, p) under parity to mean that player p has to get minimal color parity p at the *first* time she reaches X after the first node in the play. Formally, player p would win a play π iff there were some $j > 0$ with π_j in X such that $\min\{c(\pi_i) \mid 0 \le i \le j\}\%2$ equals p *and* there were no k with $0 < k < j$ such that π_k would be in X. The resulting non-monotonicity of this modified acceptance condition is illustrated in Fig. 4.

Monotonicity of F_G^p means that either all its fixed points are empty or its greatest fixed point is non-empty. This suggests an algorithm that recursively computes such greatest fixed points for each player p, and removes non-empty ones as being recognized winning regions for player p from parity game G until either G is solved completely or both F_G^0 and F_G^1 have only empty fixed points. The pseudo-code for this algorithm psolC is shown in Fig. 5.

When a greatest fixed point is discovered for player p, the partial solver removes the p attractor of that fixed point in parity game G from G, not just the fixed point. This is sound since winning node sets for players in parity games are closed under attractors for those players. The pseudo-code does not show the accumulation of the removed node sets into winning regions, as these are routine administrative matters that only detract from the essence of this partial solver.

We show soundness and upper bounds on the complexity of psolC:

```
psolC(G = (V, V₀, V₁, E, c)) {
  W = tryPlayer(G, 0);
  if (W ≠ ∅) {
   return psolC(G \ W);
  } else {
    W = tryPlayer(G, 1);
    if (W ≠ ∅) {
      return psolC(G \ W);
    } else {
      return G;
    }
  }
}


tryPlayer(G, p) {
  X  =  fixedpoint(G, { v in V |  c(v)%2 = p }, p);
  if (X ≠ {}) { return Attrₚ[G, X]; }
  else { return ∅; }
}

fixedpoint(G, X, p) {
  W = V;
  repeat { X = X ∩ W;  W = X ∩  Wᵖᵣ(G, X); } until (X ⊆ W)
  return X;
}
```

Fig. 5. Partial solver psolC: in G^p_X, only $X \cap \mathsf{W}^p_r(G, X)$ needs to be computed. So this is implemented by only constructing nodes and edges in G^p_X that are reachable from $X \times \{\bot\}$ in the non-alternating sense

Theorem 2. *Let G be a parity game as above. Then* psolC(G) *runs in time* $O(|E| \cdot |\mathsf{C}(G)| \cdot |V|^2)$, *space* $O(|E| \cdot (1 + |\mathsf{C}(G)|))$, *and all node sets* Attr$_p[G, X]$ *it removes from (residual instances of) G are won by player p in the parity game G.*

Proof. Since $\mathsf{W}^p_r(G, X)$ can be computed in $O(|E| \cdot |\mathsf{C}(G)|)$, each fixed-point computation in psolC(G) runs in $O(|E| \cdot |\mathsf{C}(G)| \cdot |V|)$ as it can have at most $|V|$ iterations. But there can also be at most $2 \cdot |V|$ many such fixed-point computations in total as each subsequent such computation requires that at least one node has been removed from G beforehand.

The upper bound on the space complexity follows since the size of G^p_X is the dominating factor for space requirements of psolC – larger than the size of G, since there are at most $|E| \cdot (1 + |\mathsf{C}(G)|))$ many edges in G^p_X, and since there is no need to keep copies of G^p_X once $X \cap \mathsf{W}^p_r(G, X)$ has been computed in psolC.

The remaining soundness claim for partial solver psolC directly follows from Lemma 2 and from the aforementioned fact that winning regions of players in parity games are closed under attractors of those players. The latter also ensures that winning regions of recursive instances of G are winning regions of G. □

It turns out that reachability of (X, p) under parity cannot be solved with memoryless strategies in general, in contrast to the solving of parity games:

Theorem 3. *Solving alternating reachability under parity requires finite memory in general.*

Proof. It suffices to give an example where this is the case. Recall the simple parity game G from Fig. 1. Let p be 0 and X be $\{v_0\}$. Then $W_r^0(G, X)$ equals V and so player 0 wins all nodes for reachability of $(X, 0)$ under parity. But she cannot realize this with a *memoryless* strategy σ_0, for either $\sigma_0(v_1)$ would equal v_2 (and then player 1 can detract from X by moving from v_2 back to v_1) or $\sigma_0(v_1)$ would have to equal v_0 (in which case player 1 can move from v_0 to v_1 to generate an infinite play in which all prefixes that reach X have odd color 3). Let the strategy $\sigma_0' : V^* \cdot \{v_1\} \to V$ be defined, for all w in V^*, by $\sigma_0'(w \cdot v_1) = v_0$ if v_2 is in w; and $\sigma_0'(w \cdot v_1) = v_2$ otherwise. Strategy σ_0' has finite memory and is winning on all nodes for reachability of $(X, 0)$ under parity: σ_0' ensures that v_0 is reached, and that v_0 is reached only after v_2 has been reached. This means that the minimal color encountered until X is reached equals 2, a win for player 0.   □

The implication of Theorem 3 is that even though `psolC` identifies winning regions in the parity game the strategies that it allows us to construct, in general, require memory. At the same time, we know that there exist memoryless strategies for both players from their respective winning regions in the parity game.

Although finite memory is required in general, we note that $Y = V^0$ is the greatest fixed point of F_0^G for G from Fig. 1, and that the memoryless strategy σ_0 above *is* winning for $W_r^0(G, Y) = V$. This raises the question of whether non-empty greatest fixed points of F_G^p ever require corresponding winning strategies *with* finite memory or whether they always can be memoryless. This is also apparent in the derived games G_X^0 and X_Y^0 depicted in Figs. 2 and 3, respectively. We formulate this problem as a research question:

Question 1. Is there a parity game G and player p where the greatest fixed point X of F_G^p is non-empty and player p does not have memoryless strategies for witnessing that X is contained in $W_r^p(G, X)$?

If no finite memory is needed for greatest fixed points of F_G^p, then `psolC` might be able to compute memoryless winning strategies for parity game G. Let us next give an example of how `psolC` may solve games completely:

Example 2. Let us consider the execution of `psolC`(G) for parity game G in Fig. 4 (for the acceptance condition as in Definition 1). Initially, $p = 0$ and $X = \{v_0, v_1, v_3, v_5\} = G^0$. Then `psolC` detects in `fixedPoint` that X is the greatest fixed point of F_G^0 and removes its 0 attractor in G (which is all of V) from G. Thus `psolC` completely solves G and recognizes that all nodes are won by player 0. Note that X is a fixed point of F_G^0 since $W_r^0(G, X)$ equals V: (i) player 0 wins node v_0 as player 1 can only move to v_3 or v_5 from there and so reach X with minimal color 0; (ii) player 0 wins node v_1 since player 1 can only

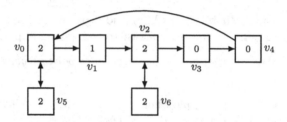

Fig. 6. Parity game G, owned by player 1, won by player 0, and where `psolC` cannot solve even a single node

move to v_0 from there and so reach X with minimal color 0; (iii) player 0 wins node v_2 since player 1 can only generate the prefix $v_2v_1v_0$ from there and so get minimal color 0 for this *second* reach of X; (iv) player 0 wins v_3 since player 1 can either move from there to v_2 and so generate a prefix $v_3v_2v_1v_0$ with minimal color 0 for his *second* reach of X or player 1 can move to v_4 from where she can only move to X with minimal color 2 for the first reach of X; (v) player 0 wins v_5 for symmetric reasons; and (vi) player 0 wins v_4 because player 1 can only reach X from here with minimal color 2 on the first reach of X.

Solver `psolC` is partial in that it may not solve even a single node in a parity game. We illustrate this with an example:

Example 3. Figure 6 shows a parity game G for which `psolC` solves no nodes at all. For $p = 0$, set X is initially $V \setminus \{v_1\}$. (i) Node v_0 is lost by player 0 since player 1 can move from there into the cycle $(v_2v_6)^\omega$ with minimal color 1. Player 0 wins all other nodes in X. Therefore, the next value of X equals $\{v_2, v_3, v_4, v_5, v_6\}$. (ii) Now, nodes v_4 and v_5 are lost by player 0, as player 1 can move from them to node v_0 (which is no longer in X) and then play as for the initial X to get minimal color 1. Player 0 wins all other nodes in X. Therefore, the next value of X equals $\{v_2, v_3, v_6\}$. (iii) Next, node v_3 is lost by player 0, as player 1 can move from there directly to node v_4 (which is no longer in X) and then enter the cycle $(v_0v_5)^\omega$ and so avoid X altogether. Player 0 wins nodes v_2 and v_6 though. Therefore, the next value of X equals $\{v_2, v_6\}$. (iv) Now, player 0 loses v_2 as player 1 can avoid reaching that node again from v_2. Player 0 still wins node v_6. Thus, the next value of X equals $\{v_6\}$. (v) Finally, player 1 can avoid reaching X again from node v_6 and so wins v_6, making X empty.

Clearly, F_G^1 computes an empty fixed point as all nodes in parity game G are won by player 0. The inability of `psolC` to solve even a single node in G seems to stem from the fact that the acceptance condition for $W_r^0(G, X)$ captures a *weak* parity acceptance condition [1] and not a parity acceptance condition.

We could extend the types of F_G^p to be $\mathbb{P}(V) \to \mathbb{P}(V)$. The proofs for monotonicity and for fixed points being won by player p in the parity game G would still carry through then. It may be of interest to compare a variant of `psolC` based on greatest fixed points for this extended type of F_G^p to `psolC`: that variant may run slower in practice but may solve more nodes in G. However, it will still be a partial solver as can be seen from Example 3: for the version of psolC based on this extended type, both v_0 and v_1 would be removed from initial $X = V$ in the first iteration and so this still would compute empty fixed points only.

5   Fatal Attractors

Our work in [13] defined and studied *monotone* attractors and built partial solvers out of them. Let X be a non-empty node set of G where all nodes in X have color c, and set p to be $c\%2$. Monotone attractors $\mathsf{MA}(X)$ were defined in [13]. For X as above, and subsets A of V this definition is as follows:

$$\mathsf{mpre}_p(A, X, c) = \{v \in V_p \mid c(v) \geq c \wedge v.E \cap (A \cup X) \neq \emptyset\} \cup$$
$$\{v \in V_{1-p} \mid c(v) \geq c \wedge v.E \subseteq A \cup X\}$$
$$\mathsf{MA}(X) = \mu Z.\mathsf{mpre}_p(Z, X, c) \tag{3}$$

where $\mu Z.f(Z)$ denotes the least fixed point of a monotone function $f\colon \mathbb{P}(V) \to \mathbb{P}(V)$. It follows that $\mathsf{MA}(X)$ is the set of nodes in G from which player p can attract to X whilst avoiding nodes of color less than c. In [13], we called such an X *fatal* if all of X is in that attractor (i.e. when $X \subseteq \mathsf{MA}(X)$). In Theorem 2 in [13], we showed that all such fatal attractors are won by player p.

To relate this to our work in this chapter, an infinite play π would be won in this monotone attractor game by player p iff there is some $j > 0$ with π_j in X and $c(\pi_i) \geq c$ for all i with $0 \leq i < j$; so X can be reached on π with minimal color c at π_j. This implies that all such fatal attractors X with node color c are fixed points of F_G^p and are therefore contained in the greatest fixed point of F_G^p. We can use this to prove that psolC is more effective than the partial solver psolB defined in [13]:

Theorem 4. *Let* psolB *be the partial solver defined in Fig. 7 and let* G *be a parity game. The call* psolC(G) *decides the winner of all nodes for which call* psolB(G) *decides a winner.*

Proof. For all players p, the acceptance condition for monotone attractors as discussed above implies that all fatal attractors for that player in G (node sets X of some color c with parity p such that $X \subseteq \mathsf{MA}(X)$) are contained in the greatest fixed point Z of F_G^p. By Theorem 5 in [13], the order of fatal attractor detection does not affect the output of partial solver psolB. Therefore, we can assume that all fatal attractors X for player p are contained in the greatest fixed point Z of F_G^p. But by monotonicity, their p-attractors $\mathsf{Attr}_p[G, X]$ are then also contained in the p-attractor $\mathsf{Attr}_p[G, Z]$ of Z. Thus, it follows that all nodes that are decided by psolB(G) are also decided by psolC(G). □

In [13], we also studied a more precise but more complex partial solver psolQ. Although the design of psolQ has superficial similarities to that of psolC, the latter is more precise: at noted in [13], psolQ does not solve even a single node for the parity game in Fig. 8. But psolC solves this game completely.

```
psolB(G = (V, V₀, V₁, E, c)) {
  for (colors d in descending ordering) {
    X = { v in V | c(v) = d };
    cache = {};
    while (X ≠ {} && X ≠ cache) {
      cache = X;
      if (X ⊆ MA(X)) { return psolB(G \ Attr_d%2[G, MA(X)])
      } else { X = X ∩ MA(X); }
    }
  }
  return G
}
```

Fig. 7. Partial solver `psolB` from [13] (figure is a reproduction of Fig. 3 in [13])

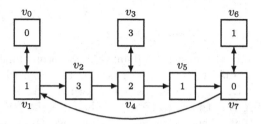

Fig. 8. A 1-player parity game that `psolC` solves completely (as $\{v_0, v_4, v_7\}$ is greatest fixed point of F_G^0) but for which `psolQ` in [13] solves no nodes (figure is Fig. 5 in [13])

6 Experimental Results

By Theorem 4, we know that `psolC` will solve completely all games that `psolB` solves completely. From [13], we know that `psolB` completely solves many structured benchmarks. Therefore, there is little value in running `psolC` over these structured benchmarks again. This is why we focused our experimental effort here an random parity games.

We now report our experiments we did on randomly generated games. The aims of these experiments are

1. to experimentally confirm that `psolC` solves all nodes that `psolB` solves, as proved in Theorem 4
2. to compare running times of `psolC` and `psolB` over a large set of random games
3. to determine game configurations for which `psolC` does not really solve more than `psolB` does.

All our experiments were conducted on a test server that has two Intel® E5 CPUs, with 6-core each running at 2.5 GHz and 48 G of RAM. Experiments were grouped into game configurations, where we generated 100,000 games for each such configuration and ran `psolB` and `psolC` against these games. We also used Zielonka's solver [29] for regression tests to ensure that psolB and psolC correctly under-approximate winning regions, all of these tests passed.

The game configurations used are shown in the "Game Mode" column of Fig. 9. Each such mode is denoted by xx-yy-aa-bb. The xx is the number of nodes in a game, and the owners (player 0 or 1) of the nodes are chosen independently at random. The color of each node is also uniformly chosen from set $\{0, 1, \ldots, yy\}$, and has between aa and bb out-going edges to randomly selected successors in the game.

We now summarize key facts that we can observe from the experimental results shown in Fig. 9:

- psolB has never solved more nodes than psolC, experimentally confirming Theorem 4 (column #10).
- For games with low edge density (i.e., when aa-bb equals 1-5), psolC solves more than psolB for around 10 % of games (#9).
- For games with higher edge density (i.e., when aa-bb is different from 1-5), psolC doesn't appear to have an effect over psolB (#9).
- psolC takes significantly more time to execute than psolB for high edge density games (#2).
- Our experimental results suggest that the psolC lapse time increases as the color cap increases, whereas we don't observe a similar increase for psolB (#2 and #3).

Game Mode	#1	#2	#3	#4	#5	#6	#7	#8	#9	#10
500-5-1-5	100000	384.17	15.64	18.63	18545	19590	18406	80410	1184	0
500-5-1-100	100000	724.14	17.91	51.76	1016	1016	1016	98984	0	0
500-5-5-10	100000	203.67	8.71	14.44	0	0	0	100000	0	0
500-5-50-250	100000	1157.37	31.06	119.10	0	0	0	100000	0	0
500-50-1-5	100000	2522.47	14.30	20.86	18166	19066	17962	80934	1104	0
500-50-1-100	100000	6807.46	18.57	54.58	992	992	992	99008	0	0
500-50-5-10	100000	2155.34	8.35	14.38	0	2	0	99998	2	0
500-50-50-250	100000	10282.66	34.36	135.29	0	0	0	100000	0	0

Fig. 9. Our experimental results for the partial solver psolC. The legend for the 10 data columns above is given in Table 1.

We note that these experiments took quite some time to complete. For example, the total running time of psolC for these 800,000 random games was more than 28 days (if converted to calendar time). The experimental data we collected suggest that the comparison between psolB and psolC is bimodal on random games: either psolC is no more effective than psolB on a given game mode, or it appears to be more effective on about 10 % of games for a given game mode.

The partial solver psolC may therefore have more theoretical than practical value. However, a staging of psolB and psolC may work reasonably well in practice: on input game G, first run psolB to obtain residual game G'; and then run psolC only on G' and only when G' is not empty.

Table 1. Legend for experimental data shown in Fig. 9: G'_B represents the number of games not completely solved by `psolB`. Similarly, G'_C represents the number of games not completely solved by `psolC`.

#1. Total number of games.	#6. How often G'_B is not 0.
#2. Average `psolC` lapse time (ms).	#7. How often $G'_C = G'_B$ and G'_C is not 0.
#3. Average `psolB` lapse time (ms).	#8. How often $G'_C = G'_B$ and G'_C is 0.
#4. Average `zlka` lapse time (ms).	#9. How often `psolC` solves more than `psolB`.
#5. How often G'_C is not 0.	#10. How often `psolB` solves more than `psolC`.

7   Other Related Work

Some easy static analyses for parity games have become part of the folklore of how to preprocess parity games. For example, the tool PGSolver can eliminate self-loops (nodes v with (v,v) in E) and dead ends (nodes v for which there is no w with (v,w) in E) [12]. The latter can be seen as justification for defining parity games not to have dead ends, as we have done in this chapter.

In [17], progress measures are defined and recognized as representations of winning strategies. A monotone function over a complete lattice is then defined such that pre-fixed points of that function capture progress measures. A least fixed-point computation therefore can compute the winning region and a winning strategy for a chosen player. This algorithm has exponential running time, since the complete lattice may be exponentially larger than the parity game. However, the algorithm runs on polynomial space, unlike some other known algorithms for solving parity games.

Our work relates to research on the descriptive complexity of parity games. In [6], it is investigated whether the winning regions of players in parity games can be defined in suitable logics. We mention two results from this paper: it is shown that this is indeed possible for guarded second-order logic (even for infinite game graphs with an unbounded number of colors); and for an arbitrary finite game graph G (the setting of our chapter), it is proved that least fixed-point logic can define the winning regions of G iff these winning regions are computable in polynomial time.

In [14], a transformation is studied that can map a partial solver ρ for parity games to another partial solver $\mathsf{lift}(\rho)$ that first applies ρ until it has no effect on the residual game. Then, $\mathsf{lift}(\rho)$ searches for some node v in V_p with more than one outgoing edge such that the commitment to one such edge (i.e. the removal of all other edges outgoing from v) would make partial solver ρ discover that node v is won by player $1 - p$ in that modified game. If so, it is sound to remove edge (v, w) from G and then try $\mathsf{lift}(\rho)$ again until no such effect can be observed for both p. It was proved in [14] that $\mathsf{lift}(\rho)$ is sound if ρ is sound, idempotent, and satisfies a locality principle; and it was shown that `psolB` satisfies these properties.

8 Conclusions

In this chapter, we studied how one may define static analyses of parity games that run in polynomial time and space and compute parts of the games' winning regions. In particular, the quality of such a static analysis could then be measured by how often it computes winning regions completely, or by what percentage of the winning region it computes across a range of random and structured benchmarks. We developed firm foundations for designing such static analyses, using a novel kind of game derived from parity games: reachability under parity. The intuition of such a game is that player p can reach a node set X whilst ensuring that the minimal color encountered en route has parity p.

We showed that such new reachability games are determined, demonstrated how one can implement their solution efficiently, and used this notion of game to define monotone functions over parity games – one for each player of the parity game. The greatest fixed-points of these functions were proved to be contained in the winning region of the corresponding player in the parity game. This insight led us to design a partial solver psolC and its experimental evaluation demonstrated that it is a powerful static analysis of parity games that can solve completely many types of random and structured benchmarks. Theoretical analysis also showed that these monotone functions generalize, in a more canonical and less ad hoc manner, work on fatal attractors that we had conducted previously [13]. In particular, we proved that psolC is more effective that the partial solver psolB in [13] that performed best in practice.

The decision problem for parity games, whether a given node is won by a given player, is in $UP \cap coUP$ [16] and so contained in $NP \cap coNP$. It is therefore perhaps no great surprise that all known algorithms that completely compute such winning regions run in worst-case exponential or sub-exponential time in the size of these games. One may therefore think of our chapter as taking a complementary approach to attempting to answer the longstanding open problem of the exact complexity of said decision problem for parity games: how to design static analyses that run in polynomial time (relatively easy to do) and that are provably computing the exact winning regions of all parity games (likely very hard to do under these constraints of efficient static analysis). We hope that the reader may find this approach to be of genuine interest so that he or she may pursue it further.

References

1. Chatterjee, K.: Linear time algorithm for weak parity games. CoRR abs/0805.1391 (2008)
2. Clarke, E.M., Grumberg, O., Long, D.E.: Model checking and abstraction. ACM Trans. Program. Lang. Syst. **16**(5), 1512–1542 (1994)
3. Cousot, P., Cousot, R.: Abstract interpretation: a unified lattice model for static analysis of programs by construction or approximation of fixpoints. In: Conference Record of the Fourth ACM Symposium on Principles of Programming Languages, Los Angeles, January 1977, pp. 238–252 (1977)

4. Cousot, P., Cousot, R.: Abstract interpretation: past, present and future. In: Joint Meeting of the Twenty-Third EACSL Annual Conference on Computer Science Logic (CSL) and the Twenty-Ninth Annual ACM/IEEE Symposium on Logic in Computer Science (LICS), CSL-LICS 2014, Vienna, 14–18 July 2014, p. 2 (2014)
5. Dam, M.: CTL* and ECTL* as fragments of the modal mu-calculus. Theor. Comput. Sci. **126**(1), 77–96 (1994)
6. Dawar, A., Grädel, E.: The descriptive complexity of parity games. In: Kaminski, M., Martini, S. (eds.) CSL 2008. LNCS, vol. 5213, pp. 354–368. Springer, Heidelberg (2008)
7. Dwyer, M.B., Avrunin, G.S., Corbett, J.C.: Patterns in property specifications for finite-state verification. In: Proceedings of the 21st International Conference on Software Engineering, ICSE 1999, pp. 411–420 (1999)
8. Emerson, E., Jutla, C.: Tree automata, μ-calculus and determinacy. In: Proceedings 32nd IEEE Symposium on Foundations of Computer Science, pp. 368–377 (1991)
9. Emerson, E.A., Clarke, E.M.: Using branching time temporal logic to synthesize synchronization skeletons. Sci. Comput. Program. **2**(3), 241–266 (1982)
10. Emerson, E.A., Jutla, C.S., Sistla, A.P.: On model-checking for fragments of μ-calculus. In: Proceedings of 5th International Conference on Computer Aided Verification, CAV 1993, Elounda, 28 June - 1 July, 1993, pp. 385–396 (1993)
11. Filipiuk, P., Nielson, F., Nielson, H.R.: Layered fixed point logic. CoRR abs/1204.2768 (2012)
12. Friedmann, O., Lange, M.: Solving parity games in practice. In: Liu, Z., Ravn, A.P. (eds.) ATVA 2009. LNCS, vol. 5799, pp. 182–196. Springer, Heidelberg (2009)
13. Huth, M., Kuo, J.H.-P., Piterman, N.: Fatal attractors in parity games. In: Pfenning, F. (ed.) FOSSACS 2013 (ETAPS 2013). LNCS, vol. 7794, pp. 34–49. Springer, Heidelberg (2013)
14. Huth, M., Kuo, J.H., Piterman, N.: Fatal attractors in parity games: building blocks for partial solvers. CoRR abs/1405.0386 (2014)
15. Huth, M., Ryan, M.D.: Logic in Computer Science - Modelling and Reasoning About Systems, 2nd edn. Cambridge University Press, New York (2004)
16. Jurdziński, M.: Deciding the winner in parity games is in UP∩co-UP. Inf. Process. Lett. **68**, 119–124 (1998)
17. Jurdziński, M.: Small progress measures for solving parity games. In: Reichel, H., Tison, S. (eds.) STACS 2000. LNCS, vol. 1770, pp. 290–301. Springer, Heidelberg (2000)
18. Kozen, D.: Results on the propositional mu-calculus. Theor. Comput. Sci. **27**, 333–354 (1983). http://dx.doi.org/10.1016/0304-3975(82)90125-6
19. Kupferman, O., Vardi, M.Y., Wolper, P.: An automata-theoretic approach to branching-time model checking. J. ACM **47**(2), 312–360 (2000)
20. Martin, D.A.: Borel determinacy. Ann. Math. **102**(2), 363–371 (1975)
21. Mostowski, A.W.: Games with forbidden positions. Technical Report 78, University of Gdańsk (1991)
22. Nielson, F., Nielson, H.R.: Model checking is static analysis of modal logic. In: Foundations of Software Science and Computational Structures, 13th International Conference, FOSSACS 2010, Held as Part of the Joint European Conferences on Theory and Practice of Software, ETAPS 2010, Paphos, Cyprus, 20–28 March, 2010. Proceedings, pp. 191–205 (2010)
23. Nielson, F., Nielson, H.R., Hankin, C.: Principles of program analysis (2. corr. print). Springer, Heidelberg (2005)

24. Queille, J., Sifakis, J.: Specification and verification of concurrent systems in CESAR. In: International Symposium on Programming, 5th Colloquium, Torino, Italy, 6–8 April, 1982, Proceedings, pp. 337–351 (1982)
25. Schmidt, D.A., Steffen, B.: Program analysis as model checking of abstract interpretations. In: Levi, G. (ed.) SAS 1998. LNCS, vol. 1503, pp. 351–380. Springer, Heidelberg (1998)
26. Steffen, B.: Data flow analysis as model checking. In: Theoretical Aspects of Computer Software, International Conference TACS 1991, Sendai, Japan, 24–27 September, 1991, Proceedings, pp. 346–365 (1991)
27. Stirling, C.: Lokal model checking games. In: CONCUR 1995: Concurrency Theory, 6th International Conference, Philadelphia, PA, USA, August 21–24, 1995, Proceedings, pp. 1–11 (1995)
28. Zhang, F., Nielson, F., Nielson, H.R.: Model checking as static analysis: revisited. In: Derrick, J., Gnesi, S., Latella, D., Treharne, H. (eds.) IFM 2012. LNCS, vol. 7321, pp. 99–112. Springer, Heidelberg (2012)
29. Zielonka, W.: Infinite games on finitely coloured graphs with applications to automata on infinite trees. Theor. Comput. Sci. 200(1–2), 135–183 (1998)

Game Theory and Industrial Control Systems

Chris Hankin[✉]

Institute for Security Science and Technology,
Imperial College London, London SW7 2AZ, UK
c.hankin@imperial.ac.uk

Abstract. Post-Stuxnet, the last couple of years has seen an increasing awareness of cyber threats to industrial control systems (ICS). We will review why these threats have become more prominent. We will explore the differences between Enterprise IT security and cyber security of ICS. Game Theory has been used to provide decision support in cyber security for a number of years. Recently, we have developed a hybrid approach using game theory and classical optimisation to produce decision support tools to help system administrators optimise their investment in cyber defence. We will describe how our game theoretic work might be used to provide novel approaches to protecting ICS against cyber attacks.

1 Introduction

Originally isolated, Industrial Control Systems (ICS) have become increasingly connected to organisational IT functions and networks, particularly as the technology necessary to deliver both has converged and proliferated. ICS-CERT provide a regular review of the growing threat[1] which shows an increase from 9 reported incidents in 2005 to 257 in 2013 and 245 in 2014. About 70 % of the reported incidents occured in the energy or critical manufacturing sectors.

Sometimes the term Operational Technology (OT) is used to refer to the ICS component of an organisation's infrastructure. Whilst offering efficiencies in terms of 'business as usual' costs, the trend towards increasing integration has exposed ICS to a greater range of vulnerabilities with potentially wider scale and inter-organisational impacts. Since major aspects of national critical infrastructure rely on the industrial exploitation of ICS, governments have taken active steps in improving this security landscape in recent years, with initiatives being represented by [3,7] and a more recent UK-focussed approach by [1].

Generally, an ICS instance may be described as a set of supervisory devices (including a single device in some cases), that control the actions and reactions of *field devices* through the acquisition of data and the issuing of commands; where the field devices are responsible for execution of a given industrial process or set of processes. An abstract representation of an ICS is shown in Fig. 1. At the heart of the system is a feedback loop which includes the physical process that is being controlled, sensors and actuators and a controller. The control room

---

[1] https://ics-cert.us-cert.gov/ICS-CERT-Year-Review-2013.

© Springer International Publishing Switzerland 2016
C.W. Probst et al. (Eds.): Nielsons' Festschrift, LNCS 9560, pp. 178–190, 2016.
DOI: 10.1007/978-3-319-27810-0_9

interface through a Human Machine Interface (HMI) is also an important aspect of any ICS. Increasingly, there is also the possibility of remote maintenance and diagnostics. Every one of these components and the communication links between them can be vulnerable to cyber attack. A typical ICS may contain multiple control loops of this kind and they may be cascaded. A key component which is not shown explicitly in this schematic diagram is the *Data Historian* which is a centralised database that logs process information from the ICS; this can be a key point of contact between the ICS and the Enterprise IT system because the data can have tremendous business value as well as being necessary for controlling the processes.

ICS can take on a range of configurations, involving diverse mixtures of hardware, software, human processess and actions, network topologies and communication protocols. Today, ICS can be found operating in organisations of all types, ranging from large multinationals to regionally focussed SMEs. Across this scale, important differences in how ICS are implemented exist and require attention, as previously isolated implementations are becoming intra-organisationlly and inter-organisationlly connected, motivated by a mixture of actual and perceived business benefits.

In large scale industrial processes, such as utilities, ICS are manifest as Supervisory Control and Data Acquisition (SCADA) systems. SCADA systems are characterised by geographically dispersed control targets requiring centralised management over typically disparate communication networks, implementing differing protocols and modalities, with varying reliability and latency. At more regional organisational scales, such as may be found in manufacturing plants, access to high reliability networks enables ICS specification to be freed of such SCADA implementation constraints, giving rise to ICS referred to as Distributed Control Systems (DCS). At the smallest scales, specialised computers known as Programmable Logic Controllers (PLC) provide control of limited numbers of devices. In recent decades, PLC have evolved from functionally rudimentary devices to highly capable independent computing systems, representing the increased sophistication of ICS systems at their *edge*. It follows from the above discussion that SCADA systems are often comprised of numerous DCS and PLC subsystems and components.

Cyber security of Enterprise IT systems often uses the acronym CIA which stands for Confidentiality, Integrity and Availability. Confidentiality is about preventing unauthorised access to data, Integrity is about the accuracy of data, and Availability is about ensuring that authorised access to data is always possible. Given national and international legislation on data protection, Confidentiality is often seen as the most important of these, so CIA does reflect this emphasis (apart from being a good security acronym!). Whilst ICS are repositories of valuable operational data, cyber attacks on ICS are often aiming to achieve sabotage rather than espionage goals – physical damage rather than exfiltration or corruption of data per se. Given this shift in emphasis, some authors have called for a reordering of the priorities to Availability (as the most important), Integrity and Confidentiality. Some go still further to suggest that Reliability, Maintainability

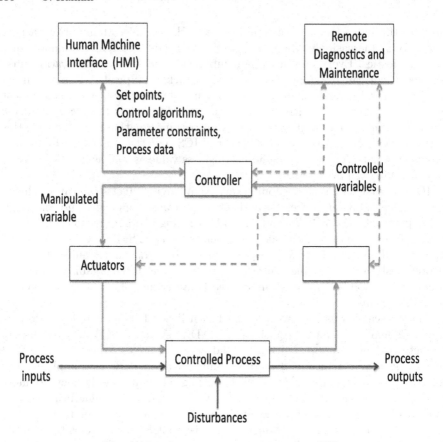

Fig. 1. An abstract representation of an ICS

and Availability should be the key criteria. Emerging standards are also beginning to recognise that Safety and Security have important interactions – can a system be safe if it is not secure against cyber attack?

Whilst ICS implementations are increasingly adopting IT solutions, there are some critical differences which must be considered when developing an ICS security programme:

- Responses from an ICS typically have to be in real-time or fixed time windows, so there is an emphasis on that rather than high data throughput which may be a goal in IT systems.
- Many industrial processes or control processes require continuous operation; if outages can be tolerated, they often have to be scheduled far in advance and any changes to the system have to be extensively tested off-line before being deployed.
- Whilst cyber security programmes for IT systems might spend a disproportionate effort on protecting the central computing facilities (servers, etc...), in ICS there is an increased importance of edge clients, such as Remote

Terminal Units (RTUs). These are likely to be easier targets for an attacker but a successful attack can have far greater impact than in a typical IT system.
- The purpose of an ICS is to control complex interactions with physical processes; a cyber attack directed at an ICS is likely to manifest itself as physical damage.
- Whilst edge clients have become more powerful, many will still be constrained by resources such as power and storage. There may also be legal constraints from the vendors which govern what solutions are deployable.
- The refresh cycle for ICS is much longer than typical IT systems. This gives rise to legacy issues: an ICS deployed today may have to be good for 15–20+ years of operation. Some of today's ICS will still be running early operating systems (DOS, Windows 9x and legacy proprietary systems). Many more recently installed sytems will be running Windows XP and be expected to be functional for many years to come.
- In a typical IT system, the device will be located in an office environment and easy to access; in contrast access to ICS components can be difficult because they may be geographically dispersed in remote, and sometimes hostile, environments.

In addition to all of these constraints, the ICS operator is likely to have a restricted budget and needs to make decisions about how to use that to best protect the system against expected attacks. In our work on cyber security of Enterprise IT systems, we have developed decision support tools based on Game Theory to address this resource allocation problem. In the next section we describe typical vulnerabilities in ICS. Section 3 reviews the types of security controls that have been proposed for ICS. Section 4 reviews the game-theoretic work and the hybrid approach to decision support that we have developed. We conclude in Sect. 5.

2 Vulnerabilities

As observed by ICS-CERT[2], a successful attacker would need to:

- gain access to the control system local area network
- gain understanding of the process
- gain control of the process

Most advice on protection of ICS suggests the use of firewalls and De-Militarised Zones (DMZ) to protect the control system from the outside world. As tools such as Shodan[3] show, there are still many systems that are exposed. One common attack route is via direct dial modems that are attached to field equipment – this provides back-up communications if the primary, high-speed lines fail; since many remote terminal units require no authentication or have default, out-of-the-box, passwords this provides the attacker a route to

---

[2] https://ics-cert.us-cert.gov/content/overview-cyber-vulnerabilities.
[3] http://www.shodanhq.com.

control part of the system. The report from ICS-CERT lists a number of other vulnerabilities which allow the attacker to gain access to the control system; these range from piggybacking on the vendor support or field service process, as reportedly used in the first version of Stuxnet [8], to SQL injection attacks via the Data Historian database.

Having gained access to a control system, the attacker must then gain an understanding of the process in order to disrupt it. The names or IP addresses of the various components in the control system are a valuable part of this discovery process. The Dragonfly group [13], also known as Energetic Bear in some circles, appear to have been collecting this kind of information from companies in the energy sector. This information is often gathered using some form of Remote Access Trojan (RAT) – the Dragonfly group use the Havex RAT for this purpose. In addition to configuration data, the second valuable target for attackers is the operator HMI; successful compromise of the HMI can be exploited in the third component described below.

The final component of the successful attack is to take control of the process. This could entail:

- Sending commands directly to the field devices. This is facilitated by the fact that power and processing restrictions, mean that the field devices perform very little authentication and are likely to act on any well-formed command.
- Exporting the Human Machine Interface console back to the attacker to allow them to behave as the current operator.
- Change the database which may result in actions in the control system for some vendors' systems.
- A man-in-the-middle attack to spoof protocol messages that may impact on HMI displays and the behavipur of the field devices such as sensors and actuators. A sophisticated attack such as Stuxnet [4,8] is likely to attack both edge devices and spoof information appearing on the control consoles.

3   Controls

The SANS Institute coordinated the maintenance of a list of the Top 20 Cyber Security Controls until 2013. The responsibility for stewardship and sustainment has now passed to the Council on Cybersecurity [2]. Their list prioritises the security functions which are effective against the latest advanced targeted threats. For each control they give advice on how to implement the control and they identify different levels of implementation which range from quick wins through to advanced implementations. For example a quick win in producing an inventory of authorised and un-authorised devices might be to deploy an automated asset discovery tool; a more advanced implementation might be to employ client certificates to authenticate devices before they are allowed to connect to the private network.

The Council identifies five tenets that underpin the security controls:

1. Offense informs defense – select controls which have been shown to be effective against real-world attacks.

2. Prioritisation – invest first in those controls that provide the greatest risk reduction; this is an area where our game theoretic approach may support the decision of where to invest.
3. Metrics – should be identified to communicate the effectiveness across the organisation and to support rapid adjustment as required.
4. Continuous diagnostics and mitigation – which helps drive the priority of the next steps.
5. Automation – where possible.

These basic tenets hold good for both Enterprise IT and ICS. The Council also highlight a "first five quick wins" which are sub-controls that have the most immediate impact:

- application whitelisting.
- use of standard, secure system configurations.
- patch application software within 48 h.
- patch system software within 48 h.
- reduce number of users with administrative privileges.

Whilst the first, second and fifth sub-controls are very effective, patching is not always possible in the ICS, as discussed earlier. More needs to be done to identify the best quick wins for ICS, but the patching sub-controls could lose out to others such as:

- Ensure that only ports, protocols, and services with valid business needs are running on each system.
- Conduct regular internal and external penetration tests.

In [2], the Council for Cybersecurity enumerate a number of attack types that have informed the development of the list of security controls. For example, one of the attacks that they describe is where the attackers scan for remotely accessible service on target systems that are unneeded for business purposes but provide an avenue for attack and compromise. They propose the following controls: malware defences (CSC 5); secure configuration for network devices such as firewalls, routers and switches (CSC 10); and limitation and control of network ports, protocols and services (CSC 11). The quick wins in this case include:

CSC 5: continuous monitoring; running of anti-malware software, if possible; configuring systems to prevent auto-running of content from removable media and external devices; scan and block e-mail attachments.

CSC 10: compare firewall, router and switch configurations against standard, secure configurations and record and deal with any deviations.

CSC 11: ensure that only ports, protocols and services with a validated business need are running on each system; apply host-based firewalls or port filtering on end systems that drop unauthorised traffic; keep all services up to date and uninstall and remove any unnecessary components.

Whilst the controls that we have discussed so far have been mainly technical, there is also the need for operational and management controls. The operational controls are protective measures that are usually implemented by humans rather than machines. They include controls such as personnel security and physical and environmental security. They also include user awareness, training and education. The management controls concern policy issues and risk management. They include supply chain security and security assessment and risk management. One of the management controls is to develop a Defence in Depth architecture.

The NIST report on ICS Security [12] includes recommendations for Defence in Depth for ICS. These range from organisational aspects to detailed technical guidance. From the former perspective, the guidance suggests the need for detailed ICS security policies and training, adopting heightened security posture as the threat level increases, providing physical access control and suitable incident reporting mechanisms. The technical measures range from a multi-layered network topology with firewalls and De-Militarised Zones to the use of modern authentication systems for identifying users and the application of standard security controls.

The SANS Institute [9] describe defence in depth as the concept of protecting a computer network with a series of defensive mechanisms such that if one mechanism fails, another will already be in place to thwart an attack.

The adversarial threat to ICS potentially comes from many different sources ranging from lone attackers, through criminal gangs and industrial spies to state-sponsored groups; it is also important not to neglect the insider threat. The script kiddie, a skilled attacker and authorised insider have some methods in common, but each presents unique problems to a secure network. For instance, a firewall does not provide any protection from an insider but should be a significant hurdle for an attacker from the outside. Likewise, policies and procedures do not mean anything to an attacker from the outside but should be part of the plan to protect a network from insiders.

The ultimate objective of implementing a strategy of defence in depth is to defeat or discourage all kinds of attackers. Firewalls, intrusion detection systems, well trained users, policies and procedures, switched networks, strong password and good physical security are examples of some of the things that go into an effective security plan. For reasons explained above, none of these mechanisms by themselves provides sufficient protection but when implemented together become much more valuable as part of an overall security plan.

In addition to understanding the different adversarial threats, defence in depth for an ICS requires a thorough understanding of the likely attack vectors:

– Backdoors and holes in the network perimeter.
– Vulnerabilities in common protocols.
– Attacks on field devices.
– Database attacks.
– Communications hijacking and man-in-the-middle attacks.

It is interesting to note that, whilst from a safety perspective defence in depth is an inside-out concept (first line defence is closest to the asset being protected), from a cyber security perspective defence in depth is an outside-in concept (successive layers of perimeter defence).

4   Game Theory and Cyber Security

We have been developing an approach to cyber defence based on game theory [5,10]. To date we have concentrated on two player, zero sum games. The two players represent a generic attacker and a system administrator. We consider any system to have a number of targets that could be vulnerable to attack. The system administrator has a budget to purchase and maintain a set of security controls. We have also concentrated on commodity style attacks – known attack patterns that target known vulnerabilities and that can be relatively easily purchased. Some vulnerabilities will require multiple security controls and some controls will address multiple vulnerabilities. The outcome of our decision support tool is advice on how to optimally use the available budget to protect against the expected attacks.

Our earlier work concerns Enterprise IT systems. We consider a typical multi-level architecture where levels are separated by firewalls or other protective mechanisms such as data diodes. The more sensitive assets are protected by being situated at deeper levels in the architecture. Advice in the ICS domain also propose multi-level architectures [12]; a schematic of such an architecture is shown in Fig. 2. The red lines from the Internet into the DMZ and the OT zones are the kind of flows that we would seek to prevent but may be enabled to allow remote maintenance and diagnostics.

Our approach involves identifying a number of targets that could be vulnerable to attack. Typical vulnerabilities are listed by organisations such as the

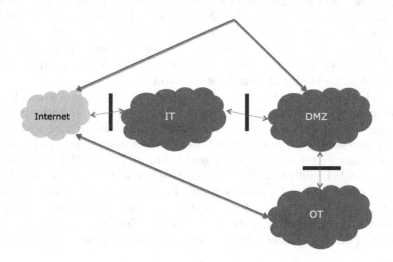

Fig. 2. An ICS architecture (Color figure online)

SANS Institute[4] and are assigned a CVE number. The SANS Institute also describes typical exploitations of these vulnerabilities which we refer to as the attack method. As an abstraction, we consider targets to be a pair of a vulnerability and the depth within the architecture at which it exists; consequently all assets at the same depth within the system which share a common vunerability are considered to be a single target.

Controls are procedures or tools that can be used to prevent the exploitation of vulnerabilities and to promote good cyber hygiene within an organisation. Controls may be implemented in a more or less effective way. For example, patching could be implemented when notified by vendor, on a regular and frequent basis (e.g. once a day), on a regular but infrequent basis, ad hoc or never. There is evidence that hackers are quick to exploit vulnerabilities as soon as they are announced – see the statistics on ShellShock exploits for example[5]. Unfortunately patching potentially conflicts with the safety requirements for ICS, so may be infrequently, if ever, performed. In general, we model the level at which each control is implemented. Of course, the purpose of implementing a control is to prevent damage and we refer to the amount of damage prevented by the control as the *mitigation*. The *direct cost* of a control is the cost to implement and maintain it. There are also *indirect costs* associated with any control. In the context of Enterprise IT systems, we have considered effects on system performance, re-training costs and the effects on staff morale as examples of indirect costs. In the context of ICS, system perfomance overheads or disruption, retraining and the costs of organisational change, such as increased physical security are examples.

The model that we developed in [10] includes an Organisational Profile parameter. In that work we considered a profile which included information about the organisation's risk appetite, the priorities assigned to the different types of indirect cost and the organisation attitude to the threat landscape – whether the organisation is more concerned about current threats or potential threats. In that work risks include the risk of data loss, business disruption and reputational risk. In the ICS arena, we would expect to include the organisation's attitude to safety incidents as part of the risk profile. We use the profile as a component in calculating the utility of a control.

We could create a large game to represent a system. In such a game the system administrator strategies would involve schedules of controls, each applied at a suitable level. In detail, if we have n controls, a schedule could be a n-tuple of integers representing the level at which each control is applied. Attacker strategies would involve the selection of targets to attack. Solving the game involves finding a Nash Equilibrium (NE): in the simplest setting, the NE involves a pure strategy – choice of a single schedule for the system administrator and a single target for the attacker – for each of the two players such that neither can improve their own payoff by unilaterally changing. In more complex situations, the NE will involve probabilistic mixtures of strategies. In our application it is

---

[4] www.sans.org.

[5] www.hackmageddon.com.

sometimes difficult to understand how to interpret mixed strategies as sensible investment plans. In [6] we provide a detailed comparison of the pure game theoretic approach with traditional optimisation and a hybrid approach; we give more detailed arguments for why the hybrid approach may be preferable. We will sketch the hybrid approach below.

4.1 A Hybrid Approach

Rather than defining a single game, we develop a set of games for each control. The individual games are referred to as control sub-games. Each sub-game includes strategies that apply that control up to a certain level. For example the third sub-game would include the following strategies: don't apply the control; apply the control to level 1 – e.g. patching on an ad hoc basis; apply the control to level 2 – e.g. patching on a regular but infrequent basis.

Since we are considering zero sum games, we just consider the utilities for one player, the defender – the attacker utility will be the negative of the defender utility. The utility for control c applied at level l for target t is defined as a combination of the damage to the target and the indirect costs. In more detail, the utility is defined as follows:

$$\mathcal{U}_D(c_l, t) :=$$
$$IMPACT \times THREAT \times (1 - MITIGATION) - IND\_COSTS$$

The first summand represents the damage to the target. The *IMPACT* is derived from the organisational profile. The *THREAT* is derived from information such as the prevalence of the particular type of attack and the likelihood that the attacker is aware that the system has an exploitable vulnerability; the SANS Institute provide estimates of these values. Finally, $(1 - MITIGATION)$ determines the residual chance of loss when the control is implemented at the indicated level.

The *IND_COSTS* are the indirect costs associated with the control when implemented at the selected level. It is worth noting that the indirect costs are important in preventing the higher level applications of a control dominating the lower levels – whilst the first summand may be less at higher levels, the indirect costs may well be significantly more.

The Nash cybersecurity plan for the Defender is computed using a maximin approach. In the control sub-game the plan will be a (mixed) strategy which selects a level at which the control should be applied.

$$D_{cl}^* = \underset{D_{cl}}{\operatorname{argmax}} \ \underset{A_{cl}}{\min} \ \mathcal{U}_D(D_{cl}, A_{cl})$$

so for the third control sub-game for control c, this might give $\langle 0, 0.7, 0.3 \rangle$: this could be interpreted as patch on a regular basis for 30 % of the most important systems and patch the other 70 % on an ad hoc basis.

Similarly, we can compute the equilibrium for the Attacker:

$$A_{cl}^* = \underset{A_{cl}}{\text{argmax}} \; \underset{D_{cl}}{\min} \; \mathcal{U}_{\mathcal{A}}(D_{cl}, A_{cl})$$

The Control Games focus on each control in isolation, the optimisation aims to show the result of combining controls to produce the best overall cybersecurity plan for an organisation. We use an approach based on the Knapsack algorithm [11]. The Knapsack algorithm is a classical optimisation algorithm which determines the optimal allocation of resources within a given budget.

The particular form of Knapsack algorithm that we have used is a 0–1, Multiple Choice, Multi-Objective Knapsack. The reasons for this choice are:

0–1: A single control sub-game must either be chosen (1) in its entirety or completely omitted (0).

Multiple Choice: For each control only a single control sub-game may be selected.

Multi-Objective: Each target will be affected differently, so we define each as an objective to be optimised.

The Knapsack optimises against a budget B. The *direct costs* of a control consume some of the budget. We consider the following direct costs: *Capital Cost* the cost of purchasing and implementing the control; and *Labour Cost* the cost of maintaining the control.

The solution to the Knapsack specifies the level at which each control should be implemented – including level 0 which means that the control is not implemented. We denote the solution:

$$\Psi = \{C_{1l_1}, \ldots, C_{ml_m}\}$$

indicating that control C_i should be implemented at level l_i.

The specification of the Knapsack is given as follows:

$$\max_{\Psi} \min_{t_i} D^*(\Psi, t_i)$$
$$\text{s.t.} \; \sum_{j=1}^{m}\sum_{l=0}^{n} \Gamma(C_{jl})z_{jl} \leq B$$
$$\sum_{l=0}^{n} z_{jl} = 1, z_{jl} \in \{0,1\}, \forall j = 1, \ldots, m$$

where

- $D^*(\Psi, t_i) = \sum_{j=1}^{m}\sum_{l=0}^{n} D^*(C_{jl}, t_i)z_{jl}.$
- z_{jl} is the 0–1 choice.
- $\Gamma(C_{jl})$ is the direct cost associated with control j at level l.

The solution effectively selects a set of control sub-games that give the best defence within the specified budget. Notice that the solution of a sub-game may be either a pure strategy or a mixed strategy. A pure strategy for a selected control will specify the level at which that control should be applied. Mixed strategies give advice about the probabilistic mix of levels at which the selected control should be applied (see above). We are currently developing a proof-of-concept web-based decision support tool based on this approach.

5 Conclusions

There are a number of critical challenges that need to be addressed when considering the security of industrial control sytems; these include:

- What physical harm arises from the cyber threats? We have written about this above but is it possible to develop a systematic framework for assessing this?
- How can we express cyber threats as business risk? Whilst increasing numbers of business leaders understand the need to protect their information assets, largely thanks to data protection legislation, the need to protect industrial control systems is less well understood. Can we develop both qualitative and quantitative methods for conveying business risk in this area?
- What novel interventions can be devised to protect ICS?

This paper addresses the third of these in suggesting a new approach to decision support for systems administrators who are defending ICS against attack. The framework described above assumes a known set of attacks. To cope with previously unseen attacks we would need to develop a more sophisticated framework possibly using Bayesian Games. This remains work for future study.

Future work will also involve considering non-zero sum games; in some of our earlier work we have considered the situation where one player's utility is an affine transformation of the others. That is, for a two-player normal form game:

$$A_{ij} = bD_{ij} + c$$

for attacker and defender utilities A_{ij} and D_{ij} and constants b and c. This does capture some realistic situations – for example, where the attacker is only able to realise a small part of the value of a compromised asset – whilst still admiting efficient solutions.

Acknowledgements. Our work on Industrial Control Systems is funded by the Research Institute on Trustworthy Industrial Control Systems (EPSRC grant EP/L021013/1) in collaboration with Deeph Chana. The work on game theory has been done in the Games and Abstraction project (EPSRC grant EP/K005790/1) in collaboration with Pasquale Malacaria, Andrew Fielder, Manos Panaousis and Fabrizio Smeraldi.

References

1. Boyes, H.: Resilience and cyber security of technology in the built environment. Techical report, IET (2013). http://www.theiet.org/resources/standards/
2. Council for cybersecurity: the critical security controls for effective cyber defense. Techical report, Council for Cybersecurity (2014)
3. Department of energy, U.: 21 steps to improve cyber security of SCADA networks. Techical report, DOE (2007). http://www.oe.netl.doe.gov/docs/prepare/21stepsbooklet.pdf
4. Falliere, N., Murchu, L.O., Chien, E.: W32.stuxnet dossier. Techical report, Symantec (2011). www.symantec.com
5. Fielder, A., Panaousis, E., Malacaria, P., Hankin, C., Smeraldi, F.: Game theorymeets information security management. In: Proceedings ICT Systems Security and Privacy Protection - 29th IFIP TC 11 International Conference, SEC 2014, 2-4 June 2014, Marrakech, Morocco, pp. 15–29 (2014)
6. Fielder, A., Panaousis, E., Malacaria, P., Hankin, C., Smeraldi, F.: Comparing decision support approaches for cyber security investment. Techical report (2015). www.archiv.org
7. ICS-CERT: recommended practice: improving industrial control systems cybersecurity with defense-in-depth strategies. Techical report, Department of Homeland Security (2009). http://ics-cert.us-cert.gov/sites/default/files/Defense_in_Depth_Oct09.pdf?
8. Langner, R.: Stuxnet: Dissecting a cyberwarfare weapon. IEEE Secur. Priv. $9(3)$, 49–51 (2011)
9. McGuiness, T.: Defense in depth. Techical report, SANS Institute (2001). www.sans.org
10. Panaousis, E., Fielder, A., Malacaria, P., Hankin, C., Smeraldi, F.: Cybersecurity games and investments: a decision support approach. In: Poovendran, R., Saad, W. (eds.) GameSec 2014. LNCS, vol. 8840, pp. 266–286. Springer, Heidelberg (2014)
11. Smeraldi, F., Malacaria, P.: How to spend it: optimal investment for cyber security. In: First International Workshop on Agents and Cyber Security (2014)
12. Stouffer, K., Falco, J., Scarfone, K.: Guide to industrial control systems (ICS)security. Techical report, NIST (2013). http://dx.doi.org/10.6028/NIST.SP.800-82r1
13. Symantec: dragonfly: cyberespionage attacks against energy suppliers. Technical report, Symantec (2014). www.symantec.com

Playing with Abstraction and Representation

Bernhard Steffen, Malte Isberner$^{(\boxtimes)}$, and Marc Jasper

TU Dortmund University, 44221 Dortmund, Germany
{steffen,malte.isberner,marc.jasper}@cs.tu-dortmund.de

Abstract. In this paper, we discuss partition refinement as an algorithmic pattern for explicating semantic properties of a system directly in the corresponding model structure in a co-inductive fashion. In particular, we review a landscape of analysis and verification approaches under this unifying perspective, which enables us to highlight their mutual profiles, while it at the same time establishes a basis for their combination: The common pattern establishes comparability, which reveals complementarity, and indicates where and under which circumstances the considered approaches may profit from one another. It can thus be regarded as a guideline for systematically exploring the benefits of the corresponding methods and their combinations.

1 Introduction and Motivation

Modern program analysis and automatic verification hinge on the interplay between three entities: (1) the considered (software) system, (2) the property to be verified/analyzed, and, last but not least, (3) a model, serving as a "mediator" in the verification process. Its very nature is what defines the actual frame conditions, like peculiarities of the system representation and the considered property, as well as the way the fact is treated that most problems are, in full, undecidable. In fact, the imposed triangle shown in Fig. 1 is an ideal structure to characterize and classify today's analysis and verification techniques, e.g., by highlighting where manual effort is needed or at which point correctness/completeness might be violated.

Traditional program analysis [18,29,40] can be characterized by, from today's perspective, simplistic algorithms that directly work on the source code (or its imposed flow graph). It was their prime role to provide program locations with information that allows for efficient code generation. Most popular are bit-vector analyses that, e.g., reveal properties like liveness of variables and availability of expressions in a syntactical fashion which can be proved to be correct: detected properties hold, but not all of them are revealed. These algorithms are typically fast enough to be integrated in compilers without impairing the compilation performance too much. Examples are dead code elimination [31], strength reduction [12,30], and partial redundancy elimination [29].

Conceptually dual is traditional program verification [14,20]. It also works on the source code, but it seeks completeness at the price of highly interactive proofs, leading to the slogan, "one verified program, one Ph.D.". In the following,

C.W. Probst et al. (Eds.): Nielsons' Festschrift, LNCS 9560, pp. 191–213, 2016.
DOI: 10.1007/978-3-319-27810-0_10

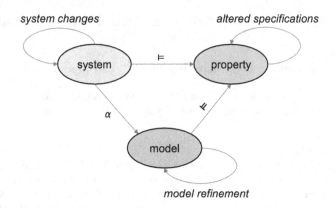

Fig. 1. High-level view of the analysis components and their dynamics

we will focus on automatic verification. Thus complex logical reasoning will only be considered as much as it can be "encapsulated" by involving SAT or SMT solvers [13].

In the eighties, model checking arose as a technique for verifying dedicated decidable system scenarios, like finite automaton models of reactive systems, or later also quite explicit models of hardware. Characteristic here were the property languages, typically temporal logics. The main precondition for applying this technology was the availability of an adequate abstract model. Indeed, the nineties were characterized by the attempt to fight the so-called state explosion problem, which is typically due to explicit modeling of data or concurrency. This fight still goes on, but the means seem to change. Approaches like statistical model checking [32], which are neither correct nor complete gain practical relevance. An early success story, where small and appropriate models can automatically be generated is the data-flow analysis via model checking approach [46]. In this approach, which nicely covers also the inter-procedural setting, models are essentially the flow graphs. To obtain more expressive models, elaborations like property-oriented expansion (POE) [47] can be used to improve the analysis results and consequently the potential for subsequent optimizing program transformations.

The idea of expanding the model according to the property to be verified was taken to its extreme in the predicate abstraction approach [15]. Characterizing the state of a model solely via properties frees one from immediate state explosion due to concurrency and explicit data modeling. In particular, combined with the CEGAR (*counterexample-guided abstraction refinement*) approach [9], it allows one to refine the model just by need. Of course, in extreme cases, many location predicates may be required, essentially reflecting the whole flow of control, but in particular in the case of distributed system verification it often leads to quite concise models.

The rules of the game change dramatically in the case of black-box systems, which can only be approached via their API or, even worse, their GUI. In this case, automata learning technology [49] proved to be adequate. Essentially, this

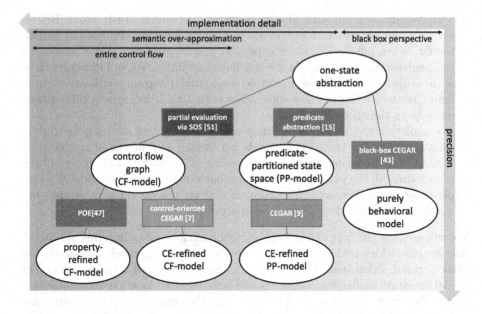

Fig. 2. Landscape of approaches based on partition refinement

leads to a test-based modeling approach, which – like statistical model checking, which also has a test character – is doomed to be neither correct nor complete, but in many cases surprisingly powerful.

2   Contribution

In this paper, we will review the described landscape of approaches (see also Fig. 2) from the very intuitive, unifying perspective of partition refinement. Looking at three quite different application scenarios, we will illustrate that partition refinement, seen as a method to explicate semantic properties directly in the model structure, is a powerful recurring theme of program analysis and verification. More concretely, we will sketch:

– A new technique called *lazy* Property-Oriented Expansion, which combines appropriate abstract collecting semantics [39] with a demand-driven (model) node-splitting algorithm for tailoring the expressive power of the underlying model structure for certain program analyses and optimizing transformations. This technique is particularly well-suited for enhancing bit vector analyses like partial redundancy elimination or partially-dead code elimination, whose very syntactic nature prohibits that it can be derived as an abstraction from the standard semantics in terms of state transformations. We will illustrate this approach by looking at partial redundancy elimination. Characteristic for this approach is that it directly works on the "what"-level, i.e., the refinement is directly driven by which property is computed rather than how.

- Two well-known variants of Counterexample-Guided Abstraction Refinement [9], which are state of the art in today's software verification, in particular, when effects like state explosion pose a problem. There refinement mechanisms directly hinge on the standard semantics. We will illustrate these approaches by considering a simple sequential program verification problem. Characteristic for these approaches is that their refinement takes places entirely on the "how"-level.
- A completely programming language-agnostic automata learning-based approach [49] to infer behavioral models via testing as a means of specification mining [3], foundation for regression testing [17], black box checking [42], or monitoring [6]. We will illustrate the approach by inferring the model of a simple registration protocol. This approach directly reflects the user perspective, making it a "what"-level/API-level approach.

We will see that the first two techniques refine initial models in terms of control-flow graphs, which means that they have the complete location information at their disposal. In contrast, the latter two techniques start with (more or less) the trivial one-state model, and automatically infer required location information via their refinement steps. However, even though the considered four scenarios are quite different in nature, they all follow the same pattern of refining partitions of the state space on the basis of *splitters*, i.e., evidence of errors in the model which need to be resolved. In the example for the first approach these are occurrences of program expressions which cannot be classified as redundant or fresh in the current model. In the examples for the second and third approach, these are so-called *false positives* or *spurious* counterexamples, i.e., paths of the model which are unfeasible according to the standard semantics in the real system. In the final example for the black-box approach, splitters are derived from counterexample traces, i.e., traces that are either allowed by the model but not in the real system or vice versa. While false positives and counterexample traces sound similar, it should be noted that the former treats splitters at the "how"-level (i.e., comprising facts about program variables and locations), whereas the latter addresses splitters at the "what"-level, and therefore only comprise knowledge about user-level observations. This has a direct impact on the refinement technology: in the first case, this generally requires an SMT-based analysis for revealing conditions that render the unfeasible path impossible also in the model, while in the other case an automata-theoretic approach is required to take care of the counterexample, either by adding or removing it from the model.

Besides these technical details, there is also a more fundamental difference between the first three (white-box) approaches and the final black-box approach. By their nature, and in contrast to most program analysis methods which are provably correct, black-box approaches are deemed to be neither correct nor complete. Nevertheless, automata learning-based techniques have proved to be very powerful in practice, and they are currently the only choice for black-box scenarios.

In the following, we will briefly sketch what we consider to be the "essence" of partition refinement in Sect. 3, before we present the three application scenarios

in Sects. 4–6. Section 7 concludes the paper with a discussion of the profile of each
of the presented methods from a practitioner's view, exploiting the established
uniform perspective.

3   The Essence of Partition Refinement: The What Perspective

From the pure "what" perspective (which contrasts the original "how"-oriented
description), partition refinement can be regarded as a systematic technique for
classifying members of (potentially very large or infinite) domains according to
some critical criteria in a co-inductive fashion. Its first occurrence [21] concerned
the domain of finite words Σ^* over a finite alphabet Σ and the considered critical
criterion was "different future behaviors" in terms of residual languages of a
given language L: two words u and u' of Σ^* should be distinguishable if there is
a continuation v revealing their difference (a *separating future*), i.e.:

$$uv \in L \Leftrightarrow u'v \notin L.$$

In essence, Hopcroft's co-inductive algorithm stepwise refines the initial two-
class partition $\{L, \Sigma^*\backslash L\}$, which distinguishes the classes of accepted words from
rejected words. It does so by refining a class C whenever it finds a symbol a
and a class C' such that $\emptyset \subsetneq \{w \in C \mid wa \in C'\} \subsetneq C$. The result of this
refinement (splitting, according to the splitter (a, C')) of C are the two classes
$C_1 = \{w \in C \mid wa \in C'\}$ and its (by definition non-trivial) complement in C,
$C_2 = C\backslash C_1$. Based on Nerode's Theorem [37], it can be shown that for regular
languages this procedure terminates after exhausting all potential splitters with
the smallest deterministic acceptor for this language. In fact, this is simply the
(unique) maximal fixpoint of the splitter functional, or, in other words, the
approach delivers the coarsest refinement of a given initial partition which is
stable under splitting.

Of course, there are some details one should be aware of:

- to be effective, one needs an adequate finite representation of all arising (intermediate) partitions, and
- the split of a class according to a given splitter needs to be effectively computable.

In Hopcroft's case, this representation problem was solved by having some finite
deterministic acceptor to start with, which can be regarded as a finite upper
bound of any chain of successive splitter-based refinements, which guarantees the
termination of the well-know minimization algorithm for deterministic automata.

The power of this approach was later applied to show that exactly the same
partition refinement procedure provides a minimization algorithm for bisimulation [36], just by dropping the determinism requirement for the initial acceptor [28].

Stepping back a bit, the "what" pattern of partition refinement can be characterized by the following requirements:

- A representation that allows to finitely represent each of the potentially arising intermediate partitions of the typically infinite domain.
- A notion of a *splitter*, which allows to effectively refine any intermediate partition (and thereby eliminate the previously revealed critical situation).
- An *oracle* that provides splitters until exhaustion. In the standard case we assume that only finitely many splits are possible, leading to a terminating algorithm that eliminates all critical situations (e.g., no word is classified incorrectly). Otherwise the process of refinement can continue indefinitely, as it would in general be the case when dealing with a non-regular scenario.

After termination (we assume that the process terminates), it results in a partition of the universe where all critical criteria are satisfied.

Rather than fully formalizing this pattern, we will formulate its ingredients and illustrate its impact for the three application scenario described above:

- Lazy Property-Oriented Expansion: The initial partition is given by the control-flow graph, the refinements by graphs arise through node splitting via successively separating the cases of availability/redundancy of an expression backwards along the transitions. The splitters are statement/location pairs, where the redundancy property of the statement cannot be determined for the location (cf. Sect. 4). The result is a model where all partial redundancies are resolved, i.e., where an expression at a location is either definitely available or definitely unavailable. Please note the underlying domain in this case: it is essentially the set of all paths through the control-flow graph leading from the initial location to some internal location.
- Counterexample-Guided Abstraction Refinement: The initial partition is given either by the control-flow graph (first case) or by a one-state abstraction. The refinements arise through node splitting via the introduction of separating predicates at the program variable/location level. Splitters are predicates deduced via SMT solving from revealed false positives (cf. Sect. 5). The result is a model where all false positives are eliminated. In this case the underlying domain is the set of all potential states, i.e., location/store pairs.
- Automata Learning: The initial partition is given by a one state abstraction. Refinements arise through node splitting on the basis of distinguishing futures, which take the role of splitters. These distinguishing futures are extracted from counterexample traces (cf. Sect. 6). Analogously to the setting of Hopcroft's original algorithm, the domain here is simply the set of all finite words over the interaction alphabet.
  After exhaustion of all splitters, the result is a minimal model of the behavioral language[1].

Thus, in fact, in all three cases an infinite domain is partitioned, however (typically) in a finitary manner. This cannot be guaranteed in general, but needs

---

[1] Note that in practice the correctness of the model cannot be guaranteed, as a perfect splitter oracle cannot be implemented but instead needs to be approximated through testing.

to be imposed by the considered scenario. Otherwise, the partition refinement process will not terminate, as it would be the case if, e.g., Hopcroft's algorithm would be applied to a context-free scenario (cf. Sect. 7).

4   Property-Oriented Expansion

Property-oriented expansion (POE) [47] is a program transformation technique based on unrolling (or expanding) the CFG. The expansion is driven by certain properties to be analyzed. An example of such a transformation is the elimination of all partial redundancies in a program: an expression e is called *partially redundant* at a certain point in the program if it has been computed on some, but not all program paths leading to this point. In [47] it was shown that POE is more powerful than traditional, motion-based approaches in eliminating partial redundancies.

POE can be regarded as the application of a *non-standard structural operational semantics* (SOS) [44]. An SOS is given as a set of inference rules describing the transformation of a configuration $\langle S, \sigma \rangle$ (consisting of a statement S and a valuation σ) to either a successor configuration $\langle S', \sigma' \rangle$, or a final valuation σ'. In the standard case, the valuation σ assigns a value to each variable in the program. However, this can be generalized to arbitrary analysis properties, which – in contrast to an abstract interpretation – need not correspond to sets of concrete valuations in any way, and in particular need not be elements of a lattice. An example of such a non-standard SOS is shown in Fig. 3. Here, σ corresponds to the set of *available expressions*. The sequential composition rule (Fig. 3a) is the same as in the standard case. The assignment rule (Fig. 3b) specifies how an assignment $x := e$ changes the set of available expressions: all expressions which contain x become unavailable, and the expression e becomes available if it does not contain x.

In traditional POE, starting with an initial property σ_0 at the initial location, the CFG is expanded by inserting a new location in the transformed CFG for each reachable pair of a location l and property σ. However, this can lead to a blow-up of the original program, which might even be unnecessary as it occurs independently of whether it is required for the analysis.

Lazy POE. To alleviate this, we propose the following, new approach (called *lazy POE*), where the CFG is expanded on demand only. Based on the (non-standard) SOS, we can define the *abstract collecting semantics*, which allow us to capture all possible sets of available expressions for each program location. If the property domain is finite, this *abstract collecting semantics* can be computed in finite time for the whole CFG using a fixpoint algorithm. For each location l annotated with $\sigma_{\mathrm{coll}}(l)$, we have $\sigma \in \sigma_{\mathrm{coll}}(l)$ if there exists a path ending in l with final property σ.

It may be desirable to ensure that at certain locations l, $\sigma_{\mathrm{coll}}(l)$ does not contain properties σ, σ' which differ according to a certain predicate. That is, for some predicate P on properties, we want to ensure that either $\forall \sigma \in \sigma_{\mathrm{coll}}(l) : P(\sigma)$

$$\frac{\langle S_1, \sigma \rangle \Rightarrow \sigma'}{\langle S_1; S_2, \sigma \rangle \Rightarrow \langle S_2, \sigma' \rangle} \qquad \frac{}{\langle x := e, \sigma \rangle \Rightarrow \{e' \in \sigma \cup \{e\} \mid x \notin \text{vars}(e')\}}$$

(a)   (b)

Fig. 3. Sample SOS-style rules. (a) Standard sequential composition rule; (b) Non-standard assignment rule for available expressions.

or $\forall \sigma \in \sigma_{\text{coll}}(l) : \neg P(\sigma)$. For example, it is useful to know that an expression e is either *definitely available* or *definitely unavailable* at some location.

As noted above, the CFG partitions the set of all possible program paths. If there exists a location l with "mixed" properties in $\sigma_{\text{coll}}(l)$ according to a predicate P, we refine this partition by splitting l into two: one location annotated with $\{\sigma \in \sigma_{\text{coll}}(l) \mid P(\sigma)\}$ and the other annotated with $\{\sigma \in \sigma_{\text{coll}}(l) \mid \neg P(\sigma)\}$. This might introduce non-determinism, which can be resolved by – in a fashion very similar to Hopcroft's algorithm – iteratively *propagating* the split to the immediate predecessors, until again a *coarsest stable partition* is obtained.

Example. Consider the program with the control-flow graph depicted in Fig. 4a. This program nondeterministically[2] executes either the action $x := a + y$ or $y := b + x$ in a loop, or it exits. Executing this program with the abstract collecting semantics for available expressions until stabilization yields the shown available expression sets.

Assume we want to ensure definite (un-)availability of the expression $b + x$ at the exit location, for example because this expression determines the exit value, and we do not want to unnecessarily recompute it. As a first step, we therefore split the exit node such that $b + x$ is in either all or none of the possible available expression sets at this location (Fig. 4b).

However, the central location of the program is still annotated with the possible available expression sets $\emptyset$, $\{a + y\}$, and $\{b + x\}$. This information is too coarse to allow the definiteness of the (un-)availability of $b + x$ at the exit locations to be derived. Thus, this location needs to be split as well (i.e., the split of the exit location *propagates* to the central location). The set $\{\emptyset, \{a + y\}, \{b + x\}\}$ is partitioned into $\{\emptyset, \{a + y\}\}$ ($b + x$ is *definitely unavailable* at the respective exit location) and $\{\{b + x\}\}$ ($b + x$ is *definitely available* at the respective exit location). The result of this second split is shown in Fig. 5, and the resulting transformed program no longer contains any uncertainties about the availability of $b + x$ at the exit node, allowing to perform the desired optimization (e.g., replacing **return** $b + x$ with **return** y).

---

[2] We assume that the non-determinism is due to presentation only: the conditions guarding the respective transitions are not displayed, since they do not matter for our example.

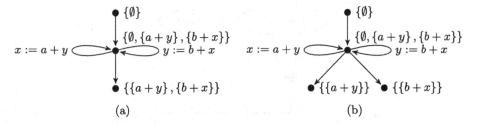

Fig. 4. (a): Initial annotated control-flow graph; (b) Annotated control-flow graph after splitting exit node

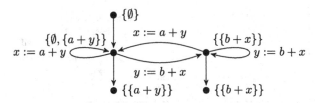

Fig. 5. Final control-flow graph after propagating split

5 CEGAR: Automated Partition Refinement

In the context of eliminating partial redundancies (cf. Sect. 4), the critical situation requiring a node split is identical throughout the coarse model. When analyzing other characteristics of a program such as whether or not a certain temporal property holds, the critical splitting criteria might vary locally. In this setting, it becomes difficult to manually describe a non-standard SOS in order to sufficiently refine the model using POE while keeping the size of the refined model small.

Counterexample-Guided Abstraction Refinement (CEGAR). In order to infer how and where to split a node in the coarse model, CEGAR [9] utilizes spurious counterexamples retrieved from model checking the desired property. This approach refines a model iteratively. Within a refinement step, the analysis increases the precision of the model by excluding the most recently retrieved spurious counterexample. The three important steps within a CEGAR approach are the initial abstraction, the counterexample analysis and the applied refinement.

Figure 6 gives a conceptual overview of CEGAR. The process starts with an initial abstract model that over-approximates the behavior of the analyzed system. A sequence of model checking attempts and refinement steps continues until the analyzed property can either be verified or falsified.

For a property that holds on the analyzed program, the final model resulting from the CEGAR loop is illustrated as its set of reachable states S_f in the Venn diagram of Fig. 7. The set S describes the reachable states in the original system under analysis. S is a subset of the overall state space represented by the trivial

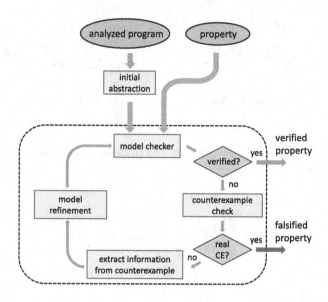

Fig. 6. Conceptual overview of a CEGAR approach

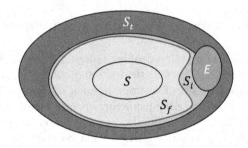

Fig. 7. Model refinement based on sets of reachable program states

one-state abstraction S_t. The CEGAR loop refines the initial over-approximating model S_i by excluding the set of error states E.

The CEGAR approaches illustrated in the following sections use a model consisting of abstract states that partition the program's state space. A transition between abstract states is introduced whenever a transition between representatives of the corresponding partitions exists in the analyzed system. This method is known by the name of existential abstraction [9,10]. It guarantees an over-approximation of the analyzed program's behavior because the set of successor states of an abstract state is the union of its representatives' successor states. As for a single refinement step, the abstract state right before the first spurious transition occurs is subdivided into two partitions.

Example. Consider the program with the control flow graph depicted in Fig. 8 that calculates the factorial of an integer value n. The *assume* statement results in an error whenever variable n is initialized to an integer less than 2.

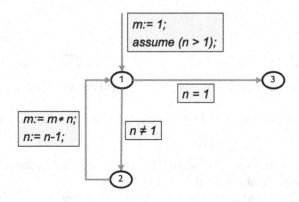

Fig. 8. Control flow graph of the exemplary factorial program

As an exemplary analysis of this factorial program, we want to prove the following property:

Analyzed property ϕ. *Variable m is even when the program terminates.*

A CFG can be seen as an over-approximating model of a program in which the state of its variables is not explicitly represented. Within this control-flow model, each node is an abstract state representing all explicit states that feature the same program location. An attempt to verify property ϕ on this control-flow model itself yields no success. The program terminates at location 3 which is reachable in the control-flow model, but the abstract state corresponding to location 3 does not specify any details of variable m's value. Section 5.1 illustrates a refinement of this coarse control-flow model using CEGAR, whereas Sect. 5.2 applies CEGAR to a further abstracted initial model.

5.1   CFG-Based CEGAR

The locations of the control-flow model do not include information about the data, instead they partition all possible states according to the value of the *program counter*. The locations therefore each represent a partition on the set of all possible valuations.

The model will be iteratively refined according to predicates that constrain the values of variables n and m. Each refinement step will introduce a distinguishing predicate that subdivides an existing partition. We will denote the negation of a predicate x by $\bar{x}$. The states are initially numbered according to the locations of the control flow graph. An additional digit is appended if a state is split due to a refinement step, meaning that, e.g., state 2.1 is split into states

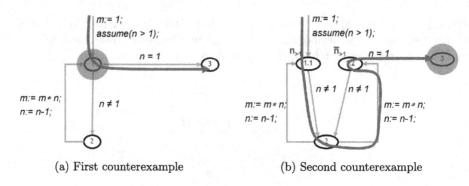

(a) First counterexample   (b) Second counterexample

Fig. 9. CFG-based CEGAR example (part 1) (Color figure online)

2.1.1 and 2.1.2. A first model checking attempt on the initial model returns the counterexample path highlighted in red in Fig. 9a.

Analyzing this counterexample, it becomes apparent that its first spurious behavior is present at location 1 (red circle). Because variable n is initially greater than 1, all feasible execution paths lead from location 1 to location 2 initially. The refinement step partitions location 1 according to the predicate $n_{>1}$ which states that the value of variable n is greater than 1. This refinement therefore separates states at location 1 that are initially reachable ($n_{>1}$ is true) from those with a successor state at location 3 ($\overline{n_{>1}}$ holds).

The result of this first refinement step is shown in Fig. 9b. For each in- and outgoing edge of location 1 that existed previously, a transition to one or both of the partitioned states is introduced based on existential abstraction. For example, in the case of state 1.2, the initial transition is not reconnected to state 1.2 because the initialization of n to an integer greater than 1 contradicts the predicate $\overline{n_{>1}}$. However, state 1.2 is reconnected to state 2: the valuation $\langle n = -3, m = 1 \rangle$ could be a representative of the partition class described by both state 1.2 and 2. Because the precise program semantics dictate that $n = -3$ at location 1 leads to location 2 in the next step, a transition is introduced here. No execution of the program can ever reach a state where variable n is less than 0, but this fact is not represented by the model yet.

While the original counterexample is no longer valid in Fig. 9b, the refined system still admits another (spurious) counterexample, again displayed as a red path. This second counterexample again reaches location 3, which until now does not specify any constraints for the value of variable m. This time, the first spurious behavior is to be found at the state representing location 3 itself. If variable n is initially set to 2, the program execution follows the marked counterexample path. This is, however, the only *real* path that meets the counterexample criterion, and it ends in a state where m is even. The second refinement step therefore splits the state representing location 3 based on whether or not m is even (predicate m_e). Because state 1.2 does not specify any information about

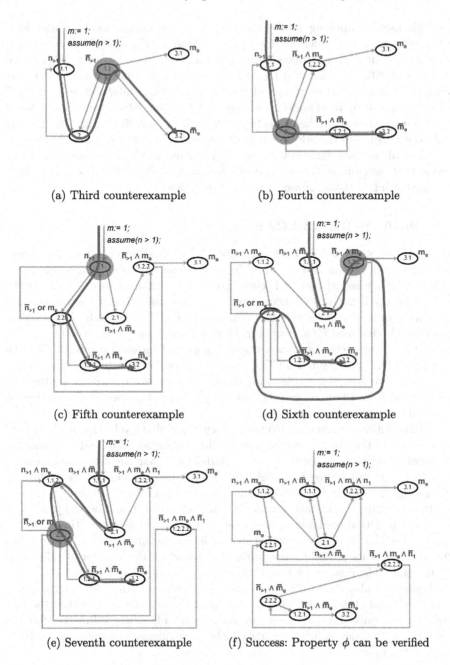

(a) Third counterexample

(b) Fourth counterexample

(c) Fifth counterexample

(d) Sixth counterexample

(e) Seventh counterexample

(f) Success: Property ϕ can be verified

Fig. 10. CFG-based CEGAR example (part 2)

the value of m, it is reconnected to both 3.1 and 3.2. The next model checking attempt finds a different counterexample and the refinement continues.

This loop comprising model checking, counterexample analysis and local refinement then continues for five more iterations (Fig. 10a–e). A refinement step of particular interest takes place after the sixth counterexample, illustrated in Fig. 10d. State 1.2.2 has a transition to state 2.2 even though no negative values of n can ever be encountered. An SMT solver can infer that n has to be 1 after the transition from state 2.1 to state 1.2.2, taking into consideration that n is decremented by 1 at the respective control-flow edge. State 1.2.2 is therefore refined according to the additional predicate n_1 meaning that n has the value 1.

After all seven refinement steps, the resulting model is precise enough to reveal that variable m is even in every reachable state at location 3 (Fig. 10f), demonstrating that the property in question holds.

5.2   Predicate-Based CEGAR

In the previous section, we have illustrated the CEGAR approach as a means of refining an initial control-flow graph by performing partition refinement on the valuation space associated with each program location. However, treating the CFG specially is not strictly necessary, as the program counter can be regarded as a (more or less) normal variable. While a single CFG is typically of a size that can easily be handled by a computer, this changes dramatically when analyzing concurrently interacting systems, where at a given time each component can be in an arbitrary location of its CFG, unleashing the full force of the state explosion (or, more adequately, "location explosion") problem. In such a situation, abstracting from the precise CFG and lazily refining the control abstraction on demand becomes a necessity.

The partition refinement then takes place at a global level, refining the overall state space of the system (where a state comprises a location and a valuation). Location predicates of form $pc_i = l_j$ (indicating that the i-th component is in location j) can be used to split classes according to their location, directly impacting the set of enabled statements that can transform a state.

In our example, we start with an initial abstraction based on the predicates m_e (signaling that variable m has an even value) and l_3 (indicating that the current location is 3, the program exit point). Transitions between these initial abstract state partitions are introduced based on the concept of existential abstraction. The resulting initial abstract model is illustrated in Fig. 11a.

Figure 11a also shows the counterexample retrieved after checking property ϕ on the initial abstract model. The first spurious behavior is present at the first state on this path: no real execution trace leads to location 3 directly after the initial step. In order to further partition the class causing the spurious behavior, we add the predicate $n_{>1}$ stating that n is greater than 1.

After applying existential abstraction locally, we retrieve a refined model that excludes the spurious counterexample (Fig. 11b). The initial state is not connected to the top-right state because any change from $n_{>1}$ to $\overline{n_{>1}}$ would imply that n held the value 2 right before the transition. In this case however, m would contain an even value afterwards. Again, this can be derived by SMT

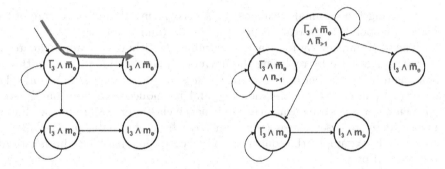

(a) Initial abstract model and spurious coun-   (b) Success: Property ϕ can be verified
terexample path

Fig. 11. Predicate-based CEGAR using data and location predicates

solvers. As a result, the state violating the property becomes unreachable and
the verification is successful.

6 Automata Learning, or Black-Box Partition Refinement

The last technique we want to take a look at is *(active) automata learning* [4,49].
Originating from the grammatical inference community [19], active automata
learning is a method of *learning* an unknown regular language by asking two
kinds of questions to a "teacher": a *membership query* corresponds to the question "is the word w in the target language $\mathcal{L}$?", and with an *equivalence query*, a
learner asks "is my hypothesis $\mathcal{H}$ [represented as a DFA] a correct model, recognizing exactly the target language?" If the answer to the latter kind of query is
negative, the teacher is expected to supply the learner with a *counterexample*,
i.e., a word $w \in \Sigma^*$ such that $\lambda_{\mathcal{L}}(w) \neq \lambda_{\mathcal{H}}(w)$.[3] The learner then *refines* the
hypothesis (possibly by asking further membership queries), and eventually sub-
mits the new hypothesis to another equivalence query. This process is iterated
until an equivalence query is met with a positive answer, or until some defined
termination criterion (e.g., exhaustion of resources) is triggered.

Technical Sketch. The "theoretical backbone" of a large class of automata
learning algorithms is the *Nerode congruence* [37]. It is a binary relation on words
over Σ, and defined as follows (for a language $\mathcal{L} \subseteq \Sigma^*$ and words $u, u' \in \Sigma^*$):

$$u \equiv_{\mathcal{L}} u' :\Leftrightarrow \forall v \in \Sigma^* : \lambda_{\mathcal{L}}(u \cdot v) = \lambda_{\mathcal{L}}(u' \cdot v).$$

The famous *Myhill-Nerode theorem* states that $\equiv_{\mathcal{L}}$ has finitely many equivalence classes if and only if $\mathcal{L}$ is regular. Furthermore, $\equiv_{\mathcal{L}}$ serves as a basis for

---

[3] Here and in the following, $\lambda_{\mathcal{L}}$ and $\lambda_{\mathcal{H}}$ denote the *labeling function* of $\mathcal{L}$ and $\mathcal{L}(\mathcal{H})$,
respectively: $\lambda_{\mathcal{L}}(w) = 1$ if $w \in \mathcal{L}$, and 0 otherwise.

constructing the minimal, canonical DFA recognizing $\mathcal{L}$, and each state of this DFA corresponds to an equivalence class of $\equiv_{\mathcal{L}}$ (and vice versa).

The idea pursued by most active learning algorithms is to approximate the Nerode congruence by replacing the universal quantification over Σ^* with considering a finite number of *distinguishing suffixes* (or *futures*) $\mathcal{D} \subset \Sigma^*$ only. The corresponding equivalence relation $\equiv_{\mathcal{D}}$ and its induced partition on Σ^* are a coarsening of Nerode equivalence. Equivalence classes of $\equiv_{\mathcal{D}}$ are further finitely identified by representatives (*short prefixes*) from the finite, prefix-closed set $\mathcal{S}p \subset \Sigma^*$. For example, the equivalence class corresponding to the initial state is represented by ε.

However, determining the equivalence class with respect to $\equiv_{\mathcal{D}}$ of an arbitrary word $u \in \Sigma^*$ requires to pose membership queries (for evaluating $\lambda_{\mathcal{L}}(u \cdot v)$ for $v \in \mathcal{D}$). To obtain a "closed-form solution", for each representative $u \in \mathcal{S}p$ and input symbol $a \in \Sigma$, the equivalence class wrt. $\equiv_{\mathcal{D}}$ of ua is determined. This equivalence class (rather: its corresponding state in the hypothesis automaton) forms the a-successor of the state represented by u. This step of obtaining a closed-form hypothesis $\mathcal{H}$, inducing a partition on Σ^*, from a finite sample of the equivalence relation $\equiv_{\mathcal{D}}$ by *extrapolation* gives rise to the synonym "regular extrapolation" for automata learning [16].

When the learner is presented with a *counterexample* $w \in \Sigma^*$, it eventually refines the equivalence relation $\equiv_{\mathcal{D}}$ by augmenting the set $\mathcal{D}$ of distinguishing suffixes. The new distinguishing suffix can usually be extracted from the counterexample w directly. Augmenting $\mathcal{D}$ (and thus refining $\equiv_{\mathcal{D}}$) leads to the set $\mathcal{S}p$ being augmented as well, and thus an increase in hypothesis size. Note, however, that the partition on Σ^* induced by the updated hypothesis is not necessarily a refinement of the previous partition, due to possible extrapolation errors.

6.1 Black-Box Checking

Peled *et al.* [43] have proposed *black-box checking* as a way to model check systems for which no model is available, i.e., which present themselves as black boxes. In this scenario, automata learning is used to infer a model of the target system. Once a stable hypothesis has been learned, this hypothesis is then checked against a specification, possibly yielding a counterexample.

Similar to CEGAR, the "nature" of the counterexample needs to be examined. If the trace, when executed on the black-box system, yields the same output as predicted by the hypothesis, it is a *real* counterexample that shows that the system violates the specification. Otherwise, if the hypothesis predicts an incorrect output, it is *spurious* and can be fed to the learner which, in turn, comes up with a refined hypothesis, leading to another iteration of the sketched process.[4]

The overall approach of black-box checking is very similar to CEGAR: here, the abstraction is imposed by substituting the Nerode congruence $\equiv_{\mathcal{L}}$ with the

---

[4] It should be noted that this approach can only be applied to specifications that admit finite counterexample traces (e.g., safety LTL formulae), as an infinite-length counterexample cannot be tested on the system.

coarser relation $\equiv_{\mathcal{D}}$ for constructing a finite-state model. A counterexample might either show a property violation, or refine our abstraction by splitting equivalence classes of $\equiv_{\mathcal{D}}$, thus reducing the gap towards $\equiv_{\mathcal{L}}$. While this notion of abstraction is somewhat different from the prevalent one in the context of CEGAR (where abstraction is employed to deal with the otherwise too large or even infinite state space), automata learning has been extended to simultaneously infer and refine abstractions in several dimensions, e.g., for dealing with large or infinite alphabets [24,25], or with data values ranging over unbounded domains [1,26].

One should, however, keep in mind an important difference (and deficiency): while the abstraction in the classical CEGAR remains sound throughout all refinement steps, the same does not hold true for automata learning. A model inferred by a learning algorithm is in general neither an over- nor an under-abstraction, and the evolution of the languages corresponding to subsequent hypotheses may be highly non-monotonic. Therefore, a positive model checking result during black-box checking does not guarantee that the whole system conforms to the specification. This is a direct consequence of the testing-based nature of automata learning, which is fundamentally incapable of making any kind of statements about parts of the system which have not been exercised during testing.

Nevertheless, automata learning and the black-box checking approach are a valuable asset when dealing with systems (or components) for which sound models cannot be generated using traditional techniques, such as binaries or web services. Important applications are regression testing [17], specification mining [3], e.g., as a way to establish runtime monitors [6], and the quality assurance of evolving system [38]. In particular in the latter case, knowledge about the systems is not established in a dedicated phase. Rather it is cumulated in a continuous learning process, which may involve the monitoring of customer site installations to continuously increase reliability. In addition, conformance testing techniques [5] may be applied for approximating equivalence queries using membership queries, in a way that guarantees correctness up to certain assumptions (e.g., assuming a concrete bound on the number of states of the target system).

Example. We want to conclude our explanation on automata learning and black-box checking with a small example, highlighting the overall approach and illustrating some key characteristics. Let us consider a simple on-line service, that allows registration of users (reg, assuming a fixed user name). Registering twice is impossible. Once registered, a user can log in (login) to the service, and eventually log out (logout). A desirable property that we would like to verify on the system might be given by the statement "once logged in, a user cannot log in again before logging out", which can be encoded into the LTL property $\phi = \mathbf{G}(\mathsf{login} \Rightarrow \mathbf{X}(\overline{\mathsf{login}}\ \mathbf{WU}\ \mathsf{logout}))$.

Learning usually starts with a one-state initial hypothesis $\mathcal{H}_0$, depicted in Fig. 12a. In the initial state, registering is the only possible action. However, in the absence of any splitters, the consequences of registering are not further

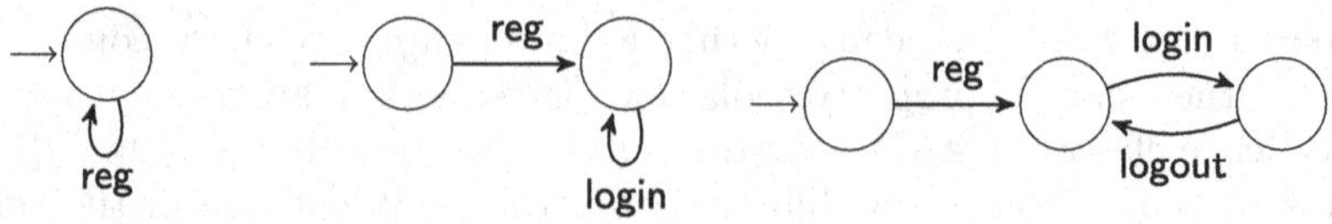

(a) Initial hypothesis (b) Second hypothesis   (c) Final hypothesis

Fig. 12. Sequence of hypotheses inferred through learning

examined, hence the target state is assumed to be the same as the initial one. Here, it already becomes apparent that the model is neither an over- nor an under-approximation: it contains paths which are not admissible by the actual system (e.g., reg reg: registering twice), and vice versa (e.g., reg login). Consequently, the fact that ϕ holds for the initial model is of little practical value.

As noted above, a *counterexample* that disproves the hypothesis is reg reg. From this counterexample, a learning algorithm would derive the splitter reg, and thus recognize that the initial state is different from the state reached via reg (as registering is possible in one state but not in the other). It will further discover that the latter state admits the action login. For the same reasons as above, however, it will not proceed to examine the impact of performing this action. The resulting hypothesis $\mathcal{H}_1$ is depicted in Fig. 12b.

This hypothesis now indeed violates the specification ϕ. Model checking "$\phi \models \mathcal{H}_1$?" would yield the counterexample reg login login. A counterexample analysis would then yield that the splitter login needs to be applied to the state reached by reg. This shows that login again moves to another state, in which logging in again is not possible (but the logout action is enabled). The resulting (final) hypothesis $\mathcal{H}_2$ (which also satisfies ϕ) is shown in Fig. 12c.

7 Discussion of the Profiles and Perspectives

Partition refinement is a technology and art for deriving tailored finite quotients of potentially infinitary systems that expose just as much detail as required for a certain analysis, verification or transformation task. This has been illustrated above along three example categories of quite different nature, which all come with specific challenges.

– For (lazy) POE everything is quite easy, as long as the domain for abstracting the store is finite, like in the case of any bit vector analysis. In this case scalability is the main concern: how can one succeed while avoiding the potential exponential state explosion? This means that at the generic level, on-demand techniques, like the lazy POE presented here, need to be developed, whereas the concrete application requires the identification of an adequate abstract domain (at the "what"-level), a precondition for many analysis and verification approaches.

POE has been successfully used, first as a means to spread out the control-flow graph in a fashion that optimally supports program transformations, like the elimination of all partial redundancies. A second application is the validation of the mutual consistency between the models of a heterogeneous system specification [48] by constructing a "unifying" operational model that obeys all the operational constraints of all sub-specifications. This is the conceptual basis underlying the One-Thing-Approach [34,45] and its corresponding tool product line [50].

- The CEGAR approaches also rely on a "what"-level specification, which needs to be provided manually and which can then be automatically model checked to provide the false positives driving the corresponding partition refinement. However, in contrast to lazy POE, where splitter identification is straightforward, this is the key problem for CEGAR for two reasons. First, it consists of (in general undecidable) "how"-level reasoning to eliminate the found unfeasible counterexample path typically with the aid of SMT solvers. Second, the derived splitters (predicates over the set of program variables and locations) should be powerful enough to guarantee that the iterative partition refinement process will eventually terminate. In fact, in contrast to the other two approaches considered here, resulting partitionings are by no means unique, and even if there exists an adequate finite partitioning, the refinement process may easily bypass it and continue forever. It should be noted, however, that, in general, we are essentially dealing with a problem here as complex as the automatic derivation of program invariants. Thus it is not too surprising that the original paper [9] considered a very special finitary scenario with the main concern to increase efficiency via this impressive SMT-based heuristic. We believe that the future research potential for CEGAR for system verification is enormous, and its success will definitely grow with the increasing power of future SMT solvers.

- The world of black-box partition refinement in terms of active automata learning looks simpler, as it, by it nature, avoids all the "how"-level problems. In essence, the user only needs to specify the interaction potential, in terms of a so-called learning alphabet,[5] and the rest is automatic. Obviously, the "is automatic" leaves a lot of room for algorithmic progress in order to be able to address problems of practical relevance [27,33], but even if we totally ignore this aspect for a moment, varying the notion of interaction potential alone is currently a hot research topic. The original setting based on deterministic finite automata soon turned out to be impractical and was replaced by the more expressive Mealy machines [41] and I/O-automata [2]. Whereas this step can be seen as a kind of optimization, the subsequent generalization to so-called register automata [22,23,26], which explicitly represent data flow, lifts automata learning technology to an entirely new level in which program

---

[5] Even this is not really necessary. Our also partition refinement-based automated alphabet abstraction technology [24,25] may be used to automatically derive an adequate level of observation. Of course, for learning realistic system it is important to provide a functioning test harness for triggering the system behavior [35,52].

behaviors are not modeled via formal languages, but via parameterized, flow graph-like models which may even be executed [26]. This approach has even been further developed involving SMT-solving with all its caveats [8] (see the discussion of CEGAR above).

However, independent of these developments, black-box partition refinement is deemed to be neither correct nor complete, which truly distinguishes it from the other two approaches which maintain a notion of over-approximation in order to guarantee correctness.

That the three considered very different approaches can all be regarded as instances of a sufficiently generalized notion of partition refinement, i.e., a special co-inductive technique realizable via maximal fixpoint computation, is not just an interesting observation. Rather it is the conceptual backbone for their mutual integration. Essentially it should allow one to smoothly combine their (chaotic) iteration processes into a common heterogeneous maximal fixpoint computation, in order to obtain a technology exploiting their mutual strength and to overcome their inherent weaknesses. An early example for enhancing verification with learning technology is the black-box checking approach [42], while the assume-guarantee approach [11] indicates a way to overcome the black box systems' inherent lack of correctness in dedicated scenarios. We hope that our discussion helps paving the way to more systematic studies in this direction.

References

1. Aarts, F., Heidarian, F., Kuppens, H., Olsen, P., Vaandrager, F.: Automata learning through counterexample guided abstraction refinement. In: Giannakopoulou, D., Méry, D. (eds.) FM 2012. LNCS, vol. 7436, pp. 10–27. Springer, Heidelberg (2012). http://dx.doi.org/10.1007/978-3-642-32759-9_4
2. Aarts, F., Vaandrager, F.: Learning I/O automata. In: Gastin, P., Laroussinie, F. (eds.) CONCUR 2010. LNCS, vol. 6269, pp. 71–85. Springer, Heidelberg (2010). http://dx.doi.org/10.1007/978-3-642-15375-4_6
3. Ammons, G., Bodik, R., Larus, J.R.: Mining specifications. In: Proceedings of the 29th ACM SIGPLAN-SIGACT Symposium on Principles of Programming Languages, pp. 4–16. ACM, Portland (2002). http://research.microsoft.com/apps/pubs/default.aspx?id=71998
4. Angluin, D.: Learning regular sets from queries and counterexamples. Inf. Comput. 75(2), 87–106 (1987)
5. Berg, T., Grinchtein, O., Jonsson, B., Leucker, M., Raffelt, H., Steffen, B.: On the correspondence between conformance testing and regular inference. In: Cerioli, M. (ed.) FASE 2005. LNCS, vol. 3442, pp. 175–189. Springer, Heidelberg (2005)
6. Bertolino, A., Calabrò, A., Merten, M., Steffen, B.: Never-stop learning: continuous validation of learned models for evolving systems through monitoring. ERCIM News 88, 28–29 (2012). http://ercim-news.ercim.eu/en88/special/never-stop-learning-continuous-validation-of-learned-models-for-evolving-systems-through-monitoring
7. Beyer, D., Löwe, S.: Explicit-state software model checking based on CEGAR and interpolation. In: Cortellessa, V., Varró, D. (eds.) FASE 2013 (ETAPS 2013). LNCS, vol. 7793, pp. 146–162. Springer, Heidelberg (2013)

8. Cassel, S., Howar, F., Jonsson, B., Steffen, B.: Learning extended finite state machines. In: Giannakopoulou, D., Salaün, G. (eds.) SEFM 2014. LNCS, vol. 8702, pp. 250–264. Springer, Heidelberg (2014). http://dx.doi.org/10.1007/978-3-319-10431-7_18

9. Clarke, E.M., Grumberg, O., Jha, S., Lu, Y., Veith, H.: Counterexample-guided abstraction refinement for symbolic model checking. J. ACM 50(5), 752–794 (2003)

10. Clarke, E.M., Grumberg, O., Long, D.E.: Model checking and abstraction. ACM Trans. Program. Lang. Syst. 16(5), 1512–1542 (1994)

11. Cobleigh, J.M., Giannakopoulou, D., Păsăreanu, C.S.: Learning assumptions for compositional verification. In: Garavel, H., Hatcliff, J. (eds.) TACAS 2003. LNCS, vol. 2619, pp. 331–346. Springer, Heidelberg (2003). citeseer.ist.psu.edu/cobleigh03learning.html

12. Cooper, K.D., Simpson, L.T., Vick, C.A.: Operator strength reduction. ACM Trans. Program. Lang. Syst. 23(5), 603–625 (2001). http://doi.acm.org/10.1145/504709.504710

13. De Moura, L., Bjørner, N.: Satisfiability modulo theories: introduction and applications. Commun. ACM 54(9), 69–77 (2011). http://doi.acm.org/10.1145/1995376.1995394

14. Floyd, R.W.: Assigning meaning to programs. Math. Aspects Comput. Sci. (Proc. Symp. Appl. Math.) 19, 19–32 (1967). American Mathematical Society

15. Graf, S., Saïdi, H.: Construction of abstract state graphs with PVS. In: Grumberg, O. (ed.) CAV 1997. LNCS, vol. 1254. Springer, Heidelberg (1997). http://dl.acm.org/citation.cfm?id=647766.733618

16. Hagerer, A., Hungar, H., Niese, O., Steffen, B.: Model generation by moderated regular extrapolation. In: Kutsche, R.-D., Weber, H. (eds.) FASE 2002. LNCS, vol. 2306, pp. 80–95. Springer, Heidelberg (2002)

17. Hagerer, A., Margaria, T., Niese, O., Steffen, B., Brune, G., Ide, H.D.: Efficient regression testing of CTI-systems: testing a complex call-center solution. Annu. Rev. Commun. Int. Eng. Consort. (IEC) 55, 1033–1040 (2001)

18. Hecht, M.S.: Flow Analysis of Computer Programs. Elsevier Science Inc., New York (1977)

19. de la Higuera, C.: Grammatical Inference: Learning Automata and Grammars. Cambridge University Press, New York (2010)

20. Hoare, C.A.R.: An axiomatic basis for computer programming. Commun. ACM 12(10), 576–580 (1969)

21. Hopcroft, J.E.: An N log N algorithm for minimizing states in a finite automaton. Technical report, Stanford University, Stanford, CA (1971)

22. Howar, F., Isberner, M., Steffen, B., Bauer, O., Jonsson, B.: Inferring semantic interfaces of data structures. In: Margaria, T., Steffen, B. (eds.) ISoLA 2012, Part I. LNCS, vol. 7609, pp. 554–571. Springer, Heidelberg (2012)

23. Howar, F., Steffen, B., Jonsson, B., Cassel, S.: Inferring canonical register automata. In: Kuncak, V., Rybalchenko, A. (eds.) VMCAI 2012. LNCS, vol. 7148, pp. 251–266. Springer, Heidelberg (2012)

24. Howar, F., Steffen, B., Merten, M.: Automata learning with automated alphabet abstraction refinement. In: Jhala, R., Schmidt, D. (eds.) VMCAI 2011. LNCS, vol. 6538, pp. 263–277. Springer, Heidelberg (2011)

25. Isberner, M., Howar, F., Steffen, B.: Inferring automata with state-local alphabet abstractions. In: Brat, G., Rungta, N., Venet, A. (eds.) NFM 2013. LNCS, vol. 7871, pp. 124–138. Springer, Heidelberg (2013)

26. Isberner, M., Howar, F., Steffen, B.: Learning register automata: from languages to program structures. Mach. Learn. 96(1), 65–98 (2014)

27. Isberner, M., Howar, F., Steffen, B.: The TTT algorithm: a redundancy-free approach to active automata learning. In: Bonakdarpour, B., Smolka, S.A. (eds.) RV 2014. LNCS, vol. 8734, pp. 307–322. Springer, Heidelberg (2014). http://dx.doi.org/10.1007/978-3-319-11164-3_26

28. Kanellakis, P.C., Smolka, S.A.: CCS expressions, finite state processes, and three problems of equivalence. In: Proceedings of the Second Annual ACM Symposium on Principles of Distributed Computing, PODC 1983, pp. 228–240. ACM, New York (1983). http://doi.acm.org/10.1145/800221.806724

29. Knoop, J., Rüthing, O., Steffen, B.: Lazy code motion. In: Proceedings of the ACM SIGPLAN 1992 Conference on Programming Language Design and Implementation (PLDI), pp. 224–234. ACM (1992)

30. Knoop, J., Rüthing, O., Steffen, B.: Lazy strength reduction. J. Program. Lang. 1, 71–91 (1993)

31. Knoop, J., Rüthing, O., Steffen, B.: Partial dead code elimination. In: Proceedings of the ACM SIGPLAN 1994 Conference on Programming Language Design and Implementation (PLDI), pp. 147–158. ACM (1994)

32. Legay, A., Delahaye, B., Bensalem, S.: Statistical model checking: an overview. In: Barringer, H., Falcone, Y., Finkbeiner, B., Havelund, K., Lee, I., Pace, G., Roşu, G., Sokolsky, O., Tillmann, N. (eds.) RV 2010. LNCS, vol. 6418, pp. 122–135. Springer, Heidelberg (2010). http://dx.doi.org/10.1007/978-3-642-16612-9_11

33. Maler, O., Mens, I.-E.: Learning regular languages over large alphabets. In: Ábrahám, E., Havelund, K. (eds.) TACAS 2014 (ETAPS). LNCS, vol. 8413, pp. 485–499. Springer, Heidelberg (2014). http://dx.doi.org/10.1007/978-3-642-54862-8_41

34. Margaria, T., Steffen, B.: Business Process Modelling in the jABC: The One-Thing-Approach. In: Cardoso, J., van der Aalst, W. (eds.) Handbook of Research on Business Process Modeling. IGI Global, Hershey (2009)

35. Merten, M., Isberner, M., Howar, F., Steffen, B., Margaria, T.: Automated learning setups in automata learning. In: Margaria, T., Steffen, B. (eds.) ISoLA 2012, Part I. LNCS, vol. 7609, pp. 591–607. Springer, Heidelberg (2012)

36. Milner, R.: Communication and Concurrency. PHI Series in Computer Science. Prentice-Hall Inc, Upper Saddle River (1989)

37. Nerode, A.: Linear automaton transformations. Proc. Am. Math. Soc. 9(4), 541–544 (1958)

38. Neubauer, J., Steffen, B., Bauer, O., Windmüller, S., Merten, M., Margaria, T., Howar, F.: Automated continuous quality assurance. In: Formal Methods in Software Engineering: Rigorous and Agile Approaches (FormSERA), pp. 37–43 (2012). http://ieeexplore.ieee.org/xpl/articleDetails.jsp?arnumber=6229787

39. Nielson, F., Nielson, H.R.: Infinitary control flow analysis: a collecting semantics for closure analysis. In: Proceedings of the 24th ACM SIGPLAN-SIGACT Symposium on Principles of Programming Languages, POPL 1997, pp. 332–345. ACM, New York (1997). http://doi.acm.org/10.1145/263699.263745

40. Nielson, F., Nielson, H.R., Hankin, C.: Principles of Program Analysis, 2nd edn. Springer, Berlin (2005)

41. Niese, O.: An integrated approach to testing complex systems, Ph.D. thesis, University of Dortmund, Germany (2003)

42. Peled, D., Vardi, M.Y., Yannakakis, M.: Black box checking. In: Wu, J., Chanson, S.T., Gao, Q. (eds.) Proceedings of FORTE 1999, pp. 225–240. Kluwer Academic, Dordrecht (1999)

43. Peled, D., Vardi, M.Y., Yannakakis, M.: Black box checking. J. Autom. Lang. Comb. 7(2), 225–246 (2001). http://dl.acm.org/citation.cfm?id=767345.767349

44. Plotkin, G.D.: A structural approach to operational semantics. J. Log. Algebr. Program. **60**(61), 17–139 (2004)
45. Schaefer, I., Rabiser, R., Clarke, D., Bettini, L., Benavides, D., Botterweck, G., Pathak, A., Trujilol, S., Villela, K.: Software diversity - state of the art and perspectives. Int. J. Softw. Tools Technol. Transf. (STTT) **14**(5), 477–495 (2012)
46. Steffen, B.: Data flow analysis as model checking. In: Ito, T., Meyer, A.R. (eds.) TACS 1991. LNCS, vol. 526. Springer, Heidelberg (1991). http://www.springerlink.com/content/y5p607674g6q1482/
47. Steffen, B.: Property-oriented expansion. In: Cousot, R., Schmidt, D.A. (eds.) SAS 1996. LNCS, vol. 1145. Springer, Heidelberg (1996). http://dx.doi.org/10.1007/3-540-61739-6_31
48. Steffen, B.: Unifying models. In: Reischuk, R., Morvan, M. (eds.) STACS 1997. LNCS, vol. 1200. Springer, Heidelberg (1997). http://dx.doi.org/10.1007/BFb0023444
49. Steffen, B., Howar, F., Merten, M.: Introduction to active automata learning from a practical perspective. In: Bernardo, M., Issarny, V. (eds.) SFM 2011. LNCS, vol. 6659, pp. 256–296. Springer, Heidelberg (2011)
50. Steffen, B., Margaria, T., Nagel, R., Jörges, S., Kubczak, C.: Model-driven development with the jABC. In: Bin, E., Ziv, A., Ur, S. (eds.) HVC 2006. LNCS, vol. 4383, pp. 92–108. Springer, Heidelberg (2007). http://dx.doi.org/10.1007/978-3-540-70889-6_7
51. Steffen, B., Rüthing, O.: Quality engineering: leveraging heterogeneous information. In: Jhala, R., Schmidt, D. (eds.) VMCAI 2011. LNCS, vol. 6538, pp. 23–37. Springer, Heidelberg (2011)
52. Windmüller, S., Neubauer, J., Steffen, B., Howar, F., Bauer, O.: Active continuous quality control. In: 16th International ACM SIGSOFT Symposium on Component-Based Software Engineering, CBSE '13, pp. 111–120. ACM SIGSOFT, New York (2013)

Schedulers are no Prophets

Arnd Hartmanns, Holger Hermanns, and Jan Krčál[(✉)]

Computer Science, Saarland University, Saarbrücken, Germany
{arnd,hermanns,krcal}@cs.uni-saarland.de

Abstract. Several formalisms for concurrent computation have been proposed in recent years that incorporate means to express stochastic continuous-time dynamics and non-determinism. In this setting, some obscure phenomena are known to exist, related to the fact that schedulers may yield too pessimistic verification results, since *current* non-determinism can surprisingly be resolved based on *prophesying* the timing of *future* random events. This paper provides a thorough investigation of the problem, and it presents a solution: Based on a novel semantics of stochastic automata, we identify the class of schedulers strictly unable to prophesy, and show a path towards verification algorithms with respect to that class. The latter uses an encoding into the model of stochastic timed automata under arbitrary schedulers, for which model checking tool support has recently become available.

1 Introduction

The modelling of concurrent systems operating in continuous time is at the heart of several branches of computing sciences. In the *systems* world, discrete event simulation tools like OMNET [23], NS-2 or NS-3 [1,2], or GLOMOSIM [30] are routinely used to gain insight into phenomena that are difficult to study "in the wild". However, the validity of results obtained in this manner is often questionable, and comes with notorious suspicions about hidden assumptions that affect the simulation studies [3,9,19,26]. The predominant mathematical objects that such simulators operate on are classes of stochastic processes, in particular generalised semi-Markov processes [13,21] (GSMP). Stochasticity is used to conveniently reflect variations in behaviour due to mass effects.

Over the past decades, concurrent systems operating in stochastic continuous time have also received attention from a foundational perspective, especially in the formal methods community. Process calculi for stochastic timed systems have been proposed, starting with the work of Harrison and Strulo [15,27]. D'Argenio proposed stochastic automata (SA) [10] as a compositional formalism akin to timed automata. Bravetti proposed the IGSMP calculus [8] for interacting GSMP. A comparative reflection of the two latter approaches can be found in [7]. The work of D'Argenio inspired the MODEST language, which operates with stochastic timed automata (STA) [6] and is supported by the MODEST TOOLSET [16]. Lately, Zeng, Nielson and Nielson proposed the stochastic quality calculus SQC [22] as an intriguing formalism to reason about distributed systems with broadcast communication.

© Springer International Publishing Switzerland 2016
C.W. Probst et al. (Eds.): Nielsons' Festschrift, LNCS 9560, pp. 214–235, 2016.
DOI: 10.1007/978-3-319-27810-0_11

All the approaches discussed above use semantic objects that extend the model of GSMP in a particular dimension: nondeterminism. Albeit with different flavors, the nondeterminism is essentially intertwined with the concept of an interleaving semantics, which assumes that no specific temporal ordering can be assumed for events that may happen in independent components—unless the ordering is specified in some way. In fact, it might not be far fetched to claim that in the systems community much of the above mentioned criticism which has accumulated with respect to GSMP simulation results is rooted in well-hidden assumptions determining certain event orderings, yet thereby discriminating against behaviour well possible "in the wild". For instance, OPNET is known to use a default round-robin schedule between enabled processes if no other information is at hand, and so does GLOMOSIM.

The correct treatment of stochastic processes with nondeterminism can best be explained in the simplistic setting of Markov chains and their nondeterministic extension, Markov decision processes [24]. A Markov decision process turns into a Markov chain by fixing a resolution of nondeterminism. A *scheduler* is a mathematical object for this task, and the correct analysis of a Markov decision process is based on the principle of considering any Markov chain induced by any realistic scheduler. A verification task then gives rise to an entire range of quantitative results, such as an interval of reachability probabilities. Interestingly, if the class of schedulers at hand contains schedulers that can be considered unrealistic, then the analysis, albeit being correct, may become overly pessimistic in the sense that the interval returned is larger than realistically needed [12].

So, which family of schedulers is to be used for nondeterministic extensions of GSMP? This is the main question we aim at answering with this paper.

To shed some light on this, we discuss the problem in the context of stochastic automata. Roughly speaking, a stochastic automaton is a timed automaton where each clock, whenever reset, *expires* after a random amount of time. The randomness is specified by a probability measure associated to each clock. An edge is guarded by a (possibly empty) set of clocks and can be taken only when all clocks from this set are expired. When location ℓ_1 is entered in the model in Fig. 1 on the left, a clock x is reset to 0. At this moment, the (random) time until its expiration, say distributed uniformly between 0 and 1, starts. Any outgoing edge can be taken only after clock x expires. Once this happens, there are multiple concurrently enabled edges, and one of them is chosen nondeterministically. Assume we want to reach the desired state $\checkmark$. The probabilities of this to happen now depends on the scheduler we consider. In the worst case, the probability is 0, because a scheduler can just decide to take the left edge in ℓ_1. Note that a random resolution of the non-determinism (or a kind of round-robin schedule) would result in a higher probability of reaching state $\checkmark$.

The formal semantics of stochastic automata is defined by uncountable *timed probabilistic transition systems (TPTS)* where each state consists of the current location and the current valuation. As for timed automata, a valuation is used to store for each clock the amount of time elapsed since its last reset. In addition, it also stores the (randomly chosen) clock expiration times. Non-determinism in

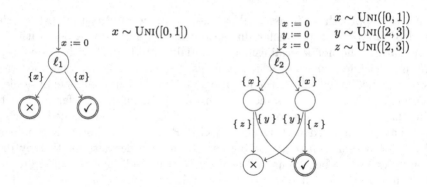

Fig. 1. Examples of stochastic automata.

the TPTS is resolved by schedulers that can base their decisions on all values in the current valuation including the clock expiration times, i.e. the information when *in the future* each individual clock expires. Therefore, in the model in Fig. 1 on the right, a scheduler can always choose in location ℓ_2 the appropriate edge so that the desired state ✓ is never reached (based on the fact whether y occurs before z). However, no *realistic* scheduler not knowing the timing of future random events can make the probability smaller than $1/2$.

The semantics indicated above is known as *residual lifetimes semantics* [7], and is the one (at least conceptually) used in MODEST, in SQC, in the works of D'Argenio, and in those of Strulo. Bravetti's IGSMP use a different and at first sight more adequate approach, based on continuous resampling. This prevents schedulers from exploiting stored sampled values, and is called *spent lifetimes semantics* [7]. However we will argue that this semantics is in fact even more pessimistic and unrealistic.

We overcome this problem by introducing a new semantics based on separating the flow of time from non-deterministic choices. The set of all schedulers of the new semantics forms a strict subset of schedulers of the standard residual lifetimes semantics. As this new subclass excludes exactly those schedulers that observe the timing of future random events, we call them *non-prophetic* schedulers. We are then interested in worst-case and best-case guarantees with respect to *non-prophetic* schedulers.

We show that verification problems for non-prophetic schedulers can be translated to verification problems with respect to *all* schedulers on an induced model from the more expressive class of *stochastic timed automata*. Stochastic timed automata come from the same theoretical background and are thus also based on residual lifetimes semantics. Their higher expressiveness nevertheless allows us to emulate the behaviour of the SA while obfuscating the knowledge of the future timing. Using this translation, the verification of probabilistic reachability and expected-reward properties for stochastic automata under non-prophetic schedulers based on extensions of STA model checking techniques [14] is on the horizon.

2   Preliminaries

For a given set S, its power set is $\mathcal{P}(S)$. We denote by $\mathbb{R}$, $\mathbb{R}^+$, and $\mathbb{R}_0^+$ the set of real numbers, positive real numbers and non-negative real numbers, respectively.

2.1   Probability Theory

A (discrete) *probability distribution* over a countable sample space Ω is a function $\mu \in \Omega \to [0,1]$ s.t. $\sum_{\omega \in \Omega} \mu(\omega) = 1$. The *support* of μ is $\text{support}(\mu) \stackrel{\text{def}}{=} \{\, \omega \in \Omega \mid \mu(\omega) > 0 \,\}$. We denote by $\text{Dist}(\Omega)$ the set of all probability distributions over Ω. Furthermore, we write $\mathcal{D}(\omega)$ for the *Dirac* distribution for ω, defined by $\mathcal{D}(\omega)(x) \stackrel{\text{def}}{=} 1$ if $x = \omega$ and $\mathcal{D}(\omega)(x) \stackrel{\text{def}}{=} 0$ otherwise.

We say that a set Ω is a *measurable space* if it is endowed with a σ-algebra $\Sigma(\Omega)$, a collection of *measurable* subsets of Ω. A (continuous) *probability measure* over Ω is a function $\mu \in \Sigma(\Omega) \to [0,1]$ such that $\mu(\cup_{i \in I} B_i) = \sum_{i \in I} \mu(B_i)$ for any countable index set I and pairwise disjoint measurable sets B_i. Each probability distribution μ induces a probability measure and we thus also use $\mathcal{D}(s)$ for the corresponding Dirac measure. We denote by $\text{Prob}(\Omega)$ the set of probability measures over Ω.

Given a a pair of probability measures μ_1, μ_2 we denote by $\mu_1 \otimes \mu_2$ the *product measure* which is the unique probability measure such that

$$(\mu_1 \otimes \mu_2)(B_1 \times B_2) = \mu_1(B_1) \cdot \mu_2(B_2) \qquad \text{for all measurable } B_1, B_2.$$

For a collection of measures $(\mu_i)_{i \in I}$, we analogously denote the product measure by $\bigotimes_{i \in I} \mu_i$. We lift the same notation to a collection of *sets* of probability measures $(M_i)_{i \in I}$ by $\bigotimes_{i \in I} M_i \stackrel{\text{def}}{=} \{\, \bigotimes_{i \in I} \mu_i \mid \mu_i \in M_i \text{ for all } i \in I \,\}$. For a probability measure F over $\mathbb{R}_0^+$ and any $c \in \mathbb{R}_0^+$ such that $F([c, \infty)) > 0$, we denote by F_c the measure F *conditioned by* $\geq c$, defined for any interval $[a, b]$ by $F_{|c}([a, b]) \stackrel{\text{def}}{=} F([a, b] \cap [c, \infty))/F([c, \infty))$.

2.2   Stochastic Automata

Definition 1. *A* stochastic automaton *(SA) is a 6-tuple*

$$\langle Loc, \mathcal{C}, A = A_d \uplus A_u, E, F, \ell_{init} \rangle$$

where

- *Loc is a countable set of locations;*
- *$\mathcal{C}$ is a finite set of clock variables;*
- *A is the automaton's finite action alphabet partitioned into a set A_d of delayable and a set A_u of urgent actions;*
- *$E \in Loc \to \mathcal{P}(\mathcal{P}(\mathcal{C}) \times A \times \text{Dist}(\mathcal{P}(\mathcal{C}) \times Loc))$ is the edge function, which maps each location to a finite set of edges, which in turn consist of a guard set, a label and a probability distribution over sets of clocks to reset and target locations;*

- $F \in \mathcal{C} \to \mathrm{Prob}(\mathbb{R}_0^+)$ *is the delay measure function that maps each clock to an absolutely continuous probability measure[1]; and*
- $\ell_{init} \in Loc$ *is the initial location.*

We also write $\ell \xrightarrow{C,a}_E \mu$ for $\langle C, a, \mu \rangle \in E(\ell)$, and for two edge functions E_1 and E_2, we define

$$E_1 < E_2 \Leftrightarrow \forall \ell \in Loc\colon E_1(\ell) \subseteq E_2(\ell) \wedge \exists \ell \in Loc\colon E_1(\ell) \subsetneq E_2(\ell),$$

i.e. an edge function is "smaller" if it maps to "smaller" sets of edges.

Intuitively, a stochastic automaton starts its execution in the initial location with all clocks expired. Any edge $\ell \xrightarrow{C,a}_E \mu$ may be taken only if all clocks in its guard set C are expired. If it is taken, the action associated to the edge is a, and the distribution μ encodes the discrete branching of this edge: when a branch $\langle R, \ell' \rangle$ is taken (which happens with probability $\mu(R, \ell')$), all clocks from the set R get *(re)started*, other expired clocks remain expired, and the process moves into the successor location ℓ'. Here, another edge may be taken immediately or the automaton may need to wait until some further clocks expire and so on.

If a clock c gets *started*, it expires again after an amount of time chosen randomly according to the probability measure $F(c)$. Implementing the abstract notions of clock start and clock expiration is the crucial step in defining a formal semantics. In this paper, we focus on what power such an implementation gives to *schedulers*—objects that choose which edge to take when several of them may be taken at the same point in time.

Defining the semantics of stochastic automata formally is the core topic of this paper. We discuss various approaches in Sects. 3 and 4. In the rest of this section, we lay the foundations for defining the semantics. First, we define probabilistic timed transition system with uncountable state and action spaces. This is needed since we need to store the current valuation of real-valued clocks and variables in each state. Second, we introduce assignments and clock expressions to simplify manipulation with these valuations.

2.3   Uncountable Transition Systems

The semantics of (non-Markovian) continuous-time stochastic models with non-determinism can be defined using the following formalism [6,7,29].

Definition 2. *A* timed probabilistic transition system *(TPTS) is a 4-tuple*

$$\langle S, A, T, s_{init} \rangle$$

where

---

[1] In this paper we restrict all $F(c)$ to absolutely continuous measures as it simplifies the overall notation and the technical treatment. Recall that a measure is absolutely continuous if it assigns 0 to any set with Lebesgue measure 0.

- S *is a (usually uncountable) measurable space of states;*
- $A = \mathbb{R}^+ \uplus A'$ *is the system's (uncountable) alphabet that can be partitioned into delays in* $\mathbb{R}^+$ *and normal actions in* A'*;*
- $T \in S \to \mathcal{P}(A \times \mathrm{Prob}(S))$ *is the transition function, which is explicitly allowed to map a state to an uncountable set of transitions; and*
- $s_{init} \in S$ *is the initial state.*

We also write $s \xrightarrow{a}_T \mu$ for $\langle a, \mu \rangle \in T(s)$, and the $<$ relation can be defined for transition functions analogously to its definition for edge functions.

A behavior of a TPTS is a *run*, an infinite alternating sequence $s_0 a_0 s_1 a_1 \ldots$ of states and actions. The system starts in the initial state $s_0 = s_{init}$. Assuming the current state is s_i, the next transition $s_i \xrightarrow{a_1}_T \mu$ is chosen non-deterministically by a *scheduler* based on the whole history $s_0 a_0 \ldots a_{i-1} s_i$ up to this point. The successor state s_{i+1} is then chosen randomly according to the probability measure μ.

Formally, a *scheduler* is a measurable function σ that maps every $s_0 a_0 \ldots s_i \in (S \times A)^* \times S$ to a measure over transitions from $T(s_i)$ (i.e. the scheduler may randomize over available transitions). Every scheduler σ defines a probability measure $\mathbb{P}^\sigma$ over the set of all runs. For a full formal definition, see e.g. [29]. Following the standard approach, we restrict to *non-Zeno* schedulers that allow time to diverge with probability one. More precisely, we require that $\mathbb{P}^\sigma(D) = 1$ where D is the set of runs where the sum of all actions from $\mathbb{R}^+$ along the run is ∞.

Inspired by [25], we define the *timed trace distribution* $\mathrm{Tr}(T, \sigma)$ of a TPTS T induced by a scheduler σ as follows. First, a *timed trace* is a finite or infinite sequence of actions, obtained as the natural projection (denoted ttrace) mapping each run $s_0 a_0 s_1 a_1 \cdots$ to a timed trace obtained from $a_0 a_1 \cdots$ by merging every maximal sequence of real numbers into its sum (a potential infinite sequence at the end of a run is simply removed, resulting in a finite trace). With this, the timed trace distribution $\mathrm{Tr}(T, \sigma)$ is a distribution over the measurable space of timed traces such that every measurable set of timed traces A has probability $\mathbb{P}^\sigma(\mathrm{ttrace}^{-1}(A))$. We denote by $\mathrm{Tr}(T)$ the set of timed trace distributions of T ranging over all schedulers of T. Finally, we say that two TPTS T_1, T_2 are *timed trace distribution equivalent* if $\mathrm{Tr}(T_1) = \mathrm{Tr}(T_2)$.

Remark 1. The example discussed in Fig. 1 works with state-based properties, in particular considering state reachability probabilities. We can encode such properties in a trace-based setting by, for example, adding a loop $\ell \xrightarrow{\varnothing, a} \ell$ to the state whose reachability probability we intend to compute, where a is a unique urgent action. We can then ask for the probability of the set of timed traces that include a instead. In this sense, timed trace distribution equivalence can be ensured to preserve timed reachability probabilities.

2.4 Variables and Expressions

In this subsection, we introduce a unified way to deal with the evaluation and modification of valuations over a set of variables. For a finite set of (real-valued) variables Var, we let $Val \stackrel{\text{def}}{=} Var \to \mathbb{R}$ denote the set of $valuations$. By $\mathbf{0} \in Val$, we denote the valuation that assigns value 0 to all variables. We now first introduce an abstract notion of $expressions$ which we use for two operations: $updates$ to modify a valuation, and (timed automata-like) $clock\ constraints$ to evaluate a valuation. Similarly to timed automata, we also define how the flow of time modifies a valuation.

Expressions. By $Exp(C)$ we denote the set of $expressions$ over the set of variables $C \subseteq Var$. We simply write Exp for the set of expressions over the whole set Var. We treat expressions in an abstract manner: We assume a standard expression $syntax$ (as in e.g. ML or C) with extensions for nondeterministic and randomly sampled values. We formally work only with the $semantics$ $[\![e]\!]$ of expressions e, which are functions that take a valuation over Var and return the value of e depending on the expression class:

- Bxp: $Boolean\ expressions$ e have $[\![e]\!] \in Val \to \{\ true, false\ \}$. Bxp include e.g.

$$i = 1, \quad tt, \quad x \geq 2.5.$$

- Axp: $Arithmetic\ expressions$ e have $[\![e]\!] \in Val \to \mathbb{R}$. Axp include e.g.

$$2.5 + x, \quad 3 + (\text{if } i = 1 \text{ then } x + 1 \text{ else } x - 1).$$

- Sxp: $Sampling\ expressions$ e have $[\![e]\!] \in Val \to \mathcal{P}(\text{Prob}(\mathbb{R}))$. These are conceptually arithmetic expression featuring two additional constructs: nondeterministic choice and random sampling. Sxp include, e.g.,

$$x + \mathsf{sample}(F) + \mathsf{any}(I), \quad 3 + \mathsf{sample}(\text{Exp}(x)), \quad x * y * \mathsf{any}([x, y))$$

where $\mathsf{sample}(F)$ denotes the random selection of a value according to the probability measure F and $\mathsf{any}(I)$ the nondeterministic selection of a value out of the interval I. In the example, $\text{Exp}(x)$ denotes the exponential distribution with rate given by the current value of variable x.

The semantics of a sampling expression maps to a set (representing the nondeterministic choice) of probability measures (representing the random sampling). For example, the semantics $[\![3 + x + \mathsf{sample}(\text{Exp}(1)) + \mathsf{any}((0, 1))]\!]$ applied to valuation $\mathbf{0}$ returns the set $\{\ \mu_i \mid i \in (3, 4)\ \}$ where each measure μ_i is the exponential distribution "shifted" by i. For a sampling expression e without nondeterminism, we denote by $[\![e]\!]_1 \in Val \to \text{Prob}(\mathbb{R})$ the function that maps a valuation v to the single probability measure in $[\![e]\!](v)$.

Updates. An $assignment$, written as $x := e$, is a pair $\langle x, e \rangle \in Var \times Sxp$. Two assignments $\langle x_1, e_1 \rangle$ and $\langle x_2, e_2 \rangle$ are $consistent$ if $x_1 \neq x_2$ or $[\![e_1]\!](v) = [\![e_2]\!](v)$ for all valuations v. The set of all assignment is denoted by $Asgn$. A finite set of pairwise consistent assignments is called an (atomic) $update$, and two updates are consistent if their union is an update. The set of all updates is denoted Upd.

Similar to sampling expressions, the semantics of an update $U \in Upd$ is a function $[\![U]\!] \in Val \rightarrow \mathcal{P}(Prob(Val))$. Due to consistency, we can treat every update $U = \{\langle x_1, e_1 \rangle, \ldots, \langle x_n, e_n \rangle\}$ consisting of $n \in \mathbb{N}$ assignments as a function $U \in Var \rightarrow Sxp$ (even though we may have $x_i = x_j$ for some $i \neq j$). Assuming some fixed total order on the variables, we can identify valuations with tuples of values. This then allows us to define straightforwardly $[\![U]\!](v) \stackrel{\text{def}}{=} \bigotimes_{x \in Var} [\![U(x)]\!](v)$.

Clocks and Clock Constraints. Later, (similarly to timed automata) we restrict operations that can be applied to *clock* variables. Let us fix a set $\mathcal{C} \subseteq Var$ of *clock* variables. *Clock constraints* over $\mathcal{C}$ are expressions constructed according to the following grammar:

$$\mathcal{CC} ::= b \mid \mathcal{CC} \wedge \mathcal{CC} \mid \mathcal{CC} \vee \mathcal{CC} \mid c \sim e \mid c_1 - c_2 \sim e$$

where $\sim \in \{>, \geq, <, \leq, =, \neq\}$, $c, c_1, c_2 \in \mathcal{C}$, and b and e are Boolean and arithmetic expressions over $Var \setminus \mathcal{C}$, respectively. The semantics of a clock constraint g is again a function $[\![e]\!] \in Val \rightarrow \{true, false\}$. Similarly, an update is called *clock update* if all its assignments to clocks $c \in \mathcal{C}$ are of the form $c := 0$. The set of all clock updates is denoted by $CUpd$. Finally, we define for any valuation v and any delay $t \in \mathbb{R}^+$ a valuation $v + t$ by

$$(v + t)(c) \stackrel{\text{def}}{=} \begin{cases} v(c) + t & \text{for } c \in \mathcal{C}, \text{and} \\ v(c) & \text{for } c \in Var \setminus \mathcal{C}. \end{cases}$$

3   Prophetic and Divine Scheduling

In this section we review two existing semantics for stochastic automata. Both map SA to TPTS with uncountable state spaces. A scheduler for an SA is then defined as a scheduler in the underlying TPTS.

In the first subsection, we introduce the more common *residual lifetimes* semantics that however allows a scheduler to be *prophetic*. Then, we address the *spent lifetimes* semantics that at first sight appears to solve this problem. We show that (a) it still allows a scheduler to be *prophetic* (though in a limited way) and more importantly (b) it allows a scheduler to act *divine* in the sense of being able to manipulate the future in unexpected and unintuitive ways.

We fix for the rest of the paper an SA $M = \langle Loc, \mathcal{C}, A = A_d \uplus A_u, E, F, \ell_{init} \rangle$. The presentation of the two semantics is closely inspired by their comparison in [7] which in turn slightly deviates from the respective original definitions [8, 10] without affecting core properties.

3.1   Residual Lifetimes [10]

In the residual lifetimes semantics, the states of the TPTS are pairs $\langle \ell, v \rangle$ of the current location ℓ and a valuation v over the set of variables

$$Var \stackrel{\text{def}}{=} \mathcal{C} \cup \{d_c \mid c \in \mathcal{C}\}.$$

For each clock c, the (non-clock) variable d_c stores the value sampled for c when c was reset most recently. For a set R of clocks, both reset and sampling can be done by the update

$$\text{Sample}(R) \overset{\text{def}}{=} \{\, c := 0, d_c := \mathsf{sample}(F(c)) \mid c \in R \,\}.$$

The value of each clock then increases with the flow of time; a clock c is called *expired* when its value reaches the value of the sampled variable d_c. An edge $\ell \xrightarrow{C,a}_E \mu$ may be taken only if all clocks from the guard set C are expired, captured by the clock constraint

$$\text{Expired}(C) \overset{\text{def}}{=} \bigwedge_{c \in C} c \geq d_c.$$

Let us now define the induced TPTS precisely:

Transition System. The *residual lifetimes* semantics of an SA M is the TPTS

$$[\![M]\!]_r = \langle Loc \times Val, \mathbb{R}^+ \uplus A, T_M, \langle \ell_{init}, \mathbf{0} \rangle \rangle$$

where T_M is the smallest (according to relation $<$) transition function satisfying the following two inference rules:

$$\frac{\ell \xrightarrow{C,a}_E \mu \qquad [\![\text{Expired}(C)]\!](v)}{\langle \ell, v \rangle \xrightarrow{a}_{T_M} \sum_{\langle R, \ell' \rangle \in \mathcal{P}(C) \times Loc} \mu(\langle R, \ell' \rangle) \cdot (\mathcal{D}(\ell') \otimes [\![\text{Sample}(R)]\!]_1(v))} \ (jump_r)$$

$$\frac{t \in \mathbb{R}^+ \qquad \forall t' \in [0,t) \colon [\![\neg\text{Urgent}_r(\ell)]\!](v + t')}{\langle \ell, v \rangle \xrightarrow{t}_{T_M} \mathcal{D}(\langle \ell, v + t \rangle)} \ (delay_r)$$

where the first rule formalizes the preconditions and effects of taking an edge and the second rule states that time may flow in a location ℓ only if there is no edge to be taken urgently where

$$\text{Urgent}_r(\ell) \overset{\text{def}}{=} \bigvee_{a \in A_u, \langle C, a, \mu \rangle \in E(\ell)} \text{Expired}(C).$$

Recall that when an edge $\ell \xrightarrow{C,a}_E \mu$ is taken, a successor location ℓ' and a set R of clocks is randomly picked according to the distribution μ. For a fixed pair $\langle R, \ell' \rangle$, the term $\mathcal{D}(\ell') \otimes [\![\text{Sample}(R)]\!]_1(v)$ appearing in the first rule is a distribution over states, say $\alpha_{R,\ell'}$. The sum $\sum_{R,\ell'} \mu(\langle R, \ell' \rangle) \cdot \alpha_{R,\ell'}$ then represents the overall distribution obtained by weighting the $\alpha_{...}$ by μ.

Prophetic Schedulers. In light of the TPTS as defined above, we consider the SA model on the right below, which is a notationally more formal variation of the one from Fig. 1. The TPTS starts in the initial state $\langle \ell_{init}, \mathbf{0} \rangle$. Since the outgoing edge from ℓ_{init} has an empty guard set and we assume action a to be urgent, no delay is possible in $\langle \ell_{init}, \mathbf{0} \rangle$ and the only outgoing transition is with action a to a probability measure over states of the form $\langle \ell_1, v \rangle$ where $v(x) = v(y) = v(z) = 0$ and the values $v(d_x)$, $v(d_y)$ and $v(d_z)$ are sampled randomly according to the continuous uniform distributions $\text{UNI}([0, 1])$, $\text{UNI}([2, 3])$ and $\text{UNI}([2, 3])$, respectively.

From any such location, there are uncountably many outgoing transitions corresponding to all possible delays $0 < t \le v(d_x)$. If a scheduler chooses some action $t_0 < v(d_x)$, then the remaining time to delay decreases by t_0 and in the next state, the choice options are reduced to actions $0 < t \le v(d_x) - t_0$ and so on. In the end, all (non-Zeno) delay sequences $t_0, t_1, \ldots$ end up in some state $\langle \ell_1, v \rangle$ where $v(x) = v(d_x)$ where a scheduler needs to choose between b and c.

$x \sim \text{UNI}([0, 1])$
$y \sim \text{UNI}([2, 3])$
$z \sim \text{UNI}([2, 3])$

In such a state $\langle \ell_1, v \rangle$, one possible scheduler σ can decide to choose action b only if $d_z < d_y$ and action c otherwise (and to choose always maximal delay whenever delaying is possible): One can then easily argue that the probability induced by scheduler σ to reach a state with location ✓ is 0, while our intuition says that less than 0.5 is not achievable. However, that scheduler can be considered *prophetic*, since its decisions are effectively based on the timing of events that *will occur in the future*.

3.2 Spent Lifetimes [8]

The spent lifetimes semantic TPTS is defined over the same state space, but in order to avoid prophetic decisions, each transition comes with a complete resampling of the variables d_c that represent the residual time for each clock c. Thereby, the current value of d_c (on which the scheduler may base its decisions) becomes irrelevant right with the execution of the decision of the scheduler, i.e. whenever taking a transition.

In order to keep the delay between resetting c and its expiration distributed according to $F(c)$, the resampling needs to take into account the time already *spent* which is captured by the value of the clock c. This is achieved by conditioning the delay measure $F(c)$ on the time spent. As an example, consider a clock c with $F(c)$ being uniform on $[1, 2]$. The clock is initially sampled to, say, 1.3. After taking a delay transition of 1.1 time units, we need to resample it according to the distribution $F(c)_{|1.1}$, which is distributed uniformly on $[1.1, 2]$. If instead the resampling were to occur already after 0.5 time units, we actually would have $F(c)_{|0.5} = F(c)$ (as knowing that the event does not occur before 0.5 does not change the chances of when it will occur in the future). Resampling of a set $C \subseteq \mathcal{C}$ can be expressed by the update

$$\text{Resample}(C) \stackrel{\text{def}}{=} \{\, d_c := \text{if } c < d_c \text{ then sample}(F(c)_{|c}) \text{ else } d_c \mid c \in C \,\}$$

where $F(c)$ should be interpreted as one literal giving a distribution that is then within the expression conditioned by the current elapsed time of c. Observe that the update resamples only values for clocks that are not expired.

Transition System. The spent lifetimes semantics of an SA M is the TPTS

$$[\![M]\!]_s = \langle Loc \times Val, \mathbb{R}^+ \uplus A, T_M, \langle \ell_{init}, \mathbf{0} \rangle \rangle$$

where T_M is the smallest transition function satisfying the following two inference rules:

$$\frac{\ell \xrightarrow{C,a}_E \mu \quad [\![\text{Expired}(C)]\!](v)}{\langle \ell, v \rangle \xrightarrow{a}_{T_M} \sum_{R,\ell'} \mu(\langle R, \ell' \rangle) \cdot (\mathcal{D}(\ell') \otimes [\![\text{Sample}(R) \cup \text{Resample}(C \setminus R)]\!]_1(v))} \; (jump_s)$$

$$\frac{t \in \mathbb{R}^+ \quad \forall t' \in (0,t) \colon [\![\neg\text{Urgent}_s(\ell)]\!](v + t')}{\langle \ell, v \rangle \xrightarrow{t}_{T_M} \mathcal{D}(\ell) \otimes [\![\text{Resample}(C)]\!]_1(v + t)} \; (delay_s)$$

where the first rule again describes that an edge is taken and the second rule again describes the flow of time. The clock constraint Urgent_s is defined by

$$\text{Urgent}_s(\ell) \stackrel{\text{def}}{=} \text{Urgent}_r(\ell) \vee \bigvee_{c \in C} \text{Expiring}(c)$$

where $\text{Expiring}(c) \stackrel{\text{def}}{=} (c = d_c)$. It differs from Urgent_r used in the residual lifetimes semantics by forcing each delay not to exceed the moment when the next clock is expiring. This condition means that whenever some clock expires, all other active clocks get resampled. The rule $delay_s$ requires $v + t'$ to satisfy $\neg\text{Urgent}_s(\ell)$ only for *positive* time points t' because $\text{Expiring}(c)$ is violated by v if the clock c has just expired.

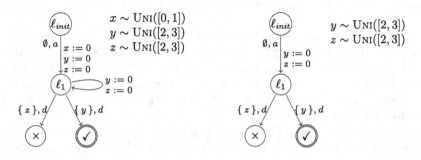

Fig. 2. Examples of prophetic and divine scheduling.

Prophetic Scheduling. We now discuss that the spent lifetimes semantics, despite its intention, is not free of prophetic power. In the SA in Fig. 2 on the left, after some delay $t \in [0,1]$, clock x expires and clocks y and z get resampled both independently according to $U[2,3]_{|t} = U[2,3]$. In other words, a state $\langle \ell_1, v \rangle$ is reached where $v(x) = v(y) = v(z) = v(d_x) = t$ and $v(d_y), v(d_z) \in [2,3]$. We can distinguish two cases:

1. If $v(d_z) < v(d_y)$, the scheduler σ may choose the maximal enabled delay $v(d_z) - t$ by which z becomes expired (in one step, i.e. z does not get resampled) and the location $\times$ is reached.
2. Otherwise, the scheduler σ repeatedly takes the enabled self-loop edge resetting y and z until a state $\langle \ell_1, v \rangle$ with $v(d_z) < v(d_y)$ is reached. In this state the scheduler behaves as described in point 1 above.

By this scheduler σ, a state with location $\checkmark$ is again reached with probability 0. In other words, the crucial property of the spent lifetimes semantics is that the scheduler observes *what* is the first clock to expire and *when* will it happen. If the scheduler prefers this observed plan, it may *let it happen* by one delay transition. Otherwise, it may *block this from happening* by taking some other (non-urgent) edge.

Divine Scheduling. Actually, the self-loop edge in the example above is *not needed* for a scheduler to guarantee that $\checkmark$ is reached with probability 0. Consider the SA in Fig. 2 on the right. Remarkably, another way how a scheduler may influence the sampled timing in this SA is to take *ever shorter* delay transition. Each of them induces a resampling of all running clocks. Thus, such a scheduler also gets arbitrarily many chances to resample the clocks by delaying, say for $1/2$, then for $1/4$, $1/8$, $1/16$, and so on.[2] In this way, a scheduler can arguably effectuate *divine* power by forcing a particular ordering of events through the way in which it lets time progress.

In general, this means that a scheduler can force one of the active clocks c in some location to expire first (unless the lower bound of the support of its associated probability measure disallows that). But the power of schedulers does not stop here: A scheduler can also use the same technique to force a clock to expire in an arbitrarily small subinterval I of its support (with $F(c)(I) > 0$); so in the example above, it could achieve probability 1 for reaching location $\times$ before 2.1 time units have elapsed.

Furthermore, a scheduler in the spent lifetimes semantics can prevent urgent actions from ever taking place, even when no alternative action is available, and without letting time converge. Consider the small example on the right, where we assume both actions a and d to be urgent. ℓ_1 must thus be reached within

ℓ_{init} $x \sim \text{EXP}(1)$

$\emptyset, a \downarrow x := 0$

ℓ_1

$\{x\}, d \downarrow$

$\checkmark$

---

[2] Note that this is *not* Zeno behaviour: An edge will eventually be taken after a finite number of steps with probability 1.

zero time units, and we would expect location ✓ to be reached after a further delay according to the exponential distribution with rate 1, i.e. after on average a further 1 time unit. However, a scheduler in the spent lifetimes semantics for this model can prevent ✓ from being reached at all: When in state $\langle \ell_1, v_1 \rangle$ with $v_1(d_x) = t_1 > 0$, it can choose to delay by $t_1 - \epsilon$ ($\epsilon > 0$) time units. The value for d_x is then resampled, and we again end up in a state $\langle \ell_1, v_2 \rangle$ with $v_2(d_x) = t_2 > 0$. Due to the unbounded support and the memoryless property of the exponential distribution (i.e. $\mathrm{EXP}_{|t}(1) = \mathrm{EXP}(1)$ for all $t \in \mathbb{R}_0^+$), this process can be repeated ad infinitum, and $\sum_i t_i = \infty$ with probability 1.

These anomalies are clearly not intended conceptually, but overarch the existing solutions. It thus appears that the concepts currently at hand for stochastic automata and related models are not adequate. We therefore aim at settling a semantics that makes sure that the schedulers are neither prophetic nor divine. We define such a semantics, that we call *non-prophetic*, in the next section.

4   Non-prophetic Semantics

This section introduces a novel semantics for stochastic automata where schedulers can neither act divine nor prophetic. It is a spent lifetimes semantics in the sense that the residual times (variables d_c for clocks c) are resampled whenever delays are to be performed. However, the choice of the actual time to delay and this resampling are performed in one atomic step. In this way, the scheduler cannot know the residual times at the point where it has to choose the delay. After the choice and resampling, the amount of time that passes is at least the minimum of the sampled residual times and the chosen delay. Only when this amount of time has passed can a jump be performed or a new delay be chosen (including another resampling of the residual times).

4.1   Definition

Technically, to achieve this kind of behaviour, we split the evolution of the system into two alternating phases, denoted as ○ and •. In the ○-phase, the scheduler may only take *jump* transitions, or it may decide to switch to the •-phase. On this switch, it chooses the next delay, and the residual times for the clocks are resampled. Then, in the •-phase, the scheduler can only let time pass via *delay* transitions or switch back to the ○-phase. However, the switch back is only enabled at the exact points in time where either a clock has just expired, or the amount of time that has passed is the delay previously chosen by the scheduler. As usual, if an edge with an urgent action has become enabled, no more time can pass and the switch back to ○ must occur immediately.

Definition 3. *The* non-prophetic *semantics of an SA M is the TPTS*

$$\llbracket M \rrbracket_n = \langle Loc \times \{ \circ, \bullet \} \times Val), \mathbb{R}^+ \uplus A \uplus \{\tau\}, T_M, \langle \ell_{init}, \circ, \mathbf{0} \rangle \rangle$$

where Val are valuations over the set of variables $Var = C' \uplus \{ d_c \mid c \in C' \}$ where $C' \overset{\text{def}}{=} C \uplus \{ w \}$ are the clock variables and T_M is the smallest transition function such that the following inference rules are satisfied:

$$\frac{\ell \xrightarrow{C,a}_E \mu \qquad [\![\text{Expired}(C)]\!](v)}{\langle \ell, \circ, v \rangle \xrightarrow{a}_{T_M} \sum_{R,\ell'} \mu(\langle R, \ell' \rangle) \cdot \mathcal{D}(\langle \ell', \circ \rangle) \otimes [\![\text{Sample}(R)]\!]_1(v)} \ (jump_\text{n})$$

$$\frac{d \in \mathbb{R}^+ \qquad [\![\neg\text{Urgent}_\text{r}(\ell)]\!](v)}{\langle \ell, \circ, v \rangle \xrightarrow{\tau}_{T_M} \mathcal{D}(\langle \ell, \bullet \rangle) \otimes [\![\text{Resample}(\mathcal{C}) \cup \text{Set}_\text{n}(d)]\!]_1(v)} \ (choice_\text{n})$$

$$\frac{t \in \mathbb{R}^+ \qquad \forall t' \in [0,t) : [\![\neg\text{Urgent}_\text{n}(\ell)]\!](v+t')}{\langle \ell, \bullet, v \rangle \xrightarrow{t}_{T_M} \mathcal{D}(\langle \ell, \bullet, v + t \rangle)} \ (delay_\text{n})$$

$$\frac{c \in \mathcal{C}' \qquad [\![\text{Expiring}(c)]\!](v)}{\langle \ell, \bullet, v \rangle \xrightarrow{\tau}_{T_M} \mathcal{D}(\langle \ell, \circ \rangle) \otimes [\![\{ d_c := 0 \}]\!]} \ (expiring_\text{n})$$

where $\text{Set}_\text{n}(d) \overset{\text{def}}{=} \{ w := 0, d_w := d \}$ *and*

$$\text{Urgent}_\text{n}(\ell) \overset{\text{def}}{=} \text{Urgent}_\text{r}(\ell) \lor \bigvee_{c \in \mathcal{C}'} \text{Expiring}(c).$$

The rules $choice_\text{n}$ and $expiring_\text{n}$ take care of switching between the phases whereas the rules $jump_\text{n}$ and $delay_\text{n}$ echo the rules of the residual lifetimes semantics. The precondition of $delay_\text{n}$ uses the predicate Urgent_n, which prevents the rule from being applied not only when the clock for an urgent action has expired (as in Urgent_r), but also when the new clock w or the clock of a delayable action is just expiring. The update $d_c := 0$ on $expiring_\text{n}$ makes sure that the clock can expire only once at a given moment of time.

4.2   Absence of Prophetic and Divine Behaviour

In light of the shortcomings of earlier approaches discussed in Sect. 3, the question arises in what sense this new semantics is any good. We argue in the sequel that the non-prophetic semantics meets its design goals. Formally, we consider a restricted class of schedulers on this new semantics $[\![M]\!]_\text{n}$ such that the schedulers in this class *clearly* only enable non-prophetic scheduling. This is because their decisions are only based on spent lifetimes. We then show that this scheduler class is no less powerful than the class of all imaginable schedulers on $[\![M]\!]_\text{n}$ w.r.t. timed trace distribution equivalence. Notably, the same does not hold for $[\![M]\!]_\text{r}$ and $[\![M]\!]_\text{s}$, as shown by our earlier examples.

Procrastination. First, we define and show one technical property that simplifies the proofs later and reveals additional structure of scheduling: we will require that after waiting for the delay previously chosen by the scheduler without being interrupted by the expiration of any clock, the scheduler cannot choose to wait further, i.e. it needs to choose some edge. We say that a scheduler σ in $[\![M]\!]_\text{n}$ is *procrastination-free* if for all histories $h = s_0 a_0 \cdots a_{n-1} s_n$ we have the following two properties:

1. if $a_{n-1} = \tau$ and $s_n = \langle \ell, \circ, v \rangle$ with $v(w) = v(d_w)$, then the scheduler σ chooses in h any τ transition with probability zero;
2. if $s_n = \langle \ell, \bullet, v \rangle$, the scheduler σ chooses in h the *delay* transition with maximum possible label value (i.e. maximum delay) with probability one.

Next, we show that we can restrict to procrastination-free schedulers.

Lemma 1. *For any scheduler σ in $[\![M]\!]_n$, there is a procrastination-free scheduler σ' in $[\![M]\!]_n$ such that the stochastic processes induced by σ and σ' have the same timed trace distribution.*

Proof (Sketch). We define the scheduler σ' for a given history h as follows. We observe the measure over sequences of several delay steps that end by choosing some non-waiting action from A. The scheduler then takes the delay according to this measure in one step. In the next step (if not interrupted by expiration of some clocks earlier), the non-waiting action is also taken according to this measure (conditioned by the chosen waiting).

Non-prophetic schedulers in $[\![M]\!]_n$ We say that a scheduler σ in $[\![M]\!]_n$ is *non-prophetic* if $\sigma(h) = \sigma(h')$ for all histories $h = s_0 a_0 \cdots a_{n-1} s_n$ and $h' = s'_0 a'_0 \cdots a'_{n-1} s'_n$ such that

- for all $0 \le i < n$ we have $a_i = a'_i$ and
- for all $0 \le i \le n$ the valuations in s_i agree on values of $\mathcal{C}$.

Lemma 2. *For any procrastination-free scheduler σ' in $[\![M]\!]_n$, there is a procrastination-free non-prophetic scheduler σ'' in $[\![M]\!]_n$ such that the stochastic processes induced by σ' and σ'' are timed trace distribution equivalent.*

Proof. We define each choice of the scheduler σ'' by randomization over choices of σ' over all sampled values of variables that a non-prophetic scheduler cannot observe. This can be easily defined locally as the variables are resampled in every step and the scheduler σ is procrastination-free.

Non-prophetic schedulers in $[\![M]\!]_r$. Next, we observe that every scheduler in a non-prophetic semantics can be mimicked by a scheduler in the standard residual lifetimes semantics. The following theorem bridges the two semantics.

Theorem 1. *For any scheduler σ in $[\![M]\!]_n$, there is a scheduler $\bar{\sigma}$ in $[\![M]\!]_r$ such that the stochastic processes induced by σ and $\bar{\sigma}$ have the same timed trace distribution.*

Proof (Sketch). Owed to the preceding lemmata, we can assume σ to be procrastination-free and non-prophetic, since otherwise we could switch to another scheduler satisfying these assumptions with the same timed trace distribution.

We define the scheduler $\bar{\sigma}$ in $[\![M]\!]_r$ with the same timed trace distribution as follows. It always takes the decision only based on the spent lifetimes of every clock (which are stored in the state space of $[\![M]\!]_r$). When a decision (say to wait for t time units) is taken, it sticks to this decision: even if some clock expires earlier (say after $t' < t$ time units), the decision is not changed up to the point where the expiration happens (so there is indeed waiting for t' time units). At this point, the observations of $\bar{\sigma}$ do change, and it may thus take another decision according to σ.

Finally, we say that a scheduler $\bar{\sigma}$ in $[\![M]\!]_r$ is *non-prophetic* if there is a scheduler σ in $[\![M]\!]_n$ such that the stochastic processes induced by $\bar{\sigma}$ and σ are timed trace distribution equivalent. In the next section, we address the problem of analysing SA w.r.t. the non-prophetic semantics, or equivalently w.r.t. the class of non-prophetic schedulers in the standard residual lifetimes semantics.

5   Towards Non-Prophetic Model Checking

In this section, we discuss how the non-prophetic semantics of stochastic automata can equivalently be encoded into the more expressive formalism of stochastic timed automata. This is possible despite the fact that STA use the residual lifetimes approach for expressing stochastic delays. We will finally discuss ways to perform model checking of non-prophetic SA based on this encoding.

We first define the formalism of STA and its semantics using TPTS. We then explain the translation from SA to STA, before we turn to the model checking discussion.

5.1   Stochastic Timed Automata [6]

The STA formalism is somewhat similar to SA, with the main difference being that the sampling from probability measures is now made explicit in the model: In addition to clock variables as in SA, an STA can also have real-valued non-clock variables. These do not change over time, but when an edge is taken, they can be set to values sampled according to probability measures. Edges in STA are decorated with a guard and a deadline. Both of these are clock constraints, and in particular, can contain comparisons between clocks and non-clock variables. In this way, the residual lifetimes semantics can be encoded explicitly in an STA, but at the same time, also nondeterministic timing is possible by simply not making use of the possibility of sampling and instead comparing a clock with constant values in guards and deadlines.

Definition 4. *A stochastic timed automaton (STA) is a 5-tuple*

$$\langle Loc, Var, A, E, \ell_{init} \rangle$$

where

- *Loc is a countable set of locations;*
- *Var $\supseteq C$ is a finite set of variables with a subset C of clock variables;*
- *A is the automaton's countable action alphabet;*

– $E \in Loc \rightarrow \mathcal{P}(\mathcal{CC} \times \mathcal{CC} \times A \times \text{Dist}(CUpd \times Loc))$ *is the edge function, which maps each location to a set of edges, which in turn consist of a guard, a deadline, a label and a probability distribution over updates and target locations; and*

– $\ell_{init} \in Loc$ *is the initial location.*

We also write $\ell \xrightarrow{g,d,a}_E \mu$ for $\langle g, d, a, \mu \rangle \in E(\ell)$.

Intuitively, an STA M evolves as follows: It starts in the initial location ℓ_{init} with all variables having value 0. When time passes, values of all *clock* variables synchronously increase. An outgoing edge $\ell \xrightarrow{g,d,a}_E \mu$ *may* be taken only when its guard g is satisfied by the current values of the variables. If the deadline d of *any* outgoing edge is satisfied, then *some* outgoing edge *must* be taken before time can pass again. Whenever an edge as above is taken, a clock update and a successor location is chosen randomly according to μ. The update is applied on the current values of variables and the process moves to the successor location.

On the right, we illustrate how an STA can be used to express stochastic delays. The edges (all of which lead to Dirac distributions here, i.e. they have a single successor location each) are annotated by their guard (in green) and their deadline (in red), their action, and the updates of their single target (if non-empty). The edge from the initial location, sampling the delay for clock c, needs to be taken immediately because its deadline is *true*. In location ℓ_1, we need to wait at least until "c expires". Note that the waiting can be longer (depending on nondeterministic choice) as the deadline occurs only 1 time unit after that.

Formally, the semantics of STA [6] is defined using TPTS:

Definition 5. *The semantics of an STA M is the TPTS*

$$[\![M]\!] = \langle Loc \times Val, \mathbb{R}_0^+ \uplus A, T_M, \langle \ell_{init}, \mathbf{0}_{Var} \rangle \rangle$$

where T_M is the smallest function satisfying the following two inference rules:

$$\frac{\ell \xrightarrow{g,d,a}_E \mu \quad [\![g]\!](v)}{\langle \ell, v \rangle \xrightarrow{a}_{T_M} \sum_{\langle U, \ell' \rangle \in \text{support}(\mu)} \mu(\langle U, \ell' \rangle) \cdot (\{\mathcal{D}(\ell')\} \otimes [\![U]\!](v))} \ (jump_{\text{sta}})$$

$$\frac{t \in \mathbb{R}^+ \quad \forall t' \in [0, t) \colon [\![\neg\text{Urgent}_{\text{sta}}(\ell)]\!](v + t')}{\langle \ell, v \rangle \xrightarrow{t}_{T_M} \mathcal{D}(\langle \ell, v + t \rangle)} \ (delay_{\text{sta}})$$

where $\text{Urgent}_{\text{sta}}(\ell) \stackrel{\text{def}}{=} \bigvee_{\langle g,d,a,\mu \rangle \in E(\ell)} d$.

Both rules above are not surprising, since they closely resemble the residual lifetimes semantics of SA.

5.2 Residual-Lifetimes Embedding of SA

Before addressing our ultimate target, the non-prophetic semantics, we start by showing that stochastic automata (with respect to the residual lifetimes semantics) are a subclass of stochastic timed automata by the following simple embedding: An SA

$$M = \langle Loc, \mathcal{C}, A = A_d \uplus A_u, E, F, \ell_{init} \rangle$$

is mapped to an STA with the same set of locations,

$$\overline{M}_r = \langle Loc, \mathcal{C} \cup \{ d_c \mid c \in \mathcal{C} \}, A, \bar{E}, \ell_{init} \rangle.$$

For each clock c, we again have one variable d_c with the sampled value. For each edge in the SA, there is one edge in the STA as given by the inference rule

$$\frac{\ell \xrightarrow{C,a}_E \mu}{\ell \xrightarrow{\text{Expired}(C),\text{Deadline}(a,C),a}_{\bar{E}} \sum_{R,\ell'} \mu(R,\ell') \cdot \mathcal{D}(\langle \text{Sample}(R), \ell' \rangle)} \quad (jump_{\bar{r}})$$

where $\text{Expired}(C)$ is the guard of the edge and $\text{Deadline}(a,C)$ is its deadline. The deadline coincides with the guard if the action is urgent, i.e.

$$\text{Deadline}(a, C) \overset{\text{def}}{=} \begin{cases} \text{Expired}(C) & \text{if } a \in A_u, \\ f\!f & \text{if } a \in A_d. \end{cases}$$

5.3 Embedding of SA with Non-prophetic Semantics

We move on to the crucial translation, namely the one that embeds the non-prophetic SA semantics into STA. The embedding proceeds similar to the embedding from the previous subsection, but makes sure that nothing but spent lifetimes are considered.

Definition 6. *The STA translation of an SA M as above is the STA*

$$\overline{M} = \langle Loc \times \{ \circ, \bullet \}, \mathcal{C}' \cup \{ d_c \mid c \in \mathcal{C}' \}, A \uplus \{ \tau \}, \bar{E}, \langle \ell_{init}, \circ \rangle \rangle$$

where $\mathcal{C}' \overset{\text{def}}{=} \mathcal{C} \cup \{ w \}$ are the clock variables and $\bar{E}$ is the smallest edge function such that the following inference rules are satisfied:

$$\frac{\ell \xrightarrow{C,a}_E \mu}{\langle \ell, \circ \rangle \xrightarrow{\text{Expired}(C),\text{Deadline}(a,C),a}_{\bar{E}} \sum_{R,\ell'} \mu(R,\ell') \cdot \mathcal{D}(\langle \text{Sample}(R), \langle \ell', \circ \rangle \rangle)} \quad (jump_{\bar{n}})$$

$$\frac{}{\langle \ell, \circ \rangle \xrightarrow{\neg \text{Urgent}_{\text{sta}}(\ell), tt, \tau}_{\bar{E}} \mathcal{D}(\langle \text{Resample}(\mathcal{C}) \cup \text{Set}_{\bar{n}}, \langle \ell, \bullet \rangle \rangle)} \quad (choice_{\bar{n}})$$

$$\frac{c \in \mathcal{C}'}{\langle \ell, \bullet \rangle \xrightarrow{\text{Expiring}(c),\text{Expiring}(c),\tau}_{\bar{E}} \mathcal{D}(\langle \{ d_c := 0 \}, \langle \ell, \circ \rangle \rangle)} \quad (expiring_{\bar{n}})$$

where $\text{Set}_{\bar{n}} = \{ w := 0, d_w := \text{any}((0, \infty)) \}$.

The update $Set_{\bar{n}}$ resets the newly introduced clock w and allows the nondeterministic selection of a value in $\mathbb{R}^+$ for d_w. It thus corresponds to the nondeterministic choice of "scheduler delay" of rule $choice_n$ in the non-prophetic semantics of SA.

Notably, this embedding is linear in the size of the original SA. The inference rules of Definitions 5 and 6 together build the very same TPTS as the rules for the non-prophetic semantics in Definition 3, as expressed by the following theorem:

Theorem 2. *We have* $[\![M]\!] = [\![\overline{M}]\!]$.

Remark 2. For decidability reasons, definitions of timed automata concepts usually avoid the possibility to read *clock* values in update assignments. We instead do read clock values, but, in fact, this is done only to simplify the exposition. Actually, as all delays are stored into (non-clock) variables *before* each waiting, we can determine the current value of any clock on expiration by accessing non-clock variables only. When adapting the STA model in such a way, the resulting TPTS would however not be identical but only bisimilar to the non-prophetic semantics of TPTS.

5.4 Analysis of STA

The above semantic translation maps on STA models, for which, in turn, two different analysis techniques are available: Simulation (also called statistical model checking), as for example implemented in the modes [5] tool, and model checking using an abstraction of the continuous measures as implemented in the mcsta tool [14]. Both are part of the MODEST TOOLSET [16].

The simulation approach is inherently restricted to models that do not contain nondeterministic choices, neither in terms of the discrete jumps nor when it comes to delays. It is thus of limited use for the cases we consider in this paper where schedulers, and thus nondeterministic choices, play an important role. Some techniques based on partial order and confluence reduction are available to simulate restricted classes of nondeterministic models [4,17] in a sound manner, however they focus thus far on the untimed model of Markov decision processes, and are limited to cases where the scheduler choices are guaranteed to not influence the analysis results. The confluence-based approach has been lifted to the Markov automata [28] model, which is semantically very close to stochastic automata [18]. If properly lifted to STA, it would then be applicable to SA models where scheduling power does not matter with respect to the non-prophetic semantics.

On the other hand, the model-checking technique implemented in mcsta is generally applicable across STA. It can deliver upper and lower bounds on maximum or minimum reachability probabilities and expected cumulative reward values. Technically, it proceeds by replacing the sampling from continuous probability measures by sampling from a discrete probability distribution over a number of intervals that cover the measure's support, followed by a continuous nondeterministic choice over the concrete values from the chosen time interval. This turns an STA into an overapproximating probabilistic timed automaton (PTA), for which existing model checking techniques such as the digital clocks approach [20] can be used to compute the values in question. That PTA analysis relies on the inability to *read* the exact values of clock variables, as mentioned above. It therefore makes it necessary to resort to the notationally more complex workaround discussed in Remark 2. When connecting this with the mcsta approach, a technical obstacle remains in the abstraction of continuous sampling by discrete sampling plus nondeterministic choices over time intervals: The resolution of the latter is in fact delegated to the PTA analysis, but the concrete values picked inside the time intervals need to be taken into account for resampling, which so far is not supported. One viable way to overcome this lifts the digital clocks semantics to STA by restricting to integer clock valuations *prior* to moving to PTA. This appears not to affect the soundness of the abstraction. We consider this approach as an interesting technical challenge, for which we have presented the foundations along with this paper.

6   Discussion and Conclusion

This paper has discussed to what extent formalisms for concurrent systems operating in stochastic continuous time can be equipped with a meaningful semantics, especially in the sense that schedulers are not supposed to be prophets. The results presented do enable us to encode the SQC calculus of Zeng, Nielson and Nielson into STA, and pave the way for non-prophetic model checking provided via the MODEST TOOLSET.

Relative to the survey paper by Bravetti and D'Argenio [7] we did, for simplicity, not consider priorities of actions. However, we see no obstacle in including this feature in our setting, since the concept is orthogonal to the other SA ingredients.

Unlike D'Argenio [10] and Bravetti [8], we only focussed on *closed* systems, i.e. systems which are not subject to composition with other systems. This is rooted in the observation that the semantics we propose is not compositional. Let us illustrate this on a simple example of two components that need to get synchronised by a delayable action a: component A needs to finish some task (modelled by the expiration of a clock c) before the synchronization, whereas component B is ready to synchronize from the start. In the SA $A\|B$ obtained by parallel composition [11] of A and B, one naturally obtains a transition with the delayable action a that can be taken at any time *after* the clock c expires.

The (natural) parallel compositions of the TPTS induced by the residual lifetimes semantics or the spent lifetimes semantics, i.e. $[\![A]\!]_r\|[\![B]\!]_r$ or $[\![A]\!]_s\|[\![B]\!]_s$, coincide with the semantics of the composed SA, i.e. $[\![A\|B]\!]_r$ or $[\![A\|B]\!]_s$: They include the possibility of action a being scheduled at any time after clock c expires. However, as we pointed out in this paper, these semantics enable undesired prophetic or divine scheduling.

Unfortunately, the parallel composition $[\![A]\!]_n\|[\![B]\!]_n$ of the TPTS induced by our non-prophetic semantics allows different behaviour than the semantics of the composed SA, $[\![A\|B]\!]_n$. The former does not allow the a-labelled transition to be freely scheduled at any time after c expires. In particular, the scheduler can take the transition *at the moment when c expires* only with probability 0. This is because the scheduler needs to choose a delay d first (for B); then the composed system needs to wait for d time units; and only then, action a can be taken (by A), provided clock c has expired in the meantime. If it has not expired yet, the scheduler needs to choose another delay d' and so on. This does not allow the scheduler to react immediately to the fact that c has just expired. On the other hand the latter approach, $[\![A\|B]\!]_n$, which applies our non-prophetic semantics to the composed SA avoids any such problems and captures exactly the desired behaviour.

We leave a compositional *and* non-prophetic semantics as an open problem and conjecture that it is not possible, unless striving for a different parallel composition operator that would circumvent the problem sketched above.

Acknowledgements. This work is partly supported by the German Research Council (DFG) as part of the Transregional Collaborative Research Center AVACS (SFB/TR 14), by the Czech Science Foundation under grant agreement P202/12/G061, by the EU 7th Framework Programme under grant agreement no. 295261 (MEALS) and 318490 (SENSATION), by the CDZ project 1023 (CAP), and by the CAS/SAFEA International Partnership Program for Creative Research Teams.

References

1. ns-2 wiki. http://nsnam.isi.edu/nsnam/
2. ns-3. https://www.nsnam.org/
3. Andel, T.R., Yasinsac, A.: On the credibility of Manet simulations. IEEE Computer **39**(7), 48–54 (2006)
4. Bogdoll, J., Ferrer Fioriti, L.M., Hartmanns, A., Hermanns, H.: Partial Order Methods for Statistical Model Checking and Simulation. In: Bruni, R., Dingel, J. (eds.) FORTE 2011 and FMOODS 2011. LNCS, vol. 6722, pp. 59–74. Springer, Heidelberg (2011)
5. Bogdoll, J., Hartmanns, A., Hermanns, H.: Simulation and statistical model checking for Modestly nondeterministic models. In: Schmitt, J.B. (ed.) MMB/DFT. LNCS, vol. 7201, pp. 249–252. Springer, Heidelberg (2012)
6. Bohnenkamp, H.C., D'Argenio, P.R., Hermanns, H., Katoen, J.-P.: MoDeST: a compositional modeling formalism for hard and softly timed systems. IEEE Trans. Software Eng. **32**(10), 812–830 (2006)
7. Bravetti, M., D'Argenio, P.R.: Tutte le algebre insieme: concepts, discussions and relations of stochastic process algebras with general distributions. In: Baier, C., Haverkort, B.R., Hermanns, H., Katoen, J.-P., Siegle, M. (eds.) Validation of Stochastic Systems. LNCS, vol. 2925, pp. 44–88. Springer, Heidelberg (2004)
8. Bravetti, M., Gorrieri, R.: The theory of interactive generalized semi-Markov processes. Theor. Comput. Sci. **282**(1), 5–32 (2002)
9. Cavin, D., Sasson, Y., Schiper, A.: On the accuracy of MANET simulators. In: POMC, pp. 38–43. ACM (2002)
10. D'Argenio, P.R., Katoen, J.-P.: A theory of stochastic systems, part I: stochastic automata. Inf. Comput. **203**(1), 1–38 (2005)

11. D'Argenio, P.R., Katoen, J.-P.: A theory of stochastic systems, part II: process algebra. Inf. Comput. **203**(1), 39–74 (2005)
12. Giro, S., D'Argenio, P.R.: Quantitative model checking revisited: neither decidable nor approximable. In: Raskin, J.-F., Thiagarajan, P.S. (eds.) FORMATS 2007. LNCS, vol. 4763, pp. 179–194. Springer, Heidelberg (2007)
13. Haas, P.J., Shedler, G.S.: Regenerative generalized semi-Markov processes. Commun. Stat. Stoch. Models **3**(3), 409–438 (1987)
14. Hahn, E.M., Hartmanns, A., Hermanns, H.: Reachability and reward checking for stochastic timed automata. In: ECEASST, 70 (2014)
15. Harrison, P.G., Strulo, B.: SPADES - a process algebra for discrete event simulation. J. Log. Comput. **10**(1), 3–42 (2000)
16. Hartmanns, A., Hermanns, H.: The Modest Toolset: an integrated environment for quantitative modelling and verification. In: Ábrahám, E., Havelund, K. (eds.) TACAS 2014 (ETAPS). LNCS, vol. 8413, pp. 593–598. Springer, Heidelberg (2014)
17. Hartmanns, A., Timmer, M.: Sound statistical model checking for MDP using partial order and confluence reduction. STTT **17**(4), 429–456 (2015)
18. Hermanns, H., Krčál, J., Křetínský, J.: Probabilistic bisimulation: naturally on distributions. In: Baldan, P., Gorla, D. (eds.) CONCUR 2014. LNCS, vol. 8704, pp. 249–265. Springer, Heidelberg (2014)
19. Kurkowski, S., Camp, T., Colagrosso, M.: MANET simulation studies: the incredibles. Mob. Comput. Commun. Rev. **9**(4), 50–61 (2005)
20. Kwiatkowska, M.Z., Norman, G., Parker, D., Sproston, J.: Performance analysis of probabilistic timed automata using digital clocks. Formal Methods Syst. Design **29**(1), 33–78 (2006)
21. Matthes, K.: Zur Theorie der Bedienungsprozesse. In: Transactions of the 3rd Prague Conference on Information Theory, Statistics Decision Functions and Random Processes, pp. 513–528 (1962)
22. Nielson, F., Nielson, H.R., Zeng, K.: Stochastic model checking of the stochastic quality calculus. In: De Nicola, R., Hennicker, R. (eds.) Wirsing Festschrift. LNCS, vol. 8950, pp. 522–537. Springer, Heidelberg (2015)
23. Pongor, G.: OMNeT: objective modular network testbed. In: MASCOTS, pp. 323–326. The Society for Computer Simulation (1993)
24. Puterman, M.L.: Markov Decision Processes: Discrete Stochastic Dynamic Programming, 1st edn. John Wiley & Sons Inc, New York (1994)
25. Segala, R.: Modeling and Verification of Randomized Distributed Real-Time Systems. Ph.D thesis, Laboratory for Computer Science, Massachusetts Institute of Technology (1995)
26. Stojmenovic, I.: Simulations in wireless sensor and ad hoc networks: matching and advancing models, metrics, and solutions. IEEE Commun. Mag. **46**(12), 102–107 (2008)
27. Strulo, B.: Process algebra for discrete event simulation. Ph.D thesis, Imperial College of Science, Technology and Medicine. University of London, October 1993
28. Timmer, M., van de Pol, J., Stoelinga, M.I.A.: Confluence reduction for Markov automata. In: Braberman, V., Fribourg, L. (eds.) FORMATS 2013. LNCS, vol. 8053, pp. 243–257. Springer, Heidelberg (2013)
29. Wolovick, N.: Continuous probability and nondeterminism in labeled transaction systems. PhD thesis, Universidad Nacional de Córdoba, Córdoba (2012)
30. Zeng, X., Bagrodia, R., Gerla, M.: GloMoSim: a library for parallel simulation of large-scale wireless networks. In: PADS, pp. 154–161. IEEE Computer Society (1998)

Replicating Data for Better Performances in X10

Marina Andrić[1], Rocco De Nicola[1]([✉]), and Alberto Lluch Lafuente[2]

[1] IMT Institute for Advanced Studies Lucca, Lucca, Italy
rocco.denicola@imtlucca.it
[2] DTU Compute, Technical University of Denmark, Kongens Lyngby, Denmark

Abstract. Linguistic primitives for replica-aware coordination offer suitable solutions to the challenging problems of data distribution and locality in large-scale high-performance computing. The data replication mechanisms that had previously been designed to extend Klaim with replicated tuples are now used to experiment with X10, a parallel programming language primarily targeting clusters of multi-core processors linked in a large-scale system via high-performance networks. Our approach aims at allowing the programmer to specify and coordinate the replication of shared data items by taking into account the desired consistency properties. The programmer can hence exploit such flexible mechanisms to adapt data distribution and locality to the needs of the application, in order to improve performance in terms of concurrency and data access. We investigate issues related to replica consistency and provide a performance analysis, which includes scenarios where replica-based specifications and relaxed consistency provide significant performance gains.

1 Introduction

Parallel and distributed computing systems are more and more frequently used to solve complex computational problems. Now, when more computing power is needed, one does not buy a faster uniprocessor but another processor or another million processors, and connects them with a high-speed communication network. Or, perhaps, one rents them instead, by resorting to cloud computing services. This gives one whatever number of computer cycles he can desire but poses the problem of how to use those computer cycles effectively by dividing the available work into chunks that can be executed simultaneously without introducing undesirable indeterminacy or waiting for conditions that may never materialize.

One of the key issues in parallel and distributed computing is the partitioning and exchange of data between computational entities. Better performances are achieved with increased data locality and minimized data communication.

Increasing data locality can be achieved by replicating data, but this comes at a high price in terms of synchronization in case replicated data need to be kept consistent. As a matter of fact the trade-off between consistency and performance is one of the big dilemmas in distributed and parallel computing and is one of the main topics of research of the High-Performance Computing (HPC) community.

© Springer International Publishing Switzerland 2016
C.W. Probst et al. (Eds.): Nielsons' Festschrift, LNCS 9560, pp. 236–251, 2016.
DOI: 10.1007/978-3-319-27810-0_12

The recent years have seen the advent of technologies that provide software engineers and programmers with flexible mechanisms to conveniently specify data locality, communication and consistency to the benefit of their applications.

A pragmatical example for large-scale distributed services is the GOOGLE CLOUD STORAGE [10] service, that allows users to geographically specify data locality (to reduce cost and speed up access) and provides different consistency levels (e.g. strong and eventual consistency) for different operations (e.g. single data and list operations). Indeed, many modern distributed systems are based on *optimistic data replication* techniques for achieving high availability and performance (see e.g. the discussion in [2]). In such systems it is vital for the programmer to know when consistency can be sacrificed for the sake of performance without compromising the application's expected functionality. One guidance for common weak memory models in distributed computing can be found in [7].

One response to this problem has been to move to a fragmented memory model. Multiple processors are programmed largely as if they were uniprocessors, but are meant to interact via message-passing middlewares such as MPI [16]. One disadvantage is that programmers must explicitly manage the interaction between multiple processes and coordinate their data exchange; large data-structures that are conceptually unitary must be thought of as fragmented across different nodes. The Partitioned Global Address Space (PGAS) model has then been proposed, see. e.g. TITANIUM [18], to permit the programmer to think of a single computation running across multiple processors, sharing a global address space and relying on zone-based memory management. All data resides at some processor, which is said to have affinity to the data. Each processor may operate directly on the data it contains but must use some indirect mechanism to access or update data at other processors. Some kind of global barriers are used to ensure that processors remain synchronized. More recently a new language, X10, has been proposed that can be considered as one of the first members of the second generation of PGAS languages. It extends the PGAS model with asynchrony (yielding the APGAS programming model) by introducing the notion of *places* as an abstraction for a computational context with a locally synchronous view of shared memory. An X10 computation runs over a large collection of places. Each place hosts some data and runs one or more activities. Activities can be dynamically created. Activities are lightweight threads of execution. An activity may synchronously (and atomically) use one or more memory locations in the place in which it resides.

This programming model facilitates the development of distributed applications having a body of data which is shared between a few or all components. Such data can range from simple variables to large arrays, structured types or multimedia objects. To reduce the number of accesses to a single point in the system, programmers often do decompose such large objects into sub-parts, which are then distributed and processed in parallel, or move a copy of the shared data to the sites that use it, thus forming local replicas at each site.

Data locality and data consistency are indeed two key aspects in the design of distributed and parallel systems and software. A proper design of those aspects can bring significant performance advantages, e.g. in terms of minimization of communication between computational entities. In our view, data locality and data consistency issues cannot be fully hidden to the programmer of the high-performance applications of the future. Programmers should be equipped with suitable primitives to deal with those aspects in a natural and flexible way. Early works presented in [6] and [9] pointed to the importance of this aspect and developed a theory of sharing which captures the behavior of programs with respect to shared data into the framework of process algebra. The core theory can describe programs performing read and write access to unitary pieces of shared data. Extensions allow shared data to be decomposed and atomic copies to be made, reflecting the common operations of parallel programs. The authors tackled the problem of decomposition strategies of shared data, from the performance perspective, and replication of commonly-read state.

Our contribution to this approach, applied to the distributed tuple space coordination paradigm, was recently presented in [1]. We introduced RepliKlaim, a tuple-based coordination language which enriches the Klaim language [5] with primitives for replica-aware coordination, in order to offer suitable solutions to the challenging problems of data distribution and locality in large-scale high performance computing. In particular, RepliKlaim allows the programmer to specify and coordinate replication of shared data items and the desired consistency properties. The programmer can hence exploit such flexible mechanisms to adapt data distribution and locality to the needs of the application, in order to improve performance in terms of concurrency and data access. We provided also a performance analysis, which includes scenarios where replica-based specifications and relaxed consistency provide significant performance gains.

In this work we describe our initial attempt at exporting our approach to X10, a general purpose object-oriented, scale-out programming language. The main motivation for turning our attention to X10 are its similarities with Klaim. Indeed, both languages consider localities as a first-class citizen and offer primitives for asynchronous parallel computations and code mobility.

We hope that the results of our preliminary work are sufficiently interesting to stimulate research on X10 aiming at adding to the language specific primitives or libraries would enable programmers to easily manipulate replicated data while choosing the appropriate level of consistency.

Structure of the Paper. The rest of the paper is organised as follows. Section 2 introduces X10, by providing an overview of the underlying programming model and by presenting the basic features of the language through small examples. Section 3 reports on a number of performance experiments by making different assumptions on the size of the data and on the number of available processing units. In Sect. 4 we draw conclusions and sketch possible directions for future work.

2   X10 in a Nutshell

X10 is a programming language primarily targeting clusters of multi-core processors linked in a large-scale system via a high-performance network, consequently concurrency and distribution are the main focus of the language design. The design philosophy of X10 is based on a belief that future server systems will consist of multi-core SMP nodes with non-uniform memory hierarchies interconnected in scalable clusters referred to as *Non-Uniform Cluster Computing* (NUCC) systems. The goal of the designers of X10 was to create a language that would combine ease of programming of object-oriented languages and efficiency of high-performance languages. Using the words of the designers, their goal was *"to increase programmer productivity for NUCC without compromising performance"*.

The programming model of X10 is called *(asynchronous) partitioned global address space*, i.e. (A)PGAS. The PGAS model combines data locality (partitioning) of a distributed memory model and global address space of a shared memory model. In PGAS each processor has private memory for local data and shared memory for globally shared data. APGAS enriches the PGAS model with two additional concepts: *places*, which provide an explicit mechanism for data and code locality, and *asynchronous invocation*, which allows forking a task, possibly at a remote place. These two notions are reminiscent of the locality/node concept and of the eval operation in Klaim [5], where the command `eval(S)@l` is used to spawn a new process at locality l to remotely execute S. The Klaim command `eval(S)@self` is instead used to execute S locally. As a matter of fact, these similarities between X10 and Klaim have inspired our interest in investigating the transfer of ideas from our work on replica-aware programming [1] to X10.

The X10 code snippet below (Listing 1.1) presents a slight simplification and adaptation of the case study used in our experimental evaluation. We shall use this simplified version of our case study in the rest of the section to introduce some key ingredients of X10, necessary to understand our work.

Listing 1.1. GlobalRef usage

```
1   val a:A = new A();
2   val y = GlobalRef[A](a);
3   val places = Place.places();
4
5   at(places(0)) async {
6       atomic y().update();
7   }
8
9   at(places(1)) async {
10      val temp = at(y.home) y().getData();
11  }
12
13  at(places(2)) async {
14      at(y.home) atomic y().update();
15  }
```

A variable **a**, actually an object of class **A**, is going to be created in a place (0) and shared with two other places (1 and 2), through a global reference **y**. Parallel computations at the three places perform different operations on **a** (through the reference **y**): an (atomic) update (local in place 0 and remote in place 2) and a remote read (in place 1).

As one can observe in the example, data items in X10 can be mutable (**var**, e.g. **a**) or immutable (**val**, e.g. the reference **y**). The set of places is fixed before program execution. Places cannot be dynamically created in the current version of X10. To set the number of places, one needs to set a value to X10_NPLACES program environment variable prior to the program execution. The program starts executing in **Place.places()(0)**, other places can be addressed in a similar fashion by their integer ranks. Each X10 place is indented to map to a hardware data-coherent unit, such as an SMP node in a multi-core machine. Functions are first-class data and as such they can be stored, passed between activities and so on. X10 provides several primitives for coordinating access to shared mutable data. Among the others we would like to mention **atomic** blocks. Specifically, **atomic S** is used to guarantee execution of a statement **S**, following certain restrictions, as if it was a single step, with respect to other concurrently executing atomic blocks in the same place. It is used for the update in the example above to avoid race situations.

The main X10 construct for concurrency within a place is the **async** construct. The main form of **async** is **async S** that starts a new activity to execute a statement **S** in the same place of the executing process. Remote execution is achieved by means of the **at** construct. For example, the activity that executes **at(P) S** is *place-shifted*, meaning that its execution is suspended in the current place and shifted to place **P** where **S** will be executed. After completion of **S** control comes back to the current place, with the result of **S**. One needs to be careful when using the **at** construct as it can potentially lead to high costs as the objects used in **S** (and depending objects) are copied to place **P**. This behavior can be altered by using global references (**GlobalRefs**) as we do in our example, which we will explain further below.

Parallelism across places can be achieved by combining **async** and **at** to spawn a new activity at a remote place, e.g. **at(P) async S** creates a new activity at place **P** to execute statement **S**. This is used in our example to spawn the parallel remote activities on places 1 and 2. To synchronize activities one of the mechanisms offered by X10 is a **finish S** construct. An activity that executes **finish S** will execute **S** and then wait for all the activities spawned by **S** to terminate.

It is worth mentioning that the activities running in a place may access (read, modify) data items located at that place with the efficiency of on-chip access. Accesses to remote places can be significantly longer, sometimes even orders of magnitude longer, as we will see in Sect. 3.

As we have already mentioned, careless use of **at** can result in copying and transmitting very large data structures. In order to avoid this copying, one has to create and use global value references **GlobalRefs**. In particular, **val ref =**

`GlobalRef[T](v)` creates a reference to a value v of type T and stores it in `ref`. Retrieval of a value is done by operation `ref()`. In such a way, manipulating data with references across different places will not involve copying, however operating on referenced values requires a place-shift to the home place of the reference, that is obtained with `ref.home`.

To illustrate this important programming concepts, we present in the code snippet below (Listing 1.2) a "wrong" variant of our previous example (i.e. the one on Listing 1.1):

Listing 1.2. Value copying

```
 1   val  a:A = new A();  val  places = Place.places();
 2
 3   at(places(0))  async {
 4         atomic a.update();
 5   }
 6
 7   at(places(1))  async {
 8         val temp = a.getData();
 9   }
10
11   at(places(2))  async {
12         atomic a.update();
13   }
```

Contrary to the previous example, no global reference is used to operate on variable a. The effect is that all places will operate on *local* copies of a, possibly introducing unwanted inconsistencies. This is due to the already explained data copying that the **at** construct entails.

As a final example, consider the following sketch of a X10 specification, which permits implementing, in a programmed manner, the kind of data replication we promote in our work:

Listing 1.3. Program replicas

```
 1   val  places = Place.places();
 2
 3   val  lock = new Lock();
 4   val  lockRef = GlobalRef[Lock](lock);
 5
 6   val  region = Dist.makeUnique(places);
 7   val  replicas : DistArray[A] = DistArray.make[A](region, (Point)=> new A());
 8
 9   for (q in places) at(q) async {
10       dataAccess();
11   }
```

To replicate an object of class **A** we use X10's built-in distributed array class, `DistArray`, that represents a generic multidimensional array distributed over multiple places. There are various strategies available for initializing such array. In this case we choose the *unique* distribution, which stores one data element (`Point`) per place in a designated region (i.e. a set of places). In order to replicate an instance of class **A** across all the available places we initialized each `Point` to an instance of class **A** and region to the set of all available places in the execution (`lines 6-7`).

All places perform the same kind of access to the data in parallel, specified by function `dataAccess`:

Listing 1.4. Data access function

```
1   for (var i:Long = 0; i < NUM_AC; i++) async {
2       with probability p {  // update
3           at(lock.home) lock().take();
4           for (r in places) at (r) async {
5               replicas(r.id()).update();
6           }
7           at(lock.home) lock().release();
8       }
9       with probability 1-p { // read
10          val temp = replicas(q.id()).getData();
11      }
12  }
```

In this model, each actual access to data is done by a separate activity, that is spawned in a loop (**line 1**). The number of concurrently running activities can be up to some pre-defined NUM_AC number. Furthermore, each activity can perform either an update or a read access, with a pre-defined probability p. Update access is performed in a way that *all* replicas are updated to ensure consistency (**lines 4–6**). Of course, such an update of all replicas can follow different strategies. For instance, one can aim at strong consistency or weak consistency with the use of appropriate locks (as shown above) or, else, one can execute the updates in sequential order or as parallel activities (as we do above). A lock variable is used to *synchronize* data accesses. The read access is simply performed against a local replica (**line 10**).

As we will show in Sect. 3, we tune parameters p and NUM_AC to compare program performances with respect to different ratios of read/update access, levels of concurrency, as well as size of accessed data. The example above is instrumental to convey our main idea: if updates are infrequent with respect to reads, then replicating data in X10 specifications yields more performant applications.

Due to the limited space, we have focused here on the main X10 constructs and concepts that are relevant to understanding the experiments we performed. X10 is still under development at IBM in collaboration with academia. There are two runtime frameworks available, Native X10 and Managed X10 that are respectively based on C++ and Java backends. The semantics of the language has been formalized in [17] along with a resilient version [4]. A core calculus with X10's main constructs for parallelism async and finish is presented in [15]. Cogumbreiro et al. developed Armus [3], a verification tool that detects barrier deadlocks for Java and X10 programs. Gligoric et al. attempted to develop a model checking tool [8] for X10 based on the JAVA PATH FINDER tool for model checking Java programs. A line of work focuses on compiling and porting programs to X10, specifically, [14] reports on compiling Matlab to X10 for high-performance computing. The work in [11] presents a kernel benchmark suite implementing distributed algorithms in X10. A complete list of X10 related publications can be found online at the official website [12].

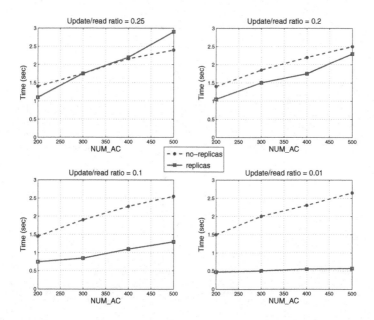

Fig. 1. (Ratio): The two strategies with shared data of size $\approx 0.4\,\text{MB}$

3   Experiments

In this section we describe the practical experiments that we have performed in X10 in order to support the claim that explicit use of replicas can provide significant performance improvements. We present a number of examples, discuss the implemented replica consistency protocol, and conclude by analyzing the obtained results.

Hypothesis. As we have already stated in the Introduction (Sect. 1) the main motivation behind our experiments is to show that better data locality and minimized communication can be achieved by replicating data in X10. In a classical, non-replicated scenario, local read access is granted only to activities residing at the same place of the data. Remote read access to data involves network data transfer cost, which is not negligible, and increases with the size of accessed data, as we will experimentally confirm. Data replication can be seen as an optimization that can remedy this problem. However, replications calls for consistency protocols, that introduce the costs of performing the same update access on each replica. We have performed a set of experiments that provide indications about the situations when such optimization is beneficial and the level of impact it can have on performance. Our experimental results show how the ratio between frequencies of updates and reads, the degree of concurrent data accesses and the size of data affects the performance of two different versions of a program: a *standard* one that does not use replicas and the one with *replicas*.

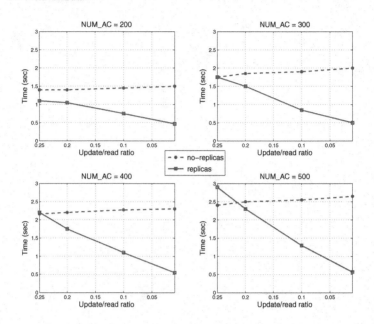

Fig. 2. (`Access number`): The two strategies with shared data of size ≈0.4 MB

For evaluating our test examples, we used the X10 compiler targeting the Java backend (a.k.a. the Managed X10), version X10-2.5.0-linux/x86_64 on OS Ubuntu 14.4. All results are obtained on hardware with 2 processors `Intel(R) Xeon(R) CPU E5620` @ 2.40 GHz, each one with 4 cores and 2 threads per core, with 40 GB of `RAM`. The full implementation of our case studies is available for download at http://sysma.imtlucca.it/wp-content/uploads/2015/05/Source_ X10_example.rar.

Experiments: Configuration of the Scenario. The main idea of the scenario we have tested is that concurrent activities running across multiple places are operating (performing read and update accesses) on the same piece of data, which is considered to be *shared* data between a number of places. We compare performances of two variants which we refer to as no-replicas and replicas. The essence of the program with replicas has been already introduced through examples Listings 1.3 and 1.4. In contrast to the replicated variant, the non-replicated one excludes creation of replicas, hence every access is directed towards a single centralized data variable, as promoted in example Listing 1.1.

As we have already mentioned, to give more elaborate results we tune three parameters in our implementations:

- The ratio of update/read rates;
- The number of shared data accesses per place `NUM_AC`; and
- The size of shared data.

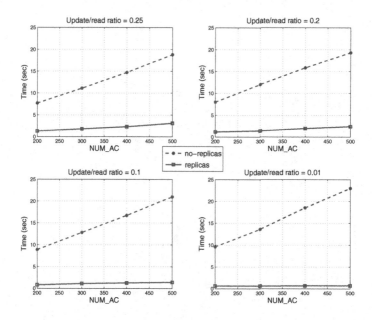

Fig. 3. (Ratio): The two strategies with shared data of size ≈4 MB

Update and read rates are used to compute the probability p with which update can happen inside our dataAccess function, and it is calculated by the formula:

p = update_rate/(update_rate + read_rate)

For calculating p we use the following pairs of update and read rates: {(1, 100), (1, 10), (1, 5), (1, 4)}. The number NUM_AC is a number of data accesses/concurrently spawned activities per place and takes values 200, 300, 400 and 500. As an example, if the update/read ratio is 1/5 and NUM_AC is 400, it means that there are approximately 80 update and 320 read accesses to shared data per place. Finally, the size of shared data in one case of our experiments is ≈0.4 MB and ≈4 MB in the other.

The two strategies (programs no-replicas and replicas) that we compare are described as follows.

Program no-replicas: the implementations of these programs are based on the standard approach that does not involve replication of shared data. The basic idea is that shared data is stored at a single place, with no replicas. Local access to the shared data is granted only to activities running at that place, while other accesses are done remotely, via place-shifting.

Program replicas: In this variant, the shared data is replicated at each place. Presence of replicas calls for the use of consistency protocols. In these implementations the level of consistency for replicated data is *weak*. This means that the interleaving of actions is allowed as update of replicas does not happen instantaneously across all the places. Particularly, when one replica is updated at a certain

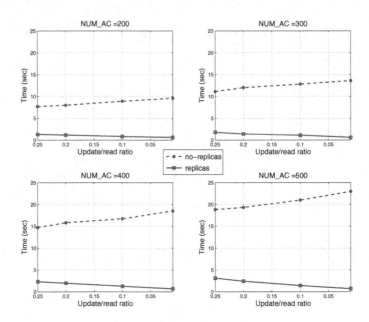

Fig. 4. (`Access number`): The two strategies with shared data of size ≈4 MB

place, multiple activities update in parallel remaining replicas in non-atomic way. During this process, local reads can occur at remote places, before all replicas have the same values. Interleaving of two or more update operations is not allowed, as this would lead to undesirable and unpredictable results. We forbid such behavior by means of a synchronization lock, that is acquired before performing the update operations, and released at the end (see Listings 1.3 and 1.4).

Experiments: Data and Interpretation. The results of our experiments are given in terms of dependencies between the ratio of updates and reads performed by all activities (Figs. 1, 3) or the number of accesses NUM_AC (Figs. 2, 4), represented on x axis, and time taken by activities to complete their computations, on y axis. Time is expressed in seconds and it is obtained as the average of 10 executions. Figures 1 and 2 correspond to results obtained for size of shared data of ≈0.4 MB, while Figs. 3 and 4 correspond to results obtained for the size of ≈4 MB.

Here we present initial results obtained for a 4 and 8 places scenario, we plan to extend the experiments in the future to 16 and larger number of places.

From the presented results we can conclude that the performance benefit of replication tends to grow with the increasing number of total accesses and decreasing update/read ratio. Furthermore, the greater the size of shared data, the more desirable it is to replicate it.

The results obtained for 8 places can be found in the Appendix. As it can be seen from the figures, preserving consistency across many replicas can be expensive. However, replication still brings good pays off when the size of data is either large enough (Fig. 5(c)) or the update/read ration is small enough (Fig. 5(a)).

We have to add that our initial attempts to scale the experiments to 16 places failed at runtime with a "`Place(0): TOO MANY THREADS`" error. We found that a similar issue with X10 was reported in [13]. By reconsidering our experiments, we came to the conclusion that the problem was mainly due to a centralized lock variable and to the large number (more than a thousand) of activities competing simultaneously for it. This should have created congestion at home place of the lock, i.e. at place 0. Initially, we did aim for high parallelism and implemented each access to shared data as a separate activity, by using the `async` feature (see Listing 1.4 `line 1`). Alternatively, one could dedicate a smaller number of activities to handle those accesses. Indeed, update accesses are atomic and hence could be sequentialized rather than parallelized. Conversely, read accesses can be interleaved and therefore should be parallelized in order to achieve high-performance. To reach this goal, one has to take into account certain limitations posed on the maximum number of activities and the amount of memory dedicated to the program.

In this work we presented a model that is based on intensive parallel data accesses. However, in the future our model will be adjusted to handle mentioned limitations in a way that would allow us to carry out experiments for 16 and more places.

4 Conclusions

Performance-vs-consistency is an inherent and classical dilemma in distributed and parallel computing, from local highly parallel systems (e.g. a multi-core machine) to widely distributed concurrent systems (e.g. a world-spread data center). The resolution of such a dilemma is often delegated to run-time frameworks and middlewares and is hidden to programmers. For some applications, however, programmers would benefit from having some control on such design decisions which significantly define the user-perception on the application's Quality-of-Service.

We are investigating programming abstractions for dealing with a key instrument in the performance-vs-consistency dilemma, namely replication of data. In a first stage of our investigation [1], we focused on a language mainly targeted at largely distributed systems, and we proposed RepliKlaim, an extension of the Klaim language [5], with the notion of replicated tuples and with specific communication operations for dealing with them.

In this paper we have tried to apply the lessons we learned when considering Klaim to highly parallel systems. In particular, we have focused on X10, a language for high-performance computing that shares with Klaim a couple of important features such as importance assigned to explicit localities and to code mobility. Like Klaim, the language X10 follows the APGAS programming model which allows for remote operation on shared data, possibly involving transfer and local replication of data. We have performed experiments similar in spirit to those we presented in [1], comparing different strategies for operating on shared data. The results we have obtained show the benefit of replicating data in specific scenarios, especially when the size of shared data is very large.

Our main goal with these investigations is to identify suitable programming abstractions for dealing with replicated data in high-performance applications. In [1], for example, we proposed a primitive $out_\alpha(t)@P$, to specify an operation that places replicas of a tuple t in all places P using the consistency level α (either weak or strong). Similarly, one could conceive convenient X10 constructs like e.g. **share X with** P to specify that the data item X is meant to be shared with the set of places P, and additional features to specify the level of consistency (e.g. weak, strong) desired when invoking methods on X. We do not necessarily advocate that programming languages like X10 should be equipped with first-class primitives supporting those abstractions. In many cases, suitable macros or libraries can be sufficient to provide programmers with mechanisms to specify and control data replication in a natural and disciplined manner.

As future work, we plan to introduce scalability tests, by extending the current framework to consider a larger number of places and of CPU cores, such as present in state of the art HPC infrastructures. We shall consider both situations where more than one place is hosted on each CPU core and the issues of lock variables on shared data that prevented us from carrying out the planned experiments for 16 cores and beyond. Along a parallel line of work we plan to focus on the implementation of case studies that show when the considered language primitives are advantageous in parallel programming. Good candidate case studies are the parallelisation of algorithms to compute functions on graphs, like maximum degree or shortest distances, and distributed algorithms run by concurrent agents connected in graph-shaped network topologies.

We are particularly interested in considering different (i.e. weaker) consistency models and implementations for obtaining such models. As we stated in the Introduction (Sect. 1) one of the most popular consistency models used in practical applications is *eventual consistency*. It is argued that this model is the weakest that can be accepted. In the present model, we restrict concurrent updates to replicas by means of a lock, while this is not the case when looking only for eventual consistency, which could be obtained by means of optimistic data replication such as those studied in [2].

Acknowledgment. This research has been supported by the European projects IP 257414 ASCENS and STReP 600708 QUANTICOL, and by the Italian project PRIN 2010LHT4KM CINA. We are grateful to the managers of the (High Performance) Computing services of IMT and DTU for their support to our experimental investigations and we would like to thank the editors of this volume for giving us the possibility of contributing. Most of all, we would like to thank Hanne and Flemming for all the discussions we have had on many occasions and for believing in the usefulness of Klaim, sometimes even more than its inventors. Without their interest in that language this paper would have never been written.

A   Results for Eight-Places Scenario

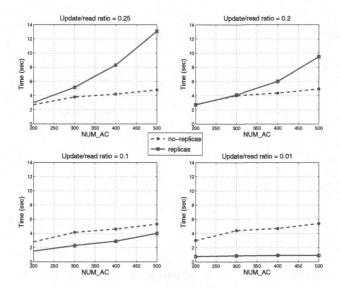

(a) (Ratio): The two strategies with shared data of size ≈ 0.4MB

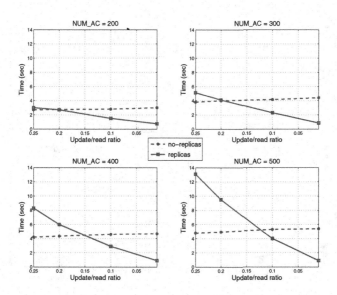

(b) (Access number): The two strategies with shared data of size ≈ 0.4MB

Fig. 5. Scenario with 8 places

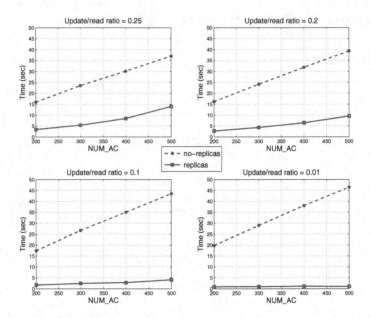

(c) (**Ratio**): The two strategies with shared data of size ≈ 4MB

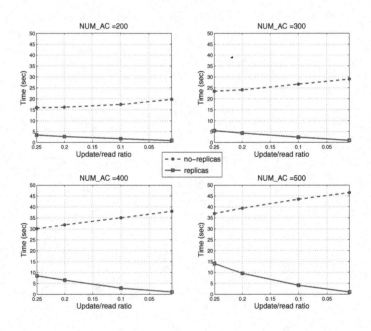

(d) (**Access number**): The two strategies with shared data of size ≈ 4MB

Fig. 5. (*continued*)

References

1. Andrić, M., De Nicola, R., Lluch Lafuente, A.: Replica-based high-performance tuple space computing. In: Holvoet, T., Viroli, M. (eds.) Coordination Models and Languages. LNCS, vol. 9037, pp. 3–18. Springer, Heidelberg (2015)
2. Bouajjani, A., Enea, C., Hamza, J.: Verifying eventual consistency of optimistic replication systems. In: Jagannathan, S., Sewell, P., (eds.) Proceedings of the 41st Annual ACM, POPL 2014, pp. 285–296. ACM (2014)
3. Cogumbreiro, T., Hu, R., Martins, F., Yoshida, N.: Dynamic deadlock verification for general barrier synchronisation. In: Cohen, A., Grove, D., (eds.) Proceedings of the 20th ACM Symposium on Principles and Practice of Parallel Programming, PPoPP 2015, pp. 150–160. ACM (2015)
4. Crafa, S., Cunningham, D., Saraswat, V.A., Shinnar, A., Tardieu, O.: Semantics of (resilient) X10. CoRR, abs/1312.3739 (2013)
5. De Nicola, R., Ferrari, G., Pugliese, R.: KLAIM: a kernel language for agents interaction and mobility. IEEE Trans. Softw. Eng. 24(5), 315–330 (1998)
6. Dobson, S.A., Wadsworth, C.P.: Towards a theory of shared data in distributed systems. In: Jelly, I., Gorton, I., Croll, P.R. (eds.) Software Engineering for Parallel and Distributed Systems, pp. 170–182. Chapman & Hall, Boca Raton (1996)
7. Fekete, A.D., Ramamritham, K.: Consistency models for replicated data. In: Charron-Bost, B., Pedone, F., Schiper, A. (eds.) Replication: Theory and Practice. LNCS, vol. 5959, pp. 1–17. Springer, Heidelberg (2010)
8. Gligoric, M., Mehlitz, P.C., Marinov, D.: X10X: model checking a new programming language with an "old" model checker. In: Antoniol, G., Bertolino, A., Labiche, Y., (eds.) 2012 IEEE Fifth International Conference, pp. 11–20. IEEE Computer Society (2012)
9. Goodeve, D., Dobson, S., Nash, J., Davy, J., Dew, P., Kara, M., Wadsworth, C.P.: Towards a model for shared data abstraction with performance. J. Parallel Distrib. Comput. 49, 156–167 (1998)
10. Google-Storage: (2015) Web site: https://cloud.google.com/storage/
11. Gupta, S., Nandivada, V.K.: Imsuite: a benchmark suite for simulating distributed algorithms. J. Parallel Distrib. Comput. 75, 1–19 (2015)
12. IBM: (2015) Web site for X10: http://x10-lang.org/x10-community/publications-using-x10.html
13. Imam, S., Sarkar, V.: A case for cooperative scheduling in X10s managed runtime. In: The 2014 X10 Workshop, X10 2014, June 2014
14. Kumar, V., Hendren, L.J.: MIX10: compiling MATLAB to X10 for high performance. In: Black, A.P., Millstein, T.D., (eds.) Proceedings of the 2014 ACM International Conference, OOPSLA 2014, pp. 617–636. ACM (2014)
15. Lee, J.K., Palsberg, J.: Featherweight X10: a core calculus for async-finish parallelism. In: Govindarajan, R., Padua, D.A., Hall, M.W., (eds.) Proceedings of the 15th ACM SIGPLAN, pp. 25–36. ACM (2010)
16. Open-MPI: (2015) Web site for MPI: http://www.open-mpi.org/
17. Saraswat, V.A., Jagadeesan, R.: Concurrent clustered programming. In: Abadi, M., de Alfaro, L. (eds.) CONCUR 2005. LNCS, vol. 3653, pp. 353–367. Springer, Heidelberg (2005)
18. Yelick, K.A., Semenzato, L., Pike, G., Miyamot, C., Liblit, B., Krishnamurthy, A., Hilfinger, P.N., Graham, S.L., Gay, D., Colella, P., Aiken, A.: Titanium: a high-performance java dialect. Concurrency Pract. Experience 10(11–13), 825–836 (1998)

Guards, Failure, and Partiality: Dijkstra's Guarded-Command Language Formulated Topologically

David A. Schmidt$^{(\boxtimes)}$

Kansas State University, Manhattan, KS, USA
das@ksu.edu

Abstract. Existing treatments of Dijkstra's guarded-command language treat divergence and failure as equivalent, even though Dijkstra clearly states they are not. We reexamine Dijkstra's language, redefining its denotational semantics with powerdomains formulated in topological terms. The results refine existing work, give a sound semantics of guards, failure, and divergence for non-flat storage domains, and reveal the important role that general topology plays in program correctness.

1 Review: The Guarded-Command Language

Dijkstra's Guarded-Command Language (GCL) [6,7] introduced nondeterministic conditional choice — and the resultant semantical complications — to the programming world. Dijsktra intended GCL and its weakest-precondition calculus to be a notation for stating succinctly and elegantly specifications, programs, and correctness proofs.

Here are two GCL-coded programs and their postconditions: the first selects the larger of two integers, X and Y, and the second codes Euclid's greatest-common-divisor algorithm:

```
if (X ≥ Y? z:=X)
   (Y ≥ X? z:=Y)
fi
// postcondition :
   z ≥ X ∧ z ≥ Y
   ∧(z = X ∨ z = Y)
```

```
if ((X > 0 ∧ Y > 0)?
   x:=X; y:=Y;
   do (x > y? x:= x − y)
      (y > x? y:= y − x)
   od)
fi
// postcondition :
   X mod x = 0 ∧ Y mod x = 0
   ∧(∀d > 0, (X mod d = 0 ∧ Y mod d = 0) ⊃ (x ≥ d))
```

The first program nondeterministically chooses either X or Y as the answer when the two integers are equal, and the second repeatedly reduces variables x or y until they hold equal values.

D.A. Schmidt—Supported by NSF CNS-1219746.

© Springer International Publishing Switzerland 2016
C.W. Probst et al. (Eds.): Nielsons' Festschrift, LNCS 9560, pp. 252–271, 2016.
DOI: 10.1007/978-3-319-27810-0_13

For postcondition, ϕ, and program, C, one calculates $wp(C)\phi$, the *weakest precondition*: the property of the initial store that ensures *(i)* C terminates and *(ii)* ϕ holds true for the store updated by C. Dijkstra proposed these laws (among others) [7] to reason about GCL:

$$wp(\texttt{skip})\phi = \phi$$
$$wp(\texttt{abort})\phi = false$$
$$wp(\texttt{v:=E})\phi = [E/v]\phi$$
$$wp(C_1; C_2)\phi = wp(C_1)(wp(C_2)\phi)$$
$$wp(\texttt{if } (G_1?C_1)\cdots(G_n?C_n)\texttt{ fi})\phi$$
$$= (G_1 \vee \cdots \vee G_n) \wedge (G_1 \supset wp(C_1)\phi) \wedge \cdots \wedge (G_n \supset wp(C_n)\phi)$$

The law for repetition, $\texttt{do}\cdot\texttt{od}$, is usually expressed with an intermediate, invariant assertion and is postponed till later. We can readily calculate the weakest precondition of the first program: Let $\phi_0 = \texttt{z} \geq X \wedge \texttt{z} \geq Y \wedge (\texttt{z} = X \vee \texttt{z} = Y)$ and $P_0 = \texttt{if}(X \geq Y?\texttt{z:=X})(Y \geq X?\texttt{z:=Y})\texttt{fi}$. Then,

$$wp(\texttt{z:=X})\phi_0 = X \geq X \wedge X \geq Y \wedge (X = X \vee X = Y) = X \geq Y$$
$$wp(\texttt{z:=Y})\phi_0 = Y \geq X \wedge Y \geq Y \wedge (Y = X \vee Y = Y) = Y \geq X$$
$$wp(P_0)\phi_0 = (X \geq Y \vee Y \geq X) \wedge (X \geq Y \supset X \geq Y) \wedge (Y \geq X \supset Y \geq X)$$
$$= true$$

The second example requires a loop invariant; see Dijkstra [7] or Gries [9] for the calculation, which produces the weakest precondition, $X > 0 \wedge Y > 0$.

In addition to its impact on program specification, refinement, and validation, GCL and its weakest-precondition calculus play key roles in implementations of boolean model checking [2,17] and counterexample-based-refinement model checking [4,28].

1.1 GCL's Model Theory

Dijkstra masterfully hid GCL's semantical complications behind his weakest-precondition calculus and the tacit assumption that primary storage was "flat" — unstructured.[1]

GCL's weakest-precondition calculus is a proof theory that deserves a model, and Plotkin's and Smyth's research on powerdomains [24,26,34] led Plotkin to define a denotational semantics for GCL based on Smyth's upper powerdomain applied to a flat domain of storage [25]. Subsequently [35], Smyth explained why the storage domain need not be flat, and in his thesis [3], Bonsangue defined denotational semantics of a GCL-variant for all of the lower, upper, and convex powerdomains (but his semantics definitions again used flat storage).

These developments were insightful and important but unfinished in that

1. the semantics of failure of the conditional and divergence of its guards were never completely developed; and
2. the semantics of GCL for non-flat domains was never completely specified.

---

[1] Not all difficulties were hidden, however, as witnessed by Chap. 9 of Dijkstra's text [7], which presented a Scott-continuity law for commands.

Mappings from location numbers to possibly uninitialized cells, modelling dynamic cell allocation/deallocation:
$$MStore = \mathbb{N} \to \mathbb{N}_\perp$$
$$\lambda n.n$$
Sample elements of $MStore$: $\lambda n.\ \perp$
$$\lambda n.n = 0 \to 1; n = 1 \to 2; \perp$$
Linear sequences of numbers, modelling storage stacks:
$$LStore = (\{nil\} + (\mathbb{N} \times LStore))_\perp$$
$$(2,(3,nil))$$
Sample elements of $LStore$: $(2,\perp)$
$$(1,(2,(3,\cdots(i,\cdots)\cdots)))$$

Fig. 1. Two non-flat storage domains and sample elements

The two omissions should be remedied because Dijkstra's description of failure is central to the semantics of the nondeterministic conditional (see Harel's thoughtful explanation in [13], Chapters 5–7), and the natural definition of storage might well be a non-flat domain that contains partial values — see Fig. 1.

1.2   What This Paper Accomplishes

This paper aims to fill these gaps and summarize existing results in a systematic manner. The unifying methodology is general topology [39], whose concepts of open set and continuous function not only provided Scott with notions he needed to solve the $D = D \to D$ problem [32,36] but also gave Smyth and others the tools needed to understand computation theory [1,3,8,15,24,26,27,29–35,38]. This paper accomplishes the following:

- It reveals the role topology plays in the construction of powerdomains and in the definition of the box and diamond modalities that define predicate transformers for GCL.
- It gives a sound denotational semantics of GCL and its wp-calculus for non-flat domains that is faithful to Dijkstra's description of guards, failure, and divergence.

Scott-domain theory and its topology are used to accomplish these results, as they were originally used to define many of the concepts. The results can also be obtained within more recent formulations, say, Kleisli morphisms and Dijkstra monads [14,18,19], but that is for another time and place.

2   Technical Background

2.1   Domains

For our purposes, a *domain* $(D, \sqsubseteq_D)$ is an algebraic, directed-complete, partially ordered set [8,26]. When discussing $(D, \sqsubseteq_D)$, we normally state just D and leave

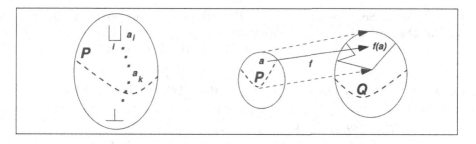

Fig. 2. Scott-open set (P is up-closed and closed under tails of directed sets) and continuous function (when $f(a)$ maps in open set, Q, then $f[P] \subseteq Q$ for some open P)

$\sqsubseteq_D$ implicit. Standard domain constructions (product, sum, function-space, lift) and their associated functions can be found in any text on denotational semantics [5, 11, 21–23, 26, 29, 36, 40].

A function f from domain D to domain E is *Scott continuous* iff for all directed $S \subseteq D$, $f(\sqcup S) = \sqcup\{f(d) \mid d \in S\}$. (Recall that nonempty set S is *directed*, if for all $d, d' \in S$, there is some $e \in S$ such that $d \sqsubseteq e$ and $d' \sqsubseteq e$.)

These subsets are useful: for domain D and $S \subseteq D$,

up closure: $\uparrow S = \{d \in D \mid \exists e \in S, e \sqsubseteq d\}$
down closure: $\downarrow S = \{d \in D \mid \exists e \in S, d \sqsubseteq e\}$
Scott closure: $cl(S) = \downarrow\{\sqcup T \mid T$ *is directed and* $T \subseteq S\}$
convex closure: $conv(S) = cl(S) \cap \uparrow S$

2.2 Scott Topology

Topology is the study of properties (*open sets*) and functions that behave well (are *continuous*) regarding the properties. For example, the real line, $\mathbb{R}$, has as open sets the open intervals, (a, b). A number $r \in \mathbb{R}$ has property (a, b) when $r \in (a, b)$, e.g., $\pi \in (3, 4)$. A function $f : \mathbb{R} \to \mathbb{R}$ is topologically continuous when it maps arguments "close together" (sharing many open sets) to answers "close together" (sharing equally many open sets), e.g., $area(r) = \pi r^2$ is continuous with respect to intervals. The continuous functions on the real line are exactly the topologically continuous functions.

Topology applies to Scott-domain theory [8, 27, 31]: For domain D, Scott defined D's open sets to be those subsets of D that are *(i)* upwards closed and *(ii)* closed under tails of directed sets.[2] See Fig. 2. Scott proved that the functions that are topologically continuous for his *Scott topology* of D are exactly the Scott-continuous functions on D. Further, to solve the domain equation,

---

[2] That is, for every directed set, S, when $\sqcup S \in O$, for open set $O \subseteq D$, then there exists some $d \in S$ such that $d \in O$ also. This means S's "tail," from d upwards, is in O. A Scott-open set is like a half-open interval, $(r, \infty]$, $r \in \mathbb{R}$.

$D = D \rightarrow D$, Scott restricted $D \rightarrow D$ to the continuous functions, limiting domain D's cardinality to the continuum.[3]

Here are some open sets ("properties") from the domains in Fig. 1:

- $O_1 = \{\sigma \in MStore \mid \sigma(1) = 3\}$ ("σ's cell 1 holds 3")
- $O_2 = \{\sigma \in MStore \mid \exists k > 0, \forall 0 \leq i < k, \sigma(i) \in \mathbb{N}\}$ ("σ has a defined finite prefix")

- $O_3 = \{(a, b) \in LStore\}$ ("the store has length ≥ 1")
- $O_4 = \{(a, (3, b)) \in LStore\}$ ("the store's second element is 3")
- $O_5 = \{(a_0, (a_1, \cdots (a_k, nil) \cdots)) \in LStore \mid k \geq 0\}$ ("the store has finite length")

Note that $(\lambda n.3)$ belongs to O_1 and O_2, as does $(\lambda n.n \leq 1 \rightarrow 3; \perp)$ — a "partial" store can belong to a "property set." Similarly, $(2, (3, \perp))$ belongs to O_3 and O_4, as does the infinite sequence, $(3, (3, \cdots (3, \cdots) \cdots))$. But neither belongs to O_5.

This variant of O_5 is not Scott-open: $\{(a_0, (a_1, \cdots (a_i, \cdots) \cdots)) \in LStore\}$ ("the store has infinite length"), nor is this variant of O_2: $\{\sigma \in MStore \mid \forall i \in \mathbb{N}, \sigma(i) \in \mathbb{N}\}$ ("σ is total") — Scott-open sets must be closed under tails of directed sets, that is, the property defined by an open set must be decided "finitely."

For domain $\mathbb{N}_\perp$, *any* subset of $\mathbb{N}$ is Scott-open — open sets are not necessarily recursively enumerable. For this reason among others,[4] Plotkin required finitely-generable sets to define the elements of his powerdomain [24].

2.3   General Topology

Here are some basic concepts; Willard [39] is a good reference. For a set, X, a *topology* $\Omega X \subseteq \mathcal{P}(X)$ is a family of sets, called the *open sets*, that *(i)* are closed under arbitrary union (for all $S \subseteq \Omega X, \bigcup S \in \Omega X$), *(ii)* are closed under finite intersection (for all finite $S \subseteq \Omega X, \bigcap S \in \Omega X$). *(iii)* includes X itself — $X \in \Omega X$. Note that $\emptyset \in \Omega X$, due to (i).

The complement, $\sim O = X - O$, of an open set $O \in \Omega X$ is a *closed set*; define $\mho X = \{\sim O \mid O \in \Omega X\}$. Note that $\mho X$ is closed under arbitrary intersection and finite union.

For topology ΩX, a *base* is a subset, $\mathcal{B}_X \subseteq \Omega X$, such that every $O \in \Omega X$ is the union of some members of $\mathcal{B}_X$; the members of $\mathcal{B}_X$ are called *basic-open sets*. The topology on the real line uses open intervals, (a, b), for $a, b \in \mathbb{R}$, as its base. A *subbase* is some $\mathcal{SB}_X \subseteq \Omega X$ such that all finite intersections of sets in $\mathcal{SB}_X$ form a base.

Given topologies for sets X and Y, there are standard definitions for the coarsest topologies for $X \times Y$, $X \rightarrow Y$, etc. [39].

---

[3] By Cantor's Theorem, the set of *all* functions from D to D has a cardinality larger than that of set D, so Scott's construction is essential to defining D as a model of the untyped lambda-calculus [32,36].

[4] Finitely generable sets ensure that Plotkin's powerdomain, $\mathcal{P}_C(D)$, is algebraic when D is algebraic.

$$O \in \Omega D \qquad \psi \in Proposition$$

$$\psi ::= O \mid false \mid \psi \wedge \psi \mid \bigvee_{i \in I} \psi_i \mid \psi \supset \psi$$

$$[\![O]\!] = O \qquad\qquad\qquad [\![\bigvee_{i \in I} \psi_i]\!] = \bigcup_{i \in I} [\![\psi_i]\!]$$
$$[\![false]\!] = \emptyset \qquad\qquad\quad [\![\psi_1 \supset \psi_2]\!] = \bigcup\{O \in \Omega X \mid O \cap [\![\psi_1]\!] \subseteq [\![\psi_2]\!]\}$$
$$[\![\psi_1 \wedge \psi_2]\!] = [\![\psi_1]\!] \cap [\![\psi_2]\!]$$

Fig. 3. Propositional logic: $[\![\cdot]\!] : Proposition \to \Omega D$

A function, $f : X \to Y$, is *(topologically) continuous* iff for all $x \in X$ and $O' \in \Omega Y$, if $f(x) \in O'$, then there exists some $O \in \Omega X$ such that $x \in O$ and $f[O] \subseteq O'$ (where $f[O] = \{f(x) \mid x \in O\}$). See Fig. 2. A crucial result is that f is continuous iff its inverse-image function maps open sets to open sets: for all $O' \in \Omega Y$, $f^{-1}(O') \in \Omega X$, where $f^{-1}(O') = \{x \in X \mid f(x) \in O'\}$. When f is continuous, then f^{-1} maps closed sets to closed sets as well.

A nonempty family of open sets, $F \subseteq \Omega X$, is *directed* if for all $O_1, O_2 \in F$ there is some $O_3 \in F$ such that $O_1 \subseteq O_3$ and $O_2 \subseteq O_3$. A set, $S \subseteq X$, is *compact* if for every directed family of open sets, F, $S \subseteq \bigcup F$ implies $S \subseteq O$ for some $O \in F$.[5] The intuition is that a compact set is "small enough" to be covered by some "finite sized" open set. Plotkin's finitely generable sets are compact [24, 26].

Open sets can be understood as logical properties, and there is a natural intuitionistic propositional logic, defined in Fig. 3 [37]. The disjunction can be infinitary. As usual, define $\neg\psi$ as $\psi \supset false$ so that $[\![\neg\psi]\!] = \bigcup\{O \in \Omega X \mid O \cap [\![\psi]\!] \subseteq \emptyset\}$. That is, $\neg\psi$ denotes the largest open set disjoint from ψ. In the Scott topology, $[\![\neg O]\!] = {\sim}(\downarrow O)$ for $O \in \Omega D$. Thus, for every open $O \neq D$, $\bot_D \notin O$, that is, $\bot_D$ satisfies no nontrivial property.

2.4 Powerdomains

Because domain D is partially ordered, the naive set-of-all subsets construction, $\mathcal{P}(D)$, does not possess standard functions that are Scott-continuous. In this paper, we generate powerdomains as equivalence classes of sets [24, 29, 34].

For domain D and $PD \subseteq \mathcal{P}(D)$, let $(\sqsubseteq_M) \subseteq PD \times PD$ be a preorder and $\equiv_M$ be its derived equivalence relation. Define equivalence classes, $[S]_M \in PD/M$, for $S \in PD$, as usual, and define $[S]_M \sqsubseteq_M [T]_M$ iff $S \sqsubseteq_M T$.

Definition 1. $\mathcal{P}_M(D) = (PD/M, \sqsubseteq_M)$ *is a* powerdomain *if the following operations are well-defined (congruences with respect to $\equiv_M$) and are Scott-continuous:*

---

[5] Equivalently, S is compact iff whenever it is covered by the union of any collection of open sets, it is covered by a finite subset of that collection.

$\{\!|\cdot|\!\} : D \to PD/M$ *is defined*
$\{\!|d|\!\} = [\{d\}]_M$
$\uplus : PD/M \times PD/M \to PD/M$ *is defined*
$[S]_M \uplus [T]_M = [S \cup T]_M$
For any Scott-continuous $f : D \to PD/M$, $f^\dagger : PD/M \to PD/M$ *is defined*
$f^\dagger[S]_M = [\bigcup_{d \in S} F_d]_M$, *where* $f(d) = [F_d]_M$

Plotkin and Smyth [24, 26, 34] showed that there are (initial) solutions to the above constraints where

1. $[S]_M \sqsubseteq_M [S]_M \uplus [T]_M$ and $[T]_M \sqsubseteq_M [S]_M \uplus [T]_M$: The solution, called the *lower powerdomain*, is $\mathcal{P}_L(D) = (PD/L, \sqsubseteq_L)$, where PD are all nonempty subsets of D and $S \sqsubseteq_L T$ iff for all $O \in \Omega D$, $S \cap O \neq \emptyset$ implies $T \cap O \neq \emptyset$.
2. $[S]_M \uplus [T]_M \sqsubseteq_M [S]_M$ and $[S]_M \uplus [T]_M \sqsubseteq_M [T]_M$: The solution, called the *upper powerdomain*, is $\mathcal{P}_U(D) = (PD/U, \sqsubseteq_U)$, where PD are all nonempty compact subsets of D and $S \sqsubseteq_U T$ iff for all $O \in \Omega D, S \subseteq O$ implies $T \subseteq O$.
3. No orderings are required between $[S]_M$, $[T]_M$, and $[S]_M \uplus [T]_M$: The solution, called the *convex powerdomain*, is $\mathcal{P}_C(D) = (PD/C, \sqsubseteq_C)$, where PD are all nonempty compact subsets of D and $\sqsubseteq_C = \sqsubseteq_L \cap \sqsubseteq_U$.

D's topology identifies which sets possess equal information content. The initial solutions have well-known canonical representations [15, 16, 26, 35]:

lower powerdomain: $(CL(D), \sqsubseteq_{CL})$, where $CL(D) = \{S \subseteq D \mid S = cl(S) \neq \emptyset\}$ and $S \sqsubseteq_{CL} T$ iff for every $d \in S$ there is some $e \in T$ such that $d \sqsubseteq_D e$. (Indeed, $\sqsubseteq_{CL}$ is $\subseteq$.) Define $\{\!|d|\!\} = \downarrow\{d\}$, $S \uplus T = S \cup T$, and $f^\dagger(S) = cl(\cup\{f(d) \mid d \in S\})$.

upper powerdomain: $(UC(D), \sqsubseteq_{UC})$, where $UC(D) = \{S \subseteq D \mid S$ *is compact,* $S = \uparrow S \neq \emptyset\}$ and $S \sqsubseteq_{UC} T$ iff for every $e \in T$ there is some $d \in S$ such that $d \sqsubseteq_D e$. (Indeed, $\sqsubseteq_{UC}$ is $\supseteq$.) Define $\{\!|d|\!\} = \uparrow\{d\}$, $S \uplus T = S \cup T$, and $f^\dagger(S) = \cup\{f(d) \mid d \in S\}$.

convex powerdomain: $(CONV(D), \sqsubseteq_{CL} \cap \sqsubseteq_{UC})$, where $CONV(D) = \{S \subseteq D \mid S$ *is compact,* $S = conv(S) \neq \emptyset\}$. Define $\{\!|d|\!\} = \{d\}$, $S \uplus T = conv(S \cup T)$, and $f^\dagger(S) = conv(\cup\{f(d) \mid d \in S\})$.

Note that $f^\dagger$ is well defined for $\mathcal{P}_U(D)$ and $\mathcal{P}_C(D)$ because $f^\dagger$ is binary additive and the domains' elements are compact sets [20].

When working with these representations, care should be taken when performing set-theoretic reasoning. For example, in $\mathcal{P}_L(\mathbb{N}_\perp)$, $\{\!|2|\!\}$ is the equivalence class, $[\{2\}]_L$, whose canonical representation is the Scott-closed set, $\downarrow\{2\} = \{2, \perp\}$. It is tempting to conclude that $\perp \in \{\!|2|\!\}$, but this is not the case for all sets in the equivalence class, $[\{2\}]_L$.[6]

---

[6] For this reason, among others, Smyth claimed that the elements of a (power)domain are "bundles of properties" — completely prime filters in a Sober space [35]. Or, one can construct the elements of a (power)domain as ideal completions of directed sets of finite elements [11, 12, 26].

An operation, $f : \mathcal{P}(D) \to E$, is an *M-congruence* with respect to $(\sqsubseteq_M) \subseteq PD \times PD$, for $PD \subseteq \mathcal{P}(D)$, if for all $S, T \in PD$, $S \equiv_M T$ implies $f(S) = f(T)$; we define $f : PD/M \to E$ as $f[S]_M = f(S)$.

For domain D, $PD \subseteq \mathcal{P}(D)$, $(\sqsubseteq_M) \subseteq PD \times PD$,

- If $(\sqsubseteq_M) \subseteq (\sqsubseteq_L)$, then the property, "$\_ \cap O \neq \emptyset$," for $O \in \Omega D$, is an *M*-congruence. For $[S]_M \in PD/M$, we write "$[S]_M$ *meets* O" to denote $S \cap O \neq \emptyset$.
- If $(\sqsubseteq_M) \subseteq (\sqsubseteq_U)$, then the property, "$\_ \subseteq O$," for $O \in \Omega D$, is an *M*-congruence. For $[S]_M \in PD/M$, we write "O *covers* $[S]_M$" to denote $S \subseteq U$.

2.5   Powerspace Topologies and Multifunctions

Smyth [35] developed useful characterizations of topologies on powersets, and they apply to powerdomains, too. For set X, let ΩX be its topology. Then, for $PX \subseteq \mathcal{P}(X)$,

1. PX's *upper powerspace*, $\Omega_U PX$, is the topology generated from a base consisting of sets of form *(i)* $\{S \in PX \mid S \subseteq O\}$ for each $O \in \Omega X$.
2. PX's *lower powerspace*, $\Omega_L PX$, is the topology generated from a subbase consisting of sets of form *(ii)* $\{S \in PX \mid S \cap O \neq \emptyset\}$ for each $O \in \Omega X$.
3. PX's *convex powerspace*, $\Omega_C PX$, is the topology generated from a subbase consisting of sets of form *(i)* and *(ii)* above.

A (pre)ordering underlying a powerspace's elements is defined as follows: for $s, t \in PX$, $s \sqsubseteq t$ iff for all $O \in \Omega PX, s \in O$ implies $t \in O$.

Smyth proved that the Scott topologies for the three canonical powerdomains coincide with the powerspaces on domain D:

1. $\Omega \mathcal{P}_U(D)$, the Scott topology of $\mathcal{P}_U(D)$, is topologically isomorphic (*homeomorphic*) to $\Omega_U UC(D)$, the upper powerspace of $UC(D)$.
2. $\Omega \mathcal{P}_L(D)$ is homeomorphic to $\Omega_L CL(D)$.
3. $\Omega \mathcal{P}_C(D)$ is homeomorphic to $\Omega_C CONV(D)$.

Further, the underlying orderings for each of the three powerspaces are order-isomorphic to the orderings on the powerdomains. For this reason, *from here on we always understand ΩD to mean the Scott-topology on domain D.*

Smyth also studied set-valued functions. Again, for set Y, let $PY \subseteq \mathcal{P}(Y)$. Smyth called function $f : X \to PY$ a "multifunction"[7] [35]. There are two inverses of f:

upper: $[f] : PY \to \mathcal{P}(X)$, defined $[f]S = \{x \in X \mid f(x) \subseteq S\}$
lower: $\langle f \rangle : PY \to \mathcal{P}(X)$, defined $\langle f \rangle S = \{x \in X \mid f(x) \cap S \neq \emptyset\}$

Say that sets X and Y have topologies ΩX and ΩY. Smyth proved these crucial results for multifunctions, $f : X \to PY$:

---

[7] a.k.a. "Kleisli morphism" [18].

1. $[f]$ has functionality $\Omega Y \to \Omega X$ (that is, it maps open sets to open sets) iff f is a topologically continuous function of functionality $f : X \to \Omega_U PY$ iff $\langle f \rangle$ has functionality $\mho Y \to \mho X$ (that is, it maps closed sets to closed sets).
2. $\langle f \rangle$ has functionality $\Omega Y \to \Omega X$ iff f is a topologically continuous function of functionality $f : X \to \Omega_L PY$ iff $[f]$ has functionality $\mho Y \to \mho X$.
3. Both $[f]$ and $\langle f \rangle$ have functionality $\Omega Y \to \Omega X$ iff f is a topologically continuous function of functionality $f : X \to \Omega_C PY$ iff $\langle f \rangle$ and $[f]$ have functionality $\mho Y \to \mho X$.

3   Properties of $[\,\cdot\,]$ and $\langle\,\cdot\,\rangle$

In this section, let D be a domain, $PD \subseteq \mathcal{P}(D)$, and preordering $M \subseteq PD \times PD$ generate the powerdomain, $\mathcal{P}_M(D) = (PD/M, \sqsubseteq_M)$.

Proposition 2. *For $f : D \to \mathcal{P}_M(D)$ and $(\sqsubseteq_M) \subseteq (\sqsubseteq_U)$,*

1. $\bigcap_{i \in I} [f]O_i = [f]\bigcap_{i \in I} O_i$, for $(O_i)_{i \in I} \subseteq \Omega D$
2. $[f]O \cup [f]O' \subseteq [f](O \cup O')$, for $O, O'' \in \Omega D$

Proof. (1): $\bigcap_{i \in I} [f]O_i = \bigcap_{i \in I} \{d \in D \mid O_i \text{ covers } f(d)\} = \{d \in D \mid \text{for all } i \in I, O_i \text{ covers } f(d)\} = \{d \in D \mid \bigcap_{i \in I} O_i \text{ covers } f(d)\}$.

(2): The proof for $\subseteq$ looks like (1)'s. But $\supseteq$ fails: Let $D = \mathbb{N}_\perp$, $O = \{0\}, O' = \{1\}$, $f_0(n) = [\{0,1\}]_M$, for all $n \in D$. Then, $[f_0]\{0,1\} = D$, but $[f_0]\{0\} = [f_0]\{1\} = \emptyset$. QED

These useful facts are proved in the Appendix:

- If $(\sqsubseteq_M) \subseteq (\sqsubseteq_U)$, then $\{E \in \mathcal{P}_M(D) \mid O \text{ covers } E\}$ is Scott-open in $\Omega \mathcal{P}_M(D)$, for every $O \in \Omega D$.
- If $(\sqsubseteq_M) \subseteq (\sqsubseteq_L)$, then $\{E \in \mathcal{P}_M(D) \mid E \text{ meets } O\}$, is Scott-open in $\Omega \mathcal{P}_M(D)$, for every $O \in \Omega D$.

Proposition 3. *If all sets in $\mathcal{P}_M(D)$ are compact with respect to ΩD, and $(\sqsubseteq_M) \subseteq (\sqsubseteq_U)$, then $[f]O$ is continuous in both its arguments, $f : D \to \mathcal{P}_M(D)$ and $O \in \Omega D$.*

Proof. For the first argument, f, we show monotonicity as follows: say that $f \sqsubseteq_{D \to \mathcal{P}_M(D)} g$. Then $f(d) \sqsubseteq_M g(d))$ implies $f(d) \sqsubseteq_L g(d))$, and then $O \text{ covers } f(d)$, and then $O \text{ covers } g(d)$.

To show continuity, let $(f_i)_{i \in I}$ be a directed family of functions. We show that $[\bigsqcup_{i \in I} f_i]O \subseteq \bigcup_{i \in I} [f_i]O$. First, $[\bigsqcup_{i \in I} f_i]O = \{d \mid O \text{ covers } (\bigsqcup_{i \in I} f_i)(d)\} = \{d \mid O \text{ covers } \bigsqcup_{i \in I} (f_i(d))\}$.

When $O \text{ covers } \bigsqcup_{i \in I} (f_i(d))$ holds true, then $\bigsqcup_{i \in I} (f_i(d))$ belongs to the open set, $\{E \in \mathcal{P}_M(D) \mid O \text{ covers } E\}$. The family, $f_i(d)$, $i \in I$, is directed in $\mathcal{P}_M(D)$, so there is some $f_k(d)$ in that same open set, that is, $O \text{ covers } f_k(d)$ holds.

For the second argument, O, monotonicity is immediate. To prove continuity, first $[f](\bigcup_{i \in I} O_i) = \{d \mid \bigcup_{i \in I} O_i \text{ covers } f(d)\}$. When $\bigcup_{i \in I} O_i \text{ covers } f(d)$

holds, it means $F \subseteq \bigcup_{i \in I} O_i$ holds, for $f(d) = [F]_M$, $F \in PD$. Since set F is compact and is covered by the union of the directed family of open sets, $(O_i)_{i \in I}$, it is covered by some O_k, that is, $F \subseteq O_k$, implying O_k covers $[F]_M$. Hence, $d \in \bigcup_{i \in I}\{d \mid O_i \text{ covers } f(d)\}$. QED

We have the dual results (and proofs) for $\langle \cdot \rangle$:

Proposition 4. *For $f : D \to \mathcal{P}_M(D)$ and $(\sqsubseteq_M) \subseteq (\sqsubseteq_L)$,*

1. $\bigcup_{i \in I} \langle f \rangle O_i = \langle f \rangle \bigcup_{i \in I} O_i$, for $(O_i)_{i \in I} \subseteq \Omega D$
2. $\langle f \rangle (O \cap O') \subseteq \langle f \rangle O \cap \langle f \rangle O'$, for $O, O' \in \Omega D$.

Proposition 5. *If $(\sqsubseteq_M) \subseteq (\sqsubseteq_L)$, then $\langle f \rangle O$ is continuous in both its arguments, $f : D \to \mathcal{P}_M(D)$ and $O \in \Omega D$.*

In his thesis [3], Bonsangue uses $[\cdot]$ and $\langle \cdot \rangle$ as isomorphism maps between programs (Scott-continuous functions) and predicate transformers: For domains X and Y,

1. $X \to \mathcal{P}_L(Y)$ is order isomorphic to the domain of completely additive functions, $\Omega Y \to \Omega X$, where the isomorphism takes program f to $[f]$.
2. $X \to \mathcal{P}_U(Y)$ is order isomorphic to the domain of binary-multiplicative functions, $\Omega Y \to \Omega X$, where the isomorphism takes program f to $\langle f \rangle$.
3. A pair of Scott-continuous functions, (bx, di), both of functionality $\Omega Y \to \Omega X$, is *jointly multiplicative* if *(i)* bx is multiplicative, *(ii)* di is completely additive, and for all open sets $O, O' \in \Omega Y$, *(iii)* $bx(O \cup O') \subseteq bx(O) \cup di(O')$ and *(iv)* $bx(O) \subseteq di(O)$. The collection of jointly multiplicative pairs forms a domain that is order isomorphic to $X \to \mathcal{P}_C(Y)$, where the isomorphism takes program f to $([f], \langle f \rangle)$.[8]

Bonsangue's work augments Plotkin's and Smyth's characterizations of $X \to \mathcal{P}_U(X_\perp)$ (Result 2, above) by Results 1 and 3.

4   Predicate Transformers

The preceding developments suggest that we define correctness properties/predicates as open sets and use $[\cdot]$ and $\langle \cdot \rangle$ as predicate transformers.

But we approach the situation from first principles: *Program/function f's weakest-precondition map is its inverse-image map.* This is readily apparent for a deterministic program/function $f : Store \to Store_\perp$, where a correctness property is a set, $\psi \subseteq Store$, and $wp(f)\psi = f^{-1}[\psi] = \{s \in Store \mid f(s) \in \psi\}$.

This principle should also apply when D is a non-flat domain and $f : D \to \mathcal{P}(D)$ denotes a nondeterministic program. But D's ordering complicates matters — correctness properties can no longer be mere sets, and f's range is a set-of-sets so that $f^{-1}\psi$, for $\psi \subseteq D$, is no longer well defined. Smyth [35] made these two assertions:

---

[8] The definition of "jointly multiplicative pair" given here applies when Y's topology is a *coherent space* [3,8].

1. A correctness property/predicate is an open set, $U \in \Omega D$, in the Scott topology for non-flat domain D.
2. A nondeterministic program is a multifunction, more precisely, a Scott-continuous function of functionality $f : D \to \mathcal{P}_U(D)$,[9] and its inverse image is restricted to $wp(f) = [f] : \Omega D \to \Omega D$.

Smyth's choices are eminently sensible for $D \to \mathcal{P}_U(D)$. Do Bonsangue's results, stated above, suggest that $\langle f \rangle$ is "wp" for $f : D \to \mathcal{P}_L(D)$? And what about $D \to \mathcal{P}_C(D)$?

4.1   Predicate Transformers are Inverse-Image Maps

For non-flat domain D, $PD \subseteq \mathcal{P}(D)$, and nondeterministic program $f : D \to PD$, we can define $wp(f) = f^{-1} : \Omega \mathcal{P}_M(D) \to \Omega \mathcal{P}_M(D)$ for each of the three canonical powerdomains (that is, when $M \in \{U, L, C\}$). The topologies show us how:

Theorem 6. *For (non-flat) domain D and open set $O' \in \Omega \mathcal{P}_U(D)$, function $f : D \to \mathcal{P}_U(D)$'s inverse can be defined as $f^{-1}[O'] = \bigvee_{i \in I} [f]O_i$, for some family, $(O_i)_{i \in I}$, of open sets in ΩD.*

Proof. Recall that the base of the Scott topology on $\mathcal{P}_U(D)$ are those sets of form $B_O = \{S \in \mathcal{P}_U(D) \mid S \subseteq O\}, O \in \Omega D$. Thus, each open $O' = \bigcup_{i \in I} B_{O_i}$, for some family of open sets, $(O_i)_{i \in I}$. So, $f^{-1}[O'] = f^{-1}(\bigcup_{i \in I} B_{O_i}) = \{d \in D \mid f(d) \in \bigcup_{i \in I} B_{O_i}\} = \{d \mid f(d) \in B_{O_k}, \text{for some } k \in I\} = \{d \mid O_k \text{ covers } f(d), \text{for some } k \in I\} = \bigcup_{i \in I}\{d \mid O_i \text{ covers } f(d)\} = \bigvee_{i \in I} [f]O_i$, using the definitions of $\bigvee$ and $[f]$. QED

Theorem 7. *For (non-flat) domain D and open set $O' \in \Omega \mathcal{P}_L(D)$, function $f : D \to \mathcal{P}_L(D)$'s inverse can be defined as $f^{-1}[O'] = \bigvee_{i \in I} \bigwedge_{j \in J} \langle f \rangle O_{ij}$, for some family, $(O_{ij})_{i \in I, j \in J}$, of open sets in ΩD, where J must have finite range.*

Proof. Recall that the subbase of the Scott topology on $\mathcal{P}_L(D)$ are those sets of form $S_O = \{S \in \mathcal{P}_L(D) \mid S \cap O \neq \emptyset\}, O \in \Omega D$. Thus, open set $O' = \bigcup_{i \in I} \bigcap_{j \in J} S_{O_{ij}}$, for some family of open sets, $(O_{ij})_{i \in I, j \in J}$, where J has finite range. The proof proceeds like the one above. QED

Theorem 8. *For (non-flat) domain D and open set $O' \in \Omega \mathcal{P}_C(D)$, function $f : D \to \mathcal{P}_C(D)]$'s inverse can be defined as $f^{-1}[O'] = \bigvee_{i \in I} \bigwedge_{j \in J} (\!(f)\!)O_{ij}$, where $(\!(f)\!)$ may be either of $[f]$ or $\langle f \rangle$, and $(O_{ij})_{i \in I, j \in J}$ is a family of open sets in ΩD, where J has finite range.*

Proof. The subbase of the Scott topology on $\mathcal{P}_C(D)$ are those sets of form $B_O = \{S \in \mathcal{P}_C(D) \mid S \cap O \neq \emptyset\}$ and $S_O = \{S \in \mathcal{P}_C(D) \mid S \cap O \neq \emptyset\}, O \in \Omega D$. The proof proceeds like the ones above. QED

---

[9] or $f : D \to \mathcal{P}_U(D_\perp)$.

These results assert that the propositional logic of open sets along with $[\,\cdot\,]$ and $\langle\,\cdot\,\rangle$ express all preconditions (inverse images) on open sets.

When program/function f has codomain $\mathcal{P}_M(D_\perp)$, and $O \in \Omega\mathcal{P}_M(D)$, then $f^{-1}[O]$ remains defined as above for $f : D \to \mathcal{P}_M(D_\perp)$ — the Scott topology on $\mathcal{P}_M(D)$ is exactly the relative topology [39] taken from $\mathcal{P}_M(D_\perp)$.

4.2   Predicate Transformers for the Powerdomains

The previous theorems justify why Plotkin and Smyth [25,35] can use $[f] : \Omega D \to \Omega D$ as the weakest-precondition transformer for $f : D \to \mathcal{P}_U(D)$.

It is less evident that $\langle f \rangle : \Omega D \to \Omega D$ defines a total or partial-correctness transformer for $f : D \to \mathcal{P}_L(D)$. Indeed, $\langle f \rangle \phi \wedge \langle f \rangle \neg \phi$ is satisfiable for program f and predicate (open set), ϕ. But $\langle f \rangle$'s *dual* defines partial correctness: For $f : D \to \mathcal{P}_L(D)$, $O \in \Omega D$, $[f] \sim O = \sim \langle f \rangle O$. Thus, the partial correctness (weakest liberal precondition) of f with respect to ϕ, $wlp(f)\phi$, is defined as $[f] \sim (\neg\phi)$, which is the well-defined *closed set*, $\sim \langle f \rangle \neg \phi$.

That is, f is partially correct with respect to ϕ if there is no execution whose output satisfies property $\neg\phi$, where $\neg$ is intuitionistic negation. Since $\perp \notin [\![\neg\phi]\!]$ for all $[\![\phi]\!] \in \Omega D$, a diverging answer is partially correct.

Recall that $\langle f \rangle : \Omega D \to \Omega D$ implies $[f] : \mathcal{U}D \to \mathcal{U}D$, so we can define a closed-set logic that uses $[f]$ with finite disjunction and arbitrary conjunction to form partial-correctness propositions. And since the convex powerdomain, $\mathcal{P}_C(D)$, possesses both $[f]$ and $\langle f \rangle$, for $f : D \to \mathcal{P}_C(D)$, we can perform both total and partial correctness reasoning. Dijkstra's claim [7], Page 21, that $wp(f)\phi \equiv wlp(f)\phi \wedge wp(f)\mathit{True}$ is expressed as follows:

Proposition 9. $[f]\phi = \sim\langle f \rangle\neg\phi \wedge [f](\phi \vee \neg\phi)$.

Proof. First, $\sim \langle f \rangle\neg\phi =\sim \{\sigma \mid f(\sigma)\,meets\,\neg\phi\} = \{\sigma \mid not(f(\sigma)\,meets\,\neg\phi)\} = \{\sigma \mid \downarrow\phi\,covers\,f(\sigma)\}$.

This means that $\{\sigma \mid \downarrow\phi\,covers\,f(\sigma)\} \cap [f](\phi \vee \neg\phi) = \{\sigma \mid (\downarrow\phi \cap (\phi \cup \neg\phi))\,covers\,f(\sigma)\} = \{\sigma \mid \phi\,covers\,f(\sigma)\}$. QED

This result is lifted to nonflat domains — the second conjunct asserts that the (partially defined) answer is sufficient for deciding ϕ.

5   Execution Semantics of GCL

Dijkstra's Guarded-Command Language (GCL) is distinguished by its conditional statement, which admits nondeterministic choice. The syntax of GCL goes as follows:

$$C : Command \qquad P : PrimitiveCommand \qquad G : Guard$$

$$C ::= P \mid \mathtt{skip} \mid \mathtt{abort} \mid C_1; C_2 \mid \mathtt{if}\ (G_i?C_i)_{i\in I}\ \mathtt{fi}$$

Primitive comands, P, include assignment. Guards, G, name open sets and represent boolean-valued test expressions. The conditional's syntax means to say,

$$\llbracket \cdot \rrbracket : Command \rightarrow Store \rightarrow \mathcal{P}_M(Store_{fail,\perp})$$

$$\llbracket skip \rrbracket \sigma = \{|\sigma|\}$$

$$\llbracket abort \rrbracket \sigma = \{|fail|\}$$

$$\llbracket C_1; C_2 \rrbracket = \llbracket C_2 \rrbracket^\dagger_{fail,\perp} \circ \llbracket C_1 \rrbracket, \quad where \quad \begin{array}{l} f_{fail,\perp}(\perp) = \{|\perp|\} \\ f_{fail,\perp}(fail) = \{|fail|\} \end{array}$$

$$\llbracket if\ (G_i?C_i)_{i \in I}\ fi \rrbracket \sigma = \begin{cases} \{|fail|\}, & if\ \bigwedge_{i \in I}(\sigma \in \llbracket \neg G_i \rrbracket). \\ Otherwise: \\ \biguplus_{i \in I} \begin{cases} \llbracket C_i \rrbracket \sigma, & if\ \sigma \in \llbracket G_i \rrbracket \\ \{|\perp|\}, & if\ \sigma \notin \llbracket G_i \rrbracket\ and\ \sigma \notin \llbracket \neg G_i \rrbracket \end{cases} \end{cases}$$

$$\llbracket \cdot \rrbracket : Guard \rightarrow \Omega Store \quad See\ Figure\ 3$$

Fig. 4. Semantics of guarded-command language

$if(G_1?C_1)(G_2?C_2)\cdots(G_n?C_n)fi$, for $n \geq 0$. We add the looping construction, $do \cdot od$, momentarily.

In Chap. 4 [7], Dijkstra explains that a program's execution is nondeterministic and can terminate (with a store) or fail or diverge. Here is a semantics that matches Dijkstra's narrative: As before, we use $\mathcal{P}_M(D)$ to denote the powerdomain generated from preordering $M \subseteq PD \times PD$, for $PD \subseteq \mathcal{P}(D)$.

A program has functionality, $Store \rightarrow \mathcal{P}_M(Store_{fail,\perp})$, where set-or-domain $Store$ represents "proper" outcomes, and $fail$ and $\perp$ denote failure and divergence, respectively. The ordering within $Store_{fail,\perp}$ is $\perp \sqsubseteq fail \sqsubseteq \sigma$, for all $\sigma \in Store$ (in addition to the ordering internal to $Store$).

Figure 4 gives the semantics of GCL. The semantics of the guarded-if construction, $if\ (G_i?C_i)_{i \in I}\ fi$, expresses that the outcome may be any C_k such that G_k is decided true. If all guards, G_i, are decided false, then the construction fails. If any guard can diverge, so can the if-construction.

We treat the iteration construction, $do \cdot od$, as this recursively defined $if \cdot fi$ construction, interpreting it with the usual least-fixed-point semantics [10]:

$$do\ (G_i?C_i)_{i \in I}\ od \equiv w, \quad where\ w \equiv if\ (G_i?C_i; w)_{i \in I}\ ((\bigwedge_{i \in I} \neg G_i)?skip)\ fi$$

Note that the last guarded command, $((\bigwedge_{i \in I} \neg G_i)?skip)$, of the conditional forces termination when no proper guard holds true.

The Scott-continuity of the above denotational semantics is immediate, except for the $if \cdot fi$ construction:

Proposition 10. $\llbracket if\ (G_i?C_i)_{i \in I}\ fi \rrbracket$ *is well defined, that is, it has functionality* $Store \rightarrow \mathcal{P}_M(Store_{fail,\perp})$, *and it is Scott-continuous.*

Proof. First, a cases analysis on the possible outcomes of $\llbracket G_i \rrbracket \sigma$, for all $i \in I$, shows that the empty set is never an outcome, so the construction is well defined.

Next, monotonicity is verified by checking the possible outcomes of $\llbracket G_i \rrbracket \sigma_j$, for $j \in \{0,1\}$, $\sigma_0 \sqsubseteq_{Store} \sigma_1$. (Note that $\{|\perp|\}$ is the least element.)

For continuity, consider the outcomes of $[\![\text{if } (G_i?C_i)_{i\in I} \text{ fi}]\!](\sqcup S)$, for directed set, $S \subseteq Store$: *(i)* If the outcome is $\{\!|fail|\!\}$, then it is the same for $\sqcup_{\sigma\in S}[\![\text{if } (G_i?C_i)_{i\in I} \text{ fi}]\!]\sigma$, because $\bigcap_{i\in I}[\![\neg G_i]\!]$ is a Scott-open set (and $\{\!|\perp|\!\}$ is least). *(ii)* If the outcome includes $\{\!|\perp|\!\}$, then so must $\sqcup_{\sigma\in S}[\![\text{if } (G_i?C_i)_{i\in I} \text{ fi}]\!]\sigma$, because $\{\!|\perp|\!\}$ is least. *(iii)* Finally, when $[\![C_i]\!](\sqcup S)$ is included in the outcome, so must be $\sqcup_{\sigma\in S'}[\![C_i]\!]\sigma$, for some "tail", S', of S. By the continuity of $[\![C_i]\!]$, $[\![C_i]\!](\sqcup S) = \sqcup_{\sigma\in S'}[\![C_i]\!]\sigma$. QED

The semantics in Fig. 4 can be used with each of the three canonical power-domains. Consider these example programs, where $[\![\text{True}]\!] = Store$:

1. $[\![\text{if } (\text{True?skip}) (\text{True?abort}) \text{ fi}]\!]\sigma = \{\!|\sigma|\!\} \uplus \{\!|fail|\!\}$
2. $[\![\text{if True?skip fi}]\!]\sigma = \{\!|\sigma|\!\}$
3. $[\![\text{if True?abort fi}]\!]\sigma = \{\!|fail|\!\}$

For the powerdomains,

- $\mathcal{P}_L(Store_{fail,\perp})$'s elements denote "what may be achievable." Examples 1 and 2 above have the same denotation, that is, $[\{\sigma, fail\}]_L = [\{\sigma\}]_L$. Any ordering $(\sqsubseteq_M) \subseteq (\sqsubseteq_L)$ uses $\langle \cdot \rangle$ to define partial-correctness behavior.
- $\mathcal{P}_U(Store_{fail,\perp})$'s elements denote "what must be achievable." Examples 1 and 3 above have the same denotation, that is, $[\{\sigma, fail\}]_U = [\{fail\}]_U$. Any ordering $(\sqsubseteq_M) \subseteq (\sqsubseteq_U)$ uses $[\cdot]$ to define total-correctness behavior.
- $\mathcal{P}_C(Store_{fail,\perp})$'s elements denote both "may" and "must" achievability. The three Examples have distinct denotations — $[\{\sigma, fail\}]_C$, $[\{\sigma\}]_C$, and $[\{fail\}]_C$, respectively — and an ordering $(\sqsubseteq_M) \subseteq (\sqsubseteq_C)$ uses both $\langle \cdot \rangle$ and $[\cdot]$.

It is tempting to define $\text{if } (G_0?C_0) (G_1?C_1)\cdots\text{fi}$ as $(G_0;C_0) \mid (G_1;C_1) \mid \cdots$ and use these nondeterministic-choice and guard-as-command constructions:

$$[\![C_1 \mid C_2]\!]\sigma = [\![C_1]\!]\sigma \uplus [\![C_2]\!]\sigma \qquad [\![G]\!]\sigma = \begin{cases} \{\!|\sigma|\!\}, \textit{if } \sigma \in [\![G]\!] \\ \{\!|fail|\!\}, \textit{if } \sigma \in [\![\neg G]\!] \\ \{\!|\perp|\!\}, \textit{otherwise} \end{cases}$$

An alternative semantics of $[\![G]\!]\sigma$ is that it equals $\{\!|\perp|\!\}$ (or even $\emptyset$, if allowed) when $\sigma \in [\![\neg G]\!]$. In any case, $[\![\text{if } (G_i?C_i)_{i\in I} \text{ fi}]\!]$ does *not* equal $[\![|_{i\in I}(G_i; C_i)]\!]$, because of Dijkstra's description of failure.[10] The next section develops the consequences.

5.1   Failure and Divergence

In Chap. 4 [7], Dijkstra states that failure is the outcome of an $\text{if} \cdot \text{fi}$ construction when all guards are decided false. What's more, an empty $\text{if} \cdot \text{fi}$ has failure as its outcome and is semantically identical to the **abort** command. Further, evaluation of a guard can diverge and in doing so forces the $\text{if} \cdot \text{fi}$ construction to diverge. Dijkstra does *not* state that guards themselves can fail — only commands are indicated to have failure as a behavior.

---

[10] Indeed, on Page 33 of [7], Dijkstra states that a guard is *not* a command.

There are multiple treatments of failure in the literature: For set, *Store*, Plotkin [25] gives a structured-operational semantics of GCL, where failure is a blocked ("stuck") configuration that cannot be written futher. Plotkin ignores failure in his denotational semantics of GCL, equating it with divergence.

Harel [13] maps a program to a computation tree whose paths represent executions. Failure can appear as a leaf in the computation tree, and divergence appears as an infinite path. Individual guards can fail, and if · fi fails when all its guards fail. Like Plotkin, Harel assumes that a guard never diverges. Harel's modelling of failure prevents him from characterizing $wlp(f)\phi$ as $[f]\phi \cap \langle f \rangle True$, as he had hoped [13], Chap. 5.

Bonsangue's denotational semantics [3] also uses a set *Store* and total guards. A guard's failure is "no output," denoted by the empty set. (His powerdomains include $\emptyset$.) In principle, this should make the semantics of if $(G_i?C_i)_{i\in I}$ fi into a union of the semantics of the $G_i; C_i$ pairs, but Bonsangue makes the conditional construction *diverge* when all of its guards fail [3], Sect. 3.3. This is done because $\emptyset$ is the least value in the lower powerdomain (denoting both failure and divergence); the topmost value in the upper powerdomain (meaning it belongs to all open sets of the powerdomain — possessing all possible properties — which is unacceptable for failure); and an isolated element in the convex powerdomain (meaning that logical negation in the powerdomain is neither set complement nor intuitionistic negation).

If failure, *fail*, is a "stuck configuration" that "aborts" [7], Page 34, then we have the ordering, $\perp \sqsubseteq fail \sqsubseteq \sigma$, for all $\sigma \in Store$, which we use for the domain $Store_{fail,\perp}$. Thus, *fail* never interferes with any Scott-open set (predicate) in $\Omega Store$ and never interferes with the characterizations of inverse image in Theorems 6–8. This also explains why Plotkin conveniently "merged" *fail* with $\perp$ in his denotational semantics of GCL.

6   Correctness of Dijkstra's Laws

Here are Dijkstra's five properties for wp [7], Chaps. 4,5,9, stated and proved in terms of $[\cdot]$ and $\langle \cdot \rangle$. For domain *Store*, predicates $\phi, \psi \in \Omega Store$, and program $f : Store \to \mathcal{P}_M(Store_{fail,\perp})$:

Proposition 11. *When* $(\sqsubseteq_M) \subseteq (\sqsubseteq_U)$:

1. $[f]\emptyset = \emptyset$.
2. $(\phi \supset \psi) = Store$ *implies* $([f]\phi \supset [f]\psi) = Store$
3. $[f](\phi \wedge \psi) = [f]\phi \wedge [f]\psi$
4. $[f]\phi \vee [f]\psi \subseteq [f](\phi \vee \psi)$;
5. *For all directed families* $S \subseteq \Omega Store$, $[f](\bigvee S) = \bigvee_{O \in S}([f]O)$

When $(\sqsubseteq_M) \subseteq (\sqsubseteq_L)$:

1. $\langle f \rangle \emptyset = \emptyset$
2. $(\phi \supset \psi) = Store$ *implies* $(\langle f \rangle \phi \supset \langle f \rangle \psi) = Store.$
3. $\langle f \rangle(\phi \vee \psi) = \langle f \rangle \phi \vee \langle f \rangle \psi$

4. $\langle f \rangle (\phi \wedge \psi) \subseteq \langle f \rangle \phi \wedge \langle f \rangle \psi$

5. For all directed families $S \subseteq \Omega Store,$ $\langle f \rangle (\bigvee S) = \bigvee_{O \in S} (\langle f \rangle O)$

Proof. We state the proofs for $[\,\cdot\,]$; the ones for $\langle\,\cdot\,\rangle$ are similar.
(1) is immediate, since $f(\sigma)$ is a nonempty set.
(2) When $\phi \supset \psi = Store$, this implies $\phi \subseteq \psi$, because $\phi \supset \psi = \bigcup \{O \in \Omega Store \mid O \cap \phi \subseteq \psi\}$. This equals $Store$, which is an open set, so $Store \cap \phi \subseteq \psi$, implying $\phi \subseteq \psi$. By monotonicity of $[f]$, $[f]\phi \subseteq [f]\psi$. Next, we must prove for all $\sigma \in Store$, $\sigma \in \bigcup \{O \in \Omega Store \mid O \cap [f]\phi \subseteq [f]\psi\}$, that is, we must find some $O_\sigma \in \Omega StoreS$ so that $O_\sigma \cap [f]\phi \subseteq [f]\psi$. Choose $O_\sigma = Store$, and this yields the result.

(3)–(5) have been proved earlier, as Propositions 2 and 3. QED

Dijkstra's laws for GCL are expressed and proved as follows:

Theorem 12. *For domain Store, property* $\phi \in \Omega Store$, *and program* $f : Store \to \mathcal{P}_M(Store_{fail,\perp})$: *When* $(\sqsubseteq_M) \subseteq (\sqsubseteq_U)$:

1. $[\mathtt{skip}]\phi = \phi$
2. $[\mathtt{abort}]\phi = \emptyset$
3. $[C_1; C_2]\phi = [C_1]([C_2]\phi)$
4. $[\mathtt{if}\,(G_i?C_i)_{i \in I}\,\mathtt{fi}]\phi = (\bigwedge_{i \in I}(G_i \vee \neg G_i)) \wedge (\bigvee_{i \in I} G_i) \wedge (\bigwedge_{i \in I}(G_i \supset [C_i]\phi))$

When $(\sqsubseteq_M) \subseteq (\sqsubseteq_L)$:

1. $\langle \mathtt{skip} \rangle \phi = \phi$
2. $\langle \mathtt{abort} \rangle \phi = \emptyset$
3. $\langle C_1; C_2 \rangle \phi = \langle C_1 \rangle (\langle C_2 \rangle \phi)$
4. $\langle \mathtt{if}\,(G_i?C_i)_{i \in I}\,\mathtt{fi} \rangle \phi = \bigvee_{i \in I}(G_i \wedge \langle C_i \rangle \phi)$

Proof. Proofs are given for $[\,\cdot\,]$; the ones for $\langle\,\cdot\,\rangle$ are similar.
(1)$[\mathtt{skip}]\phi = \{\sigma \mid \phi \text{ covers } [\mathtt{skip}]\sigma\} = \{\sigma \mid \phi \text{ covers } \{|\sigma|\}\} \supseteq \phi$. If $\sigma' \notin \phi$, then it is not the case that $\phi \text{ covers } \{|\sigma'|\}$.
(2) $[\mathtt{abort}]\phi = \{\sigma \mid \phi \text{ covers } [\mathtt{abort}]\sigma\} = \{\sigma \mid \phi \text{ covers } \{|fail|\}\} = \emptyset$.
(3) The cases when $\perp$ and *fail* arise are straightforward. Now consider $[C_1; C_2]\phi = \{\sigma \mid \phi \text{ covers } [C_2]^\dagger([C_1]\sigma)\} = \{\sigma \mid \phi \text{ covers } [\bigcup_{\sigma' \in [C_1]\sigma}([C_2]\sigma')]_M\} = \{\sigma \mid \forall \sigma' \in [C_1]\sigma, \phi \text{ covers } [C_2]\sigma'\}$. But then, $[C_1]([C_2]\phi) = [C_1]\{\sigma' \mid \phi \text{ covers } [C_2]\sigma'\} = \{\sigma \mid \{\sigma' \mid \phi \text{ covers } [C_2]\sigma'\} \text{ covers } [C_1]\sigma\} = \{\sigma \mid \forall \sigma' \in [C_1]\sigma, \phi \text{ covers } [C_2]\sigma'\}$.
(4) (outline): $\bigwedge_{i \in I}(G_i \vee \neg G_i)$ ensures that all guards are decidable so that $\perp$ is not an outcome. $(\bigvee_{i \in I} G_i)$ ensures that *fail* is not an outcome. For all $\sigma \in Store$, when $\sigma \in [G_i]$, then $\sigma \in [C_i]\phi$ must hold, which is $(G_i \supset [C_i]\phi)$. QED

The weakest-liberal-precondition transformer for the conditional is

Corollary 13. $\sim \langle \mathtt{if}\,(G_i?C_i)_{i \in I}\,\mathtt{fi} \rangle \neg \phi = \bigwedge_{i \in I}(\sim G_i \vee \sim \langle C_i \rangle \neg \phi) = \bigwedge_{i \in I}(\sim G_i \vee [C_i] \sim (\neg \phi))$.

Here is the semantics of do · od, simplified to use one clause in its body:

$$\text{do } G?C \text{ od} \equiv w, \text{ where } w \equiv \text{if } (G?C; w)(\neg G?\text{skip}) \text{ fi}$$

$$[\![w]\!] = \bigsqcup_{j \geq 0} f_j, \text{ where } \begin{array}{l} f_0\sigma = \bot \\ f_{j+1}\sigma = \begin{cases} f_j^\dagger([\![C]\!]\sigma), & \text{if } \sigma \in [\![G]\!] \\ \{\!|\sigma|\!\}, & \text{if } \sigma \in [\![\neg G]\!] \\ \{\!|\bot|\!\}, & \text{otherwise} \end{cases} \end{array}$$

Therefore, when $(\sqsubseteq_M) \subseteq (\sqsubseteq_U)$:

$$[w]\phi = \bigcup_{j \geq 0} [f_j]\phi, \text{ where } \begin{array}{l} [f_0]\phi = \emptyset \\ [f_{j+1}]\phi = (G \vee \neg G) \wedge (G \supset [C; f_j]\phi) \wedge (\neg G \supset \phi) \end{array}$$

When $(\sqsubseteq_M) \subseteq (\sqsubseteq_L)$:

$$\langle w \rangle \phi = \bigcup_{j \geq 0} \langle f_j \rangle \phi, \text{ where } \begin{array}{l} \langle f_0 \rangle \phi = \emptyset \\ \langle f_{j+1} \rangle \phi = (G \wedge \langle C; f_j \rangle \phi) \vee (\neg G \wedge \phi) \end{array}$$

The weakest-liberal-precondition transformer for the loop is

$$\sim \langle w \rangle \neg \phi = \bigcap_{j \geq 0} \sim \langle f_j \rangle \neg \phi = \bigcap_{j \geq 0} [f_j] \sim (\neg \phi)$$

7   Conclusion

Dijkstra prefered proof theory, specifically equational algebra, to reason about programs, and GCL is an especially elegant and useful theory. But model theory cannot be avoided, as Reynolds demonstrated in Chap. 9 of Dijkstra's text. Reynolds's observation was merely the "tip" of the semantical "iceberg," and this paper has meant to expose the model theory that underlies GCL.

Acknowledgements. Hanne Riis Nielson and Flemming Nielson have been friends and inspirational colleagues for many decades, and this paper, building on material that was developed and presented by Mike Smyth in Edinburgh in 1982–83 when all of us were resident there, is dedicated to them. I thank Mike for his clear, intuitive papers and explanations. The referees are thanked for their helpful comments.

Appendix

Assume D is a domain, ΩD its Scott topology, and $PD \subseteq \mathcal{P}(D)$. Recall that $[S]_U \sqsubseteq_U [T]_U$ iff for all $O \in \Omega D, S \subseteq O$ implies $T \subseteq O$. The following is an unproved exercise in [26] that is useful here:

Lemma 14. $[S]_U \sqsubseteq_U [T]_U$ iff for every $t \in T$, there exists $s \in S$ such that $s \sqsubseteq_D t$.

Proof. Only if: assume $S \subseteq O$ implies $T \subseteq O$ but also that there is some $t_0 \in T$ for which no $s \in S$ satisfies $s \sqsubseteq_D t_0$. Since $\downarrow\{t_0\}$ is a closed set, then $\sim(\downarrow\{t_0\})$ is open and covers S. But T is not covered by this open set, which is a contradiction. If: Assume $S \subseteq O$. Since O is up-closed, it is immediate that $T \subseteq O$ as well. QED

Let $(\sqsubseteq_M) \subseteq PD \times PD$ generate the powerdomain, $\mathcal{P}_M(D) = (PD/M, \subseteq_M)$, where PD consists of compact sets.

Lemma 15. *If* $(\sqsubseteq_M) \subseteq (\sqsubseteq_U)$, *then* $\{E \in \mathcal{P}_M(D) \mid O \text{ covers } E\}$, *for* $O \in \Omega D$, *is an open set in the Scott topology,* $\Omega\mathcal{P}_M(D)$.

Proof. The set is up-closed because, when $[S]_M \sqsubseteq_M [T]_M$ and $S \subseteq O$, then for every $t \in T$ there is some $s \in S \cap O$ such that $s \sqsubseteq_D t$. Since O is up-closed, $T \subseteq U$.

The set is closed under "directed tails": Assume O covers $\bigsqcup_{i \in I}[S_i]_M$. Assume that no O covers $[S_i]_M$ holds, for all $i \in I$. This causes a contradiction: First, for every S_i, there is an element, $s_i \in S_i$, such that $s_i \notin O$. Since $(\sqsubseteq_M) \subseteq (\sqsubseteq_U)$, for every $[S_j]_M \sqsubseteq_M [S_i]_M$, there is some $s_j \in S_j$ such that $s_j \sqsubseteq_D s_i$, where $s_j \notin O$. By the Axiom of Choice, one can construct a directed set, $NO = \{s_i \in S_i \mid s_i \notin O\}$, and we have $\sqcup NO \notin O$.

We now show that $(\bigsqcup_{i \in I}[S_i]_M) \uplus \{\!\{NO\}\!\}$ is an upper bound of the $([S_i]_M)_{i \in I}$: First, the underlying set is compact, because adding NO preserves compactness. Next, for each $[S_k]_M$, $[S_k]_M = [S_k \cup \{s_k\}]_M = [S_k]_M \uplus \{\!\{s_k\}\!\}_M$. This implies $[S_k]_M \sqsubseteq_M (\bigsqcup_{i \in I}[S_i]_M) \uplus \{\!\{NO\}\!\}$ by the monotonicity of $\uplus$ and $\{\!\{\cdot\}\!\}$.

But $\bigsqcup_{i \in I}[S_i]_M \not\sqsubseteq_M (\bigsqcup_{i \in I}[S_i]_M) \uplus \{\!\{NO\}\!\}$, because there is no $t \in D$ in any set represented by equivalence class $\bigsqcup_{i \in I}[S_i]_M$ such that $t \sqsubseteq_D NO$. This contradicts the existence of the least upper bound. QED

Let $(\sqsubseteq_M) \subseteq PD \times PD$ generate the powerdomain, $\mathcal{P}_M(D) = (PD/M, \subseteq_M)$.

Lemma 16. *If* $(\sqsubseteq_M) \subseteq (\sqsubseteq_L)$, *then* $\{E \in \mathcal{P}_M(D) \mid E \text{ meets } O\}$, *for* $O \in \Omega D$, *is an open set in the Scott topology,* $\Omega\mathcal{P}_M(D)$.

Proof. The set is up-closed because $(\sqsubseteq_M) \subseteq (\sqsubseteq_L)$. The set is proved closed under "directed tails" as follows: Let $(E_i)_{i \in I}$ be a directed subset of $\mathcal{P}_M(D)$. Assume $\bigsqcup_{i \in I} E_i$ meets O and assume that no E_i meets O holds, for all $i \in I$. We generate a contradiction by constructing a discontinuous function using the powerdomain operations (which are all continuous). First, we observe that for any nontrivial domain D, any nontrivial $\mathcal{P}_M(D)$ must possess at least two distinct elements, A_0 and A_1, such that $A_0 \sqsubseteq_M A_1$ implying that $A_0 \sqsubseteq_M A_1 \sqsubseteq_M A_0 \uplus A_1$ (because $(\sqsubseteq_M) \subseteq (\sqsubseteq_L)$). We use these two elements to define this continuous function, $f : D \to \mathcal{P}_M(D)$: $f(d) = \begin{cases} A_1, & \text{if } d \in O \\ A_0, & \text{if } d \notin O \end{cases}$. By the definition of powerdomain, there is a continuous function, $f^\dagger : \mathcal{P}_M(D) \to \mathcal{P}_M(D)$, defined as $f^\dagger[S]_M = [\bigcup_{d \in S} F_d]_M$, where $f(d) = [F_d]_M$.

Because $\bigsqcup_{i \in I} E_i$ meets O holds, it must be that $f^\dagger(\bigsqcup_{i \in I} E_i) \sqsupseteq_M A_1$. But we assumed that no E_i meets O holds, for all $i \in I$, so it must be that $\bigsqcup_{i \in I} f^\dagger(E_i) = \bigsqcup_{i \in I}\{A_0\} = A_0$. Since $A_0 \neq A_1$, this contradicts the continuity of $f^\dagger$. QED

References

1. Abramsky, S.: Domain theory in logical form. Ann. Pure Appl. Logic **51**, 1–77 (1991)
2. Ball, T., Podelski, A., Rajamani, S.K.: Boolean and cartesian abstraction for model checking C programs. In: Margaria, T., Yi, W. (eds.) TACAS 2001. LNCS, vol. 2031, pp. 268–283. Springer, Heidelberg (2001)
3. Bonsangue, M.: Topological duality in semantics. Electr. Notes Theor. Comput. Sci. **8**, 1–274 (1998)
4. Clarke, E., Grumberg, O., Lu, Y., Jha, S., Veith, H.: Counterexample-guided abstraction refinement. In: Emerson, E.A., Sistla, A.P. (eds.) CAV 2000. LNCS, vol. 1855, pp. 154–169. Springer, Heidelberg (2000)
5. de Bakker, J.: Mathematical Theory of Program Correctness. Prentice Hall, Upper Saddle River (1980)
6. Dijkstra, E.W.: Guarded commands, nondeterminacy and formal derivation of program. Comm. ACM **18**, 453–457 (1975)
7. Dijkstra, E.W.: A Discipline of Programming. Prentice Hall, Upper Saddle River (1976)
8. Gierz, G., Hoffmann, K., Keimel, K., Lawson, J., Mislove, M., Scott, D.: Continuous Lattices and Domains. Cambridge University Press, Cambridge (2003)
9. Gries, D.: The Science of Programming. Springer, New York (1989)
10. Guessarian, I. (ed.): Algebraic Semantics. LNCS, vol. 99. Springer, Heidelberg (1981)
11. Gunter, C.: Semantics of Programming Languages. MIT Press, Cambridge (1992)
12. Gunter, C., Scott, D.S.: Semantic domains. In: van Leeuwen, J. (ed.) Handbook of Theoretical Computer Science, vol. B, pp. 633–674. MIT Press, Cambridge (1991)
13. Harel, D.: First-Order Dynamic Logic. LNCS, vol. 68. Springer, New York (1979)
14. Hasuo, I.: Generic weakest precondition semantics from monads enriched with order. In: Bonsangue, M.M. (ed.) CMCS 2014. LNCS, vol. 8446, pp. 10–32. Springer, Heidelberg (2014)
15. Heckmann, R.: Power domain constructions. Ph.D thesis, University Saarbrücken (1990)
16. Heckmann, R.: Set domains. In: Jones, N.D. (ed.) ESOP 1990. LNCS, vol. 432, pp. 177–196. Springer, Heidelberg (1990)
17. Henzinger, T., Jhala, R., Majumdar, R.: Counterexample-guided control. In: Baeten, J.C.M., Lenstra, J.K., Parrow, J., Woeginger, G.J. (eds.) ICALP 2003. LNCS, vol. 2719, pp. 886–902. Springer, Heidelberg (2003)
18. Jacobs, B.: Measurable spaces and their effect logic. In: Proceedings of 28th Symposium on LICS, pp. 1043–6871. IEEE Press (2013)
19. Jacobs, B.: Dijkstra monads in monadic computation. In: Bonsangue, M.M. (ed.) CMCS 2014. LNCS, vol. 8446, pp. 135–150. Springer, Heidelberg (2014)
20. Main, M.: A powedomain primer. Technical report, University of Colorado CU-CS-375-87 and Bull. EATCS (1987)
21. Milne, R., Strachey, C.: A Theory of Programming Language Semantics. Chapman and Hall, New york (1976)
22. Nielson, H.R., Nielson, F.: Principles of Program Analysis. Springer, Heidelberg (1999)
23. Nielson, H.R., Nielson, F., Hankin, C.: Semantics with Applications. Wiley, New york (1992)

24. Plotkin, G.: A powerdomain construction. SIAM J. Computing **5**(3), 452–487 (1976)
25. Plotkin, G.: Dijkstra's predicate transformers and Smyth's powerdomains. In: Bjorner, D. (ed.) Abstract Software Specifications. LNCS, vol. 86. Springer, Heidelberg (1980)
26. Plotkin, G.: Domains. Lecture notes, University of Pisa/Edinburgh (1983)
27. Reynolds, J.C.: Notes on a lattice-theoretic approach to the theory of computation. Technical report, Computer Science, Syracuse University (1972)
28. Saïdi, H.: Model checking guided abstraction and analysis. In: Palsberg, J. (ed.) SAS 2000. LNCS, vol. 1824, pp. 377–396. Springer, Heidelberg (2000)
29. Schmidt, D.A.: Denotational Semantics. Allyn and Bacon, Boston (1986)
30. Schmidt, D.A.: Abstract interpretation from a topological perspective. In: Palsberg, J., Su, Z. (eds.) SAS 2009. LNCS, vol. 5673, pp. 293–308. Springer, Heidelberg (2009)
31. Scott, D.S.: Continuous lattices. In: Proceedings of Dalhousie Conference, LNM 274, pp. 97–136. Springer Lecture Notes in Mathematics (1972)
32. Scott, D.S.: Lectures on a mathematical theory of computation. Technical report prg-19, Programming Research Group, Oxford University (1980)
33. Smyth, M.B.: Effectively given domains. Theoretical Comp. Sci. **5**, 257–274 (1977)
34. Smyth, M.B.: Power domains. J. Comput. Syst. Sci. **16**(1), 23–36 (1978)
35. Smyth, M.B.: Powerdomains and predicate transformers: a topological view. In: Díaz, J. (ed.) ICALP 1983. LNCS, vol. 154, pp. 662–675. Springer, Heidelberg (1983)
36. Stoy, J.: Denotational Semantics. MIT Press, Cambridge (1977)
37. van Dalen, D.: Intuitionistic logic. In: Gabbay, D., Guenther, F. (eds.) Handbook of Philosophical Logic, vol. III, pp. 225–340. Kluwer, Dordrecht (1986)
38. Vickers, S.: Topology via Logic. Cambridge University Press, New York (1989)
39. Willard, S.: General Topology. Dover Publications, New York (2004)
40. Winskel, G.: Formal Semantics of Programming Languages. MIT Press, Cambridge (1993)

Enhancing Top-Down Solving
with Widening and Narrowing

Kalmer Apinis[1]([⊠]), Helmut Seidl[2], and Vesal Vojdani[1]

[1] Deptartment of Computer Science,
University of Tartu, J. Liivi 2, 50409 Tartu, Estonia
`{kalmer.apinis,vesal.vojdani}@ut.ee`
[2] Lehrstuhl für Informatik II, Technische Universität München,
Boltzmannstraße 3, 85748 Garching, Germany
`seidl@in.tum.de`

Abstract. We present an enhancement of the generic fixpoint algorithm **TD** which can deal with widening and narrowing even for non-monotonic systems of equations. In contrast to corresponding enhancements proposed for other standard fixpoint algorithms, no extra priorities on variables are required. Still, a mechanism can be devised so that occurrences of the widening/narrowing operator are inserted as well as removed dynamically.

1 Introduction

Many analysis problems can be formalized as (post)-solutions to systems of equations $x = f_x, x \in V$, where V is a set of unknowns each denoting and f_x is a function specifying how x depends on the values of other unknowns in V. In the simplest setting of context-insensitive analysis of sequential imperative programs, the set of unknowns is given by the set of program points, for which the equation system provides a specification of valid invariants. In the more elaborate case of context-sensitive analysis, though, the unknowns are no longer plain program points but also incorporate information about the calling contexts of the respective functions.

A *solver* of systems of equations is an algorithm which determines such post-solutions. It is *local* if it is started with a query to the value of some unknown and then tries to explore the system only as much as is necessary to determine the answer to the query. Local solving has attracted attention in particular for interprocedural analysis of recursive programs [3,9,15,21,23,24] where the potential number of abstract calling contexts can be extremely high, if not *infinite*, while the number of those contexts which are really required for describing all occurring contexts for each function may be quite small. Local solvers are also the method of choice to realize *incremental* program analysis, e.g., when updating the analysis result after an incremental modification of the source program in question [14,22]. Particularly useful, from a software engineering perspective, are *generic* local solvers [12,13,16,19,21] which make only minimal assumptions

© Springer International Publishing Switzerland 2016
C.W. Probst et al. (Eds.): Nielsons' Festschrift, LNCS 9560, pp. 272–288, 2016.
DOI: 10.1007/978-3-319-27810-0_14

about the domain of values to compute with, e.g., that it has an ordering relation $\sqsubseteq$ as well as an upper bound operation $\sqcup$, while right-hand sides of equations are taken as black boxes. This means that the right-hand side f_x of a variable x is *not* considered as some kind of syntactical expression which can be inspected beforehand and must be interpreted by the solver. Instead, the right-hand side is considered as a function implemented in some programming language which can be called for another function σ representing the current information about the unknowns and returns a contribution to the left-hand side x of the equation. Interestingly, quite competitive generic solvers have been proposed. Among these, the *top-down* solver **TD** [19] or the solver from GOBLINT [16]. Since they are completely ignorant of the concrete analysis problem in question, they conveniently allow the analysis designer to separate the algorithmic concerns of solving from the design of a suitable domain of abstract values (corresponding to potential invariants) and the realization of the abstract semantics by means of equations. Accordingly, they are at the heart of modern analysis frameworks such as the CIAO system [15] or GOBLINT [4,24].

One key problem for solving systems of equations is that many interesting analysis problems require lattices with *infinite* strictly ascending chains. This is already the case for interval analysis [7] which tries to determine for each numerical program variable and program point a suitably small interval superset of all runtime values, but also the case for more elaborate numerical properties such as octagons [20] or polyhedra [11]. One general technique to deal with such problems is the widening and narrowing approach as proposed by Cousot and Cousot [7]. The idea is to accelerate the Kleene-type fixpoint iteration for the system of equations by rapidly increasing the values of the unknowns through a *widening* operator. In this way, a guarantee of termination is traded against a severe loss in precision—some of which may later be recovered by means of a subsequent *narrowing* iteration. Technically, a widening produces a larger value than the ordinary least upper bound operator. Thus it may reach a post-solution more quickly (and hopefully in finitely many steps), whereas narrowing when applied to a post-solution (perhaps produced by over-enthusiastic widening) may return a better post-solution.

While local solvers such as the *top-down* solver **TD** or the solver from GOBLINT can easily be extended to work with widening, it has been observed in [5], that they do not go well with narrowing. There are two reasons for this behavior. First, during the narrowing phase, further unknowns may be encountered which may not yet been considered so far. More severely, however, is that the application of context-sensitive analysis may result in *non-monotonic* systems of equations, while narrowing in the original sense can only be applied when all right-hand sides are monotonic. As a remedy, therefore, Apinis et al. introduce a new operator $\boxtimes$ which combines a widening operator ∇ with a narrowing operator Δ into one [5]. By means of this operator, variants of several standard solvers are derived and sufficient conditions are provided for which these algorithms are guaranteed to terminate. In particular, variants of the generic local solvers underlying the GOBLINT system are presented. The key idea for enforcing termination is to maintain an ordering on the names of the unknowns which is respected during fixpoint iteration.

In this paper, we present a variant of the solver **TD** which also supports widening and narrowing. It turns out that **TD** iterates according to an ordering on unknowns as provided by the iteration strategy. This means that it suffices to insert the operator ⊠ into the base algorithm for combining old values with newly computed values and additionally always trigger reevaluation of an unknown, whenever its value has changed. Already for this minimalistic enhancement, termination can be guaranteed—at least for equation systems where all right-hand sides are monotonic, and only finitely many unknowns are encountered. Beyond that, we enhance the algorithm so that the operator ⊠ is not applied for each equation when its right-hand side is evaluated, but only for a small subset of these. This subset is dynamically established by means of the set of unknowns under evaluation by the solver, which is explicitly maintained by **TD** anyway.

2   Equation System

Assume that D is a set of values. Usually, we assume that D is a complete lattice, but weaker assumptions would do as well. The *minimal* requirements are that D is equipped with a partial ordering $\sqsubseteq$, that there is a designated least element $\bot$ with $\bot \sqsubseteq d$ for all $d \in D$, and that there is a binary upper bound operation $\sqcup$, i.e., $a \sqsubseteq a \sqcup b$ and $b \sqsubseteq a \sqcup b$. Let V denote a set of variables or unknowns. Then a system $\mathcal{C}$ of equations over the values D with variables from V is a collection of equations:

$$x = f_x , \quad x \in V$$

where the right-hand side f_x of an unknown x specifies how the value of x depends on the values of all other unknowns in the system. Thus, f_x can be understood as a function $f_x : (V \to D) \to D$, which for every assignment $\sigma : V \to D$ of values to unknowns, returns a value in D for the left-hand side x. A mapping $\sigma : V \to D$ is a *post*-solution to S if the values of σ for the left-hand sides are upper bounds to the values returned by their respective right-hand sides for σ, i.e., if $\sigma x \sqsupseteq f_x \sigma$ for all $x \in V$.

Example 1. As a running example, consider the following equation system with two equations

$$x = (x < 2^{32} \ ? \ y \ : \ 2^{32})$$
$$y = x + 1$$

where the set D of values is given by $D = \mathbb{N} \cup \{\infty\}$, equipped with the natural ordering and extended with ∞. The right-hand side of x returns the value of y, if x is less than 2^{32}, otherwise it returns 2^{32}. The right-hand side of y, however, always returns the value of $x + 1$. Then the mappings $\{x \mapsto 2^{32}, y \mapsto 2^{32} + 1\}$ and $\{x \mapsto \infty, y \mapsto \infty\}$ are post-solutions for the given equation system.   ■

In static program analysis, equation systems are used for specifying data flow [18] or the abstract semantics of a programs [3,11]. The value domains in such cases typically are (complete) lattices where the right-hand side functions are monotonic.

In the practical application within a program analyzer, the function f_x is not given as a mathematical object, but as a piece of code realizing the mathematical function. This code can be implemented in any language. We only make the assumption that the realized function is terminating and *pure* in the sense of [17]. This means that operationally, every evaluation of $f_x \, \sigma$ consists of a finite sequence of *steps* which eventually returns a value, where each step consists of a look-up of the value of an unknown, followed by some computation solely depending on the sequence of values read so far.

For some analysis problems, the set of potential unknowns and thus the resulting systems of equations may be very large, or even *infinite*. In order to deal with such a situation, the system of equations is more conveniently assumed to be represented implicitly by means of a single function $f \in V \to (V \to D) \to D$ so that $f \, x$ returns the right-hand side f_x for each unknown x. Using this representation, the mapping $\sigma \in V \to D$ is a post-solution if $\sigma x \sqsupseteq f \, x \, \sigma$ for all $x \in V$.

A *solver* for a class of equation systems is an algorithm that for each system $\mathcal{C}$ of equations in that class, upon termination, returns a post-solution. Various solvers have been proposed for equation systems where the set of unknowns is finite and the partial ordering D is *Noetherian*, i.e., has no infinite strictly increasing chains. One example of such a solver is *Round Robin* iteration with accumulation. For other solvers, such as the *worklist* iterator, further information about the right-hand side functions is required—namely the set of unknowns whose values are queried during their evaluations. In some cases, though, the system of equations is queried for the values of a few *interesting* unknowns only. Consider, e.g., inter-procedural analysis in the style of [9], e.g., for C. In this application, the unknowns are pairs of program points and abstract calling contexts in which these points are analyzed. The equation system then is queried for the value of the *end point* of the call to the *main* function for the *initial* abstract calling context. From the remaining unknowns only those must be inspected which directly or indirectly contribute to the result of the initial query. A *local* solver is an algorithm meant to deal with such queries. When started with the initial query to an unknown x, it returns a *partial* solution σ. The mapping σ is a partial solution if it provides values for a subset $V' \subseteq V$ of unknowns such that the following holds:

- $x \in V'$;
- For every unknown $y \in V'$, f_y when evaluated on σ, only queries the values of unknowns in V';
- $\sigma x \sqsupseteq f_x \sigma$ for all $x \in V'$.

Note that the equation system in Example 1, when started with a query of x, has a partial solution of only $\sigma = \{x \mapsto 2^{32}\}$. This is because the short-circuit evaluation of the ternary operator :? does not require to inspect the value of y to determine the value of the right-hand side of x for σ.

In this paper we are concerned with the Top-Down local solver **TD** from Le Charlier and Van Hentenryck [19] as depicted in Fig. 1. The solver **TD** operates on a partial assignment σ of unknowns to values which initially is empty. Each unknown for which σ does not provide a value, implicitly is assumed to be mapped to the least value $\bot$. The solver **TD** consists of two functions: solve, and destabilize. The main function of **TD** is the function solve—which when called with an unknown x, is meant to compute a partial solution σ that provides a value for x. Furthermore, **TD** maintains a subset called of unknowns which consists of all unknowns for which the evaluation of the right-hand side has been started but is not yet completed. It also maintains a set stable receiving the unknown x as soon as solving for x has started, where x is only removed when some unknown onto which x recursively depends has changed its value. Initially, both called and stable are empty. A call to solve for the unknown

```
void solve(var x) {
  D eval(var y) {
    solve(y);
    infl y ← infl y ∪ {x};
    return σ y;
  }
  if (x ∈ stable ∪ called) return;
  else {
    called ← called ∪ {x};
    stable ← stable ∪ {x};
    tmp ← σ x ⊔ fₓ (eval);
    called ← called \ {x};
    if (tmp = σ x) return;
    else {
      σ x ← tmp;
      destabilize(x);
      solve(x);
    }
  }
}

void destabilize(var x) {
  W ← infl x;
  infl x ← ∅ ;
  forall (y ∈ W) {
    if (y ∈ stable) {
      stable ← stable \ {y};
      destabilize(y);
    }
  }
}
```

Fig. 1. The original solver **TD**.

x first checks if x is contained in **stable** or **called**. If this is the case, **solve** immediately returns. Otherwise, x is inserted into **stable** and **called** to indicate that solving of x has now started. Then the right-hand side f_x for the unknown x is evaluated for the local function **eval** (instead of σ directly).

When within a call **solve** x, the argument function **eval** is queried for the value of an unknown y, it ultimately returns the value of y. Before that, however, the solver tries to compute the best possible value for y by calling the function **solve** for y. Furthermore, **eval** y keeps track of detected influences between unknowns. All currently known dependences are maintained by **TD** in a mapping **infl** which, initially, is empty. The function **eval** records the fact that the variable y was required for computing the value for x, by adding the unknown x in the mapping **infl** to the value for y. Only then is the value of y (as stored in σ) returned.

In the next step, the function **solve** joins the old value of σ for x with the new value returned by f x **eval**. Since now the evaluation of the right-hand side is finished, x is removed from the set **called**, and the joined new value is compared to the old value for x as provided by σ. If these two values are equal, no increase of x has occurred and **solve** returns. Otherwise, the value of x in σ is updated to the new value. Since the value of x has changed, all unknowns which directly or indirectly may be influenced by x, can no longer be considered as **stable** and therefore are marked for potential reevaluation. This is the task of the function **destabilize**.

The function **destabilize** when called for an unknown x, iterates through all unknowns in the set **infl** x. Each of the unknowns y which are found to be in **stable** are removed from **stable** and then recursively destabilized. Moreover, the value of **infl** for x is updated to the empty set. In particular this means that before every call of **solve**, all **infl** sets of unstable unknowns, i.e., unknown not **stable**, are empty. Once destabilization has terminated, function **solve** re-evaluates x by calling itself tail-recursively.

Assume that initially, σ is the empty map, all sets **stable**, **called** and **infl** x for all $x \in V$ are empty. Then we consider the following invariant I:

1. Whenever $y \notin$ stable $\cup$ called, then infl $y = \emptyset$;
2. Whenever $y \in$ stable\called, then $\sigma y \sqsupseteq f_y \sigma$, and for every unknown z whose value is queried during the evaluation of f_y w.r.t. the current σ, $z \in$ stable $\cup$ called and $y \in$ infl z.

Then we have the following properties:

Lemma 1. *1. The invariant I holds in the beginning and is re-established by each call to* **solve** *or* **eval**. *Likewise, the set* **called** *is preserved and only increased intermediately.*

2. After each call of **eval** y *inside a call of* **solve** x, $x \in$ infl y, $y \in$ stable$\cup$called *and the current value of σy is returned.*

3. After each call of **solve** x, *the variable x is in the set* **stable**. *Moreover, if σx has been updated, then x does not recursively influence any unknown in* stable $\cap$ called. ∎

By Lemma 1, the program **TD** when started with a call `solve` x, returns a partial post-solution σ for some set V' of unknowns which contains x — whenever it terminates. That set V' then is given by all unknowns x which are accessed when recursively re-evaluating the right-hand side of x starting from σ. Technically, this re-evaluation can be triggered by re-setting the set `stable` to the empty set and again calling `solve` x.

Lemma 1 also implies that the call `solve` x is guaranteed to terminate whenever the domain is Noetherian and only finitely many distinct unknowns are encountered during the evaluation.

We remark that one important step in proving Lemma 1 is to prove that conceptually, the evaluation of $f_x\,\sigma$ of the right-hand side of x in a call to `solve` x for the present mapping σ can be considered as if it happened atomically after evaluation of the unknowns whose values are queried during the evaluation of f_x. For that, it suffices to convince ourselves that every direct query to an unknown $y \notin$ `called`, during this evaluation, will add y and all unknowns by which it is influenced and that are not in called, into the `stable` set— ensuring that a second query of y or any unknowns by which y is influenced will return exactly the same result. Note that the unknowns in `called` are not changed during the evaluation of $f_x\,\sigma$.

Solving the equation system of Example 1 with **TD** produces the following sequence of updates:

	y	x	y	x	$\cdots$	x
x	0	0	1	1	2	$\cdots$	2^{32}
y	0	1	1	2	2	$\cdots$	$2^{32}+1$

We notice that the solving process, although it theoretically terminates after 2^{33} updates, is not efficient. Such inefficiency is typical for equation systems where the value domain contains long increasing chains.

3 Widening and Narrowing

Solving systems of equations usually is based on some form of Kleene iteration, meaning that it consists of a sequence of evaluations of right-hand sides, followed by updates of the unknowns on the corresponding left-hand sides—until all equations in question are satisfied. In case when the partial ordering D of values is not Noetherian, termination of the iteration, though, can no longer be guaranteed. For such cases, Cousot and Cousot [7] propose to first accelerate the iteration by introducing another upper bound operator $\nabla : D \to D \to D$ (the *widening*) to accumulate intermediate values. Conceptually, the idea can be seen as replacing the accumulating version:

$$x = x \sqcup f_x$$

of each equation with the equation:

$$x = x \, \nabla \, f_x$$

where ∇ is an upper bound operator which guarantees that every (post) solution of the new system is also a post-solution of the original system. Beyond that, the widening operator must ensure that values only be increased finitely often. Accordingly, if the set of unknowns which is encountered is finite, **TD** equipped with ∇ (instead of $\sqcup$) will be guaranteed to terminate.

Solving the equation system in Example 1 with **TD** where widening is defined as

$$x \, \nabla \, y = \begin{cases} \infty & \text{if } y > x \\ x & \text{otherwise} \end{cases}$$

produces the following sequence of updates:

	y	x	
x	0	0	∞
y	0	∞	∞

Accordingly, the solving process terminates already after two updates, the resulting values for x and y, though, seem unnecessarily large.

In general, many heuristics have been proposed for various domains widening operators which guarantee termination, while at the same time retain enough precision to return useful results. Still, in many cases the results obtained by widening alone, are unsatisfactory. Therefore, Cousot and Cousot propose to perform a second iteration on the system of equation which subsequently may improve a given post-solution [8,10]. The second iteration starts at a post-solution of the system. Given that all right-hand sides represent monotonic functions, the second iteration will result in a *decreasing* sequence of assignments to unknowns—each of which now forms a post-solution. In order to enforce termination of this second iteration, a *narrowing* operator $\Delta \in D \to D \to D$ is introduced. Again, the first argument of this operator is meant to be the former value of an unknown, while the second argument corresponds to the value newly provided by evaluating the corresponding right-hand side. Then the following property should hold:

$$b \sqsubseteq a \quad \Longrightarrow \quad b \sqsubseteq a \, \Delta \, b \sqsubseteq a$$

As before, the narrowing operator should enforce that all possibly resulting decreasing chains are finite.

For our running example, we use the following narrowing operator:

$$x \bigtriangleup y = \begin{cases} y & \text{if } x = \infty \\ x & \text{otherwise} \end{cases}$$

Starting with the post-solution $\{x \mapsto \infty, y \mapsto \infty\}$, downward iteration produces the following sequence of updates:

	x	y
x	∞	2^{32}	2^{32}
y	∞	∞	$2^{32}+1$

Thus, the solving process terminates already after two updates.

In general, narrowing operators can only be applied if the evaluation of a right-hand side returns less or equal value than currently provided by the left-hand side. If right-hand sides are *not* monotonic, this is not necessarily the case. Non-monotonic right-hand sides, however, inevitably occur in the systems of equations for inter-procedural analysis in the style of Cousot and Cousot in [9].

Example 2. Consider the equation for a call to a procedure g at an edge in the control-flow graph of the calling procedure f from program point u to program point v. For simplicity, assume that all procedures operate on a global state (full treatment of this kind of constraint system together with a discussion of variations, e.g., for partial contexts is discussed in [3]). For every abstract calling context α of f, we then obtain the equation:

$$\langle v, \alpha \rangle = \langle g, \langle u, \alpha \rangle \rangle$$

where $\langle u, \alpha \rangle, \langle v, \alpha \rangle$ are unknowns representing the abstract values attained at program point u, v when analyzing f for context α, and $\langle g, \beta \rangle$ is the abstract state attained at the exit of the procedure g when called in the abstract context β. Note that in this equation, the context β for which $\langle g, \beta \rangle$ provides the value for the left-hand side $\langle v, \alpha \rangle$, equals the current abstract value for $\langle u, \alpha \rangle$. This means that in a first evaluation of $\langle u, \alpha \rangle$ could return a value β_1, while a later evaluation might return another value β_2, and there is no reason why the values of the two distinct unknowns $\langle g, \beta_1 \rangle$ and $\langle g, \beta_2 \rangle$ should always be related.

Likewise, as elaborated by Apinis et al. in [5], local solving and the two-phase approach to widening/narrowing does not go well together. As a remedy, Apinis et al. propose to *combine* the two operators into one update operator $\boxtimes : D \to D \to D$:

$$a \boxtimes b = \begin{cases} a \bigtriangleup b & \text{if } b \sqsubseteq a \\ a \bigtriangledown b & \text{otherwise} \end{cases}$$

Let us call this new operator a *warrowing*. Plugging the warrowing operator into a local solver results in a fixpoint iteration which not necessarily performs a single widening iteration followed by a single narrowing iteration. Instead, widening and narrowing is applied in an intertwined manner—with the additional benefit of increasing precision.

We recall from Apinis et al. [5] that every variable assignment σ such that

$$\sigma x = \sigma x \boxtimes f_x \sigma \qquad (x \in V)$$

is also a post-solution of the original system. In general, though, when plugging the combined operator into an arbitrary solver, termination can no longer be guaranteed—even if the original system of equations has monotonic right-hand sides only.

The following sequence of updates that may be exhibited by some solver (not **TD**) for the equation system in Example 1, when the warrowing operator $\boxtimes$ is applied for every right-hand side.

	y	y	x	x	y	y	...	y
x	0	0	0	∞	1	1	1 ...	2^{32}
y	0	∞	1	1	1	∞	2 ...	$2^{32}+1$

Although the iteration terminates, the solving process turns out to be even less efficient than if no widening/narrowing were used. In general, even termination of the iteration can no longer be guaranteed. Therefore, Apinis et al. [4,5] provide a modifications to several standard solvers so that termination guarantees are retained. The key idea for these modifications is to introduce some kind of ordering on the unknowns which is obeyed during fixpoint iteration. In the following, we show that the enhancement of the top-down solver **TD** by means of the warrowing operator $\boxtimes$ is possible — without resorting to such artificial change in the iteration ordering.

4   Enhancing TD

Intuitively, adding an extra ordering on the unknowns for **TD** can be omitted as top-down iteration already imposes an ordering by which unknowns are re-evaluated: no unknown, once called, will be reevaluated before each of the unknowns onto which it depends are stabilized. Surprisingly, this already suffices to ensure termination for equation systems with monotonic right-hand sides, given that the least upper bound operator in **TD** is replaced with the warrowing operator $\boxtimes$.

Consider again the equation system in Example 1. When x is solved with the enhanced **TD**, we obtain:

Now, the solving process terminates after a few steps. Note that **TD** does not update the value for y as the value of y is not required for verifying the answer to the initial query of x.

	y	y	x	y	x	
x	0	0	0	∞	∞	2^{32}
y	0	∞	1	1	∞	∞

Practical evidence shows, however, that performing widening (and narrowing) for every program point throws away too much information [6]. Therefore, the set of unknowns in whose right-hand sides ☒ is applied, should be chosen to be as small as possible. Figure 2 shows the proposed modified top-down solver where the additions are highlighted. The first point to note is that accumulation with ⊔ is now replaced with accumulation by means of the warrowing operator ☒. Also, once ☒ is involved for computing the next value for an unknown x, the unknown x is also added to the set `infl` x in order to trigger reevaluation of x once x changes its value. The second point to note is that, by default, the new values provided by the respective right-hand sides are *directly* used to update the value of the unknown on the right-hand side. The warrowing operator ☒ is used to combine old values of unknowns with the new values only for dedicated unknowns, namely, those from the set `wpoint`.

The insight is that in order to enforce termination, widening (and likewise also narrowing) need not be applied everywhere in the system but only for at least one unknown within each cyclic influences of unknowns [6]. For systems of equations originating from control-flow graphs of programs (without recursive procedures), a reasonable choice is to use loop heads as widening points only. In our setting, though, the solver is unaware of the application where the system of equations originates from. Moreover, preprocessing of influences between unknowns is not possible—also due to potential changes of influences between unknowns during the iteration of the solver. This means that a *dynamic* method must be provided which detects a sufficiently large set of widening points.

In our modification of **TD**, detection of widening points happens inside of the local function `eval`. Assume that `eval` is called for unknown y inside a call of `solve` for an unknown x. Then the variable y is added to `wpoint` whenever y is found to be already in `called`. As **TD** is a demand-driven local solver, we have, therefore, dynamically detected a cycle in the dependency graph for the unknowns of the equation system.

As a second improvement, the variable y is *removed* again from `wpoint` as soon as the iteration on y has stabilized. Such dynamic shrinking of the set `wpoint` not only accounts for dynamic changes of influences between unknowns, but also may significantly increase precision. Consider, e.g., the unknowns corresponding to a loop in a control-flow graph. Assume that the loop head has been removed from `stable`, but is no longer contained in `wpoint`. Then the prior iteration on the loop must have stabilized. Thus, the destabilization of x must have been triggered from outside the loop—implying that applying ☒ in the right-hand side of x is not necessary [1,2].

```
void solve(V x) {
  D eval(V y) {
    if (y ∈ called) wpoint ← wpoint ∪ {y};
    solve(y);
    infl[y] ← infl[y] ∪ {x};
    return σ[y];
  }
  if (x ∈ stable ∪ called) return;
  called ← called ∪ {x};
  stable ← stable ∪ {x};
  if (x ∈ wpoint) {
    wpoint ← wpoint \ {x};
    tmp ← σ[x] ☐ f (x) (eval);
    infl[x] ← infl[x] ∪ {x};
  }
  else tmp ← f (x) (eval);
  called ← called \ {x};
  if (tmp = σ[x]) return;
  else {
    σ[x] ← tmp;
    destabilize(x);
    solve(x);
  }
}

void destabilize(V x) {
  W ← infl[x];
  infl[x] ← ∅ ;
  forall (y ∈ W) {
    if (y ∈ stable) {
      stable ← stable \ {y};
      destabilize(y);
    }
  }
}
```

Fig. 2. The enhanced solver $\mathbf{TD}^{\boxtimes}$.

Theorem 1. *Consider* $\mathbf{TD}^{\boxtimes}$ *for a system* $\mathcal{C}$ *of equations with set* V *of unknowns. Assume that initially, both* `stable` *and* `called` *are empty, and* `solve` x *has been called for some unknown* $x \in V$. *Then the following holds:*

1. *Upon termination, a partial solution for* $\mathcal{C}$ *is obtained for some subset* $V' \subseteq V$ *with* $x \in V'$.
2. *The call is guaranteed terminate if only finitely many unknowns are encountered and one of the following assumptions are met:*
   (a) $a \, \Delta \, b = a$, *i.e., narrowing is effectively switched off, or*
   (b) all right-hand sides are monotonic.

Clearly, Theorem 1 is unsatisfactory, as it does not provide a termination guarantee for the case where right-hand sides are *not* monotonic. With contrived non-monotonic systems, virtually every solver using ⊠ as is, can be forced into non-termination. In that sense, the second assertion for monotonic right-hand sides cannot easily be improved. It gives an indication, though, that *practically* termination can be hoped for. At the price of giving up some opportunities for further narrowing steps, we can always *enforce* termination. We could, e.g., modify the warrowing operator ⊠ so that the number of switches from widening to narrowing is bounded at each occurrence of ⊠ in the equation system.

For the proof of Theorem 1, we remark that the properties stated in Lemma 1 for solver **TD** also hold true for the program **TD**$^{⊠}$. From that, the statement 1 of Theorem 1 immediately follows. Therefore here we concentrate on the proof of termination.

5   Proof of Termination

We perform an induction on the number n of unknowns queried during the evaluation of the unknown x and which are either equal to x or not contained in the set `called`. For $n = 0$, the evaluation immediately terminates. Now assume that $n > 0$. To establish a contradiction, assume that the call `solve` x does not terminate. Since by inductive hypothesis, each recursive call to `eval` terminates, the tail-recursive call to `solve` x is executed infinitely often. This means that the value of x must be updated infinitely often, and thus its right-hand side also be re-evaluated infinitely often.

We claim that then during each evaluation of the right-hand side of x, x is added to the set `wpoint`—implying that each new value is obtained by application of the operator ⊠. Assume for a contradiction that this were not the case. Let V_i denote the set of unknowns which are not in `called` which are queried during the ith evaluation of the right-hand side of x. If before the $(i + 1)$th evaluation, x is *not* contained in `wpoint`, then for none of the unknowns $y \in S_i$, the evaluation of their right-hand sides may have queried the value of x. After the ith evaluation of the right-hand side of x, each unknown $y \in S_i$ is stable and none of them is contained in the set `infl`(x). Therefore, none of them is removed from the set `stable` when the value of x in σ is updated. Therefore, the next as well as any subsequent evaluation of the right-hand side will query always the same set of unknowns, i.e., $S_j = S_i$ for all $j \geqslant i$, and all the unknowns in there will be stable. But then the $(i+2)$th value returned for x will equal the $(i+1)$th value for x—in contradiction to our assumption.

Let $d_1 \neq d_2 \neq \ldots$ be the sequence of values for x after the ith update. In particular, between any two updates, x must have been destabilized (otherwise, `solve` x would have terminated immediately), implying that x recursively has been found to influence itself. To establish this influence, x will have been inserted into the set `wpoint`, the latest during the first evaluation of its right-hand side and will stay there until its value has stabilized. Therefore, for each $i \geqslant 1$ it holds that $d_{i+1} = d_i ⊠ b_i$ for suitable values b_i.

First assume that narrowing returns its first argument, i.e., is effectively switched off. Then $d_{i+1} = d_i \nabla b_i$ (for all $i \geqslant 1$). Since the operator ∇ is a widening, the sequence d_i must eventually be stable—contradicting the assertion that $d_i \neq d_{i+1}$ for all i.

Therefore, now consider the second sufficient condition for termination as stated in the theorem, namely, that all right-hand sides are monotonic. Let m denote the maximal index such that for all $i < m$, $d_{i+1} = d_i \nabla b_i$. Since ∇ is a widening, such an m exists. For that m, we claim:

Claim. For all $j \geqslant m$, $d_j \sqsupseteq d_{j+1}$.

Given that the claim holds, $d_{j+1} = d_j \Delta b_j$ for all $j \geqslant m$. Now since Δ is a narrowing operation, the sequence $d_j, j \geqslant m$ must become ultimately stable— again contradicting the assertion that $d_i \neq d_{i+1}$ for all i.

It remains to prove the claim. In order to do so, we introduce a few extra notions. For a set V and a lattice $(D, \sqsubseteq)$, let g be a function $(V \to D) \to D$. Given a mapping $\sigma \in V \to D$, the function g *depends* on the set $V' \subseteq V$ of unknowns (relative to σ) if for all $\sigma' \in V \to D$ such that V' is the smallest subset such that $\sigma|_{V'} = \sigma'|_{V'}$ implies that $g\,\sigma = g\,\sigma'$. We say that g *references* unknowns from $R(g, \sigma) \subseteq V$ w.r.t. the mapping σ if the evaluation of the strategy tree [17] for g for the mapping σ queries exactly the unknowns $R(g, \sigma)$. It can be shown that referencing is an over-approximation of dependency, i.e., all mappings σ' such that $\sigma|_{R(g,\sigma)} = \sigma'|_{R(g,\sigma)}$ implies $g\,\sigma = g\,\sigma'$. We have:

Lemma 2. *If g is monotonic then for all $\sigma, \sigma' : V \to D$,*

$$\forall x \in R(g, \sigma).\ \sigma' x \sqsubseteq \sigma x$$

then

$$g\,\sigma' \sqsubseteq g\,\sigma \ .$$

Proof. Assume for a contradiction that there are mappings σ, σ' such that $\forall x \in R(g, \sigma).\ \sigma' x \sqsubseteq \sigma x$, but $g\,\sigma' \not\sqsubseteq g\,\sigma$. We construct

$$\sigma'' x = \begin{cases} \sigma x & \text{if } x \in R(g, \sigma) \\ \sigma' x & \text{otherwise.} \end{cases}$$

We have

$$\forall x \in V.\ \sigma' x \sqsubseteq \sigma'' x$$

and therefore, by monotonicity of g,

$$g\,\sigma' \sqsubseteq g\,\sigma'' \ .$$

Because reference is an over-approximation of dependence we also have that $g\,\sigma'' = g\,\sigma$. Thus, we conclude that $g\,\sigma' \sqsubseteq g\,\sigma$ holds—in contradiction to our assumption. ∎

Now we are ready to prove our claim:

Lemma 3. *During a call to* solve *(x), for some unknown x, once the sequence of values u_j provided by evaluating the right-hand side for the unknown x starts to descend, it will stabilize or keep descending, i.e., $d_j \sqsupseteq d_{j+1}$ for all $j \geqslant m$.*

Proof. Evaluation of the right-hand side of the unknown x, when solving x generates a sequence $(z_1, \sigma_1), \ldots, (z_r, \sigma_r)$, where the first components z_i are the unknowns that are re-evaluated and the second components σ_i are the respective mappings at the time when the evaluation of the right-hand side of z_i has been completed, and the ordering is the ordering in which the new values for the unknowns are determined. In particular, the last unknown in this sequence z_r equals x. Let us call this the *trace* of the evaluation of x.

Assume that the evaluation of the right-hand side of the unknown x returned a smaller value u than the value currently stored in σ. At that point in time, all referenced unknowns $R(f\, z_i, \sigma)$ that are not in the set called are stable. Assume that $\sigma\, x \,\Delta\, u \sqsubseteq \sigma\, x$. After evaluation of x has been completed, destabilize is called for x, as we assume that the value for x continuously changes. The function destabilize will remove all unknowns from stable that might need to be updated, as they are (transitively) influenced by x. Subsequently, solve is again called for the unknown x.

As before, evaluation of the right-hand side of x will generate a trace $(q_1, \sigma'_1), \ldots, (q_n, \sigma'_n)$. Recall that the last unknown to be updated again will be x. Now we show that those unknowns q_i that have already occurred in the sequence $z_1, \ldots, z_r$ will receive a smaller value or stay the same. For the proof, we perform induction over the prefixes of the trace $(q_1, \sigma'_1), \ldots, (q_n, \sigma'_n)$.

Base Trivial.
Step Assume that the values of $q_1, \ldots, q_{i-1}$ that occurred already in the sequence $z_1, \ldots, z_r$ stayed the same or decreased—according to the induction hypothesis. As for the update to q_i, we only need to consider the case that q_i has already occurred, i.e., that $q_i = z_j$ for some index j.
As TD solves all unknowns occurring in the right-hand side of q_i beforehand, except when they are in called or in stable, only unknowns which did not occur among the $z_1, \ldots, z_r$ may receive a larger or incomparable value. This means that the last evaluation of z_j did not depend on these unknowns. By Lemma 2, however, the value returned for the right-hand side of $q_i = z_j$ then will be smaller or stay the same. This concludes the proof of the claim and hence of Theorem 1.   ∎

6   Conclusion

We have presented a moderate improvement of the generic local solver **TD** which enables the solver to use widening and narrowing in a convenient way. Upon termination, the resulting algorithm always returns a partial solution from which a partial post-solution can be extracted. Moreover, termination can be guaranteed whenever only finitely many unknowns are encountered and either no narrowing is used or right-hand sides are all monotonic. During fixpoint iteration, it dynamically not only detects dependences between unknowns but also those unknowns which require widening/narrowing. Compared to the solvers presented in [2,4,5], the solver $\mathbf{TD}^\boxtimes$ is simpler as no explicit priorities of unknowns need to be maintained. The latter solvers, however, can be enhanced to deal with *side-effects* inside systems of equations. Side-effects allow to generate contributions to unknowns different from the left-hand side. This mechanism is convenient, e.g., for combining flow-insensitive analysis with inter-procedural analysis [3]. It is still open whether the solver $\mathbf{TD}^\boxtimes$ can be enhanced to deal with such systems as well. Also, in the application of $\mathbf{TD}$ inside the CIAO system, extra measures are taken to limit the number of unknowns to be considered [14]. It would be interesting to see how the plain version considered here works together with such extra methods.

Acknowledgements. The research leading to these results has received funding from the ARTEMIS Joint Undertaking under grant agreement no 269335 and from the German Science Foundation (DFG). This work was funded by institutional research grant IUT2-1 from the Estonian Research Council.

References

1. Amato, G., Scozzari, F.: Localizing widening and narrowing. In: Logozzo, F., Fähndrich, M. (eds.) Static Analysis. LNCS, vol. 7935, pp. 25–42. Springer, Heidelberg (2013)
2. Amato, G., Scozzari, F., Seidl, H., Apinis, K., Vojdani, V.: Efficiently intertwining widening and narrowing (2015). arXiv:1503.00883 [cs.PL]
3. Apinis, K., Seidl, H., Vojdani, V.: Side-effecting constraint systems: a Swiss army knife for program analysis. In: Jhala, R., Igarashi, A. (eds.) APLAS 2012. LNCS, vol. 7705, pp. 157–172. Springer, Heidelberg (2012)
4. Apinis, K.: Frameworks for analyzing multi-threaded C, Ph.D. thesis, Institut für Informatik, Technische Universität München (2014)
5. Apinis, K., Seidl, H., Vojdani, V.: How to combine widening and narrowing for non-monotonic systems of equations. In: 34th ACM SIGPLAN Conference on Programming Language Design and Implementation (PLDI), pp. 377–386. ACM (2013)
6. Bourdoncle, F.: Interprocedural abstract interpretation of block structured languages with nested procedures, aliasing and recursivity. In: Deransart, P., Małuszyński, J. (eds.) PLILP 1990. LNCS, vol. 456. Springer, Heidelberg (1990)
7. Cousot, P., Cousot, R.: Static determination of dynamic properties of programs. In: Robinet, B. (ed.) 2nd International Symposium on Programming, Paris, pp. 106–130. Dunod (1976)
8. Cousot, P., Cousot, R.: Abstract interpretation: a unified lattice model for static analysis of programs by construction or approximation of fixpoints. In: 4th Annual ACM Symposium on Principles of Programming Languages (POPL), pp. 238–252. ACM Press (1977)
9. Cousot, P., Cousot, R.: Static determination of dynamic properties of recursive procedures. In: IFIP Conference on Formal Description of Programming Concepts, pp. 237–277. North-Holland (1977)

10. Cousot, P., Cousot, R.: Systematic design of program analysis frameworks. In: Aho, A.V., Zilles, S.N., Rosen, B.K. (eds.) 6th Annual ACM Symposium on Principles of Programming Languages (POPL), pp. 269–282 (1979)

11. Cousot, P., Halbwachs, N.: Automatic discovery of linear restraints among variables of a program. In: 5th Annual ACM Symposium on Principles of Programming Languages (POPL), pp. 84–96. ACM Press (1978)

12. Fecht, C., Seidl, H.: Propagating differences: an efficient new fixpoint algorithm for distributive constraint systems. Nord. J. Comput. 5(4), 304–329 (1998)

13. Fecht, C., Seidl, H.: A faster solver for general systems of equations. Sci. Comput. Program. 35(2), 137–161 (1999)

14. Hermenegildo, M., Puebla, G., Marriott, K., Stuckey, P.: Incremental analysis of constraint logic programs. ACM Trans. Program. Lang. Syst. (TOPLAS) 22(2), 187–223 (2000)

15. Hermenegildo, M.V., Puebla, G., Bueno, F., López-García, P.: Integrated program debugging, verification, and optimization using abstract interpretation (and the Ciao System preprocessor). Sci. Comput. Program. 58(1), 115–140 (2005)

16. Hofmann, M., Karbyshev, A., Seidl, H.: Verifying a local generic solver in Coq. In: Cousot, R., Martel, M. (eds.) SAS 2010. LNCS, vol. 6337, pp. 340–355. Springer, Heidelberg (2010)

17. Hofmann, M., Karbyshev, A., Seidl, H.: What is a pure functional? In: Abramsky, S., Gavoille, C., Kirchner, C., Meyer auf der Heide, F., Spirakis, P.G. (eds.) ICALP 2010. LNCS, vol. 6199, pp. 199–210. Springer, Heidelberg (2010)

18. Kildall, G.A.: A unified approach to global program optimization. In: ACM Symposium on Principle of Programming Languages (POPL), pp. 194–206. ACM (1973)

19. Le Charlier, B., Van Hentenryck, P.: A universal top-down fixpoint algorithm. Technical report 92–22, Institute of Computer Science, University of Namur, Belgium (1992)

20. Miné, A.: The octagon abstract domain. Higher-Order Symb. Comput. 19(1), 31–100 (2006)

21. Muthukumar, K., Hermenegildo, M.: Deriving a fixpoint computation algorithm for top-down abstract interpretation of logic programs. Technical report ACT-DC-153-90, Microelectronics and Computer Technology Corporation (MCC), Austin, TX 78759 (1990)

22. Puebla, G., Hermenegildo, M.: Optimized algorithms for the incremental analysis of logic programs. In: Cousot, R., Schmidt, D.A. (eds.) SAS 1996. LNCS, vol. 1145. Springer, Heidelberg (1996)

23. Seidl, H., Fecht, C.: Interprocedural analyses: a comparison. J. Log. Program. 43(2), 123–156 (2000)

24. Vojdani, V.: Static data race analysis of heap-manipulating C programs, Ph.D. thesis, University of Tartu, (2010)

Modal Intersection Types, Two-Level Languages, and Staged Synthesis

Fritz Henglein[1]([✉]) and Jakob Rehof [2]

[1] DIKU Department of Computer Science,
University of Copenhagen, Copenhagen, Denmark
henglein@di.ku.dk
[2] Faculty of Computer Science,
Technical University of Dortmund, Dortmund, Germany
jakob.rehof@cs.tu-dortmund.de

Abstract. A typed λ-calculus, $\lambda^{\cap\square}$, is introduced, combining intersection types and modal types. We develop the metatheory of $\lambda^{\cap\square}$, with particular emphasis on the theory of subtyping and distributivity of the modal and intersection type operators. We describe how a stratification of $\lambda^{\cap\square}$ leads to a multi-linguistic framework for staged program synthesis, where metaprograms are automatically synthesized which, when executed, generate code in a target language. We survey the basic theory of staged synthesis and illustrate by example how a two-level language theory specialized from $\lambda^{\cap\square}$ can be used to understand the process of staged synthesis.

1 Introduction

Two-level languages have been proposed for capturing a number of different, often related, properties of metaprogramming systems, including staged computation by Jones [1] and binding-time properties by Nielson and Nielson [2]. In this paper we introduce a two-level framework, $\lambda^{\cap\square}$, for the intersection typed λ-calculus [3]. In $\lambda^{\cap\square}$ we extend System $\lambda_e^{\rightarrow\square}$ of Davies and Pfenning [4] for simple types to intersection types. The calculus $\lambda_e^{\rightarrow\square}$ of Davies and Pfenning can be seen as a logical formalization of Jones' ideas [1] of expressing staging at the type level, essentially by giving a modal interpretation of the act of reifying (indeed, quoting) code at a metalevel of computation. It is a remarkable fact discovered by Davies and Pfenning, that staged computation thereby endows an intuitionistic fragment of Gödel's provability logic, **S4**, with a Curry-Howard interpretation[1].

Our motivation for studying $\lambda^{\cap\square}$ arises in the context of introducing staging into the area of program synthesis. A basic idea in *staged composition synthesis* [6] comes from the observation that, instead of directly synthesizing programs in some target language, L1, we may consider synthesizing metaprograms

---

[1] The literature on various fragments and interpretations of modal logic is enormous, and we can not attempt here to do any justice to that broader context of related work. For the immediate context of staged computation the reader is referred to [4], and for comparison with other interpretations related to staging we refer to [5].

© Springer International Publishing Switzerland 2016
C.W. Probst et al. (Eds.): Nielsons' Festschrift, LNCS 9560, pp. 289–312, 2016.
DOI: 10.1007/978-3-319-27810-0_15

in a metalanguage, L2, which when executed generate programs in L1, leading to a number of advantages we illustrate in the paper. Another central idea in staged composition synthesis is the insight that type theoretical foundations for component-oriented synthesis [7] can fruitfully be developed based on combinatory logic [8] with *intersection types* [3], which are used to specify semantic properties of components.

We focus on the basic theory of $\lambda^{\cap\Box}$ and its use in staged composition synthesis. The main new theoretical issue considered is the status of distributivity properties of the modal and intersection type operators, which turn out to be of fundamental interest in our applications to synthesis.

The paper is organized as follows. The $\lambda^{\cap\Box}$-calculus is introduced in Sect. 2 including basic metatheoretic properties, most of which can be transferred from or are analogous to corresponding properties of the $\lambda_e^{\to\Box}$-calculus. In Sect. 3 we introduce a theory of intersection type subtyping, by extending standard intersection type theory [3] to encompass the modal operator, and we analyze the status of distributivity in that setting. In Sect. 4 we stratify the $\lambda^{\cap\Box}$-calculus into two distinct language levels, L1 and L2, thereby integrating possibly quite different languages (an object language, L1, and a metalanguage, L2) into a single formal framework suitable as a foundation for staged composition synthesis. In Sect. 5 we introduce the main ideas in staged composition synthesis and illustrate how the two-level approach may support the method of staged composition synthesis.

2   Modal λ-calculus with Intersection Types

We introduce a modal extension of the standard intersection type system [3] following the design of the $\lambda_e^{\to\Box}$-calculus of Davies and Pfenning [4], which extends simple types [9] with a modal operator, $\Box$.

2.1   System $\lambda^{\cap\Box}$

The set $\mathbb{T}$ of *types* of $\lambda^{\cap\Box}$ are defined as follows.

$$\mathbb{T} \ni \tau, \sigma, \rho := \alpha \mid \tau \to \sigma \mid \tau \cap \sigma \mid \Box\tau$$

where α ranges over a set of type variables. We assume that $\cap$ binds stronger than $\to$, and $\Box$ binds stronger than $\cap$. Terms of $\lambda^{\cap\Box}$, ranged over by M, N, P, Q, are the same as the terms of the $\lambda_e^{\to\Box}$-calculus [4] (the only difference being that we consider here an implicitly typed system, whereas in [4] bound variables carry type annotations):

$$M := \mathbf{box}\ M \mid \mathbf{let\ box}\ u = M\ \mathbf{in}\ N \mid x \mid u \mid \lambda x.M \mid (MN)$$

The terms of $\lambda^{\cap\Box}$ are assigned types by the inference system in Fig. 1. This type system extends the $\lambda_e^{\to\Box}$-rules of Davies and Pfenning [4] with the introduction and elimination rules for $\cap$ in the intersection type calculus [3].

λ-calculus Fragment

$$\frac{x : \tau \ \text{ in } \ \Gamma}{\Delta; \Gamma \vdash x : \tau}(\text{ovar})$$

$$\frac{\Delta; (\Gamma, x : \tau) \vdash M : \sigma}{\Delta; \Gamma \vdash \lambda x.M : \tau \to \sigma}(\to\text{I}) \qquad \frac{\Delta; \Gamma \vdash M : \tau \to \sigma \quad \Delta; \Gamma \vdash N : \tau}{\Delta; \Gamma \vdash (MN) : \sigma}(\to\text{E})$$

$$\frac{\Delta; \Gamma \vdash M : \tau_1 \quad \Delta; \Gamma \vdash M : \tau_2}{\Delta; \Gamma \vdash M : \tau_1 \cap \tau_2}(\cap\text{I}) \qquad \frac{\Delta; \Gamma \vdash M : \tau_1 \cap \tau_2}{\Delta; \Gamma \vdash M : \tau_i}(\cap\text{E})$$

Modal Fragment

$$\frac{u : \tau \ \text{ in } \ \Delta}{\Delta; \Gamma \vdash u : \tau}(\text{mvar})$$

$$\frac{\Delta; \emptyset \vdash M : \tau}{\Delta; \Gamma \vdash \mathbf{box} \ M : \Box\tau}(\Box\text{I}) \qquad \frac{\Delta; \Gamma \vdash M : \Box\tau \quad (\Delta, u : \tau); \Gamma \vdash N : \sigma}{\Delta; \Gamma \vdash \mathbf{let \ box} \ u = M \ \mathbf{in} \ N : \sigma}(\Box\text{E})$$

Fig. 1. Type inference rules for $\lambda^{\cap\Box}$

Following [4] the type system shown in Fig. 1 uses two type environments, Δ and Γ, distinguishing between bindings of type assumptions to *modal* and *ordinary* term variables, ranged over by u and x, respectively, where Γ is the ordinary λ-calculus environment, and Δ is the modal environment.

We briefly explain the modal rules of the system, referring the reader to [4] for more details. The introduction rule ($\Box$I) corresponds to (indeed, it implements) the modal logical *rule of necessitation*, by which we can introduce the modal proposition $\Box\tau$, intuitively understood as the statement that the proposition τ is provable. We can do so provided that, indeed, we have a proof M of τ (possibly under the condition that other propositions are provable). Notice that the premise of the rule requires the ordinary environment Γ to be empty, thereby implementing the requirement that there exist a *proof* of τ, a proof being a closed term with respect to the ordinary environment. The proof term M may contain free *modal* variables, intuitively because such will ever only be bound to other proof terms, as implemented in the elimination rule ($\Box$E). From a programming perspective, we can understand the type $\Box\tau$ as meaning "code of type τ", and the distinction between modal and ordinary environments as exploited in the rules ($\Box$I) and ($\Box$E) ensures that substitution of code for modal variables u is guaranteed to be hygienic (it cannot lead to the capture of free ordinary program variables), under any computation starting from a well typed program. In the applications considered later in this paper, it is useful to think of a term M with free modal variables as *code templates* which can be used to generate new pieces of code by substituting different pieces of code into the template.

The operational semantics of $\lambda^{\cap\Box}$ is the reduction relation $\longmapsto$ of $\lambda_e^{\to\Box}$, the smallest relation containing

$$(\lambda x.M)N \longmapsto M[x := N] \qquad (\beta)$$
$$\textbf{let box } u = \textbf{box } M \textbf{ in } N \longmapsto N[u := M] \qquad (\Box\beta)$$

and closed under all contexts except **box** [] [4, p. 565].

Because $\longmapsto$ is *not* a congruence with respect to **box**-expressions (reduction does not "go under" the box), the type system ensures that computation is *staged*. We refer the reader to Davies and Pfenning [4] for full details of the semantics of $\lambda_e^{\to\Box}$.

The following (Substitution, Subject Reduction, Eliminability, Strong Normalization) are analogues in $\lambda^{\cap\Box}$ of properties shown for $\lambda_e^{\to\Box}$ in [4].

Lemma 1 (Substitution).

1. If $\Delta; \Gamma \vdash M : \tau$ and $\Delta; (\Gamma, x : \tau) \vdash N : \sigma$, then $\Delta; \Gamma \vdash N[x := M] : \sigma$.
2. If $\Delta; \emptyset \vdash M : \tau$ and $(\Delta, u : \tau); \Gamma \vdash N : \sigma$, then $\Delta; \Gamma \vdash N[u := M] : \sigma$.

Theorem 1 (Subject Reduction). *If $\Delta; \Gamma \vdash M : \tau$ and $M \longmapsto N$, then $\Delta; \Gamma \vdash N : \tau$.*

The type system imposes a strict phase distinction, in that only terms that are *not* nested inside a **box**-constructor can be reduced under $\longmapsto$. Subterm occurrences in the scope of a **box**-constructor are, in the parlance of Davies and Pfenning [4], *persistent*, in that they cannot be reduced under the relation $\longmapsto$. Term occurrences other than persistent term occurrences are called *eliminable*. By Subject Reduction, expressions cannot "go wrong" under reduction, for example by applying a boxed term, or by unboxing an unboxed term.

Theorem 2 (Eliminability). *If $\emptyset; \emptyset \vdash M : \Box\tau$ and $M \longmapsto^* N$ and N is irreducible, then N contains no eliminable term occurrences.*

Strong normalization can be shown by an embedding into the intersection typed λ-calculus [3], just as strong normalization can be shown for $\lambda_e^{\Box\to}$ by embedding into simply typed λ-calculus [4].

Theorem 3 (Strong Normalization). *If $\Delta; \Gamma \vdash M : \tau$ then M is strongly normalizing under $\longmapsto$.*

Notice that we have in particular the consequence:

Corollary 1. *If $\emptyset; \emptyset \vdash M : \Box\tau$, then $M \longmapsto \textbf{box } N$ for some N such that $\emptyset; \emptyset \vdash N : \tau$.*

Proof. Apply Theorem 3 to obtain a normal M' from M, then apply Theorem 2 to conclude that $M' \equiv \textbf{box } N$, and inversion of the rule ($\Box$I) allows us to conclude that $\emptyset; \emptyset \vdash N : \tau$.

As in $\lambda_e^{\to\Box}$ we have in $\lambda^{\cap\Box}$ the following combinator types[2] characteristic (reading types as propositions under the Curry-Howard isomorphism) of the modal logic **S4**; see, e.g., Boolos [10]:

$\lambda f : \Box(\alpha \to \beta).\lambda x : \Box\alpha.$
   let box $u = f$ **in let box** $v = x$ **in box** $(uv) : \Box(\alpha \to \beta) \to \Box\alpha \to \Box\beta$

$\lambda x : \Box\alpha.$ **let box** $u = x$ **in box box** u $\qquad\qquad : \Box\alpha \to \Box\Box\alpha$

$\lambda x : \Box\alpha.$ **let box** $u = x$ **in** u $\qquad\qquad\qquad : \Box\alpha \to \alpha$

In addition, we have in $\lambda^{\cap\Box}$:

$$\lambda x : \Box(\alpha \cap \beta). \text{ \textbf{let box} } u = x \text{ \textbf{in box} } u : \Box(\alpha \cap \beta) \to \Box\alpha \cap \Box\beta$$

This typing judgement is derived as follows, where we take $\Delta = [u : \alpha \cap \beta]$ and $\Gamma = [x : \Box(\alpha \cap \beta)]$. First, we have the subderivation $\mathcal{D}_1$:

$$\cfrac{\cfrac{\cfrac{\overline{\Delta; \emptyset \vdash u : \alpha \cap \beta}\,(\text{mvar})}{\Delta; \emptyset \vdash u : \alpha}(\cap\text{E})}{\Delta; \Gamma \vdash \textbf{box } u : \Box\alpha}(\Box\text{I}) \qquad \overline{\emptyset; \Gamma \vdash x : \Box(\alpha \cap \beta)}(\text{ovar})}{\emptyset; \Gamma \vdash \textbf{let box } u = x \textbf{ in box } u : \Box\alpha}(\Box\text{E})$$

Similarly, we have the subderivation $\mathcal{D}_2$:

$$\cfrac{\cfrac{\cfrac{\overline{\Delta; \emptyset \vdash u : \alpha \cap \beta}\,(\text{mvar})}{\Delta; \emptyset \vdash u : \beta}(\cap\text{E})}{\Delta; \Gamma \vdash \textbf{box } u : \Box\beta}(\Box\text{I}) \qquad \overline{\emptyset; \Gamma \vdash x : \Box(\alpha \cap \beta)}(\text{ovar})}{\emptyset; \Gamma \vdash \textbf{let box } u = x \textbf{ in box } u : \Box\beta}(\Box\text{E})$$

Putting these together we get

$$\cfrac{\cfrac{\overline{\mathcal{D}_1} \qquad \overline{\mathcal{D}_2}}{\emptyset; \Gamma \vdash \textbf{let box } u = x \textbf{ in box } u : \Box\alpha \quad \emptyset; \Gamma \vdash \textbf{let box } u = x \textbf{ in box } u : \Box\beta}}{\cfrac{\emptyset; \Gamma \vdash \textbf{let box } u = x \textbf{ in box } u : \Box\alpha \cap \Box\beta}{\emptyset; \emptyset \vdash \lambda x. \textbf{let box } u = x \textbf{ in box } u : \Box(\alpha \cap \beta) \to \Box\alpha \cap \Box\beta}}$$

where we use ($\cap$I) followed by ($\to$I) in the last two steps.

In contrast, there is no closed term in $\lambda^{\cap\Box}$ of type

$$\Box\alpha \cap \Box\beta \to \Box(\alpha \cap \beta)$$

To see this, consider that the existence of such a term would imply (by normalization and subject reduction) the existence of a normal form N of type $\Box\alpha \cap \Box\beta \to \Box(\alpha \cap \beta)$. This term must (by generation of its typing) be of the

---

[2] In the following we will sometimes write explicit type annotations in terms in order to indicate particular typings.

form $\lambda x.\mathbf{box}\ N'$ where x occurs free in N', which is impossible by the typing rules: the subterm $\mathbf{box}\ N'$ does not type, since N' is not closed with respect to the λ-calculus environment, so rule ($\Box$I) is not applicable.

The fact that such a term does not exist is closely connected with the special property of intersection which requires the *same* term to have both types of an intersection. Compare with a standard extension of our calculus to include product types $\sigma \times \tau$. Writing $\langle M, N \rangle$ for the pairing constructor with component terms M and N and π_i ($i = 1, 2$) for the projections, and assuming that we add standard rules for the product type, we certainly have:

$$\lambda x : \Box\alpha \times \Box\beta.\ \mathbf{let\ box}\ u_1 = \pi_1 x\ \mathbf{in\ let\ box}\ u_2 = \pi_2 x\ \mathbf{in\ box}\ \langle u_1, u_2 \rangle$$

of type

$$\Box\alpha \times \Box\beta \to \Box(\alpha \times \beta)$$

as well as

$$\lambda x : \Box(\alpha \times \beta).\ \mathbf{let\ box}\ u = x\ \mathbf{in}\ \langle \mathbf{box}\ (\pi_1 u), \mathbf{box}\ (\pi_2 u) \rangle$$

of type

$$\Box(\alpha \times \beta) \to \Box\alpha \times \Box\beta$$

3   Subtyping and Distributivity

We introduce modal intersection type subtyping (Sect. 3.1), an extension to the standard theory [3] of subtyping for intersection types which encompasses modal types. In particular, our extended theory of subtyping postulates distributivity of $\Box$ over $\cap$. We then discuss the status of distributivity and various η-principles in Sect. 3.2.

3.1   Modal Intersection Type Subtyping

We now extend the standard theory of intersection type subtyping [3] with modal types[3]. In following definition of subtyping axioms $S1$–$S5$ are standard for intersection types [3]; they will be referred to as the *standard axioms*. Axioms $S6$ and $S7$ are added to accomodate modal types. These axioms will also be referred to as the *modal axioms* of subtyping.

Definition 1. Subtyping $\leq$ *is the least preorder (reflexive and transitive relation) on types closed under the following axioms and rules:*

($S1$) $\tau \cap \sigma \leq \tau$
($S2$) $\tau \cap \sigma \leq \sigma$
($S3$) $(\tau \to \sigma) \cap (\tau \to \rho) \leq \tau \to \sigma \cap \rho$
($S4$) $\tau \leq \tau' \wedge \sigma \leq \sigma' \Longrightarrow \tau' \to \sigma \leq \tau \to \sigma'$

---

[3] In some variants of the intersection type theory there is a special type ω which we leave out here.

($S5$) $\tau \leq \tau' \wedge \sigma \leq \sigma' \Longrightarrow \tau \cap \sigma \leq \tau' \cap \sigma'$
($S6$) $\tau \leq \sigma \Longrightarrow \Box\tau \leq \Box\sigma$
($S7$) $\Box\tau \cap \Box\sigma \leq \Box(\tau \cap \sigma)$

Intersection types are tacitly considered modulo commutativity, associativity and idempotence of the intersection type operator $\cap$. We say that τ and σ are equal, written $\tau = \sigma$, if $\tau \leq \sigma$ and $\sigma \leq \tau$. We write $\tau \equiv \sigma$, if τ and σ are syntactically identical.

We add the rule of subtyping to $\lambda^{\cap\Box}$ and denote the resulting derivability relation as $\vdash^*$.

$$\frac{\Delta; \Gamma \vdash^* M : \tau \quad \tau \leq \sigma}{\Delta; \Gamma \vdash^* M : \sigma}(\leq)$$

We have the greatest-lower-bound property

$$\tau \leq \sigma \wedge \tau \leq \rho \Rightarrow \tau \leq \sigma \cap \rho$$

by Axiom S5, monotonicity of $\cap$, since $\tau \leq \sigma \wedge \tau \leq \rho$ and therebye $\tau \cap \tau \leq \sigma \cap \rho$ and $\tau \leq \sigma \cap \rho$ by idempotence of $\cap$.

The following distributivity properties are consequences of the standard axioms of subtyping for intersection types:

$$(\tau \to \sigma) \cap (\tau \to \rho) = \tau \to \sigma \cap \rho$$
$$(\tau \to \sigma) \cap (\tau' \to \sigma') \leq (\tau \cap \tau') \to (\sigma \cap \sigma')$$

Distributivity of $\Box$ over $\cap$

$$\Box(\tau \cap \sigma) = \Box\tau \cap \Box\sigma \tag{1}$$

follows from the axioms of modal intersection type subtyping. To wit, consider each distributive subtyping relationship contained in (1) separately:

$$\Box(\tau \cap \sigma) \leq \Box\tau \cap \Box\sigma \tag{2}$$
$$\Box\tau \cap \Box\sigma \leq \Box(\tau \cap \sigma) \tag{3}$$

We can see that (3) is postulated by Axiom S7, and (2) follows by the greatest-lower-bound property: Assuming $\tau \cap \sigma \leq \tau$ and $\tau \cap \sigma \leq \sigma$, monotonicity of $\Box$ (Axiom S6) gives $\Box(\tau \cap \sigma) \leq \Box\tau$ and $\Box(\tau \cap \sigma) \leq \Box\sigma$, hence by greatest lower bound, $\Box(\tau \cap \sigma) \leq \Box\tau \cap \Box\sigma$.

In contrast to the situation mentioned at the end of Sect. 2.1, as a consequence of postulating the subtyping relation (3) we now have

$$\emptyset; \emptyset \vdash^* \lambda x.x : \Box\tau \cap \Box\sigma \to \Box(\tau \cap \sigma)$$

for all σ, τ.

Every type σ can be written in a (not necessarily unique) standard form as

$$\sigma = \bigcap_{i \in I} (\tau_i \to \tau_i') \cap \bigcap_{j \in J} \Box\rho_j \cap \bigcap_{k \in K} \alpha_k$$

where at least one of the index sets I, J, K is nonempty and an empty index set denotes a missing conjunct. The following lemma is a generalization, to include modal types, of a standard lemma [3] for intersection type subtyping (sometimes referred to as "β-soundness").

Lemma 2. *Let σ be given in a standard form as*

$$\sigma \equiv \bigcap_{i \in I} (\tau_i \to \tau_i') \cap \bigcap_{j \in J} \Box\rho_j \cap \bigcap_{k \in K} \alpha_k$$

Then the following conditions hold for all τ, τ', α:

1. *$\sigma \le \tau \to \tau'$ if and only if the set $\{i \in I \mid \tau \le \tau_i\}$ is nonempty and $\bigcap\{\tau_i' \mid \tau \le \tau_i\} \le \tau'$.*
2. *$\sigma \le \Box\tau$ if and only if $J \ne \emptyset$ and $\bigcap_{j \in J} \rho_j \le \tau$.*
3. *$\sigma \le \alpha$ if and only if $\alpha \equiv \alpha_k$ for some $k \in K$.*

Proof. The implications from left to right are proven by induction on the derivation of the subtyping relations. The implications from right to left follow easily by the axioms of subtyping.

3.2   Subtyping and η-principles

It is well known (see, e.g., [3]) that the standard intersection type system allows its standard notion of subtyping to become representable by a derived rule, if we add rules to the system that ensure the preservation of types under η-reduction, and, conversely, subtyping ensures subject reduction under η-reduction. As we will show now, the situation is more complicated for modal intersection type subtyping, and this is mainly caused by the principle of distributivity shown as (3).

Let $\le^\circ$ denote the relation generated by the axioms $(S1)$ through $(S6)$ from Definition 1. Let $\vdash^\circ$ denote the restriction of $\vdash^*$ arising by restricting the subtyping relation $\le$ to be $\le^\circ$ in the rule $(\le)$ and call the resulting rule $(\le^\circ)$.

Let $\vdash_{\eta 1}$ denote the system arising from adding the rules (η) and $(\eta\Box 1)$ shown in Fig. 2 to those of $\lambda^{\cap\Box}$ shown in Fig. 1. Let $\vdash_{\eta 2}$ denote the extension of $\vdash_{\eta 1}$ by adding the rule $(\eta\Box 2)$. Let us define the notions of η-reduction

$$
\begin{array}{lll}
\lambda x. M x & \mapsto_\eta & M, \text{ provided } x \notin \mathsf{FV}(M) \\
\textbf{let box } u = M \textbf{ in box } u & \mapsto_{\eta 1} & M \\
\textbf{box (let box } u = M \textbf{ in } u) & \mapsto_{\eta 2} & M, \text{ provided } \mathsf{FV}(M) = \emptyset
\end{array}
$$

Notice that $\mapsto_{\eta 1}$ is considered in the context of $\lambda_e^{\to\Box}$ in [4]. Let $\twoheadrightarrow_{\beta\eta 1}$ denote the reflexive, transitive reduction relation generated from the union of $\to_\beta$, $\mapsto_{\beta\Box}$, $\to_\eta$ and $\mapsto_{\eta 1}$ and let $\twoheadrightarrow_{\beta\eta 2}$ be generated by adding $\mapsto_{\eta 2}$.

$$\frac{\Delta; \Gamma \vdash \lambda x. Mx : \tau \to \sigma, \quad x \notin \mathsf{FV}(M)}{\Delta; \Gamma \vdash M : \tau \to \sigma} \, (\eta)$$

$$\frac{\Delta; \Gamma \vdash \text{let box } u = M \text{ in box } u : \Box\tau}{\Delta; \Gamma \vdash M : \Box\tau} \, (\eta\Box 1)$$

$$\frac{\Delta; \emptyset \vdash \text{box (let box } u = M \text{ in } u) : \Box\tau}{\Delta; \Gamma \vdash M : \Box\tau} \, (\eta\Box 2)$$

Fig. 2. η-rules

Theorem 4. *1. If $\Delta; \Gamma \vdash_{\eta 1} M : \tau$ and $M \twoheadrightarrow_{\beta\eta 1} N$, then $\Delta; \Gamma \vdash_{\eta 1} N : \tau$.*
2. If $\Delta; \Gamma \vdash_{\eta 2} M : \tau$ and $M \twoheadrightarrow_{\beta\eta 2} N$, then $\Delta; \Gamma \vdash_{\eta 2} N : \tau$.

We will now show that subtyping can to some degree be "internalized" into the type system via η-rules, such that subtyping becomes (to some degree) a derived rule when the η-rules are added. The most problematic case is the derivability of axiom $(S7)$ for subtyping. Before we consider the full system of subtyping including $(S7)$, we consider its restriction $\leq^\circ$, for which we can show full internalization of subtyping as a derived rule under the η-principle $(\eta\Box 1)$.

Proposition 1. *$\sigma \leq^\circ \tau$ implies, for all Δ, Γ, M:*

$$\Delta; \Gamma \vdash_{\eta 1} M : \sigma \Rightarrow \Delta; \Gamma \vdash_{\eta 1} M : \tau$$

Proof. By induction on the derivation of $\sigma \leq^\circ \tau$. We consider two cases and leave the rest to the reader.

In case we have $\sigma \equiv \sigma_1 \cap \sigma_2$, $\tau \equiv \tau_1 \cap \tau_2$ with $\sigma \leq^\circ \tau$ by $(S5)$, where $\sigma_i \leq^\circ \tau_i$ $(i = 1, 2)$, assume $\Delta; \Gamma \vdash_{\eta 1} M : \sigma_1 \cap \sigma_2$. By $(\cap E)$ we get $\Delta; \Gamma \vdash_{\eta 1} M : \sigma_1$ and $\Delta; \Gamma \vdash_{\eta 1} M : \sigma_2$. Applying the induction hypothesis to the former of these judgements, we get $\Delta; \Gamma \vdash_{\eta 1} M : \tau_1$, and applying it to the latter yields $\Delta; \Gamma \vdash_{\eta 1} M : \tau_2$. The claim follows by an application of $(\cap I)$.

In the case where we have $\sigma \equiv \Box\sigma'$ and $\tau \equiv \Box\tau'$ with $\sigma' \leq^\circ \tau'$ by $(S6)$, assume $\Delta; \Gamma \vdash_{\eta 1} M : \Box\sigma'$. We have (for u fresh) that $(\Delta, u : \sigma'); \emptyset \vdash_{\eta 1} u : \sigma'$. Hence, by induction hypothesis, $(\Delta, u : \sigma'); \emptyset \vdash_{\eta 1} u : \tau'$, and so by $(\Box I)$, $(\Delta, u : \sigma'); \Gamma \vdash_{\eta 1} \text{box } u : \Box\tau'$. By $(\Box E)$, we have $\Delta; \Gamma \vdash_{\eta 1} \text{let box } u = M \text{ in box } u : \Box\tau'$. Therefore, by $(\Box\eta 1)$ we get $\Delta; \Gamma \vdash_{\eta 1} M : \Box\tau'$.

Notice that the corresponding property for simple typed λ-calculus can be obtained there as a corollary of the following property (where we momentarily let $\leq$ and $\vdash$ denote the system of simple types): if $\sigma \leq \tau$, then there exists a term M such that $\vdash M : \sigma \to \tau$ and $M \twoheadrightarrow_{\beta\eta} \lambda x.x$. The term M can be constructed by induction on the derivation of $\sigma \leq \tau$. This property cannot be proven for $\vdash_{\eta 1}$, because the induction cannot be carried out in the case of $(S5)$.

With regard to the relationship between full modal subtyping $\leq$ as given by Definition 1 and the system $\vdash_{\eta 2}$, we have the further restriction that the η-principle $(\eta\Box 2)$ only applies to closed terms, because the premise of the rule requires a term M which type correctly appears in the scope of box. Consequently, we cannot internalize the relation $\leq$ fully in the system $\vdash_{\eta 2}$ of $\lambda^{\cap\Box}$. But we can show that the distributive property (3) can be internalized into $\lambda^{\cap\Box}$ itself on closed terms, in the sense of Theorem 5.

The following lemma is an extension to $\lambda^{\cap\Box}$ of a property which is true of the standard intersection type system (see [11] for an exposition of this).

Lemma 3. *Let* $M \longmapsto N$ *by contracting the redex occurrence* R, *with* $R \equiv$ $(\lambda x.P)Q$ *or* $R \equiv$ **let box** $u =$ **box** Q **in** P, *in* M. *If* $\Delta; \Gamma \vdash M : \sigma$ *and* Q *is typable in the context of* Δ *and* Γ, *then* $\Delta; \Gamma \vdash N : \sigma$.

Theorem 5. $\emptyset; \emptyset \vdash M : \Box\tau \cap \Box\sigma$ *if and only if* $\emptyset; \emptyset \vdash M : \Box(\tau \cap \sigma)$.

Proof. If $\emptyset; \emptyset \vdash M : \Box\tau \cap \Box\sigma$, then (Theorems 1 and 3) we have $M \longmapsto^* N$ with N a normal form (irreducible) and $\emptyset; \emptyset \vdash N : \Box\tau \cap \Box\sigma$. Therefore, by $(\cap E)$, we have $\emptyset; \emptyset \vdash N : \Box\tau$ and $\emptyset; \emptyset \vdash N : \Box\sigma$. Since N is irreducible, it follows by Theorem 2 that N is persistent, and by inversion applied to both judgements, we obtain $N \equiv$ **box** P for some P with $\emptyset; \emptyset \vdash P : \tau$ and $\emptyset; \emptyset \vdash P : \sigma$. By $(\cap I)$ it follows that $\emptyset; \emptyset \vdash P : \tau \cap \sigma$. Then, using $(\Box I)$ applied to this judgement we obtain $\emptyset; \emptyset \vdash N : \Box(\tau \cap \sigma)$. Finally, an induction in the reduction length of $M \longmapsto^* N$ using Lemma 3 yields $\emptyset; \emptyset \vdash M : \Box(\tau \cap \sigma)$.

On the other hand, if $\emptyset; \emptyset \vdash M : \Box(\tau \cap \sigma)$, we find a normal form $N \equiv$ **box** P with $\emptyset; \emptyset \vdash N : \Box(\tau \cap \sigma)$ such that $\emptyset; \emptyset \vdash P : \tau \cap \sigma$, hence by (1) we have $\emptyset; \emptyset \vdash P : \tau$ and $\emptyset; \emptyset \vdash P : \sigma$, so by $(\Box I)$, $\emptyset; \emptyset \vdash N : \Box\tau$ and $\emptyset; \emptyset \vdash N : \Box\sigma$, hence by $(\cap I)$ $\emptyset; \emptyset \vdash N : \Box\tau \cap \Box\sigma$. Finally, an induction in the reduction length of $M \longmapsto^* N$ using Lemma 3 yields $\emptyset; \emptyset \vdash M : \Box\tau \cap \Box\sigma$.

Proposition 2. $\Delta; \emptyset \vdash_{\eta 2} M : \Box\sigma \cap \Box\tau \Rightarrow \Delta; \emptyset \vdash_{\eta 2} M : \Box(\sigma \cap \tau)$

Proof. Assume $\Delta; \emptyset \vdash_{\eta 2} M : \Box\sigma \cap \Box\tau$. By $(\cap E)$, we get $\Delta; \emptyset \vdash_{\eta 2} M : \Box\sigma$ and $\Delta; \emptyset \vdash_{\eta 2} M : \Box\tau$. Then, by $(\Box E)$, we have $\Delta; \emptyset \vdash_{\eta 2}$ **let box** $u = M$ **in** $u :$ σ and $\Delta; \emptyset \vdash_{\eta 2}$ **let box** $u = M$ **in** $u : \tau$. Hence, by $(\cap I)$, we have $\Delta; \emptyset \vdash_{\eta 2}$ **let box** $u = M$ **in** $u : \sigma \cap \tau$. By $(\Box I)$ we then get

$$\Delta; \emptyset \vdash_{\eta 2} \textbf{box (let box } u = M \textbf{ in } u) : \Box(\sigma \cap \tau)$$

By $(\eta\Box 2)$ we have $\Delta; \emptyset \vdash_{\eta 2} M : \Box(\sigma \cap \tau)$.

As a variation on the system $\vdash_{\eta 2}$, we could also introduce the restricted *commuting conversion*:

$$\textbf{box (let box } u = M \textbf{ in } u) =$$
$$\textbf{let box } u = M \textbf{ in box } u, \quad \text{provided } \mathsf{FV}(M) = \emptyset$$

Incorporating this principle into the system $\vdash_{\eta 1}$ would evidently lead to rule $(\eta\Box 2)$ being derivable.

Notice carefully that the equivalent of the property in Proposition 1 can not be shown for $\vdash_{\eta 2}$ and $(\leq)$. An attempt to extend the induction from the proof of that proposition to $\vdash_{\eta 2}$ and $(\leq)$ will fail in the case where $\sigma \leq \tau$ is derived by $(S4)$, because one is forced there to consider open terms.

4   Two-Level Language

We introduce our two-level *metalanguage*, L2, which is suitable for computing over expressions of a given *object language*, denoted L1 (strictly speaking, L1 will be a mild extension of the object language, see below). In our formal development we wish to keep the language L1 fairly abstract, since L1 is to a large extent interchangeable. For the present purposes we will assume that both L1 and L2 are suitably typed in a standard intersection type system [3], to accomodate for *semantic types* as used in the type-theoretic approach to synthesis [6,12]. In this usage of intersection types we do not assume that intersection types are defined in the language L1 itself, but rather that they are superimposed onto L1-types as specifications that are used to direct synthesis. Thus, L1 could be a standard programming language such as Java or ML, and intersection types may be used only to expose type interfaces of components (understood as combinators in [6]) to synthesis. We will feel free to use concrete L1-expressions in examples, relying on them to be readily understood by familiarity with typical programming language constructs and their typing rules.

As in the approach to staged composition synthesis [6], the metalevel language L2 and the object level language L1 will be combined into a single type system. We will do so by stratifying $\lambda^{\cap\square}$ into a two-level system in which L1 plays, roughly speaking, the rôle of the λ-calculus fragment (non-modal level), and L2 is the intersection typed modal calculus of $\lambda^{\cap\square}$. We will sometimes refer to the resulting system as L2/L1 (pronounced "L2 over L1"). Although the approach can in principle be used to stratify an arbitrary number of levels of modalities and metalevels, we only consider the case of two levels here.

4.1   Object Language L1

We assume a language called L1, which denotes the object language under consideration extended with *template variables*. Expressions of L1 will be ranged over by e, e' etc. Template variables, ranged over by u, are metalanguage variables that act as placeholders for expressions of L1. Note that template variables are distinct from *program variables* of L1, ranged over by v. For example, we may consider an expression such as

$$e \equiv \mathtt{if}\ (u)\ \mathtt{then\ 0\ else\ 1}$$

assuming that conditional statements (as shown) can be formed in L1, where the template variable u stands (in this case) for a suitable expression that could appear in the test of a conditional. We shall sometimes refer to expressions of L1 possibly containing template variables as *template expressions* or *code templates*. Informally, template variables u will be used to perform abstraction, in the metalanguage, over code templates in the object language in such a way that other code templates can be hygiencially substituted into template variables, that is, without problems of variable capture with respect to L1-program variables. As already mentioned in Sect. 2.1, the hygienic discipline is enforced by the modal type system of $\lambda^{\cap\Box}$. As in the $\lambda_e^{\to\Box}$-calculus, this is achieved by treating template variables as modal variables which, according to the modal type discipline, can only be bound to expressions that do not contain any free L1-program variables. The rule of modal necessitation ($\Box$I)together with the elimination rule ($\Box$E) ensure that code substitution results in expressions that are closed with respect to ordinary program variables. Under the Curry-Howard isomorphism, such expressions denote proofs in the corresponding logic.

Let $A, B, \ldots$ range over a set of type expressions of L1, denoted $\mathbb{T}_1$, given by

$$\mathbb{T}_1 \ni A, B ::= b \mid \alpha \mid A \to B \mid A \cap B$$

where b ranges over type constants and α ranges over type variables. We assume that L1 has a type system formalized by judgements of the form

$$\Delta; \Sigma \vdash_{\mathsf{L1}} e : A$$

where Δ is a type environment containing type assumptions on template variables of the form $(u : A)$, and Σ is a type environment containing type assumptions on program variables of L1 of the form $(\mathsf{v} : A)$. So, for instance, we would expect the following judgement to be derivable in the type system of L1:

$$\{u : \mathtt{bool}\}; \{\mathtt{v} : \mathtt{int}\} \vdash_{\mathsf{L1}} \mathtt{if}\ (u)\ \mathtt{then}\ 0\ \mathtt{else}\ \mathtt{v} : \mathtt{int}$$

4.2   Metalanguage L2/L1

The metalanguage L2 is the $\lambda^{\cap\Box}$-calculus with the addition that L1-template expressions can be injected into the metalanguage via the modal rule of necessitation ($\Box$I). We obtain this discipline by stratifying the type language of $\lambda^{\cap\Box}$ into two levels, corresponding to L1 and L2, as follows. Let the set $\mathbb{T}_2$ denote *metalanguage types* of L2, ranged over by τ, σ, defined by:

$$\mathbb{T}_2 \ni \tau, \sigma ::= \Box A \mid \tau \to \sigma \mid \tau \cap \sigma$$

where $A \in \mathbb{T}_1$. Notice that L2-types are generated from "boxed" types (appearing under the $\Box$ constructor) of L1. We can think of the modal type constructor as injecting types of the object language into the metalanguage, and we can intuitively understand an L2-type $\Box A$ ($A \in \mathbb{T}_1$) as meaning "the type of a metaprogram in L2 which produces L1-code with L1-type A".

The type system of the metalanguage L2 is shown in Fig. 3. The rule ($\Box$I) together with the environment Δ provide the interface between L1 and L2. According to this rule, template expressions that are well typed in L1 can be injected into L2 by being placed in the scope of the **box**-operator. Importantly, the rule requires that we only inject object language expressions e with no free *program variables* of L1 (but possibly with free template variables) into L2. As we have seen in Sect. 2.1, this discipline ensures that we can soundly substitute L1-expressions into L1-expressions under L2-computations, provided that the corresponding Substitution Lemma and Subject Reduction property holds

$$\frac{}{\Delta;(\Gamma,x:\sigma)\vdash_{L2} x:\sigma}(\text{var}) \qquad \frac{}{(\Delta,u:\tau);\Gamma\vdash u:\tau}(\text{mvar})$$

$$\frac{\Delta;(\Gamma,x:\sigma)\vdash_{L2} M:\sigma'}{\Delta;\Gamma\vdash_{L2}\lambda x.M:\sigma\to\sigma'}(\to\text{I}) \qquad \frac{\Delta;\Gamma\vdash_{L2} M_1:\sigma\to\sigma' \quad \Delta;\Gamma\vdash_{L2} M_2:\sigma}{\Delta;\Gamma\vdash_{L2}(M_1 M_2):\sigma'}(\to\text{E})$$

$$\frac{\Delta;\emptyset\vdash_{L1} e:A}{\Delta;\Gamma\vdash_{L2}\textbf{box }e:\Box A}(\Box\text{I}) \qquad \frac{\Delta;\Gamma\vdash_{L2} M_1:\Box A \quad (\Delta,u:A);\Gamma\vdash_{L2} M_2:\sigma}{\Delta;\Gamma\vdash_{L2}\textbf{let box }u=M_1\textbf{ in }M_2:\sigma}(\Box\text{E})$$

$$\frac{\Delta;\Gamma\vdash_{L2} M:\tau \quad \Delta;\Gamma\vdash_{L2} M:\sigma}{\Delta;\Gamma\vdash_{L2} M:\sigma\cap\tau}(\cap\text{I}) \qquad \frac{\Delta;\Gamma\vdash_{L2} M:\sigma \quad \sigma\le\tau}{\Delta;\Gamma\vdash_{L2} M:\tau}(\le)$$

Fig. 3. Metalanguage L2/L1

for L1. In practical applications, one will need to discipline the use of template variables in such a way that these properties are ensured. The dual rule ($\Box$E) discharges assumptions in Δ using the **letbox** construct. As detailed in Sect. 2.1, this construct performs substitution of L1-expressions for template variables in L1-expressions under L2-computation.

As a consequence of the properties Subject Reduction and Eliminability, which must be ensured in applications to particular languages L1 in practice, typability in system L2 implies that computation can be *staged* into metalevel computation followed by object-level computation, by first reducing, in L2, an expression of type $\Box A$ to normal form resulting in a well typed L1-expression in the scope of a **box**-operator. It is guaranteed for a well-typed closed L2-term of type $\Box A$ that metalanguage reduction to normal form in L2 computes all L2-term occurrences away and leaves only a well typed boxed L1-expression as a result. That L1-expression can then be executed at the next stage (object-level runtime).

In comparison with other multi-level systems, a distinguishing feature of our construction of L2/L1 lies in the fact that it uses modal logic to construct a staged, *multi-linguistic* system. A key observation here is that the rule of necessitation ($\Box$I) together with the injection of metalevel template variables (modal variables u) into L1 provides a very simple interface between the language- and type-systems of L1 and L2, in which the nature of L1 is as close to being a "black box" to the metalevel as one could possibly imagine. This feature is not only theoretically pleasing, but it is also of great utility in practical applications where the internal complexity of L1 can be challenging in itself. All that is needed for the construction of L2/L1, in principle, is a type-safe discipline for abstracting templates out of L1-code (the application specific details of which are not dealt with here). Some example expressions can be found in Sect. 5, where applications to synthesis are considered.

4.3 Logical Considerations

A special case of the construction of L2/L1 is the case where L1 is the intersection typed λ-calculus [3]. This case is obtained by stratifying the type system of $\lambda^{\cap\Box}$

into the intersection type system [3] as the nonmodal object-level subsystem L1 and the modal intersection typed calculus at the metalevel L2, according to the method of construction of $\mathbb{T}_1$ and $\mathbb{T}_2$ introduced above together with the stratified rules of Fig. 3. The resulting system is a restriction of $\lambda^{\cap\square}$ in which the modal axioms

$$\square A \to \square\square A$$

and

$$\square A \to A$$

are no longer valid (the types are not inhabited). The former axiom is not valid, because the rule $(\square I)$ in the system L2/L1 injects the type A into the L2-level where this rule is not available, since the premise of the rule requires a judgement derivable in L1. The latter axiom is not valid, because L1-types A are disjoint from L2-types (all of which have boxed L1-types at the leaves) and are not in the range of the types σ in the rule of modal elimination $(\square E)$. The resulting logic is characterized, in the simple typed fragment, by the modal axiom

$$\square(A \to B) \to \square A \to \square B$$

which is known to the modal logician as the axiom of normal modal logic $\mathbf{K}$ (see, e.g., [10]).

As already mentioned, it is not difficult to see that we can generalize the construction of L2/L1 to arbitrary numbers of levels n (each of them distinguished by modal types $\square_n\tau$), where the rules $(\square I)$ and $(\square E)$ would enable passage up and down between the levels. The case considered here, $n = 2$, is not only useful (due to its relative simplicity) for illustrative purposes but is also paradigmatic for the applications in the type-theoretic approach to component-oriented synthesis [6], which motivated its construction.

5   Application to Staged Composition Synthesis

We give a brief introduction to the main ideas in staged composition synthesis and illustrate the application of the two-level approach in that context with an example. The reader interested in understanding the theory of staged composition synthesis in detail would probably need to consult the references given below.

5.1   Staged Composition Synthesis

A basic idea in *staged composition synthesis* [6] comes from the observation that, instead of directly synthesizing programs in some target language, L1, we may consider synthesizing metaprograms in a metalanguage, L2, which when executed generate programs in L1.

An advantage of this approach is that it allows metaprogramming technology to be integrated into synthesis in a principled way. In particular, when the target language L1 is low-level or otherwise unsuited for metaprogramming tasks, the introduction of a metalanguage L2 into synthesis is clearly helpful. In our development here we focus on a paradigmatic case where L1 is a first-order imperative monomorphic language and L2 is the modal λ-calculus. The modal λ-calculus is suitable as (the theoretical kernel of) a metaprogramming language because, among other things, it allows the construction and manipulation of code templates of the target language, as we have seen.

The advantages of the two-level approach becomes even clearer when we consider the other main idea of staged composition synthesis, which is to consider synthesis not "from scratch" but as a process of automatic composition from a given collection ("repository") of components. In *component-oriented synthesis* (see [6] with further references there, and also [7]) it is a central concern to be able to design component repositories containing flexibly reusable components as the raw material for synthesis. In this setting, flexible code abstraction mechanisms (such as templating) as well as other abstraction mechanisms, e.g., higher-order functional abstraction and polymorphism, are valuable. More generally, our two-level approach shows that synthesis can in principle be carried out in a functional programming language at the metalevel, even though the target language is quite different.

Composition synthesis is based on the theory of *combinatory logic synthesis* [6,12], in which components are exposed to synthesis in the form of typed combinators [8], where each combinator symbol names a component, and its type represents a semantically enriched decoration, using intersection types, of the type of the component. The basic idea here is that the theory of combinatory logic in arbitrary combinatory theories is a natural foundation for component-oriented synthesis. Synthesis is reduced to solving problems of *relativized type inhabitation* in fragments of combinatory logic with intersection types [13]. The problem of relativized inhabitation in a combinatory logic is the decision problem which takes as input a collection $\mathscr{C}$ of typed combinators and a goal type τ and asks whether there exists a combinatory term e, an applicative combination of combinators from $\mathscr{C}$, such that $\mathscr{C} \vdash e : \tau$ holds in the theory of combinatory logic with intersection types. Such a term e is called an *inhabitant* in the type τ. Formally, the inhabitation problem is the decision problem, given $\mathscr{C}$ and τ, to decide

$$\exists e.\ \mathscr{C} \vdash e : \tau$$

where $\vdash$ is defined by the rules of combinatory logic (see [8,12,13]). We sometimes abbreviate an instance of the relativized inhabitation problem as

$$\mathscr{C} \vdash ? : \tau$$

The relativized inhabitation problem is a generalization, to an arbitrary collection of typed combinators, from the standard case of a fixed set of combinators **S**, **K** and **I**. The standard, fixed case of **SKI**-calculus corresponds to the λ-calculus (see [8]) and its inhabitation problem is PSPACE-complete in simple types by Statman's theorem [14]. It should be emphasized here that the relativized inhabitation problem – inhabitation relative to an *arbitrary*, given set of combinators, or, equivalently, provability in arbitrary propositional theories – is undecidable, even in *simple* types. This follows from classical results of Linial and Post. A discussion of this important fact can be found in [12], see also [13].

An algorithm (or semi-algorithm) for computing inhabitants from $\mathscr{C}$ and τ can be used to synthesize the program e. The framework of combinatory logic synthesis and the staged approach has been implemented in a tool, (CL)S (Combinatory Logic Synthesizer) [15]. At the core of the framework is an algorithm that solves bounded fragments of the relativized inhabitation problem with intersection types [13]. The framework and its application is still very much an active research area, but it has already been used in a number of experiments [15–17]. Among ongoing research directions are the application of the framework to object-oriented code repositories [18,19] and applications to product line synthesis [20].

In combinatory logic synthesis, intersection types are used as *semantic types* [12,21,22], to specify semantic properties of combinators understood as interface types of components, as will be illustrated by the example below. In practical applications of composition synthesis, in broad lines following the overall approach of [21,22], types are not necessarily mechanically checked against the implementations of combinators (although this might be done for suitable fragments or explicit versions of intersection type systems). This is regarded as an issue orthogonal to composition synthesis.

Still, the framework of $\lambda^{\cap\square}$ may serve as a useful foundational reference point for an idealized relation between combinator implementations in L2/L1, semantic interface types, and metalevel code generation. By studying $\lambda^{\cap\square}$, we distilled mathematically sound principles which can provide guidance in practical applications, even though they might have to be adjusted or restricted in practice. An important aspect of this is provided by the distributivity properties in Sect. 3. The moment we combine two different languages L1 and L2 into a framework L2/L1, distributivity becomes a mediating principle between different type systems. The defining equation should really be written (at least, understood) as

$$\square(A \cap_1 B) = (\square A) \cap_2 (\square B)$$

where $\cap_1$ and $\cap_2$ are operators in two different type systems, that of L1 and that of L2. Moreover, the modal axiom **K** would more precisely be written as

$$\square(A \Rightarrow B) \to \square A \to \square B$$

where we use $\Rightarrow$ to denote the type of functions in L1 and $\to$ denotes the type of functions in L2. Using the explicit notation, we clearly see that the principles of distribution amount to assumptions of the existence of certain homomorphic (or, categorically, functorial) relations between type operators in different languages. This viewpoint may give a mathematical handle on certain issues of integrating languages L1 and L2 into a framework L2/L1. For example, if L1 is an imperative language, we know that subtyping and polymorphism present special challenges for type soundness, sometimes leading to the need for restrictions. An interesting observation [23] is that type soundness of intersection types in the presence of references may be achieved by restricting the axiom of functional distributivity (axiom $S3$ from Sect. 3), although various other approaches are also possible [24,25]. Finally, recalling that distributivity is an important component in the standard notion of intersection type subtyping, let us note that subtyping may affect expressiveness at finer levels of granularity. Thus, it is known that intersection type subtyping may be surprisingly expressive in restricted settings as witnessed by the result shown in [26] that, in the absence of the intersection introduction rule, inhabitation in λ-calculus is EXPSPACE-complete with subtyping but PSPACE-complete without subtyping. As an example (taken from [26]) suggesting the specific impact of distributivity, consider the λ-calculus inhabitation question

$$\{x : \alpha \cap \beta, y : (\alpha \to \gamma) \cap (\beta \to \delta)\} \vdash ? : \gamma \cap \delta$$

In the absence of intersection introduction, this problem has the solution inhabitant (yx), provided we have access to distributivity (applied to the type of y). We can see that, in the restricted setting, distributivity allows to recover some of the expressiveness of intersection introduction. A more general understanding of the specific impact of distributivity both in theory and in practice is an interesting question for future work which could be pursued based on $\lambda^{\cap\square}$.

5.2   Example

To illustrate the approach, we consider an example. The example is a further development of a similar but simpler example from [12], where staging had not yet been introduced into synthesis. The reader may want to consult the examples in [12] to see how the theory of subtyping supports interesting features in combinatory synthesis which we cannot, for space reasons, describe here.

Consider the L1-implementation of Quicksort written in a first-order monomorphic Java-like language shown in Fig. 4. We use the form

```
def B foo(A1 x1,..., An xn) {  ... }
```

for locally scoped definitions, as in def ... { ... } in e. Such a definition is given the type

```
(A1,..., An) → B
```

In Fig. 5 we have the type declaration (shown as $\mathbf{Q} : \tau_\mathbf{Q}$ where $\tau_\mathbf{Q}$ is the type shown) and implementation (shown as $\mathbf{Q} \overset{\Delta}{=} M$) of an L2-combinator named $\mathbf{Q}$ which abstracts a code template out of the L1-implementation shown in Fig. 4. The type of the combinator $\mathbf{Q}$ is followed by its implementation in L2/L1. The combinator abstracts the L1-implementation in two respects. Firstly, it parameterizes over the order relation, using higher-order abstraction in L2. The abstract order relation must satisfy the parametric semantic type

$$\square(((\alpha, \alpha) \to \texttt{bool}) \cap TotalOrder \cap id(\epsilon))$$

The component $id(\epsilon)$ is used to track a functional relationship between the first and the second argument to the implementation M of $\mathbf{Q}$, requiring the latter

```
         def int partition(int arr[], int left, int right)
         {
           int i = left, j = right; int tmp;
           int pivot = arr[(left + right) / 2];
           while (i <= j) {
             while (arr[i] < pivot) i++;
             while (arr[j] > pivot) j--;
             if (i <= j) {
               tmp = arr[i]; arr[i] = arr[j];
               arr[j] = tmp; i++; j--;
             }
           };
           return i;
         }
       in
       def void QuickSort(int arr[], int left, int right) {
           int index = partition(arr, left, right);
           if (left < index - 1)
             QuickSort(arr, left, index - 1);
           if (index < right)
             QuickSort(arr, index, right);
       }
       in
       def void Sort(int arr[]) {
           Quicksort(arr, 0, sizeof(arr)-1);
       }
```

Fig. 4. L1-implementation of Quicksort

argument to be the reversal of the order relation given in the former argument. Secondly, consistent with the type of the order relation, it abstracts the element type of the array to be sorted, into an arbitrary type α. This makes sense because all we need to carry out quicksort is indeed an arbitrary total order (and its reversal) on the elements to be sorted. Notice the use of the type variable α in the template in addition to the template variables p and q. For function definitions D we assume a metasyntactic L2-operation of the form

$$D.\text{FUN}$$

which extracts the function name defined in expression D,

$$(\text{def B foo(A1 x1}, \ldots, \text{ An xn}) \{ \ldots \}).\text{FUN} \longmapsto \text{foo}$$

and with type (A1, ..., An) $\rightarrow$ B identical to that of D. We also assume a metalevel operation

$$D.\text{NID}$$

which assigns a gloablly unique identifier to the definition D and applies the renaming in the scope of D.

$$\mathbf{Q} \ : \ \Box(((\alpha, \alpha) \to \text{bool}) \cap \textit{TotalOrder} \cap \textit{id}(\epsilon)) \to$$
$$\Box(((\alpha, \alpha) \to \text{bool}) \cap \textit{TotalOrder} \cap \textit{id}(\textit{rev}(\epsilon))) \to$$
$$\Box((\alpha\,[] \to ()) \cap \textit{SortingFunction})$$

$$\mathbf{Q} \triangleq$$
$$\lambda P : \Box(((\alpha, \alpha) \to \text{bool}) \cap \textit{TotalOrder} \cap \textit{id}(\epsilon)).$$
$$\lambda Q : \Box(((\alpha, \alpha) \to \text{bool}) \cap \textit{TotalOrder} \cap \textit{id}(\textit{rev}(\epsilon))).$$

```
let box p : (α, α) → bool = P in
let box q : (α, α) → bool = Q in
box(
    p.NID
    in
    q.NID
    in
    def int partition(α arr[], int left, int right)
    {
        int i = left, j = right; α tmp;
        α pivot = arr[(left + right) / 2];
        while (i <= j) {
            while p.FUN(arr[i], pivot) i++;
            while q.FUN(arr[j], pivot) j--;
            if (i <= j) {
                tmp = arr[i]; arr[i] = arr[j];
                arr[j] = tmp; i++; j--;
            }
        };
        return i;
    }
    in
    def void QuickSort(α arr[], int left, int right) {
        int index = partition(arr, left, right);
        if (left < index - 1)
            QuickSort(arr, left, index - 1);
        if (index < right)
            QuickSort(arr, index, right);
    }
    in
    def void Sort(α arr[]) {
        Quicksort(arr, 0, sizeof(arr)-1);
    }
)
```

Fig. 5. Combinator for Quicksort implemented in L2/L1

In Fig. 6 we show a few other L2-combinators, which wrap order relations on integers and strings ($\mathbf{O_{int}}$, resp. $\mathbf{O_{str}}$) by injecting L1-implementations into L2. The combinator $\mathbf{R}$ implements reversal of a total order. Its semantic type

$$\Box(((\alpha, \alpha) \to \text{bool}) \cap \textit{TotalOrder} \cap \textit{id}(\epsilon)) \to$$
$$\Box(((\alpha, \alpha) \to \text{bool}) \cap \textit{TotalOrder} \cap \textit{id}(\textit{rev}(\epsilon)))$$

$\mathbf{O_{int}}$: $\square(((\mathbf{int}, \mathbf{int}) \to \mathbf{bool}) \cap TotalOrder \cap id(intord))$
$\mathbf{O_{int}} \triangleq$
    box(
        def bool intord(int x, int y) { return (x < y); }
)

$\mathbf{O_{str}}$: $\square(((\mathbf{string}, \mathbf{string}) \to \mathbf{bool}) \cap TotalOrder \cap id(strord))$
$\mathbf{O_{str}} \triangleq$
    box(
        def bool strord(string x, string y) {
            return (strlen(x) < strlen(y));
        }
)

$\mathbf{R}$: $\square(((\alpha, \alpha) \to \mathbf{bool}) \cap TotalOrder \cap id(\epsilon)) \to$
        $\square(((\alpha, \alpha) \to \mathbf{bool}) \cap TotalOrder \cap id(rev(\epsilon)))$
$\mathbf{R} \triangleq$
    $\lambda P : \square((\alpha, \alpha) \to \mathbf{bool}).$
    let box $p : (\alpha, \alpha) \to \mathbf{bool} = P$ **in**
    box(
        p.NID
        in
        def bool revord(α x, α y) { return p.FUN**(y,x); }**
)

Fig. 6. Other L2 combinators in the repository

expresses this functionality: it maps a total order to a total order, and the result of reversing a relation ϵ satisfies the descriptor $rev(\epsilon)$.

We can now synthesize from the combined repository by collecting the type declarations of the combinator symbols shown in Figs. 5 and 6 into a combinatory type environment $\mathscr{C}$, that is

$$\mathscr{C} = \{\mathbf{Q} : \tau_\mathbf{Q}, \mathbf{O_{int}} : \tau_{\mathbf{O_{int}}}, \mathbf{O_{str}} : \tau_{\mathbf{O_{str}}}, \mathbf{R} : \tau_\mathbf{R}\}$$

To synthesize a sorting program on arrays of strings we execute the combinatory logic synthesizer on the input inhabitation goal:

$$\mathscr{C} \vdash ? : \square((\mathbf{string}[] \to ()) \cap SortingFunction)$$

The reader may like to verify that indeed we have

$$\mathscr{C} \vdash \mathbf{Q}\ \mathbf{O_{str}}(\mathbf{R}\ \mathbf{O_{str}}) : \square((\mathbf{string}[] \to ()) \cap SortingFunction)$$

Normalizing the inhabitant we get

$$\mathbf{Q}\ \mathbf{O_{str}}(\mathbf{R}\ \mathbf{O_{str}}) \longmapsto^* \mathbf{box}\ N$$

for a well-typed L1-expression N, in accordance with the property of Eliminability. Figure 7 shows the term **box** N resulting from the reduction.

```
box(
   def bool strord1(string x, string y) {
      return (strlen(x) < strlen(y));
   }
   in
   def bool strord2(string x, string y) {
      return (strlen(x) < strlen(y));
   }
   in
   def bool revord1(string x, string y) { return strord2(y,x); }
   in
   def int partition(string arr[], int left, int right)
      {
         int i = left, j = right; string tmp;
         string pivot = arr[(left + right) / 2];
         while (i <= j) {
            while strord1(arr[i], pivot) i++;
            while revord1(arr[j], pivot) j--;
            if (i <= j) {
               tmp = arr[i]; arr[i] = arr[j];
               arr[j] = tmp; i++; j--;
            }
         };
         return i;
      }
   in
   def void QuickSort(string arr[], int left, int right) {
      int index = partition(arr, left, right);
      if (left < index - 1)
         QuickSort(arr, left, index - 1);
      if (index < right)
         QuickSort(arr, index, right);
   }
   in
   def void Sort(string arr[]) {
      Quicksort(arr, 0, sizeof(arr)-1);
   }
)
```

Fig. 7. Quicksort implementation synthesized from the repository

6   Conclusion and Further Work

We have introduced a calculus $\lambda^{\cap\Box}$ combining intersection types and modal types, and we developed basic properties in the metatheory of $\lambda^{\cap\Box}$. We presented particular observations and results concerning the theory of subtyping and derivability of distributivity properties of the modal operator and the intersection type operator. We then introduced a stratification of $\lambda^{\cap\Box}$ to obtain a multi-linguistic framework for staged program synthesis. In this setting, metaprograms (of a metalanguage L2) are automatically synthesized from components represented as typed combinators. When metaprograms are executed they generate code in a target language (L1) to be executed in a later stage. We explained and illustrated by example how staged synthesis is supported by the combination, characteristic of $\lambda^{\cap\Box}$, of intersection types – to specify semantic properties of components and synthesis goals – and modal types – to enable type-theoretic control over staging under synthesis. We briefly introduced background from combinatory logic synthesis, where the relativized inhabitation problem in combinatory logic is used as a foundation for component-oriented synthesis.

Future work includes several directions in the further development of the framework (CL)S (Combinatory Logic Synthesizer) and applying staged synthesis to problems of practical interest. But we also see interesting questions arising specifically from the development described in the present paper. We believe in particular that it would be interesting to consider questions concerning the relation between the type systems of L1 and L2. It is an interesting feature of the construction of L2/L1 that we can have a higher-order functional language at L2 that computes over a possibly very different language at L1, and we have emphasized that our multi-level and multi-language framework and its foundational formalization in $\lambda^{\cap\Box}$ leads, via distributivity properties, to questions of homomorphic or functorial mappings between the levels. Of both theoretical and practical interest is the question: how much structure of the type system of L1 should be reflected at the L2-level and in which form? Could we develop a more systematic understanding of how to employ general algebraic or categorical structures at the L2-level in order to control the composition of programs at the L1-level? A related set of questions concern the logical expressiveness and the computational complexity of distributivity properties in the context of inhabitation problems, as was discussed in Sect. 5.1. We might hope to understand the impact of such phenomena on staged synthesis more generally by considering $\lambda^{\cap\Box}$.

Acknowledgement. The authors should like to thank Dominic Orchard, Jan Bessai, Boris Düdder and Andrej Dudenhefner for very helpful discussions and comments on the paper.

References

1. Jones, N.D.: Efficient algebraic operations on programs. In: Proceedings of AMAST 1992, Algebraic Methodology and Software Technology, pp. 393–420. Springer (1992)
2. Nielson, F., Nielson, H.R.: Two-Level Functional Languages. Cambridge University Press, New York (1992)
3. Barendregt, H., Coppo, M., Dezani-Ciancaglini, M.: A filter lambda model and the completeness of type assignment. J. Symb. Log. **48**(4), 931–940 (1983)
4. Davies, R., Pfenning, F.: A modal analysis of staged computation. J. ACM **48**(3), 555–604 (2001)

5. Pfenning, F., Davies, R.: A judgmental reconstruction of modal logic. Math. Struct. Comput. Sci. **11**(04), 511–540 (2001)
6. Düdder, B., Martens, M., Rehof, J.: Staged composition synthesis. In: Shao, Z. (ed.) ESOP 2014 (ETAPS). LNCS, vol. 8410, pp. 67–86. Springer, Heidelberg (2014)
7. Rehof, J., Vardi, M.Y.: Design and synthesis from components. In: Dagstuhl Seminar 14232. Dagstuhl Reports, vol. 7941 (2014). http://dx.doi.org/10.4230/DagRep. 4.6.29
8. Hindley, J.R., Seldin, J.P.: Lambda-Calculus and Combinators, an Introduction. Cambridge University Press, New York (2008)
9. Barendregt, H., Dekkers, W., Statman, R.: Lambda Calculus with Types. Perspectives in Logic. Cambridge University Press, New York (2013)
10. Boolos, G.: The Logic of Provability. Cambridge University Press, New York (1995)
11. Ghilezan, S.: Strong normalization and typability with intersection types. Notre Dame J. Form. Log. **37**(1), 44–52 (1996)
12. Rehof, J.: Towards combinatory logic synthesis. In: BEAT 2013, 1st International Workshop on Behavioural Types. ACM (2013)
13. Düdder, B., Martens, M., Rehof, J., Urzyczyn, P.: Bounded combinatory logic. In: Proceedings of CSL 2012, vol. 16, pp. 243–258. LIPIcs, Schloss Dagstuhl (2012)
14. Statman, R.: Intuitionistic propositional logic is polynomial-space complete. Theor. Comput. Sci. **9**, 67–72 (1979)
15. Bessai, J., Dudenhefner, A., Düdder, B., Martens, M., Rehof, J.: Combinatory logic synthesizer. In: Margaria, T., Steffen, B. (eds.) ISoLA 2014, Part I. LNCS, vol. 8802, pp. 26–40. Springer, Heidelberg (2014)
16. Düdder, B., Garbe, O., Martens, M., Rehof, J., Urzyczyn, P.: Using inhabitation in bounded combinatory logic with intersection types for GUI synthesis. In: Proceedings of ITRS (2012)
17. Düdder, B.: Automatic synthesis of component & connector-software architectures with bounded combinatory logic, Ph.D. thesis, Technische Universitt Dortmund, Fakultät fr Informatik, Dortmund (2014)
18. Düdder, B., Bessai, J., Dudenhefner, A., Chen, T.C., de'Liguoro, U.: Typing classes and mixins with intersection types. In: Proceedings of ITRS 2014, Intersection Types and Related Systems. EPTCS Electronic Proceedings in Theoretical Computer Science, vol. 177, pp. 79–93. Springer (2014)
19. Bessai, J., Dudenhefner, A., Duedder, B., De'Liguoro, U., Chen, T.C., Rehof, J.: Mixin composition synthesis based on intersection types. In: Proceedings of TLCA 2015, Typed Lambda Calculi and Applications, Warsaw, June 29–July 3 2015. To appear
20. Düdder, B., Heineman, G.T., Rehof, J.: Towards migrating object-oriented frameworks to enable synthesis of product line members. In: Proceedings of SPLC 2015, 19th International Software Product Line Conference: New Directions in Systems and Software Product Line Engineering. ACM International Conference Proceeding Series (2015)
21. Haack, C., Howard, B., Stoughton, A., Wells, J.B.: Fully automatic adaptation of software components based on semantic specifications. In: Kirchner, H., Ringeissen, C. (eds.) AMAST 2002. LNCS, vol. 2422, pp. 83–98. Springer, Heidelberg (2002)
22. Wells, J.B., Yakobowski, B.: Graph-based proof counting and enumeration with applications for program fragment synthesis. In: Etalle, S. (ed.) LOPSTR 2004. LNCS, vol. 3573, pp. 262–277. Springer, Heidelberg (2005)
23. Davies, R., Pfenning, F.: Intersection types and computational effects. In: ICFP, pp. 198–208 (2000)

24. Dezani-Ciancaglini, M., Giannini, P., Della Rocca, S.R.: Intersection, universally quantified, and reference types. In: Grädel, E., Kahle, R. (eds.) CSL 2009. LNCS, vol. 5771, pp. 209–224. Springer, Heidelberg (2009)
25. Dezani-Ciangaglini, M., Ronchi Della Rocca, S.: Intersection and Reference Types. Essays dedicated to Henk Barendregt on the occasion of his 60th birthday, pp. 77–86 (2007)
26. Rehof, J., Urzyczyn, P.: The complexity of inhabitation with explicit intersection. In: Constable, R.L., Silva, A. (eds.) Logic and Program Semantics, Kozen Festschrift. LNCS, vol. 7230, pp. 256–270. Springer, Heidelberg (2012)

Rule Formats for Bounded Nondeterminism in Structural Operational Semantics

Luca Aceto[(✉)], Álvaro García-Pérez, and Anna Ingólfsdóttir

ICE-TCS, School of Computer Science,
Reykjavík University, Menntavegur 1, 101 Reykjavík, Iceland
luca.aceto@gmail.com

Abstract. We present rule formats for structural operational semantics that guarantee that the associated labelled transition system has each of the three following finiteness properties: finite branching, initials finiteness and image finiteness.

Keywords: Structural operational semantics · Labelled transition systems · Rule formats · Bounded nondeterminism

1 Introduction

Structural operational semantics (SOS) [25,27] is a widely used formalism for defining the formal semantics of computer programs and for proving properties of the corresponding programming languages. In the SOS formalism a transition system specification (TSS) [13], which consists of a signature together with a set of inference rules, specifies a labelled transition system (LTS) [16] whose states (i.e., processes) are closed terms over the signature and whose transitions are those that can be proved using the inference rules.

Rule formats [2,21] are syntactically checkable restrictions on the inference rules of a TSS that guarantee some useful property of the associated LTS. The properties ensured by such rule formats vary from compositionality of behavioural equivalences [7,13,14,30] to finiteness of the number of outgoing transitions from a given state [6,9,32]. This paper focuses on the finiteness property, which is referred to as bounded nondeterminism in [12]. Broadly, bounded nondeterminism is taken as a synonym of finite branching [9]. Finite branching breaks down into the more elementary properties of initials finiteness and image finiteness [1] (see Sect. 2 for formal definitions).

Vaandrager [32] introduced the notion of bounded TSS and proved that a bounded TSS in de Simone format [30] induces an LTS that is finite branching. Bloom [6] used a notion of bounded TSS reminiscent of that of Vaandrager and showed that a bounded TSS in his higher-order-GSOS format [6] induces an LTS that is finite branching. Finally, Fokkink and Vu [9] used yet another notion

This research has been supported by the project 'Nominal Structural Operational Semantics' (nr. 141558-051) of the Icelandic Research Fund.

C.W. Probst et al. (Eds.): Nielsons' Festschrift, LNCS 9560, pp. 313–343, 2015.
DOI: 10.1007/978-3-319-27810-0_16

of bounded TSS and introduced a less restrictive rule format that they called 'bounded nondeterminism format'. They adapted the notion of strict stratification from [14] and showed that a bounded TSS in bounded nondeterminism format that has a strict stratification induces an LTS that is finite branching.

In this paper we take Fokkink and Vu's programme further and present rule formats for initials finiteness and for image finiteness. For initials finiteness we relax the requirement that the η-types of [9] be finitely inhabited and we introduce the initials finite format, which replaces the bounded nondeterminism format of [9]. For image finiteness, we introduce the notion of θ-type. Unlike the η-types of [9], which carry information about the sources of positive premisses in rules, the θ-types also keep track of the actions that label positive premisses. Moreover, we introduce a uniformity requirement on the targets of positive premisses, which strengthens the requirement in [9] that the variables in a rule have to be used uniformly. We introduce the accompanying notions of initials-bounded TSS and image-bounded TSS and show the following results.

- An initials-bounded TSS in initials finite format that has a strict stratification induces an LTS that is initials finite (Theorem 2).
- An image-bounded TSS in bounded nondeterminism format that has a strict stratification induces an LTS that is image finite (Theorem 3).

The results and the techniques we employ in this paper touch upon some of the main topics in the research of Flemming Nielson and Hanne Riis Nielson over the years, namely operational semantics [23], static analysis [22] and type systems [3]. This study contributes to the development of a general theory of operational semantics based on rule formats, which may be seen as providing some statically checkable, largely syntactic, conditions guaranteeing that the specified languages afford some semantic properties of interest. The various notions of 'types' that we use in the definition of the rule formats discussed in this paper allow us to classify the inference rules in a language specification. Informally, types contribute to guaranteeing that composite processes have the finiteness property of interest, if their components do so.

The rest of the paper is organised as follows. Section 2 revisits preliminaries and basic notions from [9] and adapts some of its definitions. Definition 10 formalises the notion of uniform TSS and Proposition 2 shows that a closed term p unifies only with finitely many rules in a uniform TSS. Section 3 provides an alternative proof of Theorem 1 in [9] that removes the *reductio ad absurdum* argument that is used there. Theorem 1 shows that a bounded TSS in bounded nondeterminism format that has a strict stratification induces an LTS that is finite branching. The proof of Theorem 1 here is direct and fully constructive. Section 4 discusses the variable flow in a transition rule and Definition 18 introduces the initials finite format, which requires that each variable in the source of a positive premiss occur also in the source of the rule. Definition 20 introduces the notion of initials-bounded TSS, which relaxes the η-types of [9] by requiring that the actions of an η-type are finite, instead of requiring the η-type to be finitely inhabited. Theorem 2 shows that an initials-bounded TSS in initials finite format that has a strict stratification induces an LTS that is initials finite.

Section 5 discusses the logical content of the η-types under the prism of intuitionistic logic [19], and shows that the η-types realise the intuitionistic interpretation of the property of initials finiteness. Definition 21 introduces the θ-types, which are analogous to the η-types in that they realise the intuitionistic interpretation of the property of image finiteness. Definition 22 introduces uniformity in the targets of positive premisses, which prevents the θ-types to be infinitely many as a result of using infinitely many different names for a variable occurring in the target of some positive premiss, and Definition 23 introduces the notion of image-bounded TSS. Theorem 3 shows that an image-bounded TSS in bounded nondeterminism format that has a strict stratification induces an LTS that is image finite. Section 6 discusses avenues for future work and concludes.

2 Preliminaries

We give an overview of the structural operational semantics formalism (SOS for short). We follow the notation and the presentation in [9].

For a set S, we write $\mathcal{P}(S)$ for the collection of all the subsets of S, and $\mathcal{P}_\omega(S)$ for the collection of all the finite subsets of S.

Definition 1 (Signature and Term). *We assume a countably infinite set of variables V, ranged over by x, y, z. A signature Σ is a set of function symbols, disjoint from V, together with an arity map that assigns a natural number to each function symbol. We use f to range over Σ. Function symbols of arity zero, which may be ranged over by c, d, are called constants. Function symbols of arity one and two are called unary and binary functions respectively.*

The set $\mathbb{T}(\Sigma)$ of (open) terms over a signature Σ, ranged over by t, u, v, is the least set such that:

1. *each variable is a term, and*
2. *if f is a function symbol of arity n and $t_1, \ldots, t_n$ are terms, then $f(t_1, \ldots, t_n)$ is a term.*

The function $\mathrm{var} : \mathbb{T}(\Sigma) \to \mathcal{P}_\omega(V)$ delivers, for a term t, the set of variables that occur in t. A term t is closed iff $\mathrm{var}(t) = \emptyset$. The set of closed terms over Σ, ranged over by p, q, is denoted by $T(\Sigma)$.

Definition 2 (Formula). *We consider a set of actions A, ranged over by a, b (and c when no confusion arises with the constants). The set of positive formulae over signature Σ and actions A is the set of triples $(t, a, t') \in \mathbb{T}(\Sigma) \times A \times \mathbb{T}(\Sigma)$. We use the more suggestive notation $t \xrightarrow{a} t'$ in lieu of (t, a, t'). The set of negative formulae over signature Σ and actions A is the set of pairs $(t, a) \in \mathbb{T}(\Sigma) \times A$. We use the more suggestive notation $t \xrightarrow{b}\!\!\!\!/ \;$ in lieu of (t, b).*

Definition 3 (Substitution). *A substitution is a partial map $\sigma : V \to \mathbb{T}(\Sigma)$. The substitutions are ranged over by σ, τ. A substitution is closed if it maps variables to closed terms. A substitution extends to a map from terms to terms* *in the usual way, i.e., the term $\sigma(t)$ is obtained by replacing the occurrences in t of each variable x in the domain of σ by $\sigma(x)$. When applying substitutions σ and τ successively, we may abbreviate $\tau(\sigma(t))$ to $\tau\sigma(t)$. We say term u is a substitution instance of t iff there exists a substitution σ such that $\sigma(t) = u$.*

In what follows, we shall sometimes use the notation $\{x_i \mapsto t_i \mid i \in I\}$, where I is an an index set and the x_i's are pairwise distinct variables, to denote the substitution that maps each x_i to the term t_i $(i \in I)$.

A substitution σ extends to formulae $t \xrightarrow{a} t'$ and $u \xnrightarrow{b}$ in the usual way, by applying the substitution to the term components of the formulae, i.e., $\sigma(t) \xrightarrow{a} \sigma(t')$ and $\sigma(u) \xnrightarrow{b}$ respectively. The notion of substitution instance extends similarly.

Definition 4 (Labelled transition system). *Let Σ be a signature and A a set of actions. A labelled transition system (LTS for short) is a pair $(T(\Sigma), \to)$ where $T(\Sigma)$ is the set of processes, i.e., closed terms, and $\longrightarrow \subseteq T(\Sigma) \times A \times T(\Sigma)$ is the set of transitions, i.e., closed positive formulae. We say that $p \xrightarrow{a} p'$ is a transition of the LTS iff $(p, a, p') \in \longrightarrow$.*

Labelled transition systems [16] are a fundamental model of computation and are often used to describe the operational semantics of programming and specification languages—see, for instance, [20,26,27,29]. Transition system specifications, which we now proceed to define, describe the LTS giving the semantics of a language by means of a signature (namely, the collection of term constructors offered by the language) and a set of inference rules that can be used to prove the valid transitions between terms in the language.

Definition 5 (Transition system specification). *Let Σ be a signature and A a set of actions. A transition rule (a rule, for short) ρ is of the form*

$$\frac{H}{t \xrightarrow{a} t'}$$

(abbreviated as $H/t \xrightarrow{a} t'$) where H is a set of positive premises of the form $u \xrightarrow{b} u'$ and negative premises of the form $v \xnrightarrow{c}$, and $t \xrightarrow{a} t'$ is the conclusion of the rule (with $t, t', u, u', v \in \mathbb{T}(\Sigma)$ and $a, b, c \in A$). We say t is the source, a is the action, and t' is the target of ρ. We say ρ is an axiom iff ρ has an empty set of premises, i.e., $H = \emptyset$.

A transition system specification (TSS for short) is a set of transition rules.

A substitution map extends to a rule ρ by applying the substitution to the formulae in ρ. The notion of substitution instance extends similarly to rules.

Definition 6 (Unify with a rule). *Let R be a TSS. We say that transition $p \xrightarrow{a} p'$ unifies with rule $\rho \in R$ iff ρ has conclusion $t \xrightarrow{a} t'$ and $p \xrightarrow{a} p'$ is a substitution instance of $t \xrightarrow{a} t'$.*

Definition 7 (Proof tree). *Let R be a TSS without negative premisses. A proof tree in R of a transition $p \xrightarrow{a} p'$ is an upwardly branching tree without paths of infinite length whose nodes are labelled by transitions such that*

1. *the root is labelled by $p \xrightarrow{a} p'$, and*
2. *if K is the set of labels of the nodes directly above a node with label $q \xrightarrow{b} q'$, then $K/q \xrightarrow{b} q'$ is a substitution instance of some rule $H/t \xrightarrow{b} t' \in R$.*

We say that $p \xrightarrow{a} p'$ is provable in R iff $p \xrightarrow{a} p'$ has a proof tree in R.

The set of provable transitions in R is the least set of transitions that satisfies the rules in R. Notice that if $p \xrightarrow{a} p'$ unifies with an axiom (i.e., a rule of the form $\emptyset/t \xrightarrow{a} t'$) then, trivially, $p \xrightarrow{a} p'$ has a proof tree in R which consists of a root node labelled by $p \xrightarrow{a} p'$.

A TSS without negative premisses induces an LTS in a straightforward way.

Definition 8 (TSS induces LTS). *Let R be a TSS without negative premisses and T an LTS. R induces T (or T is associated with R) iff the set of transitions of T is the set of provable transitions in R.*

The phrases

1. *$p \xrightarrow{a} p'$ is provable in R,*
2. *$p \xrightarrow{a} p'$ is a transition of T, and*
3. *p can perform an a-transition to p' in T*

are synonyms. For brevity, we may omit the R and/or the T when they are clear from the context.

In [28], Przymusinsky introduced *three-valued stable models*, which can be used to associate an LTS to a TSS with negative premisses. Each TSS has a least three-valued stable model, which coincides with the well-founded semantics from [11]. We consider the set of *sentences that are certainly true* in the least three-valued stable model, which, for a TSS without negative premisses, coincides with the set of provable transitions in Definition 8. As Fokkink and Vu noticed in [9], if R is a TSS and R' is obtained by removing all the negative premisses from the rules in R, then the LTS associated with R is included in the LTS associated with R'. In particular, if the LTS associated with R' has any of the finiteness properties considered in this paper, then the LTS associated with R has the property too. We follow [9] and ignore the negative premisses in the TSSs. None of the rule formats that we introduce here impose any restrictions on negative premisses.

The notion of *uniform TSS* stems from [9]. We introduce the notion of *structure of a term*, and provide a formal definition of uniform TSS, to which we refer as *uniform TSS in the sources* because the focus is on the sources of the rules.

Definition 9 (Structure of a term). *Let R be a TSS. The terms t and u have the same structure iff*

1. $t = x$ and $u = y$, where x and y are variables, or
2. $t = f(t_1, \ldots, t_n)$ and $u = f(u_1, \ldots, u_n)$, where f is a function symbol of arity $n \geq 0$, and the terms t_i and u_i have the same structure for each $1 \leq i \leq n$.

Intuitively, two terms t and u have the same structure iff their syntax trees differ only in the name of the variables. For example $f(x, y)$ and $f(x, x)$ have the same structure. Two closed terms have the same structure iff they are the same term.

Definition 10 (Uniform in the sources). *A TSS R is uniform in the sources iff $t = u$ holds whenever t and u have the same structure and are sources of any two rules in R.*

In Sect. 5 we will introduce the analogous notion of *uniform TSS in the targets of positive premisses*, in which the focus is on the targets of positive premisses. When no confusion arises, we may abbreviate and say 'uniform TSS' for 'uniform TSS in the sources'.

The rationale behind uniformity in [9] is to enforce that in a uniform TSS, each closed term is a substitution instance of the sources of at most finitely many transition rules. In order to show this property, we introduce the notion of *partial term* and the *less-defined-than* relation.

Definition 11 (Partial term). *The set $\mathbb{T}_\perp(\Sigma)$ of partial terms over a signature Σ, ranged over by r, s, is the set of terms that results by extending Σ with the constant symbol $\perp$. The symbol $\perp$, which stands for 'undefined', is different from the other symbols in Σ.*

Notice that $T(\Sigma) \subset \mathbb{T}(\Sigma) \subset \mathbb{T}_\perp(\Sigma)$. The notion of structure of a term from Definition 9 is extended to partial terms in a straightforward way by considering the symbol $\perp$ as a variable. For instance, $f(x, y)$ has the same structure as $f(\perp, z)$.

Definition 12 (Less-defined-than relation). *The relation $\sqsubseteq$ (which we refer to as the less-or-equally-defined-than relation) is the least binary relation over partial terms such that*

1. *$\perp \sqsubseteq r$ for each partial term r,*
2. *$x \sqsubseteq x$ for each variable x, and*
3. *$f(s_1, \ldots, s_n) \sqsubseteq f(r_1, \ldots, r_n)$ where f is a function symbol of arity $n \geq 0$ iff $s_i \sqsubseteq r_i$ for each $1 \leq i \leq n$.*

We say s is an approximant of r iff $s \sqsubseteq r$.

   The less-defined-than relation $\sqsubset$ is the binary relation over partial terms defined thus: $s \sqsubset r$ iff $s \sqsubseteq r$ and $s \neq r$.

It is easy to see that $\sqsubseteq$ induces a partial order and $\sqsubset$ induces a strict partial order over partial terms.

Proposition 1. *The less-defined-than relation, $\sqsubset$, is a well-founded relation.*

Proof. We prove that there exists no infinite decreasing chain $r_1 \sqsupset r_2 \sqsupset \ldots$. To this end, we first define the size of a partial term r as follows:

1. the size of $\bot$ is zero,
2. the size of a variable is one, and
3. the size of $f(r_1, \ldots, r_n)$ with f a function symbol of arity $n \geq 0$ is one plus the sum of the sizes of the r_i's with $1 \leq i \leq n$.

Let r and s be partial terms. If $s \sqsubseteq r$ then s is obtained by replacing by $\bot$ one or more maximally disjoint subterms of r that are different from $\bot$, and hence the size of s is strictly smaller than that of r. Since the size of every partial term is finite, each decreasing chain is also finite and we are done. □

Proposition 2. *Let R be a uniform TSS. For each closed term p the set of pairs (t, σ) with $\sigma : \mathrm{var}(t) \to T(\Sigma)$ such that $\sigma(t) = p$ and t is the source of some rule in R is finite.*

Proof. We prove the generalised proposition:

> *Let R be a uniform TSS. For each pair (p, r) where p is a closed term and r is an approximant of p (i.e., $r \sqsubseteq p$), the set of pairs (t, σ) with $\sigma : \mathrm{var}(t) \to T(\Sigma)$ such that there exists r' an approximant of r (i.e., $r' \sqsubseteq r$) with the same structure as t, and $\sigma(t) = p$ and t is the source of some rule in R, is finite.*

The original proposition follows from the generalised proposition by fixing $r = p$. We construct the set S of pairs (t, σ) that meet the conditions of the generalised proposition and show that S is finite. We proceed by well-founded induction on the set of approximants of r ordered by the less-defined-than relation ($\sqsubseteq$).

We first check that the generalised proposition holds for the $\sqsubseteq$-minimal partial terms in the set of approximants of r. The only such partial term is $r_0 = \bot$. There exists only one r'_0 an approximant of r_0 (i.e., $r'_0 = \bot \sqsubseteq \bot = r_0$) and the only terms that have the same structure as r'_0 are the variables. Since R is uniform, all the rules whose source is a variable (if there are any) have the same variable x as source. If there exist no rules whose source is a variable, then the set we are looking for is the empty set. Otherwise, the set we are looking for is $S = \{(x, \{x \mapsto p\})\}$. Both sets are finite.

Now we check that the generalised proposition holds for an arbitrary partial term $r_a \neq \bot$ in the set of approximants of r. Notice that the partial term r_a is such that $r_a \sqsubseteq r \sqsubseteq p$. By the induction hypothesis, for every r_x such that $r_x \sqsubset r_a$, the set S_x of pairs (t, σ) such that there exists r'_x an approximant of r_x (i.e., $r'_x \sqsubseteq r_x$) with the same structure as t, and $\sigma(t) = p$ and t is the source of some rule in R, is finite. Since R is uniform, all the rules whose source has the same structure as r'_x (if there are any) have the same source u. Since $r'_x \sqsubset r_a$, then r'_x is obtained by replacing by $\bot$ one or more maximally disjoint subterms of r_a that are different from $\bot$. We let x_j (with j ranging over some index set J) be the variables that occur in u in the positions corresponding to the occurrences of $\bot$ in r'_x. (Notice that no other variables could occur in u, since u has the same structure as r'_x, and $r'_x \sqsubseteq p$.) We let t_j be the terms such that p results from replacing respectively the x_j by the t_j in u. If there exist no rules with source u, then the set we are looking for is $S = S_x$. Otherwise, the set we are looking for is $S = S_x \cup \{(u, \{x_j \mapsto t_j \mid j \in J\})\}$. Both sets are finite. $\square$

The next example shows that Proposition 2 does not hold for TSSs that are not uniform.

Example 1. Let Σ consist of a constant c and assume $A = \{a\}$. Let the x_i with $i \in \mathbb{N}$ be infinitely many distinct variables. Consider the TSS with rules

$$\frac{}{x_i \xrightarrow{a} c} \, , \qquad i \in \mathbb{N}.$$

All the x_i in the instantiations of the rule template above have the same structure, but $x_j \neq x_k$ for $j, k \in \mathbb{N}$ and $j \neq k$. Therefore, the TSS is not uniform. Notice that for c there exist infinitely many pairs (x_i, σ_i) (with $i \in \mathbb{N}$ and $\sigma_i = \{x_i \mapsto c\}$) such that $\sigma_i(x_i) = c$.

We focus on the properties of finite branching, initials finiteness, and image finiteness [1], which we define next.

Definition 13 (Bounded nondeterminism). *Let T be an LTS and p a closed term in T. We say*

1. *p is finite branching iff the set $\{(a, p') \mid p \xrightarrow{a} p'\}$ is finite,*
2. *p is initials finite iff the set $\{a \mid \exists p' \text{ s.t. } p \xrightarrow{a} p'\}$ is finite, and*
3. *p is image finite iff for every action a, the set $\{p' \mid p \xrightarrow{a} p'\}$ is finite.*

An LTS T is finite branching (resp. initials finite and image finite) iff every closed term in T is finite branching (resp. initials finite and image finite).

We call $\{a \mid \exists p' \text{ s.t. } p \xrightarrow{a} p'\}$ the set of initials of p. We call $\{p' \mid p \xrightarrow{a} p'\}$ the set of images of p for action a.

3   Finite Branching

The rule format in [9], which restricts a TSS to be bounded, to be in bounded nondeterminism format, and to have a strict stratification, ensures that the associated LTS is finite branching. Intuitively, the restrictions such a format places on the allowed rules ensure that, for each closed term p,

1. the rules in the TSS do not allow one to simulate 'unguarded recursion' for p,
2. only finitely many rules can be employed to derive transitions from p, and
3. each rule can only be used to infer finitely many transitions from p.

The third property is checkable for each rule in isolation and is embodied in the requirement that the TSS be in bounded nondeterminism format (see Definition 16 to follow). On the other hand, the first and the second properties are 'global' and need to be checked for sets of rules. The existence of a strict stratification (see Definition 17) enforces the first property, while the second is guaranteed by the requirement that the TSS be bounded (see Definition 15 below). In order to define the notion of bounded TSS, Fokkink and Vu classify the transition rules in a TSS according to their so-called η-types. Intuitively, rules having the same η-type are those that could potentially be used to derive transitions from a closed term p that unifies with the source of the rules. The requirement that the TSS be uniform and that the η-types be finitely inhabited ensures therefore that only finitely many rules can be employed to derive transitions from p.

We now adapt the definition of η-types in [9], on which the notion of bounded TSS is based, and recall the bounded nondeterminism format and the notion of strict stratification in [9].

We let $\eta : \mathbb{T}(\Sigma) \to \mathcal{P}(\mathbb{T}(\Sigma))$ be the maps that parametrise the η-types of Definition 14 to follow. The maps η deliver, for a given term t, a predefined set of sources of positive premises in rules that have source t. We say that $\eta(t)$ is the support of the sources for source t.[1]

Definition 14 (η-type). *Let R be a TSS, $\rho \in R$ a rule with source t and positive premises $\{t_i \xrightarrow{a_i} t_i' \mid i \in I\}$, and η a map with type $\mathbb{T}(\Sigma) \to \mathcal{P}(\mathbb{T}(\Sigma))$. We define $\psi : \eta(t) \to \mathcal{P}(A)$ as the map that delivers, for each term u in the support of the sources for t, i.e., $u \in \eta(t)$, the actions of the positive premises of ρ with source u. More formally,*

$$\psi(u) = \{a_i \mid i \in I \ \wedge \ t_i = u\}.$$

The tuple $\langle t, \psi \rangle$ is said to be the η-type of rule ρ.

Differently from [9], our definition of η-type does not require that each set in the codomain of ψ be finite. This requirement is not necessary for the rule format to ensure finite branching, as we explain in Remark 1 to Theorem 1.

The η-types distinguish rules based on their source and on the set of actions of their positive premises whose source belongs to the predefined set specified by the map η. For instance, all the rules without positive premises that have the same source belong to the same η-type, regardless of their action and target.

Intuitively, as mentioned above, rules that have the same η-type might all be used to derive transitions from a closed instantiation of their source. As the following example indicates, the presence of infinitely many rules with the same η-type might yield infinite branching.

---

[1] We beg the reader to bear with us in the repetition of 'sources' and 'source' in sentences like the above. The 'sources' refers to the positive premises and the 'source' to the conclusion of the rule.

Example 2. Let A be an infinite set of actions and $\Sigma = \{c\}$. Consider the TSS

$$\frac{}{c \xrightarrow{a} c} \, , \qquad a \in A.$$

All the infinitely many instantiations of the rule template above have η-type $\langle c, \psi \rangle$, where ψ maps each term in $\eta(c)$ (if any) to the empty set. Note that c is not finite branching.

Definition 15 (Bounded). *A TSS R is bounded iff R is uniform and there exists η with codomain $\mathcal{P}_\omega(\mathbb{T}(\Sigma))$ (i.e., the set $\eta(t)$ is finite for each t) such that for every rule $\rho \in R$ with η-type $\langle t, \psi \rangle$, the η-type $\langle t, \psi \rangle$ is finitely inhabited.*

The requirement that the function η have codomain $\mathcal{P}_\omega(\mathbb{T}(\Sigma))$ in Definition 15 means that in a bounded TSS only a finite support of the sources for a source can be distinguished. Consider Example 5 on page 508 of [9], which we reproduce next.

Example 3. Let A be an infinite set of actions and Σ consist of constants $A \cup \{c\}$ where $c \notin A$. Consider the TSS

$$\frac{}{a \xrightarrow{a} a} \, , \qquad a \in A \qquad\qquad \frac{a \xrightarrow{a} y}{c \xrightarrow{a} y} \, , \qquad a \in A.$$

If we allowed η to have codomain $\mathcal{P}(\mathbb{T}(\Sigma))$, e.g., $\eta(a) = \emptyset$ (with $a \in A$) and $\eta(c) = A$, then it would be possible to distinguish the infinite support of the sources in the rule template on the right, and each η-type $\langle c, \psi_a \rangle$ (with $a \in A$), where $\psi_a(a) = \{a\}$ and $\psi_a(b) = \emptyset$ for $b \neq a$, would correspond to exactly one rule. If instead we require η to have codomain $\mathcal{P}_\omega(\mathbb{T}(\Sigma))$, e.g., $\eta(a) = \emptyset$ with $a \in A$ and $\eta(c) = B$ for some $B \in \mathcal{P}_\omega(A)$, then an infinite number of sources of premises $a \in A \setminus B$ will be excluded from the support for source c, i.e., $\eta(c) \cap (A \setminus B) = \emptyset$. The sources $a \in A \setminus B$ cannot be distinguished, and thus the infinitely many instantiations of the rule template on the right with sources of premises $a \in A \setminus B$ will have the same η-type $\langle c, \psi \rangle$ where $\psi(t) = \emptyset$ with $t \in B$. Therefore, the TSS is not bounded. Notice that c is not finite branching.

Definition 16 (Bounded nondeterminism format). *A rule*

$$\frac{\{u_i \xrightarrow{b_i} u_i' \mid i \in I\}}{t \xrightarrow{a} t'}$$

is in bounded nondeterminism format iff

1. $\mathrm{var}(u_i) \subseteq \mathrm{var}(t)$ *for each $i \in I$, that is, all the variables occurring in the source of its positive premises also occur in its source, and*
2. $\mathrm{var}(t') \subseteq \mathrm{var}(t) \cup \bigcup\{\mathrm{var}(u_i') \mid i \in I\}$, *that is, all the variables occurring in its target also occur in its source, or in the target of some of its positive premises.*

A TSS R is in bounded nondeterminism format iff every rule in R is in bounded nondeterminism format.

The bounded nondeterminism format enforces that the target of a transition ultimately comes from the source, i.e., the rules cannot introduce variables spuriously. The following example illustrates this fact.

Example 4. Let Σ consist of a constant c and a binary function symbol f, and let $A = \{a\}$. Consider the TSS

$$\frac{}{c \xrightarrow{a} c} \qquad \frac{x \xrightarrow{a} z}{f(x,y) \xrightarrow{a} f(z,y)}.$$

The TSS is in bounded nondeterminism format. Note that variable z in the premiss of the rule on the right comes neither from the source of the premiss nor from the source of the rule. However, in every application of that rule in proof trees allowing one to derive transitions from closed terms of the form $f(p,q)$, the variable z will always be instantiated to some closed term p' such that $p \xrightarrow{a} p'$. Therefore, the rule does not introduce variables spuriously.

On the other hand, consider the rule

$$\frac{}{f(x,y) \xrightarrow{a} z}.$$

Such a rule is not in bounded nondeterminism format because the variable z in the target of the rule does not appear in its source. The above rule can be used to prove transitions of the form $f(p,q) \xrightarrow{a} r$ for all closed terms p, q and r, so the target r of a transition does not necessarily stand for a process that can be reached from either p or q. Therefore, the rule introduces the variable z spuriously.

Definition 17 (Strict stratification). *Let R be a TSS. A strict stratification of R consists of a map S from closed terms $T(\Sigma)$ to ordinal numbers such that for every transition rule $H/t \xrightarrow{a} t' \in R$ and for every closed substitution σ, $S(\sigma(u)) < S(\sigma(t))$ for every $u \xrightarrow{b} u' \in H$.*

The conditions of Theorem 1 on page 509 of [9] define the rule format for finite branching. We paraphrase Theorem 1 of [9] and its proof, and remove the *reductio ad absurdum* argument that is used there, providing a direct and fully constructive proof.

Theorem 1 (Theorem 1 of [9]). *Let R be a bounded TSS in bounded nondeterminism format that has a strict stratification S. The LTS associated with R is finite branching.*

Proof. We prove that each closed term p in the LTS associated with R is finite branching. Since R is uniform, for a given p there are only finitely many distinct terms t_i and substitutions $\sigma_i : \mathrm{var}(t_i) \to T(\Sigma)$ (i.e., the i ranges over a finite index set I) such that $\sigma_i(t_i) = p$ and the rules that unify with transitions from p have some t_i as source. We proceed by induction on $S(p)$.

The initial case is when $S(p) = 0$. Since $S(\sigma_i(t_i)) = 0$, the rules with source t_i are axioms of the form

$$\frac{}{t_i \xrightarrow{a_j} t'_j} \, , \qquad i \in I, \ j \in J_i$$

where the J_i are taken to be disjoint to avoid proliferation of indices. Since R is bounded, there exists η such that for each i and for each $j \in J_i$ the instantiation of the rule template above has η-type $\langle t_i, \psi_j \rangle$, and $\langle t_i, \psi_j \rangle$ is finitely inhabited. By Definition 14, all the ψ_j map each term in $\eta(t_i)$ (if any) to the empty set. Since R is in bounded nondeterminism format, $\text{var}(t'_j) \subseteq \text{var}(t_i)$, and thus the $\sigma_i(t'_j)$ are closed. Since the rules above are axioms, the transitions $\sigma_i(t_i) \xrightarrow{a_j} \sigma_i(t'_j)$ are provable in R. Since all the ψ_j in the η-types $\langle t_i, \psi_j \rangle$ with $j \in J_i$ are equal, and since the η-types are finitely inhabited, then the J_i are finite. Therefore, for each $i \in I$ the set

$$\{ (a_j, \sigma_i(t'_j)) \mid \sigma_i(t_i) \xrightarrow{a_j} \sigma_i(t'_j) \}$$

is finite. By the finiteness of I it follows that the set $\{ (a, p') \mid p \xrightarrow{a} p' \}$ is finite and we are done.

The general case is when $S(p) > 0$. The rules with source t_i such that $\sigma_i(t_i) = p$ are of the form

$$\frac{\{ u_k \xrightarrow{b_k} u'_k \mid k \in K_j \}}{t_i \xrightarrow{a_j} t'_j} \, , \qquad i \in I, \ j \in J_i$$

where the J_i and the K_j are taken to be disjoint to avoid proliferation of indices. Since R is bounded, there exists η such that for each i and for each $j \in J_i$, the instantiation of the rule template above has η-type $\langle t_i, \psi_j \rangle$, the set $\eta(t_i)$ is finite, and $\langle t_i, \psi_j \rangle$ is finitely inhabited.

For each i, we show that there are only finitely many distinct ψ_j with $j \in J_i$ such that rules with η-type $\langle t_i, \psi_j \rangle$ give rise to transitions from $\sigma_i(t_i)$. By Definition 14, each rule of η-type $\langle t_i, \psi_j \rangle$ contains a premiss of the form $v \xrightarrow{c} v'$ for each $v \in \eta(t_i)$ and each $c \in \psi_j(v)$. Since R is in bounded nondeterminism format, $\text{var}(v) \subseteq \text{var}(t_i)$, and thus the $\sigma_i(v)$ are closed. By Definitions 7 and 8, for each transition in the node of a proof tree, if the transition unifies with a rule of η-type $\langle t_i, \psi_j \rangle$ then for each $v \in \eta(t_i)$ the process $\sigma_i(v)$ can perform, at least, a c-transition for each $c \in \psi_j(v)$. The ψ_j giving rise to transitions from $\sigma_i(t_i)$ are dependent functions of type $\Pi_{v \in \eta(t_i)} \{ c \mid \sigma_i(v) \xrightarrow{c} \tau \sigma_i(v') \}$ with substitutions $\tau : (\text{var}(v') \setminus \text{var}(v)) \to T(\Sigma)$. For each i the refined type of the ψ_j with $j \in J_i$ is finitely inhabited, since the codomain of a dependent function depends on the inputs of the function. Each image of ψ_j cannot be an arbitrary subset of A, but only the one that is determined by the input v and by the associated LTS. That is, the only elements in the codomain of ψ_j are the sets $\{ c \mid \sigma_i(v) \xrightarrow{c} \tau \sigma_i(v') \}$ where $v \in \eta(t_i)$. Since the $\eta(t_i)$ are finite sets, both the domain and the codomain of ψ_j are finite. Therefore, for each i there are only finitely many distinct ψ_j with $j \in J_i$ such that rules with η-type $\langle t_i, \psi_j \rangle$ give rise to transitions from $\sigma_i(t_i)$.

Since R is in bounded nondeterminism format, $\mathrm{var}(u_k) \subseteq \mathrm{var}(t_i)$ and therefore the $\sigma_i(u_k)$ are closed terms. As S is a strict stratification, $S(\sigma_i(u_k)) < S(p)$. By the induction hypothesis the $\sigma_i(u_k)$ are finite branching, and therefore for each $i \in I$ the set

$$\{(b_k, \tau_\ell \sigma_i(u'_k)) \mid \sigma_i(u_k) \xrightarrow{b_k} \tau_\ell \sigma_i(u'_k)\}$$

is finite, with $\tau_\ell : ((\bigcup_{k \in K_j} \mathrm{var}(u'_k)) \setminus \mathrm{var}(t_i)) \to T(\Sigma)$ closed substitutions where ℓ ranges over some index sets L_j and where $j \in J_i$. Since R is in bounded nondeterminism format, $\mathrm{var}(t'_j) \subseteq (\mathrm{var}(t_i) \cup (\bigcup_{k \in K_j} \mathrm{var}(u'_k)))$ and therefore the $\tau_\ell \sigma_i(t'_j)$ are closed terms. Since for each i there are only finitely many distinct ψ_j with $j \in J_i$ such that rules with η-type $\langle t_i, \psi_j \rangle$ give rise to transitions from $\sigma_i(t_i)$, and since the η-types $\langle t_i, \psi_j \rangle$ are finitely inhabited, then the L_j are finite. Therefore, for each $i \in I$ the set

$$\{(a_j, \tau_\ell \sigma_i(t'_j)) \mid \sigma_i(t_i) \xrightarrow{a_j} \tau_\ell \sigma_i(t'_j)\} \quad (j \in J_i, \ell \in L_j)$$

is finite. By the finiteness of I it follows that the set $\{(a, p') \mid p \xrightarrow{a} p'\}$ is finite and we are done. □

Remark 1. The requirement in [9] that each set in the codomain of ψ in an η-type $\langle t, \psi \rangle$ must be finite (i.e., the codomain of ψ must be $\mathcal{P}_\omega(A)$) is superfluous. In a TSS that induces a finite-branching LTS such that η witnesses that the TSS is bounded, there could be rules with η-type $\langle t, \psi \rangle$ where each set in the codomain of ψ is infinite, but since the LTS is finite branching, the transitions in the nodes of a proof tree will never unify with these rules.

Remark 2. The proof above follows that of Theorem 1 in [9], with the most notable difference being that [9] uses a *reductio ad absurdum* argument to show that the distinct ψ_j for a given i are finitely many. The proof in [9] assumes that there exists $m \in I$ such that there are infinitely many ψ_n with $n \in J_m$ such that rules with η-type $\langle t_m, \psi_n \rangle$ give rise to transitions from $\sigma_m(t_m)$, and then shows that this assumption contradicts the induction hypothesis.

We believe a direct proof is preferable over a proof by contradiction. Our proof not only establishes the desired conclusion above, but also the intermediate conclusion that the ψ_j such that rules with η-type $\langle t_i, \psi_j \rangle$ give rise to transitions from $\sigma_i(t_i)$ are dependent functions of type $\Pi_{v \in \eta(t_i)}\{c \mid \sigma_i(v) \xrightarrow{c} \tau \sigma_i(v')\}$ with substitutions $\tau : (\mathrm{var}(v') \setminus \mathrm{var}(v)) \to T(\Sigma)$. This is an interesting observation in its own right that could be used to draw further conclusions. Besides, our proof is fully constructive, and thus it is better suited for the purpose of mechanising it.

Example 5. Let A consist of an action a. Consider a TSS whose signature contains the constants c_i, with $i \geq 1$, and whose rules are

$$\frac{x \xrightarrow{a} y \quad y \xrightarrow{a} z}{x \xrightarrow{a} z} \qquad \frac{}{c_i \xrightarrow{a} c_{i+1}}, \qquad i \geq 1.$$

This TSS is neither in bounded nondeterminism format nor strictly stratified, and therefore does not satisfy the conditions of Theorem 1. It is easy to see that every constant c_i ($i \geq 1$) has infinitely many outgoing transitions. Indeed, $c_i \xrightarrow{a} c_j$ is provable for all $j > i \geq 1$.

Several examples of applications of the rule format defined by the conditions of Theorem 1 can be found in [9]. In the next section we adapt the conditions of Theorem 1 to account for initials finiteness.

4   Initials Finiteness

As shown by Example 4 in Sect. 3, the bounded nondeterminism format enforces that no variables are introduced spuriously, thus preventing infinite branching coming from replacing the variables in the target of a rule by infinitely many distinct terms. In a transition rule, there are three kinds of 'variable flow' that it is worth considering:

1. variables from the source of the rule that flow to the sources of the positive premisses,
2. variables from the source of the rule that flow to the target of the rule, and
3. variables from the targets of positive premisses that flow to the target of the rule.

By the bounded nondeterminism format, all the variables in a rule (except for the variables in the source of the rule and in the targets of positive premisses) come from some of the variable flows described above. By induction on the proof tree, it is easy to show that the 'circulation' of the variables is closed in the leaves of the proof tree (i.e., by the second kind of variable flow above) and thus no variables can be introduced spuriously. This requirement is too strong for initials finiteness, which is only concerned with the *actions* of transitions that are provable from a given process. For initials finiteness it is immaterial whether the rules introduce variables in the target spuriously, and the bounded nondeterminism format can be relaxed. However, as the following example shows, dropping all the requirements on the variable flow does not ensure initials finiteness.

Example 6. Let A be an infinite set of actions and let $\Sigma = A \cup \{c, f\}$ with c a constant, f a unary function symbol and $f, c \notin A$. Consider the TSS

$$\frac{}{f(a) \xrightarrow{a} f(a)} \, , \qquad a \in A \qquad\qquad \frac{f(x) \xrightarrow{a} y}{c \xrightarrow{a} y} \, , \qquad a \in A.$$

The TSS is uniform and has a strict stratification given by

$$S(c) = 1$$
$$S(f(p)) = 0.$$

We let $\eta(f(a)) = \emptyset$ (with $a \in A$) and $\eta(c) = \{f(x)\}$. For each $a \in A$, the instantiation of the rule template on the left has η-type $\langle f(a), \emptyset \rangle$, and the instantiation of the rule on the right has η-type $\langle c, \psi_a \rangle$ where $\psi_a(f(x)) = \{a\}$. However, the associated LTS is not initials finite because the set of initials of c is A.

Variable x in the rule template on the right does not come from the source of the rule. Thus, there exist infinitely many substitutions $\tau : \{x\} \to A$ such that the transitions from $\tau(f(x))$ unify with some instantiation of the rule template on the left. For initials finiteness, it is enough to prevent spurious variables in the sources of positive premises.

We now introduce the initials finite format, which takes care of the first kind of variable flow described above.

Definition 18 (Initials finite format). *A rule*

$$\frac{\{u_i \xrightarrow{b_i} u_i' \mid i \in I\}}{t \xrightarrow{a} t'}$$

is in initials finite format iff all the variables occurring in the sources of its positive premisses also occur in its source, that is, $\mathrm{var}(u_i) \subseteq \mathrm{var}(t)$ *for each* $i \in I$.

A TSS R is in initials finite format iff every rule in R is in initials finite format.

The following example shows that the requirements on the variable flow, except for the one enforced by the initials finite format, can be dropped.

Example 7. Let $A = \{a\}$ and Σ consists of infinitely many constants $\{c, d, \ldots\}$. Consider the TSS with rule

$$\frac{}{c \xrightarrow{a} x} .$$

The system is uniform and has a trivial strict stratification. The rule above has η-type $\langle c, \psi \rangle$ where ψ maps each term in $\eta(c)$ (if any) to the empty set, and thus the TSS is bounded. Variable x comes neither from the target of any positive premiss, since there are none, nor from the source of the rule, and hence the TSS is not in bounded nondeterminism format. However, the TSS is in initials finite format. Notice that the associated LTS is initials finite.

However, replacing the bounded nondeterminism format by the initials finite format is not enough to cover all the TSSs in which we are interested. Some initials-finite LTSs are induced by TSSs which are not bounded, despite being in initials finite format. This is shown in the following example.

Example 8. Let $A = \{a\}$ and let Σ consist of infinitely many constants $\{c, d, \ldots\}$. Let $P = \{p_i \mid i \in I\}$ (with the p_i distinct and I an infinite index set) be a proper subset of $T(\Sigma)$, i.e., $P \subset T(\Sigma)$. Consider the TSS with rules

$$\frac{}{c \xrightarrow{a} p_i} , \qquad i \in I.$$

All the rules above have η-type $\langle c, \psi \rangle$ where ψ maps each term in $\eta(c)$ (if any) to the empty set, and hence the η-type $\langle c, \psi \rangle$ is infinitely inhabited and the TSS is not bounded. However, the associated LTS is initials finite.

Example 8 implements *bounded quantifiers* by means of a rule template and an *ad hoc* infinite index set I. The use of bounded quantifiers[2] is different from the implicit universal quantifiers for variables in the rules of a TSS, as illustrated in Example 7. The TSS of Example 7 consists of a single rule whose target x ranges over the set of closed terms $T(\Sigma)$. On the contrary, the TSS of Example 8 consists of a rule template such that the targets p_i with $i \in I$ range over an infinite proper subset of the set of closed terms, i.e., $\{p_i \mid i \in I\} \subset T(\Sigma)$. Technically, the sentences $\forall x.\ c \xrightarrow{a} x$ and $\forall x \in \{p_i \mid i \in I\}.\ c \xrightarrow{a} x$ are respectively a Π_1-sentence and a Π_0-sentence in the Lévy hierarchy [18].

Bounded quantifiers are conventional and useful, and we wish our rule format to allow for TSSs like the one of Example 8. To this end, we need a more refined notion of bounded TSS, which disregards the cardinality of the set of inhabitants of an η-type and takes into account the actions of rules.

We now define the actions of an η-type and introduce the notion of initials-bounded TSS.

Definition 19 (Actions of an η-type). *Let R be a TSS. We define $\chi : \eta\text{-type} \to \mathcal{P}(A)$ as the map that delivers, for each η-type $\langle t, \psi \rangle$, the set of actions of the rules that have η-type $\langle t, \psi \rangle$. More formally,*

$$\chi(t, \psi) = \{a \mid \rho \text{ has } \eta\text{-type } \langle t, \psi \rangle \text{ and } a \text{ is the action of } \rho\}.$$

The set $\chi(t, \psi)$ is said to be the actions of η-type $\langle t, \psi \rangle$.

Definition 20 (Initials bounded). *A TSS R is initials bounded iff R is uniform and there exists η with codomain $\mathcal{P}_\omega(\mathbb{T}(\Sigma))$ (i.e., the set $\eta(t)$ is finite for each t) such that for every rule $\rho \in R$ with η-type $\langle t, \psi \rangle$, the η-type $\langle t, \psi \rangle$ has finitely many actions, i.e., $\chi(t, \psi) \in \mathcal{P}_\omega(A)$.*

In the TSS of Example 8, the η-type $\langle c, \psi \rangle$ is infinitely inhabited but it has finitely many actions as $\chi(c, \psi) = \{a\}$. Therefore, the TSS of Example 8 is initials bounded.

Intuitively, since rules having the same η-type are those that could potentially be used to derive transitions from a closed term p that unifies with the source of the rules, requiring that η-types have finitely many actions can help one to ensure that p be initials finite. However, as the following example shows, having a strict stratification is also needed to ensure initials finiteness as it intuitively disallows 'unguarded recursion'.

Example 9. Let Σ consist of a constant c and a unary function symbol f, and let $A = \{a_1, a_2, \ldots\}$ be an infinite set of actions. Consider the TSS with rules

$$\frac{}{f(x) \xrightarrow{a_1} c} \qquad \frac{f(x) \xrightarrow{a_i} y}{f(x) \xrightarrow{a_{i+1}} y}, \qquad i \in \mathbb{N}.$$

---

[2] Notice that 'bounded' in 'bounded quantifiers' does not have the connotation of 'finite' that is present in 'bounded nondeterminism'. The bounded quantifiers restrict the range of the quantified variable, but this range could still be infinite. Examples 7 and 8 illustrate the difference between universal quantifiers and bounded quantifiers with an infinite range.

The TSS is uniform and in initials finite format. We let $\eta(f(x)) = \{f(x)\}$. The rule on the left has η-type $\langle f(x), \psi \rangle$ where $\psi(f(x)) = \emptyset$, and for each $i \in \mathbb{N}$, the instantiation of the rule template on the right has η-type $\langle f(x), \psi_i \rangle$ where $\psi_i(f(x)) = \{a_i\}$. The set of actions of $\langle f(x), \psi \rangle$ is $\{a_1\}$, and for each $i \in \mathbb{N}$ the set of actions of $\langle f(x), \psi_i \rangle$ is $\{a_{i+1}\}$. Therefore, the TSS is initials bounded. However, the TSS does not have a strict stratification. Notice that the associated LTS is not initials finite, since the set of initials of $f(c)$ is A.

The conditions of the following theorem define the rule format for initials finiteness.

Theorem 2. *Let R be an initials-bounded TSS in initials finite format that has a strict stratification S. The LTS associated with R is initials finite.*

Proof. We prove that each closed term p in the LTS associated with R is initials finite. Since R is uniform, for a given p there are only finitely many distinct terms t_i and substitutions $\sigma_i : \text{var}(t_i) \to T(\Sigma)$ (i.e., the i ranges over a finite index set I) such that $\sigma_i(t_i) = p$ and the rules that unify with transitions from p have some t_i as source. We proceed by induction on $S(p)$.

The initial case is when $S(p) = 0$. Since $S(\sigma_i(t_i)) = 0$, the rules with source t_i are axioms of the form

$$\frac{}{t_i \xrightarrow{\ a_j\ } t_k'}\ , \qquad i \in I,\ j \in J_i,\ k \in K_j$$

where the J_i and the K_j are taken to be disjoint to avoid proliferation of indices. Since R is initials bounded, there exists η such that for each i, for each $j \in J_i$, and for each $k \in K_j$, the instantiation of the rule template above has η-type $\langle t_i, \psi_k \rangle$, and $\langle t_i, \psi_k \rangle$ has finitely many actions, i.e., $\chi(t_i, \psi_k) \in \mathcal{P}_\omega(A)$. By Definition 14, all the ψ_k map each term in $\eta(t_i)$ (if any) to the empty set, so all the rules above with source t_i have the same η-type. Since the rules above are axioms, the transitions $\sigma_i(t_i) \xrightarrow{\ a_j\ } \tau\sigma_i(t_k')$ are provable in R for each substitution $\tau :$ $(\text{var}(t_j') \setminus \text{var}(t_i)) \to T(\Sigma)$. Since all the ψ_k in the η-types are equal, and since the η-types have finitely many actions, the sets J_i are finite. Therefore, for each $i \in I$ the set

$$\{a_j \mid \exists p' \text{ s.t. } \sigma_i(t_i) \xrightarrow{\ a_j\ } p'\} = \chi(t_i, \psi_k)$$

is finite. By the finiteness of I it follows that the set $\{a \mid \exists p' \text{ s.t. } p \xrightarrow{\ a\ } p'\}$ is finite and we are done.

The general case is when $S(p) > 0$. The rules with source t_i such that $\sigma_i(t_i) = p$ are of the form

$$\frac{\{u_\ell \xrightarrow{\ b_\ell\ } u_\ell' \mid \ell \in L_k\}}{t_i \xrightarrow{\ a_j\ } t_k'}\ , \qquad i \in I,\ j \in J_i,\ k \in K_j$$

where the J_i, the K_j, and the L_k are taken to be disjoint to avoid proliferation of indices. Since R is initials bounded, there exists η such that for each i, for each $j \in J_i$, and for each $k \in K_j$, the instantiation of the rule template above has η-type $\langle t_i, \psi_k \rangle$, the set $\eta(t_i)$ is finite, and $\langle t_i, \psi_k \rangle$ has finitely many actions.

For each i, we show that there are only finitely many distinct ψ_k with $k \in K_j$ and $j \in J_i$ such that rules with η-type $\langle t_i, \psi_k \rangle$ give rise to transitions from $\sigma_i(t_i)$. By Definition 14, each rule of η-type $\langle t_i, \psi_k \rangle$ contains a premiss of the form $v \xrightarrow{c} v'$ for each $v \in \eta(t_i)$ and each $c \in \psi_k(v)$. Since R is in initials finite format, $\text{var}(v) \subseteq \text{var}(t_i)$, and thus the $\sigma_i(v)$ are closed. By Definitions 7 and 8, for each transition in the node of a proof tree, if the transition unifies with a rule of η-type $\langle t_i, \psi_k \rangle$, then for each $v \in \eta(t_i)$ the processes $\sigma_i(v)$ can perform, at least, a c-transition for each $c \in \psi_k(v)$. The ψ_k giving rise to transitions from $\sigma_i(t_i)$ are dependent functions of type $\Pi_{v \in \eta(t_i)} \{ c \mid \sigma_i(v) \xrightarrow{c} \tau \sigma_i(v') \}$ with substitutions $\tau : (\text{var}(v') \setminus \text{var}(v)) \to T(\Sigma)$. For each i the refined type of the ψ_k with $k \in K_j$ and $i \in J_i$ is finitely inhabited, since the codomain of a dependent function depends on the inputs of the function. Each image of ψ_k cannot be an arbitrary subset of A, but only the one determined by the input v and by the associated LTS. That is, the only elements in the codomain of ψ_k are the sets $\{ c \mid \sigma_i(v) \xrightarrow{c} \tau \sigma_i(v') \}$ where $v \in \eta(t_i)$. Since the $\eta(t_i)$ are finite sets, both the domain and the codomain of ψ_k are finite. Therefore for each i there are only finitely many distinct ψ_k with $k \in K_j$ and $j \in J_i$ such that rules with η-type $\langle t_i, \psi_k \rangle$ give rise to transitions from $\sigma_i(t_i)$.

Since for each i there are only finitely many distinct ψ_k with $k \in K_j$ and $j \in J_i$ such that rules with η-type $\langle t_i, \psi_k \rangle$ give rise to transitions from $\sigma_i(t_i)$, and since the η-types $\langle t_i, \psi_k \rangle$ have finitely many actions, then for each $i \in I$ the set

$$\{ a_j \mid \exists p' \text{ s.t. } \sigma_i(t_i) \xrightarrow{a_j} p' \}$$

is finite. By the finiteness of I it follows that the set $\{ a \mid \exists p' \text{ s.t. } p \xrightarrow{a} p' \}$ is finite and we are done. $\qquad \square$

Remark 3. In Theorem 2 the TSS R is not required to be in bounded nondeterminism format. The terms t'_k may have variables which are neither in t_i nor in $\bigcup_{\ell \in L_k} \text{var}(u'_\ell)$. Consider $\tau_m : (\text{var}(t'_k) \setminus \text{var}(t_i)) \to T(\Sigma)$ closed substitutions with m ranging over index sets M_k such that $\sigma_i(t_i) \xrightarrow{a_j} \tau_m \sigma_i(t'_k)$. For each $\sigma_i(t_i)$ there may be infinitely many transitions $\sigma_i(t_i) \xrightarrow{a_j} \tau_m \sigma_i(t'_k)$ because the M_k may be infinite. This is illustrated by Example 7.

Remark 4. In Theorem 2 the η-types are not required to be finitely inhabited. For each η-type $\langle t_i, \psi_k \rangle$ there could be infinitely many rules with conclusions $t_i \xrightarrow{a_j} t'_k$, and the K_j need not be finite. The TSS R could be in bounded nondeterminism format, and then there would be $\tau_m : ((\bigcup_{\ell \in L_k} \text{var}(u'_\ell)) \setminus \text{var}(t_i)) \to T(\Sigma)$ closed substitutions with $m \in M_k$ and M_k are finite index sets such that $\sigma_i(t_i) \xrightarrow{a_j} \tau_m \sigma_i(t'_k)$. But, although the M_k may be finite, for each $\sigma_i(t_i)$ there may be infinitely many transitions $\sigma_i(t_i) \xrightarrow{a_j} \tau_m \sigma_i(t'_k)$, because the K_j may be infinite. This is illustrated by Example 8.

We now present an example of application of the rule format defined by the conditions of Theorem 2.

Example 10. Let Σ contain constants c and $\mathbf{0}$ and the unary action prefixing operation $a.\_$ from Milner's CCS [20]. Consider the TSS with rules

$$\frac{}{a.x \xrightarrow{a} x} \qquad \frac{}{c \xrightarrow{a} \underbrace{a.\dots.a.}_{i \text{ times}} \mathbf{0}} \,, \qquad i \geq 0.$$

Intuitively, the constant c is akin to a random assignment [4]. The TSS is uniform and has a trivial strict stratification. We let $\eta(a.x) = \emptyset$ and $\eta(c) = \emptyset$. The rule on the left has η-type $\langle a.x, \emptyset \rangle$ and each instantiation of the rule template on the right has η-type $\langle c, \emptyset \rangle$. The rule template on the right implements bounded quantifiers as illustrated in Example 8. Although the η-type $\langle c, \emptyset \rangle$ is infinitely inhabited, the set of its actions is $\{a\}$. The associated LTS is initials finite.

In the next section we develop a rule format for image finiteness.

5 Image Finiteness

Consider the properties of an LTS in Definition 13, which we paraphrase here in mathematical notation:

Finite branching: $\forall p. \ \{(a, p') \mid p \xrightarrow{a} p'\} \in \mathcal{P}_\omega(A \times T(\Sigma))$.
Initials finiteness: $\forall p. \ \{a \mid \exists p'. \ p \xrightarrow{a} p'\} \in \mathcal{P}_\omega(A)$.
Image finiteness: $\forall p. \forall a. \ \{p' \mid p \xrightarrow{a} p'\} \in \mathcal{P}_\omega(T(\Sigma))$.

We consider the Brouwer-Heyting-Kolmogorov interpretation of intuitionistic logic (BHK interpretation for short) [15]. According to the BHK interpretation, the proof of any of the properties above consists of a function that takes one argument for each of the universally quantified symbols and returns a proof of the trailing proposition after the quantifiers,[3] which asserts that some set is finite. As a proof of each assertion, it is enough to exhibit the set in point. For example, given a TSS R the proof that the LTS associated with R is initials finite consists of a function that takes an element $p \in T(\Sigma)$ and delivers the finite set of actions a such that $p \xrightarrow{a} p'$ (with $p' \in T(\Sigma)$) is provable in R. The BHK interpretation provides a profitable insight on the notion of η-types. In essence, the η-types are a sort of syntactic fingerprint of the BHK interpretation of initials finiteness. Recall from Definition 14 that in an η-type $\langle t, \psi \rangle$ the map ψ takes a term and delivers a set of actions. This map represents the function corresponding to the BHK interpretation. The disciplined focus on the positives premisses (e.g., through the finite support of the sources defined by η and with the variable flow enforced by the initials finite format) is only an instrument to construct the intuitionistic proof from ψ, by induction on the strict stratification of the TSS. This is exemplified by our proof of Theorem 2.

It may seem odd that the η-types, which correspond to the BHK interpretation of initials finiteness, are also used in the rule format that ensures finite

---

[3] Recall that in intuitionistic logic a universal quantifier '$\forall x.$' is akin to a big lambda '$\Lambda x.$', i.e., a binding operator at the level of types.

branching. The map ψ delivers a set of *actions* b, instead of the set of *pairs of actions and terms* (b, u') that would be expected from the BHK interpretation of finite branching. The reason lies in the fact that the additional requirements of the rule format make keeping track of the targets u' redundant. To see this, let the positive premises be of the shape $u \xrightarrow{b} u'$. Since the TSS is required to be in bounded nondeterminism format, then $\mathrm{var}(u) \subseteq \mathrm{var}(t)$ and the $\sigma(u)$ are closed. Thus, for each $u \in \eta(t)$ there are at most finitely many pairs (b, u') such that $b \in \psi(u)$ and $\sigma(u) \xrightarrow{b} \tau\sigma(u')$ with substitutions $\tau : (\mathrm{var}(u') \setminus \mathrm{var}(u)) \to T(\Sigma)$. Therefore, keeping track of the targets u' of positive premises is redundant because the requirements of the rule format ensure that the associated LTS is finite branching.

The different requirements for bounded TSS and for initials-bounded TSS complete the picture, respectively for the BHK interpretation of finite branching and of initials finiteness. In a bounded TSS, it is required that there exists an η such that each η-type $\langle t, \psi \rangle$ is *finitely inhabited*. This enforces that if for each term t and for each substitution σ such that $\sigma(t)$ is closed there are only finitely many ψ such that the rules that give rise to transitions from $\sigma(t)$ have η-type $\langle t, \psi \rangle$, then the set of pairs (a, t') such that $\sigma(t) \xrightarrow{a} \tau\sigma(t')$ with substitutions $\tau : (\mathrm{var}(t') \setminus \mathrm{var}(t)) \to T(\Sigma)$ is finite. The bounded nondeterminism format ensures that there are only finitely many substitutions τ, and then the set of pairs $(a, \tau\sigma(t'))$ is also finite and the associated LTS is finite branching. In an initials-bounded TSS, it is only required that there exists an η such that each η-type $\langle t, \psi \rangle$ has *finite actions*. This enforces that if for each term t and for each substitution σ such that $\sigma(t)$ is closed there are only finitely many ψ such that the rules that give rise to transitions from $\sigma(t)$ have η-type $\langle t, \psi \rangle$, then the set of actions a such that $\sigma(t) \xrightarrow{a} \tau\sigma(t')$ with substitutions $\tau : (\mathrm{var}(t') \setminus \mathrm{var}(t)) \to T(\Sigma)$ is finite. The bounded nondeterminism format can be replaced by the initials finite format because the number of substitutions τ is immaterial in order to keep the number of actions a finite, and thus for the associated LTS to be initials finite.

We now introduce the θ-types, which are gleaned from the BHK interpretation of image finiteness. Unlike the η-types of [9], which carry information about the sources of positive premises in rules, the θ-types also keep track *of the actions* that label positive premises.

We let $\theta : (\mathbb{T}(\Sigma) \times A) \to \mathcal{P}(\mathbb{T}(\Sigma) \times A)$ be the maps that parametrise the θ-types of Definition 21 to follow. The maps θ deliver, for a given term t and action a, a predefined set of sources and actions of positive premises in rules that have source t and action a. We say that $\theta(t, a)$ is the support of the sources and of the actions for source and action (t, a).[4]

Definition 21 (θ-type). *Let R be a TSS, $\rho \in R$ a rule with source t, action a, and positive premises $\{t_i \xrightarrow{a_i} t_i' \mid i \in I\}$, and θ a map with type $(\mathbb{T}(\Sigma) \times A) \to$*

---

[4] We beg the reader to bear with us in the repetition of 'sources', 'actions', 'source', and 'action' in sentences like the above. The 'sources' and 'actions' refer to the positive premises, and the 'source' and 'action' to the conclusion of the rule.

$\mathcal{P}(\mathbb{T}(\Sigma) \times A)$. *We define* $\phi : \theta(t, a) \to \mathcal{P}(\mathbb{T}(\Sigma))$ *as the map that delivers, for each term* u *and action* b *in the support of the sources and of the actions for* (t, a), *i.e.,* $(u, b) \in \theta(t, a)$, *the targets of the positive premisses of* ρ *with source* u *and action* b. *More formally,*

$$\phi(u, b) = \{t_i' \mid i \in I \ \wedge \ t_i = u \ \wedge a_i = b\}.$$

The triple $\langle t, a, \phi \rangle$ *is said to be the* θ-*type of rule* ρ.

The θ-types distinguish rules based on their source, their action, and on the set of targets of their positive premisses whose source and action belong to the predefined set specified by the map θ. Let us illustrate this with an example.

Example 11. Let Σ consist of a constant c and a unary function symbol f and let A be an infinite set of actions. Consider the TSS

$$\frac{}{c \xrightarrow{a} c} \, , \qquad a \in A \qquad\qquad \frac{x \xrightarrow{a} y}{f(x) \xrightarrow{a} y} \, , \qquad a \in A.$$

For each $a \in A$, we let $\theta(c, a) = \emptyset$ and $\theta(f(x), a) = \{(x, a)\}$. For each $a \in A$, the θ-types of the instantiations of the rule templates on the left and on the right are $\langle c, a, \emptyset \rangle$ and $\langle f(x), a, \phi_a \rangle$ respectively, where $\phi_a(x, a) = \{y\}$. Notice that the associated LTS is image finite, because the target of every transition is c. However, it is neither finite branching nor initials finite, since every process can do an a-transition for each $a \in A$.

Intuitively, the θ-types play for image finiteness the role that the η-types play for finite branching. Rules having the same θ-type $\langle t, a, \phi \rangle$ are those that could potentially be used to derive a-transitions from a closed term p that is an instantiation of t. In order to ensure that the set of processes that are the targets of a-transitions from a closed term p is finite, it is reasonable to require that each θ-type be finitely inhabited. However, for image finiteness, the variables occurring in the targets of positive premisses of rules have to be used uniformly. The following example illustrates this fact.

Example 12. Let Σ consist of a constant c and a unary function symbol f, and assume $A = \{a\}$. Let the y_i with $i \in \mathbb{N}$ be infinitely many distinct variables. Consider the TSS

$$\frac{}{c \xrightarrow{a} c} \qquad\qquad \frac{x \xrightarrow{a} y_i}{f(x) \xrightarrow{a} f^i(x)} \, , \qquad i \in \mathbb{N}$$

where f^i stands for applying i times the function symbol f. The TSS is uniform in the sources (recall Definition 10) and has a strict stratification given by

$$S(c) = 0$$
$$S(f(p)) = 1 + S(p).$$

We let $\theta(c,a) = \emptyset$ and $\theta(f(x),a) = \{(x,a)\}$. The rule on the left has θ-type $\langle c, a, \emptyset \rangle$, and for each $i \in \mathbb{N}$, the instantiation of the rule template on the right has θ-type $\langle f(x), a, \phi_i \rangle$, where $\phi_i(f(x),a) = \{y_i\}$. However, the associated LTS is not image finite, because process $f(c)$ can perform infinitely many a-transitions to $f^i(c)$ (with $i \in \mathbb{N}$).

In the TSS of Example 12 there are infinitely many different variables y_i, and thus there are infinitely many different θ-types that morally should be the same. The inhabitants of each of these θ-types give rise, for a given source and action, to transitions with different targets, and the associated LTS is not image finite. To address this issue we introduce the notion of *uniform TSS in the targets of positive premisses*. This notion extends that of *uniform TSS in the sources*, which is the *uniform TSS* from [9] that we adapted in Definition 10.

Definition 22 (Uniform in the targets of positive premisses). *A TSS R is uniform in the targets of positive premisses iff $t' = t''$ holds whenever t' and t'' have the same structure and $t \xrightarrow{a} t'$ and $t \xrightarrow{a} t''$ are positive premisses of any two (not necessarily different) rules.*

The TSS of Example 12 is not uniform in the targets of positive premisses. Indeed, $x \xrightarrow{a} y_1$ and $x \xrightarrow{a} y_2$ are positive premisses of rules and y_1 and y_2 have the same structure, but $y_1 \neq y_2$. However, the LTS induced by the TSS of Example 12 can be specified by a TSS that is uniform in the targets of positive premisses as follows.

Example 13. Let Σ consist of a constant c and a unary function symbol f, and assume $A = \{a\}$. Consider the TSS

$$\frac{}{c \xrightarrow{a} c} \qquad \frac{x \xrightarrow{a} y}{f(x) \xrightarrow{a} f^i(x)}, \qquad i \in \mathbb{N}.$$

The TSS is uniform both in the sources of rules and in the targets of their positive premisses and has a strict stratification given by

$$S(c) = 0$$
$$S(f(p)) = 1 + S(p).$$

We let $\theta(c,a) = \emptyset$ and $\theta(f(x),a) = \{(x,a)\}$. The rule on the left has θ-type $\langle c, a, \emptyset \rangle$, and for each $i \in \mathbb{N}$ the instantiation of the rule template on the right has θ-type $\langle f(x), a, \phi \rangle$ where $\phi(x,a) = \{y\}$. Therefore, the θ-type $\langle f(x), a, \phi \rangle$ is infinitely inhabited. Notice that the associated LTS is equal to that in Example 12, which is not image finite.

Next we prove a proposition that resembles Proposition 2 of Sect. 2, which states that for a uniform TSS in the targets of positive premisses, each transition is a substitution instance of at most finitely many positive premisses of the TSS.

Proposition 3. *Let R be a uniform TSS in the targets of positive premises. For each transition $p \xrightarrow{a} p'$, and for each term t and substitution $\sigma : \mathrm{var}(t) \to T(\Sigma)$ such that $\sigma(t) = p$, the set of pairs (t', τ) with $\tau : \mathrm{var}(t') \setminus \mathrm{var}(t) \to T(\Sigma)$ such that $\sigma(t) \xrightarrow{a} \tau\sigma(t') = p \xrightarrow{a} p'$ and $t \xrightarrow{a} t'$ is a positive premiss of some rule in R is finite.*

Proof. We prove the generalised proposition:

> Let R be a uniform TSS in the targets of positive premises. For each pair $(p \xrightarrow{a} p', r)$ where $p \xrightarrow{a} p'$ is a transition and r is an approximant of p' (i.e., $r \sqsubseteq p'$) and for each term t and substitution $\sigma : \mathrm{var}(t) \to T(\Sigma)$ such that $\sigma(t) = p$, the set of pairs (t', τ) with $\tau : \mathrm{var}(t') \setminus \mathrm{var}(t) \to T(\Sigma)$ such that there exists r' an approximant of r (i.e., $r' \sqsubseteq r$) with the same structure as t', and $\sigma(t) \xrightarrow{a} \tau\sigma(t') = p \xrightarrow{a} p'$ and $t \xrightarrow{a} t'$ is a positive premiss of some rule in R, is finite.

The original proposition follows from the generalised proposition by fixing $r = p'$. We fix a t and a σ such that $\sigma(t) = p$ and construct the set S of pairs (t', τ) that meet the conditions of the generalised proposition and show that S is finite. We proceed by well-founded induction on the set of approximants of r ordered by the less-defined-than relation ($\sqsubseteq$).

We first check that the generalised proposition holds for the $\sqsubseteq$-minimal partial terms in the set of approximants of r. The only such partial term is $r_0 = \bot$. There exists only one r'_0 an approximant of r (i.e., $r'_0 = \bot \sqsubseteq \bot = r_0$) and the only terms that have the same structure as r'_0 are the variables. Since R is uniform in the targets of positive premises, all the positive premises of R with source t, action a, and whose target is a variable (if there is any) have the same variable x as target. If there exist no positive premises as described before, then the set we are looking for is the empty set. If there exist positive premisses as described before, we distinguish two cases. If $x \in \mathrm{var}(t)$, then the set we are looking for is $S = \{(x, \emptyset)\}$. Otherwise, the set we are looking for is $S = \{(x, \{x \mapsto p'\})\}$. All three sets are finite.

Now we check that the generalised proposition holds for an arbitrary partial term $r_a \neq \bot$ in the set of approximants of r. Notice that the partial term r_a is such that $r_a \sqsubseteq r \sqsubseteq p'$. By the induction hypothesis, for every r_x such that $r_x \sqsubset r_a$ the set S_x of pairs (t', τ) such that there exists r'_x an approximant of r_x (i.e., $r'_x \sqsubseteq r_x$) with the same structure as t', and $\sigma(t) \xrightarrow{a} \tau\sigma(t') = p \xrightarrow{a} p'$ and $t \xrightarrow{a} t'$ is a positive premiss of some rule in R is finite. Since R is uniform in the targets of positive premises, all the positive premises with source t, action a, and whose target has the same structure as r'_x (if there is any) have the same target u. Since $r'_x \sqsubset r_a$, then r'_x is obtained by replacing by $\bot$ one or more maximally disjoint subterms of r_a that are different form $\bot$. We let x_j (with j ranging over some index set J) be the variables that occur in u in the positions corresponding to the occurrences of $\bot$ in r'_x. (Notice that no other variables could occur in u, since u has the same structure as r'_x, and $r'_x \sqsubset p'$.) We let t_j be the terms such that p' results from replacing respectively the x_j

by the t_j in u. If there exist no rules with a positive premiss whose target is u, then the set we are looking for is S_x. Otherwise, the set we are looking for is $S = S_x \cup \{(u, \{x_j \mapsto t_j \mid j \in J \land x_j \notin \mathrm{var}(t)\})\}$, which is finite.   □

The notion of image-bounded TSS, which we introduce next, collects the requirements that we have discussed so far.

Definition 23 (Image bounded). *A TSS R is image bounded iff R is uniform in the sources of rules and in the targets of their positive premisses, and there exists θ with codomain $\mathcal{P}_\omega(\mathbb{T}(\Sigma) \times A)$ (i.e., for each pair (t, a) the set $\theta(t, a)$ is finite) such that for every rule $\rho \in R$ with θ-type $\langle t, a, \phi \rangle$, the θ-type $\langle t, a, \phi \rangle$ is finitely inhabited.*

For image finiteness, the restrictions on the variable flow have to be enforced again, and the bounded nondeterminism format is needed. Example 7 in Sect. 4 shows that the variables in the target of a rule have to occur in either the source of the rule, or in the targets of its positive premisses. The LTS induced by the TSS in Example 7 is not image finite because $c \xrightarrow{a} d$ holds for each of the infinitely many constants d. The following example is a variation on Example 6 in Sect. 4 that shows that for image finiteness, the variables in the sources of positive premisses have to occur in the source of the rules.

Example 14. Let Σ consist of a constant c and a unary function symbol f, and assume $A = \{a\}$. Consider the TSS

$$\frac{}{f(x) \xrightarrow{a} f(x)} \qquad \frac{f(x) \xrightarrow{a} y}{c \xrightarrow{a} y} \ .$$

The TSS is uniform both in the sources of rules and in the targets of their positive premisses and has a strict stratification given by

$$S(f(p)) = 0$$
$$S(c) = 1.$$

We let $\theta(f(x), a) = \emptyset$ and $\theta(c, a) = \{(f(x), a)\}$. The rule on the left has θ-type $\langle f(x), a, \emptyset \rangle$, and the rule on the right has θ-type $\langle c, a, \phi \rangle$ where $\phi(f(x), a) = \{y\}$, and thus the TSS is image bounded. However $c \xrightarrow{a} f(p)$ for every $p \in T(\Sigma)$ and thus the associated LTS is not image finite.

In an image-bounded TSS, it is required that there exists a θ such that each θ-type $\langle t, a, \phi \rangle$ is finitely inhabited. This enforces that if for each term t, for each action a, and for each substitution σ such that $\sigma(t)$ is closed there are only finitely many ϕ such that the rules that give rise to a-transitions from $\sigma(t)$ have θ-type $\langle t, a, \phi \rangle$, then the set of targets t' such that $\sigma(t) \xrightarrow{a} \tau\sigma(t')$ with substitutions $\tau : (\mathrm{var}(t') \setminus \mathrm{var}(t)) \to T(\Sigma)$ is finite. The bounded nondeterminism format ensures that only finitely many τ exist, and thus the set of targets $\tau\sigma(t')$ is also finite and the associated LTS is image finite.

The following example shows that having a strict stratification is needed to ensure image finiteness.

Example 15. Let A consist of an action a, and let $\Sigma = A \cup \{f\}$ with f a unary function symbol f. Consider the TSS

$$\frac{}{f(x) \xrightarrow{a} a} \qquad\qquad \frac{f(x) \xrightarrow{a} y}{f(x) \xrightarrow{a} f(y)} \ .$$

The TSS is uniform in both the sources of rules and the targets of their positive premises, and it is in bounded nondeterminism format. We let $\theta(f(x), a) = \{(f(x), a)\}$. The rule on the left has θ-type $\langle f(x), a, \phi_1 \rangle$ with $\phi_1(f(x), a) = \emptyset$. The rule on the right has θ-type $\langle f(x), a, \phi_2 \rangle$ with $\phi_2(f(x), a) = \{y\}$. The TSS is image bounded. However, the TSS does not have a strict stratification. Notice that the associated LTS is not image finite since $f(a)$ can perform an a-transition to each of the terms $f^i(a)$.

The conditions of the following theorem define the rule format for image finiteness.

Theorem 3. *Let R be an image-bounded TSS that is in bounded nondeterminism format and has a strict stratification S. The LTS associated with R is image finite.*

Proof. We prove that for each closed term p and for each action a in the LTS associated with R the set $\{p' \mid p \xrightarrow{a} p'\}$ is finite. Since R is uniform in the sources, for a given p there are only finitely many distinct terms t_i and substitutions $\sigma_i : \mathrm{var}(t_i) \to T(\Sigma)$ (i.e., the i ranges over a finite index set I) such that $\sigma_i(t_i) = p$ and the rules that unify with transitions from p have some t_i as source. We proceed by induction on $S(p)$.

The initial case is when $S(p) = 0$. Since $S(\sigma_i(t_i)) = 0$, the rules with source t_i and action a are axioms of the form

$$\frac{}{t_i \xrightarrow{a} t'_j} \ , \qquad i \in I, \ j \in J_i$$

where the J_i are taken to be disjoint to avoid proliferation of indices. Since R is image bounded, there exists θ such that for each i and for each $j \in J_i$, the instantiation of the rule template above has θ-type $\langle t_i, a, \phi_j \rangle$, and $\langle t_i, a, \phi_j \rangle$ is finitely inhabited. By Definition 21, all the ϕ_j map each pair in $\theta(t_i, a)$ (if any) to the empty set. Since R is in bounded nondeterminism format, $\mathrm{var}(t'_j) \subseteq \mathrm{var}(t_i)$, and thus the $\sigma_i(t'_j)$ are closed. Since the rules above are axioms, the transitions $\sigma_i(t_i) \xrightarrow{a} \sigma_i(t'_j)$ are provable in R. Since all the ϕ_j are equal, and since the θ-types are finitely inhabited, then the J_i are finite. Therefore, for each $i \in I$ the set

$$\{\sigma_i(t'_j) \mid \sigma_i(t_i) \xrightarrow{a} \sigma_i(t'_j)\}$$

is finite. By the finiteness of I it follows that the set $\{p' \mid p \xrightarrow{a} p'\}$ is finite and we are done.

The general case is when $S(p) > 0$. The rules with action a and source t_i such that $\sigma_i(t_i) = p$ are of the form

$$\frac{\{u_k \xrightarrow{b_k} u'_k \mid k \in K_j\}}{t_i \xrightarrow{a} t'_j}, \qquad i \in I, \; j \in J_i$$

where the J_i and the K_j are taken to be disjoint to avoid proliferation of indices. Since R is image bounded, there exists θ such that for each i and for each $j \in J_i$, the instantiation of the rule template above has θ-type $\langle t_i, a, \phi_j \rangle$, the set $\theta(t_i, a)$ is finite, and $\langle t_i, a, \phi_j \rangle$ is finitely inhabited.

For each i, we show that there are only finitely many distinct ϕ_j with $j \in J_i$ such that rules with θ-type $\langle t_i, a, \phi_j \rangle$ give rise to transitions from $\sigma_i(t_i)$. By Definition 21, each rule of θ-type $\langle t_i, a, \phi_j \rangle$ contains a premiss of the form $v \xrightarrow{c} v'$ for each $(v, c) \in \theta(t_i, a)$ and each $v' \in \phi_j(v, c)$. Since R is in bounded nondeterminism format, $\mathrm{var}(v) \subseteq \mathrm{var}(t_i)$ and thus the $\sigma_i(v)$ are closed. By Definitions 7 and 8, for each transition in the node of a proof tree, if the transition unifies with a rule of θ-type $\langle t_i, a, \phi_j \rangle$ then for each pair $(v, c) \in \theta(t_i, a)$ and for each $v' \in \phi_j(v, c)$ the process $\sigma_i(v)$ can perform, at least, a c-transition to $\tau\sigma_i(v')$ for some substitution $\tau : (\mathrm{var}(v') \setminus \mathrm{var}(v)) \to T(\Sigma)$. The ϕ_j giving rise to transitions from $\sigma_i(t_i)$ are dependent functions of type $\Pi_{(v,c) \in \theta(t_i,a)} \{v' \mid \sigma_i(v) \xrightarrow{c} \tau\sigma_i(v')\}$ with substitutions $\tau : (\mathrm{var}(v') \setminus \mathrm{var}(v)) \to T(\Sigma)$. For each i the refined type of the ϕ_j with $j \in J_i$ is finitely inhabited, since the codomain of a dependent function depends on the inputs of the function. Each image of ϕ_j cannot be an arbitrary subset of $\mathbb{T}(\Sigma)$, but only the one determined by the input (v, c) and by the associated LTS. That is, the only elements in the codomain of ϕ_j are the sets $\{v' \mid \sigma_i(v) \xrightarrow{c} \tau\sigma_i(v')\}$ where $(v, c) \in \theta(t_i, a)$. Since the $\theta(t_i, a)$ are finite sets, both the domain and the codomain of ϕ_j are finite. Therefore, for each i, there are only finitely many distinct ϕ_j with $j \in J_i$ such that rules with θ-type $\langle t_i, a, \phi_j \rangle$ give rise to transitions from $\sigma_i(t_i)$.

Since R is in bounded nondeterminism format, $\mathrm{var}(u_k) \subseteq \mathrm{var}(t_i)$ with $k \in K_j$ and $j \in J_i$, and therefore the $\sigma_i(u_k)$ are closed terms. Since S is a strict stratification, $S(\sigma_i(u_k)) < S(p)$. By the induction hypothesis the $\sigma_i(u_k)$ are image finite, and for each i and for each b_k the set

$$\{\tau_\ell \sigma_i(u'_k) \mid \sigma_i(u_k) \xrightarrow{b_k} \tau_\ell \sigma_i(u'_k)\}$$

is finite, with $\tau_\ell : ((\bigcup_{k \in K_j} \mathrm{var}(u'_k)) \setminus \mathrm{var}(t_i)) \to T(\Sigma)$ closed substitutions where ℓ ranges over some index sets L_j. Since R is uniform in the targets of positive premisses and by Proposition 3 the L_j are finite. Since R is in bounded nondeterminism format, $\mathrm{var}(t'_j) \subseteq (\mathrm{var}(t_i) \cup (\bigcup_{k \in K_j} \mathrm{var}(u'_k)))$ and therefore the $\tau_\ell \sigma_i(t'_j)$ are closed terms. Since for each i there are only finitely many distinct ϕ_j with $j \in J_i$ such that rules with θ-type $\langle t_i, a, \phi_j \rangle$ give rise to transitions from $\sigma_i(t_i)$, and since the L_j are finite, then for each $i \in I$ the set

$$\{\tau_\ell \sigma_i(t'_j) \mid \sigma_i(t_i) \xrightarrow{a} \tau_\ell \sigma_i(t'_j)\}$$

is finite. By the finiteness of I it follows that the set $\{p' \mid p \xrightarrow{a} p'\}$ is finite and we are done.   □

In Theorem 3 the rules of R are not required to have finitely inhabited η-types. This is illustrated by Example 16 below.

Example 16. Let Σ consist of infinitely many constants $c_1, c_2, \ldots$ and assume $A = \{a_1, a_2, \ldots\}$. Consider the TSS

$$\frac{}{x \xrightarrow{a_i} c_i} \, , \qquad i \in \mathbb{N}.$$

The TSS is uniform in both the sources of rules and in their targets of premises, and it is in bounded nondeterminism format and has a strict stratification given by $S(c_i) = 0$, $i \geq 1$. We let $\theta(x, a_i) = \emptyset$ with $i \in \mathbb{N}$. For each $i \in \mathbb{N}$, the instantiation of the rule template above has θ-type $\langle x, a_i, \emptyset \rangle$. The associated LTS is image finite because for each process p and for each $i \in \mathbb{N}$, p can only perform an a_i-action to c_i. However, the LTS is neither finite branching nor initials finite.

Example 5.3 from page 515 of [9] is an example of application of the rule format defined by the conditions of Theorem 3. We reproduce it next.

Example 17 (Example 5.3 of [9]). Let $r \in \mathbb{R}_{>0}$. Consider the operator for dead-lock in real-time Basic Process Algebra [17], which can be expressed by the rule

$$\frac{}{\delta[r] \xrightarrow{\delta[s]} \checkmark} \qquad 0 < s < r.$$

Process $\delta[r]$ is infinitely branching and has an uncountable set of initials. However, it is image finite as can be checked using our format. The TSS above is uniform in both the sources of rules and in the targets of their positive premises, and is in bounded nondeterminism format and has a trivial strict stratification. Take $\theta(\delta[r], \delta[s]) = \emptyset$ for each $r, s \in \mathbb{R}_{>0}$. The θ-type of each instantiation of the rule template above is $\langle \delta[r], \delta[s], \emptyset \rangle$. By Theorem 3, the associated LTS is image finite.

6   Future Work

We say that the rule formats are *adequate* with respect to the corresponding finiteness property, i.e., the syntactic conditions ensure that the associated LTS has the property. However, the rule formats are not *complete* with respect to the corresponding finiteness property, i.e., not all the LTSs that have the property are induced by TSSs that satisfy the syntactic conditions. One direction for future work is to generalise the rule formats to cover such TSSs. In the following examples we collect some of the cases that we are aware are not covered by the rule formats.

Example 18. Consider the following TSS R_{pc} describing a fragment of an instance of the algebra for process creation from [5]. The signature for that TSS contains the following operations:

- constants a, ε and δ,
- the unary process-creation operation new, and
- the binary operations $\cdot$ and $\|$, which we write in infix style.

We set $A = \{a, \checkmark\}$ and use α to range over it. The set of rules of R_{pc}, for whose intuition we refer the reader to [5], are:

$$\frac{}{a \xrightarrow{a} \varepsilon} \qquad \frac{}{\varepsilon \xrightarrow{\checkmark} \delta}$$

$$\frac{}{\mathrm{new}(x) \xrightarrow{\checkmark} x \cdot \delta} \qquad \frac{x \xrightarrow{a} x'}{\mathrm{new}(x) \xrightarrow{a} \mathrm{new}(x')}$$

$$\frac{x \xrightarrow{a} x'}{x \cdot y \xrightarrow{a} x' \cdot y} \qquad \frac{x \xrightarrow{\checkmark} x', \; y \xrightarrow{\alpha} y'}{x \cdot y \xrightarrow{\alpha} x' \| y'} \qquad \frac{x \xrightarrow{\checkmark} x', \; x' \xrightarrow{a} x'', \; y \xrightarrow{a} y'}{x \cdot y \xrightarrow{a} x'' \| y'}$$

$$\frac{x \xrightarrow{a} x'}{x \| y \xrightarrow{a} x' \| y} \qquad \frac{y \xrightarrow{\alpha} y'}{x \| y \xrightarrow{\alpha} x \| y'} \qquad \frac{x \xrightarrow{a} x', \; y \xrightarrow{a} y'}{x \| y \xrightarrow{a} x' \| y'} \; .$$

Note that the third rule for the operator $\cdot$ is not in bounded nondeterminism format because of the premise $x' \xrightarrow{a} x''$. Therefore the TSS R_{pc} does not meet the requirements of Theorem 1. On the other hand, it is not too hard to show that the LTS induced by R_{pc} is finite branching. (This is also a consequence of the more general Elimination Theorem from [5, Theorem 4.9].)

Example 19. Let Σ consist of a constant c and a unary function symbol f, and let $A = \{a\}$. Consider the TSS with rules

$$\frac{}{f(x) \xrightarrow{a} c} \qquad \frac{f(x) \xrightarrow{a} y}{c \xrightarrow{a} y} \; .$$

This TSS is uniform and has a strict stratification given by

$$S(f(p)) = 0$$
$$S(c) = 1.$$

We let $\theta(f(x), a) = \emptyset$ and $\theta(c, a) = \{(f(x), a)\}$. The rule on the left has θ-type $\langle f(x), a, \emptyset \rangle$, and the rule on the right has θ-type $\langle c, a, \phi \rangle$ where $\phi(f(x), a) = \{y\}$. Variable x in the premiss of the rule on the right does not occur in the source of the rule, and hence the TSS is not in bounded nondeterminism format and does not meet the rule format for image finiteness. However, the set of images of any process p for action a is $\{c\}$, and therefore the associated LTS is image finite. Notice that the TSS does not meet the rule format for finite branching either, but the associated LTS is finite branching.

Example 20. Let A consist of infinitely many actions $a_1, a_2, \ldots$ and let $\Sigma = A \cup \{f, g\}$ where f and g are unary function symbols. Consider the TSS with rules

$$\frac{}{g(a_1) \xrightarrow{a_1} a_1} \qquad \frac{g^i(x) \xrightarrow{a_i} x}{f(x) \xrightarrow{a_i} x}, \qquad i \in \mathbb{N}$$

where g^i stands for applying the function symbol g to its argument i times. The TSS is uniform, in bounded nondeterminism format, and has a strict stratification given by

$$S(g^i(p)) = 0$$
$$S(f(p)) = 1.$$

Notice that there exists no η such that the η-types are finitely inhabited. No matter how one picks η, for every finite set $\eta(f(x))$ there would be an infinite number of instances of the rule on the right that have the same η-type. Thus the TSS is not bounded and the TSS does not meet the rule format for finite branching. However, the associated LTS is finite branching because the only possible transitions are $g(a_1) \xrightarrow{a_1} a_1$ and $f(a_1) \xrightarrow{a_1} a_1$.

Example 21. Let Σ consist of a constant c and a unary function symbol f, and assume $A = \{a_1, a_2, \ldots\}$ with infinitely many actions. Consider the TSS

$$\frac{}{f(x) \xrightarrow{a_1} f(x)} \qquad \frac{f(x) \xrightarrow{a_i} y}{f(x) \xrightarrow{a_{i+1}} y}, \qquad i \in \mathbb{N}.$$

The TSS is uniform in both the sources of rules and the targets of their positive premises, and it is in bounded nondeterminism format. We let $\theta(f(x), a_1) = \emptyset$ and $\theta(f(x), a_{i+1}) = \{(f(x), a_i)\}$ for each $i \in \mathbb{N}$. The rule on the left has θ-type $\langle f(x), a_1, \emptyset \rangle$. For each $i \in \mathbb{N}$, the instantiation of the rule template on the right has θ-type $\langle f(x), a_{i+1}, \phi_i \rangle$, where $\phi_i(f(x), a_i) = \{y\}$. The TSS is image bounded. Notice that the TSS does not have a strict stratification and therefore it does not meet the rule format for image finiteness. However, the associated LTS is image finite, since c has no outgoing transitions and the image of each process of the form $f(p)$ for action a_i (with $i \in \mathbb{N}$) is $f(p)$.

Another direction for future research is the study of algorithmic aspects of the rule formats discussed in this paper. Indeed, whereas the conditions pertaining to single rules, such as those imposed by the bounded nondeterminism format, are purely syntactic and easy to check, those related to the various notions of types have a global nature. It would be interesting to study ways to enforce those global constraints and to develop algorithms for checking them over classes of TSSs.

Nominal structural operational semantics (NoSOS) [8] enriches the SOS formalism by using some of the nominal techniques from [10,24,31] to deal with names and binders within the SOS framework. We are currently investigating how to adapt the results in this paper to NoSOS. The main challenges there are to treat transition labels that may contain variables and the effect that the so-called freshness assertions may have on the finiteness properties of interest. In NoSOS, it is conventional to consider special administrative transitions for freshness conditions, for substitution, and for α-conversion [8]. The transitions for freshness conditions in isolation induce an initials-finite LTS. There are two kinds of substitution, atom-for-atom and term-for-atom substitution, which taken in isolation induce image-finite LTSs. The transitions for α-conversion taken in isolation induce an initials-finite LTS. One of the problems in extending our results to NoSOS is to abstract from these administrative transitions in order to focus on the finiteness properties of the remaining transitions.

Acknowledgements. We thank two anonymous referees for their careful reading of our paper and their constructive comments.

References

1. Abramsky, S.: Domain theory and the logic of observable properties. Ph.D. thesis, Department of Computer Science, Queen Mary College, University of London (1987)
2. Aceto, L., Fokkink, W., Verhoef, C.: Structural operational semantics. In: Bergstra, J., Ponse, A., Smolka, S. (eds.) Handbook of Process Algebra, Chap. 3, pp. 197–292. Elsevier, Amsterdam (2001)
3. Amtoft, T., Nielson, F., Nielson, H.R.: Type and Effect Systems. Imperial College Press, London (1999)
4. Apt, K.R., Plotkin, G.D.: Countable nondeterminism and random assignment. J. ACM **33**(4), 724–767 (1986)
5. Baeten, J.C.M., Vaandrager, F.W.: An algebra for process creation. Acta Inf. **29**(4), 303–334 (1992). http://dx.doi.org/10.1007/BF01178776
6. Bloom, B.: CHOCOLATE: Calculi of Higher Order COmmunication and LAmbda TErms (preliminary report). In: Boehm, H.J., Lang, B., Yellin, D.M. (eds.) Conference Record of the 21st ACM Symposium on Principles of Programming Languages, Portland, Oregon, pp. 339–347. ACM Press (1994)
7. Bloom, B., Istrail, S., Meyer, A.R.: Bisimulation can't be traced. J. ACM **42**(1), 232–268 (1995)
8. Cimini, M., Mousavi, M.R., Reniers, M.A., Gabbay, M.J.: Nominal SOS. Electron. Notes Theoret. Comput. Sci. **286**, 103–116 (2012)
9. Fokkink, W., Vu, T.D.: Structural operational semantics and bounded nondeterminism. Acta Inf. **39**(6–7), 501–516 (2003)
10. Gabbay, M.J., Pitts, A.M.: A new approach to abstract syntax involving binders. In: Longo, G. (ed.) Proceedings of the 14th Symposium on Logic in Computer Science, Trento, Italy, pp. 214–224. IEEE Computer Society Press (1999)
11. van Gelder, A., Ross, K.A., Schilpf, J.S.: The well-founded semantics for general logic programs. J. ACM **38**(3), 620–662 (1991)
12. van Glabbeek, R.J.: Bounded nondeterminism and the approximation induction principle in process algebra. In: Brandenburg, F.J., Wirsing, M., Vidal-Naquet, G. (eds.) STACS 1987. LNCS, vol. 247, pp. 336–347. Springer, Heidelberg (1987)
13. Groote, J.F., Vaandrager, F.W.: Structured operational semantics and bisimulation as a congruence. Inf. Comput. **100**(2), 202–260 (1992)

14. Groote, J.F.: Transition system specifications with negative premises. Theoret. Comput. Sci. **118**(2), 263–299 (1993)
15. Heyting, A. (ed.): Constructivity in Mathematics. North-Holland Publishing Company, Amsterdam (1959)
16. Keller, R.M.: Formal verification of parallel programs. Commun. ACM **19**(7), 371–384 (1976)
17. Klusener, A.S.: Models and axioms for a fragment of real time process algebra. Ph.D. thesis, Department of Mathematics and Computing Science, Technical University of Eindhoven (1993)
18. Lévy, A.: A hierarchy of formulas in set theory. Mem. Am. Math. Soc. **57**, 76 (1965)
19. Martin-Löf, P.: Intuitionistic Type Theory. Studies in Proof Theory: Lecture Notes, Bibliopolis, Napoli (1984)
20. Milner, R.: Communication and Concurrency. PHI Series in Computer Science. Prentice Hall, Upper Saddle River (1989)
21. Mousavi, M.R., Reniers, M.A., Groote, J.F.: SOS formats and meta-theory: 20 years after. Theoret. Comput. Sci. **373**(3), 238–272 (2007)
22. Nielson, F., Nielson, H.R., Hankin, C.: Principles of Program Analysis. Springer, Heidelberg (2005)
23. Nielson, H.R., Nielson, F.: Semantics with Applications: An Appertizer. Springer, London (2007)
24. Pitts, A.M.: Nominal Sets: Names and Symmetry in Computer Science. Cambridge Tracts in Theoretical Computer Science, vol. 57. Cambridge University Press, Cambridge (2013)
25. Plotkin, G.D.: A structural approach to operational semantics. Technacal report. DAIMI FN-19, Department of Computer Science, Aarhus University, Denmark (1981)
26. Plotkin, G.D.: An operational semantics for CSP. In: Salwicki, A. (ed.) Logic of Programs 1980. LNCS, vol. 148, pp. 250–252. Springer, Heidelberg (1983). http://dx.doi.org/10.1007/3-540-11981-7_17
27. Plotkin, G.D.: A structural approach to operational semantics. J. Logic Algebraic Program. **60–61**, 17–139 (2004)
28. Przymusinski, T.C.: The well-founded semantics coincides with the three-valued stable semantics. Fundamenta Informaticae **13**(4), 445–463 (1990)
29. Sangiorgi, D., Walker, D.: The pi-calculus: A Theory of Mobile Processes. Cambridge Universtity Press, Cambridge (2001)
30. de Simone, R.: Higher-level synchronising devices in Meije-SCCS. Theoret. Comput. Sci. **37**(3), 245–267 (1985)
31. Urban, C., Pitts, A.M., Gabbay, M.J.: Nominal unification. Theoret. Comput. Sci. **323**(1–3), 473–497 (2004)
32. Vaandrager, F.W.: Expressiveness results for process algebras. In: de Bakker, J.W., de Roever, W.-P., Rozenberg, G. (eds.) REX 1992. LNCS, vol. 666, pp. 609–638. Springer, Heidelberg (1993)

Author Index

Printed in the United States
By Bookmasters